Classroom Measurement & Evaluation

Second Edition

Charles D. Hopkins

Richard L. Antes

both of
INDIANA STATE UNIVERSITY

F.E. PEACOCK PUBLISHERS, INC.
ITASCA, ILLINOIS 60143

Contents

Preface ix

Chapter 1. Role of Measurement and Evaluation
         in Education 1
    Functions of measurement and evaluation 3
    Educational objectives 4
    School program 12
    Collection of information 12
    Measurement 14
    Evaluation 20
    Relationship of measurement and evaluation 24
    Summary 25
    New technical terms listed in the glossary 26
    Activity exercises 27
    For discussion 27
    References and knowledge extenders 28

Chapter 2. Integrating Testing with Instruction 29
    Appraisal 31
    Diagnosis 33
    Formative evaluation 35
    Summative evaluation 38
    Other techniques 40
    Summary 40
    New technical terms listed in the glossary 40
    Activity Exercises 41
    For discussion 41
    References and knowledge extenders 41

Chapter 3. Using Observation in the Classroom 43
    The nature of observation 44
    Effective classroom observation 48
    Aids to direct observation 51
    Supplementing direct observation 61
    Planning observation 63
    Valid observations 67
    Summary 69
    New technical terms listed in the glossary 70
    Activity exercises 71
    For discussion 71
    References and knowledge extenders 72

Chapter 4. Evaluation of Classroom Performance 73
The classroom situation 74
Procedure and product 76
Building reliability into evaluation of performance 91
Summary 98
New technical terms listed in the glossary 99
Activity exercises 99
For discussion 99
References and knowledge extenders 100

Chapter 5. Planning for Classroom Testing 101
What is a test? 102
The test as a sample 104
The table of specifications 105
Test construction considerations 110
Other test planning considerations 122
General considerations in construction of test items 125
Summary 127
New technical terms listed in the glossary 128
Activity exercises 128
For discussion 129
References and knowledge extenders 129

Chapter 6. Constructing Selected–Response Items 131
Selection 132
Strengths of selected-response items 133
Weaknesses of selected-response items 134
True-false items 134
Multiple-choice items 140
Matching items 149
Classification items 160
Summary 165
New technical terms listed in the glossary 165
Activity exercises 166
For discussion 166
References and knowledge extenders 166

Chapter 7. Constructing Constructed–Response Items 169
Written expression 170
Strengths of constructed-response items 170
Weaknesses of constructed-response items 171
Completion items 172
Short-answer items 177
Essay items 179
Summary 183
New technical terms listed in the glossary 184
Activity exercises 184

For discussion 185
References and knowledge extenders 185

Chapter 8. Constructing Problem Items 187
  Problem solving 189
  Mathematical problems 189
  Technical problems 198
  Summary 203
  Activity exercises 204
  For discussion 204
  References and knowledge extenders 205

Chapter 9. Assembling, Administering, and Scoring
            the Classroom Test 207
  Test assembly 207
  Administration of the test 216
  Scoring 218
  Summary 231
  New technical terms listed in the glossary 232
  Activity exercises 232
  For discussion 233
  References and knowledge extenders 233

Chapter 10. Test Appraisal 235
  Why appraise a test? 236
  Important test characteristics 237
  Item analysis 240
  Using appraisal information for revision and
     selection of items 255
  Using appraisal information to improve test quality 258
  Using appraisal information to help students
     and teachers 259
  Summary 261
  New technical terms listed in the glossary 262
  Activity exercises 262
  For discussion 262
  References and knowledge extenders 263

Chapter 11. Establishing Test Reliability 265
  Ways of estimating rest reliability 267
  Standard error of measurement 282
  Increasing reliability 287
  Summary 292
  New technical terms listed in the glossary 294
  Activity exercises 294
  For discussion 295
  References and knowledge extenders 295

Chapter 12. Establishing Test Validity 297
  Types of validity 299
  Determination of test validity 302
  Tests as operational definitions 310
  Improving validity for data-collecting devices 311
  Summary 313
  New technical words listed in the glossary 314
  Activity exercises 314
  For discussion 314
  References and knowledge extenders 314

Chapter 13. Reference Systems 317
  Criterion-referenced evaluation 319
  Norm-referenced evaluation 329
  Should CRM or NRM be used? 334
  Summary 337
  New technical terms listed in the glossary 338
  Activity exercises 338
  For discussion 338
  References and knowledge extenders 338

Chapter 14. Interpreting Test Scores 341
  Interpretation by criterion 343
  Interpretation by percentages 344
  Norm-referenced interpretation 345
  Graphic representation of frequency distributions 348
  Measures of central tendency 353
  Relationships within a distribution 359
  Measures of variability 361
  Other characteristics of distributions 365
  Standard scores 369
  The normal curve 373
  Percentile rank 380
  Stanines 382
  Whadjagit? 384
  Summary 388
  New technical terms listed in the glossary 390
  Activity exercises 390
  For discussion 391
  References and knowledge extenders 391

Chapter 15. Marks and Marking Plans 393
  Philosophical issues 394
  Using marks 396
  Inadequacy of marks 397

Purposes of marking 397
Types of marks 399
Alternatives to marks 405
Multiple marking and reporting systems 410
Computerized reporting of marks 418
Technical issues 419
Considerations in determination of marks
   and writing reports 420
Summary 421
New technical term listed in the glossary 422
Activity exercises 422
For discussion 423
References and knowledge extenders 423

Chapter 16. Published Tests 425
Classification of published tests 426
Standardized achievement tests 428
Standardized aptitude tests 438
Readiness tests 444
Screening tests 445
Selecting standardized tests 449
Norms for standardized tests 453
Summary 460
New technical terms listed in the glossary 463
Activity exercises 463
For discussion 463
References and knowledge extenders 464

Glossary 466
Appendix A Affective and Psychomotor Domains 482
Appendix B Writing Behavioral Objectives 489
Element 1: Who 489
Element 2: Action 490
Element 3: Product 492
Element 4: Conditions 493
Element 5: Minimum acceptance 494
Appendix C Correction for Guessing 498
Appendix D Kuder–Richardson Formulas for
                Test Reliability 502
Appendix E Outline of a schoolwide standardized
                testing program 503
Appendix F Ethics Code — Standards for
                Published Tests 506
Appendix G Information Needed to Evaluate a
                Standardized Test 509

Appendix H   Data Collection Procedures 510
Appendix I   Areas of the normal curve in terms of x/σ 513
Appendix J   Squares and square roots of numbers
              from 1 to 120 515
Name Index 517
Subject Index 519

Preface

Classroom Measurement and Evaluation, Second Edition, is written to direct preservice and all levels of inservice teachers to a meaningful integration of measurement procedures and evaluation techniques into the ongoing classroom instructional activities. The text does not assume any previous course as a prerequisite and begins at the basic level, thus providing both preservice students and inservice teachers with direction on how to build a sound ingredient of evaluation into the teaching-learning process.

Though this is largely a how-to-do-it book, the direction is supported by theory and tested procedures. Understanding of the art attached to measurement and evaluation is developed by articulation of topics and bridging the specifics into a well-coordinated presentation for the student. The science of the topics supports the art of application of principles of measurement and evaluation in the classroom.

The emphasis of the first edition on topics used at the classroom level has been retained, while important changes have been included. Psychological testing for the most part has not been discussed, however the basic principles of test construction are the same for educational and psychological tests and a knowledgeable teacher will be able to understand reports of psychological tests given to students. Psychological tests used in collecting information for the classroom teacher are reviewed in chapter 16 on published tests.

Six new chapters have been written. Three of these (chapters 6, 7, and 8) have been added on writing and construction of: *(a)* selected-response items — true-false, multiple-choice, matching, classification; *(b)* constructed-response items — completion, short-answer, essay; and *(c)* problem items — mathematical and technical. In each of these chapters a section concerning the strengths and weaknesses of each category and specific types of item is included. Example items have been added to provide more helpful illustrations of the guides for writing each specific type of item. In addition, exemplary items for the elementary and secondary schools are provided for each type of item.

Chapter 2 directs teachers to collection and use of information to support learning and promote student literacy. A basic premise that testing should benefit those who take the tests remains from the first edition and the text material reflects the need to support instruction by collection of adequate information about what students know and can do. The integration of testing with instruction is individual and classroom specific, thus the chapter centers around testing for appraisal, diagnosis, formative evaluation, and summative evaluation as they support student cognitive and skill learning.

Chapter 13 gives a clear description of criterion-referencing and norm-referencing. The need to use both referencing systems in the classroom is supported by explanation of how each referencing system is to be used to support the instructional program.

Chapter 15 overviews marking plans and attends to the problem of giving marks to student achievement.

Chapter 16 incorporates the first edition coverage of "Using Published Tests in the Classroom" and "Screening for Learning Disabilities." Revision and rewriting of the discussion of standardized tests to be used in the classroom setting and teacher-administered screening tests for learning disabilities has been undertaken.

The text is organized around the following broad topics:

Orientation to basic understandings:	Chapters 1, 2, 3
Evaluation of performance:	Chapter 4
Planning, constructing, administering tests:	Chapters 5–9
Appraisal of the testing instrument:	Chapters 10–12
Interpretation of test results:	Chapters 13–15
Using published tests in the classroom:	Chapter 16

The topics of reliability and validity have been divided for presentation. Before the student commences the study of test construction the concepts of reliability and validity are developed and a working knowledge is established. After further study of testing, the need to establish the levels of each of these with a particular test is used as a basis for presentation of the ways to determine how a test rates in reliability and its degree of the important type of validity associated with the test instrument. Content validity is given in-depth study because it is the most important type of validity for classroom tests.

Suggestions from users of the first edition have given input that has allowed further clarification where needed and helped us better tune this edition to the needs of the classroom teacher. Substantial rewriting of some sections has allowed us to more fully express ideas and points. William R. Merz, California State University, Sacramento, and William Wiersma, University of Toledo, were especially helpful in preparation of the first edition. We are grateful for the opportunity to build on the foundation of that edition.

Key T. Lee, Harley Erickson, Bruce Rogers, and Marlene Strathe from the University of Northern Iowa have read this manuscript and made suggestions that aided us to avoid errors of omission and commission. Key T. Lee, James S. Terwilliger and Jerry L. Gray made a final review and helped reorganize the sequence of the material into a firmly knit succession of topics. However, the final manuscript and text material contain our personal choices and reflect our biases. We must live with these and hope that they are either your biases, or biases that you can live with.

C. H. and R. A.

Chapter 1. Role of Measurement and Evaluation in Education

After study of Chapter 1, you should be able to:

1. Describe how educational objectives are stated and used at the national, state, local, and classroom levels.
2. Indicate the primary difference between measurement and evaluation and the direct relationship of the two processes.
3. Summarize how collection of information from students supports educational evaluation.
4. Understand the purpose of evaluation and its relationship to decision making.
5. Describe how classroom measurement and physical measurement are alike, and how they are different.
6. Define the terms *reliability* and *validity,* as they apply to interpretation of information collected from students.
7. Describe how to use reliability and validity to increase the meaningfulness of information collected from students.
8. Explain how the items on a test formulate an operational definition of the characteristic the test is to measure.
9. Describe how measurement and evaluation contribute to student learning.
10. Explain how each glossary term listed at the end of the chapter is used in classroom measurement and evaluation.

Appraisal of student progress has been a part of the educational scene for as long as there has been a teacher-learner relationship. Assessment of the effectiveness of a classroom instructional program has been a more recent addition to the process of education. These two major components of **evaluation*** —appraisal and assessment—provide information that a teacher uses to

---

*The first time a word that is listed in the glossary is used in the text it will appear in **boldface** type. As indicated, use of **evaluation** is described in the glossary. You should now turn to the glossary and find out how **evaluation** is used in this book. Do this each time a **boldface** word appears in your reading.

make instructional decisions for an individual student and make decisions for a classroom. The terms *appraisal* and *assessment* have been used interchangeably to refer to either students or programs. For clarity, in this book the term *appraisal* is used to refer to evaluation of students and the term *assessment* is used to refer to evaluation of programs.

The need for educators to be answerable for their professional decisions has become evident to teachers and administrators at all levels as the question of **accountability** arises. Other questions about competency at various stages of the educational process, competency for certification, or licensing of practitioners for an ever-expanding list of professions, arts, and trades continue to be issues not only for educators but also for licensing agencies and state legislatures as laws are enacted and enforced. Educational evaluation enhances the likelihood of attaining sound answers to these questions, and supports instruction by supplying data for making decisions. The sequence is: *(a)* an abundance of information, *(b)* meaningful evaluation, and *(c)* sound decisions. Logical decisions in education must be formed from sound evaluation. In turn, those evaluations must be based on accurate information that is relevant to the evaluation. This information must be collected in sufficient quantity to encompass the scope of whatever is being evaluated. The major purpose of this book is to prepare classroom teachers to make well-grounded instructional decisions about a student individually and about students collectively.

Evaluation and the closely related process of **measurement** have expanding importance in education as educators collect data and form judgments about student progress toward prescribed goals and the effectiveness of activities designed to facilitate student learning. The judgments made about students and their learning have a pervasive effect on each student's development of knowledge and skill. The importance of the development of techniques to supply information about students and their status cannot be overemphasized because educators at all levels use this information to make judgments about students and school programs. The information used in evaluation is, in general, supplied by students, and most of this information is collected in the classroom.

Parents, administrators, and prospective employers as well as students make decisions based on information generated from within the classroom. Parents' decisions about school-related situations must be made in light of how the student is performing academically, physically, psychologically, and socially. Student decisions about future schooling are based on how others perceive performance as well as how the student views himself or herself. A decision to employ a particular person may rest almost entirely on past school performance as reported by school records of academic, social, and skill development. A decision to continue, revise, or to discard a school program will be determined largely from information about how well students perform in the program and how well it has prepared them to meet situations outside the classroom after completion of the course of study. Since so many decisions are based on information provided from within the classroom, data collection, and evaluation should be integral parts of classroom activities.

The kind of data collected and the kind of evaluation of educational progress employed are also important in directing learning. As information is gathered and results are discussed with students, they begin to understand teacher goals and expectations. The types of knowledge and skill deemed important are clearly indicated by what teachers emphasize in class exercises, **test** items, and data collection in the classroom. For example, if the teacher wants students to learn to apply the principles of mathematics the exercises should include application of math knowledge. Likewise, when a **classroom test** is given students should be required to apply knowledge and go beyond computation and recall of facts and bits of information when responding to test tasks. Test items that measure understanding, application, and higher cognitive processes indicate to the student that these are important to learning and that future study should be directed into higher levels of the **cognitive domain.**

The authors consider all forms of data collection to be appropriate if each is employed in proper articulation with the situation and information needed. Although testing is expected to continue to be the primary vehicle for collecting information from students it takes many forms. A host of other collection techniques are also available for the classroom teacher. Many of these alternatives are presented in this textbook so that professional educators can make proper choices when called on to do so. Those who support good schools should be able to use data collection techniques compatible with good decision-making procedure. The major objective of this book is to improve knowledge and understanding for anyone who collects data, interprets data, or makes educational decisions to enhance student learning.

FUNCTIONS OF MEASUREMENT AND EVALUATION

Historical development of present-day evaluation procedures shows that ways are needed to provide objective information that allows for sound judgments about student progress and school program effectiveness. Sound judgments are based upon systematically collected student information in maximum quantities. For this reason measurement and other data-collecting procedures become a prerequisite for evaluation.

The two terms—*measurement* and *evaluation*—refer to two different sets of procedures that generate products with a close relationship. Awareness of the separate functions of measurement and evaluation as well as differences and similarities in procedures can best be explained by pointing up relationships that exist among the basic components of education (see Figure 1.1). These components are:

1. Educational needs of the students.
2. Educational objectives.
3. A school program of instructional activities.
4. Collection of information (includes measurement).

5. Appraisal of students and assessment of the school program (evaluation).

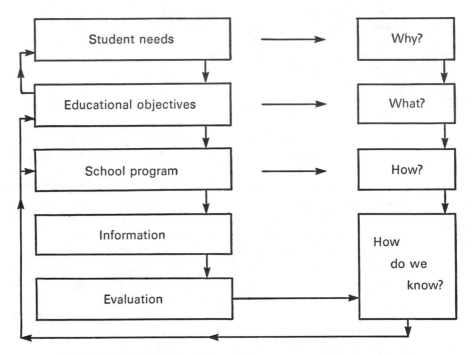

FIGURE 1.1. Relationships of five components of education

The first of these, student needs, can be viewed as the reason *why* the educational institution exists; the second, educational objectives, can be viewed as *what* the educational process is to accomplish; the third, school program, can be viewed as *how* the educational process is to accomplish the goals to serve the needs of students. The fourth and fifth are needed to see how well the school program is functioning for the students. They should answer the question: "*How do we know* if students' needs are being met?"

The educational needs of students and a school program of instructional activities are important elements of education. The objectives to be attained by students are set from needs and the program of instruction is designed to move students toward the fulfillment of these objectives, and in turn meet the educational needs of the students.

EDUCATIONAL OBJECTIVES

Educational objectives stated as desired student learning outcomes are deduced by the classroom teacher prior to commencing instruction and they provide direction to the teaching-learning process. These **instructional objectives** state what knowledge and skill are to be developed in a course and provide standards for evaluating student progress. Instructional objectives may be written to cover a course, a specific unit of instruction, or an assignment, and serve as guides to measurement as well as directing teaching and learning. The description of what to measure is established directly or indirectly in the statements of instructional objectives as developed by the classroom teacher.

Objectives have been developed at several levels in the educational institution. For example, objectives are set by national and state committees, county or city school officials, committees of teachers in a school, and the individual classroom teacher. Figure 1.2 shows how the scope of an objective for the classroom narrows from the broad base that reflects the general nature of national objectives to the classroom level where the operational level is reached and the objective becomes specific. **General educational objectives** expressed at the national level reflect broad concerns of society for the education of citizens, and classroom objectives reflect the special needs of students in a specific classroom. Two examples of sets of general objectives developed at the national level are the *Cardinal Principles of Secondary Education* (Na-

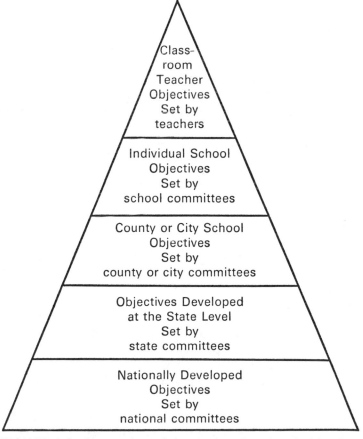

FIGURE 1.2. Narrowing of the scope of national objectives
to classroom objectives

tional Education Association, Commission on Reorganizing Secondary School Education, 1918) and *Elementary School Objectives* (Kearney, 1953) developed by the Mid-century Committee on Outcomes in Elementary Education.

The objectives at the various levels serve as guides for school systems and teachers since use of objectives from authoritative sources is a helpful way to begin thinking about production of specific objectives for the classroom, a subset of that classroom, or an individual. Instructional objectives vary in degree of complexity, depending on student experiential level, maturation level, content studied, and presentation of the subject matter. Our concern is with instructional objectives that guide learning and those that can be used to assess student progress toward goals and the effectiveness of instruction; therefore, each bit of information collected for evaluation should be related to one or more of the instructional objectives established for the classroom or for an individual.

Since teacher-made tests are based on objectives that direct teaching, the teacher should develop a set of objectives to meet the learning needs of students in a classroom. Objectives developed within the classroom are better understood by the teacher and serve measurement procedures better than a set of objectives prepared outside the classroom and handed to the teacher. Student learning should be enhanced with the integration of objectives into each classroom educational program. Noll and Scannell (1972) point up the importance of instructional objectives when they state:

> Definition of goals comes first—as it must if teaching is to have purpose and direction. To try to teach and evaluate without defining objectives is like starting out on a journey without knowing where you want to go. It may be pleasant to wander around for a while, but it is doubtful that any sort of progress can be made without some direction. (p. 166)

Classification of Objectives

Objectives can be considered to be general or specific in nature. General objectives deal with learning outcomes that focus on learning in a broad sense. General instructional objectives a teacher could state for particular courses might be like the following:

1. Develop understanding of mathematics for everyday life.
2. Understand measurement to the nearest half inch.
3. Comprehend the basic needs of animals.
4. Understand the background of the American revolution.

These generally stated objectives are helpful in giving direction to instruction that has a broad base and where students may be successful, but at varying levels. For use in evaluation, clearly defined domains of behavior need to be established so that data can be collected for each clearly defined domain.

Behavioral objectives deal with specific
tion. The following are illustrative of behaviora
learning to specifics and establish minimum levels

1. Using 10 minutes of class time, the student will
   essay acceptable to the teacher concerning the
   needs of animals.
2. The student will demonstrate knowledge of measurem
   16-foot steel tape to measure the classroom accurately in fee
3. The student will write from memory five important events
   tributed to the colonies' Declaration of Independence and the
   American revolution.

These objectives are explicit because they give direction for a specific
student action. In addition, each indicates who will perform a particular
action, the conditions under which the action will be observed, the product to
be created, and the minimum acceptance level for goal attainment. A synthesis
of procedures for writing behavioral objectives is presented in Appendix B as
a review for teachers who previously have written behavioral objectives, and
a reference for those who need to write objectives at that level of specifics.

A preferable way to write objectives may be by stating them in general
terms and listing the specific types of behaviors desired as outcomes.

Example

General outcome: Students will understand the concept of set as
related to the four basic arithmetic processes.

Specific outcomes:
1. Learn to associate a number with a set of objects.
2. Be able to draw an array for a given number.
3. Join sets in addition and separate sets in subtraction.
4. Join sets in multiplication and separate sets in division.
5. Solve fractional problems using parts of sets.

Both general instructional and behavioral objectives can help provide direction
to the teaching-learning program, and neither should be used to the exclusion
of the other. It is also important to keep in mind that not all objectives can
or should be stated as behavioral objectives, nor can the outcomes of all
objectives be directly measured by tests. **Direct observation, checklists, scorecards, rating scales, unobtrusive observation,** and **anecdotal records** are useful
when collecting data to be used in evaluating learning outcomes that cannot
be measured through a testing device.

Learning outcomes also can be classified into a **taxonomy** to help teachers determine instructional objectives which relate to the expected student
behavior. Taxonomies for the cognitive, affective, and psychomotor **domains**
provide the teacher with a common reference for classifying student behavior
in instructional objectives. Each domain is subdivided into categories arranged
in hierarchical order from simple to complex. The cognitive domain is con-

and concrete aspects of instruc-
objectives that direct student
of acceptable performance:

write a two-paragraph
asic growth-related

ent by using a
t and inches.
hich con-
sulting

y
ts
leans of dealing with specifics

equences
and categories

and abstractions in a field
generalizations
tructures

...erpretation
      2.30 Extrapolation
3. Application
4. Analysis
      4.10 Analysis of elements
      4.20 Analysis of relationships
      4.30 Analysis of organizational principles
5. Synthesis
      5.10 Production of a unique communication
      5.20 Production of a plan, or proposed set of operations
      5.30 Derivation of a set of abstract relations
6. Evaluation
      6.10 Judgments in terms of internal evidence
      6.20 Judgments in terms of external criteria

FIGURE 1.3. A condensed version of the taxonomy for cognitive domain (Bloom 1956, pp. 201-254)

cerned with intellectual outcomes, the **affective domain** with interests and attitudes, and the **psychomotor domain** with motor skills.

The affective domain has five levels in hierarchical order moving from "receiving" through "responding," "valuing," and "organization," to the highest category, "characterization by value or value complex." The summary outline has been placed in Appendix A. When writing classroom objectives for this domain and for evaluation of their attainment, the taxonomy should be consulted.

The psychomotor domain consists of six major levels moving from "reflex movement" through "basic fundamental movements," "perceptual abilities," "physical abilities," and "skilled movements" to the highest category "nondiscursive communication." The summary outline has been placed in Appendix A. When writing classroom objectives for physical skill development and for judging attainment, the taxonomy should be consulted.

An instructional objective may involve more than one domain or classification of behavior, but cognitive behaviors are most closely related to achievement in academic subjects and factors of cognition associated with skill development. The summary outline in Figure 1.3 of a condensed version listing behaviors in the cognitive domain (Bloom, 1956, pp. 201–254) consists of six major levels arranged in hierarchical order moving from "knowledge" to "evaluation." When writing classroom objectives for academic achievement and skill development that include a component of cognition and judgment of attainment after instruction the taxonomy should be consulted.

Objectives based on the six major levels of the cognitive domain encompass objectives which emphasize intellectual learning, problem-solving tasks, and the element of cognition associated with skill development. Discussion of the six levels follows:

1. *Knowledge* is the simplest level of complexity and requires a student to recall facts or remember previously learned material. The knowledge objective and its 12 subcategories expect the student to store and remember information.

   Illustrative behavioral terms for stating specific learning outcomes include:

choose	define	describe	identify
label	list	match	name
outline	reproduce	select	state

   Illustrative educational objectives:

   — Identify how many hundreds, tens, and ones are represented by any numeral.
   — List the names of the states and the capital of each.

2. *Comprehension,* the lowest level of understanding, involves translating material from one form or level to another. Individuals are able to change information from one form to another by restating it in their own words: The emphasis is on the grasp of meaning and intent of the material.

   Illustrative behavioral terms for stating specific learning outcomes include:

convert	defend	distinguish	estimate
explain	extend	generalize	give examples

infer	order	paraphrase	predict
rename	rewrite	summarize	

Illustrative educational objectives:

— Given a set of numbers less than 100, order them from least to greatest.
— Convert mathematical verbal material into symbolic statements.

3. *Application* requires the ability to apply abstracts and learned material in new and concrete situations. The emphasis is on remembering and bringing to bear upon material the appropriate generalizations or principles.

Illustrative behavioral terms for stating specific learning outcomes include:

change	compute	demonstrate	draw
discover	make	modify	operate
predict	prepare	produce	relate
show	solve	use	

Illustrative educational objectives:

— Solve problems using multiplication and division factors 1 to 9.
— Solve a problem which requires the computation of the area of a square given the dimensions.

4. *Analysis* requires ability to break down material into its component parts so that its organizational structure can be understood. The emphasis is on detection of the relationships of the parts and analysis between parts of a communication.

Illustrative behavioral terms for stating specific learning outcomes include:

break down	diagram	differentiate	discriminate
distinguish	identify	illustrate	infer
outline	point out	relate	select
separate	subdivide		

Illustrative educational objectives:

— Identify by sound and name the common musical instruments

(violin, clarinet, trumpet, piano, cello, French horn).

— Point out the pros and cons concerning slavery as viewed by people from the North and South.

5. *Synthesis* requires the ability to put parts together, to form a new whole which is something unique. This involves the process of combining elements or parts to develop a pattern not clearly there before. A recombination of parts or previous experience with new material is necessary for synthesis.

Illustrative behavioral terms for stating specific learning outcomes include:

categorize	combine	compile	compose
create	devise	design	explain
generate	modify	organize	plan
rearrange	reconstruct	reorganize	revise
rewrite	summarize	tell	write

Illustrative educational objectives:

— Complete a story which incorporates four of the six thoughts in the following sentences.

— Design and construct a poster to communicate three views concerning safety.

6. *Evaluation* involves the ability to make judgments about the value of material and requires a combination of elements of the other categories of behavior included in the cognitive domain. The value of material for a given purpose is included.

Illustrative behavioral terms for stating specific learning outcomes include:

appraise	compare	conclude	contrast
criticize	decide	describe	discriminate
evaluate	explain	interpret	justify
relate	summarize	support	

Illustrative educational objectives:

— Compare the number of faces, edges, and vertices of a cube.

— Critique and appraise another student's paper concerning great leaders in America on the basis of organization of the paper.

The cognitive domain is categorized by complexity from the "knowl-edge" subcategory through "evaluation," and each higher level requires attain-ment at each level beneath it. The vast number of alternatives illustrated by the taxonomy makes the teacher aware of alternative goals and objectives. There is a tendency to employ those objectives at the lower level and write fewer objectives relating to the succeeding levels. Serious attention and concen-tration are necessary to overcome that tendency and to employ higher-level categories of objectives when appropriate. Many objectives in addition to knowledge of facts should be included in the teacher's repertory of stated objectives. The illustrative behavioral terms for stating specific learning out-comes and the illustrative educational objectives facilitate the writing of behav-ioral objectives.

To be of value in the classroom, an objective must be stated specifically and include enough information to indicate what is to be accomplished, and how to determine whether the objective has been reached. Students, teachers, parents, school officials, legislators, and individuals at all levels require infor-mation to guide them in decision making. Educational objectives direct the school program and give evaluation something to use as a sounding board when judgments are being made in the educational setting.

SCHOOL PROGRAM

After the direction is clearly set by objectives, a school program of instructional activities is designed to move students toward goal fulfillment. Since development of school programs falls to the lot of curriculum specialists no attempt will be made here to cover program development. Our approach will be to develop ways to determine program effectiveness by comparing students' accomplishments to the objectives.

COLLECTION OF INFORMATION

The first major topic for our study is the collection of information, largely by testing and structured direct observation of students to support the total educational process. Collection of information becomes important as teachers and other interested persons make judgments about student progress and effectiveness of classroom instruction. A large part of *Classroom Measure-ment and Evaluation* is devoted to ways of making the data about students meaningful for evaluative purposes. The thrust is to support study of ways to do that by generating information that is reliable and valid for evaluation.

Meaningful Data

A quick reference back to Figure 1.1 reveals a feedback mechanism within the schema of the educational process. Feedback can be only as good as the information that is collected to evaluate student progress toward the goals of instruction. For this reason strong emphasis is given to generating data/information that is accurate and meaningful for evaluative purposes. Much direction is given in this book to help teachers learn how to collect meaningful data—data that are useful to inform educators how students have progressed and in turn how well the school program served the needs of students.

If information is to be useful for evaluation the data must be at acceptable levels of two important characteristics—**reliability** and **validity.** The soundness of evaluation depends on how well data-collection procedures generate consistent data and how meaningful the data are.

Reliability

The focus of reliability is on how consistent the data are. To formalize a definition:

Reliability is the consistency of observations yielded over repeated recordings either for one subject or a set of subjects.

Validity

The focus of validity is not only on the consistency of the data but also on the meaningfulness of the data. To formalize a definition:

Validity is the degree to which an observation consistently describes or quantifies whatever is being observed.

Using Reliability and Validity

As teachers collect data they plan and execute procedures to meet high levels of reliability and validity. After data collection a further check is made to see how successfully acceptable levels of these two important characteristics have been met. After study of how to plan data collection in Chapters 3 through 8 you will turn to in-depth study of these two important characteristics in Chapters 11 and 12 and ways to determine levels of reliability and validity.

An important concept to develop now is the relationship between reliability and validity, and why it is more important to give validity top attention. Data collection may generate information that is highly reliable but rates low on the characteristic of validity. It may be consistent in that the same results are generated again and again but do not have the right information. For example, a weighing scales may record the weight of a 10-pound object again and again as 9 pounds. This set of scales would generate very reliable data, but the data would not be valid. If the scales were adjusted or repaired so that readings of 10 pounds were recorded over many times then the data are both reliable and valid. As you can see, reliability is necessary to establish validity but validity goes one step further. To formalize the relationship:

Reliability is a necessary, but not sufficient, condition for validity.

In one way or another all characteristics and practices of data collection are related to the main characteristics of reliability and validity, and all procedures of data collection must be constantly checked for reliability and validity. Ways to do this for direct observation are dealt with in Chapter 3. Chapters 5–10 on test construction are directly related to building tests that generate valid data. After the necessary background of construction techniques has been covered, Chapter 11, Establishing Test Reliability, and Chapter 12, Establishing Test Validity, provide in-depth studies of how to determine the degree of success the test-builder has had in meeting acceptable levels for validity and reliability.

MEASUREMENT

The idea of measurement has been developed to such a degree that everyone interprets distances on maps, heights of mountains, capacities of containers for liquids, and reported weights of popular screen and television stars as well as professional boxers in much the same way. There is less agreement and understanding about measures of many of the human **attributes** that are important to educators. Measures of mental ability, scores on achievement tests, ratings of attitudes, levels of motivation are likely to have as many interpretations as there are interpreters. Physical attributes are easier to measure than cognitive and affective attributes, and measures for physical properties are easier to interpret.

The major reasons for the differences associated with interpretations of measures lie not only in the nature of the attributes being measured but also the level of development and degree of sophistication of instruments that are used in measurement. Another difficulty associated with understanding measurement is the many different uses of the word *measure* (Jones, 1971, p. 335). Because of ambiguity attached to a word with so many different uses, it becomes necessary to indicate what measure and measurement mean in this presentation. The noun **measure** refers to the number value obtained from the process of measurement, and the verb **measure** refers to the actual process of measurement. Proper use of the two terms:

A measure of 64 inches was obtained for John's height.
Sam measured the distance from the golf ball to the cup with a steel tape.
Debbie's teacher measured her history achievement with a paper-and-pencil test.
Debbie's teacher obtained a measure of 127 for her history achievement.

In the preceding paragraph the term *measurement* was used to clarify two different uses of the word measure. What is measurement? Basic to a full comprehension of measurement is the understanding that measurement is a way of making **observations.** For this book *measurement* is defined as:

A process that assigns by rule a numerical description to observation of some attribute of an object, person, or event.

In classroom measurement the attribute most often measured is cognitive or skill achievement. The attribute of achievement should be limited to achievement in a well-defined domain of content or a specific skill. Measurement might be as specific as measuring achievement of naming the capitals of the states or as broad as measuring how well a student reads and understands French literature. Measurement of skill is usually oriented to a specific skill but could be broadly based as in the case of measuring skill in automobile driving.

In general, an observation made by a measurement process involves a measuring instrument. Rather than making a judgment about an observation, the observer uses an instrument to **quantify** the attribute of concern. The instrument is used because of the objectivity provided by the properties of the instrument. Rather than reporting that Debbie had a high temperature, a nurse would be expected to measure the body temperature as accurately as possible with a thermometer. Rather than reporting that Debbie is knowledgeable about the Civil War period of United States history, a teacher could measure the achievement in that area as accurately as possible with a test. Both the nurse and the teacher use an appropriate measuring instrument to **observe** a particular attribute, and supply objective data for evaluation through measurement.

Objects, persons, and events as such are not measurable, but as the above definition indicates, some attribute of something is acted upon by the process of measurement. For example, a room cannot be measured. However, characteristics of length, width, volume, number of windows, and such can be expressed as measures.

Physical measurement has been developed to a high level of sophistication. As physical scientists discovered that their native senses did not permit making precise measures of size, speed, distance, and such, they took steps to extend their senses through devices called measuring instruments. Weighing scales were devised, and measurement of mass developed to a high degree of refinement. Even today the weight guesser on the midway at fairs and at the beach uses a measuring instrument as a more objective and reliable device to ascertain the precise measurement for a check on his subjective estimation of weight. Why does he use a set of scales? He uses the weighing instrument because it can quantify the attribute of weight better than he can. Why does a civil engineer use a steel tape to measure the dimensions when laying out a foundation for a building? Why do pharmaceutical companies spend large sums of money for delicate instruments to measure amounts of chemicals and drugs? These questions must seem rather inappropriate and the answers obvious. Why? There seems to be general agreement that the range and clarity of observation can be extended by utilizing specially devised and appropriately chosen measuring instruments to quantify physical attributes under study.

Associated with physical measurement is **error.** No measurement procedure produces a measure which is exact. In general, the measure is close—but how close? The answer depends on the accuracy of the instrument and the **unit** employed to report the measure. Error in measurement is not to be thought of as a mistake. Error can best be thought of as the variation produced by the inaccuracies of the measures. If an accurate measuring device is employed, the value will be within one-half of the unit used to report the results of the measurement. Physical measurement can be made more precise by reducing the size of the measuring unit. The more accurate the instrument and the reading of the instrument, the less variation associated with physical measurement and in turn the less error.

The units used in physical measurement by their nature are approximate. The basic unit of the metric system—*the meter*—is at best approximate. When defining a meter, it becomes difficult to determine where it begins and where it ends. At one time the meter was defined as the distance between two tiny marks on a piece of platinum stored in a bank in France. This definition seems all right until you inspect the marks under a microscope. The tiny marks now look wide enough to be crayon marks. Where does the mark begin and end? Another difficulty is differences in temperature and their effect on the metal. There are other uncertainties. Nevertheless, physical measurement seems to be quite acceptable for general use and functions well in the everyday world; however, ordinary good sense is needed to overcome some definite shortcomings of physical measurement.

Classroom Measurement

A human being cannot be measured, but the properties of achievement, height, weight, motivation, creativity, and such can be described by assigning numerals which indicate differences in the attribute being measured. In general, the numerals carry with them quantitative meaning, and as used in the educational setting, measurement supplies accurate information not attainable in other ways.

Measurement of human **constructs** has the same shortcomings as physical measurement. In fact, the doubt associated with the uncertainties of measurement in these areas is greater than that of measurement in the physical sciences. The greater doubt about measurement in psychology and education is based on two factors.

First, the attributes being studied are more difficult to conceptualize and in turn to define. Physical attributes are more visible and open for agreement by observers about what they are than are those attributes most closely associated with the classroom. Definitions and measurement for attributes such as achievement, motivation, creativity, and aptitude require that a construct be created to explain something that cannot be observed with the natural senses. This makes agreement about what the attribute is more difficult. A construct, assembled with sense data to explain some aspect of human behavior, may not enjoy the same degree of agreement about its nature that some more visible physical characteristics would. For example, motivation must be explained in actions before motivation becomes a meaningful construct. Since constructs are created without physical form, they may mean different things to different people.

Second, the instruments used to measure constructs have not been developed to the refinement level of devices used to measure physical characteristics. The relatively low level of scientific precision for psychological and educational measurement demands additional ordinary good sense to overcome shortcomings of those measurement procedures. It is difficult to arrive at agreement as to what a given construct means as well as to find a set of operations that will isolate and define the characteristic to be measured.

Measurement as Quantification

The assignment of numbers to attributes of objects, persons, or events is made to point up differences in amount. The question asked is basically how much or how many. How much height does Lynne have? How much spelling (or history, physics, etc.) achievement does Lynne have? How many record albums does Lynne have? How many free throws can Lynne make in one minute? Answers to these questions require that determination be made about the amount of something. The operation of quantifying—**quantification**—gives answers to questions like these.

Before the assignment of numbers to attributes, there must be a clear understanding of what is to be measured. Associated with physical, educational, and psychological measurement is the interpretation of what the measures mean. For example, some agreement must be made about how relative size is to be interpreted. How is size defined? How can a decision be made when comparing two individuals—Dave and Dan?

Name	Weight	Height
Dave	154 lbs.	70 ins.
Dan	184 lbs.	67 ins.

Which boy is larger?
Is Dave larger than Dan?
Is Dan larger than Dave?

The dilemma presented in these questions (each of which has no *one* right answer) is based in the idea of quantification. A football coach would probably say that Dan is larger while a basketball coach would probably say that Dave is larger. Common agreement could be obtained if a particular attribute were associated with larger. Either of the questions—

Which boy is taller? or
Which boy weighs more?

should be answered the same by everyone. The agreement results from common understanding of "tall" and "weigh."

Rich and Daniel were arguing about which state was larger—Alaska or Texas. Rich said that Alaska is larger because it has more square miles. Daniel said that Texas is larger because it has more people. Rich said that there could be no agreement about who was right until they decided what "larger" meant. Daniel agreed and said that a decision must be made about quantification before the dilemma could be resolved.

Two of the aspects of measurement are: (*a*) *decide* what is to be measured, and (*b*) *define* what is to be measured. When decisions about how to quantify something have been made, these two aspects should be clear enough for general interpretation about what is being measured. With common understanding of what is to be measured and a clear definition, interpretation of the measures can be made.

Quantification also involves two distinct aspects. First, the attribute must be defined, and second, a device must be constructed to measure it. A unique property of most educational measuring instruments is the definition of the attribute (what) by the procedures of measurement (how). Measuring instruments explain operationally what is being measured. This property of an **operational definition** is especially valuable when a descriptive *word* definition is too general to explain the property adequately to allow for its measurement. A paper-and-pencil test used to measure history achievement will define history achievement through the tasks demanded from the test taker. As will be seen later, this is a very important property of educational measuring instruments.

Measuring Units

A unit of measure for physical measurement provides a vehicle that allows equality throughout a measurement scale. Any centimeter equals any other centimeter by a direct proof. Some other measurement instruments establish equality by an **isomorphic** definition. For example, equal increases in temperature any place on the scale of the thermometer result in equal increases in the expansion of a column of mercury. If an increase of temperature from 15°C to 25°C results in an increase of one centimeter in the length of the mercury in the tube, any other 10-degree increase (say 75° to 85°) will result in an increase of one centimeter in the height of the mercury column.

Measuring devices for educational and psychological attributes rarely, if ever, have units that allow the property of equality between pairs of measures the same way that centimeters and degrees can. Use of a test to measure nonphysical characteristics, those which are not directly observable, involves an assumption. It is assumed that all tasks are equivalent or, in other words, each task completed is equal to any other task that is presented to the person whose trait is being measured. Accompanying the assumption is a concerted effort to create conditions to meet the assumption. The tasks on a spelling test are chosen so that the assumption is met as nearly as possible. A spelling list appropriate for a typical fourth grade class would not include both "cat" and "encyclopedia" with the assumption that they are equally difficult to spell. The list would include a range of difficulty for words to be included, but compared to the total range of difficulty for all of the words in the dictionary, the range of difficulty of the words on the test would be relatively small. Quantification of spelling achievement by counting words correctly spelled permits a definition of amount, but equivalence of tasks is not established beyond the assumption and efforts of the constructor of the measuring device to supply equal tasks.

None of the human characteristics of importance to the educator can be measured with the soundness of physical measurement, because establishing correspondence to some external reality is highly unlikely. However, sharp definitions and highly valid measurement devices can provide valid information about characteristics which are important to the educational process.

Tests as Operational Definitions

An *operational definition* gives meaning to a construct by specifying in terms of tasks what attribute is being measured. Examples of operational definitions are:

> *Popularity* is determined by the number of choices each member of the group receives from the peer group when each is asked, "Whom would you like to have as a partner for the science project?"
> *American History Achievement* is determined by the number of correct answers the student receives on the *Cooperative Social Studies Tests: American History,* Grades 10–12, Form A.
> *American History Achievement* is determined by the number of correct answers the student receives from the following true-false test devised by the teacher.

Although general agreement about whether the test is or is not a good operational definition may be difficult to obtain, the tasks on any true-false test or other testing device define for the reader what the test maker believes is important in order to demonstrate the attribute being measured. For example, a score on the *Cooperative Social Studies Tests: American History,* Grades 10–12, Form A, or a score on the teacher-made true-false test is a measure of American history achievement in operational terms of successfully completed test tasks.

Educators need to develop classroom tests which reflect accurate measurement of the content areas and learning skills desired. This can be accomplished only if the test maker has a good understanding of the content area and strives to build tests that are good definitions of what they *should* measure. Teachers must strive to make the tasks on their tests represent a sample of what is considered to be important to exhibit significant aspects of the trait being measured. A social studies teacher who has taught a unit on the Civil War may have as a major goal the student's development of a thorough understanding of the relationships of political, economic, and societal aspects of the conflict. For a test to reflect the objectives in these terms, the test's tasks must require the student to respond with understanding about the relationships. A test that asks the student to tell what happened on 25 different dates between 1859 and 1865 provides an entirely different operational definition of achievement over the Civil War period.

Teachers of Civil War units may have somewhat different ideas about what outcomes they desire. Differences in objectives will result in differences in measuring devices. Each classroom teacher should strive to make tests better operational definitions of what is to be measured. In addition the test should fit closely to what other academicians in the tested area feel is important.

The thrust of this book is toward ways to develop for the classroom teacher better quantification procedures (measurement) and to improve the interpretation of measures of students through teacher judgments (evaluation). Even teachers with an excellent command of the subject matter may have difficulty developing tests which represent good definitions of the trait to be measured; however, the command of subject matter is assumed before good testing practices can be initiated.

Although educational test scales may always leave something to be desired and quantification procedures may fall short of what is ideal, classroom teachers can overcome basic problems of classroom measurement by developing skill in test planning and item writing. Skill in selecting **published tests** is also necessary for comprehensive classroom measurement programs. There are also nontesting techniques which should be considered equally valuable in providing information for educational evaluation.

EVALUATION

Historically the terms *measurement* and *evaluation* have been used loosely and, at times, interchangeably. A distinction is made in contemporary educational literature. Evaluation has been broadly defined (Stufflebeam, 1971) as:

> the process of delineating, obtaining, and providing useful information for judging decision alternatives. (p. 15)

According to Thorndike and Hagen (1977, pp. 1–5), measurement provides only information such as a test score and not the judgment of insight which is required for reaching a sound conclusion or plan of action. The judgment of insight is to be considered as the set of evaluative procedures used to interpret information into an appraisal.

Robert Ebel (1979) clarifies the difference between "measurement" and "evaluation":

An evaluation is a judgment of merit, sometimes based solely on measurements such as those provided by test scores but more frequently involving the synthesis of various measurements, critical incidents, subjective impressions, and other kinds of evidence. (p. 376)

In practice, evaluation is specific in terms of function and each type of evaluation uses this general definition in a special way. Common to all evaluation is the use of adequate information to make judgment about someone or something.

Each of these interpretations points out that judgment and introspection are necessary when evaluating. One should clearly understand that evaluation goes beyond measurement, measuring, and measures. To formalize the definition:

Evaluation is the continuous inspection of all available information concerning the student, teacher, educational program, and the teaching-learning process to ascertain the degree of change in students and form valid judgments about the students and the effectiveness of the program.

Focus of Evaluation

In making decisions about students and questions concerning the effectiveness of the educational program, the school, and its personnel, it is necessary to: (*a*) identify and formulate the goals, (*b*) select and devise tools for measuring progress toward the goals, (*c*) employ the tools to quantify, and (*d*) formulate judgments based on the results obtained. The last element comprises the evaluative process. For example, at the end of the fourth-grade two students could be performing at the fourth-grade level in mathematics. At the beginning of the year one student was at the third-grade level and the other at the second-grade level. Does our evaluation of the students' progress and the outcomes mean the same thing? No, because one student progressed at an above average rate and the other at the expected rate. The example illustrates how evaluation utilizes all data but goes beyond terminal measurement.

Evaluation aids the decision maker who is concerned about all aspects of the educational endeavor. The key point to consider and keep in mind is that evaluation involves appraisal in view of particular goals or purposes. Useful information may be obtained for evaluation procedures by both formal and informal means and should include information collected during instruction as well as end of the course data. Evaluation during an ongoing program is referred to as **formative evaluation** while terminal evaluation is called **summative evaluation.**

Purpose of Evaluation

Why evaluate? It is natural to want to determine the degree to which goals are being reached and evaluation procedures do this. Students, teachers, administrators, parents, and the public labor toward student achievement of educational objectives and they wish to see if the goals are reached. In addition to assessment for the direct benefit of the student, another major purpose of contemporary evaluation is to provide relevant information which decision makers need about inputs, outputs, operations of programs, and placement of students in programs. Levels of understanding can be assessed and future educational objectives set based on student needs. Appropriate activities can be planned by the teacher based on the knowledge of the attributes of the students and their achievement of objectives which have been set for them. Formation of objectives, selection of content, and planning for learning experiences appropriate to student achievement can be facilitated. Clues may be obtained about all aspects of the teaching-learning process and student learning supported and teaching guided by continuous evaluation.

Educational decision making utilizes evaluative judgments to make valid choices when developing school programs. Continued thrusts will be oriented toward making sound educational decisions concerning the entire academic endeavor. Public pressure has been applied to educators to report to the public what they are attempting to accomplish within the educational enterprise and accountability continues to be a controversial topic in education. The process of gathering and interpreting information concerning the effectiveness of our schools is a necessary response to public demand. Blaine R. Worthen and James R. Sanders (1973) stated that evaluation is one of several little-used but widely discussed processes in educational systems. The role and use of evaluation has become increasingly important as attempts to make educational systems accountable to their publics expand at a rapid pace. When large sums of federal money have been invested in curriculum projects, the funding agency has required that the projects be evaluated and that directions of the programs be within the guidelines of the funding agency. Legislative bodies at both national and state levels have authorized funds to be employed for evaluating the effectiveness of educational programs. New evaluation units are being established in many public schools, state departments of education, and institutions of higher education while more writing and discussion of evaluation appear in educational circles.

It is difficult to identify how educators are meeting the needs of students and society, since a general consensus has not been developed in regard to what education is to encompass. This leads to the question, "What aspects of education can educators control?" If this question can be answered satisfactorily, movement in the direction of professional educational responsibility will be made.

For the student, evaluation provides feedback regarding strengths and weaknesses and as a fringe benefit should encourage good study and increase motivation. This feedback is made possible by the teacher communicating the goals of instruction to students prior to instruction so that the goals will allow the student opportunity to see where instruction and associated learning are directed. Improvement of the teacher's teaching and the students' learning through judgments using available information is the ultimate function of the evaluative process.

Types of Evaluation

To clarify further the concept of evaluation, some educators have divided evaluation into formative and summative aspects based on how the results are to be used. This separation resulted from thrusts to understand the evaluation process better, and to expand and organize knowledge of evaluation as a systematic problem-solving effort when choice-making is called for.

Formative evaluation is used to provide information for curriculum review, identification of the effectiveness of the instructional process, and assessment of the teaching process during the period of instruction. Formative evaluation takes place during the forming stage and provides for analysis during the learning process. Formative evaluation facilitates curriculum construction, improves teaching, and supports learning. As applied to the school curriculum, short-term evaluation is provided during the development of the total curriculum. In the case of evaluation of the teaching process, which may be the main intent of formative evaluation, continuous feedback provides the teacher and the student with a basis for instructional changes and learner progress. The teacher and learner can detect on a day-to-day basis, over a teaching unit or short period of time, those areas which need further or different instruction.

Summative evaluation is used to ascertain the degree to which the larger outcomes have been obtained over a substantial part of or all of a course and is a cumulative terminal judgment. The purposes of summative evaluation are the assignment of grades; certification of skills, knowledges, and abilities; prediction of success in subsequent courses; and to provide an initiation point of instruction in a subsequent course, feedback to students, and comparisons of outcomes of different groups. Description of the level of achievement at the close of a semester or academic year would be summative in nature. When determining whether or not the learner has achieved the objectives set in advance, the summative concept of evaluation is employed. Grades given over an entire course and reported to students and parents are examples of outcomes of summative evaluation. The most prominent use of summative evaluation as related to the classroom is the use of test results and other information as bases for assigning grades (Bloom, Hastings, & Madaus, 1971, pp. 66–68). A summing process is required where judgments are made concerning the terminal or semiterminal nature of the evaluation.

As applied to the curriculum, formative evaluation is employed in building a curriculum whereas summative evaluation is used to evaluate a completed curriculum. Bloom et al. (1971, p. 28) state that the distinction between the concepts of summative and formative evaluation is not clear-cut; and furthermore, the main difference is not in the amount of content covered, but in the purpose of the evaluation. Therefore, a terminal evaluation is referred to as summative while an evaluation of an ongoing program is formative, although either process has the functional goal of determining the worth or merit of something.

Evaluation, whether formative or summative, by necessity includes consideration of a great variety of evidence in addition to the usual terminal paper-and-pencil examination scores. Meaningful judgments must be based on a wide base of information generated by tests spaced throughout instruction, direct observation, unobtrusive observation, anecdotal records, checklists, scorecards, rating scales, **rankings, mechanical instruments, conferences, written assignments,** or terminal examination. Evaluation is an aid to clarification of the significant objectives of education as well as a process for determining the extent to which students are developing in desired ways. Improvement of teaching and of students' learning occur through acquiring and processing all evidence available. Because questions of whether the teaching-learning process is effective and what changes may be needed are determined through evaluation, teachers must realize the tremendous influence evaluation has on the lives of their students, and it should not be taken casually or lightly. Teachers must also be cognizant of the variety of sources and methods for gathering information about students and the total educational process to allow for valid judgments and, in turn, valid decisions about students and programs.

RELATIONSHIP OF MEASUREMENT AND EVALUATION

The two elements of measurement and evaluation tell how effective the school program has been and refer to collection of information, appraisal of students, and assessment of programs. These are most directly related to our study. Much information about the educational process is collected through measurement that quantifies human attributes by administration of tests. This procedure collects data directly from the objects of concern—the students. Other information is collected from students by nontesting procedures. Information provided by testing and nontesting procedures is best thought of as the material to be used in the evaluation process.

All *measurement* involves deciding what is to be measured, defining what is to be measured, and translating what is to be measured into symbolic representation. The major function of all measurement in schools is to describe student attributes through objectively obtained quantification. **Educational measurement** deals primarily with characteristics closely related to achievement. Other important characteristics of the classroom scene such as intelligence, emotion, and personality are dealt with in **psychological measurement.** Much, but by no means all, of the information is collected through the use of tests. Data from measurement plus information collected by direct observation and other nontesting procedures supply the input for evaluation.

Evaluation includes any set of procedures designed to determine how well the school program moves students toward educational goals and in turn how well their needs are met. *Student evaluation* uses information about a particular student to appraise individual growth. *Program evaluation* uses all available information about the students to make judgments about school program effectiveness. A characteristic of evaluative techniques is the disciplined inquiry made into a question based in the need to choose among alternatives. The evaluator takes all information available as raw materials and through a logical process develops an assessment that is credible. Evaluation may best be thought of as the determination of the worth of something. Evaluation is also used to assign **marks,** and for grouping students for instruction, counseling, and guidance. **Diagnostic evaluation** and formative evaluation give the classroom teacher opportunities to adjust the school program to meet student needs. **Instructional evaluation** gives the teacher the opportunity to reflect on total program effectiveness during teaching and after the educational sequence is completed.

The major function of evaluation is to take all information about students and form a judgment using a set of objectives as a sounding board. Although the process itself utilizes the logical structure mentioned before, subjective judgment is implied when an evaluation is made.

Most educators, as well as parents and other taxpayers, feel that any attempt to educate children or adults is incomplete without discerning how well the school does what it is supposed to do. Sound decisions are also needed to direct further educational activities for students and educational evaluation becomes an integral part of the educational process. To summarize the presentation so far, let us take a look at the answers to the question:

Why should educators go beyond merely providing a school program based on sound educational objectives? The reasons are to:

1. aid in the forming stages of learning,
2. evaluate accomplishments of students at the end of an instructional sequence,
3. evaluate effectiveness of school programs, and
4. make rational, valid decisions about future school programs.

Specific decisions should be based on functional judgments provided through proper evaluative procedures that use a wide information base.

SUMMARY

Direction of student learning through appraisal is important if students are to gain an understanding of what is expected of them. Professional educators strive to improve their skills and understanding of the evaluation process as they relate to their students individually and collectively. The importance of measurement and evaluation has developed as they contribute to valid educational decisions.

Functions of measurement and evaluation point out differences and relationships of measurement and evaluation in an educational context. The discussion of physical measurement developed an understanding of measurement in general and the difficulties inherent in measuring with the accuracy and soundness desired. The nature of measurement procedures associated with human attributes of concern to educators—motivation, achievement, and similar human characteristics—magnifies difficulties associated with physical measurement.

The assignment of numbers to indicate differences involves two aspects of quantification—a definition of the characteristic and development of some device to measure it. Major emphasis on classroom measurement is directed toward overcoming problems associated with needed definitions and construction of test instruments to measure achievement. Test constructors are encouraged to consider the tasks on each test instrument as giving an operational definition of the trait being measured. Measurement has been defined as:

> a process that assigns by a rule a numerical description to observation of some attribute of an object, person, or event.

Evaluation in contemporary educational literature is associated with judgments to aid in decision making. Evaluation has been defined as:

> the continuous inspection of all available information concerning the student, teacher, educational program, and the teaching-learning process to ascertain the degree of change in students and form valid judgments about the students and the effectiveness of the program.

Evaluation is considered as establishing the worth of something in view of specific aims. Although evaluative procedures appear to be much the same, a distinction is made in how the judgment is used. Direct feedback into an ongoing program is referred to as *formative evaluation* while a terminal judgment is called *summative evaluation*. The emphasis of the difference is how the judgment is used.

Educational objectives serve to give direction not only to program development but also to direct data collection and support the evaluation process as a systematic problem-solving effort used when choice-making is called for.

NEW TECHNICAL TERMS LISTED IN THE GLOSSARY

Accountability	Evaluation
Affective domain	Formative evaluation
Anecdotal record	General education objective
Attribute	Instructional evaluation
Behavioral objective	Instructional objective
Checklist	Isomorphic
Classroom test	Marks
Cognitive domain	Measure (noun)
Conference	Measure (verb)
Construct	Measurement
Diagnostic evaluation	Mechanical instrument
Direct observation	Objective
Domain	Observation
Educational measurement	Observe
Educational objective	Operational definition
Error	Physical measurement

Psychological measurement
Psychomotor domain
Published test
Quantification
Quantify
Ranking
Rating scale
Reliability

Scorecard
Summative evaluation
Taxonomy
Test
Unit
Unobtrusive observation
Validity
Written assignment

ACTIVITY EXERCISES

1. Write an operational definition for each of the following:
    a. Achievement
    b. Intelligence
    c. Mathematics achievement
    d. History achievement
2. For each of the following general objectives write two or more behavioral objectives. Check against the five elements from Appendix B.
    a. Develop reading comprehension
    b. Use a dictionary
    c. Learn the multiplication facts
    d. Learn to use a hammer (or other tool)
    e. Understand the Constitution
3. State objectives for a unit of instruction for a course you are preparing to teach. State the subject and grade level.
4. Throughout this book the focus is on how teachers use measurement and evaluation to support student learning in the classroom. While engaged in this study you may want to expand a topic or read about a current question in education that relates to this study. Select from the following, using personal interest or need. Read throughout the semester and write a synthesis that reflects contemporary views or present status.
    Accountability
    Competency based testing
    Criterion-referencing
    Evaluation in kindergarten
    Evaluation in a subject area
    Mastery learning/testing
    Minimal competency testing

    National Assessment of Educa-
        tional Progress
    Norm-referencing
    Use of the Buros *Mental Meas-
        urements Yearbook* series
    Using standardized tests
    Other topic of interest or need

FOR DISCUSSION

1. Explain in general terms how each of the topics, *measurement* and *evaluation,* relates to the other four components of education.
2. Why is a distinct statement of specific objectives important as the basis for planning measurement and evaluation?

3. Your use of classroom time to administer a test has been challenged. Defend the use of classroom time to administer a test as a data collection device.

4. As a teacher of United States history you have administered a test over the Civil War period. Discuss how administration of a test can be considered as a process of quantification.

5. As a classroom teacher how do you view evaluation as contributing to the classroom instructional program?

6. Explain how sets of objectives at the national, state, regional, and local levels can help a classroom teacher establish goals for students.

REFERENCES AND KNOWLEDGE EXTENDERS

BLOOM, B. S. (Ed.). *Taxonomy of educational objectives: The classification of educational goals, Handbook I: Cognitive domain.* New York: David McKay, 1956.

BLOOM, B. S., HASTINGS, J. T., & MADAUS, G. F. *Handbook on formative and summative evaluation of student learning.* New York: McGraw-Hill, 1971. Chap. 2, pp. 19–42; chap. 4, pp. 61–80; chap. 6, pp. 117–138; Appendix, pp. 271–277.

EBEL, R. L. *Essentials of educational measurement* (3rd ed.). Englewood Cliffs, NJ: Prentice-Hall, 1979. Chap. 1, pp. 1–14; chap. 2, pp. 18–31.

HARROW, A. J. *Taxonomy of the psychomotor domain: A guide for developing behavioral objectives.* New York: David McKay, 1972.

HOPKINS, C. D., & ANTES, R. L. *Classroom testing: Administration, scoring and score interpretation.* Itasca, IL: F. E. Peacock, 1979. Chap. 3, pp. 41–59; chap. 7 and 8, pp. 112–147.

HOPKINS, C. D., & ANTES, R. L. *Classroom testing: Construction.* Itasca, IL: F. E. Peacock, 1979. Chap. 1, pp. 1–15; chap. 8, pp. 165–179.

JONES, L. V. The nature of measurement. In R. L. Thorndike (Ed.). *Educational measurement* (2nd ed.). Washington, D.C.: American Council on Education, 1971. Chap. 12, pp. 335–355.

KEARNEY, N. C. *Elementary school objectives.* New York: Russell Sage Foundation, 1953.

KRATHWOHL, D. R., BLOOM, B. S., & MASIA, B. B. *Taxonomy of educational objectives: The classification of educational objectives, Handbook II: Affective domain.* New York: David McKay, 1964.

NATIONAL EDUCATION ASSOCIATION, COMMISSION ON REORGANIZING SECONDARY EDUCATION. *Cardinal principles of secondary education.* Washington, D.C.: U.S. Office of Education, 1918. (Bulletin No. 35)

NOLL, V. H., & SCANNELL, D. P. *Introduction to educational measurement* (3rd ed.). Boston: Houghton Mifflin, 1972. Chap. 1 and 2, pp. 1–44.

STUFFLEBEAM, D. L. (Ed.). *Educational evaluation and decision making.* Itasca, IL: F. E. Peacock, 1971.

THORNDIKE, R. L. Educational measurement for the seventies. In Robert L. Thorndike (Ed.). *Educational measurement* (2nd ed.). Washington, D.C.: American Council on Education, 1971. Chap. 1, pp. 3–14.

THORNDIKE, R. L., & HAGEN, E. *Measurement and evaluation in psychology and education* (4th ed.). New York: John Wiley, 1977. Chap. 1, pp. 1–22.

WORTHEN, B. R., & SANDERS, J. R. *Educational evaluation: Theory and practice.* Worthington, OH: Charles A. Jones, 1973. Chap. 1 and 2, pp. 1–39.

Chapter 2. Integrating Testing with Instruction

After study of Chapter 2, you should be able to:

1. Identify the relationship between appraisal and the instructional program.
2. State what information is needed from students to assure effective appraisal.
3. Discuss diagnosis as it relates to individual learners and its place in an instructional sequence.
4. Define formative evaluation.
5. Define summative evaluation.
6. Differentiate between formative and summative evaluation as each is used to integrate testing with instruction.
7. Discuss what is meant by *testing fluidity* and *data-collection fluidity*.
8. Explain how each glossary term listed at the end of the chapter is used in classroom measurement and evaluation.

A historical examination of the American educational institution from Colonial days to the present reveals that the central purpose of education has been to foster literacy. In recent years some individuals and some groups of citizens have viewed the school as being able to solve social and economic problems. As these problems remained or worsened they blamed the schools. Conflicts about the purpose of education and related school activities have led to questioning whether education is serving the needs of the present set of students. In addition, questions about the place of testing in schools have been raised. Few of these questions relate to testing that supports learning, and the influence of testing on teaching is likely to receive the continued attention of both teachers and testing experts, as they use measurement and evaluation to support decision making within the classroom.

Literacy comes about when students are able to read, write, manipulate symbols mathematically, and develop independence in making decisions and establishing courses of action. Happiness, life adjustment, morality, and economic gain cannot be considered as goals of education but they can come about as students become literate. They may be goals for students but still not be direct purposes for the process of education. Unless the educational institution remains basically single purpose—fostering cognitive learning—the worth of education will be questioned. The contribution of a high level of cognitive functioning to each of the other goals places literacy as means to an end rather than an end in itself. The contribution of testing lies in its support of the instructional programs established for students.

As you know, educational testing serves many purposes. Some of those purposes do not directly foster literacy in the students who take the tests. For example, tests are given to supply data to compare effectiveness of different schools, evaluate results of experimental programs, establish norms for **standardized tests,** and meet state/federal requirements for evaluative reports. Testing that does not make a direct contribution to the *literacy of those who take the test* should be held to a minimum. Testing for **appraisal, diagnosis,** formative evaluation, or summative evaluation can be supported for the contribution it makes to student literacy through educational diagnosis and guidance of those who take the tests. Integration of testing with instruction must be done where instruction takes place—in the classroom. Careful examination of this kind of testing reveals that the focus is on students as individuals or collectively as classes.

This discussion of integrating testing with instruction is based on the postulates: (*a*) the purpose of the schools is to promote student literacy, and (*b*) testing can support learning. Furthermore, testing should be subordinate to, but provide support for, the gain students can obtain from classroom instructional sequences. This is accomplished when the classroom teacher uses testing to aid in diagnosis and guidance of further instruction. In general, there is far too little combining of the knowledge about measurement and the collection of pertinent student data with the betterment of instruction. There is a need for measurement people to become more knowledgeable about instruction and for instructional people—teachers and curriculum developers—to become more knowledgeable about how measurement and evaluation can support student learning. The contribution of measurement to instruction, and in turn to student literacy, depends largely on how well each procedure of information collection fits with the information the teacher and student need to make sound decisions about how to proceed in teaching and learning.

The idea of integrating testing with instruction is not new. The topic was presented as early as 1939 by Purnell and Davis as they wrote about using classroom tests to direct learning. In 1951 Tyler pointed out that:

> Educational measurement can have a profound influence in the improvement of instruction; but to do so, it must be viewed as an integral part of instruction, its planning must go hand in hand with instructional planning, and the results must be used continuously to guide the planning and development of curriculum. (p. 64)

Now, more than 30 years later, teachers have too little help to guide their efforts to make testing an integral part of the everyday classroom program;

nevertheless, many are able to make the connection through good teaching. Although emphasis is being given to development of general guidelines for testing in mastery learning and the referencing of tests to criteria is better understood, the need to adjust for a specific situation leaves many decisions to the classroom teacher. The integration of testing with instruction is individual and classroom specific. The rest of the chapter centers around using testing for appraisal, diagnosis, formative evaluation, and summative evaluation as they support student cognitive learning.

APPRAISAL

"You have to take each child where he is." This often-repeated phrase by elementary school teachers also applies to the other levels of the educational process. Even at the doctoral level, committees of faculty members direct a student's study to degree completion by an individually designed course of study. The first step is to ascertain the student's educational and professional experience and with that information tailor a course of study designed for a specific individual. In varying degrees teachers from preschool through graduate school are called on to make appraisal of their students to direct an educational sequence.

Many questions arise when a teacher meets a new set of students. What can they do? What do they know? What does Mary know? What can Billy do? Formal determination of needs and informal appraisal serve to establish a basis from which to build. Depending on the decisions to be made, data collection might be as simple as giving a five-minute quiz on the addition facts or the administration of a standardized reading readiness test, or as complex as a full-blown individual appraisal of cognitive, affective, and psychomotor functioning.

Appraisal must be complete because many factors affect cognitive learning and they must be considered. Teachers can best judge what information they need because they have preconceived notions about where students should be at the conclusion of an instructional sequence and how that status is to be reached. Information needed about students includes:

1. present knowledge level. (What the student knows.)
2. present skill level. (What the student can do.)
3. performance of prerequisites.
4. understanding the mechanics of tasks.
5. capability.
6. personality factors.

With this information the teacher can: *(a)* specify what instructional or skill development procedures to implement, *(b)* establish the level of expected development, and *(c)* establish ways to ascertain when the development is considered as complete.

The input information for appraisal can come in part from professionals outside the classroom—school psychologists, counselors, other teachers—but for the most part the data will come from efforts of teachers as they collect data in the classroom. Information from outside the classroom is likely to be from formal testing using standardized instruments and interpretations of outside professionals, or cumulative records that contain test results and teachers' observations. Within the classroom, structured observation and informal observation provide current information about students.

Data from standardized tests can compare an individual with peer group performance using **norms,** or they can compare performance in one area with performance in other areas. In either case what a standardized test measures must be fully understood by the teacher, and the data interpreted with the idea of establishing a student's present status to insure a more effective instructional program.

Teacher appraisal in the classroom is used to establish student status when no published test is available to provide needed information. Informal classroom appraisal uses procedures that range from general observations made on a day-to-day basis to a complete case study of a student. Many techniques can be used to establish a level of performance for a student on a task, skill, or level-of-concept development. Appraisal can be made, for example, from information about whether or not a student has adequately completed a task, or has met a criterion level set for a series of tasks.

The procedures used should identify present student needs and status and point up for the teacher where instruction should begin and the direction instruction should take. Use of **norm-referenced** tests will separate performances of individuals to allow the teacher to order and discriminate levels of the performances. Use of **criterion-referenced** tests allows the teacher to identify specific skills that the student has and those that the student lacks. With such appraisal information the school program is developed for individual, small group, or classroom instruction.

After the information is collected the next consideration should be given to translating it into instructional objectives. In an ideal situation each student has a set of educational objectives. In real-world classroom situations a teacher has from 15 to 25 or more students and managing a set of objectives for each student becomes difficult. Usually some adjustments are made—not in the overall instructional objectives but in the way they are to be reached.

Given a set of objectives the next consideration is to establish an appropriate set of practical and manageable classroom strategies. The type of instruction to be implemented may also give further direction to how objectives are to be written. For example, individualized instruction in fourth-grade mathematics directs the writing of very specific objectives while in a junior high school science class the objectives would be expected to be more broadly based. In sum, the appraisal must mesh with the writing of objectives and the selection of the type of instruction that is planned. At the same time appraisal information can direct the type of program that can best foster learning. If used as intended, appraisal supports learning and facilitates teaching by evaluating student behavior for entry into an instructional sequence.

DIAGNOSIS

When working with a student in an ongoing instructional sequence the teacher needs to identify learning difficulties peculiar to that learner. In this sense diagnosis is appraisal but it is used here to refer to the determination of specific difficulties and deficiencies in learning during instruction. Diagnosis is most commonly used in reading or mathematics but other areas have need for feedback that pinpoints specific difficulties. Diagnostic use of tests requires information about what difficulties each student is experiencing. Although diagnostic materials may be administered to a group or an entire class the diagnosis is applied individually. In this way diagnosis gives direction to decisions about needed remediation.

The purpose of classroom diagnosis is to allow the teacher to meet specific learning needs of students. After completion of a learning sequence, remediation allows specific teaching to overcome any deficiencies pointed up in diagnosis. It is not enough to know that a student is unsuccessful as a reader. To effect remediation requires more specific data. For example, a student may have a satisfactory reading rate but have poor comprehension of material read. If the teacher knows this, instruction can be directed to increase comprehension. Or a student may be having difficulty using the division algorithm. Diagnosis of a few division problems attempted may point up the problem of multiplying the divisor by the trial digit for the quotient. If this specific problem is uncovered in diagnosis and corrected in teaching the rest of the process of division by the algorithm may be no problem for the student. If there is further difficulty another deficiency may be identified by further diagnosis.

Corrective teaching requires not only a teacher who understands the learning processes, is able to apply diagnostic techniques, and can develop appropriate learning experiences to overcome any learning difficulty, but also one who can recognize when clinical help is needed. A learning deficiency may be caused by a factor other than instruction. For example, a student may not be able to learn because of a physical, psychological, or social handicap. Physical handicaps may be apparent but a teacher must also be familiar with symptoms of poor hearing or vision, and any symptoms that indicate physical illness. Psychological or social bases of a problem may need a specialist from one or both of these disciplines to support remediation of an identified deficiency.

In most cases what a classroom teacher needs to expedite diagnosis are practice exercises and tests that can point up when a student can or can not complete a task and indicate the specific barrier to noncompletion. Diagnostic procedures are so diverse and specific to the topic of study that coverage here is impossible. In addition to their own materials teachers can find standardized **diagnostic tests** for many subject areas listed in the *Mental Measurements Yearbook* (Buros, 1978) series and in *Tests in Print III* (Mitchell, 1983).

When constructing or selecting a diagnostic test the teacher should keep in mind that the student should supply the responses rather than select them. Other considerations are:

1. Procedures should be such that student weaknesses will be revealed.
2. Weaknesses that have been uncovered must be confirmed by further observation by the classroom teacher.
3. Diagnostic tests are not intended to indicate a level of overall proficiency. If a standardized diagnostic test reports norms they can be used the same way that norms for a survey test are used.
4. Errors made by students must be analyzed to isolate the cause or, if the deficiency is complex, the causes.

When developing or using diagnostic materials for the classroom the teacher must strive to get as accurate an estimate of the students' levels of learning as possible and to isolate any deficiencies. For elementary school teachers this means devising material specific to the topic being taught. The purpose of each diagnostic checkup must be clear before the test or informal technique is administered. Many skills, e.g., reading and spelling are closely related and particular care is needed to generate data that will, indeed, identify any deficiency. Within a subject the type of errors may direct the teacher to identify one deficiency that is to a great extent responsible for difficulty in learning. For example, a speech disability or mispronunciation could be the cause of a large portion of spelling errors. Either inability to use phonics skills or overdependence on phonics may be the underlying cause of poor spelling. When isolated, the deficiency can be attacked by remediation through further corrective instruction.

Secondary school teachers should also be prepared to administer diagnostic tests to their students and also identify specific deficiencies informally. Inability to successfully meet objectives in a course in United States history could be the result of one or more of several deficiencies. Poor background in physical geography, poor reading skills, poor reading comprehension, lack of cultural opportunities through travel, disinterest, no personal reward are only a few of the possible reasons why history achievement may be low. When the deficiencies are identified for an individual, the teacher may be able to deal with the difficulty on a one-to-one basis or if the difficulty is spread widely through a class it could be dealt with at the class level. By grouping students with like problems, remediation can be carried out for subsets of a class.

The teacher's art in teaching, to a great extent, incorporates much diagnosis on a day-to-day basis of conducting the ongoing classroom instruction. The contribution of diagnostic materials is their ability to do what direct observation may not be able to do. What a good diagnostic test can do is provide information for forming a hypothesis about why a student has failed to learn and direct decisions for remediation of a deficiency by corrective teaching. Use criterion items to find out if an objective has been reached. Use diagnostic items to find out why the objective has not been reached. Most diagnostic tests incorporate both of these functions by using criterion items that have diagnostic components.

Computer programs written for instruction can often incorporate diagnosis as a part of the learning sequence. As this new technology is more widely used, teachers and students will benefit from the great capability of the computer to give direction for remediation in specific difficulties in tightly structured subjects such as reading and mathematics. As supplements to regular classroom instruction, new technologies may be able to incorporate new knowledge of human learning processes to allow the adjustment of the rate and style of teaching to each specific learner and to the particular difficulties each student encounters.

FORMATIVE EVALUATION

Many tests are designed to ascertain whether one or more educational objectives have been accomplished within a learning sequence. A criterion-referenced test of this type incorporates appraisal not as a starting point for instruction or diagnosis but to identify where instruction has been successful and learning accomplished and where intended outcomes have not been met. Some diagnosis may be extracted from the results of the test but the emphasis for tests that supply information for formative evaluation lies in their determination of attainment of objectives. Decisions about further instruction can be based on information about success in the preceding instruction. In general, formative evaluation is conducted over small bodies of content or a specific skill.

To serve in formative evaluation the conditions established in test items and the performance required of students must correspond with the conditions and behavior called for in the objective. The operational definition established by a test or a set of test items should tie directly to an educational objective or a clearly defined domain of content. Using test results as feedback, teachers are able to modify instruction, undertake remediation, or introduce prescriptive teaching as needed. The principle of formative evaluation is to test with a criterion-referenced instrument over small units to permit analysis of each student's performance in order to direct further individual instruction. This is somewhat different from the use of quizzes or tests of progress used as motivation or for assignment of marks.

By connecting the number of errors on an item to its related objective a teacher can identify where further instruction is needed. Tabulation of the errors can be done quickly by placing student response sheets side by side and counting incorrect responses for each item by the group. Further analysis of *what* incorrect responses were given is helpful in directing further instruction. Analysis by proportion of students who miss an item can help identify whether errors are student centered or instruction centered. If a large portion (teachers decide criterion for a "large portion" as some point, say 60 percent) have missed the item the difficulty is likely to be found in a deficiency of the instructional sequences, or maybe a concept that is too difficult for the developmental level of the students. Assuming the latter is not the case a different approach in teaching is employed to explain the ideas in new ways. Results of tests that connect items directly to objectives are also used to direct curriculum development for other sets of students by altering instructional procedures and rearranging the content.

Given a well-constructed criterion-referenced test over a small unit of material the teacher, after administering the test, analyzes the results. If only a few students have errors in responses to an item, correction is based individually. If a large portion erred then correction is made by group instruction. Correction could also be by subgroups of students who missed a specific set of items. Corrective teaching should begin as soon as possible and when completed another criterion-referenced test administered. By structuring the process very tightly (Bloom, Hastings, & Madaus, 1981; pp. 174–176) classes are organized as mastery-learning classes, but formative evaluation is a tool for integrating testing with instruction in any structure of teaching.

The question of how many items should be used to test for objective attainment arises. If the action or performance is open to view by direct observation one example of performance may be enough. Consider the objective:

> When supplied with a set of tools the student will be able to remove the spark plugs from an eight-cylinder automobile and replace them with a set of new plugs with proper torque on each plug within 20 minutes.

One example of performance would be enough to check for objective attainment. If the objective were written differently the performance under test conditions would probably be different. For example, an objective could be written the same as the one above with one exception. The phrase "an eight-cylinder automobile" could be replaced with "any 1985 General Motors car." One example of performance is no longer enough because of the differences in the many models of GM cars produced in one year. Should the student be tested for each GM model for all makes? Should attainment be assumed if the spark plugs of four randomly selected GM models are replaced satisfactorily? The objective could be written with different conditions—e.g., the student could be required to select the correct wrench the first time, within two tries, within three tries. . . . Look to the objective statement and match the item to the action of the objective. The way the objective is written will to a great extent direct the testing. Enough examples of performance are needed to sample the actions and conditions supplied by the objective. Operationally the teacher makes the final decision about the size of the sample of student performance.

Where the action is not directly observable, the level of minimum acceptance of the objective should give directions about expected proficiency on test items in reasonable terms. The objective may set conditions as: "with no errors," "with 90 percent accuracy," or some logically derived proportion of possible test items. This "range of stimulus conditions" (Mager, 1973) is also used when a student is to perform the same thing under different conditions, or engage in different performances under the same conditions. An objective directs the writing of an item and each item must be tied to an objective. To answer the question of how many items to use: The teacher must write as many items as are needed to sample the range of action and the range of conditions. The teacher as a subject-matter expert can decide how many items are required to ascertain that a student has reached objective attainment. Most standards of school achievement must be set by classroom teachers; however, a standard itself may be determined somewhat subjectively.

The frequency of testing in the forming stages of learning is determined by how instruction is broken down. At times a test may be needed for one lesson and at other times a test may cover a chapter in the textbook or the material covered over a specific time period. Ideally the test would be given at natural breaks in the instructional sequence. The time between tests should be spaced so that deficiencies can be readily and quickly remedied. Testing in formative stages is usually frequent and by necessity specific. To improve testing, tests for formative evaluation must be designed specifically for the purpose for which they are used and those who use them need to know when to use a norm-referenced test and when to use a criterion-referenced test.

Of particular interest to testing in the forming stages is the recent progress in information-handling technology that utilizes computer capabilities. In addition to allowing increased individualization of instruction at all levels computer capability allows a testing component to be incorporated in an instructional sequence. The use of computers for test scoring and to construct tests from item banks to be given at a later time are mature fields. The use of computers to monitor students and direct instruction from student responses is more recent and not yet widely used in classroom instruction. When the computer is used testing can be easily integrated with instruction.

The revolution in the technology of information-handling is giving the public school many devices useful for instruction. In addition to the instruction element of programs is the component of testing. Computer use allows further integration of testing with instruction. By combining a sophisticated computer and a video tube the personal computer becomes a learning aid when programmed for instruction. By adding the element of computer-aided diagnostic and performance testing, data are generated for formative evaluation.

As the demand for better tests to serve formative evaluation increases, teachers will be called upon to work closely with experts in psychometrics, psychologists, other experienced teachers, and curriculum developers. Continued cooperation between schools and colleges to establish the needed integration of testing with instruction will develop principles needed to make testing more and more a tool of learning. Tyler & White (1979) says:

> It [program of research, test construction, and pilot studies] can accomplish in the next 20 years what was done for sorting tests in the 20 years following World War I. We need this intellectual guidance in order to derive the potential benefits of testing as a tool of learning. (p. 46)

In the meantime each teacher can do much to use "testing as a tool of learning" by continuing to be informed about how to build good tests and utilize reports from the literature, supporting staff, and pilot studies to make testing support instruction during the forming stages of learning.

SUMMATIVE EVALUATION

Many tests are designed for assessment of the larger outcomes of an extended instructional sequence over an entire course or a large part of it. A test of this type may serve one of several purposes but has no intended component of feedback for formative evaluation or diagnosis. Often-mentioned uses of summative tests as they relate to the students who took them are:

1. report a student's overall achievement.
2. licensing and certification.
3. appraisal for a starting point in a following grade or course.
4. prediction of success in related courses.
5. assignment of marks.
6. report overall achievement of a class.

If these uses of test information seem familiar to you it is probably because most tests that have been given were summative in nature. Any use of summative test data to direct learning or for diagnosis would be in addition to the major purposes given above.

The diverse purposes of test data for formative evaluation and test data for summative evaluation preclude the use of one test for both evaluations. It has been tried but the combination of the two violates the spirit of one or the other if not both. It is not recommended procedure; however, commercial test publishers have marketed tests that they feel serve both evaluation systems.

Tests for summative evaluation are also useful for a loosely structured subject where satisfactory progress could be at one of several levels of achievement or for a part of a larger scope of subject matter. For example, social studies courses tend to be less sequential than say mathematics or reading courses and are not structured as tightly.

When assigning marks or giving feedback about the degree of success in a course a component should be a measure of the student's overall achievement. Although any mark or report should be based on a wide base of information, summative test results should be included as a part of those data. Depending on the philosophy of the school or teacher the summative test can be either norm-referenced or criterion-referenced; however, the norm-referenced test seems to be more appropriate as a terminal indication of success unless the information is for certification, licensing, or appraisal for beginning instruction in a subsequent course or a new class. Then criterion-referencing may be in order. A score on a norm-referenced test can point up for a student the level of achievement attained in the context of group successes, and seems to be more appropriate for a large block of subject matter and wide coverage of behavior.

If a terminal test is to be used as a determining factor in certification or issuance of a license the test is most likely criterion-referenced. Since the test is to dichotomize a population into those students who qualify and those who do not, the **table of specifications** must have specific behavior/content cells that match with on-job performances. Anything less is invalid for the intended purpose of the test.

As students move from one elementary school class to the next grade level, new teachers can gain general information about them from end-of-the-year test scores. Certain appraisal information can be gleaned from scores on cumulative records and should be used as general indicators of where students are in their learning. More specific information is needed to locate points for beginning instruction unless there is a continuing system of individualized instruction from grade to grade. Secondary teachers, however, will rarely find use for test scores to determine initiation points for instruction since the division of subject matter is clearly defined in the course title and description.

If there is a close relationship between the course being completed and a following course, the terminal test score for the first may be used to predict the degree of success in the second. Since end-of-course tests are not designed to predict, prediction from those tests may have little meaning except that those students who do well in one study tend to do well in other courses. If prediction is particularly important a prognostic test should be located or developed.

Although results of summative tests given in a classroom serve varying intents their major purpose is to give each student an overall indication of how objectives were met. By combining the test scores summative evaluation procedures also can be used to judge the effectiveness of the school program. For our purposes the concern will be for a classroom instructional program, not a schoolwide curriculum. The assessment of the worth of the classroom program requires that judgments of quality and value be made.

The best way for the classroom teacher to make a judgment of effectiveness of a program is to make an accounting of how the class as a whole met overall and specific objectives. If successful formative procedures feed back into instruction then successful corrective teaching will support a successful program. Also, given the operational definition of the instructional objectives, the degree of overall attainment is measurable and should reflect the worth of the classroom instructional program. The major contribution of summative evaluation to better instruction is the data that can be used to ascertain the effectiveness of the overall instructional program. Decisions about needed changes in the curriculum can be directed largely through evaluation of how well the previous school program served to meet the objectives set for the students.

Summative evaluation also allows the teacher to reflect on the objectives of instruction. Were the objectives obtainable by these students? Were the objectives defined clearly enough to serve as a sounding board for achievement? Although some reflection is in order, the writing of objectives must continue to be in regard to meeting the needs of students.

OTHER TECHNIQUES

When integrating testing with instruction the teacher must make testing a part of the ongoing natural classroom milieu. To paraphrase the term *methodological fluidity* (Jones, Bagford, & Wallen, 1979, p. 1) what is needed for a teaching-testing system envisioned here is data-collection fluidity. "Methodological fluidity refers to the ability of the instructor to better serve students' subject matter needs" (p. 1). The same can be said for testing fluidity or data-collection fluidity. In all cases teachers need to vary strategies given different classroom situations, subjects, or students.

In addition to utilizing a variety of test strategies a well-rounded data collection plan will also include qualitative information from as many sources as possible. This seems to be one of the greater challenges for teachers and supporting professionals during the next several years. In addition more information is needed about why responses were wrong—not merely which responses were wrong. Data that allow a listing of specific methodological errors are much more valuable than data that allow only a listing of incorrect responses.

SUMMARY

The primary function of evaluation in the classroom is to improve learning by supporting the instructional program. Evaluation supports the goal of literacy for students in four ways: *(a)* It aids in assessment of students' abilities and needs through *appraisal.* This information is useful in proper placement of students in learning sequences, or for initial placement of a student in a new study. *(b)* It aids in identifying specific deficiencies in student learning through *diagnosis.* This information allows for prescriptive teaching to overcome learning difficulties. *(c)* It assists in keeping track of student progress during instruction through *formative evaluation.* This information is used to direct further learning for students during the instructional sequence. *(d)* It allows for judgments about the effectiveness of instruction through *summative evaluation.* This information is used to look back on materials and procedures of instruction to see how the program met its intended effect of moving students to attainment of the objectives. Development of student literacy is enhanced by provision of valid evaluation information that further sound decision making for individual and classroom instruction.

These four processes are applied somewhat differently according to the instruction plan—conventional, mastery, individual, or such—but each of these needs a firm informational base. The next chapter begins the study of data collection to support well-grounded educational evaluation and in turn sound decisions for students individually or as classes.

NEW TECHNICAL TERMS LISTED IN THE GLOSSARY

Appraisal	Diagnosis
Criterion-referenced	Diagnostic test

Norm   Standardized test
Norm-referenced   Table of specifications

ACTIVITY EXERCISES

For each of the instructional decisions listed below state how data may be obtained for effective evaluation and valid decisions.

a. The needs of a set of students in reference to the subject(s) to be taught.
b. Grouping for effective learning.
c. Student readiness for a next learning experience.
d. Extent that students are attaining the minimal essentials of a course.
e. Extent that students are progressing beyond the minimum essentials of the course.
f. Point where review would be beneficial.
g. General learning difficulties students are encountering.
h. Specific learning difficulties students are encountering.
i. Which students are underachievers.
j. Students to be referred to special classes or remedial programs.

FOR DISCUSSION

1. Explain how diagnosis can be used to support learning in an ongoing instructional sequence.
2. Contrast the uses of formative evaluation and summative evaluation to integrate testing with instruction.
3. State the relationship between appraisal and the instructional program making clear which is antecedent to the other.

REFERENCES AND KNOWLEDGE EXTENDERS

BERK, R. A. (Ed.). *Criterion referenced measurement: The state of the art.* Baltimore: Johns Hopkins University Press, 1980.

BLOOM, B.S., HASTINGS, J. T., & MADAUS, G. F. *Evaluation to improve learning.* New York: McGraw-Hill, 1981.

BUROS, O. K. *The eighth mental measurements yearbook.* Highland Park, NJ: Gryphon Press, 1978.

CRONBACH, L. J., & SNOW, R. E. *Aptitudes and instructional methods.* New York: Irvington, 1977.

GLASER, R., & NITKO, A. J. Measurement in learning and instruction. In R. L. Thorndike (Ed.). *Educational measurement* (2nd ed.). Washington, D.C.: American Council on Education, 1971. Chap. 17, pp. 625–670.

JONES, A. S., BAGFORD, L. W., & WALLEN, E. A. *Strategies for teaching.* Metuchen, NJ: Scarecrow, 1979.

MAGER, R. F. *Measuring instructional intent.* Belmont, CA: Fearson, 1973.

MANN, P. H., SUITER, P. A., & McCLUNG, R. M. *Handbook in diagnostic prescriptive teaching* (2nd ed.). Boston: Allyn & Bacon, 1979.

MITCHELL, J. V., Jr. (Ed.) *Tests in print III.* Lincoln: University of Nebraska Press, 1983.

POPHAM, W. J. *Criterion-referenced measurement.* Englewood Cliffs, NJ: Prentice-Hall, 1978.

POPHAM, W. J. *Modern educational measurement.* Englewood Cliffs, NJ: Prentice-Hall, 1981.

PURNELL, R. T., & DAVIS, R. A. *Directing learning by teacher-made tests.* Boulder: University of Colorado, 1939.

TYLER, R. W. The functions of measurement in improving instruction. In E. F. Lindquist (Ed.). *Educational measurement.* Washington, D.C.: American Council on Education, 1951, pp. 47–67.

TYLER, R. W., & WHITE, S. H. (Ed.). *Testing, teaching, and learning: Report of a conference on research on testing.* (HE 19,202: T28). Washington, D.C.: DHEW/NIE, 1979.

WALLACE, G., & LARSEN, S. C. *Educational assessment of learning problems: Testing for teaching.* Boston: Allyn & Bacon, 1978.

Chapter 3. Using Observation in the Classroom

After study of Chapter 3, you should be able to:

1. Discuss the nature of observation and how it is used differently in artificial and natural situations.
2. Identify the strengths and weaknesses of direct observation.
3. Construct checklists, scorecards, and ratings scales.
4. Make entries into anecdotal records and perform unobtrusive observation.
5. Explain how direct observation can be supplemented by mechanical instruments, classroom tests, and published tests.
6. State why testing is considered an observational procedure.
7. Summarize reliability checks and validity checks for direct observation.
8. Explain how each glossary term listed at the end of the chapter is used in classroom measurement and evaluation.

Instructional objectives direct the choice of strategies for a school program and provide a sounding board for evaluation of that program. Information used in evaluation to ascertain students' progress and the effectiveness of the school program must come from observation of the central figures of the educational institution—the students. The input information (data) for evaluation is collected by observing students individually and collectively. Teachers observe their students; teachers make observations; teachers collect data about students through observation.

For our purposes observation has two meanings. Observation can mean that the teacher is collecting information. In this usage of the term *observation* is a *process*. The term observation also refers to a fact or bit of information that has been collected about the student. In this usage of the term *observation* is a *product*. The use of the term will be clear in context. Any observation (the product) used as a basis for evaluation results from observation (the process). Since a classroom teacher is concerned with a wide range of student characteristics, an observation (product) may be generated by one of several procedures of observation (process). For example, the two facts that Debbie has red hair and Debbie scored 73 on a history test are generated by two different observational procedures. The first observation of hair color being red is generated by direct observation. The second observation of 73 on a history test is generated by test administration.

Historically, crude observation of physical characteristics was first used to gather certain information about an individual. Belief that a certain physical characteristic indicates a certain personality trait seems to be a part of our heritage. A receding hairline is viewed as an indication of high intelligence, a square chin as a mark of fortitude, and everyone knows that a heavy person is pleasant—or is it lazy? There is little, if any, scientific evidence to support the idea that physical appearance provides reliable clues about traits of personality, aptitudes, or achievement in school subjects.

Observation in the classroom must reach much farther than physical observation. Since observation provides the means to collect data, procedures must be developed to make all observation as objective as possible. It must probe deeply for information about constructs important to success in school. As more refined observational procedures developed, educators had more meaningful data to work with. Continued refinement of observation is important to help teachers learn as much as possible about students. Present behavior is observed to indicate effectiveness of previous instruction, reveal current status, and aid in predicting future behavior. Teacher observation must be organized so that information collected supports sound judgments formed in evaluation and, in turn, valid decisions about future education of the students and the classroom curriculum.

Observation is a natural part of the interaction process and occurs whenever people get together. Teachers observe students and students observe teachers. The approach to the study of observation in this chapter will be to discuss those principles of observation that have maximum potential for furthering the educational process and student educational growth.

THE NATURE OF OBSERVATION

The type of observational procedure used in data collection varies according to the nature of the characteristic being measured. The carpenter observes the length of a board by placing a steel tape directly on the board. The chemist observes (measures) the weight of a chemical by weighing it directly on a balance scale, and milk at the dairy is packaged into gallons, quarts, and pints by direct allotment. The educator deals with many attributes such as achievement, aptitude, and motivation of human beings that do not allow for direct observation.

For our purposes, observational procedures include: *(a)* direct observation and use of devices to aid direct observation—checklists, scorecards, rating scales, unobtrusive observation, anecdotal records, mechanical instruments, and *(b)* use of devices to measure—classroom and published tests.

Observation of students is made in a variety of environmental circumstances and may be recorded or unrecorded. Most classroom observations that teachers make in day-to-day schoolroom events are unrecorded and are interpreted and acted upon in a few seconds. It logically follows that an element of good teaching is the ability to make, interpret, and act on unrecorded observations. Recorded observations originating from direct observation and testing procedures are also important for reference by students, teachers, and others when total appraisals of students and assessments of school programs are being formed.

Sense Data

Although "to see is to believe" is considered as fundamental, simple optical illusions demonstrate that interpretations can vary. Distortion of figures and drawings that appear curved when they are straight, longer than they actually are, or out of proportion occurs within the psychological framework or mental set of the observer. (Figure 3.1 shows examples of drawings that appear to be distorted.) Another type of optical illusion appears to change before one's eyes without any change in the drawing. A set of stairs which appears to change direction, or two faces looking at each other which may lose that relationship and become a vase are examples of this type of optical illusion. Life-size illusions have been created where all objects in a room appear to be the wrong size. To see this may depend on knowing that a child is smaller than a man regardless of how far away he is and other relationships of size. This type of illusion is more psychological than visual.

These illusions point up the fact that sometimes our senses cannot be trusted directly. Steps must be taken to objectify observation by extension of the senses and improvement in the use of the senses. Scientists in all disciplines have seen the need to structure direct observation carefully and to overcome some of the limitations of direct observation by use of **instrumentation** and

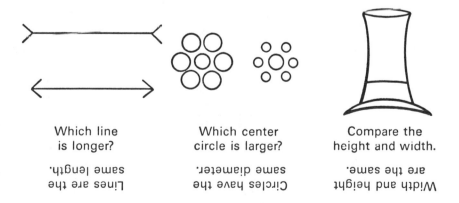

Which line is longer?	Which center circle is larger?	Compare the height and width.
Lines are the same length.	Circles have the same diameter.	Width and height are the same.

FIGURE 3.1. Illustrations of optical illusions

establishment of rules for observational procedures. The classroom teacher needs the same kind of help and practice in the collection and interpretation of information about students.

A mere look at the phenomena within a schoolroom will generally not reveal what is relevant. Observations must be created with purposeful direction if they are to generate data for making sound judgments. If the teacher wishes to determine how well a student is achieving in a subject, the data gathered should relate to topics about that subject—not about social adjustment, speed of reading, attitude toward the principal, or achievement in other subjects. A frame of reference establishes a system for interpretation. For example, a test for physics should measure only factors associated with physics. Reading skills, psychological factors, achievement in other subjects, luck in responding, or scoring should not be major contributors to the test scores. Systematically planned observation provides the needed frame of reference for interpretation of the results.

Educational data-gathering procedures for collecting observations are designed to overcome difficulties in interpretation when only sense data are used by:

1. Objectifying direct observation through a structure of rules.
2. Instrumentation.

Nontesting procedures are most helpful in building objectivity into direct observation while tests are the most widely used measuring instruments for classroom observation.

Artificial or Natural Situation?

The classroom is a unique situation. Nowhere else will you find such a combination of circumstances. For this reason the environment for collecting information about how students perform may be less than ideal if the classroom is used as a place to observe. When generalizing from the classroom to the real world an implied assumption is made—the student will perform in the real world the same way as in the classroom.

Natural situations should be used whenever possible to make observations. Natural situations exist within the educational setting, and the teacher should take advantage of them whenever possible. For example, the kindergarten teacher who has set the objective of students being able to put on their outer clothes without help has the natural situation for observation within the classroom routine. Whether a student has learned to tell time also can be observed within the classroom as can attainment of many other objectives.

Attempts to ascertain how a student will perform in natural situations from actions in an artificial situation such as the classroom may or may not be entirely satisfactory. The driver education course includes objectives devoted to maintenance, troubleshooting, and handling emergencies as well as maneuvering an automobile. A 50-item multiple-choice test on how to change a tire could be used to measure how well a person would actually perform if required to do so on an interstate highway, but a better way to judge would be to ask the student to change a tire on a car. Given the same tools, the student could probably do as well if the change had to be made on the road. However, road conditions would not be exactly the same as those at the time the tire was changed at school. A student may be able to multiply fractions on a test but still not be able to apply the needed mathematics to solve a problem in the real world. The assumption associated with gathering data in an artificial situation and generalizing to the natural situation must be considered.

Home economics, industrial arts, business, and physical education have areas for learning where nearly natural conditions for observation may be created. Subjects like history, English literature, philosophy, and psychology are difficult to structure for observation in the natural situation.

If a natural situation does not exist for observation, near natural conditions can be set for some data collecting. The attainment of skill and physical development objectives can often be observed under conditions much like the real world (see Chapter 4 under "The Classroom Situation"). If a business letter is to be written, conditions much like a typical office can be created for the composition of the letter. Any office, however, will have its own peculiarities of setting, overseers, and physical arrangement. These differences may or may not change the behavior of the student. The degree to which the assumption that the student will do the same under both conditions is met determines the degree of usefulness of the data.

Although students use the English language in the classroom, objectives directed to development of acceptable language usage and observation of how a student uses the language require more than a paper-and-pencil test. All people have more than one language which they use—golf course or tennis court language may be quite different from in-school language. Students may also have an in-school language and an entirely different going-home-from-school language. Observation for objectives devoted to usage of correct English may be difficult to manage, and the assumption may not be met to a high degree because of the differences in conditions.

Objectives and Data-collecting Procedures

Part of the planning of observational procedures must take place while the educational objectives are being formulated. When stating the objective, the conditions of observation and the type of data to be produced are clearly stated.

The direction of the relationship between objectives and data-collection procedures is important to the contribution of measurement *and* evaluation to the total educational process. Objectives are set first. Only after the goals have been determined should the educator look for ways to reach them and ways to determine how successful students have been in attaining goal fulfillment. When writing objectives, the many observational techniques must be considered to choose the most appropriate form of observation for each stated objective.

Educational objectives employed to state general learning outcomes allow the use of nonaction verbs such as "knows," "applies," "appreciates," "understands," and "analyzes." Gronlund (1970) suggests that the broad objectives are the instructional objectives that guide education in general. While these terms are adequate for their purpose of giving general direction to the educational process, they do little to aid in evaluation.

When general outcomes have been indicated, a list of student behaviors that exemplify the specific objective should be listed. Then the corresponding observational device or procedure is chosen to provide appropriate data. The sequence is: first, the broadly based instructional objective, second, the specific desired learning outcomes, and last, the selection of the proper way to look for examples of the indicated behavior through observation.

EFFECTIVE CLASSROOM OBSERVATION

Since "seeing is in the eye of the beholder," perceptions of individuals and situations may vary among observers. Although informal observation may be helpful, formal observation permits a structure for study of behavior and performance not possible with informal observation.

Teachers have used observation of students to aid in drawing conclusions and making decisions for many years, but they have taken relatively little advantage of the contribution that systematic and controlled observation can make. Observation is valuable because proper use of it permits the educational process to serve the needs of students better. The teacher observes students in a wide variety of situations, and if these observations are well planned out and structured, the quality and value of the information increases. Structured observation needs: *(a)* a frame of reference, and *(b)* a recording scheme appropriate for whatever is being observed.

Teacher observation is used to determine the *needs* of students which can be attended to in the classroom. Using professional knowledge and observation of relationships of cause and effect, educators set *objectives* to direct students by listing educational objectives to serve identified student needs. Professional experience and further observation allow the teacher to develop a relevant and meaningful *program* to meet educational objectives. Without discounting the importance of informal observation previously mentioned, structured observation is most valuable in education as judgments about students' progress and school program effectiveness are made.

All facts needed to make judgments are collected by some form of observation, and the judgments themselves come from evaluators' observation and interpretation of the data. From the beginning of data-collection procedures to the final evaluation, measurement and evaluation people rely on several ways of observing to guide them to sound judgment by using both tests and nontesting strategies to gather observations.

Direct Observation

When using direct observation something or someone is monitored without any intervening factor. Direct observation allows the actions to speak for themselves in a natural way. Although the human element of interpretation sooner or later becomes involved, a natural setting for studying behavior offers the best *opportunity* to obtain meaningful data. The best way to find out how well a student uses the English language is to observe his language in a number of natural settings. To determine how well the kindergarten pupil has conceptualized the principle of one-to-one correspondence, ask the child to decide how many cartons of milk will be needed for the class at lunchtime. Direct observation can be carried out at almost any time and proves to be quite versatile; however, as will be pointed out, there are practical difficulties associated with collecting data this way.

Although some school subjects allow a near natural setting for classroom evaluation, the teacher usually is required to base evaluation on data collected in an artificially created environment. The business teacher can establish a situation much like an office to find out how well a student can prepare a typewritten report. However, the artificially created scene is different from an operating office, and each difference works to lessen the validity of the data. Likewise, vocational and home economics teachers find opportunities to create an artificial situation very close to natural conditions.

Each time data are collected special efforts should be made to see that the situation is as near to a natural one as possible. Anytime an artificial situation is used in place of the natural situation the data collector assumes that the information gathered is the same as would be obtained if the observation were made under natural conditions.

The process of direct observation requires that the observer be trained to know what to look for and to control for the **halo effect.** Several devices are available to assist the observer. They focus attention on important aspects of behavior, supply appropriate data, and increase the quality of that data.

Strengths of direct observation

Direct observation has the following strengths:

1. Allows action to speak for itself
2. Can be carried out at almost any time
3. Is versatile
4. Allows a record for future interpretation
5. Provides for direct comparison over time
6. Is useful with nonreaders, young children, and the mentally handicapped
7. Identifies the level of skill development
8. Permits for direct feedback and immediate redirection of learning
9. May be less threatening than some other types of data collection

Direct observation allows a record of what actually happened to be made. The data can be generated to avoid rationalizations and artificial presentation. When looking for behavior change, direct comparisons can be made over a time span. If objectives have been stated in terms of observable behavior, certainly some of them will be apparent in direct observation. Varying quantities can be determined, and change over time can be ascertained.

When an individual is limited in ability to communicate through language, direct observation may be the only means of collecting needed data. Direct observation is especially valuable with very young children, nonreaders, and severely mentally retarded persons, and is appropriate in determining the level of skill development. Probably the best way to find out how well a student can read orally would be to observe that student performing the task. Skills like welding, sewing a garment, tying shoes, counseling clients, and others can be appraised through direct observation of performance. Direct observation supports immediate changes in the school program and redirection of student learning. This feature is especially helpful in formative evaluation where judgments are made in an ongoing program for benefit of those in the program.

Relative to other ways of collecting data, direct observation may be less threatening. This would be especially true for those students who may feel intimidated by a testing situation. On the other hand some students might be more threatened while under the eyes of someone considered to be an authority figure.

Weaknesses of direct observation

Direct observation has the following weaknesses:

1. Is time-consuming
2. May be too expensive
3. May not be possible until after the student has left the classroom
4. May use supplementary devices which alter natural, ongoing events
5. May reflect observer biases

In spite of its strengths some very practical considerations place limitations on the use of direct observation. To determine how learning in a course in educational measurement and evaluation is being implemented in the classrooms of inservice teachers, the course instructor could observe or have an observer view each class member over a one-month period of time to see how classroom procedures compare with acceptable techniques. Obviously this is going to take too much time and money to be practical. Some compromise must be made. Classroom teachers at all levels find it impractical to gather all their data for all students on all topics by direct observation because of the cost in time and money.

Another limitation is associated with objectives that relate to future performance—possibly after the student has left the classroom. For example, attainment of objectives of developing responsibility as an adult citizen can be investigated only after the student becomes an adult if the teacher waits for a natural situation for direct observation.

If observation requires that something be added to the scene (a movie or television camera, a human observer, or such), the question of how that addition changed the behavior is never clearly answered. Introduction of a new person or instrument to the natural situation alters that situation. If the classroom teacher or other familiar person makes the observation without noticeable change in procedure, then little if any effect would be expected. If two television cameras with an operating crew are introduced into the classroom scene, considerable change in classroom phenomena may be noted. The observational data thus obtained must be carefully screened for effects of the change, because major changes may invalidate the collected data.

The possibility always exists that a human observer may knowingly or unknowingly generate biased data. Although the former is not likely, the human elements that could unconsciously bias the data are ever present. Following sections give special emphasis to direct data collection so that the mentioned limitations of observation by human beings may be largely overcome.

AIDS TO DIRECT OBSERVATION

Just as the physical scientist uses **devices** to extend his senses for direct observation (microscopes, radar and sonar beams, oscilloscopes, and the like), classroom teachers use devices to aid direct observation of students in the school settings. The need to use devices rests in the limitations associated with the senses of the human being whether that person be a scientist, educator, or other observer of phenomena. The attention can then be focused on specific attributes that escape observation through the natural senses. The following sections may introduce the reader to new ways to structure classroom observation or may bring to mind tools which have not been utilized as much as they should have been.

Checklist

A device that organizes observation by listing relevant items grouped in categories is called a checklist. The categories contain lists of behaviors, traits, or characteristics to be observed. The arrangement is usually in the order that occurrences are expected to happen. Space is provided after each item for recording the presence, absence, or frequency of occurrence of the expected happening.

Systematic observation utilizing a checklist to observe a student requires that a frame of reference be established and a recording scheme developed. One student should be observed at a time, and a checklist should be available for each student.

Consideration should be given to each of the following points when constructing a checklist:

1. Specific points to be observed are listed.
2. The order of the list should be in the expected sequence of actual happening.
3. The reaction can be made by a tally mark or check.
4. Space should be provided for compilation of the data on the checklist itself.

As an illustration a description of play could be categorized into six activities as follows:

_____1. Unoccupied behavior
_____2. Solitary play
_____3. Onlooker behavior
_____4. Parallel play
_____5. Associative play
_____6. Cooperative play

The observation can be standardized across observers by further description of the categories. For example, the six activities may be described as:

_____1. Sits quietly doing nothing while others play
_____2. Plays by self when others are not around
_____3. Sits with other children but only watches them play
_____4. Plays well next to another youngster but separately
_____5. During play talks with other child but does not choose the same play activity
_____6. Plays with children with cooperative behavior and mutual activity

Observation of play could be recorded in regard to amount of time the child devoted to each type of play or could be recorded as the number of occurrences of each type. The checklist should be constructed to fit the manner of recording that was chosen—either by time or by frequency of occurrence.

Use of the checklist allows a quick recording and should help to avoid overlooking relevant phenomena. It can be used for a simple action such as determining a student's control for writing movements. Five movements and a measure of knowledge about them could be organized in a checklist as presented in Figure 3.2.

Given objectively defined categories, the recorded data are high in objectivity, and the system gives a uniform classification to the information. If more than one person is observing, the checklist should be designed to control for between-observer differences or for the same-observer differences from one time to another. For direct observation the checklist allows the teacher or instructor to look at all of the parts and subparts of the phenomenon. Thus, the observer has a grasp of the total picture, the interrelatedness of the separate parts, and meaningful information for basing evaluation. The checklist in

_____	Draws vertical lines
_____	Draws sharp peaks
_____	Draws wavy lines
_____	Draws circles
_____	Draws half-circles
_____	Reproduces different shapes at the teacher's request

FIGURE 3.2. Checklist of control for
writing movements

Figure 3.3 was developed to aid an instructor of a physical education class to observe a student of tennis. Checklists are especially helpful in keeping a record of an ongoing event which would lose its continuity if stopped for discussion. The record can then be referred to at a later time. All classrooms have aspects of instruction involving a continuous sequence, and teachers can find uses for checklists in all grades and subject areas.

DIRECTIONS: Below are definable aspects that are important to successful volley return. Check each one for each volley for one set. Determine the percentage of attainment for the set.		Percentage
Number of volleys	1̸ 2̸ 3̸ 4̸ 5̸ 6̸ 7̸ 8̸ 9̸ 1̸0̸ 11 12 13 14 15 16 17 18 19 20 21 22 23 24 25 26 27 28 29 30 31 32 33 34 35 36 37 38 39 40 41 42	
Racket in FRONT	𝖳𝖧𝖫 ///	80
Racket head HIGH	𝖳𝖧𝖫	50
Knees BENT, but head UP	𝖳𝖧𝖫 /	60
LEAN or STEP into shot	𝖳𝖧𝖫 ////	90
Keep racket head moving FORWARD	𝖳𝖧𝖫 //	70
Watch the ball CONTACT the racket face	///	30
NO FOLLOW-THROUGH	𝖳𝖧𝖫 𝖳𝖧𝖫	100
BE AGGRESSIVE	𝖳𝖧𝖫 ///	80

FIGURE 3.3. Checklist for volley returns in tennis

Checklists provide the recorder of ongoing events with a way to keep up with happenings. The use of the checklist avoids making judgments while an observer is actively engaged in observation, thus making this a particularly effective device for the classroom. Classroom teachers find that a checklist can facilitate direct observation and generate well-organized and objective data if care and skill are used in preparation.

Scorecard

A device that extends the concept of a checklist to include a weighting of each aspect rather than merely noting a presence or absence of detail is called a scorecard. In general, a scorecard supplies a total score for the subject being considered allowing a comparison with established standards. The worth of a scorecard can be found in analysis of the components that make up the total rather than the total itself. Scorecards have limited use in the classroom but may be valuable if no other device can give the desired data or a standard is needed for comparison. Scorecards are most often used to gather data about school buildings, school programs (see Figure 3.4), accrediting schools, selection of textbooks, and other complex situations.

Scorecards which are more directly related to observation of students are discussed in Chapter 4. Classroom teachers find a scorecard especially useful in evaluating **products** of students. The complexity of a product can be broken down into observable components and each component assigned a weight. When the product is being assessed for quality, each component will be judged and a point value assigned on the scorecard. The total number of points is then assigned as the measure of quality.

Schoolroom uses of the scorecard are most valuable when the observation is of a particular complex undertaking. The overall procedure can be observed through a weighting of important facets to the total outcome. Where a weight should be given to aspects in regard to their relative importance a scorecard can extend the principle of the checklist. For example, the apparatus which has been set up for a chemistry laboratory experiment could be scored in this way to indicate the overall probability of completing the experiment. A classroom teacher could use a scorecard to aid in determining the ability of a new reading program to serve the needs of specific students.

Rating Scale

A rating scale is a device that permits an observer the opportunity to record the intensity or degree of impressions made while observing a subject or setting. Scaling is used in informal conversation such as, "Place that car on a scale of 1 to 10," or "Rate that brunette on a scale of one to eight." The teacher can find many opportunities to collect information from students by the use of scales. A second use of scaling allows self-rating by a subject on perceptions or impression of self. Self-reports are widely used in psychological measurement where personal attributes are of concern.

Score Card Summary Sheet (Continued)

Division IV—Program (Activities)	Points Possible	Points Scored
A—Activity Emphasis (Instructional Period)	58	
B—Activities Taught (Instructional Period)	342	
C—Intramural Athletic Program	60	
D—Achievement Tests in Individual Athletic Events	40	
Total	500	

Total Scores	Points Possible	Points Scored
Division I—Instructional Staff	500	
Division II—Facilities	500	
Division III—Program (Organization)	500	
Division IV—Program (Activities)	500	
Total for Score Card	2000	
Divide Score by 2	1000	
Percentage Score for School (Divide by 10)	100	

School _____

Date _____

Scorer _____

A. Activity Emphasis (Instructional Period)

Classification of Activity

GRADE	Story Plays R Pts	Hunting & Active Games R Pts	Stunts R Pts	Relay Races R Pts	Dance Activities R Pts	Indiv. Athletic Events R Pts	Athletic Games R Pts	Points Possible	Points Scored
First	(1) 1	(1) 2			(1) 4			12	
	(2) 2	(2) 4			(2) 2				
	(3) 4	(3) 2			(3) 1				
Second	(1) 1	(1) 3		(1) 2	(1) 4			16	
	(2) 2	(2) 4		(2) 3	(2) 3				
	(3) 3	(3) 3		(3) 4	(3) 2				
	(4) 4	(4) 2		(4) 3	(4) 1				
Third		(1) 3	(1) 1	(1) 2	(1) 4		(1) 0	20	
		(2) 4	(2) 2	(2) 3	(2) 3		(2) 1		
		(3) 3	(3) 3	(3) 4	(3) 2		(3) 2		
		(4) 2	(4) 4	(4) 3	(4) 1		(4) 3		
			(5) 3	(5) 2	(5) 0		(5) 4		
Fourth		(1) 0	(1) 3	(1) 1	(1) 4		(1) 2	115	
		(2) 1	(2) 4	(2) 2	(2) 3		(2) 3		
		(3)	(3) 3	(3) 3			(3) 4		
			(4) 4	(4) 3	(4) .	(4) 3	(4) 2		
		(4) 2	(5) 3	(5) 4	(5) 0	(5) 2	(5) 1		
		(5) 3	(6) 2	(6) 3	(6) 0	(6) 1	(6) 0		
		(6) 4					**Total Points** 115		

* R—Rank in Emphasis; Pts—Points.

The total points scored _____, divided by two, equals the score given.

Possible Score	Score Given
58	

FIGURE 3.4. Sections from a scorecard used to evaluate an elementary physical education program.

Source: N. P. Neilson and Glenn V. Arnett, *A Scorecard for Use in Elementary Physical Education Programs in Elementary Schools* (Salt Lake City, Utah: University of Utah Press, 1955).

Important reasons for using rating scales are: *(a)* to eliminate reflection of what happened through memory, *(b)* to give a way of structuring a recording process that is efficient for the observer and that does not interfere with what is being observed, and *(c)* to get a detailed record of behavior.

To construct a scale for any given factor or trait such as an attitude, a skill, or an appreciation, certain categories are arranged in hierarchical order to differentiate varying amounts or intensities. The number of points to use on a scale should be a compromise between too few categories that turn out a crude measure and too many categories that make discriminations between categories difficult. In general, four or six categories or points allow adequate discriminations without making selection difficult. Two examples of rating scales are:

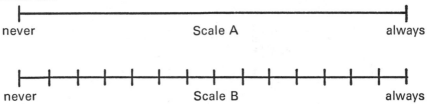

Scale A with only two points will do little beyond reporting the presence or absence of the factor or identifying extreme circumstances. Scale B, on the other hand, with so many points requires very fine discrimination by the scorer —an impossible position of choosing with confidence.

Scale C with six points is a compromise and allows precise determination without being concerned with very small differences. Some descriptive phrase or number should be associated with each point or category in the scale. Figure 3.5 illustrates a rating scale of items concerning class discussion skills. Notice that the same descriptive words are employed in describing the degree. This is known as the constant-alternative form. The changing-alternative form provides separate descriptions for each degree of each trait or factor.

Likert (1932) used a five-point scale in an early study that used the descriptions "strongly approve," "approve," "undecided," "disapprove," "strongly disapprove." When necessary for clarity, a phrase can be used to describe each of the points. Likert-type scales (Oppenheim, 1966; Babbie, 1973) are widely used to gather personal data from subjects by presenting a series of statements and having each statement judged by the student at one point on the scale. A composite score made up of all of the reactions is used as a measure of the trait.

Consideration should be given to each of the following points when constructing a rating scale:

DIRECTIONS: Indicate the degree to which this student participates in class discussion by placing a check at one of the designated points on the scale. Record your reaction below.

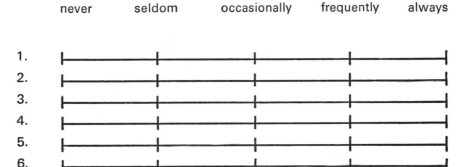

1. To what extent does the student prepare for class discussion?
2. To what extent does the student listen during classroom discussion?
3. To what extent does the student volunteer information during the discussion?
4. To what extent does the student defend his points of view?
5. To what extent does the student accept points of view of other participants?
6. To what extent does the student assume a leadership role in class discussion when asked to do so?

FIGURE 3.5. Rating scale for class discussion skills using the Likert-type five point scale

1. Avoid the use of too few or too many points on the scale. Too few points results in a crude measure. Too many points make discrimination difficult, and the procedure becomes time-consuming for the observer.
2. Use an even number of points on the scale. This avoids a completely neutral response. Rarely, if ever, is the exact midpoint of a hierarchical arrangement a proper response. The even number of points forces a response off dead center. A center point can be used if a neutral point is necessary for data collection.
3. Allow reactions at only the designated points. Marks between points require interpretation and may be ambiguous to the interpreter.
4. Select meaningful descriptors for the points on the scale. Careful selection of adjectives and modifying adverbs give direction to the observer. The descriptors should carry common meaning for all who use the scale.

Examples of different ways to set up descriptive (Cliff, 1972; pp. 176–184) and numerical rating scales to be used by an observer of students' listening behavior follow:

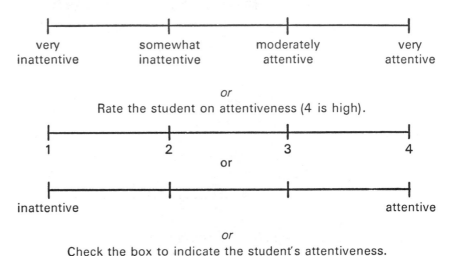

very
inattentive

somewhat
inattentive

moderately
attentive

very
attentive

or

Rate the student on attentiveness (4 is high).

1   2   3   4

or

inattentive   attentive

or

Check the box to indicate the student's attentiveness.

Never	Sometimes	Most of the time	Always

An adaptation of the scale (see Chapter 4) allows specimens of completed work with varying degrees of merit to be assigned points on the scale. Completed work by each student is compared to models to assign it to a particular rating. For example, the secondary instructor for a class in welding could prepare six welds which vary from "very poor" to "excellent." As each student's weld is judged, it could be associated with the example which is closest to it. The student's rating would be the classification of the example chosen for it. The possible six ratings could be—very poor, poor, low average, high average, very good, excellent.

Rating on overall merit usually lacks the reliability of measurement of a single attribute that is well defined, but skilled persons are able to use this technique successfully where more precise measurement is not possible. *A Scale for Measuring the Quality of Handwriting of School Children* (Ayres, 1912) and other handwriting scales for standardized tests are widely used to measure handwriting skill and use adaptation of the points on a rating scale to judge the mechanical aspects of an individual's script. When the global aspect of a complex situation is to be judged, a rating scale may be the best tool to use.

Unobtrusive Observation

No matter how carefully procedures for data collection are planned, the mere fact that the situation has been altered may cause differences that affect the data collected. When students are being administered a test or someone is taking notes in school, the students' behavior may change. Although the attributes of the affective domain seem to be most vulnerable to effects of the change introduced by data gathering, cognitive aspects may be influenced especially by administration of a test. A student may make a different response than would be made under a more normal situation.

Anytime that a person's usual performance level is changed by collection procedure, the usefulness of the data is lessened. An unobtrusive (Webb, Campbell, Schwartz, & Sechrest, 1966) observation is one that is made in such a way that the person being observed does not know it. There can be *no* interaction between performer and observer or performance and the observation. Anything that happened during the observation would have happened exactly the same way without the observation process. Unobtrusive observation is used to supplement direct observation or to gather information without possible bias. A student may give a response that is obviously the expected answer when asked about a personal feeling. Another effect is possible when students know what is expected but respond in the opposite direction to annoy the teacher. This backlash as a way of revenge has been referred to as the "boomerang effect" by Joseph Masling (1966). Either or both of these difficulties may affect the meaningfulness of the data.

Unobtrusive observation could be used when the teacher sees the need to improve the attitude of students toward mathematics, for example. By presenting new work in the classroom in a real-world context and placing new concepts into a basic mathematical structure, the teacher hopes that students' attitude toward mathematics will be enhanced. Special attention was given to presentation of mathematics and its study, so that students can relate work in the classroom to the real world. The need now is to determine the effects of the new approach on students' attitudes toward mathematics. An attitude test could be administered. Another approach could be to ask the question—Do you like your mathematics class?—to determine the impact of the change. Since the teacher has initiated the question and the desired answer is probably apparent to the one being questioned, the responses may be biased in the positive direction.

Rather than administering an attitude test or asking a question, the teacher could capitalize on opportunities to observe attitudes about mathematics within the context of actual behavior with an unobtrusive measure. The number of student entries in the mathematics division of the science fair could be used as an indicator of attitude toward mathematics. The manner in which students approach mathematics practice sessions or opportunities to do extra work in mathematics could reflect attitudes. An elementary schoolroom that has an appropriate "math corner" would provide a situation to determine attitudes through its use by the students.

The number of books checked out of the library on a topic studied in social studies class could be used as an unobtrusive measure of interest created by a particular topic or country studied. If a large number of books on the topic or country is being read by the students, then this would be considered to reflect interest. These are examples of unobtrusive observation—data collection which has been structured in such a way that no change is created in the real-world conditions. Innovative teachers have devised many ways of determining attitudes and interests without administering a scale or asking a direct question by using unobtrusive methods to collect data.

If you have reason to believe that the data might be distorted in either direction by more direct procedures, an unobtrusive measure should be considered. Establishment of a direct relationship between the measure and the characteristic being studied is as important here as in other measurement procedures.

There must be good reason to believe that more entries in the mathematics division of the science fair is indeed a result of the classroom change and not some other reason, or that the large increase of interest in a particular country being studied is a result of the classroom activities and not a movie or television program that appeared at the same time.

Anecdotal Records

At times informal methods of observation are employed to gather information about students. A behavioral diary of a student's activities may give increased understanding of development and adjustment of that student. A report of informal observation by teachers is called an anecdotal record.

Such reports can be used to increase the understanding of student behavior for the teacher and others who deal with the student presently or who may do so later. Although a single entry may have little meaning in isolation, a series of such records can contribute considerably to a teacher's understanding of the student. These accounts may be most valuable when there is little agreement about the definition of a characteristic which appears in an educational objective. By speaking in terms of occurrences, behavior is placed in operational terms. By careful reporting of the happening without interpretation, judgments can be made objectively about changes over time.

The record is intended to be a factual statement about a particular event that involved the student. The statement should accurately describe a specific event and its setting. The event should also be identified as either being typical behavior or unusual (atypical) behavior of the student. Collectively the records should reveal patterns of behavior that give insight to important areas of development. Selection of what to report must not be influenced by prejudgments or biases. By careful selection of what to report and avoidance of certain other reports, anecdotal records can probably be used to show almost anything that the teacher wants to show.

Objective reporting and interpretation must be incorporated in the use of anecdotal records to guard against misinterpretation of student behavior. Thorndike and Hagen (1977, pp. 524–525) have listed three common *deviations* from proper reporting for anecdotal records:

1. *The anecdote evaluates instead of reporting.* It tells the teacher's reaction to the child.

2. *The anecdote interprets instead of reporting.* It gives teacher's conclusions as to the reasons for behavior instead of or as well as a report of what actually occurred.
3. *The anecdote describes in general terms, rather than being specific.* A report of this type would be the following: "Mary is not well accepted by the other children in the class. She usually stands on the sidelines at recess and does not take part in the games." This summarizing statement may be of some value in providing a picture of the child. However, it lacks the objectivity and concreteness that characterize the description of a specific event. It incorporates more selection and evaluation than we would like in our basic raw material.

A good way to file a record is on a three-by-five card. A more useful reporting of a recess period might read like this:

```
Student: Mary          Date: Monday, Nov. 12, 10 A.M.
Grade: 5               Place: Recess

Incident: This morning Mary stood by the sidelines at
          recess. She did not participate in the games
          and interacted with no other child.
```

A single entry like this would in itself have little meaning, but if four entries are found in eight school days, some action is probably needed.

An anecdotal record is made on one student at a time; the whole situation must be recorded and observations continued over an extended period of time. Anecdotal records can be of value to classroom evaluation if: *(a)* the incidents are objectively chosen to provide a representative sample of behavior, *(b)* they remain factual, *(c)* the logistics of recording allow summarization and trend development, *(d)* they are used to assess attainment of educational objectives set for the student, and *(e)* judgments are based on more than one entry.

SUPPLEMENTING DIRECT OBSERVATION

Many of the techniques of direct observation are too time-consuming to be used with all members of a class. Some problems associated with direct observation involve the psychological factors discussed earlier. To overcome some of the limitations of direct observation, certain extensions can be used to supplement direct observation. In general, these extensions—mechanical instruments and classroom or published tests—are used because they are more efficient in the use of time or measure in areas where direct observation is not appropriate.

Mechanical Devices

Instruments designed to measure or gather information about a student or event may be used by the classroom teacher to extend the scope of data collection. Mechanical instruments are not affected by human characteristics which knowingly or unknowingly reduce the accuracy and in turn the validity of human observation. Although mechanical instruments are essentially tools for the researcher, a classroom teacher should become familiar with devices which have utility for measurement needs. Educational objectives that deal with physical and skill development may be investigated for degree of attainment by mechanical devices. To determine how fast or accurately something can be done may require a sophisticated mechanical device.

Movie cameras, television cameras, and tape recorders preserve a situation to allow for interpretation by repeated study. A complex set of phenomena such as often appears in the classroom may best be observed by making a permanent record and having several persons analyze what has been recorded.

Tests

Classroom objectives relating to achievement in subject-matter areas form a large proportion of all educational objectives. Although not the only way to gather information about achievement, paper-and-pencil tests are used widely in classroom observation to measure student achievement. Teachers' tests as well as published tests are good ways to gather much of the data needed for classroom evaluation. Cognitive outcomes of the educational process that relate to mathematical and verbal aspects can best be measured through well-written tests. Tests are to be considered as a way of supplementing direct observation by use of instruments that extend the teacher's observational sensitivity to hidden attributes, especially achievement.

Like all measuring instruments the classroom test must measure what it is designed to measure with the highest possible degree of accuracy and consistency if it is to be valuable as a tool. Three questions must be attended to when developing educational tests to supplement direct observation. They are:

What should I be measuring?
How can I best measure it?
How do I know that I am measuring
what I intended to measure?

There should be a direct relationship between those tasks the test demands of the student and those things the educational process set out to teach the student to do. In this way each test becomes an operational definition of the trait that is being measured, and indicates in actions what the trait means to the test maker. If the teaching is based on sound educational objectives and the tasks on tests are directly related to that teaching, the data from the test will be appropriate for basing evaluations for both student performance and program effectiveness.

The major role of educational tests is to measure in the cognitive domain. Although the classroom teacher establishes goals in the three domains of cognitive, affective, and psychomotor, *classroom-prepared tests* will not serve to measure educational objectives associated with the process of internalization (affective) or the performance of physical movements (psychomotor) with precision. Certain published tests are useful to aid classroom observation in the affective and psychomotor domains.

Observation by Testing

Through the years teachers have found that a well-prepared test, if administered and scored properly, is an efficient means of collecting information about their students. The major function of classroom testing is to measure student achievement but other characteristics are measured from time to time as information is needed to support education. There seems to be little question about how teachers view the teacher-prepared test—nearly every teacher finds uses for tests that they construct and consider them to be effective.

There seems to be less agreement about use of standardized tests. "Probably the most vocal and sustained criticism has been aimed at the value of standardized tests" (Stetz & Beck, 1981; p. 1). Predictions of teacher reactions to standardized tests have been far more negative than actually found. Results of their survey of teachers reveal:

.... that teachers find standardized achievement tests to be difficult, but generally helpful, useful, and fair. . . . Teachers generally rated standardized tests more helpful, fair, and useful, less biased, and difficult than NCME [National Council on Measurement in Education] members expected them to. (p. 8)

As long as a test score is not used as a single criterion for decision-making, scores on standardized tests can supplement other data collection and support sound decisions. Although any important outcome of education is measurable it does not follow that a paper-and-pencil test can be developed as a measuring instrument for any occasion. If used properly and for appropriate outcomes, tests are effective observation instruments for the classroom.

PLANNING OBSERVATION

After careful classification of objectives into appropriate domain categories, a series of data-collection procedures must be devised and implemented at proper times and in sequence to generate information on which evaluations can be made. The plan should be comprehensive and integrated with a total classroom program so that the instructional program, data collection, and evaluation complement each other. Equal importance should be given to understanding of human development, the psychology of learning, content of subject matter, data-collection procedures, and evaluation techniques.

There is a tendency to place greater importance in areas where data can be collected easily. Human nature seems to tell us to take the easiest path, and if it is difficult to collect data in a particular domain, objectives in that domain may be overlooked. Classroom teaching may weight some aspects heavier because it is easier to secure information about progress there. Observation should include plans to gather data for all objectives. Each student must be given the opportunity to exhibit the degree to which each objective is reached. Proper tools for collecting the information are needed. Selection of each tool must be made with an eye not only to the content but also to the type of behavior being observed. In general, achievement, knowledge, and intellectual aspects will be observed by administration of paper-and-pencil tests, both teacher-made and published. These can be supplemented by selected nontesting devices. Measurement of psychomotor skills depends heavily on performance tests supplemented by direct observation. Student adjustments, attitudes, and interests can be observed by nearly all techniques mentioned for observation. Paper-and-pencil scales of attitude and interest, anecdotal records, and sociometric devices provide the bulk of information about the affective domain.

Sampling Observation

Since the teacher cannot have a complete record of behavior for all students on all aspects of growth, a **sample** of behavior must serve as a basis for observation. Enough information must be gathered to provide a **representative sample.** A sample is considered to be representative when collected data reflect the total behavior on a specified characteristic for a student.

Sampling of behavior for direct observation is controlled through use of a sampling plan. Three sampling plans appropriate for some classroom observation are **time sampling, event sampling,** and **trait sampling.** To answer the question:

Can this behavior be recorded and interpreted best by dividing into units of time or units of occurrences of behavior (event or trait)?

the observer should be directed by the type of behavior being observed and recorded.

Time sampling selects a patterned sequence of points in time to record what is happening at those times. A checklist may be used to record what is happening every so many seconds—15 or 30—over a designated time span. Time sampling could make a record at each half hour for one school day, a week, or other appropriate block of time (see Figure 3.6). The time should be patterned and extended over a period long enough to give a representative sample. Decisions about the frequency and length of time span should be based on the kind of behavior and the type of data desired.

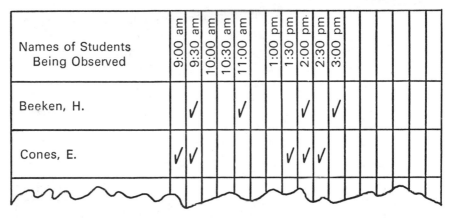

Names of Students Being Observed	9:00 am	9:30 am	10:00 am	10:30 am	11:00 am		1:00 pm	1:30 pm	2:00 pm	2:30 pm	3:00 pm					
Beeken, H.	√		√						√	√						
Cones, E.	√	√					√	√	√							

FIGURE 3.6. Time sampling showing check marks for attentive behavior

Event sampling uses occurrences of a particular behavior of an individual, or interaction between and among individuals. Event sampling might be used by a teacher who wants certain students to ask more questions. A count could be made of the number of questions asked and comparisons made to measure change (see Figure 3.7). If the concern is to have students use their talents of creativity, the number of times the student exhibits creative acts could be analyzed. Other examples of individual behavior that might be observed are: errors in arithmetic facts, completion of assignments on time, and acts of hostility. Event sampling has the advantage of a setting that is natural and ongoing. If a child has a temper tantrum, event sampling allows observation throughout the happening. Sampling by events allows continuity through an integral happening that is not possible when the sampling is broken into time units.

Names of Students Being Observed	1st week					2nd week				
	Monday	Tuesday	Wednesday	Thursday	Friday	Monday	Tuesday	Wednesday	Thursday	Friday
Anker, R.	//		/		///					
Borno, C.	///	//	/	/	/					

FIGURE 3.7. Event sampling showing tallies of questions asked each day by certain students

Trait sampling is much like event sampling except that specific behaviors are reported rather than events. The observer may be looking for exhibitions of aggressiveness and record aggressiveness according to a predetermined set of criteria (see Figures 3.8 and 3.9). The observation system used for sampling student behavior can best be devised according to these points.

Name of Students Being Observed	Bites or Kicks	Hits or Shoves	Calls Others Dirty Names	Teases Gently
David, R.	///			/
Geener, A.		///	/	

FIGURE 3.8. Trait sampling — aggressiveness showing tally marks

Another type of sampling will be discussed later and the basic principles of creating a representative sample will be used. When selecting items for a test instrument the test maker uses **content sampling** to guide selection of the items for a test so that the relative importance of topics of study receive proper emphasis on the test. A few multiple-choice items over material studied during a two-week unit will not provide a representative sample. The test should include enough items to give coverage, and guided selection of items by topics should make the test representative as to content studied and behaviors presented in instructional objectives. Material in Chapter 5 gives direction for building a test that is representative.

A major obstacle to generation of sound data is the tendency of educators at all levels to choose one approach and use it for all situations regardless of whether it is appropriate or not. Some teachers find use only for tests while others never give tests but use informal observation exclusively. It is safe to say that the use of only one type of observation will rarely be appropriate for all situations when gathering data about students. Many different ways to structure observation are available. Why not use the strengths that can be found in each when choosing observational data-collecting procedures?

TYPE OF OBSERVATION		
Procedure	Behavioral Occurrence	Record Made
Unobtrusive observation	Open to diverse phenomena	Describes accountable behavior without observer intervention
Anecdotal record		Describes intensive and continuing behavior sequence
TYPE OF SAMPLING		
Time sampling	Open to only specified phenomenon	Records selected aspects in a timed sequence
Event sampling		Records specific behavior events (e.g. arguments) as they occur
Trait sampling		Records specific behavior (e.g. aggressiveness) as it occurs

FIGURE 3.9. Description of natural events

VALID OBSERVATIONS

There are two factors that contribute to generation of significant observations. The meaningfulness and usefulness of observations relies on: (a) the consistency of the process of observation in production of the data—how reliable is the information? and (b) the soundness of the interpretation made from the data—how valid is the information?

Acceptable levels of reliability and validity for observations generated by direct observation can be maintained by careful planning for and structured procedures of observation. Without structured attention to the process of direct observation interpretation of the data will probably result in invalid evaluation. The checks for reliability and validity for direct observation are listed below as direction to planning and executing observation by direct means. (Chapter 11 and 12 summarize testing procedures to support valid measures.)

Reliability Checks

A check on reliability is focused on how procedures contribute to consistency in observations. When planning for direct observation in the classroom consider:

1. *How the data will be used.* Knowing the purpose of direct observation allows the person who plans the observational procedure to structure data collection to supply sound data for the selected evaluation technique.
2. *How observation is to be conducted.* After selection of the best way to collect the data the rest of the procedures can be organized.
3. *Selection of a device.* Prompt recording of data is facilitated by the instrument selected and allows data to be collected as it is generated rather than relying on memory. Data collection is structured around the device to aid observation and data organization can begin as data are recorded.
4. *Training of observers.* Practice in actual observation should begin well before time for data collection. When there will be more than one observer special care should be taken to insure consistency among observers, so that collected data are not a function that reflects the differences among observers.
5. *Observer effects.* Care should be taken to structure observation to keep to a minimum any extraneous effects of the collection, per se. The presence of an observer or mechanical device, e.g. a video camera, might change the natural scene and supply atypical data. Sometimes introduction of new procedures several days before actual data collection begins will avoid this difficulty.
6. *Quantity of data.* Data collection must continue long enough to generate data in adequate amounts. Reliability is increased as the amount of data is increased.

Validity Checks

A check on validity is focused on how procedures contribute to meaningful data. When planning for direct observation in the classroom consider:

1. *What is to be observed.* The attribute should be carefully defined and delineated. Observers should know precisely what is being observed, and how observation of behavior is tied to the trait.
2. *The sample of observations.* The collected data should be representative of the total amount of data being generated about the trait of concern.
3. *Closeness of a natural situation.* Observation should take place in a natural situation. If an artificial situation must be used care should be taken to approximate as close as possible a natural setting for data

collection. This is especially important when using a school setting for judging on-the-job performance.

4. *Tied to objectives.* Since objectives have directed the planning of the instructional sequence they should be considered when data are collected. Data must be tied to the behavior called for in the objective.

5. *Specific data without judgment.* Data must be collected objectively with personal judgment being held to a minimum. Although judgment must enter the decision process at some point, that is reserved for evaluation.

6. *Reliability checks.* Keep in mind that all checks on reliability support increased validity. Anything that can be done to increase reliability will support high validity if the observation is tied to the characteristic of concern.

SUMMARY

Providing for the needs of students is a tenet of the educational process, since without needs education has no purpose. Observation provides the awareness of changes within students and further information about the effectiveness of school programs. Teachers of young children must be particularly sensitive to indicators of unhappiness, distress, or disinterest, and attempts must be made to accommodate the needs of individuals. As students become older, developmental and educational goals change. Evaluative procedures need an abundance of information for appraisal of students on important attributes and to determine how well the school's program has served to move students to attainment of objectives.

Information for evaluative purposes is collected through observation. Any fact used as a basis for making judgments is called an observation. The observation (the fact) may be obtained by a testing instrument or by procedures classed as nontesting.

Distortions of observations result from instruments used to gather the data and from errors in interpretation. All observational procedures are designed to overcome such limitations by:

1. Refining the instruments
2. Objectifying direct observation through a structure of rules for observing

Checklists, scorecards, rating scales, anecdotal records, mechanical instruments, and unobtrusive observation are used to objectify direct observation. The refinement of data-collection instruments is the major thrust for the rest of this book.

Direct observation can be used at all times in the classroom and may be the only way to collect some needed data. Direct observation is supplemented by certain devices to gather data. These are mechanical instruments and test instruments.

The planning of observational procedures must include enough scope to assure that all important aspects of the educational process are reviewed. Since

Tools for Observation

Direct	Indirect
1. Checklists	1. Psychological tests
2. Rating scales	2. Educational tests
3. Scorecards	3. Rating scales
4. Mechanical devices	4. Self-reports
5. Anecdotal records	5. Questionnaires
6. Unobtrusive	6. Personal interviews

a representative sample of behavior is needed for valid evaluation, observational procedures use systematic sampling along dimensions of time, event, trait. The content of a test is also selected to provide a representative sample of course coverage.

Plans should also arrange for a situation to collect the data that is as close to natural conditions as possible. When true natural conditions cannot be used for data gathering, an assumption must be made—that observed behavior in the artificial setting is the same as what would be observed in the natural setting.

Observation must be reliable and valid. Special care is taken to see that observation has the highest possible degree of these two characteristics.

Coordination of data-collecting procedures with statements of educational objectives is necessary for evaluation of student progress and program effectiveness. Strengths of each observational procedure should be considered when selecting data-collecting procedures.

This chapter completes an orientation to the broad base of measurement techniques and evaluative procedures. The remaining chapters zero in on more specific problem areas of each of these aspects of the educational process. Chapter 4 covers topics related to evaluation of skill development. Chapters 5–8 are devoted to planning and constructing a classroom test which will do what you want that test to do. The administration and scoring of the test will then be discussed, followed by ways to decide how successful you were in building the test and ways of improving tests in general. Selection from published tests and special topics are included in later chapters.

NEW TECHNICAL TERMS LISTED IN THE GLOSSARY

Content sampling	Product
Device	Representative sample
Event sampling	Sample
Halo effect	Time sampling
Instrumentation	Trait sampling

ACTIVITY EXERCISES

1. Develop a checklist. For a behavior or skill that can be directly observed, write a clearly stated objective. Break the objective down into six or more identifiable components and present them in a checklist. Use the checklist to collect data on the behavior or skill and revise the checklist from the feedback from field testing.

2. Develop a rating scale. Assume that each student is reading a poem to a set of peers. List the points to be considered when evaluating the presentation and expand these into a rating scale that generates objective data to be used in evaluating the readings. Field-test to ascertain the utility of the rating scale and revise.

3. Using your teaching area choose a student behavior that can be viewed by direct observation for typical performance, atypical performance, or behavioral change. Select a technique for structuring direct observation, and develop a tool and specific directions for collecting and recording the data, keeping in mind the needs of the evaluation process for this behavior.

4. Describe a situation in which the data collected through observation would be biased by the procedure of data collection. Explain how unobtrusive observation could be conducted to overcome the above difficulty. How do you expect your procedures of data collecting to eliminate bias that might distort student responses or behavior?

FOR DISCUSSION

1. Explain in your own words why the process of observation is so important to the functions of educational measurement and evaluation. Consider direct observation and the several ways that teachers supplement observation made through the senses.

2. Explain the differences between informal observation and formal (structured) observation. How is each used to support instructional programs in the classroom?

3. Choose any mechanical device that can be used to collect data on students. Explain in detail how it could aid a classroom teacher in data collection. Include what data would be collected and how it would be collected, recorded, and interpreted.

4. Choose a psychological trait that is important to students you teach, or expect to teach, and explain how anecdotal records would be helpful to you as a classroom teacher. Explain how incidents should be recorded and how teachers should use the information.

5. The typical classroom is often considered to be an artificial situation for collecting data about students. Explain why it is considered to be different from a real-world (natural) situation. What can classroom teachers do to overcome some of the difficulties associated with collection of data in the classroom? What aspects of your teaching lend themselves to creation of

real-world conditions? Which aspects, by their nature, are such that real-world conditions can not be established for in-school measurement?

6. Explain why a teacher would use a test rather than some other observational procedure to collect data about students.

REFERENCES AND KNOWLEDGE EXTENDERS

AYRES, L. P. *A scale for measuring the quality of handwriting of school children*. New York: Russell Sage Foundation, 1912.

BABBIE, E. R. *Survey research methods.* Belmont, CA: Wadsworth, 1973. Pp. 269–278.

CARTWRIGHT, C. A., & CARTWRIGHT, G. P. *Developing observational skills* (2nd ed.). New York: McGraw-Hill, 1984.

CLIFF, N. Adverbs multiply adjectives. In J. M. Tanur (Ed.), *Statistics: A guide to the unknown.* San Francisco: Holden-Day, 1972.

GRONLUND, N. E. *Stating behavioral objectives for classroom instruction.* New York: Macmillan, 1970.

GRONLUND, N. E. *Measurement and evaluation in teaching* (4th ed.). New York: Macmillan, 1981. Chap. 16, pp. 433–455.

HOPKINS, C. D. *Understanding educational research: An inquiry approach.* Columbus, OH: Merrill, 1980, pp. 43–82.

HOPKINS, C. D.. & ANTES, R. L. *Classroom testing: Administration, scoring, and score interpretation.* Itasca, IL: F. E. Peacock, 1979. Chap. 3 and 4, pp. 41–80.

JONES, L. V. The nature of measurement. In R. L. Thorndike (Ed.), *Educational measurement* (2nd ed.). Washington, D.C.: American Council on Education, 1971. Chap. 12, pp. 335–355.

LIKERT, R. A technique for the measurement of attitudes. *Archives of Psychology,* 1932, *140,* 1–55.

LORGE, I. The fundamental nature of measurement. In E. F. Lindquist (Ed.), *Educational measurement.* Washington, D.C.: American Council on Education, 1951. Chap. 14, pp. 533–559.

MASLING, J. Role related behavior of the subject and psychologist and its effects upon psychological data. In *Nebraska symposium on motivation.* Lincoln: University of Nebraska Press, 1966.

MEHRENS, W. A., & LEHMANN, I. J. *Measurement and evaluation in education and psychology* (2nd ed.). New York: Holt, Rinehart, & Winston, 1978. Pp. 345–369.

OPPENHIEM, A. N. *Questionnaire design and attitude measurement.* New York: Basic Books, 1966.

STETZ, F. P., & BECK, M. D. Attitudes toward standardized tests: Students, teachers and measurement specialists. *NCME Measurement in Education,* 1981, *12*(1), 1–12.

TANUR, J. M. (Ed.). *Statistics: A guide to the unknown.* San Francisco: Holden-Day, 1972, Pp. 176–184.

THORNDIKE, R. L., & HAGEN, E. *Measurement and evaluation in psychology and education* (4th ed.). New York: John Wiley, 1977.

WEBB, E. J., CAMPBELL, D. T., SCHWARTZ, R. D., & SECHREST, L. *Unobtrusive measures: Nonreactive research in the social sciences.* Chicago: Rand McNally, 1966.

Chapter 4. Evaluation of Classroom Performance

After study of Chapter 4, you should be able to:

1. Describe the uniqueness of performance in cognitive and physical skill development.
2. Discuss procedure as process.
3. Indicate how to set standards, collect data, and evaluate procedures.
4. Construct devices to collect data important to evaluation of procedures.
5. Discuss product as result.
6. Indicate how to set standards, collect data, and evaluate products.
7. Construct devices to collect data important to evaluation of products.
8. Describe aspects of data collection about performance that contribute to reliable data and valid evaluations.
9. Explain how each glossary term listed at the end of the chapter is used in classroom measurement and evaluation.

The ongoing, everyday activities in classrooms require teachers to use many techniques to assess the progress of students. The most often used technique is the administration of a paper-and-pencil test which presents selected tasks to students in writing and requires the student to respond symbolically. Since many educational objectives deal with the cognitive domain—knowledge of facts, understandings, application of knowledge, and the higher mental processes of analysis, synthesis, and evaluation—the paper-and-pencil test is an appropriate and valuable device to gather information for student appraisal during the formative stages of learning and also in summative evaluation.

Some objectives are oriented primarily toward the affective domain, and psychological tests are proper devices to measure characteristics of emotions, feelings, intelligence, motivation, and such. However, some objectives are not oriented primarily to the cognitive or affective domains but to the psychomotor domain. An important facet of the learning may be *(a)* a series of actions (**process** or **procedure**), or *(b)* an outcome from the action which is either impalpable or physical (**result** or **product**). There are classroom objectives of learning that can be evaluated only by determination of what students can do rather than what they know or feel. Collection of information about what students can do may require that they be observed as they perform or that the product which is a result of performance be viewed and evaluated. Skill development in all domains, but more especially in the psychomotor domain, must be evaluated in terms of what the student can do.

In the sense that a paper-and-pencil test measures performance, the usual classroom achievement test is a performance test. However, performance is not the main interest of the teacher in that testing situation. The discussion of performance in this chapter centers around measurement where skill development overshadows the cognitive and affective aspects of functioning.

Appraisal for preschool classes, primary grades, and severely handicapped students relies extensively on evaluation of performance, since those students have not developed the verbal and writing skills necessary for taking paper-and-pencil tests. Vocational, business, physical education, speech, foreign language, drama, journalism, home economics, art, and music class appraisal is likely to have a large component of **performance evaluation.** In addition many other classes such as chemistry, biology, physics, general science, and social studies use performance evaluation. Teachers employ assignments and projects to help students apply information they are acquiring and to develop good work attitudes and social skills, and to enhance physical as well as cognitive development at all educational levels. Thus evaluation of student performance becomes an integral part of all classroom activities.

THE CLASSROOM SITUATION

In Chapter 3 the point was made that a teacher's opportunities to determine how well students have met objectives are largely limited to gathering data in a classroom which in many instances is an artificial situation for data collection. Depending on the nature of the subject being studied the artificial situation may not be the ideal setting to provide highly valid data. When collecting data in the classroom it is assumed that the data reveal the same information that would be generated if students were in a natural setting outside the classroom. The classroom may be very similar to the natural situation in some special subject areas except that the student is enrolled in an educational program. However, teachers must often strive to simulate natural environments for students to learn in and make application of what has been taught. As Fitzpatrick and Morrison (1971, pp. 237–270) summarized, good simulation of natural situations involves four steps to aid in replicating real-world conditions, namely:

1. Determine through careful analysis the critical aspects of the criterion situation it is desired to simulate in view of the purpose of the simulation.
2. Determine the minimum of fidelity [degree of realism] needed for each aspect and estimate the worth of increasing fidelity beyond the minimum.

3. Develop a scheme for representing a reasonably comprehensive set of aspects, within the limits of available resources.
4. Adjust comprehensiveness and fidelity, compromising as necessary to achieve a balancing of considerations but with primary attention to the aspects shown by analysis to be most critical for the purpose at hand. (p. 241)

By simulating real-world conditions, requiring the student to act in that context, and collecting data about the process and the result, the teacher can extend data collection beyond administration of a paper-and-pencil test that measures the cognitive aspect of performance. In this way teachers can overcome a tendency in education to make the test the only device used to gather data for judgment of levels of accomplishment.

Some of the ideas developed here about judging process and result may also be used to extend information collection about students' achievement in content subjects. Rarely does a student's cognitive knowledge of a complex matter of concern allow prediction about that student's ability to act when implementing the knowledge. Study and complete understanding of the principles of skiing does not guarantee that once the first trip down the slope is started, safe arrival at the base is assured. Likewise, cognitive knowledge of the principles of cooking and memorized steps of a recipe do not assure success in the kitchen.

Evaluation of a process and the result can be used to add information beyond a student's cognitive understanding as well as to determine psychomotor outcomes stated in terms of quality of a finished product. For example, a student may have a deep understanding of human behavior and social forces at work in the modern world and still not be able to function in day-to-day living without alienating nearly everyone around. Information about a student's cognitive knowledge alone does not necessarily allow high-level prediction of performance in a real-world situation. A complete look at the student's accomplishments includes performance as well as cognitive knowledge. The major concern should be with implementation of the knowledge, and teachers must deal with evaluation of performance if there is a way to see how well the student can implement knowledge at the performance level. In cases where subject matter does not permit creation of natural situations for evaluation of the student's implementation of knowledge, other alternatives should be considered and the best technique used. Information about performance should be collected whenever possible and used to augment data gathered by paper-and-pencil tests and nontesting techniques. The selection of appropriate test and nontesting data-collection devices should be fostered if teachers have a full understanding of how to assess performance within the classroom. The next two sections focus on an understanding of performance as viewed in two parts:

1. The actual act of performing.
2. The results of that act.

Procedure as Process

Procedure or process is the action exhibited by the student in bringing forth the product or results. For example, a kindergarten child may be learning to tie a bow for a shoe. The actual movements which are required to produce the bow make up the process and the bow is the product. Many other examples of performance learning can be found throughout the levels and divisions of formal education.

When the series of actions is of particular importance, teachers are concerned about how to assess the procedure that the student used. Since there is no tangible aspect of action, special techniques are used to aid in making judgments about procedure. These include planned direct observation, use of devices to record information during action, and inspection of a physical object for evidence of what procedures were used in the creation of the product.

Product as Result

The outcome of an educational objective may imply or state an entity as an end product. That product may be tangible or intangible. A tangible product could be a typewritten business letter, a ceramic vase, a hand-knitted sweater, or one of hundreds of objects which could be created by a student in a school setting. An intangible product could be a speech, a violin solo, a pantomime, or one of hundreds of different actions which could be an outcome for an educational objective.

Teachers find it necessary to assess the quality of students' products, since they are produced from classroom activities. If the product is tangible, assessment may consist of comparing it to those of fellow students, by scoring it against a weighting of important aspects, by checking for inclusion of important features, by rating on a scale, or by comparison to preconstructed objects. If the product is intangible, appraisal consists of judging the worth of the product by viewing and interpreting data generated by direct observation structured by data-collecting devices.

PROCEDURE AND PRODUCT

When instruction deals with performance a student is asked to produce, create, construct, fabricate, build, or in some way to bring forth something as evidence of meeting some specific objective. Although the result of performance is usually of primary importance the indication of the degree of accomplishment is better evaluated by: (a) the process used, (b) the result itself, or (c) a combination of process (procedures) and result (product).

There are two commonly used standards for judging performance: (a) predetermined standard criteria, and (b) peer performance. The former is set by the teacher based on training and experience and is more commonly used. Minimum acceptance levels are established for products, and appraisal is made about relative value of the student's product compared to the expected level. The judgment of correctness of procedure and of the worth of products involves the same basic elements of evaluations placed on other student achievement; however, certain principles need to be applied differently because of the nature of the outcome. For clarification the two are discussed separately; however, procedure and product are inseparable in evaluation of performance.

Procedure

Procedure is something that must be considered when assessing performance. Although procedure and product are interdependent, procedure may be second in importance to the product. It is especially important when making decisions about why a product rates high or low. Poor procedures are associated with poor products and good procedures with good products. Certain classes in school are more likely to have objectives which deal with procedure than others. Those especially involved with procedures are art, music, shorthand, typewriting, physical education, home economics, and speech. Science laboratories, courses within vocational training, and industrial arts programs are by their nature highly directed toward procedure and its contribution to performance and product.

The component of procedure includes all actions which contribute to creation of the product. Separation of procedure from product for intangible products may be difficult. For example, procedures for singing would include voice placement, projection, control of the diaphragm, muscle control, shape of mouth and throat, and breath control. Product evaluation of singing includes the outcomes of process such as tone, pitch, timbre, volume, and the overall results which reach a listener's ear. Separation of the two factors of process and result, although difficult for intangible products, is important to the evaluation of performance. Separation of procedure and product for creation of physical objects is easier because the properties of the objects which result from the procedures are physical in nature. An intricately designed piece for an automobile motor which has been turned out on a metal lathe remains in physical form, and judgments about proper procedures can be discerned from the physical properties of the final product. Such is not the case for a song, speech, or other intangible product.

Evaluating procedure

When collecting data about student procedure, the teacher must: *(a)* decide what information is needed to evaluate the procedure, *(b)* determine what information can be collected, and *(c)* formulate ways to record the data. Since most procedures are quite complex, each of these aspects must be considered in relation to the other two factors so that the data will be useful to make valid judgments. On rare occasions the evaluator may be able to gather all the important data and collect it in a form that is easily interpreted. In general, real-world or near-real-world conditions allow for something less than the ideal. For example, the evaluation of the rendition of a short aria from a classic opera may not allow enough time for a voice teacher to gather all the desired data on all procedural aspects of the performance. A 100-yard dash lasts only a few seconds and may not cover enough time for the coach to examine and gather data on all important aspects of the runner's procedural actions. In addition, data collecting may be further complicated because essential aspects of the performance may be difficult to judge. All in all, adjustments must be made if ideal conditions do not exist for all aspects mentioned above.

Evaluation of procedure is usually formative in nature but could be summative if judgment is to be made in terms of how well procedures have been refined at the end of a course of instruction. The techniques for formative and summative evaluation are much the same, but for performance the evaluation will be used differently in the decision process. The voice teacher or athletic coach will be interested in using the evaluation to further refine procedures much the same way that a classroom teacher does when using evaluation while teaching students during an ongoing educational sequence. Terminal evaluation of procedures is important for at-the-end of instruction assessments, possibly for assignment of marks, licensing, writing credentials, or meeting requirements for a further course of action.

Setting standards

Each teacher must, using training, professional experience, knowledge, and the help of other knowledgeable persons, establish a set of standards for student performance to serve as a comparison for the collected data. A teacher who wants to establish standards for students may find further help in one or more standardized performance tests designed to measure a person's procedures in the same area because the test authors have considered what standards to set when developing their tests. In some cases minimal criteria are established independently of the individual, as in the case of the way a musical instrument is held during a performance. In some cases, certainly with individualized programs, realistic criteria may be established according to the capabilities of a specific individual. If a student has a physical handicap usual procedures may be adjusted in the way a musical instrument is held. The wheel-chair bound student may need to use different procedures in a woodworking shop class than an ambulatory student.

When standards are being set, decisions are made about what data are needed and whether they can be collected. In setting standards for procedure the major features and components are identified. For example, in evaluation of writing procedures the major features of position of the body and writing arm may be identified. In addition under "position of the body" the following component parts may be listed: face the desk squarely, sit in a comfortable, erect position, and take a forward-leaning position with the lower back touching the back of the chair. For the features of the writing arm for a right-handed individual the forearm is on the desk, elbow just off the edge of the desk, and the arm in position to use the large muscle under the forearm. The area of efficiency and accuracy of procedure can be attended to in judging the procedure. Subjective judgment can be used for those aspects that are difficult to specify in precise terms. Examples of procedure evaluation are included in the next sections.

When the standards have been established, data collection about each student's procedures are judged as objectively as possible in relation to the established standard. Use of guidelines should result in highly accurate information to use in evaluation of students' procedures.

Collecting data

After deciding what needed information can be gathered about procedure, the appropriate devices must be selected for recording observation of the student's actions. Most of the collection of data will be made by structured direct observation. In Chapter 3 the point was made that unless direct observation is highly structured, it is considered to be the least precise of all data-collection techniques. Particular effort and planning must go into overcoming deficiencies of unstructured human observation. The most commonly used devices for gathering data about procedures are presented next. Each reader must consider the general statements and relate them to special needs for evaluating a specific performance.

Mechanical devices.   Certain mechanical devices may be used to make a record of procedure for consultation later. Possibly a tape recorder, movie camera, or a television camera could be used to make a permanent record of the student's actions.

Mechanical devices are particularly useful when the teacher is dealing with procedures and intangible products because they are not observable in the final product except as the characteristics of that final product reflect procedures. The coach who must advise and train the 100-yard-dash runner could use a movie camera or better yet an instant replay attachment for a television camera unit to freeze the action for his assessment and for viewing with the runner. To know that a sprinter completed the 100-yard-dash in 10.7 seconds (the intangible product) gives little for the coach or runner to employ in evaluation of procedure. Much the same process could be used by the elementary reading teacher when a child's oral reading is filmed and viewed later for eye movements and general reading skills. Teachers fortunate enough to have access to instant replay equipment have a very valuable tool for evaluating procedure when performance is important to meeting objectives.

Checklist-rating scale.   The use of a checklist or rating scale can be valuable to creation of valid data for evaluation. Each device must be designed so that procedure on each important characteristic will be observed and data recorded. If sequence of the actions is crucial to procedure, it will need to be recorded. Assistance in sharpening a specific device can be found in a review of constructing checklists and rating scales (Chapter 3). Further aid for nearly all areas can be found through an investigation of how checklists and rating scales have been used to observe procedure for your specific subject and content area.

A checklist or rating scale which has been developed for judging procedure allows attention to be directed to important aspects of procedure and assures that the same things are considered and judged for all students. Since a device is used to focus the teacher's attention on important aspects, the same device may be used to focus student attention on the same important aspects. If the checklist or scaling device is made available to a student at the beginning of a new undertaking, it can serve as a guide to learning. The expected performance will be defined operationally for the student during the forming stages while instruction takes place and serve as a sounding board for summative evaluation at the end of instruction.

A checklist for recording important procedural actions for skill in tennis is presented in Figure 4.1 and serves as an example for other areas. The extension of the point total by use of the multiplier is optional. If a total is used, an estimation of the appraisal of the procedure can be made from that value.

DIRECTIONS: Below are definable aspects that are important to successful volley return. Check each one for each volley for one set. Determine the percentage of attainment for the set.		Percentage	Multiplier	Points
Number of volleys 1 2 3 4 5 6 7 8 9 10 11 12 13 14 15 16 17 18 19 20 21 22 23 24 25 26 27 28 29 30 31 32 33 34 35 36 37 38 39 40 41 42				
Racket in FRONT			2	
Racket head HIGH			1	
Knees BENT, but head UP			1	
LEAN or STEP into shot			2	
Keep racket head moving FORWARD			.5	
Watch the ball CONTACT the racket face			1	
NO FOLLOW-THROUGH			1	
BE AGGRESSIVE			.5	
			Total	

FIGURE 4.1. Procedure checklist for tennis volley return

The final appraisal must be made for the product but as mentioned before good products are associated with good procedures. If the multiplier and point total are used, a checklist functions much as a scorecard. Some teachers may use a checklist to report only the presence or absence of a characteristic rather than frequency of occurrence. Figure 4.2 can be used in this way to record the observation of the procedure of overhead projector operation. Since the technical points of operation are not to be judged beyond the point of whether they did or did not happen, this simple checklist seems suitable.

Actions	Occurrence	
	Yes	No
Position projector		
Plug projector into receptacle		
Place sample transparency on table		
Turn on projector		
Adjust machine position		
Focus projector		
Turn off projector		
Insert first transparency		
Turn on projector		
Turn off projector while changing transparencies		

FIGURE 4.2. Checklist for observing an individual using the overhead projector

Source: Adapted from R.C. Erikson & T.L. Wentling. *Measuring student growth.* Boston: Allyn & Bacon, 1976, pp. 137–138.

Rating scales extend the ideas incorporated in checklists by allowing for some judgment during the recording process. The judgment factor may be helpful but, if time for recording is short, may lessen objectivity by requiring the recorder to become involved in the evaluation while recording the data. If ratings can be made without losing objectivity, devices incorporating a rating scale can be useful to record student procedure. A typical rating scale is presented in Figure 4.3, and since the action is over a relatively long period of time, the judgment factor should not affect the objectivity of the data.

Recording the data

Although there is no basic difference between the **performance test** and other categories of tests, the performance test is intended to find out what

RATING SHEET

Date: _____

Name: _____   Composition: _____

Score each item by circling numbers at left. 5 = Outstanding; 4 = Excellent; 3 = Acceptable, could be improved; 2 = Somewhat weak, needs considerable improvement; 1 = Very weak, needs much improvement

A. 5 4 3 2 1 *General manner* (confident, authoritative, energetic, positive)
B. 5 4 3 2 1 *Posture* (erect, relaxed, confident, commanding)
C. 5 4 3 2 1 *Starting position* (commanding, easily visible, positive); maintained distinctive movement
D. 5 4 3 2 1 *Visual contact* (not score-bound, especially at opening)
E. 5 4 3 2 1 *Beginning* (together, in tempo, good dynamic level, spirit)
F. 5 4 3 2 1 *Baton technique* (correct pattern, character, size, position)
G. 5 4 3 2 1 *Clarity* (pulsation clear, definite, regular, commanding)
H. 5 4 3 2 1 *Cues* (adequate number, effectiveness, clarity, accuracy)
I. 5 4 3 2 1 *Balance* (attention shifts among prominent sections, supportive)
J. 5 4 3 2 1 *Left hand* (reserved for special effects, cueing, dynamics)
K. 5 4 3 2 1 *Phrasing* (shape not ignored, nuance, variability of beat size, speed)
L. 5 4 3 2 1 *Facility* (graceful, well-coordinated, accurate)
M. 5 4 3 2 1 *Efficiency* (size and energy of beat appropriate, no excess)
N. 5 4 3 2 1 *Dynamics* (markings observed, good taste indicated)
O. 5 4 3 2 1 *Accuracy* (general freedom from conducting errors)
P. 5 4 3 2 1 *Expressiveness* (interpretation, feeling, freedom, musicianship)
Q. 5 4 3 2 1 *Tempo* (appropriate for expressive character, marking observed)
R. 5 4 3 2 1 *Ensemble* (rhythmic unity, articulative unity, neatness)
S. 5 4 3 2 1 *Quality* (intonation, tone quality, balance, unity)
T. 5 4 3 2 1 *How well did the group follow your conducting?*
U. 5 4 3 2 1 *Score study* (detailed, thorough, well fixed in mind)
   (Be as honest as possible with yourself on this point.)
V. 5 4 3 2 1 *Individual practice* (with tape, other recording, conducting own singing of parts of the score, anticipating difficulties)
   (Again, be honest with yourself.)
W. 5 4 3 2 1 *Overall conducting effectiveness*

FIGURE 4.3. Procedure scale for conducting an orchestra (May be self-administered)

Source: R. Colwell. *The evaluation of music teaching and learning.* Englewood Cliffs, NJ: Prentice-Hall, 1970, pp. 108–109.

students can do, while most other classroom tests are intended to find out how they can function in the cognitive domain. Because of the need to know about performance the data for assessing procedures will, in most cases, be more complex than a single score as with most tests. In addition, the data must be recorded while the procedure is underway, rather than scoring a paper sometime after the test session. For this reason the observer must know before the observation takes place exactly what to look for and the sequence of the several actions which are expected.

The scoring of a set of test papers for a class can be delayed without altering the score for the students' papers. A delay in recording data about a student's performance requires the observer to depend on memory about the actions in the performance. Even a short time delay can be expected to distort the data about what happened as compared to what actually happened. The longer the time interval and the more intervening happenings the greater the difference and the less the validity of the data.

A device for recording data about procedures must be organized in sequence of expected actions. The checklist and rating scale are especially valuable tools for recording data about procedures because the notation can be sequenced and recorded quickly, as illustrated in preceding figures. Any device which requires the observer to make written notation will probably not be effective for recording the data, since part of the action will be missed while writing the statement.

Data recorded by mechanical devices allows more freedom for interpretation because time is not a major factor. The action can be viewed again and again. However, a device for structuring the organization of the data for interpretation from the recording must be made according to the above guidelines.

Product

In general, the most important aspect of performance is the result—the *product*. Teachers have been involved in assessment of students' products for many years, and as early as 1917 books were written about ways to bring objectivity into such assessments. In an early work (Chapman & Rush, 1917), scales were presented for arithmetic, handwriting, reading, spelling, English composition, language, and drawing. Although product is considered to be separate from achievement today, the scales in the Chapman and Rush book dealt with the same principles as those which concern teachers today in assessment of products.

Accepted procedures can be expected to result in acceptable products especially when a sequence of steps is crucial to performance success. For example, if sulphuric acid is added to an experiment in the wrong sequence, the outcome may be severely altered. Sequence in this instance is of utmost importance and should be so viewed. However, in some instances sequence of steps may be varied and not affect the outcome. For example, if chocolate bits and pecans are to be added to cookie dough, the order of addition is arbitrary and the outcome is not affected.

Exceptions to this generalization should be expected and not totally discounted as a possibility. New techniques may be superior to older ones. Furthermore, each person has a unique set of characteristics, and therefore, certain digressions from common consent about procedures are to be anticipated. For example, few track coaches would have expected Dick Fosbury to develop his procedure of high jumping with his back to the bar and become a contender in that event. After he made several record jumps including the one for the gold medal in the 1968 Olympics with a high jump of 224 centimeters, the "Fosbury flop" became a technique used by other high jumpers who applied the principle successfully. His unorthodox procedure resulted in a superior product for him. Solely judging his procedure against accepted standards or incorporating procedure as a part of the evaluation of the product would be a serious error. In this particular case the product is the height that he jumped, and any low rating of his procedure would be overshadowed by a superior product—a record high jump.

Not all products are so easily judged as a high-jump attempt. Although the actual jump might be only a few seconds and the jump itself intangible, the product can be judged in terms of how high the bar is after the jump. There is no other criterion for judgment of the product, and that judgment can be made objectively. Of course, the level of competition would be a part of the assessment of the product. Junior high school students would not be judged against Olympic standards. In the same way student products should not be compared to professionally produced products, unless the student is expected to be able to perform at that level, as in advanced vocational classes. Judgment of products should have appropriately chosen standards, but the judgment remains primarily highly subjective, although hopefully it is as objective as possible.

Evaluating products

When collecting data about products, the teacher must *(a)* decide what information is needed to evaluate the product, *(b)* determine what information can be collected, and *(c)* decide how to compare students' products with standards. The method of judging products can take much the same form as judging procedures. However, the collection of data is supported by a wider selection of devices. In addition to mechanical devices, checklist, and rating scale, data about products can be generated by ranking student products, by use of a scorecard, or by comparison to a **product scale.**

The judgment of tangible products is not as severely limited in time for collecting data as is the collecting of data about procedures. For example, a student's written paper could be judged on how it meets the standards set for mechanics of handwriting. In this case the example of writing to be evaluated is in physical form, and it can be evaluated, basing the judgment on the age and experience of the student and using as much time and care as needed. This may not be true for judgment of intangible products like a musical selection or speech where nothing remains for continued observation unless an actual record or tape is made so that the product can be reproduced as often as needed to formulate the evaluation. The assessment examination of intangible products may be as severely limited by the time factor as are procedures.

Setting standards

Standards for products must be set using professional knowledge—the teacher's and colleagues'—taking into consideration the age of the student, level of maturity, and experiential background. When appropriate standards have been established, data must be collected from the product and comparison of the student's product made to standards as objectively as possible. The structure is designed to result in highly valid evaluation of students' products. In setting standards for judgment of the product of handwriting measurable characteristics are listed by breaking the product into component parts and analyzing each part. For example, the size and form of letters, stroke, spacing, line quality, and alignment of letters can be identified in the product.

That which should be considered when setting standards for products is not always easily discernible. Since the two parts of performance—procedure and product—are so closely related, separation is often more helpful pedagogically than it is in practice. Someone who is knowledgeable about a product and its creation may be able to detect much about procedure by looking at the product. For this reason standards may be somewhat difficult to arrive at with full objectivity. Each student's product could be compared to an ideal product developed by the teacher. For example in typing a letter, the student's product can be checked for format, length, and number of errors, and judged in comparison to the standards. The bead of a weld can reveal to an experienced welder whether a proper selection of a rod was made, whether the welding material was fed constantly and evenly, and other equally important characteristics of procedure which are reflected in the product. The carpenter, the cook, the concrete block layer, and all other artisans can analyze procedure by viewing product characteristics.

Teachers also have this opportunity when dealing with student products. Many teachers are able to detect instances of good or poor procedure by examination of student products. For example, an essay which is built from important ideas and material may lose its effectiveness because of lack of logical arrangement and sequence. Thus the poor procedural actions resulted in a poor product. The artisan's and teacher's expertise can be used to fuse the procedure with the product when evaluating performance.

Collecting data

When the teacher knows what information is to be collected about the product, appropriate devices must be selected to assure that the information is in usable form. The critical decisions to be made about product evaluation relate to what data are needed, what data can be collected, and how comparison of students' products with standards is carried out. The data should be collected on specific characteristics rather than formulated as a general and encompassing description. The final judgment is then made about the product through analysis of important information. Objectively obtained and valid data must be supplied for the final judgment of the product if valid evaluation is to occur. The most commonly used devices for gathering data about products are presented below.

Ranking. If a class of students has been given an assignment requiring each student to create the same tangible product, a ranking of the student products can be made by ordering them from best to poorest. The ranking should take into consideration all important characteristics and their relative importance. Ranking can be highly reliable if only one characteristic of the product is being considered. As more characteristics are included for consideration, the reliability can be expected to drop. The fewer the characteristics being considered and the more clearly each characteristic is defined the higher the expected reliability.

A teacher who is making a ranking of products should list the aspects to be considered and order them in a hierarchical arrangement according to their relative importance. More meaning can be attached to a rank if more than relative placement is included in assignment to a place in a ranking. A weighting of the characteristics according to the hierarchy should be made and a scorecard used to get a composite value. The final ranking would be made according to the composite numbers which are assigned to the products by the scoring device. Meaning in absolute terms can be attached to the rank by basing each rank on a weighting of points according to relative importance.

Scorecard. A scorecard (Chapter 3) can be useful if the points to be awarded are distributed to weigh important aspects heavily and less important aspects are given fewer points according to the hierarchy. The device can be as simple or as complex as needed for the particular product being assessed.

Use of the scorecard for assessing the quality of tangible products also allows: *(a)* assignment of each product to a predetermined class if predetermined standards (criterion-referenced) have been established, or *(b)* judgment of performance according to how others in the class have scored (norm-referenced). Scorecards are particularly effective devices in view of the complexity of the interrelatedness of the many characteristics which make up most products. Figures 4.4 and 4.5 present two scorecards used in assessment of products from cooking. In each one the judge weights each characteristic on a scale of one to three. Scales for scorecards can be extended to more points if needed to give a finer weighting of the characteristics. If all characteristics are not of equal value, a multiplier (see Figure 4.1) factor can be added to the scoring of the card. For example, it is not likely that characteristics numbered 12 and 13 in the scorecard for canned meat are of equal importance. The scorecard might be improved by weighting number 12 much more than number 13. The use to be made of the data can give direction to the need for use of a multiplier. The weighting principle of the score-

MINNESOTA SCORE CARD FOR CANNED MEAT AND POULTRY
University of Minnesota — Division of Home Economics
(Devised by Helen J. Swinney, Emma Du Bord, and Clara M. Brown)

Rating of _____ Rated by _____ Date _____ Average Score _____

	1	2	3	Score
COLOR	1.			
Seared		Pale or burned	Well browned	
Unseared		Red	Natural	1.
EDIBILITY		2. Much gristle and bone*	All meat edible; small bone in center for flavor and heat penetration	2.
TEXTURE		3. Cooked to pieces	Firm	3.
GRAIN		4. Cut lengthwise or without regard to grain*	Cut crosswise	4.
SIZE OF PIECES		5. Size not appropriate for meat*	Appropriate size for kind of meat and purpose	5.
AMOUNT OF FAT		6. None or too much	Layer about 1 inch thick	6.
LIQUID Clearness	7.			
Seared		Much sediment	Little sediment	
Unseared		Cloudy or much sediment	Clear with no sediment	7.
Consistency		8. Watery	Jellied	8.
PACKING Amount in jar		9. Two or more inches below neck of jar	Full to neck of jar	9.
Compactness		10. Very compact	Medium pack	10.
Arrangement		11. Disorderly	All meat slices packed flat or chicken packed skin side out	11.
CONTAINER Seal		12. Doubtful seal	Perfect seal	12.
Label		13. None	Complete	13.
Appearance		14. Soiled	Shining	14.
FLAVOR		15. Flat or too highly seasoned	Well seasoned and flavor developed	15.

Total Score _____

Average Score _____

*Not applicable to chicken
To find average score divide total score by the number of items rated.

FIGURE 4.4. Product scorecard for canned meat and poultry

Source: C. M. Brown. *Evaluation and investigation in home economics.* New York: F.S. Crofts, 1941, pp. 178–179.

	1	2	3		Score
APPEARANCE	1. Dull	Shiny		1.	_____
	2. Fine pieces	Large masses		2.	_____
MOISTURE CONTENT	3. Dry or watery	Slightly moist		3.	_____
TEXTURE	4. Lumpy	Smooth		4.	_____
	5. White and yolk not well-blended	Homogeneous mixture		5.	_____
LIGHTNESS	6. Compact	Fairly light		6.	_____
TENDERNESS	7. Leathery	Tender		7.	_____
TASTE AND FLAVOR	8. Flat or salty	Well seasoned		8.	_____
	9. Raw or burned	Flavor developed		9.	_____

Score _____

FIGURE 4.5. **Product scorecard for scrambled eggs**

card allows each aspect to be viewed singly or in relationship to all other listed characteristics.

Checklist-rating scale. A checklist is especially helpful in judging intangible products. The checklist allows an objective recording of information about an ongoing event such as a speech, race, or musical rendition without making judgments during the action. Since it is difficult to separate procedure and product of intangible products, a checklist allows one to collect data on both aspects during the performance and to separate later those aspects which deal with procedure and those which deal with product for evaluation separately. The checklist in Figure 4.6 allows the user to collect data on performance in speaking according to broad criteria broken into subparts. Consideration of the subparts individually according to each one's contribution to either procedure or product can be done after the performance, thus assuring more confidence that evaluation of performance is at a high level, and supports formative evaluation of the learning process.

Rating scales can be used to collect data for evaluation of intangible and tangible products. Important characteristics of the product should be decided on and listed. Each of the important characteristics can be scored on the rating scale according to the point values. The guidelines for constructing rating scales as given in Chapter 3 should be followed. After each characteristic has been rated, the composite score must be totaled and an overall assessment made. Difficulty in combining the information according to the relative importance of separate characteristics reduces the reliability of composite ratings. The fewer the characteristics being considered the higher the expected reliability; however, most products must be considered using many characteristics. Figure 4.7 illustrates the use of a rating scale for an intangible product. Either letters A, B, C, D, E or numerals may be used for the adjudicator's assessment

GENERAL SPEECH PERFORMANCE CHECKLIST

Name _____ Date _____ Rater _____

Project _____ Time _____

Subject _____ Grade _____

Criteria		*Comments*

Speech attitudes and adjustments

Indifferent _____	Antagonistic _____
Tense _____	Apologetic _____
Flustered _____	Posed _____
Irresponsible _____	Immature _____

Voice and articulation

Weak _____	Loud _____
Fast _____	Slow _____
Monotonous _____	Excess vocalization _____
Poor quality _____	Indistinct _____
Poor pitch _____	Dialect _____
Not rhythmic _____	Mispronunciation _____
Poor phrasing _____	Misarticulation _____

Bodily postures and action

Indirect _____	Monotonous _____
Inexpressive _____	Not integrated _____
Random _____	Exaggerated _____
Slovenly _____	Weak _____

Language

Inaccurate _____	Monotonous _____
Ambiguous _____	Inexpressive _____
Wordy _____	Stilted—Technical _____
Colloquial _____	Immature _____

Content

Not clear _____	Inaccurate _____
Insignificant _____	Lacks originality _____
Dull _____	Lacks movement _____
Insufficient _____	Abstract _____
Too much _____	Lacks units _____

Organization

Poorly purposed _____	Weakly supported _____
Questionable central idea _____	Poor transitions _____
	Poor sequence _____
Poorly introduced _____	Poorly concluded _____
Poorly analyzed _____	

Audience interests and adaptation

Attention not arroused _____	Beliefs not considered _____
Interest not maintained _____	Obviously solicitous _____
Knowledge not considered _____	Confidence not secured _____

General Effectiveness

FIGURE 4.6. Checklist for an intangible product.

Sources: Adapted from J.D. Ragsdale. Evaluation of Performance. In W. Braden *Speech methods and resources* (2nd ed.). New York: Harper & Row, 1972, p. 432.

for each major category. Numerals allow for totaling or averaging as an overall measure of the performance.

VOCAL SOLO

Order or time of appearance _____   Event No. _____

Class _____   Date _____   19 ____

Name _____

Voice classification _____

School _____   District _____

City _____   State _____

Selections _____

_____

_____

Adjudicator will grade principal items A, B, C, D, or E, or numerals, in the respective squares. Comments must deal with fundamental principles and be constructive. Minor details may be marked on music furnished to adjudicator.

Tone (beauty, control) .... ☐

Intonation .... ☐

Diction (clarity of consonants, naturalness, purity of vowels) .... ☐

Technique (accuracy of notes, breathing, posture, rhythym) .... ☐

Interpretation (expression, phrasing, style, tempo) .... ☐

Musical effect (artistry, fluency, vitality) .... ☐

Other factors (choice of music, stage presence, appearance) .... ☐

Adjudicator _____
                          Signature

FIGURE 4.7. Rating scale for an intangible product

Source: R. Colwell. *The evaluation of music teaching and learning.* Englewood Cliffs, N.J.: Prentice-Hall, 1970, p. 116.

Product scale.   A highly successful technique for judging tangible products where the physical characteristics are most important utilizes specimens of varying quality. A product scale is much like a rating scale except the points to be marked on the scale from inferior to superior are represented and explained by a series of preconstructed objects which vary in quality from a very low rating to a very high rating. As with other scales equal intervals are kept between points on the product scale.

When the product scale has been made by selecting the four or more examples to represent the points on the continuum, each student product is compared to the scaled examples. The score value is reported to the student according to a set of symbols to indicate the assessment. Product scales have been used for many years to judge products, and some have been standardized for general use.

Product scales are easily created by classroom teachers who deal with objects as products. All that is needed is a set of objects which vary in fulfilling the requirements of a perfect or nearly perfect example of performance. Teachers of sewing, woodworking, ceramics, mechanical drawing, and many other classes can: *(a)* create examples with varying quality, or *(b)* accumulate specimens for the scale from student work. When the physical examples have been assembled the scale can be used again and again assuming that the standards remain the same.

The product scale (see Figure 4.8) is probably most useful when a product is to be judged on overall quality rather than on specific characteristics. If the objects used as examples for the different rating points are made available to students at the beginning of learning, the students have ready-made guidelines about which features are considered to be important and what the final product should look like.

Recording the data

The recording of data for intangible products has the same difficulties which are attached to recording information about procedures. Since there is no physical object to view, the data must be recorded while the action is taking place.

A device which allows the observer to record the data without a delay between the action and the recording and which is arranged in sequence of expected action is important to measurement of intangible products. The device must also be so constructed that procedural aspects of performance do not contribute to the score given to the product. If procedures and an intangible product are to be viewed separately, one device which collects the data needed for both can be used for recording. Division of the contributing factors for products and those for procedures can be made after the performance and each viewed and reported separately.

For a tangible product the observer has much more time to record the data, since the physical characteristics are open for continued viewing. Information will need to be organized and recorded by a checklist, scorecard, or rating scale if any of these can aid the assessment. For ranking and product scales the directness of the procedures will, in general, make the recording of data unnecessary.

BUILDING RELIABILITY INTO EVALUATION OF PERFORMANCE

Judgment of student performance continues to be a necessary part of most teaching positions. Such judgment is difficult because assessment must

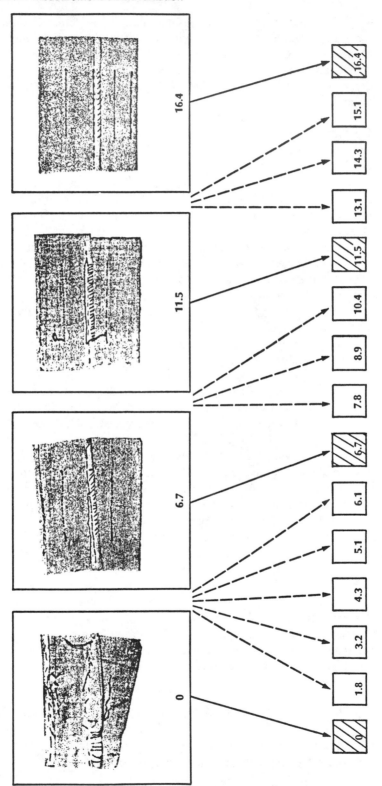

FIGURE 4.8.   Product scale for certain selected elements of sewing. Four of the 15 levels exhibit the principle of hierarchy.

Source: K. Murdoch. *The measurement of certain elements of hand sewing.* New York: Teachers College, Columbia University, 1919, p. 120 and insert.

be based on subjectively generated information which tends to reduce the reliability of the data and, in turn, affects negatively the degree of judgment validity. To keep the degree of validity high the most appropriate techniques are selected to generate information about both procedure and product as they are involved in performance.

Aspects of the overall assessment which contribute to reliable data and valid evaluations of performance must be attended to. Questions to be considered are:

1. How adequate was the sample which was taken of the performance?
2. How suitable was the technique used to select the sample?
3. How have characteristics of the observer affected the assessment?
4. How has the close interdependence of procedure and product affected assessment of either one of them or both?
5. Could use of mechanical devices have given better data?

Adequate Sample?

Evaluation of performance is often unreliable because the performance has not been successfully sampled. The sample may be less than adequate either *(a)* because of the nature of the performance, or *(b)* because the teacher did not take advantage of opportunities to collect data over several observations.

A student cannot be asked to deliver the same speech again and again, paint the same picture many times, or write an essay more than once (revision excepted). Products from woodworking, metal shop, and home economics classes may be created only once. If observation is limited to one or two performances, the teacher must assume that it is typical and representative of that student. For these situations there is not much to be done to overcome the problem other than apply the procedures suggested earlier to make sure that the data have been gathered in maximum quantity in usable form and that proper interpretive procedures are used.

Given the opportunities, the teacher should allow for several observations of student performance and use a structured device to record data on the same aspects each time. The evaluation should be a composite of the total data. If some out-of-class time is used in preparation of the product, some help may be given by other persons. If conditions can be structured, some of the observations should be made such that no outside help is possible. For example, English teachers require in addition to themes prepared over a period of time some examples of students' writings on in-class themes as a check against outside help. If great variation between the two situations is observed, some additional examples should be obtained using direct observation. Consideration should always be given to the possibility of outside help.

If the expected outcome of each performance is increased skill development, as in mathematics and reading, care should be taken not to incorporate data from early practice in a terminal evaluation. It would not be good procedure to average performance in skill development and weight the scores early in a semester the same as scores made near the end of the semester. Good procedure suggests that samples taken during the learning period be used for formative evaluation and used to support further learning. Samples taken at the termination of a learning sequence can then be used in summative evaluation.

Repeated sampling of student performance under suitable conditions is needed to increase the reliability of assessments. Careful attention to this important aspect of evaluation of procedure and product even under somewhat adverse conditions must be given if classroom assessment of performance is to be valid.

Suitable Technique?

The data to be used in judgment of performance are generated in the procedure or from characteristics of the product. Techniques for collecting the data must be such that the right kinds of data are made available in maximum quantity. This involves giving consideration to all types of ways to collect data which could be used and selection of a technique well suited for the specific situation. Teachers may find that a previously used device can be used or modified to meet present needs. If one cannot be located then the teachers should create the device.

Discussion of data-collecting devices in Chapter 3 includes possible uses for each one. A review of that coverage with an eye to increasing reliability will give the needed orientation to this section.

Observer Effects?

Whenever observations are made of performance, there is a question of how the act of observing affected the students, the procedures, and in turn the products. Unless the observation is truly unobtrusive, no clear-cut answer is available. However, some possible effects should be considered to estimate how the data that was collected might differ from data gathered with no observation effects.

If any mechanical device is used to remove personal influences and effects on data, its effects should be carefully checked to see if it introduces any change into the natural setting. A major limitation of mechanical devices is that these instruments are more effective when used in laboratories than in the classroom or a natural setting. For example, a high school sophomore may be very comfortable giving a speech before a class of peers but uncomfortable and threatened if the presentation is made before a television camera. If the device can not record usual or natural conditions it really serves no purpose in data collection.

Unless conditions are radically changed from the real world or normal classroom, the data have probably not been altered appreciably. In most cases the objectivity obtained in collecting the data more than offsets the change made by introduction of some observation procedure.

What may be a major problem in direct observation is based on the human nature of the observer. Boredom and fatigue that result when an observer must repeat the same thing again and again for all students can render data virtually useless. While these effects can never be reduced to nil, plans to spread the observation over a reasonable time period can minimize boredom and fatigue. If observation must be made in a short time span, additional observers competent in the field and trained for observation can help in data collection.

Additional observers can be used in another way to increase reliability of data. If competent observers make multiple observations and reconcile differences, more reliable information is expected. If the teacher is unable to recruit additional observers, more than one independent observation may be made and then the observations reconciled for an assessment.

Procedure-Product Interdependence?

Judgments of performance are sometimes affected by weighting either procedure or product too heavily at the expense of the other. In general, the product is more important and should be given most if not all the weight. In some classes teachers evaluate students' work by dividing credit between procedure and product. For example, a mathematical problem could be divided two-thirds credit for procedure and one-third for the correct answer. This tells the student that both are important with procedure being the more important of the two. For a geometric proof where each step is a product in itself but collectively all steps lead to the theorum proof, the teacher might consider the procedure to be worth nine times the product and divide the credit as nine-tenths for procedure and one-tenth for product. Personal opinion will be a contributing factor about division of the two parts for judgment of performance.

When judging performance in the classroom, the teacher must keep in mind that on-the-job performance will in most cases be in terms of product. A wrong answer which costs the company half-a-million dollars is likely to be viewed in terms of the product rather than the procedure even though the error was in procedure. If in the assessment of performance undue weight is given to procedure, the product may be assessed either too high or too low. In either case the degree of reliability may be lowered.

When assessing a tangible product, little if any importance should be given to the procedure. If the procedure has resulted in a superior product, then little fault can be found with process. It has been said that there is little basis for an argument against success. However, a question may remain about product improvement or production efficiency which might have been possible if more widely accepted procedures had been used.

Teachers may be reluctant to give high ratings in a terminal sense to the product if the procedure is known to violate accepted principles, and it may be difficult to be objective in this sense. The student who does not follow the teacher's suggested procedure may find it difficult to receive a high teacher rating. For example, a teacher may be concerned with developing skill in use of a thesaurus. When presenting an efficient procedure for locating a word to be used to express a certain thought, certain steps can be listed for the student. However, many different ways of locating a particular word can be used. A student who uses a different approach which is equally or more efficient should not be penalized for procedure if the product (locating the word) is equal or superior to the suggested approach.

During a period of learning or skill development the teacher may forgo a critical analysis of a student product if rightly convinced that product improvement will come from following a given set of procedures which will result in a superior product. In this case nearly all emphasis should be given to assessment of procedure with little or no attention given to the product. During learning the product may serve primarily as a way for the teacher to determine where the student erred in procedure. For example, when a second grade student is developing skill in cursive writing, certain procedural aspects such as position of the paper, holding the pencil, position of the arm and hand on the writing surface, and stroke for letter formation contribute to the quality of the writing. An example of a rating scale for handwriting performance in which procedure and product are provided is given in Figure 4.9. The most important facet of the product at that stage of learning is the investigation of procedures used rather than the product itself. Teachers feel that improved skill will result in an acceptable product. The assumption is that an improved product will result when the procedure is refined according to the given set of procedures. Product assessment can be delayed until the later stages of the period of learning or as a terminal evaluation of the objective's attainment.

Use of Mechanical Devices?

The discussion of the previous four points has been based on the assumption that mechanical devices have not been used to collect data for either process or product. Since certain recording devices are available for use with process evaluation, they should be considered and implemented if their objectivity will contribute to more reliable data. Likewise, mechanical devices can be used to measure physical characteristics of products for conformance to standards, and recording devices can make a permanent record of intangible products like speeches and musical renditions for later viewing or listening and assessment.

The objectivity associated with data collected by mechanical devices makes their use important not only to procedure but also to product evaluation. Physical characteristics of the product lend themselves to measurement by mechanical devices. If the marketable weight of an animal is important to product evaluation, a set of scales can best give that information. Measurements for seams, lapels, and hems of garments are best made by rulers and

Name _____   Date _____

For each consideration ring a number at the right using this scale.

		Low	High		
Poor	Low	Average	Average	Good	Excellent
1	2	3	4	5	6

Evaluation of the Writing Procedure

1. Body	Desk is faced squarely; sitting in a comfortable erect position, forward-leaning with the lower back touching the back of the chair.	1 2 3 4 5 6
2. Feet	Both feet on the floor	1 2 3 4 5 6
3. Arms	Both forearms on the desk with elbows just off the edge of the desk; the writing arm is in position to use the large muscle under the forearm; the nonwriting arm resting on top of the table	1 2 3 4 5 6
4. Paper	Placed directly in front of the body; the top of the paper is slanted	1 2 3 4 5 6
5. Fingers	The writing hand fingers are curved so that the tip of the third and fourth fingers rest on the paper	1 2 3 4 5 6
6. Hand and wrist	The wrist of the arm is close to the paper but neither the wrist nor the side of the hand next to the wrist is resting on the paper	1 2 3 4 5 6
7. Nonwriting hand	Palm down on the top of the paper to accommodate the writing hand	1 2 3 4 5 6
8. Pencil	Between thumb and middle finger, crosses the middle finger at the corner of the nail and crosses the hand slightly in front of the large knuckle, with the nonwriting end of the pencil pointing back toward the shoulder	1 2 3 4 5 6

Evaluation of the Quality of the Written Product

1. Form	Correct shape of alphabet	1 2 3 4 5 6
2. Size	Uniform, correct height and width of various types of letters	1 2 3 4 5 6
3. Stroke	Beginning and ending strokes joined correctly	1 2 3 4 5 6
4. Space	Uniform space between letters and between words	1 2 3 4 5 6
5. Line quality	Uniform thickness and smoothness of the line	1 2 3 4 5 6
6. Alignment	Uniformity of letter touching the line	1 2 3 4 5 6

FIGURE 4.9. Rating scale for handwriting performance

tapes. When a physical characteristic is important, a mechanical measuring device should be used.

Newly developed devices as well as time-tried instruments should be given consideration for evaluation of process and product. In general, mechanical devices give highly objective and reliable data or freeze a situation for further study which cannot be accomplished in any other way.

SUMMARY

The evaluation of student performance is necessary because some educational objectives focus directly on what a student can do. The usual paper-and-pencil test requires artificial performance because the classroom situation is removed from the places where knowledge or skill would be applied naturally. The performance test often can be arranged so that the examinee's actions will be performed in a natural-like setting. Natural situations may also be created for some subject areas to supplement test information about what a student knows with information about how that knowledge can be applied.

The process (procedure) component of performance pertains to the actual actions which the examinee exhibits. The result (product) component of performance pertains to the intangible or tangible entity which was created by the performance. Collectively they constitute a means of assessing a student's performance. Although procedure contributes highly to performance and should be given consideration, the most important aspect of nearly all performance is the result of that performance—the product.

Direct observation is necessary to collection of data about performance. The observation will include viewing the action taking place and, as with physical products, a careful look at the result of the action. To give the observation direction, standards for procedure and product must be decided upon and some structure for a data-collecting device developed so that the data are recorded in interpretable form.

Because of the human element in direct observation, measurement of performance is expected to be less precise than measurement where more objectivity can be applied. To increase the probability that reliability of the data is at the highest point, five questions are asked about techniques used to evaluate performance in the classroom:

1. Was the sample large enough to generalize to the student's usual performance?
2. Were the techniques for sample selection suitable for the situation?
3. Did the act of observing affect the milieu so that the performance was altered from natural conditions?
4. Was the assessment of either procedure or product affected by a confounding factor caused by the interdependence of a procedure and product?
5. Could the use of any mechanical device generate more valid data than the technique used?

In very early stages of skill development and in new learning situations teachers are likely to find measurement of procedure to be most suitable for performance evaluation. When assessing performance, a teacher is well advised to be concerned about procedure during learning stages and with product after the basics have been developed. In general, the product is considered to be the more important of the two factors of performance and in most cases should be given most or all of the weight in terminal performance evaluation. Professional expertise in each area can be utilized to adapt performance testing to assess student attainment levels of objectives which are based on what a student can do.

NEW TECHNICAL TERMS LISTED IN THE GLOSSARY

Performance evaluation	Product
Performance test	Product scale
Procedure	Result
Process	

ACTIVITY EXERCISES

1. Develop a checklist to be used in evaluation of an intangible product. Select a product that will be expected from your students such as a voice or instrument solo, a recitation, a speech, oral reading. Be sure to consider only those points that relate to the product itself. Construct a second checklist that also ascertains the level of the procedure used. How can you use one checklist to make separate evaluations for procedure and product?

2. Develop a product scale. Select a tangible product that will be expected from your students such as a business or personal letter, a set of bookends, an outline, a drawing, an art object. Explain how the product scale is to be used to judge a tangible product. Explain how the product itself may reveal what procedures were used and whether the procedures were correct according to class instruction and generally accepted as proper procedure.

3. Choose a performance skill that you will expect from your students sometime during the period of time of your instruction. Develop a set of guidelines needed to evaluate the level of student skill development. Considering relative importance of procedure and product, develop techniques, devices, and ways to record the data for separately assessing procedure and product and combining those assessments into overall evaluation of performance.

FOR DISCUSSION

1. Describe the two aspects of performance evaluation.
2. What should be considered when building high reliability into evaluation of performance?

3. Explain why procedure is considered to be more important than product during the learning (forming) stages of instruction. Explain why the product is considered to be more important than procedure at the conclusion of an instructional sequence.

4. Defend the use of unusual procedures if the product is satisfactory. Explain how you could attack the use of unusual procedures if the product is satisfactory.

5. Describe why procedure-product interdependence is more difficult to deal with in intangible products than it is for tangible products. How would you direct a fellow teacher who comes to you for help in evaluation of intangible products?

REFERENCES AND KNOWLEDGE EXTENDERS

BRADEN, W. W. *Speech methods and resources* (2nd ed.). New York: Harper & Row, 1972.

BROWN, C. M. *Evaluation and investigation in home economics.* New York: F. S. Crofts, 1941.

CHAPMAN, J. C., & RUSH, G. P. *The scientific measurement of classroom products.* New York: Silver Burdett, 1917.

COLWELL, R. *The evaluation of music teaching and learning.* Englewood Cliffs, NJ: Prentice-Hall, 1970.

COOPER, J. O. *Measurement analysis of behavioral techniques.* Columbus, OH: Charles E. Merrill, 1974. Chap. 1, pp. 8–23.

ERICKSON, R. C., & WENTLING, T. L. *Measuring student growth.* Boston: Allyn & Bacon, 1976. Chap. 6, pp. 125–186.

FITZPATRICK, R., & MORRISON, E. J. Performance and product evaluation. In R. L. Thorndike (Ed.), *Educational measurement* (2nd ed.). Washington, D.C.: American Council on Education, 1971. Chap. 9, pp. 237–270.

HOPKINS, C.D., & ANTES, R. L. *Classroom testing: Construction.* Itasca, IL: F. E. Peacock, 1979. Chap. 8, pp. 165–179.

LIEN, A. J., & LIEN, H. S. *Measurement and evaluation of learning* (4th ed.). Dubuque, IA: William C. Brown, 1980.

MEHRENS, W. A., & LEHMANN, I. J. *Measurement and evaluation in education and psychology* (2nd ed.). New York: Holt, Rinehart & Winston, 1978. Pp. 338–343.

MURDOCH, K. *The measurement of certain elements of hand sewing.* New York: Teachers College, Columbia University, 1919.

RYANS, D. G., & FREDERICKSEN, N. Performance tests of educational achievement. In E. F. Lindquist (Ed.), *Educational measurement.* Washington, D.C.: American Council on Education, 1951. Chap. 12, pp. 455–494.

Chapter 5. Planning for Classroom Testing

After study of Chapter 5, you should be able to:

1. Define test and state the primary purpose of a classroom test.
2. Discuss the concept of the test as a sample and relate it to validity of classroom tests.
3. Construct and use a table of specifications.
4. Summarize test construction considerations.
5. Contrast the characteristics of open-ended tests and mastery tests.
6. Describe test characteristics for selected-response items, constructed-response items, and problem items.
7. Write the eleven general considerations to be given to construction of test items.
8. List other test planning considerations that must be given attention prior to test administration.
9. Explain how each glossary term listed at the end of the chapter is used in classroom measurement and evaluation.

The basic concepts of measurement, evaluation, instructional objectives, observation, and performance evaluation have been discussed in the previous chapters. While the fourth chapter developed ways to appraise student progress in subjects where a paper-and-pencil test may not be appropriate, this chapter focuses on designing tests for subjects where the paper-and-pencil test is widely used. Very little evidence of cognitive achievement in content subjects is observable through *direct* observation of everyday, ongoing classroom events, as are some other student characteristics such as skill development and physical traits. While some aspects of achievement in all subjects may be discerned by direct observation of students' daily performance, *comprehensive* observation of achievement is not possible until a special device is administered to measure it. For years teachers have used oral or written tests to aid classroom observation of student achievement. Some tests have been given to only one student at a time while others have been administered simultaneously to a classroom of students, depending on the number of students to be tested and the coverage desired.

A teacher-made test expands the gathering of information beyond a teacher's direct observation in the milieu of usual classroom activities. In addition, published tests constructed by persons removed from the classroom where they are administered can be helpful in measurement of student achievement. Use of published tests in the classroom will be discussed in Chapter 16. The advantage of the teacher-made test over a published test is that it can be tailored to meet instructional objectives and match classroom instruction for a particular set of students. Determination of classroom achievement may be undertaken for a variety of reasons including the evaluation of student progress, ascertaining individual strengths and weaknesses, providing information for reporting to parents, continuous evaluation for reteaching, and evaluating the effectiveness of the teaching-learning process.

WHAT IS A TEST?

Instruments for educational measurement have been referred to in the school as "quizzes," "tests," or "examinations" interchangeably without much consideration about differences in procedures used to gather information about students and use of test results. For our purposes the formal presentation of test items and scoring of student responses falls under the canopy of "taking a test." Since tests can take many different forms and the results used in different ways, a working definition of a test is needed. For our purposes a test is:

> an instrument, device, or procedure that proposes a sequence of tasks to which a student is to respond—the results of which are used as measures of a specified trait.

As mentioned previously classroom tests are concerned primarily with the trait of achievement—either cognitive or skill. Psychological tests deal with other traits important to success in school—intellect, motivation, interest, creativity, and such. In general, the kind of information needed will determine the length and extent of the coverage of the measurement.

A comprehensive examination at the end of a course or semester without other tests can provide information about how much students have achieved, but the results of such an examination cannot be used to facilitate learning during the course. A series of tests spaced throughout the semester allows feedback to both students and teachers about progress, allowing for adaptations during the learning process. If one of the functions of testing is to facilitate learning, then planning for a series of tests will be much different from planning for one comprehensive examination. The classroom teacher makes decisions about frequency of testing, keeping in mind what information is required, when it is needed, and how it will be used. Combinations of quizzes, tests over units of study, and comprehensive examinations used in a well-thought-out testing program will, in general, be appropriate for most school settings.

The most important concept the test constructor must keep in mind is that an instrument is built to measure something. Just as a pump in a gasoline station is assembled to measure quantities of gasoline and weighing scales are built to measure the mass of objects, classroom paper-and-pencil tests in general are built to measure achievement in school subjects. The *primary purpose* of a classroom test is to:

> quantify the achievement that the test is designed to measure by assigning a meaningful number value to achievement for each student who takes the test.

Another important purpose of testing is to promote learning. The two purposes are *not* mutually exclusive, and planning procedures can allow for measurement of achievement and at the same time foster learning among students. Tests serve the *primary purpose* in varying degrees. Assuming that the test maker has adequate knowledge of the subject being tested, the capability of an instrument to do what it is supposed to do rests, first, on skill in construction of a test, and second, on the proper use of the test.

The better the test does what it is supposed to do, the higher it rates in validity. A physics test should measure physics achievement specifically. A test used to measure biology achievement should measure achievement in biology. As aspects other than the one being measured contribute to the student's score, the less the validity of the measuring instrument and the less confidence the teacher can place in that score. Special care is taken to keep measurement of extraneous factors to a minimum or to make the contribution constant for all students. For example, if the student is required to read test items, reading ability is going to be measured to some extent. The nonreader or poor reader may be in a position where the score (the quantification) is small because of poor reading skills rather than lack of knowledge in the topic being tested. The only techniques a test maker can use to control for poor reading ability are the vocabulary used in the items and the format within which the tasks are presented. Other possible contributors to the quantification should be identified in the planning stage and the early stages of test construction should include ways to control for them.

A measuring instrument used to determine the level of student achievement must provide a means of assigning the student's score to a scale value so that comparisons can be made between and among individual measures or to a criterion point. This is needed for criterion-referencing as well as norm-referencing although each system of referencing uses the measures differently. The paper-and-pencil test that the classroom teacher builds to measure achievement needs this characteristic as much as a thermometer or any other measuring instrument. The planning-stage decisions are crucial to development of a test which can identify differences. Whether the test is capable of doing what it is used to do is largely a function of the time and effort spent in planning and the care and attention given to factors important to building a good test. This statement assumes that any measuring device is used appropriately in a proper situation.

Even a very good test will not generate valid data if it is used improperly.

A third-grade mathematics test cannot be used to measure mathematics achievement in the sixth grade. It may be highly useful in measuring third-grade achievement, but a test is useless (loses its validity) in measuring something that it is not designed to measure. Obviously, third-grade tests are not used in sixth-grade classes; however, all users of tests must take steps to assure that each test is a proper measuring instrument for the characteristic being measured. A test cannot measure achievement in the content area if the tasks do not correspond to the instructional objectives. Special effort must be made to assure that what the test is being used to measure is what the instrument actually measures.

THE TEST AS A SAMPLE

A paper-and-pencil test used to measure achievement is made up of tasks based on the content covered. If achievement in algebra is to be measured, then the test tasks should relate to what students have studied about algebra. From any body of content many different items can be created as tasks for students who are to be measured. Even with a small number of things to be learned there is a large number of ways to present tasks to be done on the test—in most cases the number of possibilities is nearly limitless. The problem of the testmaker is to select from that very large number of possibilities those few situations to be included in the testing instrument. The test is best considered as a sample of all possible tasks. It is composed of a set of items chosen from that larger set of items that includes all possible items that could be presented from the material studied. Graphically it looks like this:

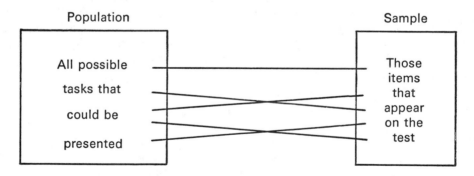

Even in a six-weeks test in spelling covering 180 newly presented words, this population of words is too large to present in its entirety for the test. If the teacher presented one word each 30 seconds, it would require a testing session of 90 minutes—much too long for a spelling test. Rather than give all the words, a portion—say 25 or 35 words—could be administered with the assumption that students will get about the same proportion of words correct in the sample that they would if given the total number of words. Graphically it looks like this:

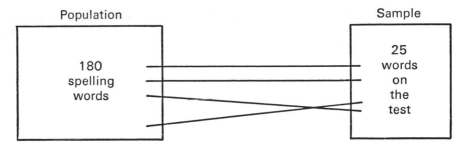

In most content areas the number of possible tasks far exceeds 180 as in the spelling test.

A major concern in preparation of a test is building a high level of **content validity** into the sample of test items. This means constructing a test that covers the subject matter studied and the appropriate weighting of the items or tasks so that each topic which was studied is stressed in the test in the proper proportion to all other topics according to relative importance. This is accomplished by making the test (the sample) representative of the population. For a sample to be representative, the items on the test, and thus the test, must reflect the population characteristics as closely as possible. Any difference between sample characteristics and population characteristics should be kept to a minimum to insure content validity. Any difference results from overemphasis on one or more topics to the exclusion or underemphasis of one or more other topics. Special attention must be given to avoid making the mistake of including too many items on one subject-matter topic and too few or none on others.

In the special case of the criterion-referenced test where a clear domain of subject-matter defines the trait to be measured, the task reduces to making a clear connection between each item on the test and an instructional objective. Since criterion-referenced tests are to tell us what examinees can or cannot do, a series of items (one item is not enough) must be written for each stated objective. The major problem to be worked out for criterion-referenced tests is determination of where the difference between "can" and "cannot" lies. The procedure for a norm-referenced test seems to be better approached by using weighting of subject-matter topics. The next section describes a procedure for sampling subject-matter topics for norm-referenced tests.

THE TABLE OF SPECIFICATIONS

The erector of a physical building relies heavily on a set of plans which synthesizes all the various factors constituting the construction of a complete and usable building. These plans are developed to provide a structure which will serve some specific function. It may be an office building, an industrial plant, a home, an oil refinery—but the capability of the structure to perform its intended purpose depends on how well the plans were drawn even before a shovel of dirt is turned. Some change can be made after getting underway, but certain basic factors are not easily altered in the building stage.

If a classroom test or any test is to be useful for a specific purpose, it must be built from a design plan much as a physical structure is built from its design plan. The building-trade people call their plans blueprints. Test constructors call a plan for a test a *table of specifications.* Because of the nature of the product, the lines and information on a true blueprint cannot be used to guide test construction. However, much the same instructions are given through the special use of a matrix where the two dimensions are: (*a*) subject-matter topics studied, and (*b*) behaviors desired. Thus, the **test blueprint** relates content and behaviors on the test to course instruction and, in turn, to the objectives.

In developing a table of specifications for a subject-matter test the horizontal dimension of a matrix is used to represent the behaviors from the cognitive domain while the vertical dimension represents a list of subject-matter topics. The skeleton table of specifications in Figure 5.1 includes the basic components needed to develop the blueprint. For convenience, the distribution of behavior classes across the top of the table should not exceed three, and subject-matter topics down the side should be three, four, or five. If the table has too many cells, the distribution of items becomes difficult. Having decided what behaviors to include and what topics to cover, the relative importance of each cell can be established.

A test over a unit on textiles will be used to illustrate how a test constructor develops a table of specifications. When planning for this unit, the general objectives were:

Behavior Topics of subject matter	1.	2.	...N	Totals % of test / No. of items
1.	?% ?	?% ?		?% ?
2.	?% ?	?% ?		?% ?
3.				
. . . N				t o t a l / t o t a l
Totals % of test / No. of items	?% ?	?% ?		100% / 100%

FIGURE 5.1. General format for a table of specifications

1. The student can name the natural and synthetic fibers used in clothing construction and knows their characteristics.
2. The student can identify the two properties of pilling and shrinking of textiles by identifying results of these two processes from provided examples.
3. The student can apply knowledge and understanding of textiles and their properties to clothing selection.

Based on these broad objectives, the topics studied and behaviors desired should be viewed as to their interrelatedness. Decisions of relative importance have been based on class emphasis on the topics and assignments made and are listed below. The percentages for desired behaviors have also been listed for the three areas to be exhibited on the test as determined by the teacher.

A. Topics studied
    1. Natural fibers   15%
    2. Synthetic fibers   20
    3. Pilling   10
    4. Shrinking   10
    5. Choosing casual clothes   45
                                              100%

B. Desired behaviors
    1. Knowledge (recall of facts)   20
    2. Understanding (comprehension)   50
    3. Application (ability to apply
        knowledge and understanding)   30
                                                100%

For selected-response, completion, and short-answer tests the most acceptable way to weight the content of a test is by the number of tasks allotted to each topic. The same value is assigned for each task, but more items are written for the more important topics. Thus the number of items for each topic is proportional to the importance it holds for the test as a whole. For example, if three topic areas have the following proportions of relative importance, Topic A—.40, Topic B—.30, and Topic C—.30, 40 percent of the items will be written for Topic A, 30 percent for Topic B, and 30 percent for Topic C. Usually one point is given for each correct response.

The percentages are incorporated into the table of specifications matrix and the cells are filled in. Figure 5.2 shows how a test maker might distribute the proportions through the matrix cells using judgments about the content and possible tasks to measure desired outcomes. Obviously fractions of test items cannot be written so some adjustments will be needed in the number of items for some cells. Also keep in mind that different test makers will come up with different numbers for the cells. When an item overlaps behaviors, for example, comprehension and application, the test constructor determines which cell is most appropriate to include the item. The values for the test on textiles have been entered as 15, 20, 10, 10, and 45 in the last column to the right. This column should always total one hundred, since 100 percent of the items represents the total test.

Topics of subject matter \ Behavior	Recall (Knowledge)	Understanding (Comprehension)	Apply (Application)	Totals % of test / No. of items
1. Natural fibers	6% / 3.6	9% / 5.4	0 / 0.0	15% / 9
2. Man-made fibers	4% / 2.4	16% / 9.6	0 / 0.0	20% / 12
3. Pilling	0 / 0.0	5% / 3.0	5% / 3.0	10% / 6
4. Shrinkage	0 / 0.0	5% / 3.0	5% / 3.0	10% / 6
5. Choosing textiles for casual clothes	10% / 6.0	15% / 9.0	20% / 12.0	45% / 27
Totals % of test / No. of items	20% / 12	50% / 30	30% / 18	100% / 60

FIGURE 5.2. A table of specifications for a selected-response test.

The behaviors which are to be exhibited on this test are listed across the top as knowledge, comprehension, and application. Across the bottom, percentages of 20, 50, and 30 are associated with the three behaviors at the top and total 100 percent. The percentages for the cells are now entered and checks made to see that the entries total to the correct amounts. When the number of items for the test has been determined (60 items for this test), it should be placed in the lowest cell of the right column. The percentages for each cell can now be transformed into the number of items to be written and entered for each cell. For example, topic number 1 (natural fibers) has 15 percent importance for this test. The teacher determined that the 15 percent should be divided between the behavior of recall (6 percent) and understanding (9 percent). For recall, 6 percent of 60 (the total number of items on the test) equals 3.6 items for that cell and for understanding, 9 percent of 60 equals 5.4 items. The teacher must now decide if recall is to have four items and understanding five items or recall three items and understanding six items.

For an essay test the weighting is best accomplished by assigning the amount of time to be spent on each test task to reflect the relative importance of the tasks and, in turn, the topics. From this weighting, points can be assigned in the same proportions as the proportions of time divisions. For example, if seven essay items contribute to three subject topics the test might be weighted as shown in Figure 5.3.

Topic	Importance	Task	Time	Points
A	40%	Item 1 Item 2 Item 3	10 minutes 10 minutes 4 minutes	20 20 8
B	20%	Item 4 Item 5	6 minutes 6 minutes	12 12
C	40%	Item 6 Item 7	14 minutes 10 minutes	28 20
Totals	100%	7 items	60 minutes	120

FIGURE 5.3. A table of specifications for an essay test

Using the Table of Specifications

When the table of specifications has been developed, the test maker has the direction needed to build a test that has a high degree of content validity while serving those objectives that are measurable. The table aids the choice of behaviors to be exhibited in the students' reactions to the prescribed tasks. In practice, the test constructor will deviate somewhat from the specific values of the table when a certain test item relates to more than one cell or when some adjustments need to be made in proportions. Since items that require only recall of facts (level of knowledge) are easier to write than other divisions of behavior, the tendency to overload that division at the expense of others must be overcome by writing at least as many items in other divisions as the table calls for. In most tests the percentage of recall items should be as small as possible depending on the material being covered. Although the specific values of the table may be changed slightly, the use of the table contributes considerably to the major thrust to building highly valid tests.

Since content validity can be estimated only by judgments rather than by statistical procedures, support for content validity can best be presented through a carefully constructed table of specifications. Although construction of a table of specifications does not guarantee a test high in content validity, without the table subsequent testing procedures lack the necessary component of a good beginning.

Tests made by classroom teachers are, in general, not as technically well-done as tests that are built by teams of test specialists who use field-study data to guide item and test revisions. Nevertheless, the classroom teacher who sets objectives for students has an advantage over the person who must build a test that serves for classes having many differences of experience and culture. No one else has the same opportunity to make a set of test tasks fit the students' learning experiences to expected achievements as the teacher who has developed a program to serve those students' educational needs.

The classroom teacher needs to be aware of the opportunity to build in content validity during the planning stage of test development. The fact that a teacher plans and builds a test for a particular class is no guarantee that the test will be valid, but success is largely a function of how well the plans are developed and followed. There is no reason why a teacher through careful attention to measurement theory, practice, and experience cannot develop the skills necessary to construct good tests. Classroom teachers who are willing to expend moderate efforts on test development will be able to build quite acceptable measuring devices for student achievement in any subject where they have a working knowledge. The test design or planning stage is the first step to that goal.

TEST CONSTRUCTION CONSIDERATIONS

Certain aspects of building tests must be given attention to assure that the result is a quality instrument and a valid measuring device. Those topics that must be considered and decisions to be made are discussed in detail in the following sections:

1. Should the test be open-ended or mastery?
2. How difficult should the items be?
3. What kinds of tasks will be presented to the students?
4. What items (the sample) are to be included in the test instrument?

Open-ended or Mastery?

In physical measurement the scale for a measuring device is selected and built with a range to include all possible values of what is being measured. Thermometers are constructed in such a way that the range of the scale is appropriate for whatever is being measured. Those used in food freezers do not use the same scale as thermometers used in ovens. The lower and upper limits of each thermometer are placed so that all possible values appropriate for the device will be measured with no actual reading reaching either of the limits. The floor and ceiling are placed such that either is rarely, if ever, reached. The person planning the measurement of a physical characteristic purposively chooses points on a scale according to the uniqueness of whatever is to be measured.

Scales for educational tests are often chosen in the same way—a lower limit which is rarely reached and an upper limit which is rarely reached, if the test is used with appropriate subjects. A fifth-grade spelling test does not contain items selected from all of the words in the English language. The lower limit is set because some words are too easy for a fifth-grade test. The upper limit is set because some words are considered to be too difficult. The knowledge of the subject matter, the ability level, and the age level of the students being tested provide a guide in determining the measurement limits of a particular test. The difficulty level of test items provides direction for setting the upper and lower limits of the test. Many **achievement tests** are built on this principle.

Educational tests built to measure the complete range of expected values are referred to as **open-ended tests** and have a top possible score so high that rarely, if ever, will a student score at the ceiling. On the other hand, **mastery tests** are constructed such that students should score at or near the ceiling. The decision of which one to use should be based on what information is being sought by the teacher, how the scores are to be interpreted, and decisions to be made. If a teacher wants to know the highest level of attainment, then the open-ended test would be used so that each student would have an opportunity to score at the highest level. If the teacher wishes to know if a particular level of attainment has been reached or if a clearly defined domain of knowledge has been mastered then the mastery test is used.

A diagnostic test attempts to identify special difficulties that students encounter in new learning. A pretest prior to instruction can determine if a particular level has been reached. A test may be given to ascertain if a particular set of skills has been developed. For the diagnostic test, the pretest, and mastery tests the concern is not in spreading the students' scores along a scale but rather to determine a given level of attainment. Whether a test should determine levels of achievement or ascertain attainment of a particular level must be decided on the basis of how test scores will be used.

Some educational tests measure knowledge, skills, and other learning outcomes that all students *must* acquire. These tests are administered to determine the extent to which students have mastered skills or knowledge fundamental for further learning of the subject or to assure that a specified body of information has been assimilated in its entirety. This type of testing is commonplace in elementary schools when the teacher tests to assess basic skills of students prior to moving on to more advanced material to be learned in progressive learning stages. It is also utilized where a certain body of knowledge is needed for successful functioning in a real-world situation. The student who is going to sell a complex piece of machinery in a highly competitive market does not need to know answers to 70 percent of the questions that prospective purchasers may ask about the construction, performance, and costs. That person needs to know *all* the answers. Classroom tests may or may not require total knowledge of a subject. The mastery type of test is a particular type of **domain-referenced** test which emphasizes behavior objectives, individual instruction, and sequencing of subject matter.

Open-ended measurement

The open-ended test assesses student knowledge, skills, or other learning outcomes when instruction is structured so that all students have the same exposure but are permitted to achieve at different levels. In general, tests of achievement in a *content subject* do not require the highest level of performance to reflect successful levels of performance. A test in this situation should be able to measure the complete spectrum of possible values. It is referred to as a *survey test*—one that is open-ended and has a possible top score so high that rarely, if ever, will a student score at the ceiling.

If a paper-and-pencil classroom test is used to quantify achievement in a subject area, the students should be given the opportunity to exhibit their true achievement levels. For this reason, many classroom achievement tests provide a ceiling high enough (be open-ended) to allow that the attainment level of the highest achiever be measured. A test that does less than that will fail in its purpose of measurement unless the need is to measure a clearly defined domain of knowledge.

Mastery measurement

An alternative to the idea of an open-ended measuring device is a test that measures with a relatively low ceiling. The mastery test requires that the student give responses only to items that everyone is expected to get right. Mastery tests are constructed to determine if a criterion has been met, and most students are expected to score at or near the ceiling to be considered as having been successful in the learning venture. The ceiling reflects only a minimum level of attainment, and a satisfactory score means that the task has been mastered at that level or higher. Mastery tests are valuable for classroom teachers when measuring an area in which all students must reach the same level. In this situation the mastery test sets a minimum standard which all students are expected to achieve. They may be permitted to work and repeat with new tests until a perfect, near perfect, or the appropriate predetermined test score is obtained. Each student works until a specified minimum level of achievement is reached.

A class in first aid would certainly have certain concepts and skills that everyone should possess to be qualified to administer treatment in an emergency situation. A mastery test which requires the student to use each of these concepts and skills would be appropriate to use when trying to determine qualification for certification or license to act as a first aid person. It is more appropriate that each student know a specific body of knowledge than a portion of a somewhat larger body of knowledge. Of course, even in a situation like this additional knowledge is to be encouraged, not discouraged. Mastery testing is not intended to put a lid on learning, but it does put a ceiling on the scale which is used to measure the learning.

The mastery test may also be appropriate for use when certain knowledge or skills are prerequisite to undertaking a new study. Before a student can work through a division algorithm, he or she must be able to multiply and subtract or the process of division will break down. Each of these processes, multiplication and subtraction, must be "mastered" before a student can work a division problem using accepted algorithms for getting right answers. Before undertaking the division algorithm a mastery test for subtraction and another for multiplication could be given to see if the student has mastered these processes.

Before a student can be expected to add he must have *mastered* the addition facts. A mastery test over addition facts should be given and passed with few mistakes by each student before being allowed to undertake the study of getting solutions to problems which require the process of addition.

For mastery tests, items must be tied directly to instructional objectives of content and behaviors. Interpretation of measures that provide information about attainment of mastery of instructional objectives is made in absolute terms. The comparison to absolute standards may be made by expert rating or by **criterion keying**, and must be a part of the planning for the test.

Mastery tests are also used in programs of individualized instruction in which the student is given a test at the end of each instructional unit. Programs of instruction which utilize a model of individual instruction measure the performance of students to determine if they are ready to start a new unit of instruction. A specified minimum level of acceptance (usually close to a perfect score) is needed to continue to the next unit. A score less than the minimum indicates that the student should spend more time on the unit being tested before going on. The better programs for individual study recycle the student through the same content but change to a new procedure or new materials. The student then studies until test performance is adequate, that is, demonstrates *mastery* of the content as determined by test performance.

Other considerations

Since teachers do not want to put limits on student learning, there are some situations where measurement at minimum levels is not appropriate. Most content courses are considered to have minimum acceptance levels but the body of content is, in general, not fixed and students are encouraged to go beyond a basic body of knowledge. When writing behavioral objectives, the minimum acceptance level can be stated as a percentage of a possible perfect score on a test. An overall understanding at a predetermined acceptance level may be all that is needed to indicate competence, but in situations where student learning is expected to exceed the minimum level, a measurement instrument which has an upper limit higher than the minimum is necessary. When students understand this type of testing, the teacher is well advised to give each student the opportunity to exhibit true achievement level by using a test with an open-ended upper scale limit. Measurement of this type requires that the test which is used as the measuring device be of the highest quality.

The discussion of open-ended, mastery, and other criterion-referenced tests has pointed up some of the similarities and differences in interpretation of test scores. Figure 5.4 presents a comparative summary of various aspects of mastery and open-ended tests. Prior to test construction, these factors as well as others should be given consideration.

Scaling scores.   Since an open-ended test is intended to measure differences among students, the tasks should allow the students' scores to vary according to the amount of the trait being measured. Each score should be in

Characteristic	Open-ended	Mastery
Purpose	Measure complete range of student attainment	Measure mastery of minimum essentials
Objectives	General or specific	Highly specific and detailed
Learning outcomes	Broad range	Limited range
Representative learning outcomes	Many	Few
Type of test items	All types	All types
Difficulty of tasks	Medium difficulty	Relatively easy

FIGURE 5.4   Comparative summary of open-ended and mastery tests.

corresponding relationship to the amount of achievement possessed by that student. The relationship is thus established among all scores. The scores of the test should be isomorphic to the amount of the trait that each student holds. This means that the scores made by the students are in the same relationship to students' possession of the trait being measured.

The readings on the scale of a weather thermometer are isomorphic to the different amounts of heat contained in the air at different times. A difference of five degrees between thermometer readings will represent the same difference at the lower, middle, or upper part of the scale. Any temperature difference in degrees within the air is reflected in the measures according to the scale. The same relationship of isomorphism is required between achievement within students and the test scores produced by the students. Needless to say, the task before a test constructor is not an easy one and remains formidable even for experts.

Need for both.   Most classroom teachers will find a need for both mastery tests and open-ended tests. Some of the specific behavioral objectives will state a minimum acceptance level best measured by a mastery test while others can best be measured by an open-ended test. Other than interpretation, the major difference between open-ended and mastery tests is in regard to the difficulty level of the task imposed on the student. The principles of good testing are the same for both kinds of tests. Since a mastery test is to be made up of tasks that all or nearly all the students are expected to get right, the tasks must be relatively easy. If the content is not fixed and a behavioral objective states a percentage of correct responses on a test over a body of content, the open-ended test ceiling would be, in general, more suitable.

The popularity of criterion-referenced measurement with emphasis on behavioral objectives has caused interest in the mastery test. Early work by educational psychologists had placed the concept of all students reaching criterion performance in an unpopular role and mastery tests were considered to be unsuitable for measurement. In the middle 1960s the idea that nearly all students could learn what the teacher has to teach but that some would take longer to complete the learning became popular. Individualized instruction, although not new to educators, more and more became a part of school instructional activities. Many individualized programs incorporated mastery tests as check points on students' progress and as guidelines for directing students to new units for study.

A strong case for mastery learning was made in the late 1960s by Bloom, Hastings, and Madaus (1971, pp. 43–60). The principle of students learning all of what the teacher has to teach them is easy to support and few, if any, would fault that concept. There are questions about whether it can be successfully implemented in all situations. Nevertheless, learning for mastery requires testing at mastery level, and mastery testing becomes a part of any program of learning for mastery.

The practice of open-ended testing has been unpopular with some educators because they felt that when a classroom sets its own norm, some are doomed to failure, and at the same time this guarantees that some will appear to do well, since there is no set of external standards. Since the resulting scale for a norm-referenced test is related to a point in the middle of the score distribution and is based on an average performance, a performance is viewed in its position and distance above or below that middle point. Whether that average as a point of reference does indeed guarantee failure for some and success for others is a matter of interpretation.

Good norm-referenced measurement must produce measures which have meaning beyond relative standings of students. The content meaning of any measure must accompany the relative position of scores one to another. This means that a score must tell the student and teacher more than just where the student stands relative to other students. The score must also indicate how much achievement in absolute terms the student has made. This is accomplished by relating the test instrument tasks to stated objectives. (Refer to the subsection "The Table of Specifications.") With this dimension the norm-based scores do not guarantee failure for some and success for others.

The opinion of the writers in regard to the choice between mastery and open-ended tests is that the open-ended test has a better chance of providing the desired information than does the mastery test unless the desired information is about a fixed body of content that should be tested in its entirety. Educators will continue to find uses for both mastery tests and open-ended tests. Where the measurement is for "minimum essentials," a form of a mastery test would be more fitting, while measurement for "maximum development" (Gronlund, 1970, p. 32) should incorporate some way of distributing values along a scale to discriminate levels of attainment. When planning for the test, most of the factors of concern will be the same for mastery tests and open-ended tests; however, if the measurement is compared to a set of predetermined standards, those aspects directed to establishing differences are irrelevant. The reader should incorporate in the plan for each individual test the ingredients appropriate for the type of test being built.

Difficulty Level of Tasks

The establishment of the difficulty level of tasks for the mastery test is easy. The only criterion for difficulty of the task is that each test taker be expected to perform satisfactorily on the task. The age level, experiential background, motivation, and interest of each student are assumed to be suitable to complete the task satisfactorily. For individualized instruction each task must be attainable at some time for each student.

Establishing the difficulty level of tasks for a test to discriminate amounts of a trait is not as straightforward as it is for a test to measure the minimum acceptance level of competence. Uncertainty associated with open-ended testing is the contribution to the total test score of the very easy items and the very difficult items. A student's achievement on an open-ended test is established in relationship to how other students achieve. To measure differences on a scale, the final quantifications must vary. An item that is answered correctly by nearly all the students does not contribute to differences, since the final score is increased the same amount for nearly all. An item that is answered incorrectly by most of the students does little to create differences, since the contribution to most total scores is about zero. Research and testing models indicate that levels of achievement can best be determined by a test that consists of items which are of medium difficulty and construction of open-ended tests is based on this principle.

Power test

First thoughts based on common sense seem to suggest that each test should include *(a)* some easy tasks that most everyone should perform satisfactorily, *(b)* some difficult tasks that only a few will perform satisfactorily, and *(c)* some tasks that students will perform with varying degrees of success. This principle is used in what measurement specialists refer to as a **power test.**

A power test is built on tasks of varying difficulty with the assumption that students will work through the tasks presented from easy to difficult until they reach the upper limit of their capabilities, and a ceiling will thus be established for each student. Relating this to a paper-and-pencil test, a student should answer all items correctly up to a point, and then beyond that point all items should be missed.

An uncertainty with this approach is that the difficulty level for any one item is not the same for all students. If a test taker knows the answer to an item, that item is easy. If the examinee does not know the answer, the item is difficult regardless of how others do on that item. For example, on a test for 50 students the better students will probably miss some items that those of lesser ability answer correctly, thus violating the basic principle of the power test. Statements about difficulty must be made in regard to how many in a group miss the item or how many get it correct, and the above assumption will not hold in every case.

In contrast to the power test some tests are designed to ascertain how quickly a student can work through a series of very easy tasks. This type of test is referred to as a *speed test,* and measures reaction speed rather than how much a student knows.

An example of a power test would be a series of mathematical computational problems ordered from simple to complex. A student should be able to work to a point successfully and then not be able to work farther. This is intended to locate a ceiling on a mathematical sequence.

An example of a speed test would be a series of addition facts that each student knows. The test would be to see how many of the facts can be recorded in a given period of time. This is intended to measure reaction time rather than whether or not a student knows the facts.

Selected-response items

Levels of achievement are best fostered by selected-response items that are answered correctly by 50 percent of the students taking the test. In practice this is not a practical or logical target for student performance. For example, if one-half of the students missed a true-false item, this would be at the chance level and would reveal nothing about how students have achieved. Multiple-choice items also have this same impracticality but not to the degree of true-false items. Most items on a selected-response test should be answered correctly by about 50 to 75 percent of the students depending on the type of item and number of possible responses from the selected-response item.

A target of difficulty for selectioned-response items is usually that point which is midway between a value obtainable by chance selection of the correct response and perfect selection of the correct response. If a multiple-choice test item with five alternatives were given to 100 students, the target would be that point where 40 students get it wrong and 60 get it right. With five alternatives one-fifth of the students (20) could be expected to get the correct answer by chance without any knowledge of the subject matter. Halfway between 20 getting it right by chance and all 100 getting it right is the ideal level of difficulty (40 wrong and 60 right). In practice the test constructor will not be able to predict exactly how difficult each item will be for a group, but with knowledge about the instructional emphases, students' capabilities, and testing procedures, the classroom teacher should be able to stay well within the range of acceptable difficulty levels. For the true-false test about 25 percent of the class should miss the item and about 75 percent of the class should get it correct. The chance level for a true-false test is 50 percent wrong by blind guessing. By dividing the range of 50 percent wrong and 00 percent wrong equally the midpoint of 25 percent incorrect is considered to be the desired level of difficulty for true-false test items.

For students and teachers who have been accustomed to tests where everyone is expected to have a correct response every time (mastery testing) the acceptance of competency attainment where 4 out of 10 students miss an item may be difficult to accept. An understanding of the principle of difficulty helps to make students more comfortable. An explanation that the test maker could prepare a test where everyone "does well" by writing easy items or could make a test where everyone "does poorly" by writing very difficult and obscure items should help students and teachers understand why tests like this are desirable. What the test maker tries to do is to level the difficulty of the items so that the scores will be distributed along the scale showing the relative positions of all students.

No one person is expected to know everything about any one topic. The best informed teachers (even authors of textbooks—even authors of textbooks on measurement and evaluation) rarely, if ever, have 100 percent knowledge about subjects that they teach or write about. This does not mean that they are incompetent. It means that every discipline has an opportunity to add more and more to that body of knowledge which is its concern. Since most students are accustomed to taking tests where they are expected to have all correct responses, some understanding of open-endedness associated with the body of knowledge is needed. Tests built to measure achievement where not everyone is expected to gain the same knowledges at the same level are then better accepted by students and teachers.

Most test constructors agree that for classroom tests a few easy items in the first part of the test can help to overcome some anxiety that students bring to a testing session. The object of test administration is to get a true measure of achievement, but test anxiety may reduce the ability of students to perform at their own levels. Although research indicates that test anxiety is not a major obstacle to educational measurement, it may be reduced within students if they have a feeling of success early in the testing session. For that reason, recommended planning procedure suggests the use of a few easy items early in the test even though those items will not contribute to any great extent to the determination of different levels of achievement.

Constructed-response items and problem items

The contribution of constructed-response and problem items to the total test score depends on the demands placed on the test taker by the item writer. The type of item utilized must be written or selected considering capabilities of test-takers and their level of understanding and ability, and can be varied to meet the expected student level of performance in the subject area and behaviors exhibited.

A teacher who is knowledgeable in the subject area and who knows student ability levels can write constructed-response and problem items at varying difficulty levels. Items can be addressed to content studied by all students when the majority would be expected to respond correctly or to measure achievement demonstrated at higher levels of learning.

What Kind of Tasks?

The choice of kind of task to use on a test should be determined taking into consideration: *(a)* the nature of the subject matter, *(b)* the specific objectives set for the students, *(c)* the type of information needed for evaluative purposes, *(d)* the age and developmental level of the students, and *(e)* the size of the group to be tested.

The test maker must decide in the planning stage what type(s) of task(s) would be most appropriate for the content and behaviors to be measured. Some content in mathematics, science, and technical aspects of other subjects can be covered by presenting specific problems for solution. Other content can be sampled better by using a test that asks students to respond in their own words to specific questions or situations created by the test maker. Some content can be sampled better by using test items such as true-false, multiple-choice, matching, and classification where the student is asked to select responses from alternatives provided by the test instrument rather than create each response. Different types of items call into play different behaviors needed to respond to tasks presented.

Tests can be divided into three divisions according to the demand placed on students as they respond to the task. Items which require the student to choose from provided alternatives are classified as **selected-response items,** and items which require the student to create a response are classified as either **constructed-response items** or **problem items.** The basic type of test items to be considered under each of the major divisions in this textbook are:

1. The selected response item:
   a. **True-false item**—students indicate whether a statement is true or false.
   b. **Multiple-choice item**—students select a correct response from a series of alternatives.
   c. **Matching item**—students indicate relationships between a set of premises and a set of responses.
   d. **Classification item**—students classify according to certain categories.
2. The constructed-response item:
   a. **Completion**—students complete a statement by filling in a blank or blanks in a sentence.
   b. **Short-answer**—students provide a short response to a direct question or direction.
   c. **Essay**—students write a paragraph or more as a complete expression of a fully developed thought.
3. The problem item:
   a. Mathematical problem—students create a response within a framework from little to much freedom concerning the problem.
   b. Technical problem—students create a response to a complex situation for a limited and specialized study.

When making the choice of the item type for the test the classroom teacher should consider the kind of information needed. The decision will have already been made that a paper-and-pencil test instrument is needed rather than some nontest procedure, but the test constructor must make the final decision about the type of item to use in the measuring instrument. Strengths and weaknesses for the three major divisions of items and each of the basic type of items included under each division are presented in separate chapters for selected-response items (Chapter 6), constructed-response items (Chapter 7), and problem items (Chapter 8). The teacher should be familiar with this information prior to test construction.

Determination of which kind of item to use depends on many considerations. Figure 5.5 provides a summary comparison of test-item characteristics that may be helpful in determining the type of item to include in the test.

Banesh Hoffman (1962) proposed that tasks which require a student to merely choose responses from those provided cannot measure understanding but are limited to testing superficial knowledge. This position is not supported by writings of experts in the field of educational measurement (Ebel, 1972, p. 100), and there seems to be general agreement that selected-response items can be used to measure more than simple recall of learned facts and knowledge. Granted most selected-response items which are written probably measure at the knowledge level, but that is the fault of the item writer not of the type of item and does not reflect a characteristic of selected-response items. High-quality tests are written by classroom teachers and testing experts, and many of them use selected-response items for tasks.

On the other hand, a test which requires that the student create the response cannot always be said to test higher levels of learning. Completion and short-answer tests are limited to the lower levels, but essay responses can require behavior at the higher levels. A high-quality selected-response test and an essay test of equally high quality will rank a sample of students in about the same order. This is as it should be for any measuring device—the better students should rank high and others leveled according to their achievement. The choice between selected-response and constructed-response items should be made in terms of what kind of data is needed and which type of item will be able to generate that information. The general characteristics of each type should be considered when making the choice.

Problem items are difficult to construct and time-consuming to score but serve quantitatively oriented learning areas. They provide a valuable way to test understanding of underlying principles or to create a real-world situation for application. The freedom of response may vary widely depending on the nature of material covered by an item. The response to a particular problem may require an in-depth investigation of a technical area.

Constructed-response tests are relatively easy to construct but difficult to score accurately and quickly. Since each response must be viewed in light of knowledge in the subject area, the scoring process will be time-consuming, and difficulty in judging the degree of adequacy of the response will tend to reduce the reliability of the measures.

Characteristic	Selected-response	Constructed-response		Problem Item
	True-false multiple-choice, matching, classification	Completion and short-answer	Essay	Mathematical and technical
Item Preparation	Tedius, difficult	Relatively easy	Difficult	Difficult
Number of Items per test	Many	Many	Few	Few
Items	Specific	Specific	General	Specific or general
Test time use	Reading, thinking	Reading, thinking	Thinking, writing	Problem solving
Responses	Symbol (letter or such)	One word or short phrase	Expressed in student's words	Expressed in figures and student's words
Responses	From provided alternatives	Brief	Extensive	Brief to extensive
Scoring	Objective	Objective or semi-objective	Reader's judgment	Objective
Scoring	Easy	Relatively easy	Time-consuming	Time-consuming
Scores	Value determined largely by the test constructor	Value determined largely by the test constructor	Value established by reader of responses	Value established largely by the test constructor
Cognitive domain	Knowledge, comprehension, application	Knowledge	All levels	Understanding and higher levels
Freedom of response	Restricted to given options	Very little	Very much	Very little to very much
Guessing	Permits, may encourage	Little	Very little	Very little
Bluffing	None	Some	Permits, may encourage	None
Implications for study	Study for facts and higher uses of knowledge	Study for facts	Study for facts and higher uses of knowledge	Study for facts, computation, and higher uses of knowledge

FIGURE 5.5. Summary comparison of test-item characteristics

Since each response is constructed by a different student, the element of guessing the correct response is reduced to a minimum. Bluffing a correct response by writing around it without a full commitment to any one answer may be a problem, but a skillful reader should be able to identify a bluff for what it is and score the response as such.

The constructed-response essay item allows the student to express ability to compare, contrast, explain, describe, and summarize, which is not possible with completion, short-answer, and all selected-response items. To allow the student to express an opinion and build a defense for it requires the freedom provided by the essay item. When interested in determining students' opinions and their ability to defend them or to measure other high levels of the cognitive process, the teacher should use the essay test.

Selected-response tests can be scored quickly and objectively but are relatively difficult and time consuming to construct. If scores from tests are needed quickly after the test has been administered and construction time is available before the test session, the teacher is well advised to use a test with selected-response items. If a teacher has a well developed **test-item file** of previously used items, construction time can be reduced.

Since more individual tasks can be provided on a selected-response test, the sample of content will be large compared to a constructed-response test. A large sampling from content allows the opportunity to build high content validity into the test. Chance selection of a small number of tasks has a higher probability of producing a large difference between the actual test items and the population of possible test items.

Tests of selected-response items are especially well suited to distinguishing among levels of achievement without the subjectivity involved in judging the quality of each response individually. The directness of the selected-response item usually presents a clearly defined task that requires no interpretation and allows students to react to a task that is the same for everyone. This makes the selected-response item suitable for measurement of knowledge, understanding, and application for all subject-matter areas.

OTHER TEST PLANNING CONSIDERATIONS

In addition to planning the actual construction of the test, other factors must be considered before the test is administered:

1. Frequency of test administration
2. Time to allot for the test administration
3. Specific time for administration
4. Selecting tasks for the test
5. Announcement of the test date
6. Scoring procedures
7. Score interpretation
8. Use of correction for guessing (Appendix C)

Frequency and Time Allotment

An overall plan for frequency of tests and time available for testing sets parameters for specific tests. If only two tests are to be given in a semester, the tests must be able to cover a much larger body of content than if tests are given weekly or every two to three weeks. School policy regarding marking and reporting may dictate how often testing will occur. In general, the more frequently testing occurs, the more reliable the base for evaluation. Formative evaluation requires a continuous flow of information, and frequent tests would be appropriate. Summative evaluation may need only one or two tests for the time period of concern. For this reason tests used for formative evaluation tend to test small bodies of content more intensely while tests used for summative evaluation need to cover a larger body of content.

The number of tasks to be presented on a test is a function of the amount of time available for testing as well as the type of item. The modules or periods used in secondary and some middle schools limit the available time. The amount of time to be spent on a test is also limited by the maturation level of younger students and their differing abilities to focus on one test for a long period of time. The attention span for young children may be only 10 to 15 minutes for classroom group testing while students in some intermediate grades could be expected to spend from 45 to 60 minutes on a test. At the other extreme, graduate students are often expected to spend as much as four or five hours in one session writing comprehensive examinations in their field of study.

Teacher understanding of students' level of development, particularly their attention spans, should give needed clues to establishment of a suitable length of time to be spent on a test for elementary school students. If it becomes necessary to go beyond these limits, the test should be divided into two or more sessions. In general, even very large blocks of content can be covered adequately within a 60-minute test period.

A specific day and time must be decided upon for actual administration of the test. Many teachers prefer midmorning of a middle-of-the-week day to give a test. There may be some advantage to a particular hour; however, "there is little if any evidence or strong logic to support preference for a particular hour of day." (Ebel, 1972, p. 100). Probably more important than these considerations is the avoidance of disturbing factors of interruptions and noise. When setting the time of administration, careful thought should be given to school schedules so that the best time to avoid disturbance is chosen. A sign on the door that says "TESTING—DO NOT DISTURB" may help to avoid interruptions that cannot be anticipated.

The teacher who has a class for only a part of a school day such as a module or a period is restricted to that time block, and little freedom is given within a day; however, attention should be given to the day of the week, since some days may have fewer disturbing factors than other days. The teacher who has a class of students for all or most of the time as in a self-contained class has the added freedom of selecting not only the day of the week but also the time of day to avoid interrupting factors.

Selecting Tasks

The major function of classroom achievement tests is to measure levels of scholastic attainment. Most educators agree that they can also be used to contribute directly to students' learning by guiding study. If a test or series of tests is to guide study, the planning stage must be coordinated with the total scope of the school program. Plans for a test need to be started when study commences. Possible tasks for tests should be identified as they are generated from day-to-day classroom activities. Specific items can be written in rough form as a part of the teacher's daily schedule. With this groundwork already laid the actual construction of the items becomes much less burdensome and stretches that job over the total time period rather than leaving it as a major problem the last few days before the test is to be given. A file of good items built from previous tests is also helpful in building better tests.

Announcing Test Date

Students should be informed as early as possible about the specific date of the test so that they can plan their preparation in view of their other commitments. Since some anxiety is attached to test taking, a test that is announced early will provide opportunity for preparation and may keep students' anxieties at acceptable levels. A moderate amount of test anxiety may be helpful to stimulate students to their highest potential, but too high a level of anxiety may actually stand in the way of measuring a student's actual achievement.

A high level of test anxiety may create a condition where an individual is unable to attend to test taking. However, a student low in motivation may be apathetic and feel free from anxiety about the test and therefore not be attentive to test taking. A certain amount of anxiety has its advantages and acts positively on school achievement testing. Early announcement of the test date and an explanation of the behavior to be exhibited (problems, essay items, etc.) allows the student to study effectively for the demands of the testing session.

Scoring Tests and Score Interpretation

After a test has been administered to students, their responses must be scored. The type of test largely dictates the scoring procedure to use. Decisions as to scoring procedures and planning for the scoring are made during the planning stage. Since the procedures themselves are discussed later in appropriate sections, they will not be presented here.

The interpretation of the scores may also be largely dictated by the type of test being administered. Score interpretation for classroom and published tests is discussed in later sections.

Since the scoring of a test and the interpretation of the scores are integral parts of the total testing process, each must be given consideration in the planning stage. As these are revealed in the several sections which follow, the reader will want to relate that material back to its place in planning the test.

GENERAL CONSIDERATIONS IN CONSTRUCTION OF TEST ITEMS

The planning stage for classroom measurement has set the direction for later steps in test construction. Plans have been developed to supply the types of information needed to make valid judgments. In addition to preliminary considerations, decisions of construction have been made about the desired difficulty level of items and type(s) of item(s) to be used, and a table of specifications was drawn up to indicate how many items would be needed for each: (*a*) subject-matter topic which is to be covered, and (*b*) behavior which is to be exhibited by the students. The next step is to prepare the items for the test instrument.

The writing of test items cannot be reduced to a set of rules which guarantees that the items will measure what the item writer wants to measure; however, there are general guides and specific considerations which should be taken into account when writing test items. Like many of the procedures associated with accepted measurement theory, much of the process of developing items for tests remains largely an art. The influence of variables which affect outcomes of research about item writing remains an unknown factor largely because our methods of study do not allow the control needed to interpret results into widely applicable generalizations. No set of rules will allow the item writer to anticipate with high accuracy how an item or set of items will perform when it is presented to a student or a group of students in the form of a test.

An overview of some illustrative studies pertaining to item writing is given by Wesman (1971) who summarizes his presentation:

> None of them [the research studies] is definitive, none supplies generalizations that may be confidently adopted. . . . Item writing continues to be an art to which some scientific procedures and experientially derived judgments make only modest contributions. (p. 86)

Theory of test-item construction can help teachers build better tests. By adding the ingredients of originality and creativity as well as a good working knowledge of subject matter to basic test theory, any teacher can become proficient in test construction.

Teachers gather a large portion of information about students through tests. They need to be able to write items and build test instruments which generate the kind of data needed. Competence in item construction is developed as items are carefully scrutinized before they are used and then critically evaluated in light of item analysis and other techniques discussed in later chapters.

Practical suggestions about writing items aid in skill development and help minimize the time and energy expended by the teacher committed to building valid and reliable tests. A set of guidelines is presented to be followed with an eye to develop the art of item writing rather than as a set of rules to be learned. Rules would probably be forgotten, but the art should remain and continue to develop at higher levels with classroom utilization.

Some factors to be kept in mind while preparing specific tasks for tests are common to all types of items. Although the study of test building includes few hard and fast rules, consideration of the following points is essential to production of a valid test instrument. Some of them may seem obvious, but they are included to make this presentation functional in all educational settings.

1. Specific test items should be written in preliminary form during the period of instruction and study. Since the testing program should be an integral part of the total classroom activities, writing items should be a part of the ongoing instructional program on a continuing basis. When writing items is concentrated into a short time period just before testing, two outcomes can be expected. First, item writing will become burdensome for the teacher, and second, the quality of items will probably be lowered. A poorly prepared test does not provide valid information to the teacher for evaluation of student learning, and it may confuse students in regard to what they think is most important to learn. If the final item-writing session starts with an abundance of items in preliminary form, selection of the best of the pool should overcome both of these difficulties to a great extent.

2. Maintain close contact with the corresponding set of educational objectives and the test's table of specifications. Any information to be used in evaluative procedures must be generated from appropriately selected tasks. The scores from the test will not be useful in judging the extent to which the objectives have been reached unless the test items are tied to objectives.

3. Base test items on important matters. Avoid items which deal with insignificant, obscure, or trivial information which is not directly related to basic understanding.

4. Write items which, when responded to correctly by students, reflect attainment of knowledge through special study of the subject matter, not from general knowledge.

5. Each task should be presented as straightforwardly as possible. Selection of the type of item to use should be based on how well that item type can generate the needed data.

6. Review items from many sources. New ideas about how to present tasks can be gleaned from colleagues' classroom tests and standardized tests.

7. Observe good language expression. This avoids ambiguity in: *(a)* presentation of the task, *(b)* instructions about how to respond, and *(c)* alternatives for selection. The intent of the writer can be conveyed in tasks for the

test only through clear and undistorted statements and questions. Rules of grammar must be followed to avoid communication breakdown.

8. Use simple and precise language. Rather than trying to impress the test taker with large or little-used words, the item writer should build the test with a vocabulary appropriate for the age and ability level of students to be tested. If students cannot understand what is written because of inappropriate vocabulary, they cannot receive credit even though they know the correct response. The measures (the scores) from the test will largely represent the size of the students' vocabularies rather than achievement in subject content.

9. Use your own original language. If the items are written in textbook language or repeated verbatim from a book, the student may be able to get correct responses by simple recall of knowledge and facts. If students meet tasks in test items the same way that they first meet them in their study, little room is left for them to go into behaviors at the level of comprehension and beyond.

10. Avoid any clues or suggestions that would help the unknowing student to get a correct response. Although this is primarily a concern of selected-response items, the essay item can be worded to give a student who does not know the correct response an indication of the direction of the intended response.

11. Recruit colleagues as editors to review items and to give constructive criticism. In addition to rewriting test items, a classroom teacher can use fellow teachers who are knowledgeable in the area to be tested for review of the items and for suggestions about how to improve the items. Their responses to the items can be used to check agreement about the correct response.

SUMMARY

Comprehensive observation of achievement is possible through the administration of teacher-made tests. Classroom tests expand the gathering of information concerning achievement by supplementing a classroom teacher's direct observation. A test is an instrument, device, or procedure that proposes a sequence of tasks to which a student is to respond—the results of which are used as measures of a specified trait.

The primary purpose of a classroom test is to quantify the characteristic that the test is designed to measure by assigning a meaningful value to each student. Tests promote learning as well as measure achievement if they are well planned and properly used.

The chapter discussed planning considerations that help the classroom teacher build meaningful and valid measures. The frequency of test administration, allotment of time, attention span of students, level of student development, scoring procedures, and other factors must be considered in test planning. Through early and careful attention to these factors a teacher can avoid unexpected contingencies later and build validity into testing procedures.

The test blueprint or table of specifications, a two-way chart relating course content to desired learning outcomes, provides a design or plan for the test. It serves those objectives that are measurable and builds content validity for the test. The table of specifications aids the teacher in test development and careful test planning.

Construction considerations included open-endedness, mastery, the difficulty of test items, the kinds of tasks to be presented, and the actual items included in the test. Whether a test is open-ended or mastery will determine the level of difficulty of the test items, and in some subject-matter topics the kinds of tasks may be different. An open-ended test is built to measure the range of expected values while mastery tests are built with a ceiling reflecting minimal level of attainment. The establishment of difficulty levels of a task for the mastery test is based on each student being expected to perform satisfactorily on the task. The open-ended test is designed to measure student knowledge along the complete range of possible values.

The content and behaviors to be measured guide the choice of item type. Three broad categories of items with their subdivisions were presented: (a) the selected-response item (true-false, multiple-choice, matching, classification), (b) the constructed-response item (completion, short-answer, and essay), and (c) the problem item. General considerations in constructing test items were provided to develop the art of item writing. Chapters 6, 7, and 8 cover item writing for selected-response, constructed-response, and problem items.

NEW TECHNICAL TERMS LISTED IN THE GLOSSARY

Achievement test
Classification item
Completion item
Constructed-response item
Content validity
Criterion keying
Domain-referenced
Essay item
Mastery test
Matching item

Multiple-choice item
Open-ended test
Power test
Problem item
Selected-response item
Short-answer item
Test blueprint
Test-item file
True-false item

ACTIVITY EXERCISES

1. Prepare a table of specifications for a selected-response test for one unit.
   a. State the objectives in behavioral or nonbehavioral terms as you would actually state the objectives for your classroom.
   b. List the subject-matter topics in the unit and establish the relative importance of the topics by assigning a percentage of the test to each subject-matter topic (total is 100 percent).
   c. Assign a percentage for each behavior in the cognitive domain (total is 100 percent).

   d. View the topics studied and behaviors desired according to their interrelatedness and incorporate this information into the cells of the table of specification as percentages.

2. With a sheet of paper cover the two columns—open-ended and mastery —in Figure 5.4, Comparative summary of open-ended and mastery tests. Complete the columns and compare your work with the figure.

FOR DISCUSSION

1. Explain the advantages of frequent testing.
2. Explain how a table of specifications contributes to the overall process of test construction.
3. Discuss open-ended and mastery teaching. Explain how classroom teacher-made tests are different as a result of the differences in teaching for open-ended or mastery learning.
4. In addition to actual construction of the test what other factors must be considered when planning for classroom testing? Why are they important to generation of valid data?

REFERENCES AND KNOWLEDGE EXTENDERS

BLOOM, B. S., HASTINGS, J. T., & MADAUS, G. F. *Handbook on formative and summative evaluation of student learning.* New York: McGraw-Hill, 1971. Chap. 3, pp. 43–60.

EBEL, R. L. *Essentials of educational measurement.* Englewood Cliffs, NJ: Prentice-Hall, 1972.

GRONLUND, N. E. *Measurement and evaluation in teaching* (4th ed.). New York: Macmillan, 1981. Chap. 5, pp. 123–153.

GRONLUND, N. E. *Stating behavioral objectives for classroom instruction.* New York: Macmillan, 1970.

HOFFMAN, B. *The tyranny of testing.* New York: Collier, 1962.

HOPKINS, C. D., & ANTES, R. L. *Classroom testing: Construction.* Itasca, IL: F. E. Peacock, 1979. Chap. 2, pp. 16–44.

MEHRENS, W. A., & LEHMANN, I. J. *Measurement and evaluation in education and psychology* (2nd ed.). New York: Holt, Rinehart & Winston, 1978. Chapter 7, pp. 159–203.

RICHARDSON, M. W., & STALNAKER, J. M. Comments on achievement examination. *Journal of Educational Research,* 1935, *28,* 425–432.

ROWLY, G., & TRAUB, R. E. Formula scoring, number-right scoring, and test-taking strategy. *Journal of Educational Measurement,* 1977, *14,* 15–22.

VAUGHN, K. W. Planning the objective test. In E. F. Lindquist (Ed.), *Educational measurement.* Washington, D.C.: American Council on Education, 1951. Chap. 6, pp. 159–184.

WESMAN, A. G. Writing the test item. In R. L. Thorndike (Ed.), *Educational measurement* (2nd ed.). Washington, D.C.: American Council on Education, 1971. Chap. 4, pp. 81–129.

Chapter 6. Constructing Selected-Response Items

After study of Chapter 6, you should be able to:

1. Recognize the strengths and weaknesses characteristic of selected-response items.
2. Recognize the specific strengths and weaknesses of true-false items.
3. Construct true-false items based on the "Guides to Writing True-False Items."
4. Critique true-false items based on the "Guides to Writing True-False Items."
5. Recognize the specific strengths and weaknesses of multiple-choice items.
6. Construct multiple-choice items based on the "Guides to Writing Multiple-Choice Items."
7. Critique multiple-choice items based on the "Guides to Writing Multiple-Choice Items."
8. Recognize the specific strengths and weaknesses of matching items.
9. Construct matching items based on the "Guides to Writing Matching Items."
10. Critique matching items based on the "Guides to Writing Matching Items."
11. Recognize the specific strengths and weaknesses of classification items.
12. Construct classification items based on the "Guides to Writing Classification Items."
13. Critique classification items based on the "Guides to Writing Classification Items."
14. Explain how each glossary term listed at the end of the chapter is used in classroom measurement and evaluation.

The choices of item types depend on the kind of information needed for evaluation, the nature of the subject matter, the specific objectives set for students, the amount of time available for testing, and the age-developmental level of the students to be tested. Selected-response items (true-false, multiple-choice, matching, and classification) present tasks that are responded to by selection of alternatives from those provided by the test itself. They are popular for classroom achievement tests because they are flexible and, when well written, can produce valid data for both formative and summative evaluation.

Selected-response items can be used in nearly all subject areas and can be tied to a wide range of instructional objectives at all levels of the cognitive domain. The items are self-contained since students make responses without going beyond the items themselves. The only freedom of response is internal because each item limits students to selection of the correct or best response from the alternatives provided, hence the term *selected-response*. A test made up of selected-response items can be scored independently by one or more scorers from a key, or electronically by an optical scanning device or similar machine. This has led to these items being referred to as **"objective items,"** because the scorer does not make judgments about the quality of the responses —only comparisons to keyed responses.

The quality of the items and also the test depends on the skill of the item writer and efforts to write effective items. The learning outcomes which can be measured by true-false, multiple-choice, matching, and classification items range from simple to complex behaviors, and through all subject areas. Standardized achievement tests rely heavily on selected-response items in test instruments to be used in a wide range of testing situations. Teachers also find selected-response items appropriate for many of the tests constructed for their classrooms.

SELECTION

Instructional activities are designed to prepare students to function in the modern world. At all ages choices must be made from two or more alternatives —situations, persons, ways of proceeding, and such. In today's media-intensive world students are increasingly being called on to make rational choices from sets of alternatives. For example, the medium of TV bombards the listener with advertising which requires the individual to bring to bear skills of choice-making to sift through the ad makers' pitches.

The game of chess could be viewed as a series of multiple-choice selections. Each time it becomes a player's turn to move, the individual must select from a finite number of possibilities. Some moves are better than other moves. The winner is conceivably the better alternative selector. Many people consider selected-response test items as apt metaphors for the "game of life."

The component of intelligent choice making is implied or stated in most lists of broad educational goals. If students are to be prepared to make intelligent choices, then the school program should have a component devoted to developing this skill.

With intelligent selection of choices receiving this attention in goal statements and programs, use of selected-response items in tests can support the instructional program. The selected-response item as used in tests provides a direct opportunity for a teacher to integrate the school program and testing activities. As the student becomes more skillful in making choices in the testing situation, teachers (as well as other concerned individuals) can assume that the student's ability to use this skill in the real world has improved. Skill in making choices developed in the school program prepares students to make rational choices.

Teachers should be able to write and judge the quality of items for their tests as well as judge the quality and appropriateness of selected-response items for published tests to be used in their classrooms. In this chapter guidelines and useful information in writing selected-response items and evaluating items written by others will be provided. The lists of strengths and weaknesses for selected-response items are presented to assist teachers to determine whether to use selected-response, constructed-response, or problem items when building tests for their own uses.

STRENGTHS OF SELECTED-RESPONSE ITEMS

The common strengths of selected-response items are related to objectivity in scoring and to the large number of items that can be responded to in a relatively short period of time. For these reasons selected-response items continue to serve tests that are criterion-referenced as well as those that are norm-referenced. Strengths associated with all selected-response items are:

1. Objectivity in scoring can be maintained because knowledge of the subject matter is not required to identify correct or incorrect responses. After the scoring key has been developed, each student's set of responses is compared to it by hand or machine.

2. Scoring of items is easy and can be carried out quickly. When a teacher wishes to provide quick feedback to students or to give a test to a large number of students and return the scored papers promptly, tests made up of selected-response items should be used.

3. Greater objectivity in scoring results since comparing sets of responses with the scoring key produces the same score for each paper unless a clerical error is made in hand scoring. Machine scoring eliminates any scoring error due to the human element.

4. A relatively short testing time is needed to obtain comprehensive coverage of subject matter. A comprehensive sample of student achievement for each subject-matter topic is possible in a reasonable time period.

5. A well-written item sets a clearly defined task and a definite correct response. This reduces ambiguity in items to a minimum.

6. The test writer provides correct responses and the quality of student handwriting and expression cannot affect scoring or reduce or inflate the measure of demonstrated achievement. In contrast, in constructed-response items, particularly essay and short-answer items, a student's handwriting and ability to express ideas and organize material may enter unintentionally into judgment of responses.

7. For selected-response items the student chooses a response which is provided, therefore the issue of bluffing is not a factor in scoring as it might be in scoring student-created or constructed responses.

8. Selected-response items are adaptable to most content areas as well as a wide range of behaviors.

WEAKNESSES OF SELECTED-RESPONSE ITEMS

The weaknesses result largely from the fact that the responses are provided for the test taker and there is no opportunity to interact or communicate beyond the provided alternatives. Weaknesses associated with all selected-response items are:

1. A student who does not know a response will guess. When guessing is involved in selection of responses, the reliability of the test is lowered. The consistency with which the test measures could be reduced below acceptable levels if a large amount of guessing occurs in a testing session.

2. Construction of good selected-response item tests is time consuming and difficult. Items at the higher levels of the cognitive domain are especially difficult to write.

3. Since items for the lower levels of the cognitive domain are easier to write there may be an overbalance of items at lower levels when the instructional objectives may call for more items at other levels.

4. The difficulty level of each item must be judged by the test writer prior to students' reactions to them. For norm-referenced tests selected-response items are written to be of medium difficulty, although the difficulty of each item for a class is unknown until students respond to that item on a test. The difficulty level of items for criterion-referenced tests must be such that a student who has learned what the objective relates to will get the item correct and others will miss the item. The problem of difficulty is large for both systems of referencing test scores.

5. There is no opportunity for originality or expression of opinion by the test taker. If these factors are important, constructed-response items should be utilized.

6. Selected-response items have been criticized because students who are testwise can pick up clues from the item and identify a correct alternative without understanding the concept being measured. A properly constructed item will not permit identification of the keyed response without understanding of the concept (guessing excepted), thus overcoming this criticism.

TRUE-FALSE ITEMS

True-false items are presented as declarative statements which propose something that the student is to discuss mentally as to its truthfulness. After making a decision about how well it conforms to reality or accepted truth, the student marks "true" if the statement is essentially true or "false" if the statement is essentially false. Other forms of the alternate-response item include: *(a)* yes-no, *(b)* right-wrong, *(c)* correct-incorrect, and *(d)* any of these forms with an added factor that the student is to correct all false statements to make them true statements. If the student is asked to correct items, then each item whether it is true or false should have a part of the words underlined to indicate what is to be changed if the item is false. Examples of the corrected true-false item are not included because procedural difficulties in writing and scoring the items make this an undesirable item except in very special cases. The use of corrected alternate-response items is not recommended by the authors.

True-false items have been criticized because of accusations (Ebel, 1979, pp. 111–121) that: *(a)* they deal with details which have little importance to the field of study, *(b)* they are ambiguous, *(c)* they are vulnerable to the effects of guessing, and *(d)* they expose students to error. The first three criticisms can be dealt with effectively by good writing procedures. Studies devoted to research of the harmful effects of false statements have not reported serious effects.

True-false items are particularly helpful in determining how well students remember facts and definitions. They are generally used to measure recall, but can be developed to measure understanding and comprehension as well as measuring a student's knowledge effectively. Criticism that many true-false items are poorly written and ambiguous should be directed toward the writer rather than the true-false item per se. Poor true-false items result from poor item writing and not because true-false items are inherently ambiguous or because they can measure only unimportant details. Avoidance of the use of the true-false item sacrifices many strengths, especially the wide range of coverage possible in limited testing time.

Special Considerations

When choosing the most appropriate item type to call forth a particular student behavior, the teacher must consider the following strengths and weaknesses of the true-false item.

Strengths

1. Students are able to respond to more true-false items in a given time period than other selected-response items. Generally students can respond to about two true-false items per minute. When a specified period of time is set for a test, quicker response allows for more extensive coverage of learning outcomes than provided by other selected-response items.

2. When responding to a true-false item, students react in much the same way as they do when answering a question in class or in a real-world situation. Students feel comfortable with well-written true-false items because of familiarity with the alternative response proposition often directed to them by parents, peers, teachers, and other people they come in contact with.

3. True-false items can be written in relatively few words so that they are easy to read and understand. This makes the true-false item useful in special situations, such as testing primary-grade children, and poor readers.

4. True-false items provide a simple and direct means of measuring

learning outcomes in the knowledge category of the taxonomy of the cognitive domain. A skillful writer can develop items which call for identification of cause-and-effect as well as items requiring distinction between fact and opinion.

5. True-false items are amenable to item analysis which enables the teacher to determine how the items functioned with the students tested.

Weaknesses

1. Guessing on true-false items may artificially increase student scores since there is a 50 percent chance of guessing the correct response thus providing a high probability of chance success.

2. True-false items presume a dichotomous relationship of being absolutely true or false. In reality, there exist degrees of correctness, and a statement may not always be totally true or totally false. As a result response to some items may be difficult for a student even when the material is familiar.

3. True-false items are susceptible to ambiguity and misinterpretation unless careful attention is given to the principles of good item writing.

4. In general, true-false items are less discriminating of levels of achievement than other selected-response items. The element of chance responses reduces the effective range of student scores, and this limits the discrimination power of true-false items.

5. Writing items which measure behaviors beyond recall of facts may be more time consuming than writing simpler recall items. However, it is probably no more time consuming than writing another type of item to measure the same concept.

Guides to Writing True-False Items

1. Long complex sentences are not acceptable for true-false statements. Base the item on one important idea which is clearly true or clearly false. If two or more matters are to be dealt with, the student may have knowledge of one and not the other. If a student is reduced to a blind guess for one, this leaves no way for knowledge of the other to contribute to the student's score. If one or more parts of the item are false but the others are true, the student is left with a situation where the correct way to respond is indeterminate. Better test procedure calls for one item for each idea to be tested.

Example A (Poor item)

T   F   Voting is an important way to express our views of government, but historically only men who owned property and paid taxes were eligible to vote.

The student may know that voting is an important way citizens may express their views of government, but may not know that men who owned property and paid taxes were the only persons permitted to vote. The student would not know how to respond to the second part of the item without guessing. The item could be broken into two items, one concerning the importance of voting and the other concerning who was permitted to vote, as in the following examples.

Example B

(T) F   Voting is an important way to express our views of government.

(T) F   Historically only male property owners were eligible to vote.

2. Avoid **specific determiners**—those unintentional signs which give clues to the correct response. Words such as "always," "never," "all," "none" are associated with false items while "usually," "often," "most," "may," "should," and the like are associated with true items. Of course, items can be written so that this pattern is broken, but this can develop into a cat-and-mouse game between the test-item writer and students thus negating the purpose of the test. Best policy suggests that these words be avoided entirely.

Example A (poor item)

T   F   Nationalism and patriotism are always used synonymously.

An alert student could get a clue that the statement is false from the word *always* and receive credit for the item without understanding the difference between "nationalism" and "patriotism."

Example B

T (F)   Nationalism and patriotism mean the same thing.

3. Direct true-false statements positively by avoiding the use of negative words. Use a negative statement *only if* an important concept cannot be tested by a positive statement and be sure to underline the negative word. When words like *no* and *not* are not underlined, they may be overlooked by students. A straightforward positive statement creates a situation in which a knowing student will respond correctly to the item.

Example A (poor item)

T   F   Undesirable family budget management means that a family should _not_ use credit.

Example B

(T) F   Fresh air as a resource has _not_ been given much thought until recent years.

Double negatives within the item are not only confusing but unacceptable grammatically and must be avoided in true-false items. The student is already involved in a decision which has a possible negative outcome in the false alternative. A second "not" or "no" further complicates the decision process and may cause a student who understands the concept to miss the item.

4. Adding the word *not* to a true statement to make it false is inappropriate.

Example A (poor item)

T F   The judicial branch of government is *not* called the Supreme Court.

Example B

T Ⓕ The judicial branch of government is called the Senate.

Example C (poor item)

T F   The state flower of Indiana is *not* the peony.

Example D

Ⓣ F   The state flower of Indiana is the peony.

5. Avoid long, complex, and involved statements. When statements are not relatively simple and direct, the students' reading ability, rather than achievement in subject matter, is tested and more than one idea may be involved.

Example A (poor item)

T F   In the late 1890s Guglielmo Marconi, an Italian inventor, developed a system of wireless telegraphy or what is now called the radio.

Example B

Ⓣ F   Guglielmo Marconi invented the radio.

Example A includes information not necessary to test whether a student knows Marconi developed a system of wireless telegraphy. An incorrect response could result from the student thinking: *(a)* that Italian was the wrong nationality, *(b)* that the date is incorrect, *(c)* someone else invented the wireless telegraphy, or *(d)* that the radio is another invention.

6. Avoid **ambiguity** by writing items so that the thought is the same for everyone. Ambiguity may be present because qualitative terms are unclear. Avoid broad generalizations as well as vague, indefinite, and certain inaccurate terms which are open to interpretation. An item which is written so that

experts in the field being tested cannot agree as to the task or the correct response (**intrinsic ambiguity**) possesses unacceptable ambiguity and is a poor item. If the student's lack of knowledge is the basis of ambiguity (**apparent ambiguity**), the quality of the item is not reduced.

7. False items should be written so that statements sound plausible to someone who has not studied in the area being tested. Common misconceptions make good bases for false items.

8. Statements used as true-false items should be about the same length in each test. Many times true statements are longer because of qualifying phrases. If items have different lengths, be sure to vary the length of both true and false items.

9. Include about the same number of false items as true items. Although false items tend to be more discriminating than true items, any tendency to have more false items on all tests gives the student who expects more false items an advantage when guessing blindly.

10. Cause-effect (if-then) relationships must be stated so that the student clearly must react to the effect and not the cause. Since two ideas come into play here, the first must be clearly stated as a given premise and not a part to be judged.

11. Statements should be written in the teacher's own words. Statements taken verbatim from textbooks encourage rote memorization. In other cases an item may be answered without having understanding of the content by remembering a phrase or sentence from the book if it sounds familiar.

12. Check the section "General Considerations in Construction of Test Items" in Chapter 5.

Exemplary Items

The following items provide models which reflect the suggestions about how to construct true-false items. Not all "Guides to Writing" or subject areas are covered.

Elementary school items

T (F) 1. Longitude lines circle the globe in an east to west direction.

(T) F 2. Sentences begin with a capital letter.

(T) F 3. There are 12 months in a year.

T (F) 4. The next numeral in the series 4, 3, 6, 5, 10, 9, 18, 17 is 26.

T (F) 5. If a girl had 11 feet of fencing material, she would have enough fence to make a puppy area 6-feet long and 4-feet wide.

Secondary school items

(T) F 1. A moist heat method of cooking should be used in the preparation of meats that contain high levels of connective tissue.

(T) F 2. The ratio of the length of the adjacent leg of angle A over the length of the hypotenuse of the triangle is called the cosine of angle A.

(T) F 3. When using a circular saw a push stick should be used with stock less than 3-inches wide.

(T) F 4. The two trends that characterized Latin American history from the 18th century through the 20th century were Europeanization and modernization.

(T) F 5. The most useful laboratory test in diagnosis of anemia is the hemoglobin test.

MULTIPLE-CHOICE ITEMS

Multiple-choice test items are presented to the student through a premise to which the student is to select a response from a set of alternatives. Students tend to understand tasks presented by well-written multiple-choice items better than they do tasks in other item types. This item type allows the writer to give more information to set the task than the true-false item. Since the scope of multiple-choice items is less than essay items, multiple-choice items tend to be more direct in setting the task than do essay items.

The student's task is usually introduced in a direct question or incomplete statement known as the **stem.** The four or five listed responses are known as **alternatives,** and the student selects one which is considered to be the best. One of the alternatives is keyed as a correct response by the writer of the item. The other alternatives are referred to as **distracters** because the item writer has deliberately developed wrong answers which would appear to be correct to a student who does *not* know the correct response.

Multiple-choice items are especially useful to the test constructor who is engaged in writing items at the levels of comprehension and application. There does not seem to be general agreement about how well the multiple-choice item functions in the higher levels—analysis, synthesis, and evaluation—of the taxonomy for the cognitive domain. Some writers have supported the use of multiple-choice items for all levels while others have reservations about the value of measuring higher-level behaviors with multiple-choice items. If through acceptable procedures, items can be written to measure complex behavior through selection in a multiple-choice format, the authors support their use. However, widespread use of the multiple-choice item to the exclusion of other types of items should be carefully evaluated to see if the desired outcomes of testing are being fulfilled.

Special Considerations

When choosing the most appropriate item type to call forth a particular student behavior, the teacher must consider the following strengths and weaknesses of the multiple-choice item.

Strengths

1. Multiple-choice items are widely adaptable to subject-matter content and to different levels of behavior of the cognitive domain. This type of item can be utilized in assessing ability to reason, discriminate, interpret, analyze, make inferences, and solve problems.

2. The stem and four or five alternatives provide less chance for guessing the correct response than in a true-false item. A well-constructed item at the appropriate level of difficulty reduces correct responses from blind guessing; therefore, only the higher achieving students should get the item correct. There is less chance of guessing the correct response because a student who does not know the correct response must guess among more possibilities than the two presented in true-false items.

3. Since there is less score variation due to guessing in a multiple-choice test as compared to a true-false test, the multiple-choice test is expected to provide greater test reliability.

4. The difficulty of each multiple-choice item can be controlled by changing the alternatives. The more homogeneous the alternatives, the more difficult it is to select the correct response from the alternatives provided.

5. The number of alternative responses helps provide information which may be utilized for diagnostic purposes. The teacher and student are able to pursue the reasons for understanding, or lack of understanding, content in specific topics, based on the alternative chosen.

6. Multiple-choice items are amenable to **item analysis** (Chapter 10) which enables teachers to determine how well the items functioned with the students tested.

Weaknesses

1. High-quality multiple-choice items are time consuming and difficult to write. Locating three or four plausible distracters for an item is arduous, and without adequate distracters the item is of limited value.

2. More skill is needed in writing multiple-choice items than any other selected-response item. The skill of the teacher in writing this type of item largely determines the quality of items and the test.

3. More time is required to respond to a multiple-choice item than a true-false item. The time needed for responding increases as the complexity of the task increases.

Guides To Writing Multiple-Choice Items

1. Set a definite task in the stem of the item. A good stem presents a task that can be responded to without seeing the distracters.

Example A (poor item)

_____ *Dress* is a term that means to
a. put in proper alignment.
b. put on clothing.
c. treat medically.
d. check diagonals.

Example B

__a__ *Dress* is a military term that means to
a. put in proper alignment.
b. put on clothing.
c. treat medically.
d. check diagonals.

This example item provides a definite task. When a student can respond without seeing the alternatives, the item would be similar to either a completion item (incomplete stem) or a short-answer item (stem as a question).

2. When the item is presented in statement form, the alternative should finish an incomplete sentence. Time is lost if the student must reread the stem.

Example A (poor item)

_____ The _____ arithmetic process should be used when deciding how many cookies each child should get when distributing 12 cookies equally among 3 children.
a. addition
b. subtraction
c. multiplication
d. division

Example B

__d__ What arithmetic process should be used when deciding how many cookies each child should get when distributing 12 cookies equally among 3 children?
a. addition
b. subtraction
c. multiplication
d. division

A student reading example A does not find the task presented directly, and there is a tendency to reread each alternative into the stem until the best response is located. In many cases the four alternatives are read into the statement before the response is selected. Presenting the task as in example B eliminates this situation.

3. When using an incomplete statement to set the task, place as much of the wording in the stem as possible. If a word or phrase is repeated in each of the alternatives, it should be moved to the stem.

Example A (poor item)

_____ Which of the following best summarizes "I Hear America Singing"?
a. The greatness of America is in its industrial strength combined with an adequate labor force.
b. The greatness of America is in the recognition of the individual's abilities.
c. The greatness of America is in the individual's working independently and yet harmoniously.
d. The greatness of America is in each individual's appropriate work choice.

Example B

___c___ In Walt Whitman's "I Hear America Singing," the greatness of America is summarized by
a. its industrial strength combined with an adequate labor force.
b. the recognition of the individual's abilities.
c. individuals working independently and yet harmoniously.
d. each individual's choice of work.

A comparison of examples A and B illustrates that attention is clearly directed to the alternatives by reducing the wording in each alternative. The readability of the alternatives is also improved.

4. The use of negative words or wording is to be avoided in the stem and alternatives. If use of the negative becomes necessary, be sure to emphasize any negative direction by underlining or writing negative words in capital letters. Never use a negatively oriented alternative with a negative stem, since double negative becomes difficult to interpret.

Example A (poor item)

_____ Which of the following is not always compatible with automobile safety?
a. four-wheel brakes
b. safety glass
c. power
d. dual brake system

Example B

___c___ All of the following are compatible with automobile safety EXCEPT
a. four-wheel brakes.
b. safety glass.
c. power.
d. dual brake system.

Students can easily overlook such words as *no* and *not* in the stem of an item. The use of a negative word usually does not reinforce what students are to learn.

5. The stem should be presented in a form to avoid making the item essentially true-false in which one alternative is true and the other alternatives are false.

Example A (poor item)

_____ Which one of the following alternatives is true?
 a. Inertia is the tendency to remain at rest or in motion unless acted on.
 b. Centrifugal force is the force tending to make rotating bodies move toward the center of rotation.
 c. Centripetal is the force tending to make rotating bodies move away from the center of rotation.
 d. Centripetal force is due to inertia.

This item reduces to four true-false items of which one is true and three are false.

Example B

__b__ What principle demonstrates that the work done in rubbing your hands together is equivalent to the amount of heat produced?
 a. inertia
 b. kinetic energy
 c. conservation of energy
 d. relativity

6. Construct all alternatives to be parallel in form with the stem of the item.

Example A (poor item)

_____ An automobile coil can be used
 a. to charge the battery.
 b. to increase the voltage of electric current.
 c. it cools the ignition system.
 d. delivering the current to spark plugs.

Both alternatives "c" and "d" are eliminated from being the correct response because they are not parallel with the stem. This can be corrected by rewriting the item with all alternatives parallel as shown in Example B.

Example B

__b__ What is the purpose of the automobile coil?
 a. charge the battery
 b. increase the voltage of electric current
 c. cool the ignition system
 d. deliver current to the spark plugs

7. Place alternatives in a vertical list to allow students to clearly compare and study the options. The following example has the alternatives arranged to follow the stem in a continuous line (tandem).

Example A (poor item)

_____ Ranchers supply food to their cattle during stormy winter snows by *(a)* carrying hay to them by airplane, *(b)* feeding them in the barn, *(c)* shipping them to farms in the North Central Plains, *(d)* driving them southward to warmer regions.

Example B demonstrates the difference in readability between the tandem and vertical arrangement of alternatives.

Example B

__a__ How do ranchers supply food to their cattle during stormy winter snows?
a. carrying hay to them by airplane
b. feeding them in the barn
c. shipping them to farms in the North Central Plains
d. driving them southward to warmer regions

8. Avoid using "all of the above" as an alternative. When "all of the above" is the correct response, students feel that they have been penalized for choosing any of the other correct alternatives without being given credit for a correct response. Better rapport with students can be developed by avoiding a possible argument about whether the student is being treated unfairly. When the teacher wishes to use an item which has all correct alternatives, the first alternative should be presented as "all of the following." In this way the test taker is forewarned about the possibility of more than one response being correct.

Example A (poor item)

_____ Which would be another name for 9?
a. $4 + 5$
b. $15 - 6$
c. $(6 + 6) - 3$
d. All of the above

For this item the student may recognize that alternative "a" is correct and make that response without continuing. If the keyed response is "d," then the student would be marked incorrect for what was indeed a correct response. The student can be alerted to the possibility of more than one correct response in the alternatives by presentation as in Example B.

Example B

___a___ Which would be another name for 9?
    a. All of the following
    b. 4 + 5
    c. (6 + 6) − 3
    d. 15 − 6

If "all of the following" is used, it should be used when it is not a correct choice as well as when it is a correct choice so as not to give a clue to it always being correct.

Example C

___c___ Which would be another name for 9?
    a. All of the following
    b. (4 + 5) − 2
    c. (9 + 9) − 9
    d. (8 + 8) − 4

9. Alternatives in each item should be about the same length. When qualifying a correct alternative, it may become longer than the distracters, which may be a signal to the alert student that the longer alternative is likely to be the best response.

Example (poor item)

_____ Why were communities in early years of history started near rivers?
    a. Roads were difficult to build and boats could travel up and down the waterways bringing people and goods.
    b. The land along waterways was beautiful.
    c. People enjoyed swimming.
    d. The horse was a slow means of travel.

In the example the longest alternative is the best response. Students tend to select detailed responses which are longer alternatives if they do not already know the correct response.

10. Eliminate verbal clues to the correct alternative or a clue which might eliminate one or more alternatives. Students not knowing the correct response may be able to respond correctly to the item by finding a clue in the stem or alternatives. For example, use of "a," "an," "is" or "are" in the stem may be a grammar clue to a correct response.

Example (poor item)

_____ If a trucking firm wants to increase its cross-country shipping rates, which of the following commissions has the job of approving or disapproving the rate increase?
    a. Federal Communications Commission
    b. Securities and Exchange Commission

    c. Federal Aviation Administration
    d. Interstate Commerce Commission

The stem specifies that the response is a "commission" and alternative "c" is eliminated as a plausible response since it is not a commission. In addition, the words *securities and exchange* in alternative "b" in relationship to the stem are verbal clues which eliminate "b" as plausible. The word *commerce* in alternative "d" may be a clue that "d" is the correct response.

    11. Each of the distracters should be plausible to a student who does not know the correct response. Each distracter should be selected by *unknowing* students about the same number of times. The example in number 10 illustrates an item in which some alternatives are not plausible.

    12. If possible, write the stem as a question which helps to clearly set the task. The incomplete statement can be used when the question is inadequate or will not serve as the stem.

    13. Control the difficulty level of the items so that the percentage of correct responses is about midway between a chance value and a perfect value (see Chapter 10). The stem can be used to make an item easier by presenting it in general terms or more difficult by making it more specific. The correct response can be made easier by making the alternatives heterogeneous or more difficult by making them homogeneous.

    14. Avoid trickery in items. Do not include in any item a component that would require a student to interpret a set of unique words, catch a slightly misspelled word, or guess how a phrase is to be interpreted. If a knowing student misses the item because of a misrepresentation, the item is unfair to the student and affects the reliability and validity of the test.

    15. "None of the above" should be employed as an alternative only if there is no absolute correct response. If the student is asked to choose a correct spelling from several possible arrangements, then "None of the above" serves as a good distracter. "None of the above" has been used by mathematics teachers who want to assure that students have an alternative if they work the problem and get an incorrect answer.

    16. Arrange alternatives in alphabetical, numerical, or appropriate order when there is a certain sequence among them.

    17. Randomly position the correct alternative so that each position is used about the same number of times. Be sure that there is no pattern to the order of correct responses which the alert student could detect.

    18. Four or five alternatives theoretically help reliability. As the number of alternatives is reduced, the chance of guessing the correct response increases. Practical considerations, such as the age of students, the content, and the time available for testing, may determine the number of alternatives feasible for a particular test. Three alternatives are commonly used with students in the first, second, and third grades.

    19. Check the section "General Considerations in Construction of Test Items" in Chapter 5.

Exemplary Items

The following recall items provide models which reflect the suggestions about how to construct multiple-choice items. The same principles apply to items designed to measure other levels of cognition. Not all "Guides to Writing" or subject areas are covered.

Elementary school subjects

1. __b__ What is the name of the grassland on which animals graze in the West?
   a. the prairies
   b. the range
   c. the dust bowl
   d. a farm

2. __c__ Where was the first permanent English settlement in the New World?
   a. Plymouth
   b. Boston
   c. Jamestown
   d. Annapolis

3. __a__ What is a man who plays a guitar called?
   a. musician
   b. dancer
   c. gambler
   d. magician

4. __a__ In what year did the first successful flight of an airplane occur?
   a. 1901
   b. 1903
   c. 1913
   d. 1928

5. __d__ What does an astronomer study?
   a. plants
   b. music
   c. history
   d. stars

Secondary school subjects

1. __c__ What determines the size of a circular saw?
   a. number of teeth on the blade
   b. coarseness of the teeth
   c. diameter of the blade
   d. size of the table

2. __d__ What is the name for the blood cells that carry oxygen to the tissues?
   a. blood plasma
   b. blood platelets

c. white corpuscles

d. red corpuscles

3. __a__ What is a common form of matter that has a definite volume but no definite shape?

a. liquid

b. solid

c. plasma

d. gas

4. __d__ In a gasoline engine where is the air mixed with gasoline?

a. distributor

b. cylinder

c. intake manifold

d. carburetor

5. __c__ The violin, viola, cello, double bass, and harp are members of what musical family?

a. percussion

b. woodwind

c. string

d. brass

MATCHING ITEMS

The matching item consists of a list of premises in one column, and a list of possible responses in another column. The two lists of phrases or terms are arranged in vertical parallel columns with the premises on the left and the responses on the right. The directions instruct the student to make an association or connection between pairs of elements, such as countries with capitals, events with dates, names of individuals with accomplishments, and so on. The nature of the matching item adapts itself to testing knowledge of names, events, conditions, places, structures, and such when recall of facts is important. The likeness to puzzles makes the task of putting the parts of matching items together fun for most test takers.

Matching items are useful in measuring students' ability to make associations, discern relationships, make interpretations, or measure knowledge of a series of facts. Many varieties of homogeneous classes are ideally suited for measurement by this type of item. Adaptations of two lists allow the principle of matching a set of responses to a set of premises to be used widely in many subjects. For example, in geography or history, places can be marked on a map to serve as premises and students asked to associate a name from a given list for each place marked.

Special Considerations

When choosing the most appropriate item type to call forth a particular student behavior, the teacher must consider the following strengths and weaknesses of the matching item.

Strengths

1. Matching items allow for a large quantity of associated factual material to be measured in a small amount of space, while student time needed to respond is relatively short. For example, a matching item of eight related terms or phrases may be utilized to measure the same things that eight multiple-choice items could measure. The amount of space necessary for the eight multiple-choice items is at least double that required of the matching item to measure the same thing.

2. The effects of guessing are reduced since the student will have one chance out of the number of responses available of guessing correctly. If all responses represent plausible options for each premise, then blind guessing should be reduced to a minimum.

Weaknesses

1. There may be a tendency to use material of little importance just to be able to construct a matching item. The item writer should use this type of item only when significant pairs of elements can be identified.

2. The item mainly measures factual information which is based on memorization. The item writer's careful attention to item writing can avoid the pitfall of overemphasizing factual memory.

Guides to Writing Matching Items

1. When a series of multiple-choice items is being utilized to measure a homogeneous area of concern, it may be possible to avoid a series of multiple-choice items by developing a matching item. An example series of seven multiple-choice items is presented to illustrate, then the matching item provided.

Example A

<u>c</u> 1. What is the name of the device used to measure specific gravity of liquids?
 a. dosimeter
 b. barometer
 c. hydrometer
 d. manometer

<u>d</u> 2. What is the name of the device used to measure atmospheric pressure?
 a. hydrometer
 b. manometer
 c. dosimeter
 d. barometer

<u>a</u> 3. What is the name of the instrument used to determine the amount of heat in a substance?

a. calorimeter
b. galvanometer
c. barometer
d. manometer

__d__ 4. What is the name of the instrument used to measure electric currents?
a. calorimeter
b. photometer
c. radiometer
d. galvanometer

__b__ 5. What is the name of the device used to measure fluid pressure?
a. hydrometer
b. manometer
c. dosimeter
d. barometer

__b__ 6. What is the name of the instrument used to study the particle nature of light energy?
a. galvanometer
b. radiometer
c. calorimeter
d. photometer

__a__ 7. What is the name of the device used to measure radiation exposure of the body?
a. dosimeter
b. hydrometer
c. barometer
d. manometer

Example B*

Directions: On the line to the left of each characteristic measured and listed in Column I, write the letter of the instrument utilized in the measurement and listed in Column II. Each instrument will be used once or not at all.

Column I	Column II
Characteristic Measured	Instrument
__b__ 1. amount of heat in a substance	a. barometer
__a__ 2. atmospheric pressure	b. calorimeter
__e__ 3. electric currents	c. closimeter
__g__ 4. fluid pressure	d. dosimeter
__i__ 5. particle nature of light energy	e. galvanometer
__d__ 6. radiation exposure of the body	f. hydrometer
__f__ 7. specific gravity of liquids	g. manometer
	h. photometer
	i. radiometer

---

*Editor's note: Items appearing in a test should *not* be divided. This rule has been violated to conform to book format.

The seven multiple-choice items included in Example A have been condensed into one matching item with seven premises and nine responses as demonstrated in Example B. Strengths of the matching item over a series of multiple-choice items in measuring homogeneous content are: *(a)* less space is needed to present the item, *(b)* less time is required in responding, and *(c)* the same knowledge is measured in a more efficient way.

2. The lists used as premises and responses should be homogeneous to prevent clues to the correct response which allows for elimination of some responses. Heterogeneous premises and responses provide an opportunity to arrive at responses based upon association. Superficial knowledge of a subject area may also provide sufficient background to arrive at the correct response if differences limit the possible responses for each premise.

Example A (poor item)

Directions: For each name in Column I, find the achievement in Column II and place the letter on the line provided. Each achievement in Column II is used one time or not at all.

Column I Name	Column II Achievement
_____ 1. Ludwig von Beethoven	a. former President of the United States
_____ 2. Alexander Graham Bell	
_____ 3. Andrew Carnegie	
_____ 4. Jimmy Carter	b. telephone
_____ 5. John Marshall	c. Chief Justice
_____ 6. Orville Wright	d. painter
	e. composer
	f. aviation
	g. steel
	h. plays

Example A does not have homogeneous content in the strict sense, since the names include inventors, government officials, men of arts, and an industrialist. The achievement column is heterogeneous, and some students can easily identify the achievements by areas which limit the name(s) that would fit the grouping by specialty. A matching item could be constructed for each of the categories or fields of endeavor if the subject content would lend itself to such an arrangement.

Example B

Directions: On the line to the left of each state listed in Column I, write the letter of the capital city in Column II. Each capital city will be used once or not at all.

	Column I States		Column II Capital Cities
f	41. Connecticut	a.	Augusta
b	42. Massachusetts	b.	Boston
a	43. Maine	c.	Burlington
d	44. New Hampshire	d.	Concord
h	45. Rhode Island	e.	Dover
g	46. Vermont	f.	Hartford
		g.	Montpeller
		h.	Providence

3. Keep the list of premises and responses to a maximum of 12. Five to eight premises provide the most efficient item since looking for a response in a long list of responses is time consuming. A long item can be broken into two or more separate items to be more efficient.

Example A (poor item)

Directions: For each of the definitions used in recipes from Column I place a letter for the term from Column II on the line. A recipe term may be used once or not at all.

		Column I Definitions	Column II Recipe Terms
_____	1.	to allow a food to stand in a liquid to soften or add flavor	a. bread
_____	2.	to beat rapidly to incorporate air and produce expansion	b. whip
_____	3.	to break lightly into small pieces	c. caramelize
_____	4.	to bring to a temperature just below boiling point	d. cut in
_____	5.	to cook in a small amount of hot fat	e. sift
_____	6.	to coat with bread crumbs, or mixture of beaten egg and milk, then crumbs	f. blanch
_____	7.	to cook by dry heat, usually in the oven	g. marinate
_____	8.	to cut in pieces with a knife, chopper, or scissors	h. pit
_____	9.	to cut food into small cubes for uniform size and shape	i. saute
_____	10.	to melt sugar slowly over low heat until it becomes brown in color	j. steep
_____	11.	to mix shortening with dry ingredients, with pastry blender, knives, or fork	k. bake
_____	12.	to moisten foods during cooking with pan drippings, water, or special sauce	l. flake
_____	13.	to pour boiling water over food	m. dice

Column II Recipe Terms (continued): n. chop, o. scald, p. knead, q. baste, r. shred, s. cream, t. score

_____ 14. to put one or more dry ingredients through a sieve

_____ 15. to remove seeds from fruits

_____ 16. to rub or beat with a spoon or electric mixer till mixture is soft and fluffy

_____ 17. to work and press dough with the palms of the hands

The following examples illustrate how the longer item may be divided into two or three separate items with a logical grouping.

Example B

Directions: Match each definition (List A) with its recipe term (List B) by writing the letter of the recipe term in the space provided on the response sheet.

List A Definitions	List B Recipe Terms
__f__ 1. to allow a food to stand in a liquid to soften or add flavor	a. chop
	b. dice
__b__ 2. to cut food into small cubes for uniform size and shape	c. dredge
	d. flake
__a__ 3. to cut in pieces with a knife, chopper, or scissors	e. grate
	f. marinate
__h__ 4. to cut narrow grooves or gashes part way through the outer surface of food	g. pit
	h. score
__g__ 5. to remove seeds from fruits	

Example C

Directions: Match each definition (List A) with its recipe term (List B) by writing the letter of the recipe term in the space provided on the response sheet.

List A Definitions	List B Recipe Terms
__g__ 1. to bring to a temperature just below boiling point	a. bake
	b. baste
__d__ 2. to cook in a small amount of hot fat	c. blanch
__a__ 3. to cook by dry heat, usually in the oven	d. saute
__h__ 4. to extract color, flavor, or the qualities from a substance by leaving it in water just below the boiling point	e. sear
	f. scald
	g. simmer
__b__ 5. to moisten foods during cooking with pan drippings, water, or special sauce	h. steep
	i. stew
__c__ 6. to pour boiling water over food	

Example D

Directions: Match each definition (List A) with its recipe term (List B) by writing the letter of the recipe term in the space provided on the response sheet.

	List A Definitions		List B Recipe Terms
h	1. to beat rapidly to incorporate air and produce expansion		a. bread
b	2. to mix shortening with dry ingredients, with pastry blender, knives, or fork		b. cut in
d	3. to put one or more dry ingredients through a sieve		c. flake
f	4. to rub or beat with spoon or electric mixer till mixture is soft and fluffy		d. sift
e	5. to work and press dough with the palms of the hands		e. knead
			f. cream
			g. shred
			h. whip

In Example B, in guide number 3 the terms and definitions relate to processes carried out generally prior to cooking. Example C, in guide number 3 involves terms and definitions in cooking which generally involve the use of heat to some degree and Example D, in guide number 3 relates to the preparation of ingredients, or doughs and batters.

4. Arrange the lists of premises and responses in a logical order. Ordering by numerical sequence for dates and numbers reduces the amount of time needed to respond. Example B in guide number 2 illustrates lists or columns containing alphabetized states and capital cities.

Example

Directions: For each number in List A choose a numeral for the same number from List B of the matching set. Enter your choice in the appropriate space provided. Use any name from List B as many times as you need to.

	List A Name		List B Numeral
h	1. $(50 \div 2) + 5$		a. 20
c	2. $(\frac{1}{2} \cdot 40) + 2$		b. 21
g	3. $32 - 3$		c. 22
d	4. $(24 + 9) - 8$		d. 25
a	5. $\sqrt{50 \cdot 8}$		e. 26
			f. 27
			g. 29
			h. 30

5. When phrases or sentences are used in a list of premises or responses, the shorter phrases should become the responses. In this way the student reads

the longer premise and then searches the shorter responses, thus saving valuable test time. This principle is illustrated in examples throughout this section.

6. Indicate the basis for establishing the relationship to be used in the matching process. At times this might be apparent from the nature of the list, but the test writer should state it clearly for the examinee.

Exemplary Items

The following items provide models which reflect the suggestions about how to construct matching items. Not all "Guides to Writing" or subject areas are covered.

Elementary school subjects

1. Directions: Find the word in Column II that matches each definition in Column I. Write the letter of the vocabulary word before the definition. Each word will be used one time or not at all.

	Column I Definition	Column II Vocabulary Word
__h__	1. an assigned job or duty	a. antic
__a__	2. a silly trick or prank	b. collide
__c__	3. join together, unite	c. combine
__b__	4. to come together with force	d. envy
__g__	5. to clean or polish by rubbing	e. fluke
__f__	6. to move slowly; fall behind	f. lag
__e__	7. a stroke of luck	g. scour
		h. task

2. Directions: Match each health profession with its description of the duties and write the letter that corresponds to the description of duties on the line provided. Each health profession will be used one time or not at all.

	Column I Duties	Column II Health Profession
__a__	1. advises diabetic patients about menu planning	a. dietician
__e__	2. diagnoses and prescribes medicines	b. hospital administrator
__b__	3. directs the work of the hospital staff	c. medical technologist
__g__	4. operates equipment that helps a doctor decide if a bone is broken	d. pharmacist
__c__	5. performs laboratory tests used in diagnosis	e. physician
__d__	6. prepares medicines according to a doctor's prescription	f. psychologist
		g. X-ray technologist

3. Directions: List A contains descriptions of the parts of the eye and List B the names of the parts of the eye. In the blank in front of each description place the letter of the part named. You may use a letter in List B once or not at all.

	List A Descriptions	List B Names of Parts
__d__	1. colored part of the eye which regulates the size of the opening	a. aqueous humor
__h__	2. jelly-like liquid on the inside of the eyeball	b. cornea
__f__	3. opening in the eye through which light enters	c. choroid
__e__	4. part of the eye that focuses light rays	d. iris
__g__	5. part of the eye containing the sensory cells	e. lens
		f. pupil
		g. retina
		h. vitreous humor

4. Directions: Read each statement carefully. Find the official of the county government listed in Column II which matches each statement of duties in Column I and write the letter of the official in front of the statement. Each official may be used as many times as needed or not at all.

	Column I Statement of Duties	Column II Official
__d__	1. arrests lawbreakers	a. assessor
__f__	2. collects taxes	b. auditor
__e__	3. determines the boundaries of lands	c. clerk
__b__	4. examines financial accounts	d. sheriff
__c__	5. issues licenses and supervises elections	e. surveyor
__d__	6. keeps the jail	f. treasurer

5. Directions: Write the letter of the word from Column II that has the opposite meaning of each word listed in Column I. Each word in Column II will be used one time or not at all.

	Column I Word	Column II Opposite
__f__	1. attract	a. insult
__d__	2. chronic	b. joyous
__e__	3. fatigue	c. plain
__a__	4. flatter	d. rare
__g__	5. lenient	e. refresh
__c__	6. ornate	f. repel
__h__	7. rapid	g. severe
		h. slow

Secondary school subjects

1. Directions: For each of the general areas of the United States where a tree would be found in its natural setting as listed in Column I, select from Column II the tree or forest that would be found in that region. Write the letter of the tree or forest beside the number of the region in the space on the response sheet.

	Column I Location	Column II Trees
__f__	1. coastal region from Alaska to California	a. hardwood for- est
__e__	2. coastal region of Northern California	b. palm
__a__	3. northeast quadrant of the United States	c. pin oak
__d__	4. semidry areas of California, Oregon, and Washington	d. ponderosa pine
__b__	5. southernmost areas from Florida to Cali- fornia	e. redwood for- est
		f. Sitka spruce
		g. willow

2. Directions: For each structure listed in A choose the city or country where it is located from List B. Write the letter for the city or country beside the number for the structure in the space on the response sheet.

	List A Structure	List B Place
__b__	1. Eiffel Tower	a. London
__h__	2. The Needle	b. Paris
__a__	3. Big Ben	c. Madrid
__l__	4. Great Wall	d. Moscow
__e__	5. The Arch	e. St. Louis
__k__	6. Taj Mahal	f. Chicago
__d__	7. Kremlin	g. San Francisco
__g__	8. Golden Gate Bridge	h. Seattle
__n__	9. Aswan Dam	i. New York City
__i__	10. Empire State Building	j. Mexico
		k. India
		l. China
		m. Italy
		n. Egypt

3. Directions: In the blank to the left of each painter listed in Column I, write the letter of the painting listed in Column II. You may use a letter in column II once or not at all.

	Column I Painter	Column II Painting
__b__	1. Leonardo DaVinci	a. *Central Park in Winter*
__e__	2. Albrecht Durer	b. *Mona Lisa*
__a__	3. William James Glackens	c. *Night Watch*
__h__	4. Pablo Picasso	d. *The Apache*
__i__	5. Odilon Redon	e. *Praying Hands*
__c__	6. Rembrandt	f. *The Gleaners*
__g__	7. Johannes Vermeer	g. *The Letter*
		h. *The Lovers*
		i. *Vase of Flowers*

4. Directions: In the blank before each life insurance phrase in Column I, write the letter of the word or phrase in Column II that is most closely associated with it. Each item in Column II may be used once or not at all.

	Column I Concepts	Column II Key Terms
__g__	1. the chance of something happening	a. annuity contract
__e__	2. a major reason for the family wage earner to have insurance	b. beneficiary
__h__	3. provides protection for a specific period of time	c. surrender value
__i__	4. also called *permanent insurance*	d. endowment
__f__	5. a dollar amount based upon mortality tables	e. premature death
__c__	6. the money the insured can get for the policy when cashed in	f. premium
		g. probability
		h. term insurance
		i. whole life

5. Directions: Match each song or slogan (List A) connected with the event (List B) by writing the letter of the event beside the number of the song or slogan in the space on the response sheet.

	List A Song or slogan	List B Event
__e__	1. "The power to tax is the power to destroy"	a. The Monroe Doctrine
__a__	2. "Europeans keep out"	b. The War Hawks
__b__	3. "On to Canada, On to Canada"	

    __f__ 4. "And the rocket's red glare, the bombs bursting in air"

c. Winter at Valley Forge
d. Defense of Washington, D.C.
e. Supreme Court decision
f. Fort McHenry bombardment

CLASSIFICATION ITEMS

The classification item consists of a list of statements or words and a key list of categories. The two lists may be arranged in parallel columns with the statements on the left and the categories on the right. Set up in this manner, the classification item resembles the matching exercise. An alternative type of form is to place the key list of categories above the list of statements or words. The directions instruct the student to classify each entry of the list by recording the letter of the category for classification. The key list of categories consists of exhaustive classes to which the student assigns each premise.

An efficient way to present a task of recall may involve the association of something with a classification system. The examinee can be given a premise and asked to identify the class to which it belongs. Specific things to be classified can be names, descriptive phrases, pictures, or statements. Part of almost every body of knowledge fits into some sort of classification system which must be understood to organize and structure all or part of the total knowledge. The classification item seems to be a direct approach to checking the student's ability to use a system with facility.

Special Considerations

When choosing the most appropriate item type to call forth a particular student behavior, the teacher must consider the following strengths and weaknesses of the classification item.

Strengths

1. Classification items require a small amount of space and provide a relatively large number of scoreable units. The single set of responses (key list) is applied to a number of situations.

2. This item type requires a relatively short period of time for students to respond to each situation presented. The small number of alternatives allows for responses to be made without a time delay caused by searching through a large set of possible responses.

3. The classification item can be used to test the ability to compare and contrast through discriminative thinking. This type of item requires the stu-

dent to make decisions concerning differences among similar things as well as to recognize similarities.

4. The effects of guessing are reduced since the student will have one chance out of the number of classes (alternatives) available of guessing correctly. For example, when five classes are available, the student has only one chance out of five of guessing the correct response.

Weaknesses

1. The item mainly measures factual information, and in some instances superficial outcomes may be measured. If the material does not lend itself to a classification system, the classification item should not be used.

2. There must be enough relationship and yet differences between key words or phrases before an item can be developed. This may make it difficult to develop classification items unless there is a natural set of classes for a system.

Guides To Writing Classification Items

1. Each of the words or statements must belong definitely to one class/category.

Example A (poor item)

Directions: Below is a list of animals doing something. Place the letter before each one that identifies the setting in which each animal is carrying out the activity.

F — in the forest   U — under an old log
O — high in an oak tree   W — in the wild grass

_____ 1. mouse running
_____ 2. rabbit keeping very still
_____ 3. bear crashing through branches
_____ 4. bear crawling on a big limb
_____ 5. chipmunk eating acorns
_____ 6. rabbits looking for supper
_____ 7. snake crawling

This item does not meet the requirement of having only one correct response class for each item. For example, a mouse may be running in the forest, under a log, or in the wild grass. The class in an item should be related to all other classes but mutually exclusive. Overlapping of classes should not occur as in example A.

Example B

Directions: Test item tasks can be classified into three general types as follows:

P — Problem S — Selected Response C — Constructed–Response

Properly categorize each of the following items according to criteria developed in this class.

____S__ 1. true-false
____P__ 2. 7 times 14
____C__ 3. essay — limited response
____C__ 4. essay — extended response
____S__ 5. multiple-choice
____S__ 6. classification
____P__ 7. "What is the mean of a distribution when the sum of the X values is 90 and the number of cases is 14?"

2. A clear explanation of the task and classification system must be provided. Without knowledge of the relationship between the key responses students may not be able to proceed in responding to the items.

3. The number of classes should be limited to the number which can be appropriately utilized. A maximum of five classes usually makes the task and judgments needed clear in classifying each item.

4. The categories in the key list of alternatives are to be exhaustive, mutually exclusive, and yet have a relationship within a structure.

5. Check the section "General Considerations in Construction of Test Items" in Chapter 5.

Exemplary Items

The following items provide models which reflect the suggestions about how to construct classification items. Not all "Guides to Writing" and subject areas are covered.

Elementary school subjects

1. Directions: All living things can be classified as either animals or plants. As I read some names, write on your paper the letter A or P. Write the letter A if what I name is an animal. Write the letter P if what I name is a plant. (To be read by the primary grade teacher for an oral presentation to the class.)

____P__ 1. tree
____A__ 2. lion
____A__ 3. bee
____P__ 4. flower

____A__ 5. butterfly
____P__ 6. grass
____A__ 7. elephant
____A__ 8. rabbit

2. Directions: Read each name below and place:

F before fruits,
V before vegetables,
FL before flowers.

___V___1. celery   ___FL___4. marigold   ___F___7. tangerine
___F___2. peach   ___V___5. turnip   ___V___8. beet
___FL___3. daisy   ___F___6. banana   ___FL___9. petunia

3. Directions: Below is a list of words which you are to read.

If *ea* sounds like *ea* in eat, place an A before the word.
If *ea* sounds like *ea* in great, place a B before the word.
If *ea* sounds like *ea* in head, place a C before the word.
Use A, B, or C as many times as necessary.

A — eat   B — great   C — head

___A___1. beat   ___A___4. cream   ___A___7. mean
___B___2. break   ___C___5. instead   ___C___8. ready
___C___3. breadth   ___A___6. leaves   ___A___9. stream

4. Directions: Write N in the blank if the word names something. Write
D if the word tells about doing something.

Example: ___D___ running   ___N___ ball

N — names something   D — does something

___N___1. cloth   ___N___5. clock
___N___2. house   ___D___6. play
___D___3. listen   ___D___7. read
___D___4. look   ___D___8. sing

5. Directions: In the blank space write M before the unit of measure if
it is used in the metric system. Write E if it is used in the English
system.

M — metric   E — english

___M___1. centimeter   ___M___7. liter
___M___2. gram   ___E___8. mile
___E___3. foot   ___M___9. millimeter
___E___4. inch   ___E___10. pint
___M___5. kilogram   ___E___11. pound
___M___6. kilometer   ___E___12. yard

Secondary school subjects

1. Directions: Each of the following scientific laws or principles is
attributed to a particular scientist. Write the letter that represents
the scientist and the law or principle connected with him in the
provided space. Use each name as many times as necessary.

A — Newton's law of gravity
B — Dalton's atomic theory
C — Boyle's law
D — Beroulli's principle

   <u>A</u> 1. The force of attraction increases as the mass of the object increases.

   <u>A</u> 2. The force of attraction decreases as the center of the mass of the object is approached.

   <u>B</u> 3. Each different kind of atom represents a different element.

   <u>B</u> 4. The atoms of different elements differ in mass.

   <u>C</u> 5. The volume of a dry gas varies inversely with the pressure on it, provided the temperature remains constant.

   <u>D</u> 6. Air pressure decreases as the velocity of the gas increases.

2. Directions: Below is a list of musical instruments. Read each one and write B, P, S, or W according to the following classification:

   B — brass   P — percussion   S — strings   W — woodwinds

<u>B</u> 1. trumpet	<u>S</u> 6. bass
<u>P</u> 2. tambourine	<u>B</u> 7. tuba
<u>S</u> 3. cello	<u>P</u> 8. bells
<u>W</u> 4. clarinet	<u>P</u> 9. snare drums
<u>S</u> 5. guitar	<u>W</u> 10. saxophone

3. Directions: For each of the phrases listed below, write the letter for the property which is described in each phrase.

   A — acid   B — base   S — salt

   <u>B</u> 1. changes red litmus to blue

   <u>A</u> 2. has a sour taste

   <u>S</u> 3. compound containing a metal and a negative ion

   <u>A</u> 4. changes blue litmus to red

   <u>B</u> 5. feels slippery or soapy to the touch

   <u>B</u> 6. has a bitter taste

   <u>A</u> 7. has a corrosive action on metal

   <u>S</u> 8. gives a tang or piquancy to anything

4. Directions: The listed crops are produced in one of the three regions listed. On the line before each crop place the letter where each crop is produced. You may use a letter more than one time.

   A — the Choa Phraya Valley
   B — the Northern Central Plains
   C — the Northern Great Plains

   <u>B</u> 1. corn

   <u>C</u> 2. flax

   <u>A</u> 3. rice

   <u>C</u> 4. sorghum

   <u>C</u> 5. spring wheat

5. Directions: Indicate the correct method of spelling the plural form of each of the following words. Record A, B, or C on the line provided using the following code system:

   A — add *s*   B — add *es*   C — change *y* to *i* and add *es*

   <u>A</u> 1. epic   <u>A</u> 6. siren

   __B__ 2. bus   __B__ 7. birch
   __A__ 3. alley   __B__ 8. thrush
   __A__ 4. highway   __C__ 9. comedy
   __C__ 5. enemy   __C__ 10. beauty

SUMMARY

Selected-response items present tasks that require the student to select the correct or best response from the alternatives provided. Varying situations can be provided to set the task. The student may be asked to indicate whether a statement is true or whether it is false (true-false), to select a correct response from a series of alternatives (multiple-choice), to indicate relationships between a set of premises and a set of responses (matching), or to classify according to certain categories (classification).

The true-false item presents a series of declarative statements and the student judges each statement as either true or false. This type of item is employed in determining how well students remember facts and definitions. In addition to measuring recall, the item can be developed to measure behaviors of understanding and comprehension. A wide range of topic coverage is possible in a limited testing time.

The multiple-choice item consists of a premise and a series of possible responses. The premise may be presented as a question and the responses as possible answers. Multiple-choice items are useful in measuring at the level of comprehension and application. This item can be written to measure higher level behaviors. A wide range of topic coverage is possible in a testing period.

The matching item presents a list of premises and a list of possible responses and the student makes an association or connection between pairs of elements. This item can be used in a situation that has a cluster of words, ideas, or such that can be used as premises. When measuring student ability to make associations, discern relationships, make interpretations, or measure knowledge of a series of facts the matching item is useful.

The classification item can be presented as a series of words, incomplete statements, or sentences. Responses are limited to a set of classes provided to the test taker. The item is useful to present a task of recall.

The strengths, weaknesses, and guides to writing the four types of selected-response items along with exemplary items were presented. Mastery of the chapter content along with conscientious application of the procedural principles of constructing items will help teachers improve test quality when using selected-response items.

The next chapter is devoted to writing constructed-response items.

NEW TECHNICAL TERMS LISTED IN THE GLOSSARY

Alternative   Apparent ambiguity
Ambiguity   Distracter

Intrinsic ambiguity　　　　　　　Specific determiner
Item analysis　　　　　　　　　Stem
Objective item

ACTIVITY EXERCISES

1. Using the table of specifications prepared for "Activity Exercise 1" from Chapter 5 as a vehicle, write 5 multiple-choice items and 10 true-false items as examples of the kinds of items to be included in the complete test. Check each item with points made about writing multiple-choice and true-false items.
2. Prepare two matching items for appropriate content of a course where associations are important. Check each item with points made about writing matching items.
3. Prepare two classification items for appropriate content of a course where associations of something are made to one of a set of categories. Check each item with points made about writing classification items.
4. "The person who is aware of shortcomings in item writing will probably be the one who is doing the best job." Be prepared to either defend or attack the above statement by explaining how item writing is viewed by testing people.

FOR DISCUSSION

1. Taking into consideration the nature of your subject area, the age-developmental level of students to be tested, and the objectives for a set of students, how have the strengths and weaknesses of each selected-response item (true-false, multiple-choice, matching, and classification) influenced the type of item you use or may use in future tests?
2. Explain: *(a)* how matching and classification are similar, *(b)* how they are different, *(c)* when the test maker would use a matching item, and *(d)* when the test maker would use a classification item.
3. Discuss how answering multiple-choice items could be considered to be a series of true-false responses.
4. Explain how the use of selected-response items supports the objective of students developing skills in selection.

REFERENCES AND KNOWLEDGE EXTENDERS

COFFMAN, W. E. Essay examinations. In R. L. Thorndike (Ed.), *Educational measurement* (2nd ed.). Washington, D.C.: American Council on Education, 1971. Chap. 10, pp. 271–302.

EBEL, R. L. *Essentials of educational measurement* (3rd ed.). Englewood Cliffs, NJ: Prentice-Hall, 1979. Chap. 7, pp. 111–134; chap. 8, pp. 135–164; and chap. 9, pp. 171–174.

GRONLUND, N. E. *Measurement and evaluation in teaching* (4th ed.). New York: Macmillan, 1981. Chaps. 6 and 7, pp. 155–200.

HOPKINS, C. D., & ANTES, R. L. *Classroom testing: Construction.* Itasca, IL: F. E. Peacock, 1979. Chap. 6, pp. 101–147.

MEHRENS, W. A., & LEHMANN, I. J. *Measurement and evaluation in education and psychology* (2nd ed.). New York: Holt, Rinehart & Winston, 1978. Chaps. 9 and 10, pp. 239–303.

WESMAN, A. G. Writing the test item. In R. L. Thorndike (Ed.), *Educational Measurement* (2nd ed.). Washington, D.C.: American Council on Education, 1971. Chap. 4, pp. 81–129.

Chapter 7. Constructing Constructed-Response Items

After study of Chapter 7, you should be able to:

1. Recognize the general strengths and weaknesses characteristic of constructed-response items.
2. Recognize the specific strengths and weaknesses of completion items.
3. Construct completion items based on the "Guides to Writing Completion Items."
4. Critique completion items based on the "Guides to Writing Completion Items."
5. Recognize the specific strengths and weaknesses of short-answer items.
6. Construct short-answer items based on the "Guides to Writing Short-Answer Items."
7. Critique short-answer items based on the "Guide to Writing Short-Answer Items."
8. Recognize the specific strengths and weaknesses of essay items.
9. Construct essay items based on the "Guides to Writing Essay Items."
10. Critique essay items based on the "Guides to Writing Essay Items."
11. Explain how each glossary term listed at the end of the chapter is used in classroom measurement and evaluation.

The choices of item types depend on the kind of information or evaluation needed, the nature of the subject matter, the specific objectives set for students, the amount of time available for testing, and the age-developmental level of students to be tested. Constructed-response items (completion, short-answer, and essay) present tasks that require the examiner to create responses within the structure provided by each item.

The demand on the student to supply information is from least to most, moving from completion, to short-answer, to essay. The level of cognition required by constructed-response-item tests is closely related to the same hierarchical order, and demanded responses follow a sequence from knowledge to understanding to application to the three highest orders of analysis, synthesis, and evaluation (Bloom, 1956). The amount of freedom in response allowed the student also increases in the same order, with the essay item allowing the greatest amount of freedom. The person who scores the essay response also has the greatest amount of freedom as increased judgment enters the scoring and cognitive demand increases.

The freedom in construction of responses may be useful when measuring the upper levels of complex behavior, but at the same time harmful to the accuracy of the measurement due to the difficulty of scoring the responses with high reliability. Too much freedom in responding erodes the common basis needed for making comparisons. The freedom allowed in the response can be controlled by the type of item used but limitation of the freedom also places a limitation on the behavior which can be measured. The planning stage of test construction allows for consideration of all contributing factors to direct the choice of the proper item type to collect the data. Construction of constructed-response items should be made in accord with general understandings about what each type can do and how each should be constructed.

WRITTEN EXPRESSION

Basic to learning at all levels of the process of education is the usefulness of what is learned. Students must be able to draw on what has been learned to serve them in daily living and to integrate learned facts to meet new and novel situations. English composition, for instance, is a vehicle which is intended to allow organization of what a student knows and to develop within the student skill in written expression.

Educational objectives from the earliest school years, even preschool age, are directed to development of a child socially. To perform in society, each individual must be able to communicate through words, either oral or written, to other human beings. Constructed-response items on tests, although not the only way of developing these skills, do allow testing sessions to support the instructional objectives directed to written expression.

Whenever possible data-collection procedures should include items which allow students to create responses. A well-written essay item can require the student to think reflectively and when creating a response the student can gain experience in organizing knowledge into a well-formulated composition. In this way measurement in the classroom becomes an integral part of the instructional activities devoted to developing skill in written expression. The lists of strengths and weaknesses of constructed-response items are presented to assist the teacher in determining whether to use selected-response, constructed-response, or problem items.

STRENGTHS OF CONSTRUCTED-RESPONSE ITEMS

Taken as a group constructed-response items have several strengths over selected-response items. In general, the strengths are related to the fact that the response is created by the student rather than by the test maker. Tests made up of constructed-response items require less time to prepare than selected-response tests because the number of items is much less. For this reason constructed-response items are probably the most widely used and most popular of all types of teacher-made test items. Strengths associated with all constructed-response items are:

1. The student becomes an active participant in the process by creating a response. Lists of general educational objectives from the national, state, or local level imply or state that students are to develop into independent beings able to function on their own, and this objective is supported when students are required to create responses.

2. Tests made up of constructed-response items are relatively easy to construct. Completion and short-answer items mainly test for recall and do not require large amounts of time or effort to construct. Since only a limited number of essay items can be presented in a testing session, essay tests require much less time to construct than do equally effective selected-response tests.

3. The possibility of getting correct responses by guessing is low. With any constructed-response item a correct response by blind guess is very unlikely. With the essay item guessing is reduced to a minimum and in some instances is eliminated entirely.

WEAKNESSES OF CONSTRUCTED-RESPONSE ITEMS

Constructed-response items also have several weaknesses. In general the weaknesses are related to scoring student responses. Weaknesses which are associated with all constructed-response items are:

1. Responses are time consuming to score since each response must be considered for its tenability. The scorer must consider each response on its own merit. Even in completion items where strict limitations are incorporated, the writer of items can not be assured that in every case one, and only one, word would encompass the response set. For short-answer and essay items the response will rarely if ever be so restricted that it can be scored objectively to a set phrase or paragraph. The scorer usually has to read for components presented by students in many different ways.

2. Scoring constructed-response items is not only time consuming but also requires that the scorer has knowledge of the subject being tested. Only rarely can aides, machines, or uninformed persons be used to relieve the teacher of the burden of scoring.

3. The student who has highly developed skills in written expression may be favored over students who have difficulty creating or expressing their knowledge and thoughts in words. If two students have the same knowledge and are at the same level on all factors except written expression, the one who rates higher in writing skills is likely to perform better on test responses.

4. Some constructed-response items may be subject to bluffing by a student who does not know the response but who can write around the task without really coming to grips with it. The scorer can be more objective in reading shorter responses, and bluffing can be controlled by writing items which set definite boundaries for responses.

5. The amount of time required for scoring responses may create a considerable time delay in returning the results to the student. If the results

are needed to guide further instruction, the delay in getting the results may be crucial.

6. The question about how to deal with the problem of misspelled words, incorrect grammar, and poor sentence structure in a response for an item in a test must be resolved. Since the test is for achievement in a subject, a component for any one or all of these may confound the purity of the final score. If spelling of certain words is important to the subject, such as in physical geography, a portion of the table of specifications should be given to spelling. If spelling, grammar, and sentence structure are not important to the subject being studied, they should not contribute to the final score. However, since all teachers deal with the general education of students, the importance of spelling could be reflected by a separate score for spelling. Two scores could be given for the test—one for content and a second for spelling. A separate score for grammar, sentence structure, or the mechanics or quality of handwriting may also be given, if the teacher decides that the measurement of content is not affected.

COMPLETION ITEMS

The completion item is the most structured of all constructed-response items and offers the least freedom of response. The task for the student is presented in a sentence in which a word, a number, a symbol, or a series of words has been omitted. The student is to finish the sentence by constructing a response that makes a complete thought in the context of the material which has been studied. The completion item calls for only one response for a blank or a specific series of responses for a series of blanks.

The incomplete sentence used for a completion item must give enough information so that the task will not be ambiguous, but worded so that the correct response is not apparent to unknowing students. Since the statement used must stand alone and the response is limited to a very short one, the completion item is limited to measuring behavior used to recall facts. Facts form the basis for the higher-level behaviors, and completion-type items provide an efficient vehicle to measure at the most basic level. If not overused or used to the exclusion of other item types, this may be the best way to measure some factual learning.

Special Considerations

When choosing the most appropriate item type to call forth a particular student behavior, the teacher must consider the following strengths and weaknesses of the completion item.

Strengths

1. Recall of information for response to completion items should not be time consuming for the test taker. Since the task is very direct, many bits of

information can be collected in a test period, thus increasing the size of the sample.

2. Well-constructed completion items can be scored more quickly than other constructed-response items. Although some time will be needed to judge certain responses, the limited domain of possible responses allows a considerable degree of objectivity in the scoring process.

3. Scorer reliability should be high for completion items. Judgments made by different scorers should be similar.

4. Because the student must recall information in order to respond at the knowledge level, this item type may be superior to one for which the response is provided. Since this level of cognition merely deals with information in the same form as it was learned, recognition may mean picking up clues from the original presentation. If the student must recall information rather than identify it, the process may be a better measure of achievement.

Weaknesses

1. The completion item usually measures the learning of facts at the recall level. Rarely does the test maker have the option of testing at a higher level than knowledge when using a completion item.

2. Writing the item may be difficult. To present a clearly defined task with only one correct response may require qualifiers which make a sentence complex. Much rewriting may be required to shorten it to an acceptable level.

Guides To Writing Completion Items

1. The omission should be placed at or near the end of the sentence. The blank at the end of the sentence allows the student to identify the task before the omitted word is called for. This allows a response without a second reading. When the omission appears first, two readings are needed: (a) to decide the task being presented, and (b) to get the response. By saving the student's time more items can be presented.

Example A (poor item)

_____ is the name of the capital of Indiana.

Example B

The name of the capital of Indiana is _____(Indianapolis)_____ .

In Example A the student has no idea of the task until the sentence is read completely. In Example B the task is clear before the examinee meets the omission, thus one reading sets the task and generates the response, assuming the examinee knows the answer.

2. Word each item so that all students have the same frame of reference. A wide range of plausible responses may result from a poorly written item.

Example A (poor item)

Marquette, Michigan, is on _____. The student may respond "Lake Superior," "a lake," "central time," or some other correct response. The item can be clarified by restating it as in Example B.

Example B

Marquette, Michigan, is geographically located on Lake _(Superior)_ .

3. Make all blank spaces the same size. Clues about the size of the expected word should not be given by providing long blanks for long words and short blanks for short words. Be sure that the response lines for recording student responses will accommodate the longest word in any item. Since younger students can be permitted to place their responses directly in the sentence, be sure that the size of the blanks is large enough for the longest word. Older students should be expected to use a separate response sheet to record their responses to facilitate scoring. If a response sheet is used, space can be saved by making small blanks in the incomplete sentence.

Example A (poor item)

The names of four states which meet at one point are _(Utah)_, _(Arizona)_, _(Colorado)_, and _(New Mexico)_ .

Example B

The names of four states which meet at one point are
____(Utah)____, ____(Arizona)____, ____(Colorado)____, and __(New Mexico)__.

For use with a separate response sheet use short blanks.

Example C

The names of four states which meet at one point are _____,
_____, _____, and _____.

4. Indicate what unit is to be used when the response requires a reporting of the response in units. Also indicate how the response is to be approximated.

Example A (poor item)

The circumference of a circle that has a diameter of twenty (20) inches is _____.

Example B

The circumference of a circle which has a diameter of twenty (20) inches is ____(5.24)____ feet. (nearest hundredth)

5. Omit only important words.

Example A (poor item)

A pulley is a grooved wheel that can lift a heavy _____ vertically 10 feet.

Example B

A grooved wheel that can lift a heavy load 10 feet vertically is the
_____(pulley)_____.

6. Write completion items with only one blank or a related series of
blanks. With too many omissions the task is more of a puzzle than a measure
of achievement.

Example A (poor item)

The   names   of   _____   _____that   have   a
_____on   the   _____   _____are
_____ ,   _____,   _____,
_____, and   _____.

Example B

The names of five states that have a border on the Pacific Ocean are
_____(Alaska)_____ , _____(Washington)__, _____(Oregon)_____ ,
_____(California)_____, and _____(Hawaii)_____.

7. There should be only one correct response to each blank. Since it is
difficult to touch all bases for correct responses, the scorer should be prepared
to give students credit for any other response(s) which do, indeed, make a
correct thought. If the item requires a series of responses, the sequence may
or may not be of critical importance. The student should be informed when
the order of the responses will be considered. When no order is asked for, then
any correct response for any blank will be considered correct. Example B in
number 6 does not ask for order. The examinee could be asked to present them
in an order, e.g., alphabetical.

8. Check the grammar of the sentence to make sure that the wording does
not: (a) include a specific determiner which implies a singular or plural word
and thus eliminate some responses, or *(b)* use an indefinite article, "a," "an,"
to indicate that the word starts with a vowel or consonant.

9. Do not lift a sentence or part of a sentence directly from any source
and leave out a word or two as blanks to be filled. Students may remember
a sentence they have read and parrot the response without real learning. More
important, the sentence out of context of supporting material may need the
surrounding sentences to give it full meaning.

10. Check the section "General Considerations in Construction of Test
Items" in Chapter 5.

Exemplary Items

The following items are models which reflect the suggestions about how to construct completion items. No attempt has been made to cover all "Guides to Writing" or subject areas.

Elementary school subjects

1. The full name of the person who invented the telephone is _(Alexander Graham Bell)_ .
2. The combined length of an automobile which is 15 feet 11 inches long and a trailer including the hitch which is 17 feet 10 inches long is equal to _____ $(33\frac{9}{12}$ or $33\frac{3}{4})$ _____ feet. (Change inches to a fraction of a foot.)
3. To locate a position on the earth's surface, a ship's captain would give reference points in regard to the ship's positions of _____(latitude)_____ and _____(longitude)_____ . (Either order is correct)
4. When there are no sharps and no flats in the key signature, the music is written in the key of _____(C)_____ .
5. Using the story you have just read, fill in the blanks in the sentences below.
   a. The last game was a very ____(important)__ game.
   b. Hank was told to _____(bunt)_____ .
   c. Hank planned to swing his _____(bat)_____ as hard as he could.
   d. Hank hit a home _____(run)_____ .
   e. Mr. Hawthorn told Hank he was not a _____(team)_____ player.

Secondary school subjects

1. Flats are placed in the key signature in the following order: __(b)__ , __(e)__ , __(a)__ , __(d)__ , __(g)__ , __(c)__ .
2. A three-speed standard transmission makes a clicking sound in low and reverse gears only. The fault is a defective _(low-reverse sliding gear)_ .
3. The clutch release bearing is controlled by the _(release fork)_ .
4. In the three-step arrangement called the syllogism, steps 1 and 2 are called ____(premises)____ , and the third step is called _(conclusion) (inference)_ .
5. Electrolysis of water creates the two gases __(hydrogen)__ and _____(oxygen)_ . (Either order)

SHORT-ANSWER ITEMS

Short-answer items are very similar to completion items, and in many cases the test maker could change a completion item to a short-answer item by phrasing it as a question or providing a direction, e.g., Define the word *caste*. The short answer does allow the test constructor to make a somewhat greater demand on the student than can be made using the completion format. Since the response is not limited to a word, a number, or a symbol, it can be extended to a short phrase. Some short-answer items could be constructed at the level of comprehension or application, but in general the short-answer item best measures facts and knowledge.

Teachers of young children who are interested in development of expression find that the short-answer item can introduce the child to written expression without requiring a complex response. The use of short-answer items for tests in primary grades supports the total instructional program because they provide a vehicle to develop written expression.

Special Considerations

When choosing the most appropriate item type to call forth a particular student behavior, the teacher must consider the following strengths and weaknesses of the short-answer item.

Strengths

1. The short-answer item which uses a phrase for a response can be used with young children to prepare them to express their thoughts in written format and to prepare them to respond to essay items at a later time.

2. Since the student must recall the response rather than recognize it, well-written short-answer items may be better than selected-response items for measuring knowledge of facts. For use in the real world, facts must be recalled by the learner. It has been suggested that application of information is as much a part of learning as putting it in the mind in the first place. A response may be apparent in a selected-response item because the test is of knowledge and the presentation is limited to presenting it in the same way that it appeared in learning. A better test of achievement may be to ask the student to recall it rather than select it.

3. Tasks are easy to set with well-written questions since directions can be made explicit. Tasks are easy to clarify, thus avoiding ambiguity.

4. The short-answer item is effective for appraising procedural steps, appropriate ordering, and listing. It is very efficient when testing for formulas and principles which must be learned in a specific form.

Weaknesses

1. In general, short-answer items measure at the knowledge level and make little demand beyond recall. There are exceptions in some, maybe most, subject areas.

2. Use of short-answer items to the exclusion of other items limits the testing to lower levels of cognitive functioning. This weakness is easily overcome by using other types of items that require other student behaviors.

Guides To Writing Short-Answer Items

1. Provide the same amount of space for each response unless you have a particular reason for specifying the length of the response. It is a good idea to arrange the order so that one-word responses are all together and phrases all together. Give the same amount of space for all one-word responses and the same amount of space for all phrases unless the intent is to direct the length of the response.

2. Include rules for responding in the item or directions. Designate units to be used, length of responses, approximation rules, and any other needed guidance.

Example A

How long is the unit formed by attaching a trailer including hitch which is 17-feet-10-inches long to an automobile which is 15-feet-11-inches long?
_____(33)_____ feet _____(9)_____ inches

Example B

In the space provided, tell the primary difference between the folk tale and the literary fairy tale. _____

3. Check the section "General Considerations in Construction of Test Items" in Chapter 5.

Exemplary Items

The following items are models which reflect the suggestions about how to construct short-answer items. No attempt has been made to cover all "Guides to Writing" or subject areas.

Elementary school subjects

1. List the three colors in the flag of the United States of America.
_____ , _____ , _____ .

2. List the two prime movers of soil which cause erosion.
_____ and _____ .

3. To whom does the title "Winners of the West" refer? _____
4. What is business which is carried on between different countries called? _____

5. What are the openings at the top of dams that let the water through called? _____

Secondary school subjects

1. Why does a gas-stove flame turn yellow when the contents of a pan spill over? _____
2. What would Newton's spectrum look like in a light source of red and violet light only? _____

3. In a long parade, the marchers far from the band may be out of step with the band members. Account for this difference. _____

4. Define caste. _____
5. Where is the Plain of Skåne? _____

ESSAY ITEMS

The essay item is the most complex of constructed-response items. The essay item demands a fully developed response from the student. The test taker must respond in a series of sentences which constitute a reasonable response to the item. The accuracy and quality of the response must be judged by someone who is knowledgeable in the subject being tested, usually the person who wrote the item. For classroom testing, the person best able to make the required judgments about responses to essay items is the classroom teacher.

The essay item can serve classroom testing in two ways, depending on how an item is written and how much freedom is given to the writer in composing the response. First, an essay item can be presented with a broad scope but a limited time allotment. This kind of item tests the writer's skill in choosing what to write and how much to write about each of the several parts. The student's abilities to organize and express a logical thesis are also called on to respond adequately. Thus the **extended-response** essay item is open-ended and does not limit the student to points for discussion, type of organization, or approach to the proposed task. This type of item is helpful in assessing written expression, especially in the language arts.

Second, an essay item can be constructed so as to put carefully designated limits on the response. The scope may be narrow or broad, but the student should know exactly what the limits are. Thus the limited-response essay item gives the student a clearly defined set of limits to establish the scope of the response to be written. The task is to write within a well-fenced-in region of the content area. This type of item is especially useful to the classroom teacher who is testing achievement in a content subject. The skills of expression and organization should be scored separately for a response to an item in an achievement test for subjects other than English. Measuring these skills can not be avoided entirely because the response must be created. In contrast to the extended-response essay item, which is intended to measure writing skill, the **limited-response** essay item is used to measure achievement in content subjects. Each has its place in classroom testing, but the test maker must keep this difference in mind when writing the items. For tests in the language arts, specifically for measurement of writing skills, the extended-response can be used; otherwise, the test maker should write limited-response essay items for all other subjects and score the content covered rather than the presentation.

Special Considerations

When choosing the most appropriate item type to call forth a particular student behavior, the teacher must consider the following strengths and weaknesses of the essay item.

Strengths

1. The essay item can be written to allow the student maximum freedom of response. The amount of freedom can be leveled by the way the item is written to set the scope of the expected response.

2. Freedom of response can be used to test the student in the higher cognitive behaviors of analysis, synthesis, and evaluation. The student can be asked to apply, compare, explain, describe, and contrast knowledge and principles.

3. The essay item allows the test maker to ask students' opinions without making a judgment about opinion. Unlike the selected-response item, which must be scored as correct or incorrect, the major factor of the response to the essay opinion item can be the student's ability to defend that opinion, not whether the student's opinion agrees with a keyed opinion.

4. A good essay test requires less time to construct than a well-prepared selected-response test. Although each essay item may take more time to prepare than, for example, a true-false or multiple-choice item, only a few items need to be written. This means that it takes less time to construct an essay test than a selected-response test.

5. The need to organize and express ideas allows the testing session to also serve as an opportunity to develop writing skills. Although the primary purpose of the classroom test is to measure achievement, the second purpose of supporting learning should be taken advantage of whenever possible.

6. By providing maximum freedom of response, the extended-response essay item can be analyzed or evaluated for written expression and organization of material.

Weaknesses

1. Judgment of student responses requires much time. Because each response must be scrutinized in scoring, the time saved in preparation of the essay test is more than used up in the time needed to score reliably the responses of students.

2. Essay responses are difficult to score with high reliability. Without special precautions in scoring, the scores on essay tests are likely to lack the objectivity needed to make the scores useful and valid measures of student achievement.

3. Essay responses are likely to provide a sample of subject matter that is less than desired because each item requires considerable time to respond. The limited sampling provided by relatively few items may cause the content validity to be reduced.

4. If a student has difficulty in expressing ideas and thoughts in writing, the student may not be able to offer a good representation of achievement. Two students who have the same level of achievement in absolute terms, but different levels of skill in expression, may receive very different scores on an essay test.

Guides To Writing Essay Items

1. Use essay items when one or more of the following student responses are expected: explanation, comparison, contrast, description, analysis, synthesis, or evaluation. The extended response essay item may be employed to measure student skill in language expression, communication, and organization of material.

2. Do NOT use an essay item to measure simple recall of facts and information. Other constructed-response and some selected-response items are more efficient for measuring at the knowledge level.

3. Prepare the item so that the question presented or implied is explicit, concise, and clear to the student. Ambiguous words and phrases leave doubt in the mind of the student about what should be responded to and provide little direction for scoring responses. If necessary, definitions of words used in setting the task can be given to clarify what is being presented to the student.

4. Include in tests only those tasks which are new and unfamiliar to the student. If a task incorporates a familiar situation, the student may be required only to recall what was learned and incorporate it in a response in the same way that it was learned.

5. Establish within each item the scope expected in the response and the detail to be included by defining and "fencing in" the expected response. The limits of the response should be established within the content studied. In addition, the length of the expected response can be indicated by the amount of time to be spent on it, by the number of points for an

entirely correct response, or by the amount of space to be used in responding. Relative weights of the several items on an essay test can be indicated in these ways.

6. Tell the student how to handle terms which have special meaning in the area being tested or which are technical in nature. The student should know whether to define or explain these in the response.

7. Each item should be written so that students spend their time on and are given credit for those aspects of the study which differentiate levels of achievement in the topics studied. The task should not be presented so that the response must include general information.

8. When setting the task, use descriptive words which are clear in their meaning. Unless the test is intended to measure the student's understanding of technical words, technical words should be defined. Directions which include words like compare, defend, trace, contrast, and explain differences give specific directions for the response. Words or phrases like "review," "tell all that you know," and "report your knowledge" are nondirective and should not be used in directions for essay items. Terms such as *discuss,* and *evaluate* should be used sparingly, and if used, the precise meaning must be clear.

9. All students should write on the same set of items without a choice from a list of possible (optional) items. Comparisons of differences in the set of scores can be made only when each score is based on the same set of items. If six items are proposed but only four are to be responded to, differences in test scores have little meaning since the combination of six items taken four at a time is sizable (15 different ways of choosing the four items to write on). Educational measurement, whether norm-referenced or criterion-referenced, needs a common base for interpretation.

However, there is an exception: individually prescribed instruction or a class organized so that students have studied in different areas by choice may cause a teacher to modify the above guide. If students have studied different content, then measures on the test should reflect achievement in appropriate content. Selection from a wide list of topics may be acceptable testing procedure under these conditions; however, the teacher should consider making a special test for each student. The teacher could have a common set of items and build the tests individually for each student by selecting from these items, basing the selection on what material each student had studied. Nevertheless, the scores must be judged for their absolute value when selection is made, rather than judged in comparison with other student scores.

10. Choose the extended-response essay item only as a vehicle to measure writing expression, communication, or organization of material. Use of this item type for content other than language arts should be limited to an in-class or take-home assignment to serve as a learning experience, or in special cases where organization of a logical thesis is required.

11. Check the section "General Considerations in Construction of Test Items" in Chapter 5.

Exemplary Items

The following items are models which reflect the suggestions about how to construct essay items. No attempt has been made to cover all "Guides to Writing" or subject areas.

Elementary school subjects

1. Describe the adobe homes and villages the Pueblo Indians lived in when the Spaniards arrived in New Mexico. (Limited-response essay.)
2. Tell what dinosaurs looked like, what they ate, where they lived, and give an explanation about why they died out. (Limited-response essay.)
3. Write what the world will be like in the year 2100. Include a section on how children's lives will change from the way you live. (Extended-response essay.)
4. Tell about George Washington. (Extended-response essay.)
5. What are basic foods? Name food sources which supply benefits for your body for each of the following: (*a*) energy (calories), (*b*) normal growth in children (protein), (*c*) aids proper formation of teeth and bones (calcium), (*d*) helps build red blood cells (iron), (*e*) promotes growth and good eyesight (vitamin A), and (*f*) promotes health, appetite, and good nerves (vitamin B). (Limited-response essay.)

Secondary school subjects

1. Trace the circulation of the blood through the parts of the human body naming the organs and their contribution to the blood. Include a labeled diagram of the heart to show the direction of blood circulation through the parts of the heart. (Limited-response essay.)
2. Describe how the introduction of railroads in a typical underdeveloped country would be expected to change the political climate of that country. (Limited-response essay.)
3. The War of 1812 has been called "the War Nobody Won." What is meant by this reference? In your opinion, how did that war change our country? Support and defend your opinion with specific examples. (Limited-response essay.)
4. Explain democracy. (Extended-response essay.)
5. Describe the three classes of musical instruments. Include three examples of each class and explain how each instrument produces sound. (Limited-response essay.)

SUMMARY

Constructed-response items present tasks that require the student to create responses within the structure provided by the item. Varying demands can be made on the student in responding to constructed-response items. The student may be asked to complete a statement by filling in a blank or blanks in a sentence (completion item), give a short response to a direct question (short-answer item), or write a paragraph or more as a complete expression of a fully developed thought (essay item).

The completion item requires the student to fill in one or more words omitted from a sentence and is limited to testing the student's recall of memorized information. This item used to the exclusion of more appropriate items may cause the student to learn only facts in isolation and neglect more advanced levels of the taxonomy of educational objectives.

The short-answer item asks for a response from the student which is usually more than one word but does not require a complete sentence. This item seems to be most useful in early grades when teachers are interested in having the student develop an expression of a thought but the child is not able to write a complex response as a task on the test. The short-answer item may be a step toward the type of response required in an essay item.

The essay item presents a question or situation with instructions which require the student to organize a complete thought in one or more sentences. The task may range from simple to complex. The limited-response essay item is appropriate for use in achievement tests. The extended-response item is more suitable for English or other language arts classes where development of skills of written expression is a primary objective. The distinguishing characteristic is the type of limits set on the response.

The strengths, weaknesses, and guides to writing the three types of constructed-response items along with exemplary items were presented. Mastery of the chapter content along with conscientious application of the procedural principles of constructing items will help teachers improve test quality when using constructed-response items.

The next chapter is devoted to writing problem items for classroom testing.

NEW TECHNICAL TERMS LISTED IN THE GLOSSARY

Extended-Response   Limited-Response

ACTIVITY EXERCISES

1. Prepare a table of specifications for a completion and/or short-answer test for one unit. Use guidelines for "Activity Exercise 1" from Chapter 5.
    Write 10 completion and/or short-answer items as examples of the kinds of items to be included in the test. Check each item with points made about writing these items.
2. Prepare a table of specifications for an essay test for one unit. Use Figure 5.3 as a guide.
    Write two limited-response essay items for the test. Check each item with points made about writing essay items. Be sure that they are appropriate for measuring achievement in the area being tested.
3. Write an extended-response essay item appropriate for measuring written expression at one or more of the following levels of education—primary,

intermediate, secondary, college. Check each item with points made about writing extended-response essay items.

4. Prepare a short essay on why extended-response essay items *are* appropriate for measuring achievement in language courses.

5. Prepare a short essay on why extended-response essay items *are not* appropriate for measuring achievement in most subjects.

FOR DISCUSSION

1. From the perspective of item construction explain how restricted-response essay and extended-response essay items differ. Which type of essay item do you feel is best for your use and why?

2. Taking into consideration the nature of your subject area, the age-developmental level of students to be tested, and the objectives for a set of students, how have the strengths and weaknesses of each constructed-response item (completion, short-answer, and essay) influenced the type of item you use or will use on future tests.

3. Explain how the freedom given to the test taker and freedom given to the scorer of essay items may reduce the accuracy of measures from an essay test.

4. Explain how the use of constructed-response items supports the objective of students developing writing skills.

REFERENCES AND KNOWLEDGE EXTENDERS

AHMANN, J. S., & GLOCK, M. D. *Evaluating pupil growth* (6th ed.). Boston: Allyn & Bacon, 1981. Chap. 5, pp. 136–156.

BLOOM, B. S. (Ed.). *Taxonomy of educational objectives: The classification of educational goals, handbook I: Cognitive domain.* New York: David McKay, 1956.

COFFMAN, W. E. Essay examinations. In R. L. Thorndike (Ed.), *Educational measurement* (2nd ed.). Washington, D.C.: American Council on Education, 1971. Chap. 10, pp. 271–302.

EBEL, R. L. *Essentials of educational measurement* (3rd ed.). Englewood Cliffs, NJ: Prentice-Hall, 1979. Chap. 6, pp. 95–110; chap. 9, pp. 165–169.

HOPKINS, C. D., & ANTES, R. L. *Classroom Testing: Construction.* Itasca, IL: F. E. Peacock, 1979. Chap. 5, pp. 82–100.

MEHRENS, W. A., & LEHMAN, I. J. *Measurement and evaluation in education and psychology* (2nd ed.). New York: Holt, Rinehart & Winston, 1978. Chap. 8, pp. 204–238.

Chapter 8. Constructing Problem Items

After study of Chapter 8, you should be able to:

1. Recognize the specific strengths and weaknesses of mathematical problem items.
2. Construct mathematical problem items based on the "Guides to Writing Mathematical Problem Items."
3. Critique mathematical problem items based on the "Guides to Writing the Mathematical Problem Items."
4. Recognize the specific strengths and weaknesses of technical problem items.
5. Construct technical problem items based on the "Guides to Writing Technical Problem Items."
6. Critique technical problem items based on the "Guides to Writing Technical Problem Items."
7. Explain how each glossary term listed at the end of the chapter is used in classroom measurement and evaluation.

The problem item refers to the mathematical problem or the technical problem. A problem is typically presented by giving: *(a)* a set of conditions to structure a situation, *(b)* descriptive information, *(c)* quantitative data, and *(d)* instruction about what responses are to be derived. Some technical problems omit the quantitative data. Demands made on the student range from a very simple situation to extremely involved circumstances. If presented in algorithmic form the examinee has little freedom, but a broad structuring may allow much freedom in a problem that is technical in nature. The problem item is a valuable way to test a student's understanding of underlying principles by creating a real-world situation for application. In fact, certain problem-solving tactics are necessary in all tests that require the student to go beyond mere recall of facts to make correct choices.

The technical problem is a somewhat involved situation created for an in-depth investigation for interpretation of data, development of relationships, use of principles, drawing conclusions, analysis, or evaluation. Since by their nature some courses are more technical than others, some instructors find more use for the technical problem than others. If real-world conditions can be approximated for the technical problem, the teacher should consider it in data collection.

Problem items are unique in that the freedom of the student in construction of the response ranges from limited to unlimited depending on how the problem is presented. The most structured of all problems is the one presented in algorithmic form where the question to be answered is implied in the presentation of the data. For example, if the student were given the following problem, the algorithm gives the conditions, the information in the form of data, and implied instructions about what response is expected.

$$647 \div 25 = \boxed{}$$

The preceding problem in algorithmic form is the special case $a \div b$, the division algorithm that eventually gives the largest whole number q such that $q \times b \leq a$. If $q \times b = a$, then q is the missing factor. If $q \times b < a$, then q is the quotient, and there is a remainder. So $a = (q \times b) + r$, where r may or may not be zero (0). (All of this is implied in the algorithm.)

The algorithm is a very convenient way to present some kinds of problems since it sets up a numerical process that can be applied again and again to reach a solution to a problem and relieves the teacher of writing extensive directions each time. The algorithm is especially useful for objectives that require the student to make computations but do not require application of the mathematics.

Presentation of a technical problem example for the "extremely involved circumstances" is not included here since it would be necessary to base it on some special area of study. Because certain technical knowledge of that special field would be needed, it would not be generally understood by readers from other disciplines. Readers are left to develop specific technical items for their test needs. The discussion in the chapter directs the writing of complex problem items for all subject areas.

Although other organizational schemes are possible, in general, the student's approach to solving problem items follows this set of steps:

1. Identify the problem by recognizing a clear question (either stated or implied).
2. Sort out and organize the needed information and data.
3. Set up a procedure for arriving at the solution.
4. Complete the sequence, and report the results and conclusions in the form of a number, symbol, or other response.

Although the problem and the above solution steps are directed specifically to mathematics and the physical sciences, nearly all fields of study can use the problem to collect information about a student's level of functioning. Problems are particularly relevant for testing student understanding of principles by requiring the student to use new data with a new set of circumstances. In this way the teacher can find out how well a student can take a set of learned principles and apply them.

PROBLEM SOLVING

Problem solving in mathematics was the theme for the 1980 yearbook of the National Council for Teachers of Mathematics, and its importance is pointed up by issues and implications for all instructional levels. Themes for special issues of professional journals have been devoted to problem solving. Conferences devoted to learning about learning have devoted a considerable amount of time and energy to learning theory as it relates to skill in problem solving. Recent research about the special functions of the two halves of the human brain has implications for learning, since each half of the brain seems to be specialized for different modes of thought. For these reasons, problem solving is becoming a major thrust of contemporary learning strategies.

Problem solving is a stated or implied objective for lists of general instructional objectives, and it is implied in statements of classroom behavioral objectives, which reflect programs stressing problem solving. Recommendations about how to teach problem solving have been a part of methods courses for teachers in both elementary and secondary schools for many years.

With problem solving receiving this attention in objectives and programs, the problem becomes a necessary item in achievement testing. Problems presented in classroom tests become vehicles to integrate the program, the test, and posttest activities, as well as assessing a particular type of learning outcome. The connection between problems and objectives is easy for students to recognize. For other types of items this connection may not be as clear as it is for the problem item.

As with all types of items the problem has been used by some teachers to the exclusion of other types of items. Some mathematics teachers have made problem tests their sole source of data. Rarely, if ever, will one type of item be appropriate for collection of all data. While encouraging those who do not use the problem at all to consider it, we want to encourage those who use it exclusively or rely on it too heavily to use other types of items also.

MATHEMATICAL PROBLEMS

There is an ongoing debate over what the thrust of mathematics teaching should be, but there seems to be little doubt that students should learn to compute and be able to deal with both theoretical and applied mathematical situations. Except for the basic facts for addition, subtraction, multiplication, and division, any arithmetic or mathematical task could be considered to be a problem item unless the student has seen the exact same problem before. Problems can relate to objectives that ask for behaviors of understanding and all higher divisions of the cognitive domain.

Special Considerations for Mathematical Problem Items

When choosing the most appropriate type of item to call forth a particular student behavior, the teacher must consider the following strengths and weaknesses of the mathematical problem item.

Strengths

1. Problem solving is the basic skill in mathematics. Learning to solve problems is the principal reason to study mathematics. These two reasons may be enough to support the use of problem items on mathematics tests.

2. Mathematical problems can be used at all levels of the educational process. A kindergarten child can be asked:

How many boxes of milk will be needed for lunch today?

This problem situation can test to see if the concept of one-to-one correspondence has been developed.

An elementary school student can be asked the following:

How much fencing would be needed to make a puppy cage which is four-feet long and three-feet wide?

This tests for concept of perimeter and addition skill (possibly for multiplication skill depending on how the student attacks the problem).

A class of advanced secondary students or college students can be asked to:

Find an algorithm suitable for minicalculator computation that can compute the length and direction of [vector] **V** directly from *a, b,* and θ (Staib, 1977, pp. 36–39). (This problem could be presented in an even more basic form by reconstructing the problem as it developed in biomedical engineering.)

This problem involves the use of many principles used in higher levels of mathematics, and the ones used are a function of the logical approach used by the student.

3. Problem tests (the test as a whole but not individual items) are relatively easy to prepare when compared to selected-response tests. Since fewer items are needed, the task of building the test is reduced considerably in both time and effort.

4. Students can be tested on how they can apply principles to a new situation. Involving students in application of principles engages them directly in the process of problem solving, hopefully fostering its transfer to real-world situations, and allows them to exhibit knowledge of the interrelatedness between factors in the problem.

5. Near-natural situations can be created to give information about how the student would be expected to perform in a real-world situation. Although the classroom continues to be an artificial environment, the problem allows creation of situations based on natural circumstances.

6. Conditions can be set up to make the problem item relevant to on-the-job performance and to make predictions about future performance. For technical subjects, especially vocational ones, the problem allows the instructor to obtain feedback about how a student would function at a later time when assuming a position after formal schooling.

7. Problem tests rate high in objectivity. The task can be clearly defined, and reasons for giving credit or "taking off" from the total points allotted for the item can be explained to students. Both procedure (the process) and product (the result) can be clearly observed, scored, and evaluated.

8. The mathematical algorithm, the most highly structured problem situation, allows the teacher to diagnose computational difficulties.

9. The problem controls for student guessing or bluffing responses to test tasks. Since the student must create the response, guessing is reduced to a minimum. The highly structured situation allows only a limited number of ways of proceeding to solution, and each can be judged objectively in terms of efficiency and the result.

10. Solving problems on a test can be a learning experience. Using learned principles in new ways generalizes the learning into new and unique circumstances and directly supports the instructional component of classroom activities.

11. Presentation of problems on tests allows the testing session to become an integral part of the total classroom program. Facility in problem solving is an acknowledged aim of social science and physical science programs as well as mathematics instruction. Inclusion of problems on tests in these subjects supports the integration of the testing program with the instructional program.

Weaknesses

The following weaknesses of the mathematical problem item are connected to the small number of items in one testing session and built-in scoring difficulties.

1. The relatively small number of problems, especially complex ones, that can be worked in a testing session may result in low content validity if the problem test is used exclusively. This should not be a weakness if the problem is used when appropriate and in conjunction with other types of items.

2. There may be more than one way to solve a problem. While an item may appear to have only one solution, knowledgeable students may uncover alternate solutions. While these may be clearly correct, an alternate solution may raise questions: (*a*) How efficient is the process? and (*b*) How important is efficiency to the total problem? Judgment of the relative importance of procedure and product must be made when reading student responses and setting rules for scoring responses.

3. The response may be correct in some aspects and incorrect in others. A logical and correct rationale may be followed to develop a procedure, but the response may be wrong because of an error in computation. All-or-none scoring should not be used for problems because information from a partially correct response is lost if credit is given when only the result is considered. The teacher must decide the relative importance of the procedure and the correct response.

4. The use of an incorrect response in computation may cause one or more subsequent responses also to be incorrect. Adjustment in scoring procedure should be made so that the student is not penalized more than one time for an error in responding to the task.

5. Considerable time may be needed to score student responses. This limitation is formidable for complex problems and when students miss several problems. Diagnostic use of the scores and procedures is also time consuming, but it should not be considered a weakness of the problem item.

6. Individual complex problems may be difficult to construct. Although a problem test may generally be easier to construct than selected-response tests, each problem is likely to be more difficult to write than individual selected-response items.

Guides to Writing Mathematical Problem Items

The special characteristics of individual mathematical problems require that the item writer give attention to the following specific points when preparing the tasks.

1. Provide enough information and direction so that students clearly understand the problem. A familiar algorithm can accomplish this purpose for many problems. If an algorithm cannot be used, then it may be necessary to give directions for a set of problems or one complex problem.

Example A

Directions: $a \cdot b = \boxed{}$ $4 \cdot 2 = \boxed{8}$

Calculate:

$43 \cdot 27 = \boxed{}$ $76 \cdot 30 = \boxed{}$ $14 \cdot 19 = \boxed{}$

$55 \cdot 11 = \boxed{}$ $23 \cdot 32 = \boxed{}$ $78 \cdot 96 = \boxed{}$

Example B

During the summer vacation Rich and Dan agreed to paint their neighbor's garage. One side of the garage is eight-meters long. The boys mark a point on the side which is four meters from each end. Each one starts at one end and paints toward the center mark, four meters from each end. Can we be sure that each painted the same area of that side if each paints to the center mark? Explain. [No. This would be true only if the side of the garage were rectangular.]

Other modifications of this item could be presented. If the second sentence is changed to read, "one side of the garage is rectangular and eight-meters long," then the response is "yes." The manner of asking the question and the expected response would vary with the purpose of the task and the age and experiential background of students. The task should not be presented in the first form for any age if the response "yes" is expected. For an expected "yes" response, the qualifier "rectangular" should be included to relieve the item of any ambiguity so that a student who visualizes that the side could be

or such is not penalized.

2. Any computational problem should indicate the degree of precision expected in the response. Indicate how to handle rounding or approximations and decimals or fractions in responses.

Example A

Directions: In the following set of exercises for figuring z-scores from the raw scores, use the mean and standard deviation values to the nearest hundredth of a raw score unit.

Example B

Directions: The proportions which you report for the ratios should be given in decimal fractions to the nearest hundredth of a point.

Example C

Directions: For this set of problems use the usual rules which this class has for rounding, approximation, and reporting fractional parts of the final responses. [This direction would be used only when the rules are clearly presented in instruction and would be used to test how well the student has remembered the ground rules.]

3. The units for reporting the response(s) must be clearly specified.

Example A

Directions: Total elapsed time should be reported in minutes and seconds.

NOT: 143 seconds

CHANGE TO: 2 minutes, 23 seconds

Example B

Directions: When reporting the perimeters, give your responses in either feet and inches or meters and centimeters, depending on the units used in each problem.

4. For primary-school students, mathematical problems of computation should be grouped according to process or other characteristic. Other situa-

tions may occur in later grades where this division should also be made. If both addition and subtraction problems are to be computed, list the addition problems together and the subtraction problems together (see Example A, below). Do not mix these through the test because the student may become confused even though each problem may be clearly marked as to the process to be used. Problems which require square root extractions should be separated from those which require the division process (see Example B). Separate as follows:

Example A

ADDITION

$24 + 18 = \boxed{}$ $\qquad$ $34 + 11 = \boxed{}$

$75 + 22 = \boxed{}$ $\qquad$ $47 + 14 = \boxed{}$

$89 + 7 = \boxed{}$ $\qquad$ $66 + 8 = \boxed{}$

SUBTRACTION

$75 - 35 = \boxed{}$ $\qquad$ $54 - 23 = \boxed{}$

$33 - 12 = \boxed{}$ $\qquad$ $78 - 52 = \boxed{}$

$46 - 37 = \boxed{}$ $\qquad$ $88 - 45 = \boxed{}$

Example B

SQUARE ROOT

$\sqrt{335}$ $\quad$ $\sqrt{440}$ $\quad$ $\sqrt{755}$

$\sqrt{867}$ $\quad$ $\sqrt{545}$ $\quad$ $\sqrt{325}$

DIVISION

$35\overline{)654}$ $\quad$ $43\overline{)768}$ $\quad$ $78\overline{)456}$

$40\overline{)976}$ $\quad$ $20\overline{)2000}$ $\quad$ $23\overline{)271}$

5. If a particular algorithm is to be used, it should be indicated. The problem could be presented in algorithmic form.

Example A

For the following division problems, use the subtractive algorithm for division to arrive at the answer.

$87 \div 34 = \boxed{}$ $\qquad$ $45 \div 13 = \boxed{}$

$96 \div 32 = \boxed{}$ $\qquad$ $56 \div 11 = \boxed{}$

Example B

Show all work for the following multiplication problems.

$$\begin{array}{ccccccc} 43 & 16 & 11 & 63 & 99 & 13 & 20 \\ \times 27 & \times 10 & \times 11 & \times 24 & \times 71 & \times 76 & \times 30 \end{array}$$

6. When using regular "everyday" words to present a mathematical situation, make sure that the connection between the structured situation and the real world is genuine and not false or ambiguous in any way.

For example, a teacher may want to build some background for permutations. Rather than saying, "Create a permutation for the three letters in TEA," a teacher may present a problem on a test without using the word permutation since it was not used in instruction. This problem might be presented as, "What words can you make from the letters in TEA?" Although the teacher is expecting to get TEA, ATE, EAT, ETA, AET, and TAE, the student could be confused in one or more ways. Since ETA, AET, TAE are not words, should they be listed? ETA is a Greek word, so it might be considered as a special case. Should the word TEA itself be listed? The directions should be written so that it is clear to the student that the task is to arrange the letters in TEA in all possible ways.

7. Check the section "General Considerations in Construction of Test Items" in Chapter 5.

Exemplary Items

Examples of problems for use at different levels are provided as further guides to writing mathematical problems, but the reader must extend the list with ideas beyond those which are given here as models to make problems relevant to a particular area of instruction. Methods books, curriculum materials, colleagues' tests, and teacher manuals are rich sources of ideas for problems. Your own creativeness is also needed for your specific class of students. Knowledge of your subject matter, examples from other sources, and creative schemes are needed to write problems which will give valid measurements in your tests. The grade level of the school which could use the items is not listed because of the great differences in school programs. You can select the appropriate level according to the group which you do, or expect to, teach.

Elementary school subjects

1. Directions: Perform the multiplication for the following exercises:

$18 \cdot 5 = \boxed{}$ $(23)(9) = \boxed{}$ $76 \times 5 = \boxed{}$

$23 \times 8 = \boxed{}$ $47 \cdot 4 = \boxed{}$

2. Directions: Perform the indicated process for the pairs numerals. [This situation could be used without violating guide number 4 if one of the knowledges to be tested is that of knowing the symbols for the four basic processes.]

$14 + 18 = \boxed{}$ $9 \times 67 = \boxed{}$ $43 - 9 = \boxed{}$

$704 \div 7 = \boxed{}$ $45 \div 4 = \boxed{}$

$(23 + 5) - (8 - 4) = \boxed{}$ $57 \times 12345 = \boxed{}$

3. Directions: Loop names for five (5) like this:

$8 - 4$ $11 - 6$ $4 + 2$ $(3 + 2)$ $10 \div 2$

$2 \div 10$ $\sqrt{25}$ $(14 + 1) - 10$

[This exercise can be leveled for many classes by adjusting the level of difficulty for the terms in the list.]

4. Directions: Find the missing number.

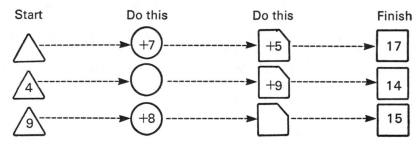

Start	Do this	Do this	Finish

5. In each exercise below, each of the letters A, B, C, D, E is to be replaced by one of the digits 0, 1, 2, 3, 4, 5, 6, 7, 8, 9. The letters may be replaced by different digits in different exercises; however, within each problem a letter has the same number for all cases. For example:

$$CC - C1 = 6$$
$$C \text{ must} = 7$$
$$77 - 71 = 6$$

Two letters together (AB, CE, or such) represent a two-place numeral.

Addition			Subtraction	

```
      Addition                    Subtraction

   47      47      DD          64       ABC
    4       D       E           A        42
   ──      ──      ──          ──       ───
   A1      CC      80          C8       153


   CC      E4                  BB       7A
    C      3C                  B2       AB
   ──      ──                  ──       ──
   60      87                   4       14
```

6. Two rectangles are placed as shown so that a larger rectangle is formed. Find the areas of both smaller rectangles and the area of the larger one in square units.

Is the larger area the sum of the other two? _____

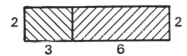

2 ... 2 Write a number sentence to represent the relationship among the three areas.

3   6

_____

What property of rational numbers does this number sentence illustrate?

_____

7. The farmer put 60 carrots in bunches of 5 carrots. How many bunches did he make?

8. A jet plane carried 42 passengers in one section and 102 passengers in another section. How many passengers were aboard the jet?

Secondary school subjects

1. Directions: Write the equations of lines having the following pairs of intercepts:

	X-intercept	Y-intercept
A.	−3.0	2
B.	0.5	3
C.	4.0	2

2. Write some of the points ( ), ( ), ( ), ( ), whose ordinate is 6 more than twice their abscissa values. Now write the relationship which represents all such points.

3. Directions: Find the midpoint of the line joining:

a. points (5, −9) and (−13, 19)
b. points (16, 0) and (0, 9)
c. points — — — — — — — —
d. — — — — — — — — — — —

4. Directions: For premises 1 and 2, form an inference or conclusion for step 3. Show the relationship for each syllogism with a Venn diagram.

1. $p \rightarrow q$ 1. Every element of p is an element of q.

2. $q \rightarrow r$ 2. Every element of q is an element of r.

3. ∴   3. ∴

In the space below show the relationship with a Venn diagram.

5. Directions: Using the graph paper provided, draw graphs for the following inequalities. Use the guidelines set for drawing graphs in this class.

1. $x + y > 6$ 2. $y \geq X - 4$ 3. $3X - 2y < 6$

The discussion of the strengths, weaknesses, and guides to writing mathematical problem items along with the exemplary items for the elementary and secondary school levels will help you develop and write items for your students. The next section is organized in the same manner as the mathematical problem item but discusses technical problems.

TECHNICAL PROBLEMS

The technical problem is presented here as the complex situation written for a limited and specialized study. Technical problems are widely used in tests for physical sciences, vocational courses, technology, engineering, and business. Other disciplines at the secondary level use the technical problem to a lesser extent. Elementary school classes rarely study a topic in sufficient depth to warrant the use of the technical problem, but some uses have been found in special materials, especially in science. However, the technical problem test usually works better at the secondary or higher levels because students at these levels tend to have stronger motivation to work through an involved test situation to a successful solution. The student may be a major in the subject, be preparing for a special job on completion of the course or series of courses, or may have formed a special interest in the topic.

The versatility of the technical problem rests in the wide scope of possible situations which can be provided. The technical problem is not to be confused with the performance test, which is used to see how well a student will perform a specific skill. The technical problem could be used to generalize on-the-job performance in a wide scope, while performance tests are more for special skills and talents.

Since each technical problem is specific to a special content area, coverage here will be limited because: *(a)* the scope of the book does not allow coverage of all possible uses, and *(b)* our knowledge in most of those special areas is limited. Exemplary items, although included, are not intended to be exhaustive even to areas which can use the technical problem.

Special Considerations for Technical Problems

When choosing the most appropriate item type to call forth a particular student behavior, the teacher must consider the following strengths and weaknesses of the technical problem item.

Strengths

Because of the similarity of the mathematical problem and the technical problem, their strengths tend to be much the same. The technical problem can test students for application of principles, control for guessing and bluffing, rate high in objectivity, and allow for learning during testing. Presentation of technical problems on a test also allows the testing session to become an integral part of the ongoing activities of the classroom. Other strengths include:

1. The technical problem allows an in-depth investigation that encompasses many related factors and allows the student to exhibit knowledge of the interrelatedness among those factors.

2. The technical problem can be used to judge how a student will attack a problem when any one of several procedures could be used. It may be that the final response is not really of great importance to this type of problem, and judgment of a student's performance may be primarily in terms of how the student reached a solution rather than the solution itself.

3. The technical problem is the most direct way to measure many outcomes and provides an adequate data base to make inferences about student competency and to predict future performance.

Weaknesses

The limitations of technical problems are similar to those of mathematical problems: both use a small number of items on the test and responses are difficult to score. The small sample of items may result in low content validity. There may be more than one solution, or the response may be partially correct, thus requiring much time to score, and may lower scorer reliability. Other possible weaknesses follow:

1. The major weakness of the technical problem is the difficulty of setting up a situation that includes the necessary aspects to solve the problem. Since the problem is so broad in scope, much thought is required to include all information needed for solution.

2. The technical problem cannot be used extensively with large classes. Even though an individual scorer tries to be objective, and scoring procedures are standardized for a set of scores, some variation can be expected because of the subjective decisions which remain in every case of scoring of a technical problem. This difficulty, coupled with the great amount of time needed to score a technical problem, makes it less useful with large classes than with small classes or individual students.

Guides to Writing Technical Problem Items

The special characteristics of the technical problem require that the item writer give attention to the following specific points when preparing tasks.

1. Be sure to include enough information and direction so that the student understands the scope of the problem and so that parameters are clear. In addition to reading the words, the student must internalize the content of the problem.

Example

Mike Mechanic ran an exhaust gas analysis on his V-8 engine and found everything okay in the left tail pipe of a dual exhaust system. He got very erratic readings on the right pipe. All of the readings were extremely lean. How do you diagnose the problem? Explain your repair schedule.

2. Indicate the degree of precision and units for reporting responses for computational parts of the problem.

Example

During computation approximate all values to the nearest hundredth, and report final responses in square feet to the nearest unit.

3. Check the section "General Considerations in Construction of Test Items" in Chapter 5.

Exemplary Items

Examples of technical problems for use at different levels are provided as further guides. Knowledge in the technical subject being tested and creative schemes are necessary for writing problems specific to each subject area.

Elementary school subjects

The elementary school teacher will rarely find use for the true technical problem because study is not sufficiently specialized at this level. A somewhat technical problem could be devised for laboratory situations in some topics of science and possibly in some other elementary school subjects.

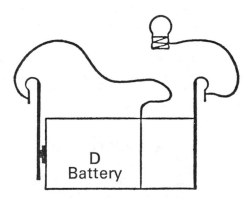

1. Use the picture above to represent an electric setup. If the battery and bulb are good, what must be done to make the bulb turn on? Explain the principle of electricity which told you how to turn on the light bulb.

2. The pointers for pulley A and pulley B are both set at zero (0). Explain how the ratio of revolutions for the two pulleys could be established.

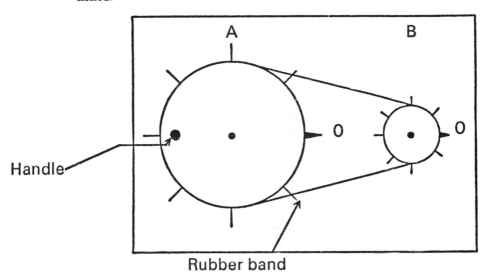

Rubber band

[This problem could be made more difficult by leaving off the scale for each pulley. The student then would need to develop some way of scaling the turns.]

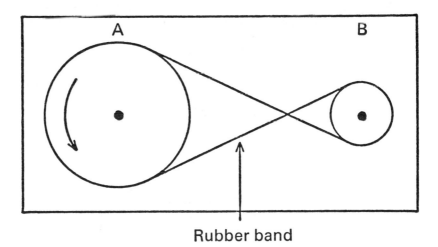

Rubber band

3. Pulleys A and B (above) are connected by a driving belt as shown. If pulley A moves in the direction indicated, show on the diagram which way pulley B will move. [This problem can be extended to three or more pulleys with many variations.]

Secondary school subjects

1. The furniture-maker is confronted often with the problem of adjusting the lengths of the four legs of a stool, table, or chair so that they all rest solidly on the floor. Explain how you could trim the length of the legs and cut off the bottoms so that all legs rest flat on the floor.

2.   Ignition Secondary "Scope" Pattern

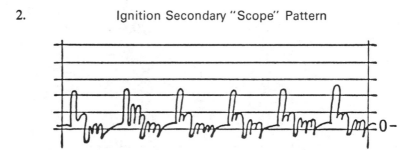

The above reading indicates possible trouble in the ignition system. How do you diagnose the problem from this reading? What replacement(s) do you suggest to overcome the difficulty?

3. Using the diagram below, connect light A with switches S_1 and S_2 so that light A can be turned on and off by either switch S_1 or switch S_2 (three-way switch).

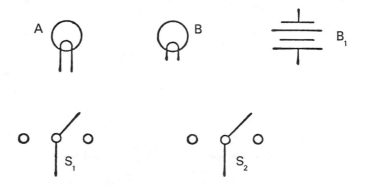

4. It is sometimes necessary in drafting to draw some special view of an object to show certain features more clearly. Through a series of 4 or 5 drawings and associated narrative extend drawing (A) to include a fourth view which is an auxiliary view showing the true size and shape of the inclined surface.

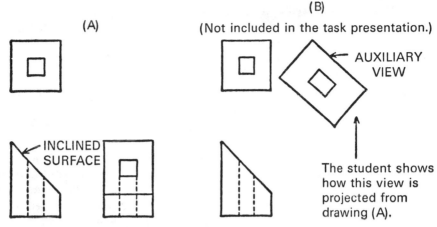

(B)

(A)

(Not included in the task presentation.)

AUXILIARY VIEW

INCLINED SURFACE

The student shows how this view is projected from drawing (A).

5. The following information for three customer accounts is taken from duplicate sales invoices. Your task is to record the sales in a Sales Journal and to post to customer accounts in the Accounts Receivable Ledger. Select forms that you need from the table at the back of the room.
A. Record in a Sales Journal these sales:

May 2 Kroftie Brothers, Jasonville, Ind.	$642.50
5 Sullins and Jessell, Linton, Ind.	$432.09
8 Allied Manufacturing, Marshall, Ill.	$173.60
10 Sullins and Jessel	$973.24
12 Allied Manufacturing	$ 43.60
15 Kroftie Brothers	$493.14
22 Kroftie Brothers	$132.90

B. Post from the Sales Journal to the debit side of the customers' accounts in the Accounts Receivable Ledger. Use terms "Net, 30 days" for all customers.
C. Find the total sales for the month for these three accounts in the Sales Journal. Pencil foot before inking the totals.
D. Find the balance due from each customer by pencil footing the debit side of each customer's account.

The problem item has much in common with the essay item, as problems serve quantitatively oriented learning areas in much the same way that the essay serves nonquantitative learning areas. Nearly all fields of study can use the problem to collect information concerning students' level of functioning and understanding of principles.

SUMMARY

Mathematical and technical problem items may be utilized for an in-depth investigation for interpretation of data, development of relationships, use of principles, drawing of conclusions, analysis, or evaluation in quantitatively oriented learning areas. The mathematical problem requires students to compute as well as deal with theoretical and applied mathematical situations. The technical problem relates to the complex situation for a limited and specialized study in subjects such as the physical sciences, vocational courses, technology, engineering, and business, although it has application to nearly all subjects at all educational levels.

Problem items are particularly relevant for testing student understanding of principles by requiring the student to use new data with a new set of circumstances. How well a student can take a set of learned principles and apply them can be determined.

For both the mathematical and technical problem items the strengths, weaknesses, and guides to writing these items along with exemplary items were presented. Mastery of the chapter content along with conscientious application of the procedural principles of construction of these items will help teachers improve test quality when using the problem item.

The next chapter is devoted to assembling, administrating, and scoring classroom tests.

ACTIVITY EXERCISES

1. Construct a set of computational problems for a principle that is appropriate for a given grade level. State the grade level, subject, and the objective.
2. Construct two mathematical word problems appropriate for a given grade level. State the grade level, subject, and objective for each.
3. Construct two technical problem test items that are appropriate for a given grade level. State the grade level, subject, and the objective for each.
4. For each mathematical problem item and technical problem item you have written refer to "General Considerations in Construction of Test Items" (Chapter 5) and the "Guides to Writing" from this chapter and check each item against these points. Make appropriate changes in items as necessary.

FOR DISCUSSION

1. Describe the problem item and how it is unique for the student.
2. Outline the strengths and weaknesses of the mathematical problem item and the technical problem item.
3. Provide examples of situations in your classroom where the mathematical problem would be appropriate. Do the same for the technical problem. Perusal of the exemplary items in the chapter can be helpful in providing ideas, but expand this into your own teaching area.
4. Explain how the use of problems on tests supports the objective of students developing problem-solving skills.

REFERENCES AND KNOWLEDGE EXTENDERS

BROWN, F. G. *Measuring classroom achievement.* New York: Holt, Rinehart & Winston, 1981. Chap. 4, pp. 71–74.

HOPKINS, C. D., & ANTES, R. L. *Classroom testing: Construction.* Itasca, IL: F. E. Peacock, 1979. Chap. 4, pp. 64–81.

STAIB, J. H. The cardiologist's theorem. *The Mathematics Teacher,* 1977, *70*(2), 36–39.

Chapter 9. Assembling, Administering, and Scoring the Classroom Test

After study of Chapter 9, you should be able to:

1. Summarize the procedures for test assembly.
2. Describe how the physical and psychological aspects of test administration affect the validity of test scores.
3. Write test directions specific to age levels of students for the several types of test items.
4. List the types of test items in hierarchical order according to demands placed on the test taker.
5. Discuss the options available for scoring selected-response items to support reliable and valid measures.
6. State the procedure for analytical scoring of essay items and its contribution to valid measures.
7. State the procedure for global scoring of essay items and its contribution to valid measures.
8. Explain how each glossary term listed at the end of the chapter is used in classroom measurement and evaluation.

The teacher selects appropriate instructional objectives for the content covered, prepares a table of specifications, and writes items appropriate for the subject and desired student behaviors. Chapter 5 directed attention to planning a test, and Chapters 6, 7, and 8 presented details about writing particular kinds of items. A teacher may take extreme care in preparation of a classroom test, but negate the efforts through lack of careful attention to details involved in assembling, administering, and scoring the teacher-made test. The discussion in this chapter develops for the teacher an understanding of the technical aspects necessary for effective classroom testing procedures. This understanding will aid the teacher to arrange for testing conditions which lead to the maximum opportunity for students to demonstrate their achievement.

TEST ASSEMBLY

Prior to **test assembly** the teacher has written and selected an appropriate sample of items based on the table of specifications to be included on a particular test. Test assembly involves the development of test directions, typing the test, arrangement of items, and reproduction of the test.

Test Directions

Test directions are important because they inform the student of what is to be done, how it is to be done, and how responses are to be recorded. Prior to the test the teacher should inform students concerning the purpose, types of items, amount of time to be allotted, desirability of guessing on selected-response items, and any other information necessary for test taking. Clear and concise directions avoid confusion in regard to test expectations. Test directions should be written so that the student who can read will be able to take the test without oral directions.

The manual of instructions must be followed for published tests because the same instructions and procedures employed with the norming group must be used in the classroom if student scores are to be compared with test norms.

The extensiveness of the directions depends on the students' familiarity with tests, particularly with the type of items on the test. General considerations in providing instructions include:

1. Set the directions off from the rest of the test by appropriate spacing and typing style, so that it is clear to the test taker that these are the directions and not test items.
2. Provide simple, clear, and specific directions for each type of item on the test as well as the general directions.
3. Make effective use of sample items and responses to help clarify the directions, particularly when an unusual or new type of item is employed.

The following examples illustrate these considerations:

1. Directions: Read each statement below. If the statement is probably a fact, write F on the line beside the item. If the statement is an opinion, write O on the line.
   Examples:
   <u>F</u> 1. Apples grow on trees.
   <u>O</u> 2. Apples are good.

2. Directions: Read the statements given below. Each statement gives an opinion. On the lines following each opinion write a statement of fact to support the opinion.
   Example:
   1. I think highways are dangerous.
      There are many cars going at high speeds on the highways.

3. Directions: Write on the line at the right of each statement the letter preceding the word or expression that best completes the statement or answers the question.

Example:

What are two important money crops grown in India?   <u>c</u>
   a. tobacco and wool
   b. bananas and coconuts
   c. jute and peanuts
   d. coffee and chicle

Primary grade students

Presentation of oral or written directions for primary students depends upon the age and grade level of the class. For the nonreader oral directions are required. Even if primary school children can read, they require verbal directions and sample items to be worked through with the guidance of the teacher prior to beginning the test. The teacher should read the directions once for primary grade students and allow questions to be raised. Students can then reread the directions as needed. Written directions for primary students help them become comfortable with seeing these in written form as well as hearing the teacher's verbal coverage. The directions should be presented on the lowest reading level represented in the group being tested. Some children at the upper level of reading ability in a classroom may find the directions childlike, but it is better to be sure that all students can read the directions than to write directions which some students may not be able to read and understand. The size of the print or type and spacing must be taken into consideration, since visual development and capabilities of primary students vary.

Providing examples which demonstrate what is to be done when responding to different types of items is a necessity for young students and advisable for any age student when a new type of item is introduced. The following directions and examples illustrate the point:

1. Directions: Read each incomplete sentence. Draw a line under the word that completes the sentence.

   Example: Some animals in the zoo are kept in _____.
            <u>cages</u>   barns   pastures

2. Directions: Circle a synonym for the underlined word.

   Example: Next to an ant, an elephant is big.
            (large)   brown   size

   How did you tear your sleeve?
            cut   (rip)   sew

3. Directions: Number the sentences in the order they happened.

Example: The Story of Columbus

   7   Columbus went on a second voyage to the New World.

   4   On October 12, 1492, Columbus saw an island in the West Indies.

   6   The king and queen of Spain welcomed him as a hero on his return.

   8   Columbus died still thinking he had found a new route to India.

   1   As a boy Columbus talked to sailors and dreamed of going to sea.

   5   Three months later he returned to Spain with Indians and tobacco.

   2   Columbus left home and soon became a good sailor.

   3   He asked Queen Isabella for ships for a voyage to India.

4. Directions: Read each question. Write a C before the correct answer.

Example: Why was Washington sent to Ohio country?

  C To ask the French to leave.

     To build a fort there.

     To take a group of settlers there.

5. Put the words where they go.

Example: cow   Joe   dog

          Dick Sally   cat

Girls	Boys	Animals
Sally	Joe	cow
	Dick	dog
		cat

6. Letters and Sounds: Circle the letter which looks like the one in the box.

Example: A   U   Ⓐ   M   D

7. Underline the word which names the picture.

Example:

her   sun

sky   ran

Responses made by very young students are usually recorded on the test page or booklet. Published achievement tests and classroom tests for older students usually use a response sheet separate from the test booklet. By the time students reach the fifth and sixth grades, they are able to follow directions and respond to a variety of types of test items with ease, because of their experience in taking tests. The following illustrations suggest ways for marking test items on the test pages themselves:

1. Mark the words on each line which rhyme like this:

Example:

2. Write the correct word which completes the sentence on the line.

Example: Shep is a good <u>sheep.</u>   (sign, sheep)

3. List the words which start with capital (S) and small (s) and capital (W) and small (w).

Example:

Sandy	with	Wilma	saw	car	Sam	was
W		w	S		s	
Wilma		with	Sandy		saw	
		was	Sam			

Older students and adults

Published achievement tests and classroom tests for older students require the student to use either the response sheet from the test booklet or a separate machine-scorable sheet. Directions for items for older students are illustrated in these examples:

1. Multiple Choice: For each of the items select the best response and mark it on the response sheet like this:

A   B   ⓒ   D

2. True-False: For each of the following items decide whether the statement is true or false. Mark your response sheet Ⓣ for a true statement or Ⓕ for a false statement like this:

T   Ⓕ

3. Matching: For each of the standardized tests listed in column A choose an appropriate use for that test listed in column B. Place the letter from column B next to the number of the premise from column A on the response sheet like this:

11. <u> h </u>
12. <u> d </u>
13. <u> a </u>

14. _g_
15. _f_
16. _c_

Specific directions will be needed for each different type of item on the test.

Clarifying directions

Clarity of directions affects the precision of the measuring instrument; therefore, the meaning of directions must be exactly the same for all students and the teacher. Whether the directions do this or not can be determined by trying out the directions with a few students similar to those who will be taking the test. Once a teacher establishes the reading level of directions required for a specific age or grade level, the instructions can become standard for all tests except for minor changes for special types of items or unique characteristics of students being tested. Well-written directions should be understood by all students of intermediate grades or above, allowing the time devoted to testing to be free of verbal discussion.

Whether the response sheets are to be hand scored, machine scored, or self-scored, written directions with graphic examples show students how responses should be recorded.

Arranging the Items

The test maker has one last chance to review and edit items and directions before moving to the final stage of the actual reproduction of the complete test. In the final assembly stage defects which have been originally overlooked such as clarity, conciseness, ambiguity, and language or verbal mistakes can be corrected in a final writing. If an item is rewritten or reworked to improve it, care must be taken to see that the intent of the implied question is not altered. It is also helpful for a colleague or two to review and criticize the items before the final assembly. The author of the items will also achieve better success in reviewing items if the test is set aside for a few days and then appraised. After final editing each item should be written on a five-by-eight-inch index card as illustrated by Figure 9.1. Recording each item on a separate card provides the opportunity to form a file which can be conveniently employed in selecting effective items for future tests. Separate item cards also facilitate changes in arrangement as the test is assembled.

The most effective method for organizing items is to arrange sections of the test first by item type, second, grouping within item types by subject topics, and third, ordering in ascending level of difficulty within each group. Subject-topic grouping is helpful for diagnostic purposes. The organization by ascending difficulty permits students to work through items which allow for early success and may provide motivation to continue, while high levels of difficulty early in the test might cause the student to become discouraged. Slower students may spend too much of their time on difficult, early tasks and never reach items which they could respond to easily. By arranging items in order

TOPIC: Scientific method									
OBJECTIVE: The student will know the purpose of a controlled experiment. ITEM: A scientist performs a controlled experiment to *a. determine the number of quantities involved. b. find a relationship between certain quantities involved. c. eliminate all the quantities involved. d. reduce the effect of the quantities involved									
TEST DATE:									
ITEM NO.									

FIGURE 9.1. Example of test-item card — physics.

of increasing difficulty within topics a better measure of the student's true achievement is obtained.

When making decisions about format which will be most efficient and helpful to students, the teacher must decide on the order of item types. A test should include no more than three types of items. A hierarchical arrangement of item types based on the overall complexity of items is:

1. Classification
2. Matching
3. Completion
4. True-false
5. Short-answer
6. Multiple-choice
7. Essay, limited response

The order is based upon the complexity of the task demanded of the student, from the simplest to the most complex. This arrangement of items leads to an economy of time in that students respond to items which take less time per item before arriving at the more involved items which usually take more thought and consideration. Specific differences between items may violate the hierarchy but, in general, these relationships hold. For example, some true-false items which measure understanding could require more time to answer than multiple-choice items which require only recall of knowledge.

The practice of grouping items by topic directs each student's thoughts to one frame of reference at a time avoiding the shift by topic from one to another as is the case when items are randomized. This is convenient also in determining the thoroughness of coverage and understanding of the material when checking for instructional effectiveness. Organization by subject topic also facilitates classroom discussion when the tests are returned to students. Within some subjects it is practical and expedient to group items according to content units or, as in a subject such as history, by time periods. For example, in a second grade science class the items in a test may be grouped in topical areas such as seasons, animals, plants, earth, or natural resources that appear in the unit being tested, and presented in ascending order of difficulty in each topical area.

The decision regarding the difficulty of items rests with the teacher's judgment and will not necessarily correspond in all instances with students' selection of items or their judgment about the degree of difficulty of items. The degree of difficulty of an item depends on the proportion of students who miss it. An easy item would be missed by only a few of the students, whereas an item is considered difficult if a large portion miss it. After a test has been administered to a class and the results analyzed, the difficulty of items for the students can be discerned from item analysis data. Item analysis of previously used objective items may be used to estimate difficulty levels of items which are to be used again. This is one of the advantages of item analysis. As data are accumulated over a number of administrations, more accurate estimates can be made.

Test items can be grouped according to instructional objectives such as knowledge of terms, application of principles, synthesis, or other behavior classes of the taxonomy. This grouping may be particularly helpful to the teacher who wishes to review the categories of a behavioral domain which are required of students as they respond to various items. Remember that the taxonomies of educational objectives are divided into three domains and subdivided into hierarchical categories ranging from the simplest to the most complex type of behavior.

Reproducing the Test

Contemporary approaches to reproduction of tests include, in addition to the conventional reproduction on paper, the placement of single items on 35-millimeter slides, reproduction of the test items on a set of transparencies, writing the items on the chalkboard, and **computer-assisted testing (CAT)** (Lippey, 1974). The method of presenting of items or questions may have an effect upon scores. Therefore careful consideration should be given to advantages and limitations of each of the possibilities.

The use of a slide projector to display the item on a screen for a given amount of time may create a time pressure and anxiety for some students. The use of an overhead projector and a transparency may be more acceptable since a number of items may be projected at one time, and a student would have a better opportunity to work an optimum pace. Another disadvantage in any of the approaches mentioned, other than reproducing items on paper, may be created if the students are not able to see the item well enough to read it and are thus limited in recording their answers correctly on the response sheet. If items are written on the chalkboard they will be erased, and no permanent record of the test items will be available for reference during class discussion of the test or to respond to a question that a student might have. Although the teacher has a record of the intended tasks, any errors in copying from the teacher's paper to the board will be lost by the erasure.

Traditionally, teachers have been able to arrange for each student to have a test copy, allowing students to respond to the items at their own pace. The employment of audiovisual equipment in testing has been encouraged because it reduces the cost of paper. This may be a practical approach to a budgeting problem by reduction of the expenditures for paper, but hopefully a teacher who wishes to supply a copy for each student will have that option.

Tests should be reproduced on one side of the paper so that print does not show through. The direct master technique of spirit duplicating and mimeograph are the most commonly used methods of test reproduction for classroom use. Usually one of these two choices will be available to teachers. The photo-offset method may be used when a large number of copies is required by wide use of a particular test.

The format of the page layout for selected-response items should allow for double spacing between items and generous margins. The alternatives for each multiple-choice item should be listed in a vertical column beneath the stem of that item. The categories for classification items should be clearly indicated to facilitate choices. The two lists for matching items must be clearly distinguishable to the reader.

For the very young child and other special cases it may be necessary for the test taker to place responses on the test booklet itself rather than on a response sheet. In the event the items are to be answered on the test booklet, the examinees can indicate choices by marking the letter of the correct response. To facilitate scoring, a set of alternatives for each item can be placed down the left side of the page if this procedure would not confuse the person selecting the responses. For example:

---

a   b   c   d   14. A school building shaped as a rectangle
has how many sides?
    a. three
  *b. four
    c. five
    d. six

a   b   c   d   15. What arithmetic process should be used?

If the response is recorded on the line next to the item, alphabetical letters should be provided for marking rather than giving a space for the student to write the letter of the chosen alternative. Carelessly written letters could be interpreted erroneously and credit given for incorrect responses, or correct responses could be interpreted as incorrect choices.

Test items numbered consecutively throughout the complete test help in discussion of test items in class as well as in item analysis. In this way there will be only one (1), one (2), one (3), and so on. Numbering the items within sections of the test generally leads to confusion since there will be more than one item with the number 1, more than one item with the number 2, and so on.

Common sense and a good typist also aid in developing a pleasing test format and reproduction of a classroom test. After the masters have been made and the pages printed, careful collation into a test booklet completes the assembly of the test, and the instrument is now ready to be administered to the students.

Use of new technology takes advantage of the capabilities of computers to administer tests to students. By combining a learning situation with a testing situation, some teachers have had good success with CAT. Students seem to like it and teachers seem to sense a reduction of test anxiety in their students. Most computer programs employ a branching for responses and also keep records of student responses, allowing a component of a test score as they work through the material. Continued increase in the use of computers in instruction has also given teachers more opportunity to collect data for formative evaluation. Progress in the technology of information handling has allowed an increase of the breadth and individualization of instruction and testing (Tyler & White, 1979). The needed fit between testing and instruction may be found or at least improved by taking advantage of the increasing availability of low-cost technology for handling information. Three examples are: computer-based item pools, computer-based testing for broader objectives, and tailored testing (Tyler & White, 1979; p. 15).

ADMINISTRATION OF THE TEST

Setting the stage for the administration of the test is the responsibility of the classroom teacher. Attention should be given to the physical arrangements and psychological aspects that could possibly affect the test session. Although the administration of the test is probably the simplest aspect of the testing procedure, proper administrative procedures are extremely important. Their effects on the students' feelings and physical comforts are reflected in the validity of the test scores. Good administrative procedures support the validity of a good test while poor procedures can reduce the validity of the results of a good test.

Physical Conditions

In administering a classroom test, the physical conditions should be favorable to all students. Room conditions are to be comfortable, examinees relaxed and attentive. The effects of the physical conditions can sometimes be discerned from student comments about room conditions. Proper attention to the elements of the physical conditions which are necessary for optimum student performance can optimize testing conditions.

Heating and ventilation

Consideration should be given to the average temperature best for the largest number of individuals. The effectiveness of the teaching-learning situation and the efficiency of students as well as school personnel are greatly influenced by the thermal environment of the classroom. Students in kindergarten and the primary grades should be in an environment which is 65° to 68° Fahrenheit or 18° to 20° Celsius at shoulder height, while students in the intermediate, junior high, and senior high school grades are most efficient when 68° to 70° Fahrenheit or 20° to 22° Celsius is maintained at shoulder height (Castaldi, p. 213).

Lighting

A discussion of detailed specifications for illumination may not be of great practical value, since the conditions which exist must be accepted. The only immediate and practical procedure in dealing with inadequate illumination is to locate the best test situation which exists within a given school facility. This might be accomplished by switching classrooms with another teacher to provide for an appropriately illuminated area.

Noise

Recess noise, band practice, lunch period noise, and other distractions from activities or classes outside the classroom testing situation can sometimes be avoided by wise planning. Teachers who meet classes on a schedule of modules or class periods may be limited in selecting an ideal time, but some days of the week may offer better conditions than others. The magnitude of the noise level may significantly affect performance, and this must be taken into consideration in testing environments. To avoid an interruption by someone entering the classroom a sign may be placed on the classroom door requesting that the class not be disturbed except in an emergency.

Acclimatization

Whenever possible testing should be carried out in the same classroom where classes meet. Students will feel comfortable at their regular desk or table since the height and general surroundings are familiar. Adequate proctoring will possibly eliminate cheating or at least remove the temptation and avoid the need for students to change the seating arrangement just during testing periods.

Many students express a feeling of not being comfortable in taking a test away from the room where the class is held. The height of the desk, color of the walls, and other environmental factors help produce the feeling of newness in a different room. Testing students in a cafeteria or study hall has an even greater effect on students.

Psychological Aspects

A relaxed atmosphere during administration of a classroom achievement test can best be developed in the regular class environment, since the teacher has an opportunity to prepare students for the testing session ahead of time. The teacher must take time to explain the purpose of testing to each student. The teacher must stress the importance for each student of giving a best effort by following the directions explicitly and giving each task a maximum effort.

Psychological aspects of test taking are largely related to test anxiety. The mental anguish is based on negative test experiences students have encountered in the past. Teachers must establish a positive mental attitude toward testing by being straightforward when explaining why evaluation is important, as well as being helpful to students by informing them early when tests will be given and by providing sample test items. How the test results are ultimately used will do more than anything else to determine the orientation students have to a particular classroom teacher's tests. The teacher may foster relief from test anxiety by assisting students to develop good test-taking skills. Robert Ebel discusses test-taking skill and **testwiseness** and supports teachers' assisting students by providing instructions in how to take tests (Ebel, 1979, pp. 180–183).

If all students have basically the same test-taking skills, this factor should be constant throughout all test scores for the class and not affect the variability of the scores. Differences among the scores will not be magnified by the components of differences in skill in test taking and testwiseness. Classroom instruction about how to take tests should occur early in each student's educational career.

A teacher who reassures students about testing situations and provides adequate time to complete the examination has gone a long way toward relieving test anxiety. Only through careful consideration and attention by each teacher who comes into contact with students throughout their schooling will anxiety in test situations be alleviated in a large portion of students.

SCORING

The task of **scoring** follows the administration of a test and may be completed with relative ease if appropriate planning has taken place. The way the responses are recorded for selected-response items, constructed-response items, and problem items influences the scoring methods available. Special attention is given to the considerations that should be taken into account as test items are scored.

Recording Responses

The method of scoring chosen by the teacher is a function of how responses have been recorded. Determining the recording scheme which is best for students is based upon the kind of items, age and grade level, and general ability of students. Primary-level students inexperienced in the school setting, immature in eye development and coordination, and lacking organizational capabilities may need to record responses on the test itself. In general, third-grade and certainly fourth-grade students are capable of recording responses on a separate response sheet if clear, precise directions and examples are provided. Even though separate response sheets provide for accurate and reliable scoring, the decision of a recording scheme rests primarily upon what is best for students.

Occasionally a student may skip a response space or record a series of responses incorrectly on a separate response sheet. This may result in a series of incorrect responses according to the key or machine scoring. This error in recording responses can be taken into consideration by making an adjustment in the score of the paper.

Scoring Procedures

The procedures for scoring a test are determined in the planning stages and vary according to the type of item and the sophistication of the student. Basically, responses to the problem item and constructed-response item should be scored by the teacher knowledgeable in the subject, and selected response items can be scored by anyone who can compare student responses with a key of correct responses or by a scoring machine.

Some teachers feel that students learn from scoring test items. After the test or during the next class period students are directed to exchange papers and class members score the test items. This procedure consumes valuable class time and the scoring may be inaccurate since students are more concerned and attentive to recalling how they responded to the test items than they are in the mechanics of scoring. This may lead to scoring errors; therefore, all papers scored by exchanging test papers must be checked by the teacher or aide. Class time can be better utilized on more meaningful activities than scoring tests.

It is recommended that teachers not have students score tests; however, in situations where teachers do have students grade papers the following should be considered to maximize the benefit to students. Each item should be read aloud and the answer given. Queries from students concerning an item should be discussed before going on to the next item.

The best procedure is to score tests outside the classroom noting student responses and which items were missed. During the next class period teaching time can be devoted to discussion of topics as indicated by test items most frequently missed. This approach provides for a meaningful teaching-learning activity which clarifies student thinking concerning the topic and produces information important to the teacher.

Initially the teacher chooses a system for scoring test items and after experience in scoring alters the procedure to meet individual needs. The basic scoring procedures presented provide alternatives which teachers may wish to adopt.

Hand scoring

Hand scoring of responses for selected-response items marked in the spaces provided on the test may be carried out with a scoring key. The key can be developed by marking the correct responses on a copy of the test. Responses on individual papers are then compared to the keyed responses. When a key is supplied to a scorer, no particular knowledge of the content being covered is required to score select-response items.

With separate response sheets or responses recorded on the test itself a scoring key can be developed by folding an 8½ by 11 inch sheet of paper lengthwise three times, providing four columns, each the length of the page. Each strip is two-inches wide allowing room for the correct responses to be recorded. If responses are recorded on the test, they are spaced on the key to correspond with the spacing of the items on the test page (see Figure 9.2). The responses are recorded near the left side of each page and the scorer lays the strip along the column of responses. The scorer may mark either the correct or incorrect responses depending upon the method of scoring. It is suggested that the incorrect response be indicated by a slash line through the response and the correct response be marked. Marking the correct responses provides feedback to correct student thinking and saves time. Classroom discussion is facilitated because the teacher does not need to provide the responses verbally.

This procedure for developing the teacher-made response sheet will result in a key similar to Figure 9.2 or Figure 9.3. The difference of spacing on Figure 9.2 represents the development of the key based on the spacing needed for the test items, since the length of items may vary. If a separate response sheet is used, equal spacing can be used and the key would look like Figure 9.3. This type of scoring key is known as the **accordion key** because it is folded along the vertical broken lines shown in the figures. If the paper is cut along the broken lines, it is called a **strip key.** Hand-scoring devices can be produced from various materials such as paper, card stock, or transparent sheet.

An overprinting process in which a separate key is developed on a stencil or spirit master can be employed when a large number of response sheets must be scored very quickly. When the key stencil is run on a duplicating machine over the completed student response sheets incorrect responses can be viewed as the response sheets are scanned. It is important to run the duplicating machine with a few blank trial response sheets prior to placing student response sheets into the machine to make sure the alignment is correct.

Another hand scoring procedure which may be employed uses a stencil which has holes punched where the correct responses appear. By laying the

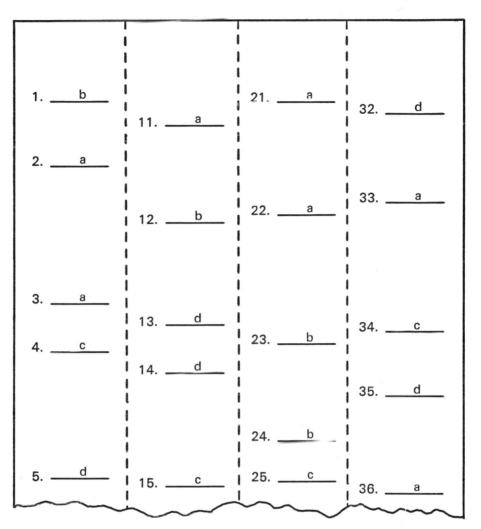

FIGURE 9.2. Accordion key for scoring responses recorded on the test sheets

stencil over the response sheet, the scorer can count the number of holes where the marks do *not* appear in the holes. The holes where nothing appears can be marked in red and the examinee will know the correct responses when the response sheet is returned. The number of red marks represents the number of items missed. Before scoring by the stencil each paper should be scanned to see if any items have more than one response marked. Any that are found should be marked across all alternatives with a red pen or pencil. In this way they will be counted as incorrect responses. Figure 9.4 presents a separate response sheet in which the correct response is to be circled and shaded. This

1. _a_	26. _a_	51. _b_	76. _a_
2. _b_	27. _c_	52. _b_	77. _c_
3. _a_	28. _c_	53. _a_	78. _a_
4. _c_	29. _b_	54. _c_	79. _d_
5. _c_	30. _d_	55. _d_	80. _b_
6. _d_	31. _a_	56. _a_	81. _c_
7. _a_	32. _c_	57. _d_	82. _b_
8. _c_	33. _c_	58. _b_	83. _d_
9. _d_	34. _a_	59. _c_	84. _a_
10. _a_	35. _d_	60. _d_	85. _c_
11. _b_	36. _b_	61. _c_	86. _d_
12. _c_	37. _c_	62. _a_	87. _a_
13. _a_	38. _d_	63. _b_	88. _d_
14. _d_	39. _b_	64. _c_	89. _a_
15. _c_	40. _a_	65. _d_	90. _d_
	41.		91. _d_

FIGURE 9.3. Accordion key for scoring responses recorded on a separate answer sheet

type of response sheet may be scored with a stencil as shown in Figure 9.5. The punched scoring key is employed in manual scoring, and the black dots represent holes which have been punched in card stock. The sample key in Figure 9.5 can be laid over a response sheet as illustrated in Figure 9.4.

Self-scoring

Self-scoring student-response devices are commercially available. They have the advantage of providing the student with immediate feedback as well

RESPONSE SHEET

Name _____

DIRECTIONS: After choosing the best response mark your choice by shading the letter which represents your choice.

Example: a b c d

1. a b c d	26. a b c d	51. a b c d	76. a b c d
2. a b c d	27. a b c d	52. a b c d	77. a b c d
3. a b c d	28. a b c d	53. a b c d	78. a b c d
4. a b c d	29. a b c d	54. a b c d	79. a b c d
5. a b c d	30. a b c d	55. a b c d	80. a b c d
6. a b c d	31. a b c d	56. a b c d	81. a b c d
7. a b c d	32. a b c d	57. a b c d	82. a b c d
8. a b c d	33. a b c d	58. a b c d	83. a b c d

FIGURE 9.4. Separate response sheet

as scoring the test for the teacher. Several different variations of the self-scoring devices are supplied by different companies. An erasure uncovers a letter which the student can interpret as a correct or incorrect response according to a code. Another type of self-scoring response sheet employs a latent image printed in invisible ink which is made visible when a light coating from a chemical marker pen "develops" the ink. Regardless of specific procedure each student response receives immediate reaction.

The teacher keys the correct response to the prekeyed response on the self-scoring sheet. The directions for the response sheet or card inform the student to erase the block or mark the space which represents his response with the chemical marker. An erasure or chemical mark reveals to the student whether the prekeyed correct response was chosen. With the use of the self-scoring sheet the student may continue to mark responses until the correct one appears. On self-scoring devices a student may have only one try or up to four or five tries depending upon the self-scoring sheet used and directions supplied by the teacher. In cases where the student has second, third, or fourth tries to obtain the correct response, a point assignment may be employed. The following table provides examples of point systems. The student or teacher uses

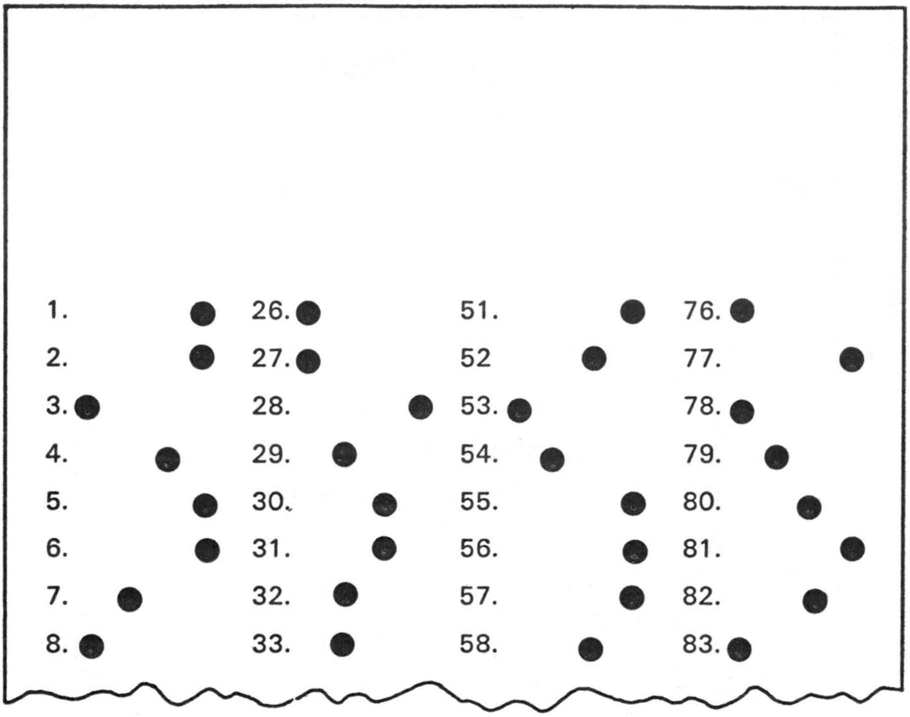

FIGURE 9.5. Punched scoring key

this table to add the points in each column and inserts the total points at the top of the response card or sheet. True-false items are scored 1 point for first erasure, or 0 for second.

Correct response upon	4-choice device; points assigned	5-choice device; points assigned
1st erasure	3	4
2nd erasure	2	3
3rd erasure	1	2
4th erasure	0	1
5th erasure		0

Machine Scoring

Machine scoring of response sheets is becoming more popular. When commercial machines are used, a special response sheet or card is required. Figure 9.6 is an example of a general-purpose response sheet which is designed primarily for multiple-choice items. This sheet may also be used with true-false

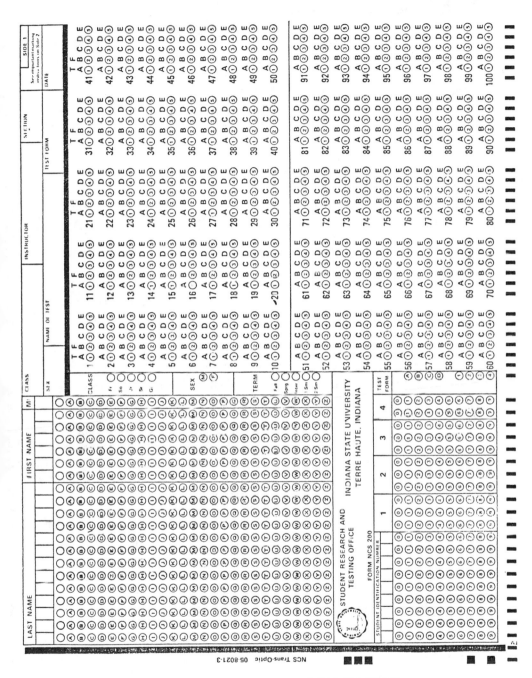

FIGURE 9.6. Machine-scorable answer sheet (IBM NCS200)

items by using only the first two spaces—usually the first space for true and the second space for false.

Several optical-scanning machines are available, each classified as a *mark scanner* or a *character scanner*. Equipment is available to read hand-printed letters or numbers as well as marks on coded sheets similar to Figure 9.6. The mark and character scanners are differentiated by the type of optical scanning they perform. The mark-scan is designed solely to read (detect) marks on response sheets while the character-scan is designed to read alphanumeric characters rather than marks (Baker, 1971, pp. 202–212).

The optical scanning systems for sensing and an electronic system for counting correct and incorrect responses are used to score classroom tests in those school systems which can afford the machines. The cost of these scoring machines is continually being reduced and machine scoring may become commonplace rather than an exception in public schools.

Scoring Selected-Response Items (true-false, multiple-choice, matching, and classification)

When selected-response items are employed and the responses are made on the test booklet, the scorer usually has more than one page to score. The more efficient way to score the pages is to score all items on the first page of all papers, all items on the second page of all papers, and so on. This facilitates the speed and accuracy of scoring since the papers can be arranged for each page and then scored rather than mixing page folding with the scoring. The scorer may, by use, memorize the part of the scoring key being used with each page thus further facilitating the scoring process.

If tests of selected-response items are hand scored, it is helpful to have a second person check the scoring. If there is not time to check all papers, checking might be done by rescoring a sample of papers in their entirety. Errors may have been made on just one section or page, and the scorer may find it necessary to recheck that page for all students.

If in the planning stage a decision was made to correct responses to selected-response items for guessing, the appropriate formula must be applied to the students' scores. The basis for the formulas lies in the assumption that if a student misses some items because the correct response could not be identified, some of the correct responses were marked by guessing. Since a correction-for-guessing formula is rarely needed for classroom tests the procedures have been placed in Appendix C: Correction for Guessing.

Scoring Constructed-Response Items (completion, short-response, and essay)

Completion items which require a one-word response or a predetermined series of one-word responses written on the test booklet may be scored by using a cutout key. It is made by cutting windows in the scoring stencil which reveal the word or words written in the blank provided on the test sheet. A teacher employing the completion item should not limit a correct response to one particular word. Students may be able to respond appropriately without using the exact word which the teacher has anticipated. Optional acceptable responses may be written above or below the cutout windows.

The problem of scoring essay responses with high reader reliability lies in the subjectivity of scorer judgments. The main criticism of essay tests concerns the judging of responses, which causes unreliability of the resulting measures. The major task associated with scoring students' essay responses is development of a set of scoring procedures which produce reliable measures of the trait being measured. Coffman points out the difficulty in achieving consistency in essay scoring when he cites evidence relative to three inescapable conclusions: *(a)* different raters tend to assign different marks to the same essay response, *(b)* a single rater tends to assign different scores to the same essay response on different occasions, and, *(c)* the greater the freedom of response the more the difference tends to increase (1971, pp. 276–277).

The clue to successful essay examination assessment lies in the ability of the teacher to develop objective procedures and techniques for scoring essay responses. There is no doubt that cognizance of techniques of planning, writing, and particularly of scoring essay items can lead to more efficient and reliable assessment of student achievement. The item should be written and framed to elicit the response desired. If the wish is to obtain the student's opinion and his ability to defend it, the item instructions might be worded:

> There seem to be two sides to the issue of building major highways through wilderness areas. State your opinion about whether the proposed new highway through the Okefenokee Swamp should be built as planned or a new route developed. Defend your stand on this issue.

The outline of the expected response must be written to reflect the elicited response based on how the task is worded and what it requests from the student. The use of descriptive words such as define, outline, select, illustrate, classify, and summarize are reasonably clear, enabling the teacher to decide in advance the factors which will be taken into consideration in judging the response.

Advocates of the essay examination employ one of two methods in scoring essay responses depending on which of the two best fits the conditions. The **analytical procedure** (also referred to as the *point procedure*) attempts to provide a detailed guide to scoring by identifying crucial elements of the ideal response. The **global procedure** (also referred to as the relative rating or *holistic procedure*) concentrates on the global ratings of the responses based on standards as determined by the overall student response to an essay item. The procedure chosen for evaluating essay responses may depend on the topic or subject being examined. A closer perusal of the aspects of each approach will help to clarify each method.

Analytical Procedure

The teacher, after writing the essay item, immediately proceeds to write a model response to the item. An outline of the major elements which are to be identified in the scoring process can then be made. The teacher may find in the process of responding that the item to be given to the students needs word changes or needs to be rewritten to generate the response the teacher expects. Development of an essay-response scoring guide provides for more stabilization of the scoring through the teacher's appraisal of each item. A listing of particular elements expected aids the scorer in assigning point or grade values. A number of additional factors may be employed in judging the essay response such as organization, method used, accuracy, completeness of response, correctness of expression, and other characteristics deemed important by the teacher.

The different factors or characteristics of the expected response may be placed in an outline form with the corresponding point values to be awarded for each of the factors in terms of the quality of response. Totaling the point values should minimize the influence on the point total of extraneous information in the response.

Most teachers find this scoring approach to be time-consuming, tedious, and tiresome if a large number of papers is to be scored. Use of analytical scoring, however, does facilitate discussion when papers are returned to students. The final score can be justified in terms of how well the responses fit with expectations.

The analytical procedure seems to be appropriate for subject or content areas whenever the response can be broken down into scorable units. For example, the relevant points which should be made on a history test can often be easily outlined and checked against student response, particularly when an item calls for a chronological resequencing of the discussion.

Global Procedure

Another way to score essay responses judges the response with an overall impression without identifying particular predetermined points to be included in the response. This procedure calls for a rapid first reading of the papers in order to form a general impression of each response and to divide the papers tentatively into categories according to varying qualities of the responses. The number of categories is contingent upon the desires of the scorer and the levels of discrimination needed. Usually a scorer reads until a response is evaluated as definitely superior and employs it as a reference point for deciding the worth of other responses.

A more careful second reading allows for a shift from the tentatively assigned category to refine the grouping of student responses if the reader feels that the original category assignment was in error. At this point the papers in each of the groups should be at about the same level of accomplishment. As a final check a third reading should be made by reading through each group to see if they are all at the same level. If one or more of the papers stand clearly above the others, it should be moved up one category. If one or more papers fall short of the rest, it should be moved down one category. The sorting before marking reduces the probability that two papers at the same level receive different final marks. After the reader is satisfied that the papers are properly categorized, the final mark can be given or other evaluation made.

The global approach is efficient with a large number of papers. However, even if the papers have been scored with high reliability, it is difficult to explain the scoring rationale to students when the papers are returned. A model response could be read to the class as a reference for each student's score.

General Considerations

Regardless of the procedure of scoring chosen for essay examinations, the teacher must realize that the time element required for scoring becomes more demanding with an increasing number of papers and for this reason may want to see if part (or all) of the test could be changed to selected-response items. Since the ease in scoring of selected-response items is one of the advantages, they may be used when the number of students is large without throwing a heavy load on readers and creating a time lag in reporting the results to the students.

Taking the following considerations into account in scoring essay responses should contribute to the increase of reader reliability and in turn to the validity of the test scores:

1. Score the responses and papers anonymously. It is only natural that teachers could, knowingly or unknowingly, be influenced by students' past performances, which could have an effect on the teachers' interpretation of the responses. A response written by a student who had previously performed at a high level may receive a higher rating than that of a student who previously performed at a low level. This and other irrelevant factors should not affect the score if the paper is read without knowledge of who the writer is. Anonymity may be achieved by using identification numbers or names written on the back of the pages or on a numbered sheet where each student can place a name after a number and then record the number on the response pages. After the teacher scores the responses the names can be matched to the papers from the numbered sheet which was circulated.

Discussion with students of the anonymity of responses for purposes of scoring should make students feel that they have not been subjected to bias in scoring. Teachers wish to treat students fairly, and students should be made aware of steps taken to provide fair reading of their responses. Although it becomes difficult to disassociate the reading from bias, the teacher is responsible for being objective in scoring essay responses.

2. When using analytical scoring, score all responses to each item before going on to another item. Scoring one response at a time provides for more consistency in judgment, since the scorer may concentrate upon one set of

scoring criteria at a time. This will also prevent the quality of a response for one item influencing the scorer's judgment of the next response.

3. Score all responses to an item in one time period. The scorer may vary from one day to another and even from morning to afternoon, and any variability will become a source of unreliability. It is also possible that some other aspect in the life of the scorer could have an effect on the scores given to responses.

The scorer must be careful to avoid being influenced by the quality of the first few papers read and thus form a mind set in reference to the responses to the question. If necessary, the scoring criteria for the item being read should be referred to often while reading responses to a question.

4. Check the scoring criteria with the responses. When the teacher prepares a model answer, it should be compared with a selection of papers in order to check the appropriateness of the model response expected. The teacher may find that expectations of student responses have been unrealistic.

5. If the mechanics of writing and the quality of expression are to be scored, they should be judged separately from the content of the response. Teachers should judge the quality of the response to the item according to its content. Separate scores for other aspects such as grammar, spelling, punctuation, or expression can be obtained by separate scoring procedures. The value assigned to a factor other than the correct answer should be clarified, so that students are thoroughly familiar with the expectations. In some essay responses factors such as accuracy and methods used may be judged. Each factor should be evaluated and scored separately. If a part of the table of specifications includes any of the mentioned factors, then they become a part of the content score for the response. For example, if the spelling of the names of cities and natural geographical features is considered as part of the educational objectives for the unit, then the component of spelling should be built into the score for content of the response.

6. All responses to each question should be written on a separate page. This will avoid the situation where the scorer sees the score on previous questions. If this seems to be uneconomical use of paper, the scores can be recorded on separate sheets of paper and then placed on the response sheets after the complete test has been scored. It is more economical timewise to start each response to an item on a separate page, but the cost of paper must be considered when making this decision. The scorer should shuffle the response sheets after each item to avoid papers appearing in the same position.

7. Provide feedback to the student by writing comments on the papers and correcting errors. The progress of the student may be assisted by analyzing strengths and weaknesses of the response and writing notes to the student. The teacher should keep a record and tally by type of error made as a diagnostic tool for planning future instruction. Remedial assistance can be facilitated by the teacher's diagnosis of student deficiencies revealed by test responses.

8. Independent reading by two or more scorers can be used as a means to build higher reader reliability for essay responses. In this procedure the teacher marks the papers independently, placing remarks and point values on

a separate sheet of paper, and then has another individual, a knowledgeable colleague, also independently score the papers. The two judgments are combined and averaged. An alternate procedure is for the teacher to score the papers as indicated and then set the papers aside for a day or two before reevaluating them. The average judgment can become the score for each paper. This procedure is much less acceptable than having two individuals independently judge the papers. The delay in returning the papers and large amount of reader time needed for scoring make this a little-used procedure; however, it is an excellent way to build scorer reliability if the scorers reconcile their differences.

If a teacher decides to give an essay test, it is essential that each student's responses be given full consideration. The teacher must take the time and care needed to judge each item on every paper adequately. Teachers who give serious consideration to the factors mentioned in scoring essay examinations will find increases in the reliability of scoring and in student morale.

SUMMARY

A knowledge of the practices and procedures involved in the assembly, administration, and scoring of classroom tests helps a classroom teacher to obtain valid measures of student achievement. The precision of the measuring instrument is affected by the clarity of directions provided for the test as a whole and for different types of items employed. Directions written to the age and grade level of students provide tasks which are the same for each student taking the test. Clear, simple, and concise written test directions for some age levels may also require brief verbal directions depending upon the testing experiences of the students. Appropriate examples should be presented where necessary. Questions which students have about procedures should be clarified before the test begins.

Test items should be grouped according to item format and ordered according to difficulty within each format. The subject-matter topics are also taken into consideration in the arrangement of the items. During the arrangement of items the teacher has a chance to review and edit items and directions prior to the reproduction of a copy of the test for each student. Items should be numbered consecutively, double spaced, and typed for reproduction.

The classroom teacher has the responsibility for setting the stage for appropriate physical conditions and psychological aspects of test administration. The students' regular classroom environment is more favorable for testing if other conditions support a desirable test atmosphere. Teachers need to give special attention to providing a room temperature which is most conducive to efficient functioning. The atmosphere should be relaxed through the teacher's early explanation of the purposes and use of testing. Teachers have an opportunity and obligation to help students learn how to take tests.

Responses may be recorded on the test or on a separate response sheet as determined by the teacher. Separate response sheets should be avoided prior to the third grade. Scoring time can be kept to a minimum through the use of scoring devices which the teacher can make. Electronic scoring is available commercially, and some schools can afford scoring devices for classroom tests. Self-scoring, immediate feedback devices are available, but somewhat expensive, and immediate feedback may be frustrating to some students. Selected-response items can be readily scored by clerical personnel or teacher aides through the use of teacher-made scoring aids such as the overprinting process, scoring strips, and other devices.

Scoring essay items is a time-consuming activity. The teacher must decide whether an analytical or global scoring procedure is most appropriate. The analytical procedure requires that the teacher develop a model response and that the major elements of the expected responses be identified. The global procedure requires a rapid first reading of the essay responses in which the papers are tentatively divided into groups based on the quality and completeness of the responses given. A second reading provides for a regrouping of the responses. A third reading further refines the grouping into a final categorization for assigning a judgment of relative worth of each of the papers.

Teachers must make a decision whether or not to correct responses to selected-response items for guessing. Published tests sometimes use a correction procedure if sufficient time is not available for each student to complete all items.

This chapter completes the discussion of obtaining the scores. The next three chapters turn to the factors of how well the test served as a measurement instrument.

NEW TECHNICAL TERMS LISTED IN THE GLOSSARY

Accordion key	Machine scoring
Analytical procedure	Scoring
Computer-assisted testing (CAT)	Self-scoring
	Strip key
Global procedure	Test assembly
Hand scoring	Test directions
Key	Testwiseness

ACTIVITY EXERCISES

1. Choose the appropriate essay scoring procedure—analytical or global—for each of the two essay items written for "Activity Exercise 2" from Chapter 7. Describe how you would proceed to score papers from students using the procedure you selected for each.
2. Develop specific directions for each type of item (completion, short-answer, true-false, and multiple-choice) that does not include the directions as part of the item.

3. Write a guideline statement that could direct a test monitor's actions (teacher or other person) to questions asked by examinees during a test session for each of the following situations:
   a. reading readiness test for kindergarten students.
   b. arithmetic computation test for primary-grade (1, 2, 3) students.
   c. arithmetic problem test for intermediate grades five and six.
   d. standardized achievement battery for fifth-grade students.
   e. classroom history test for high school sophomores.
   f. classroom history test for college sophomores.
4. Locate manuals for an achievement, a mental abilities, and one other type of standardized test. Outline procedures of administration for each one as given in the manual and compare the guidelines. In what ways can these procedures guide test administration for classroom tests?

FOR DISCUSSION

1. From your experience explain the importance of adequate (good) test directions for tests that you have taken. How much influence do you feel that test directions have in reducing test-taker anxiety? How would this be different for different levels of student development?
2. What experiences have you had with alternative approaches to reproduction of a test and its format? From your reflections, what were the strengths and weaknesses of each?
3. Distinguish between "test-taking skills" and "testwiseness."
4. Explain to a student who questions an evaluation of an essay response by global scoring how reliability can be achieved without an analysis of the response by specific points to be included in the response.

REFERENCES AND KNOWLEDGE EXTENDERS

BAKER, F. B. Automation of test scoring, reporting, and analysis. In R. L. Thorndike (Ed.), *Educational Measurement* (2nd ed.). Washington, D.C.: American Council on Education, 1971, pp. 202–212.

CASTALDI, B. *Creative planning of educational facilities.* Chicago: Rand McNally, 1969.

COFFMAN, W. E. Essay examinations. In R. L. Thorndike (Ed.), *Educational Measurement* (2nd ed.). Washington, D.C.: American Council on Education, 1971.

EBEL, R. L. *Essentials of educational measurement* (3rd ed.). Englewood Cliffs, NJ: Prentice-Hall, 1979. Chap. 10, pp. 177–201.

GRONLUND, N. E. *Measurement and evaluation in teaching* (4th ed.). New York: Macmillan, 1981. Pp. 238–253.

HOPKINS, C. D., & ANTES, R. L. *Classroom testing: Administration, scoring, and score interpretation.* Itasca, IL: F. E. Peacock, 1979.

LIPPEY, G. (Ed.). *Computer-assisted test construction.* Englewood Cliffs, NJ: Educational Technology Publications, 1974.

MEHRENS, W. A., & LEHMANN, I. J. *Measurement and evaluation in education and psychology* (2nd ed.). New York: Holt, Rinehart & Winston, 1978. pp. 304–322.

NOLL, V. H., & SCANNELL, D. P. *Introduction to educational measurement* (3rd ed.). Boston: Houghton Mifflin, 1972. Chap. 8, pp. 241–251.

ROWLEY, G. L., & ROSS, E. T. Formula scoring, number-right scoring, and test-taking strategy. *Journal of Educational Measurement,* 1977, *14,* 15–22.

SPAULDING, G. Reproducing the test. In R. L. Thorndike (Ed.), *Educational Measurement* (2nd ed.). Washington, D.C.: American Council on Education, 1971. Chap. 11, pp. 417–454.

TINKLEMAN, S. N. Planning the objective test. In R. L. Thorndike (Ed.), *Educational Measurement.* Washington, D.C.: American Council on Education, 1971. Chap. 3, pp. 46–80.

TRAXLER, A. E. Administering and scoring the objective test. In E. F. Lindquist (Ed.), *Educational Measurement.* Washington, D.C.: American Council on Education, 1951. Chap. 10, pp. 329–416.

TYLER, R. W., & WHITE, S. H. (Eds.). *Testing, teaching, and learning: Report of a conference on research on testing.* (HE 19.202: T 28). Washington, D.C.: DHEW/NIE, 1979.

WESMAN, A. G. Writing the test item. In R. L. Thorndike (Ed.), *Educational Measurement.* Washington, D.C.: American Council on Education, 1971. Chap. 4, pp. 81–129.

Chapter 10. Test Appraisal

After study of Chapter 10, you should be able to:

1. Describe the purpose of test appraisal.
2. Indicate how test balance, test specificity, and test objectivity support high levels of reliability and validity.
3. Explain how test appraisal information can be utilized to improve test quality.
4. Explain how appraisal information for selected-response items is utilized in revision of test items and in selection of items for new tests.
5. Explain how to carry out item analysis for norm-referenced and criterion-referenced tests and differentiate between the two.
6. Carry out item analysis of true-false and multiple-choice test items for both criterion-referenced and norm-referenced tests.
7. Compute difficulty indexes and discrimination indexes for norm-referenced tests.
8. Compute difficulty indexes and discrimination indexes for criterion-referenced tests.
9. Explain how each glossary term listed at the end of the chapter is used in classroom measurement and evaluation.

The specifications, skills, and procedures used to construct a test, to a large extent, determine the degree of quality for that instrument. Although the system of referencing—norm or criterion—directs test appraisal to different sets of important characteristics, the two sets have many points in common. All tests need to be reliable, valid, and have high levels of the characteristics of **balance, specificity** and **objectivity.** The **difficulty** of items is important but each referencing system uses difficulty in different ways. The **discrimination** power of an item is important if the scores are norm-referenced, but not of particular importance if the scores are criterion-referenced. The adequacy of a test is based on a composite of important test characteristics that contribute to how well the test consistently measures whatever it is designed to measure. These characteristics are discussed and illustrated in this chapter and Chapters 11 and 12.

Judgments about how well a test is serving as a measuring instrument can best be made by investigating how important characteristics have contributed to the validity of the measures. A formal mathematical approach is used to calculate a **difficulty index** (P) and a **discrimination index** (D) for each multiple-choice and true-false item, and the contribution of the item to the test's ability to discern differences in the test takers' levels of achievement. A different approach is taken to describe how well the test content reflected course content and instructional objectives (balance), how well the tasks represented the tasks that are unique to the area covered by the test (specificity), and how well the items presented clear, well-defined tasks with definite and correct responses (objectivity).

WHY APPRAISE A TEST?

A test samples behavior and performance that is representative of students' overall achievement and skill development, and the results need to be trustworthy because important decisions are based on test results. Therefore, a classroom test should be appraised to determine its effectiveness in providing accurate measures of student achievement. In **test appraisal,** the teacher asks two questions:

1. How well did the test do what it was supposed to do?
2. Which of the items were effective in terms of our purpose?

The first question pertains to appraisal of the test as a whole, and the second points to analysis of each test item. The contribution of balance, specificity, and objectivity to reliability and validity can be established before test administration. Other information supplied by student test responses gives the teacher insight into the level of reliability and further establish the degree of validity. By collecting information about how the test met important criteria, and statistical data about how individual test items functioned, the teacher finds support for the decisions based on the evaluative process. Ebel (1979) says:

> There is no better way for teachers and professors to continue to improve their skill in testing, and the quality of the tests they use, than to analyze test results systematically and to compare the findings of these analyses with ideal standards of test quality. . . . (p. 65)

In addition, a critique and discussion of test items with students can provide the teacher with information about student reaction to individual items. Students may be able to identify items that were ambiguous as well as other ways items may be improved. Although the circumstances encountered in test appraisal originate in test construction, study of the test results is a necessary component of testing procedure and allows for item improvement and ultimately test improvement. The remainder of the chapter deals with test appraisal and how it supports development of good tests.

IMPORTANT TEST CHARACTERISTICS

Balance, specificity, and objectivity require attention when judging test quality for constructed-response and selected-response items for norm-referenced and criterion-referenced tests. Balance and specificity are related directly to validity. Objectivity is directly related to reliability and indirectly to validity through the relationship of reliability to validity. In the final sense each characteristic is judged on its capability to increase the validity of test measures.

Balance

The selection of items is important in construction of a classroom test. To construct a test that reflects teaching emphasis, attention is directed to the content covered and behaviors expected from students. Consideration of balance allows a check on the sample of items to see if they are representative of important outcomes desired in instruction. Two questions are attended to:

1. Are the items selected for the test based on the instructional objectives and are they representative of the content and behaviors that are to be appraised?
2. Are there enough items on the test to sample adequately the content that has been covered and the behaviors as spelled out by the objectives?

Systematic approach to answers for these questions is a necessary step in good testing.

The needed balance for a test can be established by proper use of a table of specifications to guide the test maker's decisions about what content to test and the behavior coverage for each item. Chapter 5 provided directions for construction and use of tables of specifications for constructed-response and selected-response tests. Another type of table (Ebel, pp. 70–71) classifies test items in expressions of overt characteristics rather than educational goals or mental abilities required to respond to the test tasks. For example, a test plan could be made on the basis of content areas and type of tasks demanded of students. In Figure 10.1, each of the 35 items from a fifth-grade science test has been classified in one of four content areas and one of four types of tasks.

By using this system the construction of a test incorporates the procedures and components needed for a well-balanced test. There is general agreement that test items requiring knowledge of isolated facts appear on tests at the expense of items testing the more complex learning outcomes. This comes about primarily because the items for recall are easier to write and construction of test items appraising knowledge of facts is likely to take precedent over construction of items that measure other important learning outcomes of understanding, application, analysis, synthesis, and evaluation.

Inquiry for balance of a published or previously used test can be made

	Item Number	Number of Items
Content area		
Growth and development of animals	1, 2, 3, 4, 5, 6, 7, 8, 9, 10	10
Growth and development of plants	11, 12, 13, 14, 15	5
Systems of the body	16, 17, 18, 19, 20, 21, 22, 23, 24, 25	10
Human diseases	26, 27, 28, 29, 30, 31, 32, 33, 34, 35	10
Total		35
Type of task		
Identification of terms	2, 6, 7, 10, 12, 13, 17, 18, 20	9
Recall of factual information	1, 8, 11, 16, 19, 22, 26, 29, 34, 35	10
Generalization	3, 9, 14, 21, 23, 24, 27, 30, 32, 33	10
Explanation	4, 5, 15, 25, 28, 31	6
Total		35

FIGURE 10.1. System for classifying items according to content area and type of task

by working backward through a table of specifications. The dimension of subject matter topics on the table serves as a check on what content is covered in the tasks, and the dimension of behavior can serve as a check for the level of the cognitive demands placed on the examinee. Another way to determine balance is to classify items by content area and type of task. In either case the degree of balance of the test is established by checking the fit of the test items to the emphasis given in the instructional sequence.

Specificity

A special effort must be made when writing or choosing items for a test to include only items specific to the area studied. To determine specificity two questions are attended to:

1. Do the test items require knowledge in the content or subject areas covered by the test?
2. Can general knowledge be used to correctly respond to the test items?

When the test items are reviewed, the first question should be answered affirmatively and the second answered negatively if the test possesses the characteristic of specificity. A student should not be able to apply knowledge gathered from outside the specific study area to respond to test items and increase a test score. A student should receive credit for correct responses based on specific ability or specific knowledge in the tested area, but not for general knowledge. Obviously a teacher has no control of what students learn before study of a particular topic or what is learned outside of school while a topic is under study, but that learning can affect the specificity of the test. Since the teacher does not have full control over what the student learns and knows, each test may to some degree lack specificity. The teacher needs to prepare the items so that the student who has completed the learning tasks will not find that some students are able to obtain acceptable scores solely by basing responses on general knowledge, test-taking skill, and problem-solving ability.

Specificity of the test can be best verified by determining how someone who has not studied the specific material performs on the test. Since the achievement assessed by a test should be relevant to special competence in the particular subject covered by the test, an individual who has not studied in the area formally and who is unfamiliar with the content should score at or near a **chance level** on the test. The lower the scores of the novices the higher the specificity of the test.

Objectivity

A test item rates high in objectivity if the task to be performed is stated so that the test taker knows what is expected and the correct response is definite. Test items and the test as a whole are high in objectivity if competent scorers agree upon the correct response for each item. On a selected-response test experts in the subject covered would select the same alternative as the best response. In the event that experts disagree on the correct alternative, the teacher should reexamine the proposed task and alternatives, since the item is not communicating what the teacher wishes. A response to a constructed-response item should be scored the same by experts in the subject field to indicate a high level of objectivity.

Selected-response items,* particularly multiple-choice items, are further complicated as the tasks on the test move to higher levels of thought processes required in assessing achievement on a level other than that of gathering factual information. Testing experts attempt to stimulate teachers to prepare

---

*Most selected-response items are scored objectively, since every response is compared to a key. If given a key, any mature person can score a selected-response test. No particular knowledge about the content being tested is needed. If a test item can be scored from a key and knowledge of the subject is not needed to judge student responses, then the item is an objective item. The two terms *objective* and *objectivity* as used in educational measurement have the common element of agreement about the correct response. A selected-response test item is objective in terms of its scoring procedures. Any test item—selected-response, constructed-response, or problem—is high in objectivity if there is agreement about the correctness of a student response.

selected-response items which measure the higher cognitive processes while on the other hand these types of items provide more latitude for experts to disagree in terms of the best response. As the tasks call for behaviors corresponding with the higher hierarchical levels, the more difficult it becomes to obtain common agreement on the best alternative.

The constructed-response item, in particular the essay task, does not produce the type of objectivity found in selected-response items. The difficulty is not so much in setting the task as it is in deciding the degree of correctness of the response. The nature of the essay response does not provide the scorer great objectivity in reading responses in the content or subject areas, and this fact is taken into consideration when the teacher decides to use essay items. The methods of writing essay items which provide a more objective approach have been pointed out in Chapter 7 under the topic of "Essay Items."

To be able to use objectivity as a basis for judging test quality at least two or more experts, and preferably 5 to 10, need to respond to the test items with acceptable agreement. Classroom teachers may persuade colleagues to act as experts for determining test objectivity. It may be possible for teachers in the same grade level or in the same subject field within a school system to cooperate in this type of endeavor. Classroom teachers who cannot find other teachers who have time to respond to their tests may use their own understanding of the subject area and knowledge of correct responses to items on published tests and about how others who teach the same courses would be expected to respond, to build objectivity into classroom tests. A test made up of tasks where not even experts can agree on correct responses has little value in measuring student achievement.

ITEM ANALYSIS

The analysis of true-false and multiple-choice items generates numbers to measure the difficulty of test items and how the items discriminate between two levels of student achievement. A difficulty index and a discrimination index are utilized in analysis of criterion-referenced and norm-referenced test items. Optimum levels of difficulty and discrimination permit each student to score at the correct place on the measuring scale when norm-referencing is used. Recall that norm-referencing is intended to be used with measures that have been obtained by a scale that is open-ended. On the other hand, the criterion-referenced test is built with items written to measure minimum achievement levels and a definite ceiling is established. These differences are reflected in two different analyses. The comparative steps in the procedure of criterion-referenced and norm-referenced true-false and multiple-choice item analysis are shown in Figure 10.2. The ensuing presentation develops the two procedures for item analysis.

Analysis for Criterion-referenced Tests

Tests that are specifically designed to determine what a student knows and can do in a clearly defined domain of knowledge and performance direct

Criterion-referenced test (CRT)	Norm-referenced test (NRT)
1. Divide the scored papers into two criterion groups: a. Those who met criterion b. Those who did not meet criterion	1. Order and select the papers for the two criterion groups: a. Upper group—high scorers b. Lower group—low scorers
2. Check each paper for each item and record the number of correct responses in each group.	2. Check each paper for each item and record the number of correct responses in each group.
3. Record the total number of incorrect responses for each item in each group.	3. Record the total number of incorrect responses for each item in each group.
4. Using formulas for CRT* compute: a. A difficulty index for each item b. A discrimination index for each item	4. Using formulas for NRT* compute: a. A difficulty index for each item b. A discrimination index for each item
5. Interpret the meaning of: a. The difficulty index b. The discrimination index	5. Interpret the meaning of: a. The difficulty index b. The discrimination index

*See text.

FIGURE 10.2. Steps in item analysis for multiple-choice and true-false items on CRT and NRT

the test maker to criterion-referencing. When building the test a connection was made from an item to the instructional objective it was designed to measure. Item analysis is directed to ascertain how well each multiple-choice and true-false item contributed to identification of students who met criterion.

Basic to our study here is the tenet that each student is expected to get all, or a large portion, of the items correct, and the teacher expects nearly all students to respond correctly to each item. It is not the purpose of item writing to construct items that are so easy that success is guaranteed; however, the items are to be based on what everyone should know at the end of an educational sequence. They should be, therefore, easily answered by most students —not necessarily easy items but easily answered. A teacher who has built and administered a test for mastery over a clearly defined domain of knowledge is interested in a measure in absolute terms—how much of this domain of knowledge does each student possess.

Forming criterion groups

A standard set by the teacher before the test was administered becomes the criterion point for passing and the results of criterion-referenced tests can be used to divide students who took a test into two groups—those who met criterion (passing) and those who did not meet criterion (did not pass). These two **criterion groups** are used to make comparisons of the frequency of student errors. Applied to specific items the questions become:

1. What frequency of correct responses and incorrect responses are associated with each item?
2. Which students are responding correctly and which ones are responding incorrectly?

The teacher can answer the two questions by item analysis and a tabulation of the responses for each item by counting the number of correct and incorrect responses of students in the two criterion groups.

In general, if the test is well-constructed and serves as an adequate measuring instrument, the higher the proportion meeting criterion the better. This indicates that most of the students have met instructional objectives. Since the quality of future tests depends on the quality of individual items, item revision provides a unique opportunity to build better tests for other classes.

Item analysis procedure

Place the scored papers in two groups based on student achievement: (*a*) those who met criterion (passed), and (*b*) those who did not meet criterion (did not pass). For each of the groups record for each item the total number of correct responses. Then record the number of total incorrect responses jointly for each item. For example, the responses recorded for three four-choice multiple-choice items for 27 students who took a test look like this:

Item Number	Correct Responses		Incorrect Responses
	Above Criterion	Below Criterion	Total
5.	18	3	6
6.	21	0	6
7.	18	6	3

For convenience these three columns can be added to an extra copy of the test as:

18	3	6	5.
21	0	6	6.
18	6	3	7.

Note: The three values for each item should total 27—the number of students in the two criterion groups.

Difficulty Index.   Compute the percentage of students who missed the item. This value is directly related to item difficulty as established by the students—the more students who miss the item the larger the value. Use the formula:

$$P_D = \frac{N_w}{N_t}(100)$$

Where:

P_D = The difficulty index
N_w = The number of students who missed the item
N_t = The number of students who tried the item

$$\text{Difficulty Index (measure of difficulty)} = \left[\frac{\text{Number of students who answered incorrectly}}{\text{Number of students who tried the item}}\right] \left[\begin{array}{l}\text{Multiply by}\\ \text{100 to}\\ \text{change the}\\ \text{proportion}\\ \text{to a}\\ \text{percent}\end{array}\right]$$

The difficulty index (P_D) for items 5, 6, 7 is calculated as follows:

5. $P_D = \dfrac{6}{27}(100) = 22.22 \text{ or } 22$

6. $P_D = \dfrac{6}{27}(100) = 22.22 \text{ or } 22$

7. $P_D = \dfrac{3}{27}(100) = 11.11 \text{ or } 11$

Discrimination index.   Compute the discrimination index for each item. This index points up how the two groups perform in relation to each other. Use the formula:

$$D = \frac{U}{N_u} - \frac{L}{N_1}$$

Where:

D = Discrimination index
U = Number in group meeting criterion who answered correctly
L = Number in group not meeting criterion who answered correctly
N_u = Number in group who met criterion
N_1 = Number in group who did not meet criterion

$$\text{Discrimination index} = \frac{\begin{bmatrix} \text{Number of students who} \\ \text{passed criterion who} \\ \text{answered correctly} \end{bmatrix}}{\begin{bmatrix} \text{Number of students who} \\ \text{passed criterion} \end{bmatrix}} - \frac{\begin{bmatrix} \text{Number of students who} \\ \text{did not pass criterion} \\ \text{who answered correctly} \end{bmatrix}}{\begin{bmatrix} \text{Number of students who} \\ \text{did not pass criterion} \end{bmatrix}}$$

The discrimination indexes (D) for items 5, 6, 7 are calculated as follows:

5. $D = \dfrac{18}{21} - \dfrac{3}{6} = .86 - .50 = +.36$

6. $D = \dfrac{21}{21} - \dfrac{0}{6} = 1.00 - .00 = +1.00$

7. $D = \dfrac{18}{21} - \dfrac{6}{6} = .86 - 1.00 = -.14$

Figure 10.3 reports the analysis values for these three examples as calculated here.

Item Number	No. responding correctly		Total wrong responses	P	D
	Above Criterion	Below Criterion			
5.	18	3	6	22	+ .36
6.	21	0	6	22	+1.00
7.	18	6	3	11	− .14

FIGURE 10.3. Analysis for three criterion-referenced items

Interpretation of analysis values

Item analysis can be valuable as a guide to plan future activities that are intended to raise class members to criterion. A large difficulty index points up an item missed by many students and may indicate: *(a)* that the instruction was not adequate for the students, *(b)* that a concept was too difficult for the age group or level of development, or *(c)* that the item itself was poor. The teacher should make a judgment about why students were unable to answer the item correctly. If it is decided that instruction should be continued then prescriptive teaching for remediation is in order.

If the item is considered to be deficient, revision may salvage it, or if it appears to be beyond revision the item should be discarded. Items 5 and 6 appear to be more difficult than expected for criterion-referenced test items and the teacher should correct the items with good construction practices if it is deemed that the fault is in the item. Item 7 seems to be within the scope of expected-difficulty level for criterion-referenced test items. If the difficulty level is considered satisfactory the teacher must judge the item discrimination level as satisfactory or unsatisfactory.

High values in the D column indicate that those passing criterion did better than those who fell below criterion performance. The nearer the values are to zero the closer the performance of the groups. Negative values indicate better performance for those who did not meet the criterion than those who did. For example, item 7 has a negative value for D. Inspection of the data about the performance of each group shows that only three persons in the class missed the item, and they were in the upper group. Such a result could happen because of a deficiency in the instructional program and its effect on the students or because of a poorly prepared item. Review of both instruction and the item itself should be undertaken to make proper changes in classroom activities or the test item. D values have meaning in relation to instruction and item writing but are meaningless in and of themselves. The teacher must investigate the values that contribute to the D value and make judgments about the item and its effectiveness and in turn how it served the purpose of the test.

Analysis for Norm-reference Tests

Item analysis is especially helpful when applied to norm-referenced tests. Used with true-false and multiple-choice items in a norm-referenced test, the process of item analysis indicates: *(a)* how difficult each item was for the group, *(b)* how well each item discriminated between high- and low-scoring students, and *(c)* for multiple-choice items, how effective each alternative was for the item. Mathematical techniques assess two characteristics of each item on the test:

1. the difficulty of each item by establishing a difficulty index *(P)* which is the proportion of students who responded incorrectly to an item,
2. the extent to which each item distinguished between students with high test scores and students with low test scores by establishing a discrimination index *(D)*.

Comparisons are made of the responses of students ranking in an upper group and a lower group of the class based on total test scores for all students. These two criterion groups supply the data for item analysis for norm-referenced tests.

The level of difficulty of each item and the corresponding discrimination index are important to test improvement, since they indicate which items are: (a) too easy, (b) too difficult, (c) nondiscriminating between the high-scoring and low-scoring students, (d) in need of improvement through revision or rewriting, and (e) to be discarded. The information from item analysis can also aid in making judgments about instructional effectiveness, identification of areas of student weaknesses, and needed remediation. A practical value to the classroom teacher lies in future testing when valuable time can be saved by avoiding the construction of a test of totally new items. Test quality is also improved by the use of items which have proven to be successful on past tests if a test-item file of tried and improved items is kept for consultation when building new tests.

Forming Criterion Groups

The item analysis process is a study of how students reacted to each test item. First a level of difficulty is determined by a formula that gives a proportion of students missing an item. Second a comparison of performance for high-scoring students to low-scoring students is made according to another formula. To make the second part of the analysis, two differing groups must be selected according to total test scores. When choosing criterion groups, the teacher wants to have as many papers as possible in the groups but also to have papers from two groups that are different as to the attribute being measured. Since no measurement procedure can generate exact measures, certain middle papers should be omitted when enough papers are available to give sufficient numbers in the groups to use in the analysis. The omission of a middle group of papers provides reasonable assurance that the upper group is composed of students who differ substantially in performance from the lower group. If the papers are divided into two groups of 50 percent according to the order of high-to-low scores, there will probably be some papers in the upper group which belong in the lower group and some in the lower group which belong in the upper group because of chance factors of measurement.

In an early study, Kelley (1939) demonstrated that the selection of criterion groups based upon the upper 27 percent and lower 27 percent of the papers provides the greatest confidence that the upper group is superior in the trait measured by the test as compared to the lower group. Unless the class is small, the 27 percent figure provides the advantage of having two groups which are different in test performance, with the groups as large as possible and as different as possible. The middle 46 percent of the papers is not used when 27 percent in the upper and 27 percent in the lower groups are employed in item analysis. In practice, criterion groups of about 25 to 33 1/3 percent of the total papers are considered to be appropriate. Each of these percentages leaves out a middle set of scores, which assures the teacher that the groups are different. Four different sets of percentages that are often employed in item analysis are given in Figure 10.4.

In general, the greater the number of omitted papers, the greater the probability that the upper and lower groups are different. For a large number of papers a smaller percentage for criterion groups may be used. The larger the total number of test papers, up to a maximum of 100, in each of the upper and lower groups the more reliable the data analysis.

It is important to have enough papers in each group so that analysis becomes meaningful. When the total number of papers is very small (20 or less), practice permits the use of all of the papers with half of the papers in

Testing / Divisions	Tested Groups (%)			
	One	Two	Three	Four
Highest papers	25	27	30	33⅓
Omitted papers	50	46	40	33⅓
Lowest paper	25	27	30	33⅓

FIGURE 10.4. Dividing papers into criterion groups by total score.

each group. An odd number of papers means that the middle paper is not used. When the number in the class is between 20 and 40, 10 papers may be used in each of the criterion groups. Although these deviate from suggested practice, classroom teachers usually have fewer than 40 papers for analysis, and some adjustments need to be made. When a teacher combines classes that take the same test, the usual procedure should be used.

Item analysis procedure

When the teacher decides how many will be in each criterion group attention turns to the actual process of item analysis. Order the classroom test papers or answer sheets starting with the highest score to the lowest score. Next, decide on the number of papers to be used in each group, and select that number of highest papers and the same number of lowest papers. These form the two criterion groups. Set aside the middle group, as they will not be used in analysis. Test papers for two or more small class sections taking the same test may be combined for analysis and the criterion groups selected from the total number. This procedure will provide a larger number of papers for analysis, and the data should be more meaningful. Next, scan the papers and record the student responses.

For true-false items simply count the number of papers in each group which have the correct response. The number of correct responses subtracted from the number in both criterion groups gives the number of incorrect responses. For example, the data sheet for true-false items 1 and 2 could be compiled for 30 students who took a test as:

Item	Correct response		Incorrect response
	Upper	Lower	Both
1.	14	12	4
2.	13	10	7

For convenience these three columns can be added to an extra copy or the test as:

14	12	4	1.
13	10	7	2.

Note: The three values for each item should total 30, the number of students in the two criterion groups.

For multiple-choice items count the number of papers in the upper group who have the alternative "a." marked for the first item. Do this for each alternative in the first item (in the example: a. 9, b. 3, c. 2, d. 1). Continue this procedure for each item for the upper group. Follow the same procedure for all papers in the lower group. Combine these data on a master sheet for each multiple-choice item. For example, an item with four alternatives and 15 papers in each of the upper and lower groups could generate the following values for item 32:

32. Options	Upper group	Lower group	Incorrect
a.*	9	3	
b.	3	4	7
c.	2	5	7
d.	1	3	4
Total	15	15	18

*Indicates the correct response.

For convenience this information can be added to an extra copy of the test as:

32. What arithmetic process should be used when deciding how many cookies each child should get when 12 cookies are distributed equally among three children?

18	9	3	a.*	division
	3	4	b.	addition
	2	5	c.	subtraction
	1	3	d.	multiplication

Note: The total of the two columns should be 30—the number of students in the two criterion groups.

Difficulty Index. Compute the percentage of students who missed the item. This value is directly related to item difficulty as established by the students—the more students who miss the item the larger the value. Use the formula:

$$P_D = \frac{N_w}{N_t} (100)$$

Where:

P_D = The difficulty index
N_w = The number of students who missed the item
N_t = The number of students who tried the item

Difficulty Index (measure of difficulty) = $\left[\dfrac{\text{Number of students who answered incorrectly}}{\text{Number of students who tried the item}}\right]$ $\left[\begin{array}{l}\text{Multiply by} \\ \text{100 to} \\ \text{change the} \\ \text{proportion} \\ \text{to a} \\ \text{percent}\end{array}\right]$

The difficulty index (P_D) for items 1, 2, 32 is calculated as follows:

1. $P = \dfrac{4}{30}(100) = .1333(100) = 13.33$ or 13 percent

2. $P = \dfrac{7}{30}(100) = .2333(100) = 23.33$ or 23 percent

32. $P = \dfrac{18}{30}(100) = .60(100) = 60$ or 60 percent

The two formulas below are presently used to determine how easy or difficult an item is for a group who has taken a test. Formula A gives a percentage of those who answered incorrectly; thus it is a measure of difficulty. Formula B, the **easiness index** gives a percentage of those who answered correctly; thus it is a measure of easiness. Either one works equally well but to interpret the value reported for an item the person needs to know which formula was used. This is not a problem for the teacher who is analyzing a classroom-prepared test. However, communication about item difficulty should indicate which formula was used to measure difficulty. The authors prefer to use Formula A because it gives a direct measure of difficulty and seems more correct for measuring that characteristic.

Formula A	Formula B
$P_D = \dfrac{N_w}{N_t}(100)$	$P_E = \dfrac{N_r}{N_t}(100)$
P_D = Difficulty index	P_E = Easiness index
N_w = Number getting item incorrect	N_r = Number getting item correct

N_t = Number who tried item N_t = Number who tried the item

(Gives a *difficulty* measure)

(Gives an *easiness* measure)

$$(P_D + P_E = 100)$$

Discrimination index. Compute the discrimination index for each item. This index points up how the two criterion groups perform in relation to each other. Use this formula:

$$D = \frac{U - L}{N}$$

Where:

D = The discrimination index
U = The number in the upper group who answered correctly
L = The number in the lower group who answered correctly
N = The number in one of the criterion groups

$$\text{Discrimination Index} = \frac{\left[\begin{array}{c}\text{Number of students in} \\ \text{the upper group who} \\ \text{answered correctly}\end{array}\right] - \left[\begin{array}{c}\text{Number of students in} \\ \text{the lower group who} \\ \text{answered correctly}\end{array}\right]}{\text{Divided by the number in one of the criterion groups}}$$

The discrimination index (D) for items 1, 2, 32 is calculated as follows:

$$1. \quad D = \frac{14 - 12}{15} = \frac{+2}{15} = +.13$$

$$2. \quad D = \frac{13 - 10}{15} = \frac{+3}{15} = +.20$$

$$32. \quad D = \frac{9 - 3}{15} = \frac{+6}{15} = +.40$$

Note: Watch the sign of the numerator. If more students in the lower criterion group answered the item correctly than did the upper group, the discrimination index will be a negative number.

The data can now be transferred to an item card for a permanent record of how the item performed on this test and placed in a test-item file. Figure 10.5 illustrates the use of an item card for recording item analysis data. The front of the card contains the objective and the item, while the reverse side contains records of the item's performance on all test administrations. The card system provides the advantage of a compilation of item analysis data over extended use of the item which is helpful when selecting items to be employed in a new test.

Front Side of Card

Topic: Scientific method									
OBJECTIVE: The student will know the purpose of a controlled experiment. ITEM: A scientist performs a controlled experiment to *a. determine the number of quantities involved. b. find a relationship between certain quantities involved. c. eliminate all the quantities involved. d. reduce the effect of the quantities involved.									
TEST DATE:	Nov. 76	Mar. 77	Jan. 78						
ITEM NO:	8	11	10						

Reverse Side of Card

ITEM RECORD												
	Upper						Lower					
Date	a	b	c	d	Omit		a	b	c	d	Omit	P_D	D
Nov. 76	9	3	2	1	0		3	4	5	3	0	60	+.40
Mar. 77	12	1	1	1	0		3	4	5	3	0	50	+.60
Jan. 78	15	0	1	1	0		5	2	3	7	0	41	+.58
Comments: Distracters seem to be working properly. Good discrimination.												

FIGURE 10.5. Test-item card

Effectiveness of distracters

The final calculations use the data collected from the three alternatives of the multiple-choice items that served as distracters. Use the formula for the discrimination index (D) to calculate a discrimination coefficient for each distracter as follows:

$$D = \frac{U - L}{N}$$

Correct response	Distracter b	Distracter c	Distracter d
$D_a = \dfrac{9 - 3}{15}$	$D_b = \dfrac{3 - 4}{15}$	$D_c = \dfrac{2 - 5}{15}$	$D_d = \dfrac{1 - 3}{15}$
$D_a = \dfrac{6}{15}$	$D_b = \dfrac{-1}{15}$	$D_c = \dfrac{-3}{15}$	$D_d = \dfrac{-2}{15}$
$D_a = .40$	$D_b = -.07$	$D_c = -.20$	$D_d = -.13$

The procedure for item analysis is summarized as follows:

1. Order the scored papers from high to low by total score.
2. Choose the number of papers for criterion groups.
3. Count the number of responses marked for each alternative.
4. Record the data from the student responses.
5. Calculate: a. A difficulty index for each item; b. A discrimination index for each item.
6. Calculate a discrimination index for distracter alternatives for multiple-choice items.

The values calculated for difficulty, discrimination, and distracter efficiency direct the component of test appraisal that follows test administration. For example, the items should be checked to see if any item is discriminating negatively. If more students in the lower criterion group answered the item correctly than did those in the upper criterion group, the discrimination index will be a negative number. This points up that this item was contributing more value to low-scoring students' scores than it was to high-scoring students' scores. Since test scores are intended to measure some attribute in positive units, the negative values indicate a discrimination factor in the opposite direction from what it should be. Items with negative values should receive special attention in analysis and either be discarded from the test-item file and further tests or be revised to accommodate for deficiencies of the items. The values for difficulty and discrimination are interpreted to aid the appraisal of the test.

Interpretation of analysis values

Inspection of the two values P and D allows the teacher to see how well each item has performed compared: *(a)* to some preconceived notions about how the test maker predicted it would perform, and *(b)* to some criteria about interpretation of different P and D values. An earlier chapter developed the concepts that: *(a)* items of medium difficulty create a condition where discrimination can take place, and *(b)* very difficult and very easy items cannot generate data to allow for differences because most student responses fall into one category of either very difficult (most are classed as "wrong") or very easy (most are classed as "right") test items.

Difficulty. The difficulty index can range from zero (0) to one hundred (100). Appropriate difficulty levels are those which lie about halfway between a number that would be expected from selection by pure guess and another number that represents total correct responses (0 using Formula A). For item number 32 the data gave a difficulty index of 60. The ideal difficulty index for all four-choice multiple-choice items is 37 to 38, a value halfway between 75 (expected from chance selection) and 0.

No teacher expects to get ideal values of difficulty for all items on a test, but each test maker sets some kind of a range for desirable values. For a four-choice item the teacher would set a range of about 25 to 50 as target *P* values. How should the value of 60 for item 32 be interpreted? Since 60 percent of the students responded incorrectly, the item is somewhat more difficult than the 25 percent to 50 percent that the teacher expected. This fact alone does not cause us to interpret the item as a poor one, since the discrimination index must also be considered. Since it is very close to the desirable range, administration to another group on another test may result in a more favorable outcome in regard to both difficulty and discrimination.

True-false items have a medium difficulty level of 25 which is halfway between a chance value of 50 expected from pure guessing and perfect response of 0, obtained when no student misses an item. The range of desirable *P* values for true-false items is from 20 to 35. Since these values depart from the 50 value needed for perfect discrimination, true-false tests tend to be somewhat less discriminating than multiple-choice tests. False items, in general, are more discriminating than true items.

Discrimination. The discrimination index can take values from −1.00 to +1.00. It measures how well a test item contributes to separating the upper criterion group from the lower criterion group. The ability of a test to distinguish differences on the attribute being measured depends on the discrimination power of the test items collectively. The higher the *D* value the better the item discriminated. Any item that has a *D* value of +.40 or above is considered to be very effective in distinguishing differences. *D* values between +.20 and +.39 are usually considered to be satisfactory, but lower values in this range should be reviewed to see if some change could be made to render them more effective. Possibly a more favorable discrimination factor could be obtained by making a very difficult item somewhat easier or a very easy item somewhat more difficult by rewriting it for future use.

Any item with a value of 0.00 through +.19 has done little to differentiate among the levels of student achievement. All items in this range should be revised in some way to increase discrimination before they are used on another test. There are two exceptions to the need for revision. First, some easy items may be included in the first part of the test to help relieve students' anxiety about how they will perform, resulting in a P value of near 0 for those items. When nearly all of the students get the item correct, the numerator of the formula for D will be near 0, thus guaranteeing a low D value. Second, a low D value may be defensible for an item which has been included to determine how well students have grasped a certain important concept. If the class as a whole possesses the idea, nearly all in each group will get the item correct, thus giving a low D value.

An item with a D value of 0 provides no discrimination, since in both the low-score group and high-score group the same number of students got the item correct. Any item with a negative D value discriminates in the wrong direction, since more students in the low-score group got the item correct than in the high-score group. The item must be revised before being used in a later test. If it appears that revision is not possible, the item should be removed from the test-item file and discarded.

Discriminating power (Figure 10.6) of the test lies in the capability of test items to differentiate between persons possessing much knowledge and those having little. In reference to item alternative analysis the following points should be kept in mind:

1. Each distracter should be selected by about equal numbers of members of the lower group.
2. Substantially more students in the upper group than the lower group should respond to the correct alternative.
3. Substantially more students in the lower group should respond to the distracters.

Discrimination Index	Interpretation of Index
.40 and above	Very good
.30 to .39	Good
.20 to .29	Marginal
.00 to .19	Revise
below .00	Discard or rewrite

FIGURE 10.6. Explanation of discrimination indexes

Gilbert Sax (1980, p. 192) points out the desirability of high discrimination indexes, since reliability increases as the average value of discrimination indexes for a test's items increases. The standard deviation of scores is increased when the discrimination index increases, and if the increase measures true differences, the reliability will also increase.

Special attention should be given to the difficulty level for items which have D values near 0. An item which is responded to correctly by all or nearly all the students does not allow for differences in the numerator of the D formula since about the same number in each criterion group would get the item correct. To get large positive values for D, the numerator must be large relative to the denominator. Low D values should be investigated to see if they result from very easy or very difficult items. Since they are doing little to place students in relative standing on the trait being tested, consideration must be given to changing the difficulty or discarding the item. Item alternatives can be changed to make P and D values closer to desirable levels for all items, but special attention should be given to those with low or negative D values.

The point of our discussion concerning interpretation of difficulty indexes and discrimination indexes and examination of the alternatives for multiple-choice items is to make teachers aware of the opportunity to pick up cues which are provided by student responses to items in general and alternatives of the multiple-choice items in particular. Item analysis can indicate trouble spots in poorly functioning items, but the cause of the inferior quality must be identified by the teachers as they develop their expertise in test construction and analysis.

USING APPRAISAL INFORMATION FOR REVISION AND SELECTION OF ITEMS

The results of item analysis should be used to revise items for future tests. If tests are built from items that performed well in the past or have been revised to increase their contribution to valid measures, the quality of tests will be increased. For this section the calculation results of the three items will be used. Review of the calculation reveals these values:

32.	$P_D = 60$	$D = +.40$	Multiple-choice, four alternatives
1.	$P_D = 13$	$D = +.13$	True-false
2.	$P_D = 23$	$D = +.20$	True-false

In the example for item 32, nine students in the upper group and three students in the lower group selected the keyed option (a) as the correct response. A total of 12 of 30 students responded to the correct option, indicating that 60 percent of the students responded incorrectly while 40 percent responded correctly. Using Formula A the difficulty estimate is 60 (using Formula B, $P = 40$). Nine in the upper group and only three in the lower group responded correctly. Since more students in the upper group than the lower got the item correct, it is discriminating positively ($D = +.40$). In other words, the item is distinguishing between high and low achievers using the total test score as the criterion for achievement. Since discrimination is the more important characteristic the item has functioned adequately on this test administration. The difficulty level of 60 is higher than the optimum level of 38 for four alternative items and should be checked again after administration to another group of students. Difficulty levels for subsequent tests could vary widely because analysis values are not properties of items—only an indication of what one group of students did.

Item 1 has a very low discrimination coefficient and contributed very little to establish levels of achievement for students who took the test. The low value for D is probably a function of the low difficulty of the item. With only a few students responding incorrectly the values in the numerator of the discrimination formula are likely to be very near to the same value. It is not uncommon to find easy items in the first part of the test. The anxiety of examinees may be lessened if they can have a feeling of success in the first part of a test. The test maker who used this item could have included it knowing that it would serve that purpose.

Item 2 is somewhat more difficult than item 1 and has a better coefficient of discrimination. A D value of $+.20$ is marginal and contributes marginally to discrimination of levels of achievement. The P value of 23 is close to the optimum level for true-false items ($P = 25$). Since perfect discrimination can occur only if $P = 50$, the true-false item by its nature limits discrimination and tends to reduce reliability of true-false tests. Since item 2 is at the first of the test it may be also serving to allay anxiety of examinees.

Effectiveness of Distracters

Carrying the inspection one step further, one can tell how effectively each distracter is operating. The formula for the discrimination index can be employed to calculate an index of effectiveness for each alternative. For example recall for item 32:

Options	Upper 27 percent	Lower 27 percent	D
a	9	3	.40
b	3	4	−.07
c	2	5	−.20
d	1	3	−.13

The discrimination value for the correct response (a) is the discrimination index as defined in earlier discussion. The positive D value for the correct response shows that the item has been effective in identifying high-scoring students. Distracters b, c, and d are functioning appropriately and as intended, since they attract a larger proportion of students from the lower group, and none of them attracts a large proportion of the upper group. The negative D values for alternatives b, c, and d indicate that more low-scoring students chose each distracter than did the higher-scoring students which is what good distracters should do. For this item the test maker should consider distracter "b" to see if it should be rewritten to function better. Since three of the high-scoring group chose that alternative it may have a flaw that could easily be corrected in rewriting. The test maker must always keep in mind that distracters are there to distract the unknowing student, not the student who knows the correct response. A major tenet for tests is that all students who know the correct response and have assimilated a concept should get the item right and those who do not should get it wrong. Only in this way can tests and their scores be integrated into the instructional process.

Analysis of Student Selections

In the event that students in the upper group select an incorrect option for a multiple-choice item nearly as often as the correct option for an item, the teacher is alerted to some difficulty in the adequacy of the item. Apparently the item is vague, ambiguous, undefined, or not specific enough to allow the better students to respond correctly. For some reason students apparently lack understanding of the item's content because of lack of knowledge in the content area or a poorly written item. Each of these two possibilities should be investigated. If for some reason the instruction has not resulted in desired conceptual development, then the teacher should plan to alter the presentation. If it is found that the item is of poor quality, then it should be discarded or revised before it is used again.

When an incorrect option to an item is selected by a large number of students in the upper group, the possibility exists that the item may be keyed incorrectly. The teacher should scan the test key for all items which have been missed by a large number of students to check for this possibility. Necessary corrections must be made prior to returning the papers to students. If changes are continually made after papers are returned, students may get the idea that items are up for debate, and the result is an attitude that each should be negotiated. The best policy seems to be that of making no changes after papers have been returned. An exception would be made when a definite mistake has been made in the key and it has not been discovered prior to returning the papers. Those papers which have a correct response but have been marked wrong should be changed and the raw score increased. How to handle the returned papers which *should* be marked *wrong* after the error is discovered must be decided by the teacher. The authors suggest that any attempt to change an item which is originally scored as correct by marking a response wrong after the paper has been returned to a student, with the result of lowering the raw score, may be harmful by reducing student rapport.

When students in the upper group lack the knowledge to respond correctly to an item or the alternatives seem equally plausible, the choices may be distributed equally to the options available. An item requiring information which students have not studied for may result in guessing, and the student responses would be expected to be distributed randomly among alternatives. For a good test item the incorrect choices for the lower group should be distributed about equally among the distracters. Ideally none of the upper group would choose a distracter, and all of the lower group would; however, in practice this is a standard rather than an expectation.

USING APPRAISAL INFORMATION TO IMPROVE TEST QUALITY

Information gathered about item difficulty, discrimination power of items, balance, specificity, and objectivity can be used to improve future tests. Effective items can be developed and good testing practices determined from what has been successful in the past. Since the individual test items determine the nature of the test and the extent that the instrument measures what the teacher intends it to measure, successful testing rests first of all with a set of effective items. Improvement of the test quality rests in using appraisal information to strengthen test items through appropriate revision. This involves rewriting distracters, rewording statements, and modifying items, all of which reduce technical defects and the factors causing them.

Certain steps to increase test quality are taken before the test is constructed and administered. The table of specifications is used to provide a representative sample of items on the test. Since content validity is of primary importance for achievement tests, the use of the table allows for appraisal of the balance of the test. Further investigation of the degree of content validity is made by determination of the degree of specificity. If a test is to be valid for a particular body of content, then the parameters of topics covered should include all items on the test. If they are not directed to that body of knowledge and go beyond the parameters, then the content validity of the test is reduced because of low specificity. Concern about balance and specificity directs the test constructor to those points most directly related to validity.

The reliability of a test is directly related to the validity of a test. For a test to do what it is used to do, it must do whatever it does consistently. A human temperature thermometer which gives different readings for the same absolute temperature is of little use to the medical profession, which relies heavily on changes in the body temperature of human beings for information about patients. Educators need highly reliable readings from their measuring instruments, since they rely heavily on test scores for information about their students.

A test constructor who is concerned about the objectivity of a test instrument is directing attention to building reliability into the test. Examinee performance—although not the only contributing factor to reliability—must be consistent if the measures are to be reliable. The test constructor can do little to control student-centered variations (error) such as state of health, anxiety, emotional state, tiredness, or alertness. The test constructor can take definite steps to reduce variations (error) created by the test itself. The task (direct or implied) must be clear so that each respondent reacts to the same thing. There should be no intrinsic ambiguity attached to an item in terms of the proposed task or in alternatives provided with selection items.

After the test has been administered, analysis of the responses to selected-response items can be made to indicate to the test maker where success was achieved and where weaknesses in the test reduced the value of the results. Item analysis provides a structured procedure designed to point up items which functioned as predicted and to identify inferior items which are weak or defective on some points. These can be revised for use later or, if not salvageable, can be discarded.

Item analysis provides a difficulty level for each item and points out: (a) items that are too easy and possibly in need of revision to make them more difficult, (b) items that are too difficult and in need of revision to make them easier, and (c) those which were in the range of acceptable difficulty level. The discrimination coefficient allows the test constructor of a norm-referenced test to see which items are contributing to identifying levels of achievement. Those which are not making a contribution are in need of revision if they can be saved, and those which cannot be saved should be discarded. For the criterion-referenced test, D values point up good and poor items and places where instruction should be changed.

Poorly functioning distracters can be located and investigated for lack of plausibility or other defects. Rewriting of one or more nonfunctioning distracters may be all the item needs to make it useful.

Future tests are expected to be of higher quality if they are made up of items which have generated acceptable levels of data from item analysis, or items improved by revision. Although most classroom tests should be rebuilt each time units are taught from year to year, some teachers have found that if the content and presentation do not vary too much, a test can be used more than one time. If a test is used again in essentially the same form, any items which are revised must be checked carefully to see that they still relate to the same cell in the table of specifications after revision. Any discarded item must be replaced with an item which is associated with the same table cell as the one being replaced if the same table of specifications is used.

USING APPRAISAL INFORMATION TO HELP STUDENTS AND TEACHERS

Ultimately the appraisal of the test items benefits the student as well as the teacher, since the teacher obtains a more valid appraisal of achievement. Furthermore, the classroom discussion of test results and individual test items with students can be used as a learning experience. The teacher at the same time receives feedback concerning learning and effectiveness of instruction as well as information from students as they point out their interpretation of test tasks and the way they are presented on the test.

The teacher's appraisal of test items prior to classroom discussion assists in making the class experience more meaningful, since the teacher is aware of the technical defects of each test item before discussing it with the students. Any item which the teacher deems from analysis to be ambiguous should be presented to the class before long periods of discussion lead to negative feelings by students. It is more appropriate to discuss next the items answered correctly by only a few students. The reason(s) for missing the items may be determined as being: (a) the lack of adequate classroom coverage of material, (b) ambiguity in the item itself, or (c) lack of understanding of the information by the student.

The teacher may discover that students' poor performances on some items were due to inadequate instruction of the content involved in particular items and assign more class time to those topics in further classroom instruction. Test appraisal may provide information to point up strong as well as weak areas of learning. For example, students may be adept in vocabulary and understanding of principles in a content area but weak in ability to interpret data for practical application. Learning by particular students below that which is expected or necessary for continued progress in the subject or content can be further identified and appropriate remedial action taken.

Becoming aware that teachers are concerned with the quality of test items and that they are continually working to improve the items is a positive experience for students. They will be left with a much better feeling about the entire test experience and the part they play in assisting in the improvement of test items for current and future use if they are allowed to participate actively in test appraisal.

While improving the quality of a test through appraisal and item revision, the teacher is also improving skill in item and test development. Practice in writing and revising items is very beneficial to the development of measurement skill and supplements and refines formal cognitive development of good test appraisal. The teacher's capability in teaching the subject area is hopefully increased through careful attention and consideration of good test practices, as test building relates test tasks to the objectives and course content and causes teachers to interrelate the elements of the process of education.

Specifically test information and test appraisal help the teacher and students:

1. Provide a basis for discussing test results.
2. Provide a learning experience for students.
3. Determine why a test item is or is not discriminating between the better and poorer students.
4. Identify alternative responses which are or are not functioning appropriately.
5. Provide a basis for item improvement.
6. Determine where additional instruction or remedial work with individual students or the class is necessary.
7. Determine if the teacher has met instructional objectives in specific content areas.
8. Develop and improve the teacher's skills in test construction.
9. Develop more valid and reliable measurement of classroom achievement.
10. Provide a check against the table of specifications for balance, objectivity, and specificity of a test.
11. Help students discover errors and misunderstandings.

Only through careful test appraisal can acceptable reliability and validity be developed. The qualities of a good test are based upon adequate test appraisal which is the responsibility of the classroom teacher.

SUMMARY

The adequacy of teacher-made tests and the contributions of each item can be made by test appraisal. The validity of a test rests in the degrees of balance, specificity, and objectivity that the test possesses. These factors can be established before a test is administered but since each classroom test is directed to a specific set of students the appraisal of these points is ongoing.

Item analysis is made from responses of a class of students who have taken the test. The purpose of item analysis is to show how well each item functioned in support of accurate measurement. Every time a multiple-choice or true-false test is administered the difficulty index and discrimination index for each item should be calculated, studied, and if the item is found deficient, it should be revised for future reference and use.

The purpose of test appraisal is to improve measurement of student achievement or performance and to facilitate student learning through review and improved instruction. The appraisal should provide information to improve future tests by increasing the reliability and validity of the newer tests because increased levels of balance, specificity, and objectivity and improved items will be reflected in higher levels of reliability and validity.

Although item analysis for norm- and criterion-referenced tests are somewhat different each method is tailored to the reference system and both have the same purpose. Classification of items by content areas and type of tasks or by subject-matter topics and behaviors allows the teacher to build balance into the test. Through these references the teacher can analyze the appropriateness of test items in meeting the objective of instruction. Attention to the objectivity and specificity of the test gives the teacher a check on how clearly the tasks were presented, whether the correct response was definite, and how directly the tasks were related to the topics studied.

A caution to be observed in item analysis is that the nature and number of students who took the test affects all aspects of test appraisal. No test or test item is equally suitable for all classes or student populations. Test data gathered from one class will determine how well a test functioned in a particular situation, but item-analysis data would be expected to differ somewhat for other groups. The smaller the class size the less reliable the item analysis, and caution should be employed in interpretation of the data when very small numbers of students are involved.

Test appraisal is used to improve the overall effectiveness of the testing program and to help students to learn and teachers to teach. Guidelines for instructional improvement, remedial work, meeting instructional objectives, and improvement of the teacher's skills in test construction are made possible through careful study of a test. Eleven ways that test appraisal aids students and teachers were listed for the reader. Test appraisal is continued in the next two chapters about establishing reliability and validity for classroom tests.

NEW TECHNICAL TERMS LISTED IN THE GLOSSARY

Balance	Discrimination index (D)
Chance level	Easiness index
Criterion groups	Objectivity
Difficulty	Specificity
Difficulty index (P)	Test appraisal
Discrimination	

ACTIVITY EXERCISES

1. Here are the data from a test item on a norm-referenced classroom test used with two classes. Calculate the difficulty index and the discrimination index for this item. Analyze the data and suggest how the item should be revised to improve its contribution to the test measures.

Item 18	a	b	c	d	P_D	D
Upper group	1	16	0	3	(.30)	(+.20)
Lower group	3	12	5	0		

2. Administer (or assist a teacher who has given a test) a test that contains true-false items and complete an item analysis for the test items. Form the criterion groups, compute the level of difficulty and the discrimination index for each item. Use this information to revise the items.

3. Administer (or assist a teacher who has given a test) a norm-referenced test that contains multiple-choice items and complete an item analysis for the items. Form the criterion groups, compute the level of difficulty and the discrimination index for each item. Compute a discrimination index for each alternative. Use this information to revise the items.

FOR DISCUSSION

1. Write a summary statement that points up why a measure of discrimination is less valuable for a test that is criterion-referenced than it is for a test that is norm-referenced.

2. List and briefly describe the ordered steps for carrying out item analysis for multiple-choice items on a norm-referenced test.

3. List and briefly describe the ordered steps for carrying out item analysis for true-false items on a norm-referenced test.

4. Explain how a set of responses from novices and a set of responses from experts can be used to establish specificity and objectivity for test items.

REFERENCES AND KNOWLEDGE EXTENDERS

AMERICAN PSYCHOLOGICAL ASSOCIATION. *Standards for educational and psychological tests.* Washington, D.C.: Author, 1974.

BEGGS, D. L., & LEWIS, E. L. *Measurement and evaluation in the schools.* Boston: Houghton Mifflin, 1975. Pp. 189–206.

DOWNIE, N. M. *Fundamentals of measurement: Techniques and practice* (2nd ed.). New York: Oxford University Press, 1968. Chap. 10, pp. 182–191.

EBEL, R. L. *Essentials of educational measurement* (3rd ed.). Englewood Cliffs, NJ: Prentice-Hall, 1979. Chap. 13, pp. 258–273.

GRONLUND, N. E. *Measurement and evaluation in teaching* (4th ed.). New York: Macmillan, 1981. Pp. 253–270.

KELLEY, T. L. The selection of upper and lower groups for the validation of test items. *Journal of Educational Psychology,* 1939, *30,* 17–24.

POPHAM, W. J. *Modern educational measurement.* Englewood Cliffs, NJ: Prentice-Hall, 1981. Chap. 3, pp. 45–65.

SAX, G. *Principles of educational and psychological measurement and evaluation* (2nd ed.). Belmont, CA: Wadsworth, 1980. Chap. 7, pp. 182–207.

Chapter 11. Establishing Test Reliability

After study of Chapter 11, you should be able to:

1. Describe ways to estimate test reliability.
2. Describe the concept of correlation and how it is used to establish test reliability.
3. Calculate the Pearson r and Spearman ρ coefficients.
4. Explain how a teacher would establish reliability for a classroom test.
5. Describe how to calculate standard error of measurement and use it with a test score.
6. List the factors which can affect test reliability.
7. Explain how each glossary term listed at the end of the chapter is used in classroom measurement and evaluation.

Consistency of measures is a universal criterion of measurement. Consistency of test results is a universal criterion of educational measurement. A high degree of consistency of test scores from one test administration to another or within one set of scores is important to good measurement and to evaluations based on the measures. The classroom teacher asks the question, "How similar would each student's scores be on a first testing and a subsequent testing if the same test were used?" or "How close do two tests which were designed to test the same material actually come to giving the same results?" Answers to these questions are based on the test score reliability. If confidence is to be placed in test data, the results must be highly consistent over a period of time with the same group of students and highly consistent among scores on any one test administration. The term *reliability* as used in norm-referencing refers to and is defined as the consistency with which a test measures whatever it measures.*

---

*Reliability for criterion-referenced measurement has three different concepts: (*a*) consistency of the decisions that classify each student to mastery or nonmastery status, (*b*) reliability of test scores of criterion-referenced tests, and (*c*) reliability of domain score estimates. The first of these must be considered to be the most important concept for the classroom teacher. If a test can not separate masters and nonmasters with a high degree of consistency it can not be said to have adequate reliability. Although several methods of establishing each of the three reliabilities

Quantification of a characteristic of someone or something utilizes a measurement procedure open to some amount of chance error. The resulting scores or measures, therefore, contain an amount of chance error and vary accordingly. The variation may be small or large but all measures, whether a result of physical measurement or measurement of constructs, must be considered to be approximate. A given set of measures of an attribute for a given group of students will not be the same as another set of measures for the same attribute for the same students. Furthermore, a set of measures of an attribute for a single subject will vary over repeated measurement. Since chance error generates differences in the measures, some inconsistency is attached to those measures. Thus, interpretation of scores and differences among the scores must take into account the fact that some differences appear because of score variation from chance sources.

Test results are not expected to be impeccable, since factors such as characteristics of the student, characteristics of the test, conditions of test administration, and scoring can be sources of chance error. Since a test score contains some amount of error, it cannot be interpreted as a point, but must be interpreted as a range.

Another way to view sets of measures is to observe consistency within the measures. If a board is measured with the same steel carpenter rule by many different individuals, the measures will vary but fall within a very small range of values and cluster around one particular point. The reason they vary only slightly is that a highly developed and reliable measuring instrument was used. If a set of boards with different lengths were measured with a steel measuring tape and ordered according to the measures and measured again with the same tape and a new ordering made, the two orderings would be nearly alike. The results would be consistent. A set of test measures for a given group of students should order the students much the same as another set of measures from the same test for the same students. The relative position of each student within the reference group will remain much the same. The tendency for educational and psychological tests to measure with consistent results is known as **test reliability.**

If an average of a very large number of measures for one characteristic for one subject were calculated, that average value would be very close to what is referred to as a true score. The idea of a **true test score** is basic to an understanding of students' **obtained test scores.** Every attribute of every object or subject has one and only one value at any one point in time. Mary has a true height—that value that an all-knowing being would record for Mary. Since human beings are not all-knowing, the idea of a true score can be developed, but the true score cannot be isolated and identified as such. The

---

are presently being used, those procedures are more appropriate for standardized tests. The material in this chapter refers to reliability as it relates to norm-referenced measurement. Teachers who are interested in pursuing the question of reliability for criterion-referenced tests are referred to Hambleton, Swaminathan, Algina, & Coulson, (1978, pp. 15–23); Subkoviak (1980); and Brennan (1980).

concept of a true score as used in measurement is somewhat different from the absolute accurate value. The idea of a true score for a test is presented using the earlier developed concept of error.* Each measurement must result in a measure considered to be an estimate of some true value. The obtained score consists of the true score and the error component.

$$\text{Obtained score} = \text{True score} + \text{Error score}$$

A mathematical approach to the true score describes the true score as an average of a very large number of possible scores that an individual could conceivably make on repeated administrations of a test. With either approach the test score is to be considered as an estimate of an individual's true score. Measures of reliability for tests are based on how consistent results are within a group or how consistent individuals are in repeated measurements. An ideal condition would be for obtained and true scores to be identical. Then measurement reliability would be perfect.

Classroom tests are administered to gather information about student achievement. Published tests are administered to collect information about achievement or other characteristics. The consideration of how consistently the test measured the attribute it was designed to measure is an important aspect of establishing how well the test did what it was supposed to do. An estimate of consistency in the form of a reliability coefficient is the most useful *statistical* value in judging how successful the test maker was in building a measuring instrument. High reliability does not mean that a test is valid, but very low reliability does indicate a questionable measuring instrument. A test can rate high in reliability but at the same time not be measuring what the test maker set out to measure; therefore, a test may give data which are reliable but fall short of the primary purpose.

WAYS OF ESTIMATING TEST RELIABILITY

An estimate of test reliability may be obtained by one of several procedures: *(a)* **Test-retest** utilizes the method of administration of the same test twice to a group of students and correlating the two sets of scores, *(b)* **Equivalent-forms reliability** compares the scores made by a set of students who took two tests either concurrently or at different times, *(c)* **Split-half reliability,** a measure of **internal consistency** of a test, may be estimated by comparing two independent halves of a single test, *(d)* **Kuder-Richardson (K-R) formulas,** which measure the internal consistency, are also widely used to estimate test reliability from one administration of a test, and *(e)* **Scorer reliability** compares the scoring or reading of a set of student responses by more than one person or two sets of measures determined independently by one person. Different methods of estimating reliability determine different types of consistency as Figure 11.1 shows.

---

*In Chapter 1 the idea that error in testing is a study of variability which should not be equated with a mistake was discussed.

Method	Type of Reliability Measure	Procedure
a. Test-retest	Stability	Correlation between the scores on the same test taken twice. Measures the extent to which students hold the same relative position in the group.
b. Equivalent-forms	(1) Equivalence	Correlation between scores on two forms of the same test taken concurrently
	(2) Stability and equivalence	Correlation between scores on two forms of the same test taken at different times
c. Split-half	Internal consistency	Correlation between scores on the odd-numbered and even-numbered items of a single test
d. Kuder-Richardson	Internal consistency	Correlation is determined from a single administration of a test through a study of variances
e. Scorer reliability	Stability	Correlation between the scoring of the same test by two independent scorers

FIGURE 11.1. Ways of estimating test reliability

Using Correlation

In general, the study of consistency for a measuring instrument requires repeated measures from one element or a group of elements being studied. Physical measurement can be studied for consistency by repeating the measurement many times for a single characteristic of an element being studied. A rock may be weighed many times without changing its weight. A board may be measured for length many times without changing its length. However, when the study is of a characteristic of a human being, the object of study may be altered merely through the act of measurement. For this reason estimation of reliability associated with educational measurement must be made without many repetitions of the same measurement from the same subject. In practice, reliability for results of classroom measurement will be estimated using one score from each individual and for standardized tests using one or two scores from each individual. If the concept of repeated measures is to be used in establishing reliability for educational testing instruments, the repeated measures must be viewed across many individuals rather than many repeated measures for one individual. Typically, the estimate of reliability is made by the computation of a **correlation coefficient** for two sets of scores.

Test-retest, equivalent-forms, split-half, Kuder-Richardson, and scorer reliability have been presented as ways to approach estimation of test reliability. Although each way views reliability from a different premise, all except K-R formulas* require an inspection of the relationship of one set of scores with another set of scores each of which has been collected from the same group of elements. **Correlation** procedures are designed to investigate relationships that exist between pairs of sets of data by measuring the simultaneous variation of the several paired values. This means that correlation can reveal how much consistency is measured in regard to each subject's scores being in the same relative position in both sets of data. If each subject being measured is in exactly the same place in each set with respect to all other elements, then consistency will be measured at its maximum, giving perfect correlation. Correlation coefficients are used in determining reliability estimates for tests by comparing two sets of scores from one group of students. Later it will be shown that the two sets may come from one test administered twice, two different tests, one test which has been divided into two parts, or two scorer values for one set of responses.

Measuring Relationships by Correlation

The simplest way to look for relationships is by employing a **scattergram.** The scattergram is a graphical representation made by plotting a point for each pair of scores that has been obtained for the group of subjects. The **horizontal axis** represents the scores of one set of data as they increase from left to right while the **vertical axis** represents scores of the other set of data as they increase from bottom to top. Relationship can be revealed by the positions of points made by plotting each student's two scores as one point in a two dimensional matrix. Relationship is revealed by the pattern made when two scores for each student have been placed on the two dimensional graph. In Figure 11.2 each of the two dimensions represents values from one of the sets of data, and test information is shown as a set of points made up from two sets of data. Any relationship between the two sets will be apparent when the dots of the scattergram tend to form into a line. Figure 11.3 illustrates a set of points which forms a definite pattern. The two sets of scores are somewhat related in that there is a tendency for low scores in one set to be associated with low scores in the

---

*K-R formulas and other methods which are based on a study of variance and covariance within one set of scores are used primarily by standardized test makers and will not be given computational attention here. (See Appendix D.)

Student	X Values	Y Values
A	10	11
B	14	8
C	19	18
D	4	18
E	22	14
F	16	4
G	8	14
H	3	4
I	13	3
J	19	4
K	20	8
L	11	5
M	9	5
N	4	8
O	22	4
P	18	12
Q	12	17
R	15	17
S	14	13
T	4	11

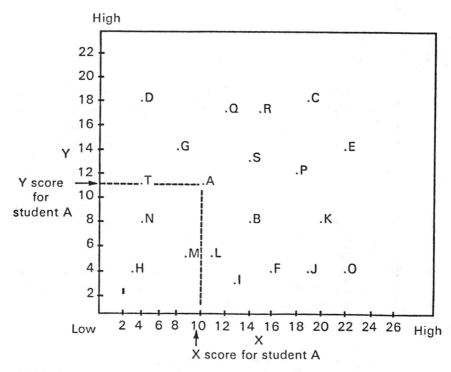

FIGURE 11.2. Scattergram with no discernible relationship

other set, middle scores in one set are associated with middle scores in the
second set, and high scores go together in each set.

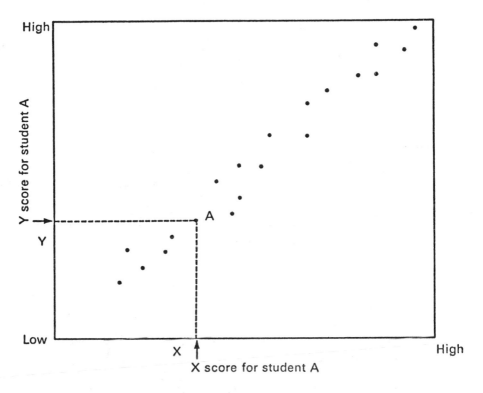

FIGURE 11.3. Scattergram with a positive relationship

The closer the dots come to fitting a line, the higher the correlation
coefficient and the more consistency within the two sets of measures. If the dots
fall on a line, then the correlation of the two sets is said to be perfect. A score
in one set of scores is in exactly the same place in that distribution as the
corresponding score for the subject in the other distribution, and all pairs meet
this condition. Figure 11.4 illustrates the condition necessary for perfect correlation.

A correlation coefficient computed from two sets of data which are
totally unrelated will be 0.00. A correlation coefficient which is computed for
two sets of data having a perfect relationship where low scores go with low
and high scores go with high will be 1.00. Correlational procedures also allow
for measurement of the relationship when the relationship is high with low and
low with high; however, with measurement of test reliability there is little
likelihood that any two sets will be so related.

The **Pearson product-moment correlation** $[\Sigma(z_x z_y)/N]$ is a method to

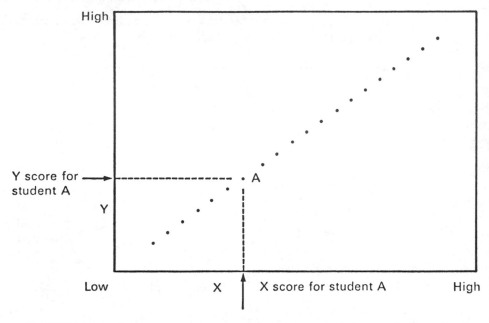

FIGURE 11.4. Scattergram for two sets of data which correlate perfectly

compute an estimate of relationship. A convenient raw score formula for use with a calculator is:

$$r = \frac{N\Sigma XY - \Sigma X \Sigma Y}{\sqrt{[N\Sigma X^2 - (\Sigma X)^2][N\Sigma Y^2 - (\Sigma Y)^2]}}$$

Where:

r = Pearson product-moment coefficient
Σ = means to add
X = score on one of the sets
Y = score on a second set
$(\Sigma X)^2$ = sum of X scores squared
$(\Sigma Y)^2$ = sum of Y scores squared
ΣX^2 = sum of squared X scores
ΣY^2 = sum of squared Y scores
ΣXY = sum of the products of paired X and Y scores

Other formulas for the Pearson r can be used to compute relationships.* This

---

*All Pearson formulas are derived from the basic formula:

$$r = \frac{\Sigma(z_x z_y)}{N} \qquad \text{Where}$$

$$z_x = \frac{X - \overline{X}}{\sigma_x} \text{ and } z_y = \frac{Y - \overline{Y}}{\sigma_y}$$

is an example of computation of r using raw scores to estimate the relationship of two sets of scores from classroom tests:

Student	Scores on		Squared		Product of
	Test X	Test Y	X^2	Y^2	$(X)\,(Y)$
Al	14	3	196	9	42
Bea	19	9	361	81	171
Carla	16	7	256	49	112
Dave	18	8	324	64	144
Eric	12	4	144	16	48
Fran	10	5	100	25	50
Gayla	17	11	289	121	187
Herm	15	6	225	36	90
	121	53	1,895	401	844

$$r = \frac{(8)\,(844)-(121)\,(53)}{\sqrt{[(8)\,(1,895)-(121)^2]\,[(8)\,(401)-(53)^2]}}$$

$$r = \frac{6,752 - 6,413}{\sqrt{(15,160 - 14,641)\,(3,208 - 2,809)}}$$

$$r = \frac{339}{\sqrt{(519)\,(399)}} = \frac{339}{\sqrt{207,081}} = \frac{339}{455.06}$$

$$r = .74$$

A somewhat simpler procedure can be used if the scores are ranked for each variable and a correlation computed using a rank correlation procedure. A convenient formula for computing a correlation from ranked data for **rho(ρ)** is:

$$\rho = 1 - \frac{6\Sigma D^2}{N(N^2 - 1)},$$

You may prefer the following formula for r:

$$r = \frac{\Sigma XY - \frac{(\Sigma X)(\Sigma Y)}{N}}{\sqrt{\left[\Sigma X^2 - \frac{(\Sigma X)^2}{N}\right]\left[\Sigma Y^2 - \frac{(\Sigma Y)^2}{N}\right]}}$$

Where:

ρ = the correlation coefficient (Spearman)
D = the difference in ranks (each student)
ΣD^2 = the sum of squared differences
N = the number of students

This is an example of computation of rho (ρ) using ranks for the same set of scores instead of raw scores:

Student	Scores on		Rank on		Difference	
	Test X	Test Y	Text X	Test Y	D	D^2
Al	14	3	6	8	−2	4
Bea	19	9	1	2	−1	1
Carla	16	7	4	4	0	0
Dave	18	8	2	3	−1	1
Eric	12	4	7	7	0	0
Fran	10	5	8	6	2	4
Gayla	17	11	3	1	2	4
Herm	15	6	5	5	0	0
						14

$$\rho = 1 - \left[\frac{(6)\,(14)}{8(64-1)} \right] = 1 - \frac{84}{504} = 1 - 17 = .83$$

Examination of each of these formulas and the accompanying computation reveals the measure of consistency as being the tendency for paired scores of a group of subjects to fall in the same position in the two different sets of measures. The second formula (rho) is a direct derivation from the first and is based on known facts about the first N integers. The size of the numerator of the formula for ranked data is a function of the differences observed in the two sets for each individual. The larger the differences the larger the value to be subtracted from 1. If the ranks in the two sets are the same for all subjects, then the D^2 column will sum to 0 and rho will be equal to 1.00 which measures the consistency at its highest level. As more and more differences appear in the data, the correlation coefficient approaches 0.00. As previously mentioned, a coefficient of 0.00 measures a complete lack of relationship.

Correlation coefficients are usually reported to the nearest hundredth—.27, .63, .89, .96, and such. Since these values are written like a proportion, there seems to be a tendency to interpret the reliability coefficient of .27, .63, .89, .96, or the like as a proportion of the pairs of points which are the same in both sets. Some interpretations are likely to be made in terms of 27 percent, 63 percent, 89 percent, or 96 percent of agreement. Neither of these explanations of the relationship is correct.

Procedurally, the use of the Pearson *r* as a reliability coefficient is based on a study of variance. The variance is a two-dimensional statistic. Therefore, to speak in terms of percentages, the percentages must be of shared variance between the two distributions. If the coefficient is squared and multiplied by 100, the result is the percentage of variance in one variable which is shared with the other variable. Figure 11.5 gives some representative percentages associated with correlation coefficients.

Pearson r Coefficient of Relationship	Percentage of Shared Variance ($r^2 \times 100$)
100	100
90	81
80	64
70	49
60	36
50	25
40	16
30	9
20	4
10	1
0	0

FIGURE 11.5. Chart of percentages of shared variance for selected Pearson r coefficients

The following discussion of ways to estimate test reliability is built on the principle of consistency as measured by the correlation of two sets of scores.

Test-Retest

Test-retest procedures are useful to builders of standardized tests as they collect data to report about their tests. The correlation coefficient is calculated by obtaining two sets of scores for the same students through the administration of the same test on two different occasions. Usually 7 to 10 days elapse between the first and second administrations of the test. The higher the relationship (larger correlation coefficient) the more consistency between the two sets of scores (see Figure 11.6). If students tend to score at about the same place on the second administration as they did on the first administration, the dots on the scattergram will fall close to an imaginary line drawn across the scattergram and the correlation coefficient will be close to 1.00. As the dots for students depart from **linear tendency,** they show inconsistency by a wider scattering on the scattergram and a resulting lower correlation coefficient.

The test-retest method of establishing reliability is as much a measure of **examinee reliability** as it is a measure of the test's reliability. Anything which causes the person being examined to be different at the two testing sessions will lower the expected coefficient. Since human beings are ever chang-

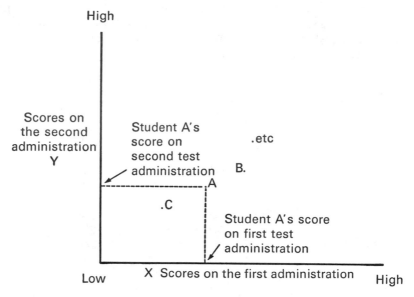

FIGURE 11.6. Test-retest correlation to establish test reliability

ing, this is a disadvantage of the test-retest procedure and causes differences within examinees to confound the estimate of the test's reliability by lowering it. A test repeated within a very short time interval introduces a memory factor, and the correlation of scores from the two testings is likely to be inflated. Repeating the test after a long time interval introduces factors of growth and intervening learning which will deflate the correlation. In either case the reliability estimate is in error to the degree that either memory or growth and intervening learning affect the coefficient.

Equivalent Forms

Equivalency of two different test forms to test the same body of content or characteristic can be established by having one set of students take both test forms contiguously. This procedure is known as the equivalent-forms method. The equivalency concept of reliability is reflected by high coefficients when the scores on the two forms of the same test are correlated (see Figure 11.7).

Rarely, if ever, should a teacher take class time to administer a classroom test twice to establish reliability estimates. Equivalent forms of classroom tests are seldom needed for the informal classroom testing program, but standardized test makers use this technique extensively. What a teacher needs is some way to estimate reliability from the scores from one administration of one test as is usually done in the classroom. Fortunately, there is a way to do this quite satisfactorily for teachers' informal tests and standardized tests as well.

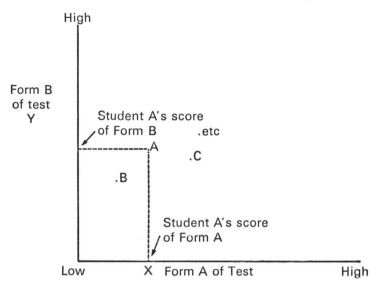

FIGURE 11.7. Correlation to establish the equivalency of two test forms

Split Halves

The split-half method of establishing internal consistency as a measure of reliability is a modification of the equivalent-forms procedure. To estimate the internal consistency of a test, two halves of the test are formed so that each half is the near equivalent of the other. The most common method for forming the halves is to consider the odd-numbered items on the test as one form and the even-numbered items as constituting the other form. Unless the test maker has some unique pattern which would tend to make one of the halves biased in some way, for example arranging the items so that easy and difficult items alternate, this procedure is quite satisfactory. In most cases the odd-even division introduces no bias between the halves which will be compared.

After the two halves have been formed a score for each half is determined for each student, thus giving two values for each student—one for the even-numbered items and another for the odd-numbered items. The student's test score will remain the total of the two half scores. A correlation of the two sets of scores, odd and even, measures the internal consistency as an estimate of the test's reliability (see Figure 11.8). Since a long test has been divided into two shortened versions, the correlation coefficient will be less for the two short forms than the coefficient for the longer test. This coefficient is biased (a constant error) toward a depressed coefficient, and it reports the consistency (reliability) of the long test at a lower level than it actually was in the longer form. A Spearman-Brown formula is used to make the correction and report the reliability estimate for the full-length test.

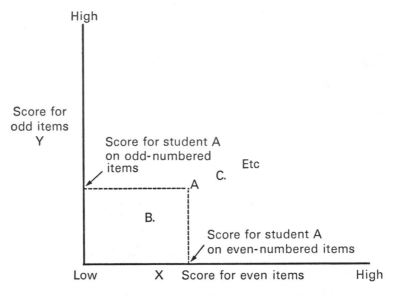

FIGURE 11.8. Correlation of odd-numbered items and even-numbered items to estimate reliability

The general **Spearman-Brown formula** which predicts the reliability for a test that has been lengthened, using the same quality of items as the original test is:

$$r_1 = \frac{N r_s}{r_s (N - 1) + 1}$$

Where:

r_1 = reliability estimate of lengthened test
N = number of times test is lengthened
r_s = reliability of the two short tests
    (the original reliability coefficient)

If the two short forms are found to have an estimated relationship of .60, the reliability estimate will be increased to .90 if the test is made six times as long:

$$r = \frac{(6)\ (.60)}{(.60)\ (5) + 1} = \frac{3.6}{3 + 1} = \frac{3.6}{4} = .90$$

When using the split-halves procedure, the formula for doubling the length of a test is:

$$r_1 = \frac{2r_{oe}}{(r_{oe})(2-1)+1}$$

Which reduces to

$$r_1 = \frac{2r_{oe}}{r_{oe}+1}$$

Where:

r_1 = reliability of the long form as administered
r_{oe} = reliability of the odd and even divisions

If the coefficient of .60 is obtained from the correlation of a set of scores from the odd items with a set of scores from the even items, the reliability estimate for the test as administered becomes .75 when the Spearman-Brown formula is used.

$$r_1 = \frac{(2)(.60)}{.60+1} = \frac{1.2}{1.6} = \frac{3}{4} = .75$$

The assumption attached to the use of the Spearman-Brown formula is that the two halves are equivalent. If they fail to be perfectly equivalent, then the coefficient of the total test will be an underestimate. The underestimate results from any difference in the sample of the subject-matter topics and behaviors for one half and the sample supplied by the other half. When the half tests are not equivalent, the scores would not be expected to correlate highly, so any tendency for the halves to be testing different bodies of knowledge and behaviors will reduce reliability estimates using the Spearman-Brown formula. Since *perfect* equivalency is rarely, if ever, achieved by procedures used to divide the test, the split-half corrected by the Spearman-Brown formula method generates coefficients for test reliability which are conservative estimates.

Kuder-Richardson Formulas

Another measure (see Appendix D) of the internal consistency of a test estimates the test's reliability based on the consistency of the student performance from item to item. If a test is scored by giving one point for a correct response and no points for an incorrect response, the Kuder-Richardson (K-R) 20 formula can be used. If the items are also of about the same level of difficulty, the K-R 21 formula can be used. K-R coefficients are used primarily to report reliability estimates for published standardized tests. Other methods which also establish the internal consistency through a study of variances and covariances are becoming more popular. Any of these methods of the analysis of variance type can be used with only one administration of a test and could be used by the classroom teacher. Since the computations involved are somewhat more demanding than other methods, most teachers will probably find that the simpler odd-even procedure is more appropriate for their use.

Scorer Reliability

Scorer reliability can be established by correlation of values for two independent scorers. Since scoring of objective tests is highly objective, scorer reliability for objective tests is at acceptable levels. Scorer reliability is particularly important for essay tests, since consistent scoring of essay responses is difficult to accomplish. Lack of reliability in scoring, as pointed out earlier, is a major disadvantage of essay items. A correlation coefficient can be determined for two sets of scores from two independent judgments on a common set of essay test responses. The obtained coefficient reflects the degree of agreement between the readings. The closer the coefficient is to 1.00 the higher the agreement of the reader scores (see Figure 11.9).

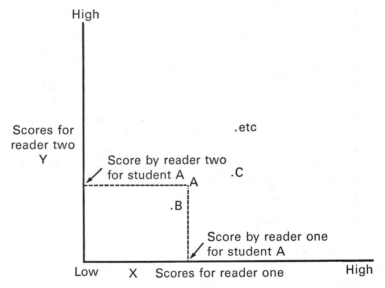

FIGURE 11.9. Scorer reliability for two readers of one set of papers.

A teacher who is fortunate enough to have someone qualified and willing to read sets of essay responses can get an estimate of how well the teacher's own evaluations of the responses agree with another person's. If a second person cannot be used, the teacher could make independent readings of the set of responses and correlate the two sets of values as a measure of consistency in scoring. Scorer reliability measures for classroom tests should be used as often as essay tests are given.

Stability and Equivalence

Through the different methods of obtaining reliability coefficients consistency may be determined:

1. over a period of time (test-retest)
2. over different forms of the test instrument (equivalent forms)
3. within the instrument itself (internal consistency)

Interpretation of the reliability coefficient is made with an eye to the type of consistency being examined.

Stability refers to the consistency of the test results over a period of time as measured by the reliability estimates using the test-retest method. Highly stable results show that the students remained in about the same relative positions in the second testing as they had in the first testing. Each subject fell at about the same place in each distribution of scores. Scorer reliability is also a form of stability, since the subjects' relative position in two distributions of scores obtained from different sources provide the data for the correlation process.

If a stability measure is used for a published standardized test, the time lapse between testing should be reported to the prospective user in the test's manual. Little change in scores would be expected as a result of time per se if the interval between test sessions is short. The longer the interval between the two test sessions, the more the reliability coefficient will be affected by the contribution of learning and other differences attributable to time.

Equivalence reflects the extent to which two tests generate comparable scores for the characteristic being measured. If the tests are measuring the same thing (equivalent) the coefficient of reliability will be high.

By administering two different tests with a time interval, a measure which combines stability with equivalence can be obtained by correlating the two sets of scores. Since the source of any error variance remains unidentified as to source (test difference or time difference), this type of reliability coefficient is not widely used in the classroom.

Choosing a Procedure

The decision to use one procedure or another for estimating test reliability cannot be made arbitrarily. A test-retest method is to be used when the score will predict for the future or the score will be referred to when making later decisions. In these cases it is important that a score remain stable over a period of time. When *stability* over time is of primary importance, then the *test-retest* method is most appropriate.

Alternate forms and internal consistency methods are studies of equivalency. Since the investigation is not over a period of time, there is no measure of stability. Concurrent validity is concerned with the ability of the test to measure the present status of students without effects of changes from time. When one form of a test is used to measure a characteristic at the beginning of the school year and another form is used at the end of the year, the comparison should be made on the basis of the test being able to measure present status without effects of other characteristics from a time interval alone. Assessment of present status and student change in status can best be assessed by procedures which use a testing instrument that rates high in equivalence.

The classroom teacher wants to measure achievement with administration of one test and to estimate the reliability of that test with as simple a procedure as possible but needs to make that estimate with reasonable assurance of accuracy. The procedure which best meets these criteria is the split-half correlation extended by the Spearman-Brown formula. Since measures of internal consistency allow reliability estimates from one test administration, they are appropriate for use with classroom tests. In this way class time is not lost by giving the same test twice or by asking the student to take two different tests. The estimate obtained in the split-half procedure compares favorably with other reliability estimates. The teacher who has the advantage of programs written for the various analysis of variance techniques and mechanical computational devices may want to derive more than one reliability coefficient. Published standardized test manuals, in general, report two or more estimates for reliability.

Each classroom teacher should understand each of the procedures well enough to interpret reported test manual values. For classroom use, the suggested split-half method of estimating test reliability should be at the computational level for the teacher. One other interpretation of consistency which estimates the amount of error in scores is useful for both the classroom test and the standardized test. A measure of unreliability as reflected in expected variation in scores over repeated testing is discussed in the next section.

STANDARD ERROR OF MEASUREMENT

Chance errors which are involved in classroom measurement reduce the coefficients of reliability. The less that chance errors are a part of the measurement the closer the coefficient is to 1.00 and the closer the measure is expected to approach the true score. Three assumptions are basic to a study of chance fluctuation of students' scores. These are:

1. Each measure (score) has been affected by chance errors associated with measurement procedures.
2. If a person could take a test again and again an uncountably large number of times completely forgetting any knowledge of the test (like taking the test for the first time again and again), those scores would vary (would not all be the same exact value each time).
3. Chance errors are independent of the actual score; some will be positive and some negative.

This discussion implies that any score on a test should be considered as an estimate of the test taker's general level. The test's measure of the characteristic represented as a score is not expected to predict a specific point on the scale but rather a range on the scale. Certainly the score is expressed as a point, but it should be interpreted taking into consideration chance error. The concept of the true score enters the formal approach to an estimate of error which is present because of test unreliability. Each score obtained from a student is considered to be made up of two parts—the true-score component and the error component. Error in statistics is considered as variation. Variation is measured by **standard error** terms.

How much of an obtained score is due to error associated with measurement? This question is asked when a test maker interprets a single obtained score as an estimate of the test taker's general level of performance.

If it were possible to test a student many times (without changing the score through boredom, practice, learning, or resistance), a frequency distribution of the individual's scores would be very near to a normal distribution. Since a student cannot take a test again and again to establish a set of scores, the error scores for the group taking the test are used to establish the standard error. The mean of that **sampling distribution** would be the true score. The standard deviation of the distribution of scores from repeated measurements is called the standard error. Standard error terms are used widely in statistics to measure fluctuation of statistics over repeated measurements. The standard deviation of the theoretical sampling distribution associated with a subject's score is the **standard error of measurement** for that measure. In practice, standard error of measurement values are estimated from test data.

The question which arises about the obtained score is in regard to its position in the sampling distribution and in turn its relationship to the true score. Since educational measurement is not amenable to repetition, the standard error of measurement cannot be obtained directly. The standard error of measurement must always be estimated indirectly by computation from a formula derived from a ratio which is a proportion of the total **variance** that is nonerror (true) variance. The standard error of measurement formula is reduced to:

$$\sigma_{se} = \sigma_t \sqrt{1-r}$$

Where:

σ_{se} = standard error of measurement
σ_t = standard deviation of the set of test scores
r = the correlation coefficient

By using the estimate of the variability of possible scores, an estimate of how far off an individual score is from the true score can be established. Let us set up a hypothetical situation to study how the standard error of measurement can help to interpret a score. Assume that repeated testings (many, many times) of a subject with no effects from learning and so on generate a frequency distribution like this:

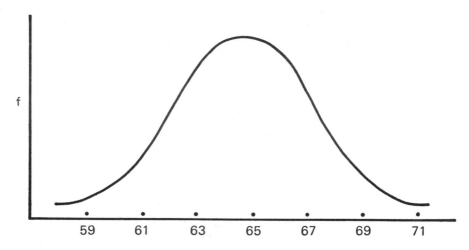

This person's true score appears to be 65, but some of the scores are less than 59 and some are more than 71. The standard deviation of this sampling distribution (the standard error of measurement) is two units; therefore, about one-third (refer to the area under the normal curve) of the scores in the distribution fall between 63 and 65, another one-third between 65 and 67, and the other one-third are divided equally below 63 and above 67. This standard deviation, 2, is the standard error of measurement for this set of scores. If one more score is obtained from this individual, the probability of that score being between 63 and 67 (65 ± 2) is .68. There is a 68 percent probability that the new score will be between 63 and 67. In other words, the chances are two out of three that any single score will be between 63 and 67. There is a 95 percent chance that any single score will be between 61 and 69. Other probabilities can be set for other intervals.

If the true score of 65 is not known but the standard error term is estimated, then judgments can be made about a single score and probabilities of where that point is in relation to the unknown true score. Since the four-unit interval from 63 to 67 includes two-thirds of the scores, the probability that any four-unit interval includes the true score is .68. If a four-unit interval is established for every score in the 63 to 67 interval (68 percent of the total N), those intervals would all include 65. For every score below 63 (16 percent of the total N) and above 67 (16 percent of the total N) four-unit intervals would *not* include 65. Try some of these and actually experience how this works. For example:

Obtained score is 66.
Standard error of measurement is 2 units.
The interval (66 − 2) and (66 + 2) or 64 to 68 *does* include the true score 65.

Obtained score is 61.
Standard error of measurement is 2 units.

The interval $(61 - 2)$ and $(61 + 2)$ or 59 to 63 does *not* include the true score 65.

Take an entirely new situation where the standard error of measurement $\sigma_t \sqrt{1 - r}$ is equal to four units, true score unknown, and a student has a score of 81. The score of 81 might fit in the person's distribution like this:

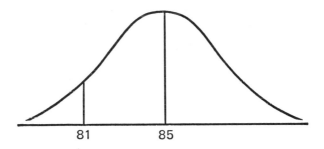

81   85

If 81 is a low score, then the true score may be 85. However, the score of 81 might fit in the person's distribution like this:

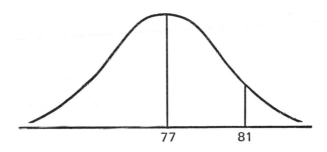

77   81

If 81 is a high score, then the true score may be 77. Figure 11.10 shows the two possibilities on the common baseline. The probability that 81 does not deviate more than four units from the true score is .68, since only 16 percent of each curve is outside the four-unit interval established by the standard error of measurement of four units.

Figure 11.10, in addition to showing how to establish an interval of confidence, points up that there is no way to know which direction the mean is in relation to the observed score. It is as likely to be below the obtained score as it is to be above the obtained score. Obviously, the limits of 77 and 85 to establish the 68 percent **confidence interval** are not the only points which could be a mean. These points are used only for setting the range. Other levels of confidence call for other pairs of points to be considered as limits. Keep in mind when using the standard error of measurement that theoretically the true

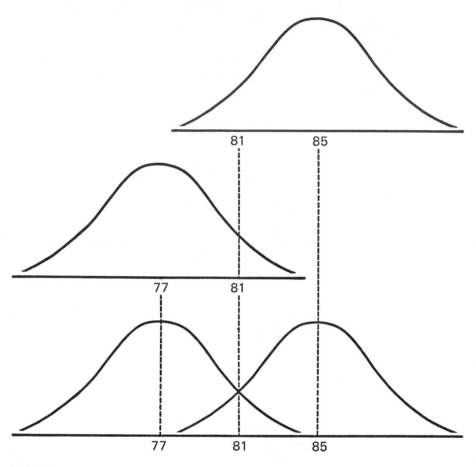

FIGURE 11.10. Using the standard error of measurement

score or the mean of the sampling distribution can take any value on the base line.

Interpretation of an obtained score with the standard error of measurement permits a person to visualize a score as a band rather than as a point. Each obtained score is made up partially of a true score, but limitations on measurement make a portion of the obtained score, error score. Since it is not known whether the error has augmented the true score or lessened it, each of these possibilities must be dealt with. If one standard error of measurement value (this is in raw score units) is added to the obtained score and one is subtracted from the obtained score, an interval is established. If many students exactly alike (have the same true score) take the test, two-thirds of these scores would fall within one standard error unit of a given true score. Likewise, if many obtained scores of the same value have a 68 percent confidence interval established for them, 68 out of 100 would be in the interval spanning the true score value. Chances for any one of the obtained scores being in the 68 percent confidence interval for a true score are also 68 out of 100. For example, if a manual for a standardized test provides a standard error of measurement of 3, the value informs us that the obtained score of 68 percent of the students tested will fall within the six-unit range associated with the true score. When a score is to be interpreted, the band permits decisions adjusted by an estimate of error and points up that in actuality the person's true score may be as low as the lowest point of the band or as high as the highest point, or any of the points between.

Two scores on the same test can be compared on the basis of possible overlapping of the bands established for the separate scores. Rather than comparing two scores directly in terms of absolute differences, the band for one score can be compared to the band for the other. Figure 11.11 shows how two scores—57 and 61—on a test having a standard error of measurement of three units can be compared in this way. Since the two bands overlap from 58 to 60, we can conclude that there is probably no difference between the students who scored 57 and 61, since both scores fall within a band for one true score. If scores as bands rather than points are compared and the two bands do not overlap, then there probably is a real difference between the scores and a real difference between students on the attribute being measured by the test.* If the two bands do overlap, then there is probably no real difference, and the difference in obtained scores appears as a result of measurement error.

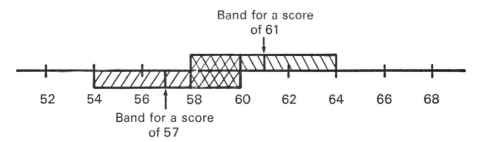

FIGURE 11.11. Use of score bands to interpret differences of two students' scores

INCREASING RELIABILITY

The reliability coefficient may be affected by: (a) length of the test, (b) degree of homogeneity of content, (c) ability range of students, (d) appro-

---

*The term *difference* as used here does not refer to a difference in the obtained scores. There is no question that 57 is different from 61. The difference which is being tested with the use of bands is a real difference between students in the attribute being measured at a specified probability level of confidence.

priateness of items, (*e*) type of scoring, (*f*) testing conditions, and (*g*) speeded-ness (see below).

Test Length

Any test can be made more reliable by increasing the length of the test with items of the same quality as those on the original test. Common sense, as well as mathematical probability, points up the increased degree of confidence associated with large samples as compared to small samples. Therefore, as large samples are taken from an area of knowledge, one expects more reliable appraisal of the area. Mathematically derived estimates of test reliability confirm the fact that longer tests tend to give more reliable results than shorter tests. This principle is used in development of Spearman-Brown formulas. Figure 11.12 shows the effects of consecutive doubling of the number of items beginning with a 10-item test with a reliability estimate of .30—a very low estimate.

Number of Items	Reliability Estimate
10	.30
20	.46
40	.63
80	.77
160	.87

FIGURE 11.12. Effects of doubling the number of items on a test

Notice that relatively small increases are obtained at the upper levels compared to the lower levels. An increase of only two times in a test with 10 items increases the *r* from .30 to .46, an increase of .16. Eighty items added to an 80-item test with an *r* of .77 adds only .10 to make the estimate for a 160-item test equal .87.

When the Spearman-Brown formula is used to estimate reliability for longer tests, the only difference between tests is the length. In addition to the assumption that any items added to the test are equivalent to the original set of items in all characteristics is the assumption that the examinees will not change in any way during the longer test session. If motivation to do well is reduced by boredom or tiredness from a longer session, the longer test may not have the expected increase in reliability. In general longer tests are more reliable than short ones but the added reliability diminishes as the number of items on the test increases.

Lengthening a test which has generated a low reliability coefficient to raise its reliability will not be practical in most cases, since a test may need to be increased as much as 3 to 10 times its original length to meet an acceptable level. If the test is very short and extending it does not exceed time limits for testing, a longer test might be used to raise the reliability estimate to an acceptable level. However, if the original test took 45 to 60 minutes, the new one will consume 3 to 10 hours—obviously too long a time.

Homogeneous Content

A content area which has sequential or tightly organized subject matter is expected to reveal higher reliability coefficients than tests in areas where subject matter is diverse and loosely organized. For example, tests in mathematics and foreign languages are more likely to have high reliability coefficients than coefficients for tests in philosophy and sociology.

A test over a limited section of a larger discipline would be expected to have a higher reliability coefficient than a test which covers the complete discipline. A high school test over algebra would probably have a higher reliability coefficient than a test over high school mathematics. Likewise, a test on high school mathematics is expected to have a higher coefficient of reliability than a test of the same length covering all subjects of secondary school.*

Higher reliability for homogeneous content results from the interdependence of principles and facts making for consistency of the responses. These statements are made with the assumption that all other factors which contribute to the degree of reliability are constant for both kinds of tests.

Ability Range

Correlational and variance techniques used to measure reliability are both affected by the heterogeneity of the group. The more heterogeneous the group is, the more opportunity there is for coefficients to reflect high test reliability. Test scores derived from a restricted age group, grade level or other selection bases cannot be expected to generate reliability coefficients as large as groups with large variances in important characteristics.

Appropriate Items

The tasks on the test must be appropriate for the experiential and maturational levels of the students. A test that is made up of tasks that are too difficult for students will cause them to guess at responses and will result in inconsistent measures. Tests that are too easy do not allow for meaningful estimates of test reliability because they do not have enough difference in measures. A well-developed test will show higher reliability estimates when administered to groups who vary widely in achievement or ability than when

---

*Test battery composite scores have higher reliability than the individual tests primarily because of the increased length of the test when the subtest scores are combined for the overall composite.

it is administered to homogeneous groups. The added reliability is a result of measures being distributed over a greater range and does not negate the need for appropriate tasks.

Difficulty levels of test items affect reliability in two ways, and to overcome effects of difficulty, items should be written so that they are of medium difficulty. First, any item which is answered correctly by all respondents or which is missed by all respondents contributes nothing to reliability. A test which allows a high percentage of correct answers or which restricts correct responses to a small percentage of students can contribute little to reliability. Second, unless an item is of medium difficulty, it has little chance to discriminate levels of achievement—discriminating items are important to increased test reliability.

Ambiguity is an enemy to reliability for two reasons. First, whenever items are ambiguous, students will guess at responses thus reducing the test's reliability. Second, unless an item is clearly written to present a well-defined task and the answer is definite, the discrimination power of the test will be reduced.

Scoring Accuracy

Any errors made in scoring a test will affect the reliability of that test. The item which is incorrectly scored wrong as well as the item that is incorrectly *not* scored wrong will affect the reliability by inserting erroneous data about the student's performance. Assuming a properly prepared key, the problem of reducing reliability of objectively scored items through scoring errors is of little concern, if it is of concern at all.

Lack of scoring accuracy for essay tests has been a major contributing factor to low reliability of those tests. If the judge (the scorer) of student responses cannot be consistent in scoring, test reliability will be drastically reduced. As mentioned earlier, objectivity in scoring responses can help overcome this major difficulty associated with essay test procedures. At best, the scoring of most essay responses is less accurate than test specialists would like, causing the reliability coefficients for many essay tests to be at less than desired levels.

Testing Conditions

If students are to be expected to perform consistently, the environmental conditions for testing must be maintained as near to ideal standards as possible and constant between testing sessions. Such things as room temperature, noise level, interruptions, and other similar distractions can affect reliability coefficients.

Classroom conditions, teacher rapport, and home conditions contribute to the motivation levels of students. Students who are at a low level of motivation may have little drive and answer items at random or with little attention to the task which has been presented on the test. Too high a motivation level may cause certain students to be too anxious and reduce their level of functioning thus affecting test reliability. Although test anxiety is not considered to be a major problem in testing, lack of motivation must be looked upon as a serious threat to reported reliability with certain populations of students and with individual students in all populations. Test consistency (reliability) is a function of consistency in student behavior.

Speededness

One other source of higher reliability coefficients is the **speededness** of a test. A test which measures how fast someone can react to test tasks is expected to have higher reliability coefficients than one which all or nearly all students can complete in the time provided for the test. Speededness is mentioned separately because the increase in the coefficient is *not* from an acceptable source as interpreted by test theory. Scores on a speeded test measure both ability and speed. When a test is divided, the component of speed appears almost identical in each part, therefore increasing the coefficient. To control for this, most students should comfortably complete all items on a classroom test. In most cases the concern of objectives is not how quickly students can perform a task but rather whether they can complete the task to satisfaction or not.

Sometimes speed is important and, of course, the reliability coefficients are not artificially inflated for these tests. In a test of a true measure of speed, examinees are often provided a series of simple tasks for which they are not being measured for any element except speed. Here ability is kept constant between groups for any reliability measure, and the reliability would not be affected. A test of speed to measure a type of reaction time could require the student to choose the larger number from a set of pairs of numerals. A partial list of 500 pairs might look like this:

List A	List B
4	9
5	4
0	14
7	3
.	.
.	.

If a middle-school examinee were asked to mark an A or a B to indicate the greater number for each pair, all students would be expected to get nearly all answers correct with only a very small number of errors. However, if the students were given only one minute to complete all 500 tasks, the scores would vary according to quickness in response. Speededness is necessary here and controlled by a very short time length and should be measured for a *speed* test.

Skill tests which involve speed as a desirable factor would include typing, shorthand, reading, and others. Reliability coefficients for tests like these are not artificially increased by the speededness of the test, since they are intended to measure how quickly a person can complete tasks.

Factors that Effect Reliability

In general the reliability coefficient will be greater for:

1. a long test than for a short one.
2. a test over homogeneous content rather than heterogeneous content.
3. a set of scores from a group of examinees with a wide ability range which causes a wide achievement score range rather than from a group which has members much alike.
4. a test composed of well-written and appropriate items.
5. measures with few scoring errors than for measures which vary from test to test or paper to paper because of scoring procedures alone.
6. test scores obtained by proper conditions for testing and students with optimum motivation.

In general the reliability coefficient will be lower for:

1. a test which is too short.
2. content which is heterogeneous.
3. a test of poorly written items.
4. many items of very low or very high difficulty.
5. poorly discriminating items.
6. a test with poor format.
7. a very homogeneous group on important contributing factors.
8. a test which has been scored with many errors or variability in evaluating responses.
9. poor testing conditions.
10. a low level of motivation for examinees.

Identification of sources which affect a reliability coefficient direct attention to these sources in the entire process of test planning. The error from the factors which adversely affect reliability must be minimized while factors which increase reliability are maximized. The unreliability of a test is a function of the variability introduced by the measurement process, and increased reliability depends on control of the variability so introduced.

SUMMARY

Test reliability has been presented as the consistency with which a test can generate measures of student attributes. Higher reliability measures are obtained as chance errors associated with the complete process of testing are reduced. The type of reliability to be investigated causes one to focus on specific sources which might reduce reliability estimates.

High reliability estimates for test-retest procedures depend heavily on the consistency of the examinees from one testing session to a second regardless of the other factors. Assuming that factors other than examinee consistency are optimum, then special steps should be taken to assure as high a level of consistency within examinees as is possible. All facets of the testing procedures should be identical in each test administration.

Reliability estimates for equivalent forms of tests will be at higher levels if the samples of the test items chosen are representative of the population of items which could be written from the content to be covered. Formats of each test should be the same. Directions and time limits must be identical.

Most important to the classroom test which uses only one test administration to supply data for estimates of reliability are those aspects affecting internal consistency. Ambiguous test items can reduce reliability estimates substantially. Length of the test is important. Both of these can be controlled by the teacher who makes the test. The heterogeneity of the group is probably already decided for classroom tests, and little if anything can be done to control this factor. Since most classrooms are composed of students appropriate for group instruction, the characteristics of importance to class instruction and to test reliability have built-in problems for obtaining high reliability estimates.

Test reliability in general will be higher when student-centered factors of motivation, health, fatigue, and emotional state, and environmental factors of temperature, noise, and such are optimal. Higher reliability will result from control of instrument-centered factors of item sampling, instrument construction, and scoring of student papers.

Study of relationships and variances generates coefficients as estimates of reliability. Correlation procedures were discussed to show the computation of reliability coefficients and Kuder-Richardson formulas were mentioned as additional ways to estimate test reliability. The standard error of measurement and its computation was discussed to allow another way to approach the study of test scores as they compare to associated true scores.

Reliability coefficients must be interpreted in the context of how certain conditions might affect the size of the coefficient. A test with a high level of speededness, a long test, or high-quality items will increase reliability estimates. A wide ability range of students will allow for high reliability estimates while homogeneous groups tend to have lower estimates for reliability. Scoring and reading accuracy are needed for high reliability estimates. Ideal testing conditions contribute to higher reliability while poor testing conditions or poor administration procedures can reduce reliability coefficients.

Coefficients of reliability are the best statistical data available to the teacher who is striving to determine the degree of success in testing and who is making efforts to improve future tests. One major aspect of test validity is the degree to which a test measures with consistency.

The next chapter will deal with an even more important factor of measuring instruments. That characteristic has to do with how well a test or any measuring instrument does what it is used to do. Within the framework of being able to do what it is used to do is the element of being able to do what it is supposed to do with consistency. Therefore, the reliability which has been discussed becomes a prerequisite for validity. However, reliability alone cannot establish the characteristic of validity. The next chapter augments consideration of the element of reliability by discussing other factors which must be present to establish validity for a test.

NEW TECHNICAL TERMS LISTED IN THE GLOSSARY

Confidence interval
Correlation
Correlation coefficient
Equivalence
Equivalent-forms reliability
Examinee reliability
Horizontal axis
Internal consistency
Kuder-Richardson (K-R)
   formulas
Linear tendency
Obtained test score
Pearson product-moment
   correlation (r)
Rho (ρ)

Sampling distribution
Scattergram
Scorer reliability
Spearman-Brown formula
Speededness
Split-half reliability
Stability
Standard error
Standard error of
   measurement
Test reliability
Test-retest
True test score
Variance
Vertical axis

ACTIVITY EXERCISES

1. Establish a reliability estimate for the following data.
   a. Calculate the correlation coefficient, r, using the odd- and even-numbered items.
   b. Figure the r for the total test using the Spearman-Brown formula.

Student	Scores	
	Odd items	Even items
Rick	10	8
Henry	14	11
Katy	16	20
Shelia	14	22
Mary	9	5
Jim	18	12
Susan	15	17

2. The standard deviation for a set of test scores is 7 and the correlation coefficient is .85. Compute the standard error of measurement and establish confidence intervals of 68 percent and 95 percent for a raw score of 40.

3. With a sheet of paper cover the two columns—Type of Reliability Measure and Procedure—in "Figure 11.1, Ways of estimating test reliability." Complete the columns and compare your work with the figure.

4. Obtain a technical report or test manual for a standardized test and peruse the reliability information provided. What is your reaction to the thoroughness of information and the reported reliability of the instrument?

FOR DISCUSSION

1. List the factors that can affect test reliability and briefly describe the sources of lowered or increased reliability.

2. Explain why the standard error of measurement is especially helpful to a teacher who wants to interpret a single test score or to compare two test scores on a test.

3. Write from memory how you as a classroom teacher could use the split-halves procedure to establish the reliability of a classroom test.

4. Use a set of scattergrams and a discussion section to explain the principle of correlation.

REFERENCES AND KNOWLEDGE EXTENDERS

ANASTASI, A. Psychological testing (5th ed.). New York: Macmillan, 1982.

BERK, R. A. (Ed.). Criterion-referenced measurement: The state of the art. Baltimore: Johns Hopkins University Press, 1980.

BRENNAN, R. L. Applications of generalizability theory. In R. A. Berk (Ed.), Criterion-referenced measurement: The state of the art. Baltimore: Johns Hopkins University Press, 1980.

CRONBACH, L. J. Essentials of psychological testing (3rd ed.). New York: Harper & Row, 1970. Chap. 6, pp. 151–193.

EBEL, R. L. Essentials of educational measurement (3rd ed.). Englewood Cliffs, NJ: Prentice-Hall, 1979. Chap. 14, pp. 274–295.

GRONLUND, N. E. Measurement and evaluation in teaching (4th ed.). New York: Macmillan, 1981. Chap. 4, pp. 93–120.

HAMBLETON, R. K., SWAMINATHAN, H., ALGINA, J., & COULSON, D. B. Criterion-referenced testing and measurement: A review of technical issues and development. Review of Educational Research, 1978, 48, 1–47.

SAX, G. Principles of educational and psychological measurement and evaluation (2nd ed.). Belmont, CA: Wadsworth, 1980. Chap. 9, pp. 255–287.

SUBHOVIAK, M. J. Decision-consistency approaches. In R. A. Berk (Ed.), Criterion-referenced measurement: The state of the art. Baltimore: Johns Hopkins University Press, 1980.

THORNDIKE, R. L. Reliability. In E. F. Lindquist (Ed.), Educational measurement. Washington, D.C.: American Council on Education, 1951. Chap. 15, pp. 560–620.

THORNDIKE, R. L., & HAGEN, E. Measurement and evaluation in psychology and education (4th ed.). New York: Wiley, 1977. Pp. 73–102.

Chapter 12. Establishing Test Validity

After study of Chapter 12, you should be able to:

1. Explain how a teacher would establish content validity for a classroom test.
2. Identify and differentiate among the four types of test validation and the particular type of testing associated with each.
3. Explain why the degree of validity must be stated in reference to the use of test scores and characteristics of the individuals who took the test.
4. Discuss how the tasks on an achievement test can be considered as an operational definition of achievement.
5. Explain how each glossary term listed at the end of the chapter is used in classroom measurement and evaluation.

In the preceding chapter reliability was developed as a necessary but not sufficient condition to establish validity for a measuring instrument. To be valid a test must not only be consistent in what it does, but more importantly, it must measure what it is intended to measure. With this in mind it follows that the most important characteristic of a test is validity. Any attempt to increase the adequacy of a test is either directly or indirectly related to the improvement of that test's validity. A well-constructed test that rates high in balance and specificity as well as having a high level of reliability will be a valid test. As you can see a large portion of the material in this book covers topics intended to increase validity of classroom test scores. *All good testing practices support validity.*

Every test is constructed to measure some characteristic. A test is valid to the degree that it accurately measures that characteristic. An intelligence test is valid to the degree that a student's score on it indicates a true measure of the capacity to function at a particular intellectual level. Two students who have different capacities should have that difference shown to the same degree in the difference between their test scores. A test of intelligence that fails to reflect those differences adequately in test scores is not performing its function and therefore lacks validity. A test that is constructed to measure achievement in Life Science I should generate test scores that reflect students' capacities to deal with topics covered in a first course devoted to study of fundamental biological concepts. The degree to which the test measures those capacities determines the degree of validity for the test.

Most classroom tests are prepared to measure student achievement. A measure for a specific student is important information about that student's progress toward stated or implied goals. If the classroom activities within the school program have been planned and sequenced with the educational objectives in mind, then the test scores collectively should give additional information about how successful the program has been in moving students toward those objectives. This can be accomplished only when a test is a highly valid instrument for measurement. Valid tests are necessary to help make useful judgments about the students who took the test and to assess the educational program designed to move those students to desired goals.

The use of published tests of achievement and tests used to measure other characteristics also requires that the tests have acceptable levels of validity. The classroom teacher has a better opportunity to build valid achievement tests for a particular class of students than standardized test makers do, because that teacher knows more than anyone else about what content has been covered and the behaviors expected. Constructors of published achievement tests are not able to build specificity into a test as well as classroom teachers, since their tests are designed for use in a wide range of classes with different objectives, different combinations of subject-matter topics studied, and different emphasis on the several topics. Published achievement tests report validity estimates for **norm groups** and usually have an acceptable level for validity. These tests tend to lose their validity as the characteristics of the group being tested depart from the characteristics of the norm group. The teacher has the best *opportunity* to build and to select standardized tests with high validity, especially when consideration is given to how well a test reflects the content which has been studied and the specific behaviors to be exhibited to show goal attainment. However, there is no guarantee that a classroom test has higher validity for a specific use than a published test.

As this implies, tests as used in the educational setting should not be classified as either totally valid or totally invalid but must be conceived as being valid to a particular degree. It stands to reason that the concept of a completely invalid test exists, but testing in schools never results in entirely invalid measures. For example, a test which is valid for measuring physics achievement loses its validity if used by the teacher of United States history to measure understanding of the contributing causes of the Civil War. Likewise, a highly valid vocabulary test is likely to lose its validity if used to measure reading comprehension, and a highly valid arithmetic test for fourth grade loses its validity if used to measure mathematics achievement in the nineth grade. The validity of a test is relative to a specific situation and depends on a unique set of circumstances. A test which has high validity for one purpose or use may have moderate or low validity for another purpose or use. The question asked in regard to validity is—How valid is this test for supplying the information needed to make the required judgment?

In summary, three points must be kept in mind when establishing the degree of validity for a test: first, validity is always specific to some particular use; second, validity is a matter of degree and does not exist on an all-or-nothing basis; and third, validity pertains to the results of a test and is only indirectly related to the instrument itself.

TYPES OF VALIDITY

When establishing validity, the type of validity becomes important. In general, three types of validity—**content, criterion-related** (includes **concurrent** and **predictive**) and **construct**— are considered for educational and psychological tests. The different types of validity are important for the classroom teacher in building tests and for selection of psychological standardized tests.

Since the degree of validity of a test indicates the usefulness and the uses of tests vary, different types of validity must be considered depending on the aims of the testing. For tests developed in the classroom the most important type of validity to be concerned about is content validity. A classroom achievement test measures how a student performs at the time of testing (concurrently). Some forecasts (predictions) may be made for the student based on the test scores. The test also deals with the concept of achievement (a construct). For these reasons the other types of validity must be given consideration, although to a lesser degree. Published achievement tests are also primarily concerned with content validity. Published tests for other characteristics of aptitude, personality, and such, on the other hand, are probably more concerned with one or more of the other types of validity although content validity remains a concern for all tests, both classroom and published.

Content Validity

For a measuring instrument of achievement to have a high degree of content validity, the test must sample the subject matter studied in such a way that the tasks on the test reflect classroom emphasis. The test should sample a cross section of content and emphasize important topics but give less attention to less important topics. In other words, the test tasks should be distributed through the subject matter topics listed vertically in the table of specifications in the same proportions as indicated by the table.

The degree of *content validity* is a result of how well the cross-sectional sample of items represents the content of instruction. A test's validity is lowered when the relative importance of topics is different for the test than the instructional emphasis given to the topics. Even in the same subject at the same grade levels, teachers may vary the emphasis they give to particular topics, thus necessitating the establishment of validity for each classroom instrument by balancing test emphasis with classroom emphasis.

In Chapter 5 the table of specifications was presented as a device to build test balance of content and behaviors to support test validity. In the table, percentages (or numbers) of test items were assigned to subject-matter topics to build within the test stress on very important topics and less coverage on less important topics. Likewise the other dimension of the table distributed behaviors across those actions deemed to be most important for the students to develop.

Test instruments other than achievement tests also need content validity. Tests for scholastic aptitude and personal-social development must be made up of a sample of all possible tasks, and therefore selection of the sample is important. But other types of validity increase in importance when dealing with measurement of psychological factors such as ability, aptitude, and interest and overshadow content validity.

Criterion-Related Validity

Two types of validity—concurrent and predictive—are referred to as criterion-related, since each is based on comparison of test scores to an external criterion of actual performance. Concurrent and predictive validity are exactly the same except for the element of time. The only difference between them is the time that the criterion variable is incorporated into the use of the test results—present performance is associated with concurrent validity while future performance is associated with predictive validity (see Figure 12.1).

Concurrent validity			Predictive validity		
Test scores of September 15	correlated with	Criterion of September 15	Test scores of September 15	correlated with	Criterion of May 15
Present	to	Present	Present	to	Future

FIGURE 12.1. Comparison of the two types of criterion-related validity

Any criterion is a standard used for comparison and serves as a direct measure of the trait performance to be used in the correlation. Disagreement over what the criterion for success may be is likely to occur. Thus the teacher who uses published tests must know precisely what the criterion was, so that the degree of validity for the test can be established for use in that teacher's classes.

Concurrent validity

A test of English usage is intended to measure how a student uses the English language. If students' test scores correlate highly with their actual use of English in a natural, real-world situation, then the test is said to have a high degree of *concurrent validity*. If those students who score low on the test are found to use poor English in natural settings and those who score high use good English, then the test may be used to generalize from test scores to real-world situations. This type of validity is of particular importance whenever artificial situations are created to replace observation in a natural setting. A test which has shown the ability to measure present performance beyond the testing situation is said to have a high degree of concurrent validity.

Predictive validity

Some tests are designed to make predictions about future performance. If students' test scores correlate highly with their actual performance some time in the future, then the test is said to have *predictive validity*. Before selecting participants for a company-sponsored class in shorthand, the personnel department would want to choose those employees who could benefit most from the course. A test could be used to identify those persons who have the best chance of high performance in taking and transcribing shorthand. For a test to do this well, it must select high future performance from test scores obtained before the study of shorthand commenced. Low test scores should indicate low future performance while high test scores should indicate high future performance. If the test can forecast well, it is said to have acceptable predictive validity.

Construct Validity

A construct is a characteristic which is deemed to exist to explain some type of behavior. Certain basic aspects of behavior appear to be located in a highly related function. That function is referred to as a construct. No one has ever seen a construct—if you could see it, it would not be a construct. Hostility is not visible. No one has seen hostility; however, some agreement has been reached about how hostility is exhibited by human actions. Underlying the construct of hostility is a psychological theory which explains this phenomenon. Hostility would be measured by the degree that someone exhibits actions considered to be hostile in nature.

Construct validity is an indication of the relationship between what a theory predicts and what test scores show. Suppose that the word "temperature" is invented to describe the amount of heat in the air. A measuring instrument to indicate the temperature should perform the way that the theory of temperature explains happenings to various substances at different levels of heat. Further suppose that a glass tube with a bulb at one end is partially filled with mercury and a numerical measuring scale is placed along the side of the glass tube and is used to measure temperature. If the measuring instrument performs the same way that a theory about temperature effects on mercury predicts, the measuring instrument would have construct validity. Most thermometers have a high degree of construct validity because they perform much the way scientists predict changes in the fluid for different temperatures.

Barometers do much the same for air pressure and also have a high degree of construct validity.*

In the classroom many constructs are employed to explain student action. Teachers are concerned with motivation, aspiration, timidness, dominance, intelligence, creativity, ad infinitum. Associated with each of these is a group of highly related student behaviors. The classroom teacher who selects published tests to be used in the classroom to measure a construct must investigate the degree that the test has construct validity. Test manuals and test inspection can be used to determine whether the test has acceptable construct validity. A measurement instrument which is believed to measure a specific construct must be validated by showing that student performance on the test demonstrates behaviors assumed by the theory to be related to the construct. If a test has high *construct validity,* scores on the test will vary from student to student the same way that the theory for that construct would predict. A high level of construct validity provides support to the theory underlying the construct and the test can then be used to measure the construct. Cronbach and Meehl (1955) say:

> Construct validity must be investigated whenever no criterion or universe of content is accepted as entirely adequate to define the quality to be measured. Determining what psychological constructs account for test performance is desirable for almost any test. (p. 282)

Construct validity for classroom achievement tests shows agreement about what constitutes achievement in the topics covered in instruction. Construct validity for standardized tests which deal with psychological traits and which are used in the educational setting must be stated by the test authors in the manual of the test by comparing test results to accepted theory.

DETERMINATION OF TEST VALIDITY

Procedures commonly used to determine the degree of validity for tests are:

1. Comparison of test content with subject-matter content.
2. Comparison of test performance with performance on a criterion.
3. Theory validation.

The degree of validity is always made by a comparison. The comparison will be different for the several kinds of validity, and since more than one type of validity is connected with most tests, the investigation of test validity will

---

*The idea of temperature and pressure as constructs may not fit the definition of psychological constructs exactly but is used here for pedagogical reasons.

be made through more than one comparison. The comparison for each type of validity is discussed in one of the sections which follow.

Content Validity

For classroom teachers who make their own achievement tests content validity is the most important type of validity. Constructors of published achievement tests are also primarily concerned with content validity; however, they are aware of the problem of establishing content validity for an achievement test used in many different classrooms.

The degree of content validity for an achievement test is determined by making a comparison of the content of the test with the content of classroom instruction. This approach is based on the premise that if the teaching has been directed by educational objectives and the test reflects the teaching, then the test will measure how well the educational objectives have been achieved by individuals and by the class as a whole.

The tasks set by criterion-referenced and other mastery tests are compared to educational objectives or a behavioral domain to see that there are test items for each objective or tied to a well-defined behavior domain. Unlike the performance objective which may be demonstrated by a single act, determination of whether a student has reached an objective through a classroom paper-and-pencil test requires more than one item for each objective or domain. In criterion-referenced measurement (CRM), test items are keyed to a set of objectives. "CRM is designed to yield information directly relevant to the level or quality of behaviors that the examinee is capable of performing" (Gilman, 1974, p. 7). This direct comparison of test items to objectives or a domain makes the determination for the degree of content validity for CRM relatively easy.

Investigation of the degree of content validity for norm-referenced measurement (NRM) becomes an exercise in inquiry about the adequacy of the sample items to reflect the total instruction. The best way to determine content validity for a norm-referenced test is to associate each item on the test with a subject-matter topic. The test has content validity if students are asked to demonstrate the skills and competencies that instruction is to develop for the learner. This procedure is much like the inverse of making a table of specifications. Rather than setting percentages for subject-matter topics and behaviors and then writing items to fit the "table," the items can be fit to subject-matter topics and behaviors. A test has content validity if the behavior and subject matter asked for in the items correspond to the subject matter and behavior identified in the specific objectives. Then actual percentages from the test can be compared to ideal percentages based on instructional emphasis. Any deviation between the two percentages reduces the degree of content validity. For example, if a test has 5 percent of its items on a subject-matter topic that has been given 20 percent of the emphasis in classroom instruction the validity of the test for measuring in that classroom is reduced considerably.

The preceding technique has been used successfully by teachers and groups of teachers who are selecting published tests to be used in the classroom or as a part of a schoolwide testing program. By working back through the test items to determine subject-matter topic emphasis, the content validity for published tests in a specific setting can be made. If several tests are being evaluated, comparisons of different emphases of the tests can be made to see which best fits the content offered and stressed in a class or throughout the school system.

The teacher who has developed a test from a table of specifications (Figure 12.2) has built in a feature for establishing content validity. A comparison of items to subject-matter topics as stated in the table is direct, and if table percentages fit well with objectives, a high degree of content validity has been

Behavior / Topics of subject matter	A Knowledge		B Comprehension		C Application		Totals	
	% of test	No. of items	% of test	No. of items	% of test	No. of items	% of test	No. of items
1. Vocabulary development	20	4	5	1	0	0	25	5
2. Reading comprehension	10	2	25	5	15	3	50	10
3. Sentence construction	0	0	0	0	25	5	25	5
Totals	30	6	30	6	40	8	100	20

___a___ 1. ¿ Que significa "rubio"?
    a. persona con puo amarillo
    b. tipo de joya
    c. del color rojo
    d. tipo de empacedado
    (Cell 1 A — vocabulary development, knowledge)

___d___ 2. ¿ Que significa "querer a"?
    a. amore
    b. amante
    c. amarrar
    d. amar
    (Cell 1 B — vocabulary development, comprehension)

FIGURE 12.2. Table of specifications and sample items for a unit in Spanish

established. A teacher should make a judgment about the degree of content validity for classroom tests. If possible a second judgment by a knowledgeable colleague can be used to supplement that judgment as a check on bias. A personal judgment supported by an outside estimate is even more valuable than either one alone and encourages teachers to construct more valid and meaningful tests.

Published test makers include test items for an achievement test which are based on components of instruction common to a large portion of classrooms throughout the region where the test is to be used. For most published tests the geographic region is the United States. Test makers survey courses of study, textbook series, teachers' emphases of topics in their classrooms, and experts in the area to be tested to direct the content of the test and the writing of specific items for the test. With this background information they build a table of specifications for the test based on the content of instruction for a typical situation. Published achievement tests are, therefore, based primarily on the core content of the subject. Since the emphasis is on the core, any published achievement test will fail to cover topics specific to a given classroom and for this reason the content validity will be reduced. Published test results should not be used as the only measure of a given student's classroom achievement nor should those results for a given class be used to assess the teacher's effectiveness in that classroom, because classroom curriculum should augment the core with topics needed for the peculiarities of the unique situation of every classroom.

Another approach to establishing content validity is used for published tests which deal with aptitude, personality, interest, and other characteristics of the affective domain. It identifies the content of testing devices through factor analysis. "This procedure identifies the underlying components of behavior and tells us to what extent each item (or subtest in a battery) reflects each component. The procedure is typically used in identifying the content of aptitude tests, interest, and personality inventories" (Chase, 1978, p. 75).

Establishment of validity for classroom tests cannot be done by any straightforward statistical procedure. It becomes primarily a matter of presenting a logical approach to establish content validity. The procedure is facilitated by clearly stated objectives and a table of specifications which bridges the test items to instruction and in turn to the objectives. The fourth component of the process of education—collection of information—provides the data needed to make judgments about effectiveness of school programs to move students to desired goals and to make judgments about individual progress. Tests without a high degree of content validity cannot be expected to provide highly valid data, and without content validity for the tests the judgments based partly or wholly on that information will also lack validity.

Criterion-Related Validity

Establishment of the degree of concurrent or predictive validity is straightforward through a study of relationships. Since each of these types is concerned about how test scores relate to some external criterion, the relationship between test scores and values on the criterion can be made by correlation. When used in this way, the correlation coefficient is referred to as a **coefficient of validity.** The higher the coefficient of validity the greater the relationship between the two sets of measures. If high test scores are associated with high criterion values, middle with middle, and low with low, high validity coefficients will result.

Concurrent validity

If the criterion is present status, then the test scores are intended to measure behavior which would be exhibited in a different situation but concurrently. The procedure for establishing the degree of validity for present status is exactly the same as the procedure for establishing predictive validity (see next section) with the exception of the time when the data on the criterion variable are gathered. The criterion measures will be collected in the present rather than in the future. The two sets of scores are correlated (see Figure 12.3) to provide a coefficient of concurrent validity as an indication of how well test scores agree with present performance.

Predictive validity

If the criterion is future performance, then the validity coefficient will reflect the ability of the test scores to forecast future performance. To estimate the predictive validity for a test's score, the test is administered to a group of subjects. Much effort already has been expended to put together a set of tasks intended to forecast some future behavior. After a considerable time interval information on the predicted variable is gathered from each subject who took the test. With two sets of data from the same set of subjects the coefficient of predictive validity can be computed.

To establish predictive validity for a test designed to forecast expected success in a shorthand class, a set of scores would be obtained from a set of subjects who are ready to undertake the shorthand course. This test will, of course, be built from items which are intended to identify those who will do well in shorthand study and those who will not do well. At the end of the course a measure of the shorthand ability of each participant will be made. The two sets of scores are correlated (see Figure 12.4) and a coefficient of predictive validity is established for the test as an indication of what forecasting power future scores on the test can be expected to have when used again.

Construct Validity

All psychological tests are designed to measure some construct but constructs are *not* tested. Properly considered, the theory behind the construct is tested. Establishment of construct validity is basically theory validation. Creativity is a construct which seems to be important to those persons engaged in the education of children. Construct validity for creativity tests is often

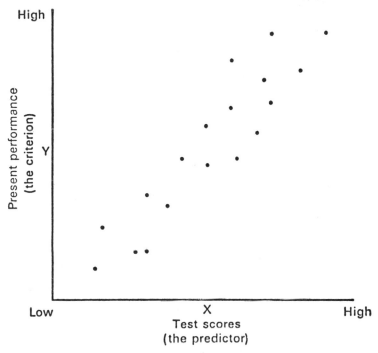

FIGURE 12.3. Test scores used to estimate present
performance

difficult to establish because it is difficult to define. Some other constructs are
equally difficult to deal with while those which can be defined so that there
is general agreement about how one exhibits the construct are easier to deal
with.

If a set of behaviors which describe a construct can be identified, then
a test to measure the behaviors should rank those who take the test in the same
degree that they possess the set of behaviors. To validate a test through
construct validity, the construct must be precisely described as a set of behaviors. The difficulty in establishing construct validity for creativity is based on
the fact that no set of behaviors which represent the construct is commonly
agreed upon. Although a high school English teacher may be speaking of a
different kind of creativity when she asks students to be creative in writing
themes than the type of creativity expected from art students who are working
in ceramics there seem to be common components to both teachers' use of the
term *creativity*. It may be that creativity is not a single construct, but one
construct underlies creativity in writing and another creativity in ceramics.
Without common agreement about what creativity is, the theory does not
permit valid predictions about behavior when conditions are manipulated.

To build a test with a high degree of construct validity, the construct
must be well described by a set of behaviors. Then the test results should agree
with predictions made from the theory. Evidence of agreement can come from

FIGURE 12.4. Test scores used to predict future performance

one or more sources. Cronbach and Meehl (281–302) indicate that evidence of construct validity could be established in one or more of many methods. Three that are widely used are:

1. Comparison of how well one sample of subjects who score high on the construct compares to another sample of subjects who score low on the construct. If a test is intended to measure anxiety, then those subjects who exhibit behaviors of anxiety should score higher on the test than those who do not exhibit behaviors of anxiety.

2. Results of a test should correlate highly with results of other tests which measure the construct. All tests which have validity for a given construct should correlate highly when compared one to another. However, if the obtained correlation is not as great as expected, there is no way to identify the source of difficulty as resting in test A, test B, or the explanation of the construct.

3. Comparison of how scores on the test change when conditions contributing to the theory are changed. Certain conditions can reduce anxiety within individuals. If anxious subjects are administered conditions to reduce anxiety, then anxiety test scores after treatment should be significantly less than test scores before treatment.

All validation of construct validity rests on one's acceptance of a test author's theory of the construct. A user of a test must accept the test writer's theory of the construct to accept the author's validation of the test. The final analysis for construct validity is made by the user of the test in regard to how well the author's theory and the related set of behaviors explains the construct to the one using the test.

Each of the four types of test validation is associated with a particular type of testing. Figure 12.5 shows the relationships of the type of validity with the respective type of testing. The procedure of validation is also presented as an aid to pointing up likenesses and differences in validation procedures.

Type of Validity	Type of Testing	Procedure for Validation
Content	Classroom achievement tests Published achievement tests	Compare the items and behaviors exhibited to the content of classroom instructional emphasis and desired behaviors
Concurrent (Criterion-related)	Tests used in selection and classification, expecially intelligence and aptitude tests	Compare the test scores to an external criterion of actual present performance
Predictive (Criterion-related)	Tests used in selection and classification, expecially intelligence and aptitude tests	Compare the test scores to an external criterion of actual performance obtained sometime after the test scores have been obtained
Construct	Any test which is to measure a psychological construct	Show that student performance on a test demonstrates behaviors assumed by the theory to be related to the construct

FIGURE 12.5. Four types of validation

What Kind of Validity?

Throughout the discussion of determination of validity, each type of validity has been discussed separately. When determining the validity of the test as a whole, the degree of validity will rest on how well it meets standards in all of the types which are important for that particular test. Content validity is of major importance for achievement tests and should receive more weight in the final analysis than concurrent, predictive, and construct validity which are of lesser importance. Certain aptitude tests (e.g., intelligence tests) and personality scales (e.g., motivation) are based on some content, but construct validity is of greatest importance. For scholastic aptitude tests the other types of validity take a back seat to predictive validity, since these test scores are used primarily to indicate expected future performance levels in the school environment or later in life.

The way the scores on the test are to be used largely determines the type of validity to be given emphasis. The degree of validity must be stated in reference to the use of test scores and characteristics of the persons who take the test. A highly valid physics test for an introductory course loses its validity when used to measure achievement levels of advanced physics students. A highly valid mathematics test for measuring levels of concept attainment for sixth-grade students would lose its validity if it were administered to second-grade students. A highly valid test for a unit in colonial history for one fifth-grade class may be a very poor measuring instrument for the same unit taught in another fifth-grade class in the same school building if different objectives and content were the basis for instructional activities.

Test validity must also be investigated as to the sampling of behaviors. A test which is constructed to measure a particular level of behavior must contain tasks which elicit that behavior. A test of understanding would not be valid if all or nearly all the test items require the student to use only recall of facts at the knowledge level. A test which is highly valid in measuring at the knowledge level will fall short of measuring in the higher cognitive levels and thus lose its validity if used to measure higher levels.

To summarize how validity for a specific administration of a specific test is to be estimated, the following points must be considered:

1. How well the test measured that which it was used to measure.
2. The appropriateness of the test for the person or persons who were measured.
3. The skill used in administering the test and interpreting the scores.

TESTS AS OPERATIONAL DEFINITIONS

A classroom teacher has another way to check validity for tests The tasks on any test define in operations what the test measures. In this way, each test is an operational definition of whatever it measures. Direct validation of the test can be made by making a comparison of what the test demands from a student with what the teacher feels is important for students to know.

If a test on the Civil War requires a student to associate an important event for each of 30 dates from the Civil War years, then that is the test constructor's definition for achievement about that time period. A test that requires students to deal with interrelationships of economics, social forces, and political aspects at work before and during the Civil War gives an entirely different definition of achievement about the Civil War. Obviously, different teachers will have different operational definitions for the same topic or topics. After constructing a test, the teacher should see if the test is a good operational definition of what should be measured. Ebel (1979) stresses this for all test makers when he says:

> Much thinking and writing about educational goals and outcomes is vaguer than it ought to be because words like "intelligence," "motivation," and "creativity" are

used freely without definite specification, and probably without any definite conception of the operational definition. (p. 301)

The heart of any validation of a test rests in clarifying what should be measured and comparing that to what the test does measure.

IMPROVING VALIDITY FOR DATA-COLLECTING DEVICES

When a teacher is faced with making judgments about student status and program effectiveness, many devices are available to collect the data needed to make those judgments. If decisions based on those judgments are to be valid, then all devices, not just tests, need to be investigated for validity of the generated data and improvements of procedures made.

Classroom Tests

Since most tests developed by classroom teachers are achievement tests, content validity is of primary importance to those persons. To increase the degree of content validity of classroom tests attention should be directed to special details of planning and constructing those tests.

A teacher must have a set of educational objectives generated from the needs of the students to form a basis for developing appropriate instructional activities and to serve as a sounding board for tasks on tests. These objectives will consist of general goals which would apply to students in widely diverse geographic and cultural divisions, and also objectives specific to the class which is being tested. If the instruction has been geared to these important goals and objectives and a test is composed of tasks that measure the degree to which the student has reached the goals and objectives, then the test can be said to be a valid test. It may be either standardized or teacher-made.

The competent teacher who is aware of the need for an adequate sample of content and behaviors will probably use a table of specifications to build a balance between those items which appear on the test and the relative importance of the content topics and behaviors. To be assured that the test's tasks do correspond to expected behaviors, the teacher must select from the types of test items those which elicit the desired behavior. Some item types (e.g., multiple-choice) are very versatile in sampling behaviors, but they also have some limitations. Some item types are limited to sampling one type of behavior (e.g., completion is limited to sampling recall of facts). All types of selected-response, constructed-response, and problem items should be considered when choosing test tasks, and the specific type chosen should be relevant to sample the type of behavior expected from the student.

Validity of classroom tests can be reduced by trying to measure aspects of student behavior which are better left to devices other than tests. Tests for classroom use are limited to measuring verbal and mathematical aspects of the desired outcomes. Classroom tests should avoid components which measure to any great extent aptitude or personal-social factors because validity may be adversely affected. It is understood that more intelligent students can be expected to do better on most tests, but the items on classroom tests are not designed to measure intelligence. Some factors are, by their nature, going to affect scores through their effects on students' approach to the learning environment. A well-organized plan for collecting information will include elements to provide all data needed for valid judgments. Classroom tests which measure adequately the verbal and mathematical aspects of students' education have fulfilled their role.

A note of warning must be given to the point about increasing test reliability and possible adverse effects on validity of attempts to increase reliability. This may seem to contradict earlier discussion which explained the importance of a test doing what it does with great consistency. An overemphasis on increasing reliability without protection for validity can result in a test which measures with consistency but does not measure what it is intended to. Some types of behavior, such as recall of facts, are easier to measure reliably than some other types such as application of classroom learning to real-world settings. A test maker who includes tasks only for those aspects that are easy to measure while neglecting others that should be measured may find that the reliability can be increased, but at the expense of lessened validity. Since validity is the more important of the two, some sacrifice of reliability may have to be made to retain the balance of behavior measurement.

Most of the theory about test construction is directed toward concepts about how a test can be built with assurance that it is valid. Any efforts to build better tests must focus on ways to make a test more valid. Therefore, most of the content of this and other texts about building better tests speaks to validity in the very basic aspects of the topic.

Finally, the last measure of validity of a test is in terms of its usage. In the strictest sense tests are not validated, but judgments are made about the validity of interpretations of the data generated by a test for a specified purpose. Evidence which supports one use may not be relevant to support another use. Since test results are to be in agreement with test purpose, validity refers to the results of the test—the measures generated by the test.

Other Data-collecting Devices

Throughout the discussion of reliability in Chapter 11 and validity in Chapter 12 reference has been made to classroom tests. Since teachers find uses for many different data-collecting procedures, what consideration should be given to reliability and validity for those other devices? Cronbach (1971) answered this question succinctly as he wrote about test validation:

> For simplicity, I refer to tests and test scores throughout the chapter. The statements, however, apply to all procedures for collecting data, including observations, questionnaires, ratings of artistic products, etc. Most statements apply to protocols and qualitative summaries as well as to numerical scores. (p. 443)

In Chapter 3 data collection was presented as making observations, where an observation was said to be any fact which could be considered as a datum or information to be used in making judgments. The most basic method of generating observations is by direct observation. To be useful in evaluation, the data must be valid; hence, aids to direct observation have been created to overcome its limitations and to increase the validity of the data.

If the aids to direct observation—the checklist, scorecard, rating scale, unobtrusive observation, and anecdotal records—are to increase the validity of direct observation, they must be valid within themselves. The concerns of test validation apply to each of these, and the need for producing valid data must be kept in mind as each device is selected and used.

Mechanical instruments are used because of the reliability associated with them. Increased reliability will increase validity assuming that the instrument measures what the teacher needs to measure. In Chapter 4 it was pointed out that evaluation of student procedures and products requires the teacher to devise ways of generating valid data about how students perform a series of actions (procedures) and the results (products) of the actions. Specific ways of approaching evaluation of student performance point directly to building validity into data-collecting procedures.

SUMMARY

Validity of a test is its most important characteristic. A test is valid to the degree that it accurately measures some characteristic. Validity does not pertain directly to the measuring instrument itself but to the results of a test or other measuring instrument. Data-collecting instruments used in an educational setting are not either valid or invalid but valid for a particular use and to a degree.

There are three basic types of validity. Content validity, which is most important for the classroom teachers' achievement tests, describes the adequacy of the test to sample the domains of a subject as stressed in classroom instruction. Both types of criterion-related validity describe the relationship between test scores and independent external criterion measures. Concurrent (current) validity compares test scores to an external criterion of actual present performance. Predictive (future) validity compares test scores to an external criterion obtained sometime after the scores have been obtained. Concurrent and predictive validity are the same except for the element of time. Construct validity is the degree to which test scores can be accounted for by certain explanatory actions which support a psychological theory.

Direct validation of a test can be made by making a comparison of what the test demands from a student with what the teacher feels is important for students to know. A test should be a good operational definition of what a teacher wishes to measure. Content validity is of primary importance to the classroom teacher, and it can be increased through control of those factors that have an adverse effect on validity.

Most of the mechanics and theory of educational measurement are directed to making tests and other measuring devices more valid. In fact, most of the content of a book on classroom measurement could be related to making tests more valid in generating meaningful data. If the reader reflects on earlier topics of study in this book, a direct bearing on validity should be discerned for each one. Steps to refine measurement procedures are steps to more valid test measures. The next chapter explains the two referencing systems: criterion-referenced and norm-referenced.

NEW TECHNICAL WORDS LISTED IN THE GLOSSARY

Coefficient of validity   Criterion-related validity
Concurrent validity   Norm group
Construct validity   Predictive validity
Content validity

ACTIVITY EXERCISES

1. With a sheet of paper cover the two columns—Type of Testing and Procedure for Validation—in "Figure 12.5, Four types of validation." Complete the columns and compare your work with the figure.
2. Obtain a technical report or test manual for a standardized achievement test and study the validity information. What information was used to establish validity for the test? How can you determine whether the test will be valid in a particular classroom?

FOR DISCUSSION

1. Explain how a teacher can best establish content validity for a classroom test.
2. Explain why it is more correct to speak of "valid measures" from a test than to speak of a "valid test."
3. Define *operational definition*. Explain how the tasks on an algebra test generate an operational definition of achievement in algebra.
4. Discuss the statement, "Reliability is a necessary but not sufficient condition to establish validity for a measuring instrument."

REFERENCES AND KNOWLEDGE EXTENDERS

CHASE, C. I. *Measurement for educational evaluation* (2nd ed.). Reading, MA: Addison-Wesley, 1978.

CRONBACH, L. J. *Essentials of psychological testing* (3rd ed.). New York: Harper & Row, 1970. Chap. 5, pp. 115–150.

CRONBACH, L. J. Test validation. In R. L. Thorndike (Ed.), *Educational measurement* (2nd ed.). Washington, D.C.: American Council on Education, 1971. Chap. 14, pp. 443–507.

CRONBACH, L. J., & MEEHL, P. E. Construct validity in psychological tests. *Psychological Bulletin*, 1955, *52*, 281–302.

CURETON, E. E. Validity. In E. F. Lindquist (Ed.), *Educational measurement.* Washington, D.C.: American Council on Education, 1951. Chap. 16, pp. 621–694.

EBEL, R. L. *Essentials of educational measurement* (3rd ed.). Englewood Cliffs, NJ: Prentice-Hall, 1979. Chap. 15, pp. 296–309.

GILMAN, D. A. *Alternatives to test, marks, and class rank.* Terre Haute, IN: Curriculum Research and Development Center, Indiana State University, 1974.

GRONLUND, N. E. *Measurement and evaluation in teaching* (4th ed.). New York: Macmillan, 1981.

SAX, G. *Principles of educational and psychological measurement and evaluation* (2nd ed.). Belmont, CA: Wadsworth, 1980. Chap. 10, pp. 288–312.

THORNDIKE, R. L., & HAGEN, E. *Measurement and evaluation in psychology and education* (4th ed.). New York: Wiley, 1977, pp. 56–73.

WICK, J. W. *Educational measurement.* Columbus, OH: Merrill, 1973. Chap. 9, pp. 199–230.

Chapter 13. Reference Systems

After study of Chapter 13, you should be able to:

1. Differentiate between criterion-referencing and norm-referencing of test scores.
2. Decide when to use a criterion-referenced test and when to use a norm-referenced test.
3. Explain how a criterion for a criterion-referenced test and how norms for a norm-referenced test are established.
4. Discuss possible decision errors when classifying students as masters or nonmasters.
5. Use criterion-referencing and norm-referencing in student evaluation and program evaluation.
6. Summarize the strengths and weaknesses of criterion-referencing.
7. Summarize the strengths and weaknesses of norm-referencing.
8. Explain how each glossary term listed at the end of the chapter is used in classroom measurement and evaluation.

When the term *measurement* is used the idea of quantification of something comes to mind. When classroom teachers use the term *educational measurement* they refer to quantification of achievement of knowledge or skill development. Differences in scores on an achievement test reflect different quantities of achievement. Thus test administration is a process of quantification. Teachers use test instruments to measure achievement for the same reason that meteorologists and physicians use thermometers to measure temperature. Each needs a measuring device.

Measures of anything must be interpreted to derive the meaning attached to each measure. To the meteorologist who is collecting information to make weather forecasts a thermometer reading of 0° C. for air temperature means something much different from a reading of 20° C. A thermometer reading of 98.6° F. for body temperature means something quite different than a reading of 102° F. to the physician who is treating a patient for a severe internal infection. A test score of 37 means something different than a test score of 63 to the teacher who has administered a history test to a class of sophomore students. Each of these situations illustrates the need for a frame of reference to give meaning to a particular measure. Meteorologists and physicians use informational charts to allow interpretation of measures that they make on many variables as they forecast weather or diagnose physical wellbeing. Comparisons are made within a particular frame of reference.

Measures generated by classroom tests also must be interpreted within a reference system to derive meaning for students, teachers, and other interested persons. Interpretation of test scores requires a reference point or reference points to give meaning to scores that students receive from tests.* The teacher will establish the reference point or points according to how the information is to be used. Measures from classroom tests may be used to: (a) direct prescriptive study for the students who took the test, (b) indicate whether a student has mastered a well-defined body of subject matter or developed particular skills, (c) indicate where a student stands in relation to others who took the test, or (d) make terminal judgments about student progress and effectiveness of programs.

In general, a classroom test will be either norm-referenced or criterion-referenced according to the evaluation being made. The tests themselves may be similar and the same item could appear in both a norm-referenced and a criterion-referenced test. In other words, you cannot distinguish the reference system to be applied solely by scanning the test items. The difference between the two referencing systems—norm-referenced and criterion-referenced—is the way that scores from a test are made meaningful for evaluative purposes. To say it another way, the fundamental difference between the two referencing systems is the manner in which test performance is interpreted. In general, interpretation for norm-referenced tests is made using performance of other students who have taken the test. Interpretation for criterion-referenced tests is made through teacher judgment about acceptable or unacceptable levels of performance on the test itself. Most classroom testing programs will need both kinds of tests to support effective school instructional decisions because each referencing system serves a different need.

Evaluation includes interpretation and analysis of test measures to determine the degree that students have met goals set for them. The meaning associated with a measure must be judged either in relation to a level of performance established by the teacher (absolutely) or to how other students perform (relatively). Gilman (1974, p. 6) points out that a criterion-referenced judgment must be made in terms of a student's performance as it relates to a certain external standard. Norm-referenced judgment is based on an internal standard set by the group who took the test or an external peer group used for norming the measures. The effectiveness of instruction is based on the extent to which students achieve objectives set for them; therefore, the choice

---

*The material in this chapter is based in part on presentation first made in Hopkins and Antes, *Classroom testing: Administration, scoring, and score interpretation,* F. E. Peacock, 1979, which gives a more in-depth presentation of the two referencing systems.

between norm- or criterion-referenced evaluation will be made on the basis of facilitating positive changes in student behavior—the ultimate purpose of instruction. For some needs criterion-referencing is appropriate but for some other needs norm-referencing is better.

CRITERION-REFERENCED EVALUATION

Criterion-referencing describes each examinee's test performance in terms of specific behaviors. The test is used to ascertain a student's status with respect to a well-defined domain of knowledge and behavior. To interpret scores within this framework, the teacher must have established a close relationship between the knowledge and behaviors that define the domain and the knowledge and behaviors demanded by the items on the test. The items are directly connected to a set of criterion behaviors.

Objectives as Referents

If the results of a test are to mean something, the test constructor must work from stated or implied objectives for the instructional sequence. It seems inconceivable that anyone would try to build a classroom test without knowing what it is supposed to measure. All tests are based on objectives, even though they may not be stated or are set forth in general terms. With criterion-referenced test interpretation, a direct relationship is established between a specific objective or set of related objectives in a domain of behavior and a series of items on the test that relate to that objective or set of objectives. Individualized instruction, need for mastery for certain bodies of subject matter, certification, and licensing require that score interpretation be made to specific objectives within a well-defined domain and criterion-referencing serves this need better than norm-referencing.

When each specific objective describes what is to be learned, the teacher knows what instruction is to produce and how to plan for it, and it becomes easier to determine the degree of student success in reaching each objective if a connection is made between each test item and an objective. By using the objectives as referents, the teacher can write test items that directly measure each set of criterion behaviors by allowing comparison of test results on a set of specific tasks to the criterion level for that objective or behavior domain. This is the principle used in building criterion-referenced tests: those tests whose measures will be interpreted by comparison to a standard set before the testing session and before results of student test performance are known.

Establishing the Criterion

The standard set by criterion-referencing provides information concerning achievement of a particular student independent of reference to achievement by other students. For this reason the teacher must determine the expected level of attainment for a particular class and each individual student based on past experience and on general capability of students to achieve in the course of study. A situation is created where the scores are interpreted in a dichotomy, and after instruction a student is considered as having met or not met the previously established standard. No student should be placed in a position where it is impossible to attain the objectives. Therefore instruction is geared toward maximizing the percentage of students who master the objectives of instruction at or above the criterion level.

The test tasks that students are asked to perform must be attainable by most of the students; therefore, the difficulty level of test items must be carefully controlled. If the objective of criterion-referenced evaluation is mastery of a body of subject matter, a set of skills, or certain performances, any test used to provide information for the evaluation must be a mastery test. When a series of tests is used in sequence, test score interpretation may include terms like *satisfactory progress toward mastery.* A test may not be a true mastery test, but the concept of mastery is still kept in mind for the content of each subtest and eventual mastery of a minimum level. At best, a mastery test is a test of a minimum level of attainment. This may or may not be appropriate depending on the type of evaluation to be used for a particular situation. The use to be made of the information obtained by the measurement process will, to a large degree, determine whether or not criterion-referencing should be employed.

Only when 100 percent mastery of subject or topic under study is needed is there a clear and well-defined acceptance level for a criterion-referenced test. Since 100 percent mastery is rarely needed, the design for interpretation must be based on either past performance of a similar group of students or professional knowledge, or both. How well have students in past years scored on a particular test? Given baseline data and information collected from past test administrations, the teacher should be able to set reasonable levels for acceptance of meeting criterion. If higher performance is deemed necessary and instructional thrust has been made to improve performance behavior, the teacher could raise the standards whereby student performance will be judged.

If data are not available, the teacher can ask other teachers who have expertise in the topic to help set reasonable levels of expectation for student test behavior. Each contributor should study the behavior domain as defined for the test and individually set a level for the absolute criterion for satisfactory performance. Teachers who make individual decisions about the level could meet collectively and reconcile the estimates needed for criterion into a single performance level to be used in interpreting the scores. When the criterion is set, each student's score is compared to that standard and is judged as meeting criterion (passing) or not meeting criterion (not passing).

Errors in Decision

A factor that must be considered when setting levels for acceptable performance is the seriousness of making certain decision errors about passing to a new study. Which is more serious—advance a student to further study (consider a learning sequence completed) when the student should not be advanced, or mistakenly hold a student for further study when he or she should be advanced?

To protect against a false positive error of advancing a student who should not be advanced, the teacher would set the standard for passing very high. To protect against a false negative error of not advancing a student who should be advanced the teacher would set the standard for passing lower. Since it is not known for sure whether pass or fail is correct for each individual student, there is a possible error attached with some decisions, and the seriousness of one error compared to the seriousness of the other error must be considered. For example, the first-aid instructor who is charged with training personnel to administer emergency treatment would set a very high standard for passing criterion to protect against sending incompetent attendants in emergency vehicles. Some competent students might be sacrificed to protect against a false positive (Type I error) as illustrated in Part A of Figure 13.1. A social studies teacher who teaches a unit on English history would probably not set criterion levels as high because the false positive (Type I error) is not as serious as a Type II error and it is not so crucial to protect against mistaken advancement. More harm might be made in mistaken retention (Type II error) so the level is lowered as illustrated by Part B of Figure 13.1.

The decision requires careful consideration about possible consequences of each type of decision error. In practice the teacher should strive to minimize errors of both kinds in real-world decisions based on criterion-referenced interpretation of student scores, but since, for one reason or another, some nonmasters may score higher than some masters, decision errors will be made under the best decision-making conditions.

Devices to Measure

Tests that are to be interpreted by criterion-referencing are intended to measure what every student is expected to know or do. Therefore, these tests should consist of minimum performance or test items written at or below acceptable level for the specific standards set in the objectives, because they are not intended to measure beyond the minimum level. The thrust of test construction for criterion-referencing is toward building a device that will generate information about whether a student can or cannot do those things expected from all students.

One of the first things a person must do when developing a criterion-referenced achievement test is to communicate in some way precisely what domain of behaviors is to be measured. As mentioned earlier, one way to do that would be through use of objectives, but conceivably a set of test specifications or some other plan could be used. In any case, statements in terms of observable behavior will be required.

A situation must be arranged to allow the student to exhibit that he or she has developed competency at or above the established standard. Since the concern here is for tests (other data-collecting situations will be needed for some objectives), a testing device must be constructed which contains items

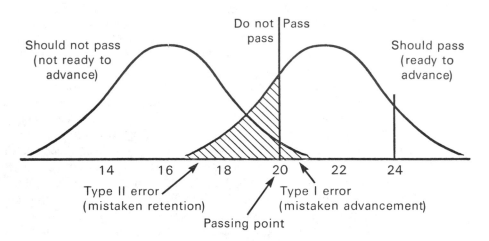

Part A
Protecting against a Type I error

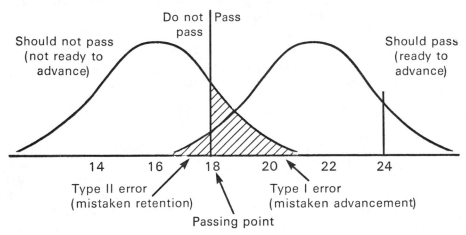

Part B
Protecting against a Type II error

FIGURE 13.1. Relationship of decision errors

at the minimum level with no items exceeding that level. The items must be homogeneous in that they are representative of the behavior to be exhibited. Say the objective is:

> A fifth-grade student will be able to compute the area of five right triangles given the lengths of the two sides with no errors.

Then each triangle must have one angle that is 90°. Likewise, items to test another objective must be relative to the behavior being measured, and there should be enough items to allow a well-grounded decision as to whether or not the student has developed the required competency level.

The results of the testing session are compared to the predetermined acceptance level. In a truly criterion-referenced interpretation, the performance is judged as either passing criterion or not passing criterion. Some tests referred to as criterion-referenced have levels of passing in addition to the single "pass–no pass" point. If a **descriptor set** is added to the satisfactory continuum, additional comparisons will need to be made. The interpretation is made by a comparison of the number of successes in the trials to the number of successes required for minimum acceptance, or some other success rate set forth in the objective statement.

When building a test to be interpreted by criterion, it is important to realize that a test is not considered to be criterion-referenced just because a cutoff point is associated with the final score interpretation. Only when a clear description of what the items are measuring is given can the test be truly criterion-referenced. The purpose of the use of a criterion as a referent is to describe the status of each student who is being assessed as either meeting minimum level or not. To merely write items which are attached to an objective does not make the test a criterion-referenced test.

The descriptive explanation (specific table of specifications or a set of criterion behaviors) of what the test is to measure serves three purposes:

1. It clarifies for the teacher what behaviors the test is intended to measure.
2. It sets the boundaries for the material and behaviors to be covered in the test.
3. It serves score interpretation by associating different verbal statements with different measures.

The definition of the behavior to be assessed by the test and the level of minimum acceptance sets the stage for test construction and score interpretation. The building of the test follows general test-building guidelines for writing directions for tests and for item construction. The items to be included on the test must be homogeneous and at the level prescribed by the descriptive explanation.

Since criterion-referencing can be employed to assess knowledge in the cognitive domain, the acquisition of attitudes and skills in the affective domain, and physical skills in the psychomotor domain, it is relevant for all three domains of instruction. The following are examples of the use of criterion-referencing in the three domains:

1. The purpose of a high school driver education class is to prepare students to drive an automobile with optimum performance levels. Prerequisite skills, abilities, and knowledge at a high level of mastery are required to attain the implicit purpose of learning to drive and to obtain a driver's license. In the cognitive domain a high level of mastery must be met in knowledge of the "rules of the road." Road signs must be recognized and understood prior to behind-the-wheel instruction. If a student does not master them, it is neces-

sary to study until all road signs are understood and criterion is met in reevaluation. The affective domain is touched upon in discussions about driver courtesy and attitudes. The development of physical driving skills involves objectives in the psychomotor domain. Objectives for driver education may include:

    a. Given a set of traffic signs without information, a high school driver education student will identify the shape and explain the meaning of the traffic signs and score 100 percent in an examination over the area. (Cognitive domain)*

    b. A student driver will demonstrate driving courtesy in a 30-minute behind-the-wheel driving test with no errors. (Affective domain)*

    c. A student driver will demonstrate in a 30-minute behind-the-wheel driving test, skill in driving in a variety of traffic situations with no errors. (Psychomotor domain)*

    d. A student driver will demonstrate the ability to parallel park within two attempts. (Psychomotor domain)*

2. In the elementary school, particularly at the primary level, numerous activities in the classroom involve the psychomotor domain and the muscular or motor behaviors necessary for physical activities such as handwriting, using crayons, and speaking. It is appropriate to employ criterion-referenced evaluation as students develop these skills. Small- and large-muscle coordination in motor and perceptual motor areas build upon one another, and appropriate kinesthetic sense is necessary for success in school subjects. Before students learn to write, they must first be able to control a pencil by making the necessary movements of the fingers, hands, and arms. Objectives may be at the behavioral level for activities necessary for printing and writing and stated as:

    a. Using a pencil and paper the student will draw four circular regions that are round and closed. (A visual picture is provided.) (Psychomotor)*

    b. Using pencil and paper the student will draw a square and a rectangle with four angles. (Visual pictures are provided.) (Psychomotor)*

Both of these examples of objectives relate to visual copying of shapes that are used in manuscript writing and later in cursive writing or drawing geometric shapes and can be considered prerequisites to those activities.

Nearly all teachers will find uses for criterion-referenced evaluation in the appraisal of students. Subject matter that is sequentially ordered relates well to criterion-referenced evaluation, since the assumption is that mastery of prerequisite skills is necessary to progress in the area of study. For example, in the study of mathematics, students must be able to add and subtract before

---

*Remember that domains overlap and only the major domain involved is listed for the above objectives.

they can use the algorithms for multiplication and division. Reading, foreign language, and history are also illustrative of subject-matter areas sequentially ordered and built on preceding tasks. At least, a minimal level of attainment is necessary in each content area, and criterion-referenced evaluation may be suitable to ascertain whether that level has been reached by a student.

Interpreting Test Performance

The intended purpose of a criterion-referenced test is to measure what the teacher has determined ought to be taught and to assess whether or not students have learned at least the minimum. If the intended competencies are clearly defined and a test operationalizes the definition, then the scores from the test should be direct measures of the described behavior. Teachers use these measures in two ways. First, the teacher wants to check each student's performance score with the criterion set for minimum acceptance. Second, the teacher wants to check the effectiveness of instruction over the entire classroom for students in general.

Student evaluation

The first thing that a teacher does with a student's score on a criterion-referenced test is to compare the test score with the criterion point set for minimum acceptance. A student who has met criterion performance has achieved an acceptable level for whatever behavior the test was designed to measure and is ready to proceed to a new learning task or instructional sequence. A student who has not met criterion has not achieved an acceptable level and is given additional prescriptive instruction on the same subject-matter topics.

A criterion-referenced test can be constructed to measure more than one objective. On a test of this kind, the items are arranged into subtests so that an item does not overlap among objectives to be measured by the test. The test would appear to the students as one test, but the interpretation of scores would be by sets of items with each set tied directly to a behavioral domain. The student could meet acceptable levels of performance on all subtests or pass some while not passing one or more other subtests.

With this interpretation scheme, the classroom must be organized for instruction at more than one level. Either individual instruction or teaching in small, homogeneous groups must be arranged for the ongoing teaching-learning process. Formative evaluation is used to direct further study, basing instruction on what the test scores reveal about student competencies.

Teaching in sequence means that each student who meets criterion will be assigned new reading, new activities, and enough practice to prepare for the next test to measure achievement of criterion for the new topic. Instruction is made up of a series of these "teaching and then measuring" episodes. Reflection on the subject matter studied and student characteristics should tell the teacher whether or not this minimum type of learning is appropriate for the subject matter and the students.

The strategies for achieving mastery learning are many, and our topic of testing does not include an in-depth study of the instructional aspects of this type of teaching. The major problem in the development of a strategy is to find ways within the structure of the classroom to allow for altering the length of time individual students need to achieve mastery and at the same time cover the material that is expected to be taught. Neither the problem of measurement nor the problem of instruction is easily solved, and much coordination is needed to take the results of testing (test scores), interpret what they mean, and then use them to direct future student study and learning.

Program evaluation

The appraisal of student progress is an important component of educational evaluation. An equally important component of educational evaluation is assessment of the overall effectiveness of the instructional program. Although judging the suitability of an education program requires information from many sources, test data must be included since that information comes directly from students. Since the schools exist to foster student literacy, the information that students give through their test scores must be considered to be of particular importance.

Program evaluation at the classroom level (the evaluation that concerns this discussion) can be made by the teacher without considering factors that have been resolved at the administrative level. Since the objectives are set at the classroom level with regard to student characteristics, the effectiveness of the program can be judged in part by the proportion of students who meet criterion on the tests and how far into the sequence students as a whole have moved. The teacher's close relationship with the components of this aspect of the evaluation process should allow a sound decision about the effectiveness of a particular program for a particular set of students.

To report to others about program effectiveness, the teacher has the problem of organizing a meaningful explanation of the results of an educational sequence. If a clear description of what students are expected to attain has been made, reports giving percentages of those who met criterion seems to be appropriate. Graphs are also descriptive and easily understood by almost everyone and can be used to explain further. A necessary part of the report will be a narrative by the teacher that gives further insight into program impact and its effectiveness. The needs will be different for different audiences, so the teacher must write in terms of those who will be reading and using the report data, and interpretation must be keyed to the audience who will be using the judgment of evaluation to make educationally oriented decisions. For example, curriculum persons will need information that differs from what parents will need.

The diagnostic element of formative evaluation also reports ongoing program effectiveness and the impact of prescriptive teaching. All in all, the teacher should be receiving continuous evaluation of program effectiveness if the system is working as expected. Certainly, the key to valid evaluation at the classroom level is valid test data. The messages discerned by the teacher as data are interpreted, form the basis for curriculum change for students in both present instruction and instruction for classes that follow.

Considerations

When deciding on the reference system to use to interpret classroom test scores, the teacher must consider the type of instruction and the nature of the subject matter. Certain strengths are associated with criterion-referenced interpretation of test scores, but certain weaknesses are also attached. The following two sections point up those aspects that all teachers must reflect on when deciding which reference system to use for a specific evaluation.

Strengths

Interpretation of scores from a criterion-referenced test should indicate precisely what each student knows and can do in terms of behaviors. Most of the strengths of this kind of interpretation are directly tied to that expectation, and others are indirectly related to the measurement of behaviors. In general, the strengths of criterion-referenced measurement (CRM) are as follow:

1. CRM can be used to measure attributes of the cognitive domain where mastery of certain material and skills is expected. For this reason, some criterion-referenced tests are needed for nearly all classrooms.
2. CRM structures the measurement process so that appraisal of affective attributes is facilitated. The close relationship of the description and the measurement in CRM overcomes the difficulty of describing an effective attribute in a word definition.
3. CRM is useful for measuring in the psychomotor domain. Use of a criterion point as reference for measurement of skill and physical competency seems to be natural for this type of performance.
4. CRM allows direct interpretation of the measure of performance. The interpretation indicates what specific tasks a student can perform.
5. Since CRM test items are at the minimum level for mastery the tasks on the test should be easily understood by students.
6. CRM works hand in hand with individualized instruction where formative evaluation directs needed changes in prescriptive teaching.
7. A score at or above criterion indicates satisfactory level of performance. CRM can be used with sequentially organized subjects since a score at or above criterion may be used to indicate a level of performance prerequisite to some other higher level of performance.
8. CRM can be used for content subjects and cognitive skill development as diagnostic procedure to point up an area of difficulty in a child's learning.

Weaknesses

Interpretation of test scores from a criterion-referenced test fails to reveal a student's level of achievement relative to other students. Although the scores indicate whether a student has achieved a certain objective or not, the scores do not allow for appraisal of overall achievement. Most of the weaknesses of CRM are either directly or indirectly tied to this deficiency. In general, the weaknesses of CRM are as follow:

1. Scores from CRM do not indicate a student's level of achievement relative to peers. At some time the idea of relative performance must enter into the interpretation. It may be included when setting the minimum acceptance level as criterion or after the scores are reported.
2. Relatively few areas of cognitive learning and only parts of other areas are amenable to being reduced solely to a list of specific instructional objectives. Since lists of objectives at any level are rarely, if ever, exhaustive, CRM cannot be used to measure large portions of subject matter in which objectives cannot be stated in specific behaviors.
3. Instruction solely to a set of specific behaviors does not allow for expansion of learning by taking advantage of ongoing classroom activities. In this sense, teaching solely to a set of specific objectives may restrict the teacher, the teaching, and in turn, the learning.
4. There is always a question about the standard set for the criterion point. The interpretation of scores by criterion is only as good as the process used to set the criterion.
5. Use of CRM exclusively does not allow a teacher to compare a student with other student performance in the class or in a larger context of the school district, region, state, or nation.

Criterion-referenced measures allow for interpretation that can be highly useful for some classroom measurement and evaluation. When the tests generate valid data about cognitive achievement or skill development, they can indicate specifically what a student can or can not do. This information is especially valuable when certain learning is:

1. Prerequisite to other learning, or
2. Requisite to special functioning.

For some learning, the need is for mastery. For example, a student must know how to subtract before using the subtraction algorithm for division. Mastery of a prerequisite is necessary to use that algorithm but in other cases mastery may be requisite for some functioning. For example, when the teacher of a first aid class decides what skills and knowledge are needed by a person who drives an emergency vehicle, instruction is pointed toward mastery of essentials for each student. CRM seems appropriate because the instructor needs information about both what the student knows and what he or she can do. Information is also needed to be sure the student has achieved mastery before being classed as qualified to serve the needs of emergencies. To know 70 percent of what is needed is not enough for on-the-job performance as a first aid person.

When there is no need for each student to learn the same things that all other students learn, interpretation to a criterion is not only undesirable but impossible. In achievement for most subjects, some learning is expected to take diverse directions; therefore, instruction, and in turn, interpretation of some test scores should allow for differences. CRM can not do that.

NORM-REFERENCED EVALUATION

A score on a norm-referenced test is intended to describe a student's test performance in relation to others who took the test at the same time or to others whose scores are used to establish external criteria for performance levels. Unless a criterion-referenced test or a problem test is used, some indication of relative standing should be reported to a student in addition to the raw score. Norm-referencing provides little information about the degree of proficiency of performance in absolute terms.

Norm-referencing employs the practice of comparing a student's performance to the performance of the class as a whole, or in the case of a standardized test, to some external population or norm group. The trait or ability measured is assumed to be present in varying degrees among students and the test is designed to ascertain the level relative to other students. Students' scores are placed in order from high to low and the arithmetical average and the variability (a measure of the dispersion of the scores) determined. With this information relative positions of scores are determined. Further interpretation of student performance is made by the teacher as he or she reflects on performance of the individual and class in relation to performance of previous classes at this level for this particular subject matter.

Quantification must be interpreted in relation to some reference point. Averages of others' performance seem to be logical reference points for interpretation of student attainment either when external criteria do not exist or when they are not suitable for a given classroom situation. A standard based on peer group performance is often most fitting for teachers to use when raw scores are to be interpreted.

Norm-referencing for classroom tests is used widely when educational objectives are based in the cognitive domain, but also serves the higher levels of the affective and psychomotor domains. Norm-referencing is widely used for psychological tests measuring in the affective domain and in skill tests in the psychomotor domain. Since a well-constructed measurement instrument used in norm-referencing assesses what students know in relationship to their classmates, it is important that the items on the test: (a) be representative of the course content covered, and (b) require the desired behaviors to be used to complete the tasks correctly.

Norms as Referents

In the strictest sense, all tests are written with an eye to what groups of students with particular sets of characteristics are expected to do. With norm-referenced test interpretation a direct relationship is established between each score on the test and the relationship of that test score to an average or set of norms. Educational objectives are the basis for the test items, but the instructional objectives may be stated without a preset level of acceptable performance and, consequently, be more general than behavioral or specific instructional objectives. If there is not a body of content or set of behaviors that must be learned in entirety (mastered) by all students, then student behavior at many levels may be considered to be satisfactory. If the test allows measurement at all levels the student has an opportunity to score at a level of highest attainment.

When teachers know in general what classroom instruction is to produce, they need to direct teaching to help each student reach full potential. Determination of how well students have achieved will need to be interpreted by something other than a criterion set as an absolute standard. By using norms as referents, the teacher can write test items and relate them more generally to objectives so that an overall picture of how a student achieved is produced rather than a list of behaviors that have been successfully attained. Comparison of the test results to peer performance becomes the system of score interpretation. The principle used in building norm-referenced tests is the same principle that is used when measuring physical properties. The resulting measure (the score) is intended to be an indication of how much someone or something has of the attribute that the measuring device is measuring. A thermometer measures the amount of heat, and a history test measures the amount of history achievement. For this type of testing, a test-score distribution should have a wide range if students being tested form a heterogeneous group. Even with a relatively homogeneous group of students, the scores that measure relative amounts of knowledge and skill should have differences and a rather wide score range.

Establishing the Norms

When use of scores directs the teacher to norm-referenced interpretation, a decision must be made about how to report performance. Many reporting systems are available, and each has certain advantages and disadvantages. The reporting system to be used is selected by giving consideration to: (a) who is to receive the data and (b) how the person will be using the data. Since more than one person may be using the data, it is conceivable that more than one system may be needed to satisfy everyone involved. When external norm groups are used for interpretation, **standard scores** and **percentile rank** bands may be the best way to report student performance on tests to administrative personnel. Students and parents might understand graphical representations or **stanines** better. More about these reporting systems will be presented in Chapter 14.

If external norms are used, the teacher will probably have tables which allow a direct comparison of each score to the norm-group performance. The tables were developed by calculating norm values for all possible test scores and listing the raw scores in one column and the associated norm scores in another column. Most tests that are normed will have tables for several different reporting systems so that interpretations can be made to fit the needs of the consumer of the test data. For classroom tests the teacher will select reporting systems that fit the needs of those using the data.

Devices to Measure

Tests that are to be interpreted by norm-referencing (average referents) are intended to measure how a student's performance compares with a peer group—either classmates or an external set of peers—which is used as a norm group. Therefore, these tests should consist of items that collectively allow a student to reveal achievement at any level. In practice the floor and ceiling for the test are set so that each student will be measured at his or her level of achievement. For example, a classroom or standardized third-grade spelling test would exclude two sets of words; first, those words that nearly all second-grade students know how to spell and, second, those words considered too difficult for most third-grade students to spell. The thrust for this kind of test would be to answer the question: What level of spelling achievement does this student have compared to third-grade students in general?

Word lists that have been assigned for study in class are expected to be mastered, and the final weekly spelling test is likely to be criterion-referenced. Six-week or semester spelling tests could be either norm- or criterion-referenced at the choice of the teacher.

One of the first things a person must do when developing a norm-referenced achievement test is to communicate in some way the content and behaviors to be covered on the test. A table of specifications is developed to direct writing of items that will weight test coverage of subject content according to relative importance and select test behaviors from appropriate behavior classes. If items of appropriate difficulty (no items that nearly all students would answer correctly and no items that nearly all students would answer incorrectly) are selected, the test should generate scores that reveal differences in levels of achievement and can be used to order students according to their differences on what is being measured.

Because criterion-referenced and norm-referenced tests measure achievement in much the same way, their formats and test items tend to be similar, and the instruments for both kinds of tests look very much alike. However, there are two major differences: *(a)* how items are selected and *(b)* the interpretation of obtained measures of student behavior. The test builder for both types of tests selects items from a domain of tasks that describe performance. The criterion-referenced test samples from a clearly defined domain of actions that exemplify minimum level of conduct. For the norm-referenced test the sample is taken from the complete domain of subject-matter knowledge and behaviors that describe the classroom instructional course of study. In contrast to criterion-referencing, norm-referencing of classroom tests does not use predetermined performance standards. After the test has been administered, the scores are organized and transformed into meaningful **statistics,** depending primarily on who will be using the scores. Reports will interpret each score in terms of how it compares to the rest of the scores from this classroom, or to scores obtained from a norm group.

Interpreting Test Performance

Since a test is a measuring instrument, its function is to quantify the amount of a specific trait that each student possesses. Measurement answers questions like: How much height does Dan have? How much spelling (or history, physics, etc.) achievement does Dan have? How many free throws can Dan make in 30 seconds? Obviously, tests cannot serve as a measuring device for all student characteristics that are of concern to teachers, but they serve to quantify many attributes important as students progress through the process of education—especially measurement of achievement.

Test scores reflect little meaning in and of themselves. As with other measures, they must be explained in meaningful terms. Even a well-understood measure of weight means little before a frame of reference is established. For example, Dan's weight of 121 pounds must be translated into meaningful terms by getting answers to such questions as: How old is Dan? How tall is he? What is his body build? A weight of 121 pounds for a slightly built 15-year-old who is five-feet-six-inches tall is a much different measure than the same reading of 121 pounds for a 10-year-old student who is four-feet-four-inches tall. A Dan who is a professional basketball player should be able to make many more free throws in a limited time period than a Dan who is a middle-fielder on a junior high school soccer team. Measures of weight and free throwing ability must be interpreted within the framework of some reference system (probably norm-referenced) that makes them understandable. Likewise, measures of achievement must be interpreted in terms of some reference system. Norm-referencing is used if the teaching has been for maximum performance. The mathematical techniques and graphical representations presented later are used to make scores meaningful for evaluative purposes.

Considerations

When deciding on the reference system to use to interpret classroom test scores, the teacher must consider the type of instruction and the nature of the subject matter. Certain strengths are associated with norm-referenced interpretation, but this interpretation also has certain weaknesses. The following two sections point up those aspects that teachers must reflect on when deciding which reference system to use.

Strengths

Interpretation of test scores from a norm-referenced test should assess a student attribute as it relates to other students. Most of the strengths of norm-referenced interpretation are directly tied to the test's ability to reveal levels of achievement, and the others are indirectly related to a report of relative student status. In general, the strengths of norm-referenced measurement (NRM) are as follow:

1. NRM can be used to measure attributes that relate to the cognitive domain where each student is allowed and encouraged to learn at maximum potential. For this reason some norm-referenced tests are needed for nearly all classrooms because teachers rarely, if ever, put a ceiling on what a student is to learn.
2. NRM is appropriate for interpreting performance at the higher levels of the affective and psychomotor domains. As performance becomes complex, comparison to others becomes increasingly important in interpretation of individual performance.
3. NRM is especially valuable for the higher levels of the cognitive domain as student development focuses on complex learning strategies. As teaching moves from mastery of the basics or material to be learned by each student, referencing to a criterion is no longer effective interpretation.
4. NRM is valuable when a set of students is moved through an instructional sequence together, but different performance levels are expected from the students. For this type of instructional scheme a test needs to be able to measure a wide range of performance.
5. NRM allows for a frame of reference not restricted to a predetermined criterion for success.
6. NRM is effective when testing for selection of candidates for particular assignments or tracks within a school system.

Weaknesses

Interpretation of test scores by norm-referencing fails to give a direct measure of achievement in absolute terms. Although a good test is built from a table of specifications to relate content taught to content measured, the test score can not be further connected to a set of observable objectives. Most of the weaknesses of NRM are either directly or indirectly tied to this deficiency. In general, the weaknesses of NRM are as follow:

1. NRM is not appropriate for measuring mastery of certain material and skills. The test score gives no indication of what a student can do in absolute terms and does not allow for judgment about performance in specifics.
2. If material or topics are sequenced, NRM can not be used satisfactorily

to indicate when a student is ready to move from one topic to another. If the ability to attain a second skill rests on being able to perform a first skill, then information other than that generated by interpreting to norms is needed.

3. NRM does not indicate specific tasks a student can perform and does not allow direct interpretation of performance from a test score.

4. Since NRM test items go beyond measurement of minimum acceptable performance, the tasks in the items are more difficult to set. Ambiguity about the task in a test item may be greater in NRM than in CRM.

Norm-referenced tests allow for interpretation that can be highly useful for some classroom measurement and evaluation. When norm-referenced tests generate valid data about cognitive achievement or skill development, they can tell what one student can do in relation to what other students can do. This information is especially valuable when:

1. teaching, and in turn, learning has been directed to the maximum level, or

2. students are to be selected according to how they perform relative to peer performance.

For some learning, the need is for maximum amounts. For example, when basic needs for knowledge and skill have been met, students are encouraged to go as far as they can to extend their performance levels. The social studies teacher wants students to understand many aspects of interrelationships of the societal, economic, and political factors that led to the Civil War and does not place a limit on any student's learning level. Students will vary in the level of learning and NRM is appropriate since study has been such that wide variance in performance is expected. Since NRM utilizes tests with no ceiling and measures over a wide range, logic tells us that it should be used when teaching has been directed the same way.

When there is the need for students to learn to a mastery level or learn a body of content in its entirety, interpretation by norms is impossible. Much learning for very young children is directed to mastery, and introductory learning in any new undertaking is pointed toward assimilation of a specific body of basic knowledge, understanding, and skill development, and interpretation should be about what specific things a student knows and can do. NRM cannot do that.

SHOULD CRM OR NRM BE USED?

In determining whether to use criterion- or norm-referenced measurement, the question of the purpose for evaluation becomes paramount. Are you planning to make decisions requiring information about individual status with reference to some criterion or individual status relative to performance of others? For example, if evaluation information will be used to determine if an individual has the necessary knowledge for study of advanced mathematics, the judgment must be made about what the individual can do and not how that individual compares with other students. Criterion-referenced measurement will answer the question as to whether or not the student has mastered the essential criterion skills or has the knowledge necessary to move to a higher level of instruction for learning. Appraisal of a senior student's academic aptitude compared to others in all graduating classes of that year calls for norm-referenced measurement. This provides information comparing that student to the norm group performance and can indicate expected performance when the student is placed in the competition of a college or university environment.

Clearly, both norm-referenced and criterion-referenced measurement are needed to make decisions about an individual and her or his status and future instruction. The decisions are made by using the strengths of each system (see Figure 13.2). When there is a degree of selectivity or the individual with the best potential is desired, norm-referencing is used. On the other hand, when the interest is in the particular competence or skill in absolute terms, criterion-referencing is used. NRM measures students' competencies in a domain of behavior in general, and CRM measures students' competencies in a domain of behavior by focusing on subparts of the domain. A choice of the type of measurement must be made by the teacher, using knowledge of the distinctions between norm-referenced and criterion-referenced evaluation when making the decision. As early as 1971 Alfred P. Garvin stated a position that makes good sense:

> In certain cases, CRM is irrelevant because, in fact, no meaningful criterion applies. In these cases, NRM must be used if there is to be any measurement at all. However, there are other cases where a meaningful criterion is inherent in the instructional objectives of the unit involved. If one measures the outcomes of such a unit at all he is, in fact, conducting CRM. Between these two extremes, we might posit a continuum of relevance between criteria and instructional objectives. (p. 56)

The norm-referenced approach allows the amount learned to vary among students, but all students proceed through subject matter at about the same pace. New material is presented to the student, progress is evaluated, and additional material is presented. To a great extent a student's performance is based upon the ability to keep up with the class. Many students may move on to succeeding units without mastering all of the material presented in the previous unit. It is not always necessary to ask all students to learn exactly the same things or a complete body of content. Norm-referenced procedures allow the teacher to teach at a maximum level and to provide a student with an opportunity to go beyond the minimum level when being measured. A strict adherence to criterion-referenced evaluation does not permit the student to be measured beyond a minimum level although the student may have learned at a much higher level. For this reason consideration should be given to norm-referencing unless criterion-referencing is needed for a fixed body of content.

Measurement notions	Norm-referencing	Criterion-referencing
1. Instruction	Cover a predetermined amount of material	Coverage determined by student mastery of objectives
2. Trait or ability to be measured	Present in varying degrees	Present in a sufficient or insufficient amount
3. Domain of instruction	Cognitive, affective, psychomotor	Cognitive, affective, psychomotor
4. Test item construction	To discriminate among students	To measure a predetermined level of proficiency
5. Difficulty of items	Medium difficulty	Relatively easy
6. Discrimination	Orders students from high to low	Separates those who met criterion from those who did not meet it
7. Validity	Content validity (items representative of materials and behaviors covered)	Content validity (items represent instructional objectives)
8. Range of scores	Low to high	High values expected
9. Score interpretation	To internally generated norms or from external norms	To external criterion

FIGURE 13.2. Summary distinctions between norm-referenced and criterion-referenced measurement

Subject matter may dictate which type of reference to use. A class in first aid when certain knowledge is crucial might best use criterion-referenced procedures while a class in philosophy where no one body of knowledge is crucial might best use a norm set by the class in making judgments about students. A mastery test for a first aid class seems appropriate, but a norm-referenced test for philosophy may be more suitable.

In the event that previous concepts are prerequisite to new ones, norm-referencing may place students at a disadvantage. In contrast, the criterion-referenced approach employs the criterion level of minimum acceptable performance for each objective as set, and the performance of each child is compared with the criterion only. The teacher starts by presenting new material and evaluates for mastery of objectives. The student who performs satisfactorily moves to new materials while the student who performs unsatisfactorily is presented with remedial and prescriptive instruction and then proceeds to the mastery of objectives. Upon successful completion of the previous material, the student moves to new materials being presented (Scannell & Tracey, 1975, pp. 37–42).

A student's progress in criterion-referenced procedures reflects the ability to exhibit the required behaviors regardless of the learning rate. Some students require more time to achieve a given set of objectives than others. In a pass-fail system, generally only a small portion of students fail to meet criterion level, and criterion-referenced evaluation can be used to reduce failure by indicating where reteaching needs to be done.

Each teacher should decide upon a model of teaching and select appraisal methods needed for the content covered and proceed from there, while realizing and understanding when and how to employ both systems of referencing. Consideration must be given to the strengths and weaknesses of both approaches to evaluation, keeping in mind that neither is to be used to the exclusion of the other. The employment of both approaches provides more flexibility and understanding of student progress and the level of instructional effectiveness. It is possible and profitable in many situations to compare student performance with a norm group as well as to provide information in reference to how a student's performance relates to a standard. The dedicated educator will want to be able to employ norm-referenced and criterion-referenced evaluation techniques as needed.

SUMMARY

Interpretation of examinees' test scores is presently made by one of two referencing systems—criterion-referenced or norm-referenced. By having these two systems a teacher can: (a) choose interpretation based on an absolute standard if teaching has been to a well-defined domain of behaviors, or (b) choose interpretation based on relative standards if teaching in the domain of behavior is more generally based. In the first, measurement is conducted by breaking a behavior domain into subsets of the domain and focusing on each part by a specific test. In the second, a test is built for the behavior domain in its total scope rather than dealing with specific subsets.

Establishment of the criterion for CRM or the norm for NRM is based in absolute or relative terms respectively. With this difference tests take on certain characteristics. Although test items are much the same for both tests and item construction is based on the same principles, items for CRM tests are relatively easy for the test taker and those for NRM are of medium difficulty. Strengths and weaknesses for each referencing system have been listed to assist classroom teachers select the type of reference system for each of the tests used in a classroom. The question about interpretation is answered by selecting the interpretation system to give meaning to student scores. One type of interpretation directs the teacher to CRM and construction of a test to measure a specific domain of minimum behaviors, and the other type of interpretation directs the teacher to NRM and construction of a test to measure a set of generally stated instructional objectives.

The next chapter discusses interpretation of test scores.

NEW TECHNICAL TERMS LISTED IN THE GLOSSARY

Descriptor set	Stanines
Percentile rank	Statistics
Standard score	

ACTIVITY EXERCISES

1. With a sheet of paper cover the two columns—Norm-Referencing and Criterion-Referencing—in "Figure 13.2, Summary distinctions between norm-referenced and criterion-referenced measurement." Complete the columns and compare your work with the figure.
2. For the following educational cases decide whether norm-referencing or criterion-referencing should be used in the process of measurement.
   a. A test is to be given to supply *some* of the data needed to certify students for summer jobs as life-guards at the city beach. Topics to be covered are cognitive in nature and do not include physical skills of swimming.
   b. The counseling staff wants to select students for a new class of 20 students who have a high interest level in protection of the natural environment.
   c. A long established dental clinic has a large number of assistants who have been on the job over five years. As a check on knowledge of contemporary procedures, all dental assistants are to be given a test to indicate which individuals need a program to update their competencies.
   d. A junior high school science teacher wants to measure in general terms how much each student knows about the topics covered during the semester.
   e. A teacher of the second-year algebra course needs to establish a point of beginning for instruction, basing it on what students now know about topics usually covered in the first year program.

FOR DISCUSSION

1. Explain in general terms how norms are established for interpretation of test scores.
2. Explain in general terms how a criterion is set to interpret test scores.
3. Describe possible decision errors associated with classification of students as masters or nonmasters.
4. Defend or attack the use of a single form of a test as both criterion-referenced and norm-referenced.

REFERENCES AND KNOWLEDGE EXTENDERS

BERK, R. A. (Ed.). *Criterion-referenced measurement: The state of the art.* Baltimore: Johns Hopkins University Press, 1980.

GARVIN, A. P. The applicability of criterion-referenced measurement by content area and level. In W. J. Popham (Ed.). *Criterion-referenced measurement: An introduction.* Englewood Cliffs, NJ: Educational Technology Publications, 1971.

GILMAN, D. A. *Alternatives to tests, marks, and class rank.* Terre Haute, IN: Curriculum Research and Development Center, Indiana State University, 1974.

HAMBLETON, R. K., SWAMINATHAN, H., ALGINA, J., & COULSON, D. B. Criterion-referenced testing measurement: A review of technical issues and developments. *Review of Educational Research,* 1978, *48,* 1–48.

HOPKINS, C. D., & ANTES, R. L. *Classroom testing: Administration, scoring, and score interpretation.* Itasca, IL: F. E. Peacock, 1979. Chaps. 7 and 8.

POPHAM, W. J. *Criterion-referenced measurement.* Englewood Cliffs, NJ: Prentice-Hall, 1978.

POPHAM, W. J. *Modern educational measurement.* Englewood Cliffs, NJ: Prentice-Hall, 1981. Chaps. 2 and 16.

SCANNELL, D. P., & TRACEY, D. B. *Testing and measurement in the classroom.* Boston: Houghton Mifflin, 1975.

Chapter 14. Interpreting Test Scores

After study of Chapter 14, you should be able to:

1. Defend interpretation of test scores by criterion-referencing.
2. Defend interpretation of test scores by norm-referencing.
3. Organize a set of scores into a frequency distribution.
4. Construct a graphic representation by histogram or frequency polygon for a frequency distribution.
5. Define, compute, compare, and understand the appropriate uses of measures of central tendency.
6. Define, compute, compare, and understand the appropriate uses of measures of variability.
7. Define, compute, compare, and understand the appropriate uses of quartiles, deciles, and percentiles.
8. Describe skewness and kurtosis and their use in interpretation of test scores.
9. Define, compute, and understand the use of standard scores and how to make test scores comparable.
10. Understand the properties of the normal curve and its use to interpret test scores.
11. Describe test scores statistically.
12. Explain how each glossary term listed at the end of the chapter is used in classroom measurement and evaluation.

After a test has been administered, each student's paper is scored for either correct or incorrect responses. The total number of items responded to correctly or points awarded is usually recorded at the top of each paper and is referred to as the student's **raw score**. When papers are returned to students, they know how many times they responded correctly, the total number of points the teacher judged their constructed responses to be worth, or a total made up of a combination of these values. However, a student is unable to determine the meaning of a **score** unless additional information is provided for interpretation. The teacher may tell the student how a score compares to a criterion point set as pass/fail, or to a set of norms established for interpretation.

For a criterion-referenced classroom test each score is compared to a predetermined criterion to judge whether the score should be considered as passing or failing. For further information the score may be compared to a scale of predetermined intervals to ascertain the degree of passing as well as either passing or failing. A certain range is considered to be the A values, another range for B values, and so forth. Other descriptions such as excellent, good, and so on can be used.

For a classroom test that is norm-referenced each score will be compared to how that score stands in relation to scores of others who have taken the test. The set of scores for a classroom may be used to establish how well a student performed compared to the peer group (internal) who took the test in the same administration. A score from a standardized test can be compared to norms established for interpretation of scores for that test. Norms are established from results of a peer group (external) who took the test under conditions like those used to administer the test in the classroom. Comparison of a score to peer-group results (internal or external) interprets a score relatively according to performance of others, rather than absolutely to a clearly defined domain of knowledge, skill, or such.

The teacher chooses the type of interpretation that best meets the needs of the evaluation process to be used. Criterion-referencing may be used for mastery learning, minimum competency, or any clearly defined domain of behaviors. Predetermined standards are most appropriate when a well-defined body of content and behaviors is to be completely or nearly completely learned. The difficulties (Hambleton, 1980) in this type of measurement are echoed in:

> The purposes of criterion-referenced testing programs can only be accomplished if technically sound criterion-referenced tests are constructed and if scores derived from the tests are interpreted and used correctly. (p. 115)

The interpretation by norm-referencing is more clearly defined by present methods than is criterion-referenced testing, but Hambleton's statement could be made about norm-referenced testing with no reservations. Trying to derive meaning from any test score is difficult at best. If students have studied within an area where a large range of performance can be considered acceptable but in varying degrees then norm-referencing is a logical choice.

For criterion-referencing the standard-setting process seems to be the most crucial aspect. For norm-referencing the attachment of a statement about how much a student knows or can do seems to be the most crucial aspect. Relating test tasks to instructional objectives or a domain of behaviors is necessary in either referencing system. The material in this chapter is based on the assumption that the relationship between test tasks and instructional objectives is sufficient to allow interpretation. Without the relationship the time spent in testing could probably be better utilized in additional learning activities.

INTERPRETATION BY CRITERION

Criterion-referenced measurement has standards set before the testing session, and a simple comparison of a score to the standards is sufficient interpretation. A score either meets criterion or it does not, and the score is interpreted as passing or not passing. If a scale is used the adequacy of a passing score may be further indicated by a number of other points and the passing score interpreted through a descriptor set. This procedure of interpretation establishes limits for varying degrees of worth for the completed test tasks. For example, descriptor sets of standards for a 70-item multiple-choice test could be:

Score Ranges	Descriptor Set A	Descriptor Set B	
69–70	Excellent	A	
67–68	Good	B	
65–66	High average	C+	
63–64	Average	C	
61–62	Low average	C–	Pass
60 and below	Below criterion		Not pass

Other descriptor sets and point values for the score ranges could be devised by a teacher. For domain-referenced interpretation the criterion point for mastery-nonmastery would be expected to be much higher than a score of 60 out of 70, and would be the only standard. Any score interpretation system should be based on the material, class characteristics, age level of the students, other important student characteristics, and the purpose of the interpretation.

Other types of standards also can be set for criterion-referenced test scores. The interpretation above is for each student across all objectives covered for the material being tested. Examinee performance also can be interpreted on each objective. The performance of all students on the set of objectives measured by the test can be interpreted. If the other standards are needed further investigation is needed. Each objective for all students could be considered. The percentage of the class meeting criterion could be compared to a standard. Each has a special meaning to educators.

Test scores compared to standards set before the test is administered place a great responsibility on the teacher in regard to test construction and administration. Absolute scales for judging performance levels assume the following:

1. The teacher can predetermine the difficulty of each test item for students and the difficulty of the test for the class.
2. The teacher can construct highly valid test items.
3. The teacher can administer the test under optimum conditions.

4. The teacher can and has fulfilled the requirements of all aspects of good testing practices.

Careful reflection on these assumptions reveals the difficulties encountered by those who build criterion-referenced tests to meet the assumptions at the desired level. Many teachers and testing experts rebel when this type of interpretation of test scores is used, but criterion-referencing is gaining in popularity with the "learn for mastery movement" of recent years. As more work is done in development of principles, procedures, and techniques for referencing to a criterion the difficulties (Berk, 1980) continue to be at least dealt with, if not entirely overcome.

INTERPRETATION BY PERCENTAGES

Information about the highest possible score on the test provides the teacher and each student with a basis to compare performance in relation to the highest possible score. A ratio, proportion, or percentage of the possible total score can be established by the student or teacher.

Classroom teachers use percentage of items correct in reporting results of classroom achievement tests. The student's score is compared with the score which is the maximum score possible. For example, Rich answered 40 items correctly on a 50-item test. His percentage of correct items is $(100 \times 40)/50 = 80$ percent.

Another way to determine the percentage is to let the highest score obtained set the percentage level. For example, Rich answered 40 items correctly on a 50-item test where 40 was the highest score. His percentage correct could be calculated as $(100 \times 40)/40 = 100$ percent. Dan answered 30 items correctly on the test and his percentage correct is calculated as $(100 \times 30)/40 = 75$. The highest score sets the reference point in this procedure.

An example of percentage of items correct applied to a descriptor set could be:

Percentage Correct	Descriptor Set
90–100%	Excellent
80–89	Good
70–79	Adequate
below 70	Unsatisfactory

Comparison of a score with the highest possible score or as a percentage of the highest obtained score provides little help in telling students about performance compared either to other student performance or to a standard. To make judgments about a percentage of a total score, the score will most likely be compared to preset percentages. This leaves the same problem of meeting the assumptions for judging performance levels for criterion-referenced tests. In addition to information about a percentage of the total score the students will want to know how their scores compare to other scores in the class, requiring that the teacher make additional data available. In either case the percentage must be interpreted further or the student is left with the same questions asked about raw scores.

NORM-REFERENCED INTERPRETATION

For some tests the best way to interpret scores is to interpret each score in context of peer-group performance. The rationale for use of norm-referencing for some tests lies in the need to get an overall estimate of how well a student has done in study of a general subject field or in some other educational undertaking. This kind of test is constructed so that students have an opportunity to reveal their highest levels of attainment.

Mathematical techniques are employed to explain what a set of scores means and to communicate meaning of individual scores for teachers, students, parents, and other interested persons. The mathematics used with test scores deals with the collection, presentation, analysis, and interpretation of test results. The accurate description of test results depends on a logical sequence of treatment of the test scores to aid in reporting them, interpreting them, and ultimately in utilizing the results in effective decision making.

The purpose of this chapter is to develop some fundamental statistical skills based upon mathematical knowledge, many of which you have already conceptualized and used. Some students are concerned about their ability to attack a study of statistics successfully because they have heard that it is difficult. Be assured that you can work comfortably not only in the study of this topic but also in the implementation of it in your classroom procedures. As you will see when you work through the chapter, many of the concepts discussed are familiar to you. New topics will be built in a context of knowledge you already have, and the integrating feature should make new learning pleasing.

The material will provide you with the skills needed to handle efficiently and effectively the results of the tests you administer, especially using scores on tests to further student learning and improve educational programs. A thorough understanding of how scores can be interpreted with a few simple procedures should clearly indicate that tests can be used to support learning and enhance instruction rather than be placed before students as some sort of hurdle to be leaped. Students are different, and test scores can be used to aid in serving those differences. What is the best way to interpret and use the test results? The answer to this question will vary depending on what information is needed, whom the teacher will be reporting to, and how the data will be used.

Ordering

Assume that you have completed the scoring of a mathematics test for your class and the raw scores on the test* are as follows:

---

*This set of data will be used to show how a classroom teacher would employ each technique in interpreting a set of test scores.

Daniel	43	Fred	53	Margaret	55
Shelia	45	Hazel	47	Sam	30
Lynne	54	Jack	40	Charles	28
Dave	41	Helen	45	Alice	49
Alison	44	Reece	52	Earl	47
Susan	38	Walt	35	Bill	43
Jim	40	Kim	46	Rene	44
Mike	46	Carole	56	Rosey	42
Sandra	43	Dick	43	Dan	44
Rich	59	Russ	42	Christopher	39
Mary	37	Joe	32	Darrell	28

Consider Dan's score of 44 and what it means. The single score of 44 on a given test is merely a number and has no meaning in and of itself. In norm-referenced interpretation Dan's score of 44 has meaning in relationship to the other scores in the list of test scores above. A look at any one of the raw scores independently of the others tells us little or nothing about any student achievement compared to how others in the class performed on the test.

Dan as well as the other students in the mathematics class will wish to know what significance is attached to scores. The teacher must answer the question, "How can the set of mathematics test raw scores be organized to provide information to aid interpretation of each student's score in the class?" The teacher may count the number of students who took the test, identify the highest and lowest scores, and compare Dan's score of 44 to them. Even though a rough idea about Dan's score can be formed, more precise information is required to make further judgments and decisions about class performance and each student's performance.

One of the simplest ways to view the score of 44 in relation to the others is to arrange the scores in order from the highest to the lowest. Known as **ordering,** this procedure places each score in a position such that all higher scores are to one side of it and all lower scores are on the other side. A view of the ordering (Figure 14.1) reveals that the score of 44 occurs three times on the test. By counting the number of scores above and below 44, 13 and 17 respectively, the meaning of the score of 44 begins to develop.

Ranking

The relative position of each score in the group may be obtained by forming a ranking. All scores are ranked with the highest being assigned a rank of 1, the second a rank of 2, the third a rank of 3, and so on until all scores have been assigned a rank number. Figure 14.1 shows an ordering of the 33 scores along with the corresponding ranks. When a score appears more than once, this indicates that two or more scores are tied for the same rank. Ranks for tied scores are averaged, and each of those scores is assigned the average rank. For example, in the set of scores in Figure 14.1 the score 47 appears twice

Score	Position	Rank
59	1	1
56	2	2
55	3	3
54	4	4
53	5	5
52	6	6
49	7	7
47	8	8.5
47	9	8.5
46	10	10.5
46	11	10.5
45	12	12.5
45	13	12.5
44	14	15
44	15	15
44	16	15
43	17	18.5
43	18	18.5
43	19	18.5
43	20	18.5
42	21	21.5
42	22	21.5
41	23	23
40	24	24.5
40	25	24.5
39	26	26
38	27	27
37	28	28
35	29	29
32	30	30
30	31	31
28	32	32.5
28	33	32.5

FIGURE 14.1. An ordering of raw scores with corresponding positions and ranks

and occupies the positions usually assigned to ranks 8 and 9. Adding ranks 8 and 9 (8+9=17) and dividing by 2 (17÷2=8.5) the rank of 8.5 is obtained for both scores of 47. The score of 46 appears twice and occupies the positions usually assigned to ranks 10 and 11. Therefore, 10 is added to 11 (21) and divided by 2. The rank of 10.5 is assigned for each score of 46. The position each score occupies is based upon counting the frequencies of scores ordered by size which are above a particular score.

The three students who scored 44 can observe that they ranked 15th out of 33 in achievement in this class. To make the rank meaningful, the number being ranked is important as well as the rank itself. For example, being 15th out of 33 is probably higher achievement than being 15th out of 16. In general, being 15th out of 90 is much better than 26th out of 90, but direct interpretation of scores in different distributions cannot be made from comparison of ranked scores.

Reporting the rank of a score and the number ranked gives information needed for placing that specific score in relation to all other scores based on order. It does not allow interpretation in absolute or equal-interval terms. To say that one horse finished second and another third in a race of seven horses does not give the information needed to decide distances between horses. Since an ordering is not concerned with distance, the space between a finish of second and a finish of third may be very small or very large. A report of a student's rank, like a report of the finish of a horse race, is limited to order, but is a very good indication of individual performance compared to general group performance. Ranks are generally well understood by students and parents.

Frequency Distribution

A **frequency distribution** (Figure 14.2) provides the classroom teacher with a systematic arrangement of raw scores by tallying the frequency of occurrence of each score in the interval or in some instances score values which have been grouped. The following steps are taken to set up a frequency distribution:

1. Find the highest score and the lowest score, and number consecutively from the highest through the lowest score in a column headed X. The X represents the raw score.
2. Head the second column *Tallies,* and record a slash or tally mark for each score. If a score value appears twice, this column will have two slashes, three values gives three slashes, and so on.
3. Count the slash marks, and place the number corresponding to the total number of tallies for each raw score value in the third column. The f column represents the frequency of each score's occurrence.
4. Sum the f column, and record the number of scores (N) as a total.

If the scores are arranged in sequential order, an alternate way to get the frequencies for the scores is by listing only those scores actually obtained on the test and count the frequency for each score and record under the f column as in Figure 14.3.

GRAPHIC REPRESENTATION OF FREQUENCY DISTRIBUTIONS

A tabular frequency distribution presents test data in an effective manner for classroom purposes, but a visual presentation may be more helpful and meaningful to others. The visual presentation may assist in communication of test data to parents and other members of the community. The two most

Raw Score X	Tallies	Frequencies f
59	I	1
58		0
57		0
56	I	1
55	I	1
54	I	1
53	I	1
52	I	1
51		0
50		0
49	I	1
48		0
47	II	2
46	II	2
45	II	2
44	III	3
43	IIII	4
42	II	2
41	I	1
40	II	2
39	I	1
38	I	1
37	I	1
36		0
35	I	1
34		0
33		0
32	I	1
31		0
30	I	1
29		0
28	II	2
		$N = 33$

FIGURE 14.2.   Tabular representation of the test scores in a frequency distribution

common graphs for this purpose are the *histogram* and the *frequency polygon;* however, many different kinds of graphs are available for special needs to represent data graphically.

Graphic representations of a frequency distribution are constructed to give the reader a picture for a quick visual analysis of the data. Although a graph does not provide an opportunity for detailed examination, a histogram or frequency polygon does allow the viewer to place a single score in relation to all other scores. Students and parents generally are more concerned about

X	f	fX
59	1	59
56	1	56
55	1	55
54	1	54
53	1	53
52	1	52
49	1	49
47	2	94
46	2	92
45	2	90
44	3	132
43	4	172
42	2	84
41	1	41
40	2	80
39	1	39
38	1	38
37	1	37
35	1	35
32	1	32
30	1	30
28	2	56
	$N = 33$	$1{,}430 = \Sigma X$

FIGURE 14.3.   Frequency distribution formed from an ordered listing

how a score is related to the total results rather than to particular other scores, and thus a graph is especially valuable to reveal the meaning of one student's score compared to the group performance.

Frequency Distribution—Grouped Data

When the interval between the lowest and highest score values exceeds about 30 units, grouping scores into intervals may aid in the analysis. **Grouped data** condense the scores into a smaller number of categories, which may aid in interpretation of a large number of scores or a set of scores with a wide **range.** Data that have been grouped into intervals greater than one are better for most graphs than ungrouped data. If a hand calculator or microcomputer is not available scores can also be grouped to facilitate hand calculation. A **cf** (cumulative frequency) column is used in later calculation. The steps in arranging the mathematics test scores into a grouped frequency distribution (Figure 14.4) are as follows:

1. Calculate the range of the distribution. The range is the difference between the highest and lowest scores. In the set of test scores in the example the highest score is 59 and the lowest is 28. The range is 31. [If Range $= (X_h - X_l) + 1$, then range $= 32$.]
2. Divide the range by 10 and 20. About 10 to 20 intervals are used for grouped frequency distributions.
3. Determine the size of the class interval to be used. In the example of test scores dividing the range of 31 by 10 gives 3.1. Dividing 31 by 20 gives 1.55. The size of the interval should be between the two values just determined. By using odd numbers of units, decimals in computation are avoided; therefore, the size of the class interval should be an odd number. In this case the class interval of 3 is selected.
4. Identify the lowest score in the distribution. In this example 28 is the lowest score.
5. Establish a lowest interval which includes the lowest score, 28. Select the lower limit of the interval by finding the multiple of the interval size which is just below the lowest score. For example, 27 (9×3) is the next multiple of 3 below 28. The lowest score is 28 and the interval width is 3, and a score of 27 which is a multiple of 3 is closest to 28. Consequently, 27 is used as the lower limit of the lowest interval, 27–29. Continue listing the intervals, 30–32, 33–35, and so on until the interval which includes the highest score is reached. For this distribution that interval is 57–59.
6. Tally each raw score according to the interval in which it falls. The frequency of each interval is the number of scores which fall within that interval as indicated by the tallies. The sum of the f (frequency) column gives the total number of scores.

Histogram

The **histogram** is a graphical representation of a frequency distribution. Through a histogram the classroom teacher may present how students scored on the mathematics test. The histogram is prepared by placing the test score values on a horizontal axis or baseline with the scores increasing in magnitude from left to right. The scale for the vertical axis on the left side of the graph is used to indicate the number of students (f) earning each score. The vertical axis begins with 0 and moves to the highest frequency appearing for any score or score interval. The data on a histogram are shown in the form of rectangular columns. The width of the base of each rectangle represents the score(s) in an interval, and the height represents the number of student scores falling within the interval.

Figure 14.5 is a histogram of the ungrouped achievement scores from the mathematics test, and Figure 14.6 presents a histogram of the grouped scores. The histogram of the grouped scores uses the limits of each interval as the

Interval	Tallies	f	cf
57–59	I	1	33
54–56	III	3	32
51–53	II	2	29
48–50	I	1	27
45–47	THL I	6	26
42–44	THL IIII	9	20
39–41	IIII	4	11
36–38	II	2	7
33–35	I	1	5
30–32	II	2	4
27–29	II	2	1
		N = 33	

FIGURE 14.4.   Grouped frequency distribution of 33 test scores

points along the baseline of the graph. The apparent score limits of the interval 27–29 contain scores 27, 28, and 29. The interval actually extends from point 26.5 to point 29.5, the next interval commences at 29.5 and extends to 32.5, the next from 32.5 to 35.5 and so on. These interval limits are called **true limits, exact limits,** or **real limits.** The real limits extend half the distance between the upper apparent limit of one interval and the lower apparent limit of the next higher interval. This way all points on the baseline are accounted for in the histogram.

The reader should note that the histogram (also frequency polygon) drawn from grouped data no longer reflects the position of the scores as they appear in the original frequency distribution. Each score is now associated with a greater baseline interval; thus, some information about the original scores is lost. However, the grouped-score histogram has an advantage in that the general characteristics of the distribution are more apparent after scores have been grouped, especially if the number of observations is relatively small. Although grouping scores for calculation is not widely used because the hand calculator has become so commonplace, grouping for graphical representation is advantageous and continues to serve as an excellent way to show how a particular score relates to all other scores.

Frequency Polygon

The **frequency polygon** is a graphical representation of a frequency distribution. It aids the understanding of the characteristics of a distribution through the visual representation of the frequency of scores associated with designated points on the baseline. A frequency polygon is constructed by locating the midpoint of each interval and recording a dot to represent the number of scores falling in that interval. This would be at the center of the

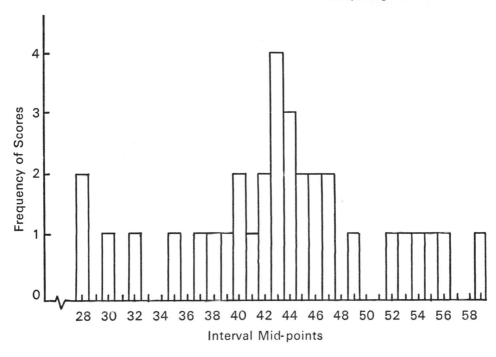

FIGURE 14.5. Histogram of ungrouped scores by frequencies

top of each rectangular column on a histogram. With grouped data the points are plotted at the midpoints of the interval and then the points are connected by lines. Figure 14.7 represents the frequency polygon of the ungrouped scores while Figure 14.8 is the frequency polygon for the grouped data.

MEASURES OF CENTRAL TENDENCY

Central tendency relates to a point in a distribution around which the scores tend to center. This point can be used as the most representative value for a distribution of scores. A measure of central tendency is helpful in showing where the average or typical score falls. The teacher can see how an individual student performance relates to the average value or make comparisons about two or more classes which took the same test. Three different procedures can be employed to obtain the most commonly used measures of central location for a distribution of test scores. If one score is to be used to represent all the scores in a distribution, then the value that appears most often (the mode), a point which divides the number of scores (N) into two equal parts (the median), or the arithmetical average (the mean) could be used. Each of these three is discussed in a following section.

A.

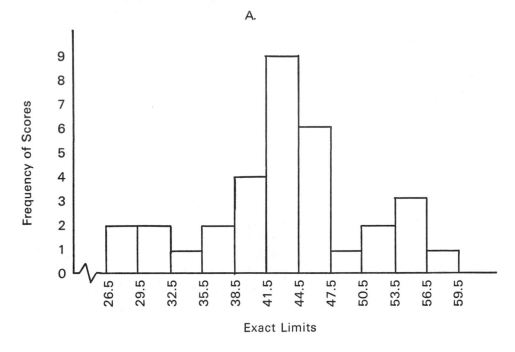

B.

Interval Limits		
Apparent	Exact	f
57–59	56.5–59.5	1
54–56	53.5–56.5	3
51–53	50.5–53.5	2
48–50	47.5–50.5	1
45–47	44.5–47.5	6
42–44	41.5–44.5	9
39–41	38.5–41.5	4
36–38	35.5–38.5	2
33–35	32.5–35.5	1
30–32	29.5–32.5	2
27–29	26.5–29.5	2

FIGURE 14.6. Histogram of grouped data (A) and tabular frequency distribution (B) using exact interval limits for grouped data

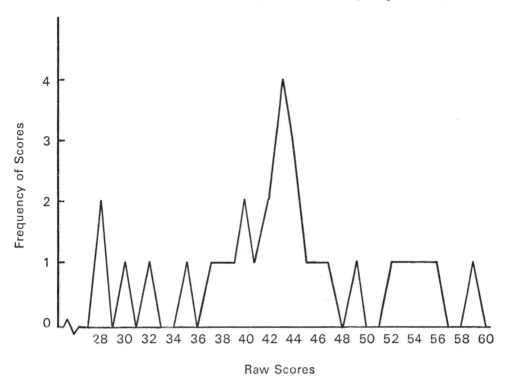

FIGURE 14.7. Frequency polygon of ungrouped scores

Mode

The **mode** is the most frequently occurring score in a distribution. From a tabular or graphical representation of a set of scores, the mode is readily identifiable. Since the mode is the score occurring most frequently, it will be the value associated with the highest point on a histogram or frequency polygon. In the tabular representation it is the score or interval with the largest frequency of occurrence. A set of scores may have two (bimodal) or more (multimodal) modes. Using the data from the mathematics achievement test scores shown in Figures 14.2 and 14.3, the mode is 43 which occurs four times. In grouped frequency distributions the mode is reported as the midpoint of the interval that has the largest frequency. From Figures 14.5 and 14.7 the mode can be observed to be 43. In Figures 14.6 and 14.8, the midpoint (43) of the interval 41.5 to 44.5 is considered to be the mode.

A.

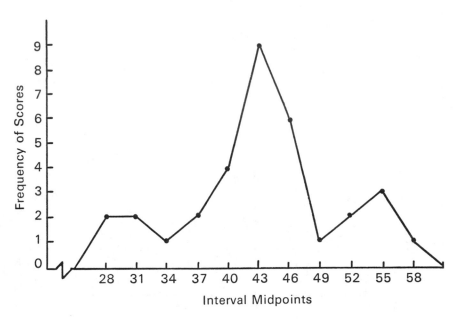

B.

| Interval Limits | | |
Apparent	Midpoint	f
57–59	58	1
54–56	55	3
51–53	52	2
48–50	49	1
45–47	46	6
42–44	43	9
39–41	40	4
36–38	37	2
33–35	34	1
30–32	31	2
27–29	28	2

**FIGURE 14.8. Frequency polygon of grouped data (A) and tabular
frequency distribution (B) using mid-points for grouped data**

The mode is employed when a quick approximate measure of central tendency is desired or when the measure of central tendency should be reported as the most frequently occurring value. The mode is a rough or coarse measure, since it depends simply upon counting the number of times each score occurs and choosing the one which is greatest. It does not take into consideration any other score values except those in the most popular interval, and other values are not reflected in the value of the mode.

Median

The **median** is the midpoint of a distribution of scores. It is the point above and below which 50 percent of the scores fall. In a distribution of ungrouped scores arranged in order of magnitude, the median is located by counting from either end of the ordered scores until the middle score is reached. When an odd number of scores appears, there is a middle score which falls in the center of the distribution of scores and is the median. For example, the median can be determined for 21 social studies test scores after they are arranged in order of magnitude.

$$44 \quad 42 \quad 42 \quad 40 \quad 39 \quad 38 \quad 37 \quad 37 \quad 36 \quad 34$$
$$33 \quad 31 \quad 30 \quad 30 \quad 29 \quad 27 \quad 26 \quad 25 \quad 23 \quad 23 \quad 22$$

There are 21 social studies test scores. Counting 11 scores, starting with either the upper or the lower end, 33 is the middle score and 33 would be reported as the *counting median.* If the score of 22 is removed from this array, 20 scores remain. When N is even, the median must be located between the two middle scores. Counting 10 ($N/2 = 20/2 = 10$) scores from either direction indicates that 34 and 33 are the two scores closest to the middle of the distribution. The average of the two scores is $(34 + 33) \div 2$, or 33.5 (the median). The median of 33.5 is halfway between 34 and 33.

The median is employed when the midpoint of the distribution is desired. It has been referred to as the *counting average,* since only the order of the scores is taken into consideration when counting to determine the median.

A special problem arises if the counting procedure for finding the median identifies a possible median score which appears more than once. For most classroom tests a median derived by counting can be used in any case, but for a procedure which covers all cases and gives the exact median point, see the later discussion of finding other points (quartiles, deciles, percentiles) in the distribution based on order.

Arithmetic Mean

The **mean** is determined by adding all the scores in a distribution and dividing by the number of scores. For example, if the five scores of 41, 45, 46, 48, and 50 are added the sum is 230. Dividing 230 by the number of scores ($230 \div 5$), the average score of 46 is computed to be the mean.

Expressed in words:

$$\text{Mean} = \frac{\text{Sum of all scores}}{\text{Number of scores}}$$

Expressed as a formula:

$$\bar{X} = \frac{X_1 + X_2 + \ldots + X_N}{N} = \frac{\Sigma X}{N}$$

Where:

X = any test score.*
$\bar{X}$ is the mean.
Σ = the sum of (uppercase Greek letter, sigma, which means add all X values which follow)
N = the number of scores

The average of 8, 5, 10, 4, 12, and 9 is computed as follows:

$$\bar{X} = \frac{\Sigma X}{N}$$
$$\bar{X} = \frac{X_1 + X_2 + X_3 + X_4 + X_5 + X_6}{N}$$
$$\bar{X} = \frac{8 + 5 + 10 + 4 + 12 + 9}{6}$$
$$\bar{X} = \frac{48}{6}$$
$$\bar{X} = 8$$

The mean is the most widely employed measure of central tendency and is used with the standard deviation which is a measure of variability or spread of the scores around the mean. Each individual score value is taken into account when determining the mean, since the scores on the test are added together and then divided by the number of scores.

The mean is sensitive to extreme scores in a distribution. If a score or a few scores are scattered to an exaggerated distance at the bottom or top of the distribution, the value of the mean can be heavily affected, distorting this measure of central tendency. For example, two or three very low or high test scores may affect the mean considerably. If extreme scores distort the mean value, the median or mode might be a better value to use as the measure of central tendency.

---

*X_1 is the first score on the variable X, X_2 is the second score, and so on. If measurement is on the Y variable, Y_1 is the first score on variable Y, Y_2 is the second score, and so on. $\bar{Y}$ is the mean of the Y variable values. The sigma (Σ) before the X indicates that all X values should be added.

Computing Measures of Central Tendency

Ungrouped data (Figure 14.3) of the mathematics achievement test scores can be used to explain computation which has been discussed in the previous section. The raw scores are listed from the highest to the lowest, and by observation the mode is identified as 43, since it appears in the distribution more times than any other value.

By substituting in the formula for the mean the computation is:

$$\overline{X} = \frac{\Sigma X}{N} = \frac{1,430}{33} = 43.33$$

To find the counting median for a set of scores where N is an odd number, add one to N and divide by 2. This gives the position in the distribution for the median. For the set of achievement scores $N = 33$.

$$\frac{N+1}{2} = \frac{33+1}{2} = \frac{34}{2} = 17$$

Counting from the lowest score to the 17th score, the counting median is 43.

Comparison of the Measures of Central Tendency

The mean is the most used measure of central tendency for testing situations. It is easy to compute and is most widely understood. It represents a logical approach to finding the average score. The mode is the crudest measure of central tendency although it is a quick estimate. The median is sometimes employed to avoid the influence of extreme scores. For example, if the test is too easy, there may be perfect scores, or if the test is too difficult, there may be very low scores. In either case, students at the extremes have not been correctly measured, and the median is the best and easiest average to use.

Looking back to the original 33 scores on the mathematics achievement test and the subsequent discussion of the measures of central tendency, the mode of the 33 scores equaled 43, the mean equaled 43.33 and the median 43. Dan's score of 44, then, is slightly above each of these measures of central tendency. Compared to the performance of the group Dan can be considered to be achieving at about an average rate in the subject of mathematics.

RELATIONSHIPS WITHIN A DISTRIBUTION

Within the interval established by the lowest score and the highest score are many points which can be used to explain relationships of scores to other scores in the distribution. When the counting median was determined for the set of test data, a point was named which had roughly 50 percent of the scores below it. Using a general formula the median and other points can be calculated precisely. A point could be located which has 25 percent of the scores below it. Another point could be located which has 75 percent of the scores below it. These two points along with the median are called **quartiles** and divide a distribution into four equal parts. Nine points which divide a distribution into 10 equal parts are called **deciles.** Ninety-nine points which divide a distribution into 100 equal parts are called **percentiles.**

The general formula for finding percentiles is:

$$P_p = L + \left(\frac{pN - f_b}{f_w}\right)i$$

Where:

P_p = any one of the 99 percentile points
L = the exact lower limit of the interval which contains P_p
N = the total number of scores
i = the interval size
p = the proportion of scores below the point
f_b = the number of scores falling below L
f_w = the number of scores in the interval which contains P_p

Expressed in words:

$$P_p = \begin{array}{l}\text{Exact lower limit}\\ \text{of the interval}\\ \text{which contains}\\ \text{the } P_p\end{array} + \left(\frac{\begin{array}{l}\text{(the proportion of}\quad\text{the number of}\\ \text{scores below the}\quad\text{scores falling}\\ \text{point) (total}\quad - \text{below the exact}\\ \text{number of scores)}\quad\text{lower limit of}\\ \text{the interval}\\ \text{which contains } P_p\end{array}}{\begin{array}{l}\text{the number of scores in the}\\ \text{interval which contains } P_p\end{array}}\right) \begin{array}{l}\text{width of}\\ \text{the class}\\ \text{interval}\end{array}$$

The following computation shows how to find P_{75}—the point that has exactly 75 percent of the distribution of scores below it. P_{25} is also calculated using grouped data in the table in Figure 14.4.

$$P_{75} = 44.5 + \left(\frac{24.75 - 20}{6}\right)3 \qquad P_{25} = 38.5 + \left(\frac{8.25 - 7}{4}\right)3$$

$$= 44.5 + \left(\frac{4.75}{6}\right)3 \qquad\qquad = 38.5 + \left(\frac{1.25}{4}\right)3$$

$$= 44.5 + (.79)\,3 \qquad\qquad\quad = 38.5 + (.31)\,3$$

$$= 44.5 + 2.37 \qquad\qquad\qquad = 38.5 + .94$$

$$P_{75} = 46.87 \qquad\qquad\qquad\quad P_{25} = 39.44$$

Another name for P_{75} is Q_3. P_{25} is also called Q_1. P_{50} is called Q_2 and the median. P_{10} is also D_1, P_{20} is also D_2, and so on. The general formula for finding percentile points can be used for any of these by varying the p value which is multiplied by N and adjusting the other formula values to the interval where the score falls. For example the exact median is calculated as:

$$\text{Median} = P_{50} = 41.5 + \left(\frac{16.5 - 11}{9}\right)3$$

$$= 41.5 + \left(\frac{5.5}{9}\right)3$$

$$= 41.5 + (.61)3$$

$$= 41.5 + 1.83$$

$$\text{Median} = P_{50} = 43.33$$

MEASURES OF VARIABILITY

In addition to finding descriptive points in a distribution, interpretation within a set of scores also requires that the property of variability be given attention. Scores which are scattered widely along the measuring scale reflect the characteristic of variability much more than a set of scores which tend to be alike with little scattering. The two distributions below have the same mean, but Set A is much more dispersed than Set B. A **measure of variability** will indicate that homogeneous groups on the characteristic being measured will reflect small measures of variability while heterogeneous groups will reflect larger measures of variability.

Set A

2 7 14 16 19 20 23 27

$$\bar{X} = \frac{128}{8} = 16$$

Set B

12 13 15 16 17 17 18 20

$$\bar{X} = \frac{128}{8} = 16$$

The measures of variability or dispersion discussed here are the range, the quartile deviation, and the standard deviation. Whereas measures of central tendency were expressed as points on a continuum, measures of variability are intervals on the scale of measurement. Each variability measure has properties which are useful in making interpretations about variations of scores within a frequency distribution and also allow for making comparisons between distributions and scores in different distributions.

Range

The range is the difference between the highest and lowest scores. (It has also been defined as the highest score minus the lowest score plus one, so both the highest and lowest scores are included, and it represents the interval to the exact limits.) It is not a dependable measure of variability, since it is calculated from only two values and extreme scores greatly influence it, but the range does provide a quick approximation of the spread of scores. The ranges for sets A and B are:

$$\text{Range}_A = 27 - 2 = 25.$$
$$\text{Range}_B = 20 - 12 = 8.$$

The difference between the highest and lowest score in Set A is more than three times that difference in Set B, reflecting that the subjects in Set A are much more heterogeneous on the characteristic measured than the subjects in Set B. For example, Set A could be one student picked at random from each of the first eight grades, and Set B could be eight students picked at random from the sixth grade. The measures could be the number of push-ups each student did. The greater differences in ages in Set A are reflected in measures of performance that are in part a function of age.

Standard Deviation

Since the range is subject to distortion by a single very low or very high score, a more sensitive measure of variation is usually calculated for test scores. Known as the **standard deviation** it is the square root of the mean of the squared deviations of all the scores from the mean.

$$\text{Standard deviation} = \sigma = \sqrt{\frac{\Sigma(X - \bar{X})^2}{N}}$$

Where:

$$\sigma = \text{Standard deviation}$$
$$\Sigma = \text{means to sum}$$
$$(X - \bar{X}) = \text{deviation of each score from the mean}$$
$$N = \text{the number of scores}$$

Expressed in words:

$$\text{Standard deviation} = \sqrt{\frac{\text{sum of}\left[\left(\begin{array}{c}\text{deviation of each score} \\ \text{from the mean}\end{array}\right)\text{squared}\right]}{\text{the number of scores}}}$$

The standard deviation is basically a measure of how far each score, on the average, is from the mean. Since the standard deviation is based on deviations from the mean, these two statistics are used together to give meaning to test scores.

To compute the standard deviation the scores are listed under the X (score) column. By subtracting the mean from each score the deviation values $(X - \bar{X})$ are obtained. Squaring each devation in the $(X - \bar{X})$ column provides the $(X - \bar{X})^2$ column values. When the $(X - \bar{X})^2$ column is summed the numerator value $[\Sigma\,(X - \bar{X})^2]$ is calculated. For the following data the mean is equal to $\dfrac{318}{6} = 53$.

Score X	$(X - \bar{X})$ $(X - 53)$	$(X - \bar{X})^2$
59	+6	36
56	+3	9
65	+2	4
52	−1	1
50	−3	9
46	−7	49
318	0	108

Substituting in the formula:

$$\sigma = \sqrt{\frac{\Sigma\,(X - \bar{X})^2}{N}} = \sqrt{\frac{108}{6}} = \sqrt{18} = 4.24$$

Using data from Figure 14.9, the steps for computation of the standard deviation from the ungrouped mathematics scores follows.

1. Set up the columns $X - \bar{X}$, score minus the mean and $(X - \bar{X})^2$, score minus the mean, squared.
2. Subtract each score from the mean, square it, and record the values in the appropriate columns as has been done in Figure 14.9.
3. When the scores are less than the mean, the negative sign precedes the difference between the raw score and the mean. Squaring the value eliminates negative numbers.
4. Sum the $(X - \bar{X})^2$ column and substitute the values in the formula.

$$\sigma = \sqrt{\frac{\Sigma(X - \bar{X})^2}{N}} \qquad \sigma = \sqrt{\frac{1894.04}{33}} \qquad \sigma = \sqrt{57.39}$$

$$\sigma = 7.57$$

Quartile Deviation

When using the statistics of percentiles, deciles, quartiles, or the median which are based on the order of the scores, the standard deviation cannot be used as a measure of variability, since the deviations used in calculation of the standard deviation are based on the mean. The variability of a distribution of scores can be shown by using the two points, Q_3 and Q_1. A measure of the variability of the middle 50 percent of the scores is considered to be a good estimate, because extreme scores or erratic spacing between scores in the upper 25 percent and lower 25 percent are excluded for computation.

Since equal intervals are not assured or expected in **ordinal data,** there is no way to base differences on the median the same way that the standard deviation used the mean as a base. Instead the value which is equal to half the distance from Q_1 to Q_3 is used and is called the **quartile deviation (Q).**

Raw Score X	$X - \bar{X}$ $X - 43.33$	$(X - \bar{X})^2$ $(X - 43.33)^2$
59	15.67	245.54
56	12.67	160.52
55	11.67	136.18
54	10.67	138.84
53	9.67	93.50
52	8.67	75.16
49	5.67	32.14
47	3.67	13.46
47	3.67	13.46
46	2.67	7.12
46	2.67	7.12
45	1.67	2.78
45	1.67	2.78
44	0.67	0.44
44	0.67	0.44
44	0.67	0.44
43	− 0.33	0.10
43	− 0.33	0.10
43	− 0.33	0.10
43	− 0.33	0.10
42	− 1.33	1.76
42	− 1.33	1.76
41	− 2.33	5.42
40	− 3.33	11.08
40	− 3.33	11.08
39	− 4.33	18.74
38	− 5.33	28.40
37	− 6.33	40.06
35	− 8.33	69.38
32	−11.33	128.36
30	−13.33	177.68
28	−15.33	235.00
28	−15.33	235.00
1,430		1,894.04

FIGURE 14.9. Ungrouped data — mathematics achievement test scores

The formula for Q and its computation for the mathematics test scores follow.

$$Q = \frac{Q_3 - Q_1}{2}$$

Where:

Q = quartile deviation
Q_3 = 75th percentile
Q_1 = 25th percentile

Expressed in words:

$$\text{Quartile deviation} = \frac{\text{75th percentile} - \text{25th percentile}}{2}$$

$$Q_3 = P_{75} = 46.87 \qquad Q_1 = P_{25} = 39.44$$

Substituting in the formula:

$$Q = \frac{46.87 - 39.44}{2} \qquad Q = \frac{7.43}{2} \qquad Q = 3.72$$

Test persons and teachers find use for the quartile deviation when reporting norms or test results in the ordinal statistic of percentiles or when they need a measure of variability of the middle 50 percent of the scores. Although the use of the quartile deviation is more limited than the standard deviation it is the measure of variability that best reflects differences in ordinal data.

Comparison of the Measures of Variability

The range is a quick measure of variability although it is the crudest measure. When the median is used as the measure of central tendency, the quartile deviation is used as the measure of variability in test interpretation. The quartile deviation, like the median, is unaffected by a few extreme scores in a distribution. The most used measure of variability is the standard deviation, since it is the most stable and varies less from one sample to another than other measures. It is expressed as a distance along the baseline of a graph which will be used later in this chapter as an aid to further score interpretation. Keep in mind that if there are no differences in the data (all scores the same) the standard deviation is 0 and serves as the minimum dispersion of scores. As differences increase the standard deviation increases.

For the 33 mathematics achievement test scores the range is 31, the quartile deviation is 3.72, and the standard deviation is 7.57.

OTHER CHARACTERISTICS OF DISTRIBUTIONS

To describe a frequency distribution by reporting its characteristics, a teacher will need to give at least one measure of *central tendency* and at least one measure of *variability.* In addition to these two values further description requires information about the **skewness** and **kurtosis** of the distribution. Skewness is the degree of *symmetry* of the scores. Kurtosis is the degree of *peakedness* or *flatness* of the distribution curve.

Both skewness and kurtosis effects are more apparent in a graphic representation of the distribution than in tabular form. Although statistical techniques exist to measure skewness and kurtosis precisely, the information needed to interpret test scores can be obtained easier from a frequency polygon or histogram.

Skewness

Skewness refers to the degree of symmetry attached to the occurrence of the scores along the score interval. When the scores tend to center around one point with those on both sides of that point balancing each other (see Figure 14.10), the distribution is said to have no skewness. If there are some scores in the distribution which are so atypical of the group that the distribution becomes asymmetrical, then that distribution is said to be skewed. The word skew means "atypical" or "not like the others"; therefore, if the atypical scores are above the measure of central tendency (in the positive direction), the distribution is said to be positively skewed (see Figure 14.10). Likewise if the atypical scores are below the measure of central location (in the negative direction), the distribution is said to be negatively skewed (see Figure 14.10). If there are no atypical scores, the two halves of a frequency polygon will appear as near mirror images of each other, and the **symmetrical** distribution is said to have no skewness. A negatively skewed distribution is shown in tabular and graphic form in Figure 14.11. A positively skewed distribution is shown in tabular and graphic form in Figure 14.12.

The skewness of a distribution is important in interpreting a set of scores from a class, since the reason for the skewness can explain something about the group tested or the test itself.

If the teacher uses norm referencing and the scores in a distribution pile up at a relatively low score and then tail out for frequencies of higher scores (positively skewed), then the test may have been too difficult for the students. If most of the scores pile up near the top of the scale and then tail out for frequencies of relatively lower scores (negatively skewed), the test may have been too easy for the group. Of course, for a test of mastery a negatively skewed distribution is expected if most of the students achieved mastery.

Criterion-referenced tests, other mastery tests, and problem tests should generate negatively skewed distributions, since students are expected to respond correctly to all or nearly all of the tasks. The most frequently occurring score may often be the highest possible score with only a few lower scores.

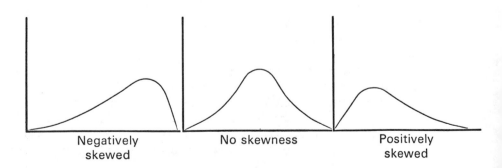

FIGURE 14.10. Three frequency distributions with varying skewness

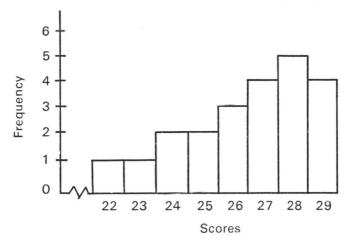

Scores	Frequency
29	4
28	5
27	4
26	3
25	2
24	2
23	1
22	1
	22

Mean = 26.59
Median = 27
Mode = 28

FIGURE 14.11. The mean, median, and mode in a negatively skewed distribution

Although most test makers of norm-referenced instruments prefer to have a smooth bell-shaped curve for distributions of test scores, a symmetrically shaped curve for a distribution does not, in itself, assure the test user that the test was a good one. If 100 students flip coins to mark answers to a lengthy true-false test, the frequency polygon would probably be very symmetrical and take the shape of a bell, since the total score for each test would be based on probability of chance occurrences. Since the symmetry can be a function of factors other than of good testing procedures, it indicates little about the quality of the test.

Kurtosis

The characteristic of kurtosis is very closely related to the characteristic of variability. Although kurtosis is not widely used in testing it can give an indication of the degree of homogeneity of the group being tested

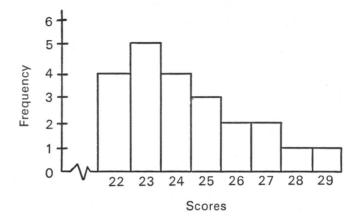

Scores	Frequency
29	1
28	1
27	2
26	2
25	3
24	4
23	5
22	4
	22

Mean = 24.41
Median = 24
Mode = 23

FIGURE 14.12. The mean, median, and mode in a positively skewed distribution

in regard to the characteristic being measured. If students tend to be much alike the scores will generate a **leptokurtic** shaped frequency polygon as represented by A in Figure 14.13, and if students are very different, a **platykurtic** distribution as represented by B in Figure 14.13. A **mesokurtic** distribution is neither platykurtic nor leptokurtic and is represented by C in Figure 14.13.

If a set of scores produces a leptokurtic frequency distribution, then the conclusion can be drawn that the group was homogeneous on the trait that the test measured. If a set of scores produces a platykurtic frequency distribution, then the conclusion to be drawn is that the group was heterogeneous on the trait which the test measured. If a set of scores produces a mesokurtic frequency distribution, then the conclusion is that the trait is normally distributed in the group tested.

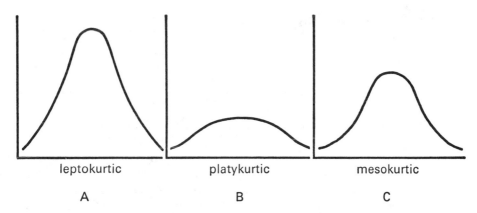

leptokurtic	platykurtic	mesokurtic
A	B	C

FIGURE 14.13. Three degrees of kurtosis for frequency distributions

STANDARD SCORES

A standard score is one of many derived scores used in testing today. Most derived scores are employed in published standardized tests, but some are also valuable to the classroom teacher, since scores from different tests can be made comparable by expressing them on the same scale. For norm-referenced tests it is meaningful to interpret classroom test scores by locating a student's score with reference to the average for the class and to describe the distance between the score and the average in terms of the spread of scores in the distribution.

Dan's raw score on the mathematics achievement test was 44. In the same class of students Dan scored 65 on a second mathematics test. To compare the raw score on one test with a raw score on another test or to add raw scores from different tests to obtain a total or average score is meaningless. The units are not comparable because the tests may have different possible total scores, means, and standard deviations. By converting raw scores on both tests to standard scores, the units become comparable, and can be averaged —a convenience for record keeping through the marking periods for classroom tests.

Using the deviation of a score from the mean $(X - \bar{X})$ and the standard deviation (σ), a teacher can build what is called a **z-score**. This linear transformation reports a score deviation $((X - \bar{X})$ in units of the standard deviation:

$$z = \frac{X - \bar{X}}{\sigma}$$

Where:

z = a standard score
X = any raw score

$\bar{X}$ = the mean

σ = the standard deviation

Expressed in words:

$$\text{Standard score} = \frac{\text{raw score} - \text{the mean}}{\text{standard deviation}}$$

If each score in a distribution is transformed into a z score and a new mean and standard deviation are calculated for the new distribution of transformed scores, the new mean will be 0 and the new standard deviation will be 1. The z score gives the teacher a common unit or standard score to use in test interpretation. The z score and other standard scores are used by test makers much the same as the standard measures of liter, inch, quart, kilometer, calorie, and such are used in physical measurement.

For example, the means and standard deviations for Dan's two test scores are as follows:

	Dan's Raw Score	Mean	Standard Deviation
Mathematics test 1	44	43.33	7.57
Mathematics test 2	65	70.00	8.50

Comparisons can be made between the two scores because the scores were earned in the same group of students. Substituting in the formula $z = \dfrac{X - \bar{X}}{\sigma}$ for mathematics tests 1 and 2:

$$z_1 = \frac{44 - 43.33}{7.57} = \frac{+.67}{7.57} = +.09$$

$$z_2 = \frac{65 - 70}{8.50} = \frac{-5}{8.50} = -.59$$

The mean for the z score distribution, as pointed out, is equal to 0, and the standard deviation is equal to 1. The z distribution and Dan's two scores look like this:

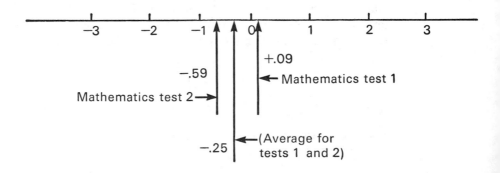

Although Dan had a higher point total on the second test, within this set of students he did less well on the second test than he did on the first.

Each of the standard measures mentioned before is standard because a unit for each measure is carefully defined so that it means the same to everyone. The volume of a quart is the same in all cases because one particular container is said to be the standard for all other quarts. The caloric is defined as the amount of heat necessary to raise the temperature of one gram of water from 14.5°C to 15.5°C when the water is at atmospheric pressure. The z score unit is defined as one standard deviation unit. Of course, the standard deviation will vary from one distribution to another, but when scores in one distribution are put in standard deviation units of that distribution, those z scores are comparable to z scores formed for scores in other distributions. Uses for, and cautions attached to the use of, the z score are discussed in a following section of this chapter.

Typically, the range of a set of scores is no more than six standard deviation units. For a set of scores from one classroom the range of the distribution is likely to be somewhat less than six standard deviation units; probably closer to four units. A set of z scores will be within the interval roughly from -3.00 to $+3.00$. This small range of scores may make differences between scores difficult to interpret. A second awkwardness associated with z scores is that some values are negative and some are positive. When recording, calculating, or reporting z scores, it is easy to drop a sign or in some way to change a value from negative to positive or vice versa. Other simple transformations can be made to a set of z score values to overcome these two difficulties. The general formula is:

$$\text{Standard score} = d(z) + c$$

where:

d = new standard deviation
c = new mean

A new set of scores which retains the original relationships but avoids the difficulties can be found by the following transformation for **Z scores:**

$$Z = 10 (z) + 50$$

This transformation has the effect of increasing the standard deviation to 10 units and moving the mean from 0 to 50. Other widely used transformations are:

(A)   100 (z) + 500
(B)   25 (z) + 150
(C)   15 (z) + 100
(D) 21.06 (z) + 100

A z score of 1 is comparable to a 600 in transformation A, to 175 in B, 115 in C and 121.6 in D. A negative two in the z score distribution is comparable to a 300 in A, 100 in B, 70 in C and 57.88 in D. See Figure 14.14 for other comparable values for the several transformations.

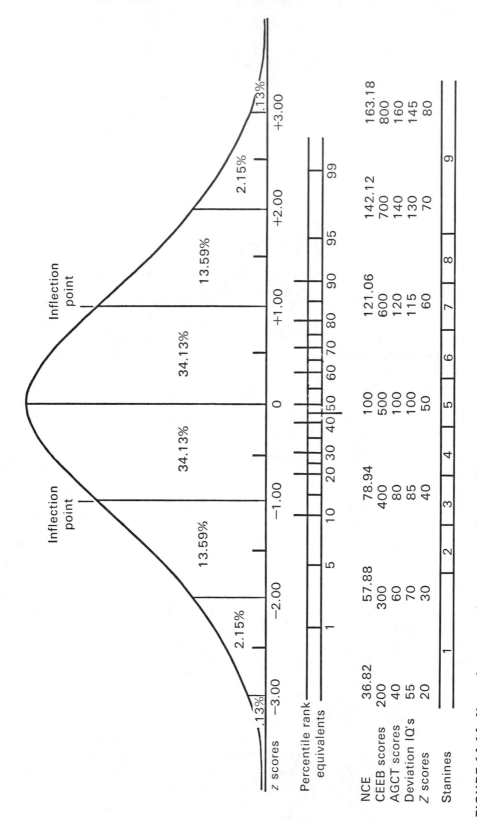

FIGURE 14.14. Normal curve and areas associated with baseline segments and equivalent values for selected transformations

A popular score for the field of testing is the **T score**. Like the Z score distribution, the T score distribution has a mean of 50 and a standard deviation of 10. The only difference between the two distributions with $\overline{X} = 50$ and $\sigma = 10$ is that the T distribution has been **normalized** to remove any skewness in the original distribution. If the normal curve is used as a model to interpret a score in a distribution which is heavily skewed, the basic assumption would be violated. By normalizing a skewed distribution by a transformation to the normal, the assumption of likeness is met. The conversion procedure* can be used for skewed distributions and for published tests. For most classroom tests where appropriate measurement procedures allow for scores to be located in proper relationship along the scale, z scores and Z scores are quite proper for school uses.

The transformation of Dan's two test scores are as follows:

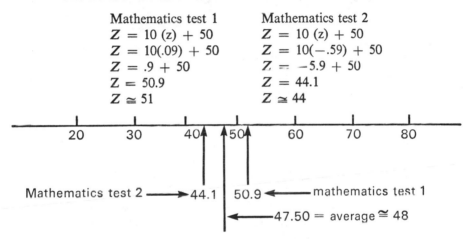

Mathematics test 1	Mathematics test 2
$Z = 10(z) + 50$	$Z = 10(z) + 50$
$Z = 10(.09) + 50$	$Z = 10(-.59) + 50$
$Z = .9 + 50$	$Z = -5.9 + 50$
$Z = 50.9$	$Z = 44.1$
$Z \cong 51$	$Z \cong 44$

Mathematics test 2 ——→ 44.1 | 50.9 ←—— mathematics test 1
←——— 47.50 = average $\cong$ 48

Dan's Z score of 50.9 for mathematics test 1 and his Z of 44.1 for mathematics test 2 can be averaged. The average of the two tests is 47.50 or about 48.

THE NORMAL CURVE

The normal probability distribution, commonly referred to as the **normal curve**, is a theoretical distribution based on an infinite number of values that vary symmetrically. The normal distribution is made up of a family of an indefinitely large number of possible distributions that are generated by different means and standard deviations. The normal curve used to interpret test scores has a mean of 0 and a standard deviation of 1 and pictorially takes the shape of a bell. It is referred to as the unit normal curve because it has a standard deviation of 1, and the area under the curve is set at unity (1) to interpret the meaning of the scores in a distribution.

---

*George A. Ferguson. *Statistical analysis in psychology and education* (5th ed.). New York: McGraw-Hill, 1981, pp. 455–458.

The normal curve is not a distribution of actual scores but a theoretical distribution plotted from a mathematical equation. The normal curve is a theoretical mathematical ideal, and its importance lies in the fact that actual distributions approximate the theoretical model of the normal curve. Sets of test scores can be made meaningful by using the unit normal curve as a model, utilizing the properties of the normal curve to interpret each score in relation to the other scores.

Properties of the theoretical normal curve used to interpret test scores are:

1. The curve is bell-shaped.
2. The curve is symmetrical.
3. In the curve the mean, median, and mode have the same value.
4. The area under the curve represents the total frequency (*N*) of the distribution.
5. The points of change of direction (inflection) of the curve occur at the points one standard deviation above and below the mean. It is at these points that the tails of the curve start decreasing.
6. In a normal curve $+1$ σ from the mean includes 68.26 percent of the cases, $+2$ σ from the mean includes 95.44 percent of the cases, and $+$ 3 σ from the mean includes virtually all of the cases.

The graphical representation in Figure 14.14 presents an opportunity for a visual study of properties of the normal curve. Each of the six listed properties of the theoretical normal curve should be observed in the frequency polygon.

Many characteristics of human beings generate sets of scores that are normally distributed, and norm-referenced interpretation of test scores uses the dimensions and characteristics of the unit normal curve. The normal curve presents an idealized distribution of scores for a group on many tests, and is used to give meaning to students' scores. The properties of the normal curve aid the interpretation of a set of test scores, allow comparisons of performances of one individual in different testing situations, and allow a student's score to be compared to scores of another group of students on the same test. A measure of central tendency (the mean) and a measure of variability (the standard deviation) have been used to transform the obtained score into the standard *z* score. The following section shows how the *z* score and the *Z* score aid in interpretation of scores of tests by use of known characteristics of the normal curve. Percentile ranks and stanines are then presented. They also use the properties of the normal curve to give further meaning to test scores.

Making Test Scores Comparable

Within the classroom the teacher makes comparisons of a student's performance among the several subject-matter fields studied. Such a student profile can show points of strength and weakness within the total school instructional program. What can a teacher do who wants to compare scores across tests and scales of measurement that are not standardized? Without some way of equating the different scales from the several tests into one scale with a common unit the comparison cannot be made.

A single raw score from a classroom test is, in and of itself, meaningless. It must be interpreted in either absolute terms or compared to other scores. Interpreting a raw score on one classroom test with a raw score on another classroom test as a comparison of a student's relative performance in the two tests is also meaningless. It is impossible to make a valid comparison between raw scores on different classroom tests, since these scores have different means and standard deviations. The following scores (the number of items answered correctly) were made by Alison, an eighth-grade student, on the six-weeks' tests in the study fields indicated:

Math	90	Social studies	115
English	85	Industrial arts	52

A teacher reviewing the scores would be unable to tell from the raw scores where the student fell in relationship to the other students taking each of the examinations. The scores do not indicate how well the student performed in any particular subject area compared to performance in any one of the other areas or to the others collectively. To be able to compare the standing in the four subject fields, some common basis of comparison must be established. Furthermore, to compare one student's scores in one area over a period of time, a common basis of comparison must be established.

In classroom tests and published standardized tests comparisons are usually made of each student's attainment in relation to the group of students taking the test or to a norm group. If scores are in comparable units the teacher can make educational and instructional decisions regarding the entire class and each student, since the teacher can interpret the data based upon group performance. Standard scores give those comparable units using measures of central tendency and variability.

Using z scores

The purpose of standard scores is to allow the teacher to combine scores to calculate a student's average achievement in one subject area or to compare a student's standing in two or more areas. It is not mathematically meaningful to compare or average raw scores from different tests, since the distributions have different possible total scores, means, and standard deviations. Let us take an extreme example. Biology test A has 10 items on the test. Biology test B has 30 items on the test. If the tests are of equivalent value, then some adjustment must be made for the difference in the contribution made by individual items. Student C and student D each missed 10 items on the two tests; therefore, they got the same percentage (75 percent) of the total correct responses of the two tests. With only this information it might appear that their

performances were the same. However, student C missed 10 on test A and
student D missed 10 items on test B.

	Student C	Student D
Test A	0	10*
Test B	30*	20

*Perfect scores

Each got a perfect score on one test, but on the other test one student missed
all of the items while the other student only missed one-third of the items. This
alone shows the folly of averaging test scores when the tests have different
numbers of items. The indicated problem has been attacked by weighting the
items on the test that has fewer items, but research indicates that this does little
to overcome the problem. In the example, test A's items could be scored as
three points rather than one thus making the total for each test the same (30).

	Student C	Student D
Test A	$0 \times 3 = 0$	$10 \times 3 = 30$
Test B	30	20
Total	30	50

Now student C has 30 points as before but student D has 50 points. Since no
common value has been set, the two values of 30 and 50 have little interpretable
relationship. This points out that two students in the same class can score the
same number of correct answers on two examinations in one subject area or
two tests in different subjects and still perform quite differently overall.

To make meaningful interpretations of students' scores, other information is needed. An analysis of mathematics test scores for the same two
students C and D can be made by use of the z score which incorporates the
mean and standard deviation values.

If student C scored 50 on test M_1 and 30 on test M_2 and student D
scored 42 on test M_1 and 38 on test M_2, then they have the same total score,
and consequently the same average score (40). If test M_1 had a mean of 50
and a standard deviation of 8, and test M_2 had a mean of 30 and a standard
deviation of 4, then the two student's scores would appear in a frequency
polygon as shown in Figure 14.15. In each distribution the score for student
C is an average score and falls in the middle of the respective distribution. The
score for student D is one standard deviation below the mean on test M_1 and
two standard deviations above the mean on test M_2. The average z score for
student C is .00. The average z score for student D is +.50. With this comparison the students are placed in the proper relationship due to the common unit
of the z score. Differences now have become clearer and allow the student and
teacher to understand better the level of accomplishment and to identify
strengths and weaknesses. By converting raw scores to standard scores, the
raw score distribution is changed into a distribution with mean and standard
deviation values common to other distributions which have been transformed

Student	C	D
Raw scores		
M_1	50	42
M_2	30	38
Total $M_1 + M_2$	80	80
Raw score average	40	40
z scores M_1	0.00	-1.00
M_2	0.00	+2.00
Total $z_1 + z_2$	0.00	+1.00
z score averages	0.00	+ .50

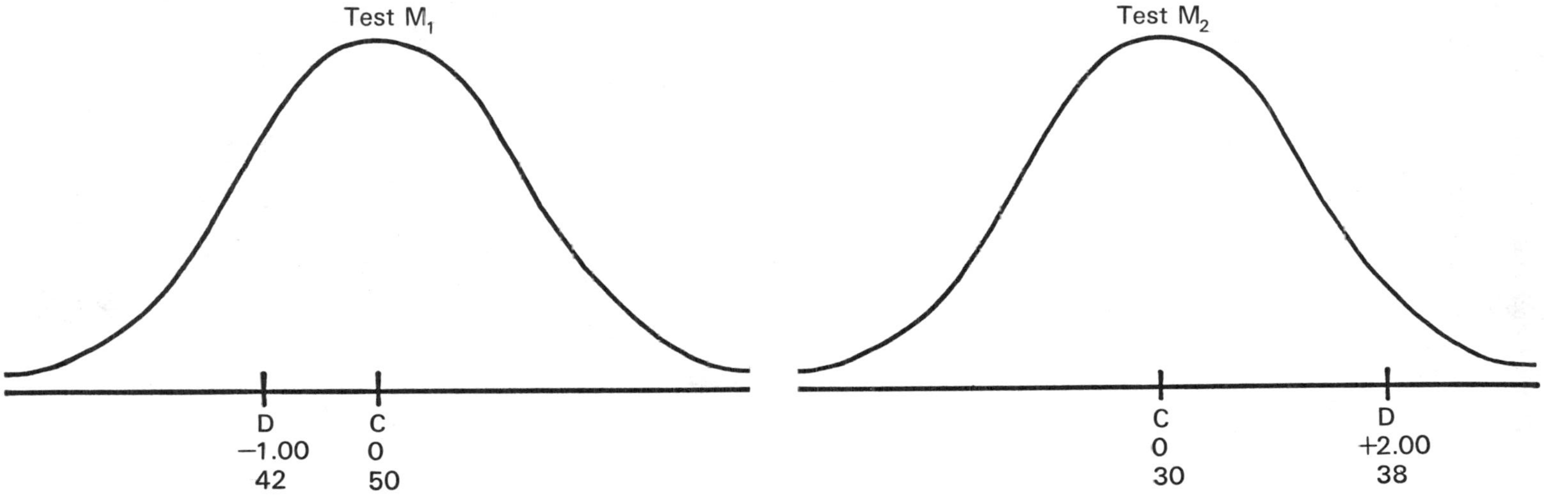

FIGURE 14.15. Comparison of scores in two frequency polygons

into z scores and allow for the differences which appear in the graph to be incorporated in the mathematics.

Remember—the z score is the deviation of a score from the mean in standard deviation units. The raw scores are changed to standard scores which express their differences from the mean in standard deviation units. Standard scores can be added, averaged, and combined as long as the raw score distributions have the same general characteristics of the normal curve.

In the example of scores for Alison, the eighth-grade student, the means and standard deviations for the subject examinations are as follows:

	X	$\bar{X}$	$X - \bar{X}$	σ
Math	90	95	−5	12
English	85	85	0	8
Social studies	115	120	−5	20
Industrial arts	52	47	5	10

The above data give the following z score values for the student's test scores.

Math
$$z = \frac{X - \bar{X}}{\sigma} = \frac{90 - 95}{12} = \frac{-5}{12} = -0.42$$

English
$$z = \frac{X - \bar{X}}{\sigma} = \frac{85 - 85}{8} = \frac{0}{8} = 0.00$$

Social studies
$$z = \frac{X - \bar{X}}{\sigma} = \frac{115 - 120}{20} = \frac{5}{20} = -0.25$$

Industrial arts
$$z = \frac{X - \bar{X}}{\sigma} = \frac{52 - 47}{10} = \frac{5}{10} = +0.50$$

All raw scores below the mean became negative z scores, and those above the mean became positive z scores. The mean has the z score value of 0. For example, Figure 14.16 shows the raw score mean, standard deviation segments on the baseline, and the z score equivalents for the four tests.

In comparing the relative standing on each of the subject areas through the process described above in viewing the z scores, the eighth-grade student is somewhat below average in math and social studies, exactly average in English, and somewhat above average in industrial arts.

An interpretation made between scores in different distributions assume that the same set of subjects is used for both distributions, or if norms are used, that the score being compared to the norms was obtained from a student who was much the same as those students who generated the norms. Without some commonality of important characteristics between distributions meaningful interpretations cannot be made.

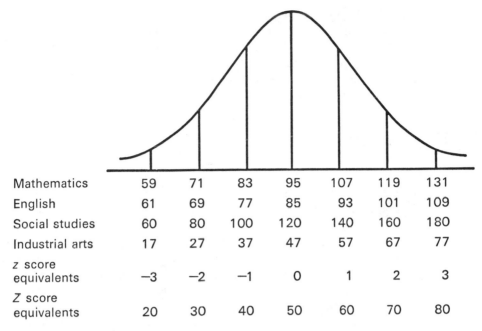

Mathematics	59	71	83	95	107	119	131
English	61	69	77	85	93	101	109
Social studies	60	80	100	120	140	160	180
Industrial arts	17	27	37	47	57	67	77
z score equivalents	−3	−2	−1	0	1	2	3
Z score equivalents	20	30	40	50	60	70	80

FIGURE 14.16. Test scores, z score, and Z score equivalents for four examinations

Using Z scores

Z scores serve the same purpose as z scores and are based on the same principle; however, they have the advantages of always being positive, being expressed in larger units, and having no decimal values. Teachers find Z scores useful for recording grades, since a particular score means the same thing in terms of student performance in a group of peers and can be conveniently averaged for a grading period, a semester, or a school year when test information is combined with other information in evaluation. Return to our example of Alison, the eighth-grade student who had a raw score of 90 in math, which is the same as a z score of −0.41. Carrying out the transformation:

$Z = 10(−.41) + 50$
$Z = −4.1 + 50$
$Z = 45.9$ or 46 (Z scores are reported to the nearest whole number)

Other Z scores calculate as:

English	50
Social studies	48
Industrial arts	55

Figure 14.17 shows the z score and Z score for the math raw score of 90. The values 90, $-.41$, and 46 are merely three different names for the same point in a distribution of scores. The shape of the original distribution and relationships among the values remain the same when raw scores are converted to z scores or Z scores. To see if you understand this important principle place the raw score, z score, and Z score for each of the other three tests on Figure 14.17.

PERCENTILE RANK

The **percentile rank** indicates the percentage of all the scores in a frequency distribution that falls below a given raw score. Percentile ranks are computed by arranging the raw scores in order of descending magnitude and finding the number of scores equal to or falling below a given score and reporting those falling below as a percentage of the total. Although the use of percentile ranks is largely a part of procedures of reporting norms for standardized tests, the computational procedure is provided to help the understanding of norms reported as percentile ranks. Charts of percentile ranks for raw score values on a standardized test allow a direct reading of the percentile rank for any given raw score. A chart of percentile ranks for the set of 33 achievement test scores reported earlier in the chapter could be organized as is the data in Figure 14.18. Since these percentile ranks are based on only 33 scores, the table would be of limited value for interpreting sets of scores for administration of the same test under the same conditions with students having like characteristics as those 33 students who gave us the scores. Charts in test manuals for published tests have many more subjects in norming groups, and the values tend to smooth out the distribution through both the raw score distribution and the percentile rank values.

The tendency for the data to concentrate in the middle values is reflected in the percentile ranks for those middle values. This phenomenon is reflected in Figures 14.14 and 14.17. For this reason percentile ranks are sometimes referred to as having rubber units—they stretch out in the center. For example, a one-point difference in raw scores at either end is worth one percentile rank difference, while in the center one raw score point difference can be worth as much as nine percentile points as can be seen in the values for raw scores 42 and 43.

This procedure allows for finding percentile ranks which correspond to given scores. Earlier a procedure for finding score values for particular percentile ranks was explained. Review of that procedure should point up the relationship between the two. When the score value associated with a proportion of the distribution is desired, the answer is a percentile. When the proportion of the distribution which falls below a score value point is needed, a percentile rank is found as an answer. For example, in the chart in Figure 14.18 the 80th percentile (P_{80}) can be read directly from the raw score column as 49 (there is some rounding error here), and the percentile rank for a score of 49

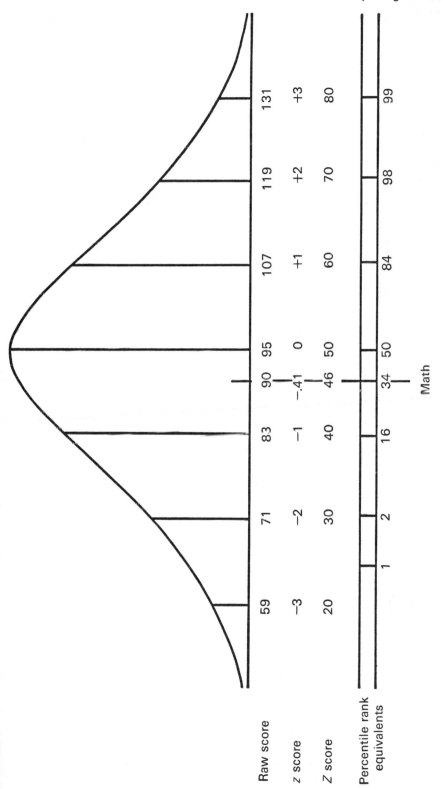

FIGURE 14.17. Normal curve with raw scores and corresponding standard scores and percentile rank equivalents

Raw Score	Percentile Rank	Number of Cases Falling Below the Score*
59	99	32.83
58	98	32.5
57	97	32.16
56	96	31.5
55	93	30.5
54	90	29.5
53	87	28.67
52	85	28
51	83	27.33
50	81	26.83
49	80	26.5
48	79	26.16
47	76	25
46	70	23
45	64	21
44	56	18.5
43	47	15.5
42	38	12.5
41	31	10.33
40	27	9
39	23	7.67
38	20	6.67
37	18	6
36	16	5.33
35	15	4.83
34	13	4.5
33	12	4.16
32	11	3.5
31	8	2.5
30	5	1.5
29	3	.83
28	2	.5
27	1	.16

FIGURE 14.18. Percentile ranks for a set of achievement scores
*The values in this column represent the number of cases using exact limits and interpolation within each interval based on cumulative frequencies from Figure 14.4.

(PR_{49}) can be read directly from the percentile rank column. (These values are also rounded to the nearest whole number for norming tables.)

STANINES

Another type of standard score allows a report of performance in general terms by reporting a stanine for a score. Since it is the teacher's intent to interpret and report performance in meaningful ways, the stanine adds another alternative to make score interpretation meaningful. Stanine, which is short for *standard nine,* has values from 1 through 9. Stanines do not represent specific points on a scale of scores, but bands of scores with a middle band having limits established by points above and below the mean. Stanines are determined by breaking the distribution of scores into groups based on intervals of one-half a standard deviation. Each stanine except 1 and 9 is one-half of a standard deviation in width, with the middle stanine of 5 extending from one-quarter standard deviation below the mean to one-quarter standard deviation above. A normal distribution of stanine scores has a mean of 5 and a standard deviation of approximately 2.

Figure 14.19 shows the percentages for each stanine in a normally distributed set of scores. Distributing 100 scores into stanines, the following values would be associated with each stanine:

Stanine 1 — 4 cases
Stanine 2 — 6–7 cases
Stanine 3 — 12 cases
Stanine 4 — 17–18 cases

Stanine 5 — 20 cases
Stanine 6 — 17–18 cases
Stanine 7 — 12 cases
Stanine 8 — 6–7 cases
Stanine 9 — 4 cases

Figure 14.20 gives the values for each stanine for different sizes (N) of distributions. These values may be used for distributions of stanines for classroom tests. If classes are larger than 35, the table can easily be extended by using the percentages in Figure 14.19.

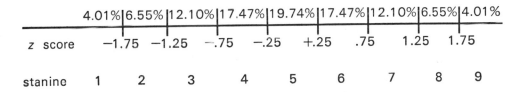

| 4.01% | 6.55% | 12.10% | 17.47% | 19.74% | 17.47% | 12.10% | 6.55% | 4.01% |

z score	−1.75	−1.25	−.75	−.25	+.25	.75	1.25	1.75
stanine	1	2	3	4	5	6	7	8	9

FIGURE 14.19. Percentages for each of the nine stanines

Stanines have the advantage of reporting performance in general categories rather than specific points. Parents and students can interpret broad categories of low, average, and high, and further break down Stanines 1, 2, and 3 into Lowest, Lower, Low; Stanines 4, 5, 6 into Low Average, Average, and High Average; and Stanines 7, 8, 9 into High, Higher, and Highest. Stanines are recommended for use in reports because of the need to communicate in a meaningful way about test performance. Norms for many published tests are

Number in group	Number in Each Stanine								
35	1	3	4	6	7	6	4	3	1
30	1	2	4	5	6	5	4	2	1
25	1	2	3	4	5	4	3	2	1
20	1	1	2	4	4	4	2	1	1
15	1	1	2	2	3	2	2	1	1
Stanine	1	2	3	4	5	6	7	8	9

FIGURE 14.20. Number of scores in stanines for selected size groups

available in stanines and make reporting about published tests more meaningful for students, parents, and other interested persons.

WHADJAGIT?

From the time teachers began returning sets of test papers to students the question of how one compared to fellow classmates has been a concern of students. The question "What did you get?" or "Whadjagit?" was in the minds of most students. When other classmates' scores were known, some idea of where a particular student's score stood could be synthesized. The thrust of this chapter has been to give the student the information about relative standing in addition to a raw score of test performance.

As pointed out in the beginning of this chapter, a raw score on a test in norm-referenced measurement is of no practical significance without additional information to aid interpretation. Test scores are indexes of measurement which must be given meaning in some way. The several ways for interpreting scores based on some mathematical principle are to be used to tell the student what a score means without the need to ask fellow students "Whadjagit?" These same procedures are also valuable when comparing a student or class to performance of other students with the same basic characteristics as is often done in standardized testing when scores are compared to a norm or norms.

Judgments made from students' scores are more likely to have increased validity if they are based on a structured approach. For example, if all the scores were reported as Z scores, the scores would have the same basic unit to aid in interpretation and would have common meaning within a classroom and throughout a school and school system.

Division at Breaks

Varying categories for test performance have been designated by what is referred to as the "eyeballing" technique. That method involves the arrangement of scores from highest to lowest and simply dividing the scores into a hierarchical arrangement of categories by drawing lines at places which seem to have natural breaking points.

For purposes of illustration the mathematics achievement test scores are presented in Figure 14.21. Applying the "eyeballing" technique, there seems to be a natural break at score 52, so a line has been drawn at that point. Beyond this point, except possibly at score 36, there seem to be no additional "natural" breaking or division points. The teacher who relies solely on this procedure must now ask, "What now?" Even if natural breaks are found, little meaning can be attached to created categories.

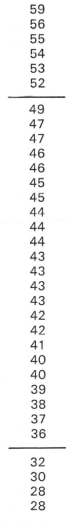

FIGURE 14.21. Mathematics achievement test scores

Predetermined Intervals

The problem of interpretation has been approached by letting particular predetermined intervals based on group performance set the hierarchical arrangement of categories. Using the set of mathematics test scores to illustrate one way this has been done, standard deviation units have been laid off along the range of scores in Figure 14.22. Before the test is administered certain points of division between categories can be designated by using standard

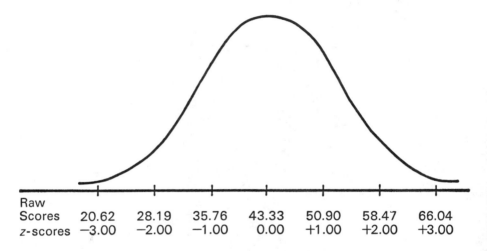

Raw Scores	20.62	28.19	35.76	43.33	50.90	58.47	66.04
z-scores	−3.00	−2.00	−1.00	0.00	+1.00	+2.00	+3.00

FIGURE 14.22. Raw score values placed on a unit normal curve

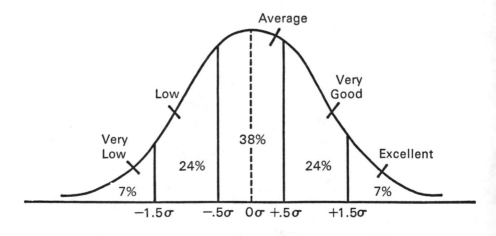

FIGURE 14.23. Distribution of achievement based on the standard deviation

deviation units or fractions thereof to assign scores. A descriptive word or phrase may be assigned to represent scores which fall in each category. For example, scores between −.5 and +.5 standard deviations could be labeled as average achievement, between +.5 and +1.5 as very good achievement, above +1.5 as excellent achievement, below −1.5 as very low, and between −1.5 and −.5 as low (see Figure 14.23). Other points in fractions of standard deviation units could be used to vary the proportions in each category using known proportions associated with particular intervals on the baseline, but their choice would be made before the test is given to students.

The mathematics achievement test had a mean of 43.33 and a standard deviation of 7.57. Employing the predetermined intervals mentioned above the scores would be assigned to categories as follows:

Achievement	Intervals	Scores	No. of Students	% of Students
Excellent	Mean+1.5 σ=43.33+11.36	54.69 and up	3	9
Very good	Mean+ .5 σ=43.33+ 3.78	47.11 to 54.69	4	12
Average	Mean− .5 σ=43.33− 3.78	39.55 to 47.11	18	55
Low	Mean−1.5 σ=43.33−11.36	31.97 to 39.55	5	15
Very low	Mean−1.5 σ and below	below 31.97	3	9

This objective approach to the problem of score interpretation appeals to most everyone until a further inspection is made. If this technique is used, obviously some students are doomed to a low category and some are guaranteed a high rating. Most educators who have given careful consideration to this problem feel this might not be a good policy for handling students. Some teachers have approached this negative aspect by assigning greater proportions to high categories and even eliminating one or more low categories for classes formed by grouping or considered in personal opinion to be made up of higher achieving students. On the other hand greater proportions for low categories and even elimination of higher categories can be made for groups considered to be made up of lower achieving students.

If these predetermined points of division are used the teacher must be aware of the difficulty of meeting the demands of using a nearly perfect measurement instrument and the likelihood that few tests can meet those rigid standards without some feedback from student performance. The authors do *not* present this as the best approach to give students a realistic answer to "Whadjagit?" for norm-referenced tests. If the difficulties of criterion-referencing can be overcome, preestablished points for standards can be used.

Relative Performance

The authors propose an approach to answering the question "Whadjagit?" with a sophistication of the original approach of finding out how others scored on the test. Unless criterion-referenced measurement, a mastery test, or problem test is being used, some indication of relative standing should be reported in addition to the raw score.

How the relative standings should be reported is largely determined by what person or group will receive the report. An elementary or secondary school faculty or administrators will expect and need more information than an elementary school student receives. Some elementary school students can understand some reports that others cannot. Since the person reporting must select the most meaningful way to report, only general guidelines can be given here. At this level of reporting, what is reported must be a part of the measurement aspect with little or no reference to evaluation or judgment.

Because of the great differences between kindergarten and the older elementary school students the reporting for elementary school tests will vary. When first used, a statistic or standard score should be explained and care taken to see that everyone understands what is being reported. Arithmetical averages are probably easiest to understand, and the first report may be in terms of average, below average, or above average.

As soon as possible, students should be introduced to a standard score distribution which is then used to report all test scores. The Z score distribution is suggested as the easiest to understand and probably the best standard score to use with young children. As standardized test results are reported and compared to test norms, other standard scores can be explained and made meaningful to students and, in turn, to parents. Some teachers have found that explanation of standard scores is a good place to augment the mathematics program with a study of averages, variance, and standard deviation in elementary school classes. By integrating those studies with score reporting purposes, study of the statistics may enhance interest and result in better understanding of a very important component of mathematics.

Percentile ranks are also easy to explain to students. Both students and parents seem to be able to interpret percentile ranks if they already understand percentages. Stanines can be used satisfactorily for reporting to parents, since the broad categories of stanines seem to be easier for some people to understand than reports in small intervals which tend to make small differences appear larger than they are. Percentile ranks and stanines seem to be best for discussion of achievement in parent conferences or for written reports to be sent to parents.

A schoolwide program for reporting scores can coordinate teachers' efforts and standardize reports of test results to students and other persons. If the Z score is chosen to report all test results, the scores begin to take on the same meaning to everyone throughout the school system as an indication of the relation of a score to all other scores in the distribution for that particular group. Thus test score interpretation has a common basis for reporting measures secured through testing, and offer a meaningful way to answer "Wadjagit?"

SUMMARY

This chapter assists teachers in development of an understanding of statistical concepts necessary to describe and interpret test scores. The discussions of ordering, ranking, and frequency distributions focus on the organization of test scores to facilitate interpretation in norm-referenced measurement. Frequency distributions simplify the presentation of data by showing how each score relates to all other scores in the class or group.

The histogram and frequency polygon demonstrate arrangements of a set of raw scores into a meaningful organization through graphing for a visual description. The shape of a distribution depends on the properties of the measuring instrument and the characteristic being measured.

The mean, median, and mode are measures of central tendency. The mean is the average and is found by adding all scores and dividing by the number of scores. The median is the middle score or the value which divides the number of scores in equal halves. The median is less stable than the mean but is not influenced by extreme scores. The mode is the most frequently appearing score. It is the least stable measure of central tendency. These three measures of central tendency provide an indication of a typical or average value in a distribution.

In addition to the median, other points which divide a distribution can be identified. Three quartile points divide a distribution into four equal parts, 9 decile points divide a distribution into 10 equal parts and 99 percentile points divide a distribution into 100 equal parts.

The standard deviation, quartile deviation, and range are measures of variability. The standard deviation is found by adding the squares of the deviation of each score from the mean, dividing that total by the number of scores and determining the square root of that figure. The more the scores vary around the mean the larger the standard deviation. The quartile deviation is found by locating the 75th and 25th percentile points, subtracting the two, and dividing by two. The range is the difference between the highest and lowest scores in a distribution. These three measures of variability provide indications of the spread of scores in a distribution.

The shape of a frequency distribution, histogram, or frequency polygon includes consideration of the skewness or the degree of symmetry of the scores, and kurtosis or the degree of peakedness or flatness of the distribution. Standard scores include the z score, which is the number of standard deviations a score is from the mean of the distribution. A Z score is obtained by multiplying a z score by 10 and adding 50 points. Other scales of standard scores are obtained by multiplying the z score by a number and adding a constant. The amount added becomes the mean of the new distribution, and the multiplier becomes the standard deviation. Standard scores allow comparison of scores on different tests when the same group is involved or to norms which are obtained from groups with characteristics much like those of the students who were tested.

The unit normal curve is a theoretical, symmetrical, bell-shaped curve that provides an idealized representation of data. The known probabilities associated with parts of the normal curve area are used to aid in interpretation of scores on a test when relative standing is important.

The percentile rank indicates the percentage of all scores in a frequency distribution that falls below a given raw score. Stanines divide the normal curve into nine areas and represent bands of scores with a middle band having limits established above and below the mean and eight other bands, four on each side of the middle band.

Test scores are indexes of measurement which are given meaning through teacher value judgments. More valid judgments can be made through perusal of test scores in relationship to the measures of central tendency, variability, skewness, and kurtosis of the distribution of those scores.

The next chapter provides a discussion of marks and marking plans.

NEW TECHNICAL TERMS LISTED IN THE GLOSSARY

Central tendency	Ordinal data
cf	Percentile
Decile	Platykurtic
Exact limits	Quartile
Frequency distribution	Quartile deviation
Frequency polygon	Range
Grouped data	Rank
Histogram	Raw score
Kurtosis	Real limits
Leptokurtic	Score
Mean	Skewness
Measure of variability	Standard deviation
Median	Symmetrical
Mesokurtic	T score
Mode	True limits
Normal curve	z score
Normalize	Z score
Ordering	

ACTIVITY EXERCISES

1. Your principal has asked you to explain to parents how you will interpret test scores of your students. Present your philosophy of measurement and list the basic points you wish to include in your discussion so that parents understand your position and know what to expect in reference to evaluation of student achievement.
2. For the following set of test scores to be norm-referenced provide:
   a. order of the scores
   b. ranks of the scores
   c. a tabular frequency distribution
   d. a histogram
   e. a frequency polygon
   f. measures of central tendency (mode, mean, median)
   g. measures of variability (range, standard deviation)

Test scores

45	58	49	53	41	53	50	51	47	52	52	45	65	48	44	42	46
49	55	51	33	38	59	55	47	45	49	53	56	51	61	37	51	

3. For the same set of scores in exercise 2, compute for each raw score:
   a. a *z* score.
   b. a *Z* score.
   Discuss how a classroom teacher can use these standard scores.

FOR DISCUSSION

1. Describe conditions that direct a teacher to criterion-referencing for some classroom tests.
2. Describe conditions that direct a teacher to norm-referencing for some classroom tests.
3. How can presentation of test scores in graphic form aid the students to understand their performances?
4. Explain how test scores on different tests can be made comparable. What limitation precludes the use of standard scores to compare scores on tests from different classes?

REFERENCES AND KNOWLEDGE EXTENDERS

BERK, R. A. (Ed.). *Criterion-referenced measurement: The state of the art.* Baltimore: Johns Hopkins University Press, 1980.

FERGUSON, G. A. *Statistical analysis in psychology and education* (5th ed.). New York: McGraw-Hill, 1981.

GRONLUND, N. E. *Measurement and evaluation in teaching* (4th ed.). New York: Macmillan, 1981. Chap. 14, pp. 367–402.

HAMBLETON, R. A. Test score validity and standard-setting methods. In R. A. Berk (Ed.), *Criterion-referenced measurement: The state of the art.* Baltimore: Johns Hopkins University Press, 1980.

HOPKINS, C. D., & ANTES, R. L. *Classroom testing: Administration, scoring, and score interpretation.* Itasca, IL: F. E. Peacock, 1979. Chaps. 3, 4, 5, 6, 7, 8; pp. 41–147.

LIEN, A. J. *Measurement and evaluation of learning* (3rd ed.). Dubuque, IA: William C. Brown, 1976. Chap. 3, pp. 55–77.

LYMAN, H. B. *Test scores and what they mean* (3rd ed.). Englewood Cliffs, NJ: Prentice-Hall, 1978.

MEHRENS, W. A., & LEHMANN, I. J. *Measurement and evaluation in education and psychology* (2nd ed.). New York: Holt, Rinehart & Winston, 1978. Chap. 4, pp. 65–86.

NOLL, V. H., & SCANNELL, D. P. *Introduction to educational measurement* (3rd ed.). Boston: Houghton Mifflin, 1972. Chap. 3, pp. 45–94, and Chap. 8, pp. 252–263.

SAX, G. *Principles of educational and psychological measurement and evaluation* (2nd ed.). Belmont, CA: Wadsworth, 1980. Chap. 8, pp. 211–250.

THORNDIKE, R. L., & HAGEN, E. *Measurement and evaluation in psychology and education* (4th ed.). New York: John Wiley, 1977. Chap. 2, pp. 25–47.

Chapter 15. Marks and Marking Plans

After study of Chapter 15, you should be able to:

1. Explain the nature of marks.
2. Explain the inadequacy of marks.
3. Understand the purposes of marking.
4. Discuss the need for marks for various audiences.
5. Describe types of marking plans and reporting systems.
6. Recognize the strengths and weaknesses of: letter marks, numerical marks, pass/fail marks, percentage marks, checklists, letters to parents, parent-teacher conferences.
7. Write the considerations in determination of marks and reports.
8. Explain how each glossary term listed at the end of the chapter is used in classroom measurement and evaluation.

Establishing levels of student achievement and reporting student progress are two duties of the classroom teacher. Creation of a plan to establish a coding of performance that serves as a communication system for several audiences is no easy task. The basis of the system—the mark—is a single symbol that summarizes a student's achievement in a course or a large portion of a study for purposes of report and record. The large number of different methods of coding achievement reflects the confusion and arguments attached to reducing a complex study to a single symbol that carries the information needed by those who use it.

Marking procedures should avoid reporting misleading information that may affect future learning, student adjustment, curricular evaluation, or administrative use of the mark. If the mark reflects the achievement level of the student—and factors such as class attendance, classroom behavior, attentiveness, and personality do not weight the mark—certain uses can be made of marks. However, present methods of assigning marks do not necessarily offer any guarantee that the mark reflects a pure image of student achievement. Marks have a high degree of validity when a teacher collects large amounts of information about knowledge and skill levels and bases a mark on those data.

Problems associated with the controversial topic of marks and **marking plans** (See Figure 15.1) continue to plague educators at all levels of education, and much teacher time and energy is expended dealing with the complicated problem of assigning marks. For many years teachers, parents, administrators, and specialists in child growth and development have argued for, and have made, changes in marking practices. Some call for changes because a present practice seems to be inadequate for communication and recording of meaningful data. Others feel that low marks could be detrimental to a child's self-concept and that marks may be interpreted and used inappropriately to a student's disadvantage (Antes & Antes, 1976, p. 13–14). Proponents of traditional marking procedures have come from the same audiences stating the point of view that marks do not affect students adversely and that individuals should learn to adjust to failure as well as success as part of the process of growing up.

Controversy concerning marking is reflected in numerous articles in professional literature and popular magazines that consider the topic of marks, points of view about how to mark, the need for reporting plans, and other related issues. In view of the differences in audiences and their varying opinions and needs, it is understandable why no single system of marking has been developed to satisfy the many needs. Since some form of reporting student progress is necessary, marks and marking plans will continue to be an area of educational concern, especially for those who object to present practice. However, when teachers recognize the shortcomings of marking, they are better able to improve their own marking procedures even when different philosophical points of view toward this highly controversial topic remain.

PHILOSOPHICAL ISSUES

Throughout the book, references have been made to the contribution of important procedural topics to the process of evaluation, e.g., Chapters 1, 13, 14. One aspect of summative evaluation may be the assignment of marks. When the evaluation is completed the marks given to students will reflect the philosophic views of the person assigning the marks and the philosophy of the school system in general. The final mark will most likely be based on one of three philosophic views. Assignment of marks by any individual teacher will most likely be directed by the perspective of a behaviorist, a humanist, or a pragmatist (Terwilliger, 1977, p. 23–26).

The behaviorist is closely attached to programmed instruction, mastery learning, or competency-based or performance-based instruction—thus the rise of criterion-referenced interpretation (Chapter 14). "The first preference of the behaviorist is not to employ differential grades [marks] at all but if there is no choice in the matter he/she will prefer to base grades [marks] upon predetermined performance criteria" (Terwilliger, 1977, p. 24). With this orientation the teacher is likely to base a mark on how well students have met criteria set for them individually or as a class before the instructional sequence.

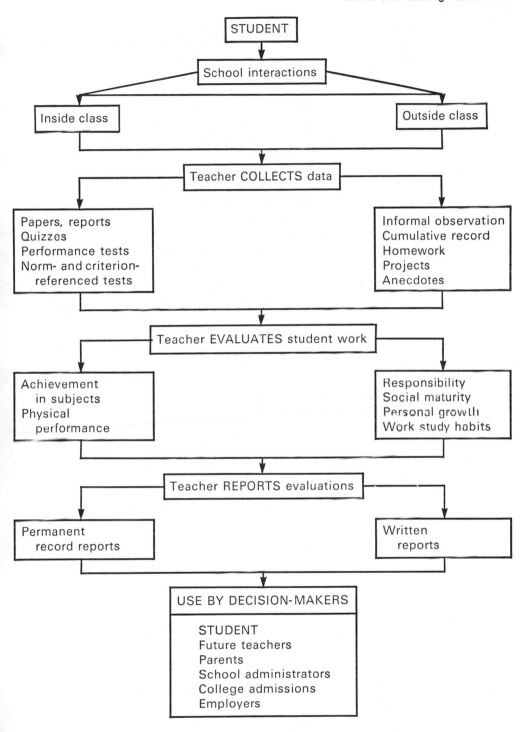

IGURE 15.1. A general model for a marking system

The humanist is closely attached to development of values, interest, and dignity of students as human beings—thus the call for abolishment of grades because they are viewed as dehumanizing. "The humanist who must assign grades [marks] to students as a matter of school policy will attempt to 'humanize' grades [marks] if at all possible" (Terwilliger, 1977, p. 25). With this teacher orientation the mark is likely to be based on growth or change within each student during the course or period of instruction.

The pragmatist is closely attached to the practical outcomes of instruction as they lead to opportunity for students to develop unique talents —thus the widespread call for norm-referenced interpretation (Chapter 14). "In fact, the pragmatist believes that grades [marks] can be very beneficial in helping an individual to make the myriad choices which are encountered in the course of development as a mature adult human" (Terwilliger, 1977, p. 26). With this teacher orientation the mark is likely to be based in reference of where a student placed in relation to other students with similar characteristics.

Recall that the purpose of instruction may direct score interpretation. Combinations of the three interpretations should be used according to the thrusts of the educational sequence. Instruction to minimums by mastery instruction points to the need for marks by criterion-referencing. Instruction to maximums or in advanced courses points to the need for marks by norm-referencing. Teachers need growth measures to foster the students' literacy by directing instruction using formative evaluation, but only in special cases do teachers find use for growth measures in assigning marks.

USING MARKS

Marks are employed to summarize cognitive achievement or skill performance over a specified period of time. A mark as a value or rating in the form of a symbol indicates an estimate of a student's achievement and is an appraisal of accomplishment in a course of study. It reports a level of quality of achievement in an academic endeavor.

The terms *mark* and *grade* are frequently used interchangeably. For clarity, it is probably better to reserve the term *grade* for a level in the educational process, e.g., first grade, second grade, but common usage of grade point average (GPA) and such is usually clear in context. Measures are assigned to tests and quantifications are given to written reports, assignments, and other activities the teacher wishes to consider. The teacher then reviews the information and judges the student's performance for a marking period based upon many observations. Usually each teacher decides what information will be used to determine the quality of student achievement, and how to report achievement in relation to either standards, norms, or growth while in the study. The reporting of attitudes, effort, deportment, and such should be done separately from achievement and the mark of record reserved for a report of achievement in the course of study.

INADEQUACY OF MARKS

The meaning of a particular mark tends to vary from one teacher to another and the source of variation is rarely communicated to the consumer. The inadequacy of marks results from the lack of clear communication regarding the factors that have been considered in arriving at a mark. However, even though the validity and reliability of marks are questionable, a consumer may view marks as accurate and invariable entities.

Robert Ebel (1979, pp. 232–233) points up that the shortcomings of marks are based upon: (a) a lack of understanding of their meaning and (b) a lack of objective evidence in assigning marks. The variability in marking standards and practices would be reduced if agreement is attained about what marks mean and objective evidence is used to assign them. If marks are to be meaningful and useful within a particular school or school system a clearly defined and uniform basis for assigning marks should exist for the teachers in the system. Attention must be given to the bases for arriving at the marks if they are to communicate valid and precise information.

PURPOSES OF MARKING

Marks and marking plans report student progress at the end of a predetermined time period or end of a course to students, parents, other teachers, and supporting personnel, such as counselors and school administrators. People in industry, business, and college admission offices request reports of marks. Each group in the varied audiences needs to be able to interpret a student's mark to make valid decisions.

Students

Marks are important to students primarily because they are utilized to facilitate student learning and development. Marks challenge many students thus stimulating them to work harder in school and to enhance their feelings of accomplishment and success. The mark provides an integrative summary of student test scores, written assignments, and other observations made in the classroom. Since they relate to classroom instructional objectives they provide a comprehensive and systematic view of expected student performance.

Every student in the classroom should know the teacher's expectations before instruction begins. Formative evaluation points out how well the student is doing as the instructional unit moves along. Then marks synthesize the information concerning achievement that students have generated and report the terminal level of performance as a summative evaluation so that the student knows how performance is viewed by the teacher.

Parents

A mark is important to parents because it communicates summative information about the level of student performance in relationship to school objectives. When parents know clearly what the school is attempting to do and what marks mean they are better able to support the school in the educational development of their children. Cooperative effort depends on good communication between home and school relative to student achievement as expressed in school marks.

To facilitate the learning and development of students more than a periodical summary of progress may be necessary. Day-to-day or at least weekly feedback to the parent of an elementary school child is vital to student learning. Parents may facilitate this feedback by encouraging children to discuss school activities daily and to share assignments, tests, and other materials. When the meaning of marks is understood by parents cooperative and sound educational and vocational planning is more likely to take place. Good communication with parents depends upon a reporting system that is clear and understandable.

Other Teachers and School Personnel

Marks are important to teachers in directing future learning experiences because they provide an overall indication of how well students have met instructional objectives. Marks provide the student's next teacher with evidence of past achievements and a general indication of status at the time the mark was recorded. Understanding past student achievement provides an opportunity to predict future success to some degree as well as to give an entry point for present study. When a mark is less than satisfactory, the deficient part of performance could have resulted from: (a) objectives that were beyond the reach of the student, (b) a student who was not motivated, (c) an instructional program that was not effective for this student, or (d) a combination of factors. The new teacher should try to determine the reasons for low marks and make adjustment when possible to improve the chance of better achievement in the future.

Cumulative records contain summative marks concerning student achievement that are helpful when a student moves from one school to another. Teachers will have marks that indicate progress made in school to help make decisions about placement of the student at an appropriate level for study. Information from the cumulative record also should aid teachers, counselors, and administrators in guiding and directing student development as a student moves through the grade levels of a school. Counselors use marks and other available information to assist students in increased self-understanding and adjustment in personal-social areas. In making realistic educational and occupational plans, information concerning student achievement and potential is essential for making valid decisions. Standardized test scores and other data in cumulative records can be helpful to supplement and complement teacher marks.

Marks and reports are important in administrative functions when determining promotion, graduation, extracurricular eligibility for athletics, band, and such, awarding honors, and reporting to other schools. Evaluations of students seeking admissions to colleges and universities are usually based in part, or in whole, on their records of school marks and ranks in class.

Employers

Hiring practices of industry and business include some indication of success levels in school subjects. The marks are usually used to communicate general levels but if the prospective job is skill oriented more precise information is needed about performance of specific skills. Marks per se are not a major determinant for hiring or not hiring unless the marks are for a specific course such as electronics, accounting, or law, and performance on qualifying examinations and tests for licenses is likely to supersede any reports of marks. Local industries and businesses are more likely to use school marks than outside sources of employment because local people tend to understand the local school and its relation to the community.

TYPES OF MARKS

The requisites for any type of reporting include clearness for interpretation, understanding, and appropriateness for the way the information will be used. Reports serve many purposes and in some cases a single mark may be adequate while in other situations a comprehensive and more detailed report may be necessary. The purpose and use to be made of marks should be given foremost consideration in determination of the type of mark to be used. Typical marks include letters of the alphabet, numerals, pass/fail, and percentages. The meaning of marks and scales varies from classroom to classroom and teacher to teacher. A scale may represent relative performance in relation to performance of classmates. A scale may represent what the student has achieved in relation to the objectives of the course or subject taught. Or a scale may represent the amount of growth during the instructional sequence.

Letter Marks

Assignment of letters, e.g., A, B, C, D, E, remains a popular plan of marking. In this five-letter plan "A" represents the highest mark and "E" the lowest. A verbal description of the qualitative meaning of each letter mark may be:

Alphabet Letter	Qualitative Description
A	Excellent
B	Good
C	Average
D	Poor
E	Unsatisfactory

Several variations of letter marks are used in schools today. The five letter symbols may be modified by being joined by plus or minus, or both. Corresponding qualitative descriptions may parallel the letter marks as follows:

Alphabet Letter	Qualitative Descriptions	
	I	II
A	Excellent	Superior
B+	Very good	Very high
B	Good	High
C+	High average	High average
C	Average	Average
D+	Weak	Low
D	Very weak	Very low
E	Unsatisfactory	Unsatisfactory

When receiving a single letter mark it is impossible to know precisely what factors were taken into account when arriving at the particular mark awarded unless this is noted. A single isolated letter mark without information relevant to the factors taken into consideration in determination of the mark contributes to misunderstanding and misuse of marks, therefore, an explanation of the factors taken into account should be made available with the mark. Factors of behavior, effort, gender, cleanliness, and such should not be considered when arriving at a letter mark for achievement in a course of study. If a report on any other factor is needed it should be made separately.

Strengths of letter marks

1. The letter mark can provide an efficient summary indication of achievement.

2. Many parents feel that they understand what letter marks for school achievement mean.

3. Letter marks are widely used and there is little confusion about the hierarchy of marks.

4. A letter mark may promote study and enhance learning.

5. The five-letter plan for marking has an optimal number (5–8) of points for judgment of capabilities.

6. Letter marks may be converted to number values and used for administrative purposes of determining grade point averages to help in decision making concerning participation in athletics, extracurricular activities and such. (See number 1 under "Weaknesses of letter marks.")

Weaknesses of letter marks

1. To determine overall average achievement, letter marks must first be converted to numerals. Since the original assignment of letters was ordinal, conversion to numerals for averaging uses an assumption that has not been met. (See number 6 under "Strengths of letter marks.")

2. An unrealistic view of student progress and educational capability may result from the temptation for a teacher to avoid giving low marks.

3. A letter mark fails to communicate specific student strengths and weaknesses.

4. The value of a letter mark depends on the factors considered when arriving at the mark and communication of those factors to users of marks.

5. The meaning of letter marks varies from one class to another.

Numerical Marks

An alternative to letter marks is a plan that assigns marks according to a series of numerals. It is not clear why some schools utilize numerals because that plan has most of the same strengths and weaknesses attached to letter grades, with one additional weakness. Confusion about what number marks mean is created because some plans use one (1) as a high value and others use one (1) as a low value. For this reason alone use of numerical marks is questionable. Some educators advocate use of numerals rather than letters because they can be averaged; however, the numerals are not assigned with equal intervals and have the same limitation for averaging that letters do. Assignment of numerals usually is to a five-point scale, e.g., 4, 3, 2, 1, 0, that corresponds directly with the letter scale (4 or A, 3 or B, 2 or C, 1 or D, 0 or E) and adds little to letter scaling. An example for a high school student enrolled in four traditionally academic classes shows how a summary index (GPA) is calculated.

Subject	Numerical Mark	Corresponding Letter Mark
English	4	A
Mathematics	2	C
History	3	B
Art	3	B
	12	

The grade point average is determined by dividing the total 12 by the number of courses taken 4. GPA = 12/4 = 3.00. When a decimal is used with a numeral mark a fraction (0.5) is included in the numerical scaling and corresponds to a plus sign (+) in letter grades. The numerical marks are summed for all courses taken and divided by the number of courses. For example:

Subject	Numerical Mark	Corresponding Letter Mark
English	3.5	B+
Algebra	2.5	C+
U.S. history	1.0	D
Music	3.0	B
	10.0	

The grade point average (GPA) for the marking period is 10/4 = 2.50. In this set of numerals 4 = A, 3.5 = B+, 3.0 = B, 2.5 = C+, 2.0 = C, 1.5 = D +, 1.0 = D, and 0 = E. Other designations may be used, for example: 6 = A, 5.5 = A−, 5.0 = B+, 4.5 = B, 4.0 = B−, 3.5 = C+, 3.0 = C, 2.5 = C−, 2.0 = D+, 1.5 = D, 1.0 = D−, and 0 = E. When a grade point average is to be determined it is simpler to use a numerical system of recording marks. One drawback is that most parents probably understand letters better than numerals. The convenience of computers to calculate the grade point average when letters are used may result in a decision to use letters to report achievement and also compute the grade point average numerically.

Another numerical scale, the 100-point marking system in which large numerals represent high achievement and low numerals represent low achievement may be utilized to assign numerals from 0 to 100 to represent student achievement. In this scale 100 is considered to be perfect achievement and 0 represents no achievement; however, teachers rarely use the lower end of the scale from 0 to 50. Using such a discriminating scale (0 to 100) implies that a teacher is capable of determining finite absolute achievement, but the distinction between adjacent points on the scale, for example, 85 and 86 or 90 and 91, is difficult to ascertain in terms of actual student achievement. For this reason using score ranges 70–74, 75–79, 80–84, . . . , 95–99 or a similar plan is preferred because of difficulty with making the fine distinctions necessary in the original 0–100 scale.

Strengths of numerical marks

1. The numerical mark can provide an efficient summary indication of achievement.
2. A scale of numerical marks provides a convenient basis for calculating grade point averages.
3. A numerical mark may promote study and enhance learning.
4. The five-point numerical plan for marking has an optimal number (5–8) of points of judgment of capabilities.

Weaknesses of numerical marks

1. It is difficult for parents to know what a score, e.g., 80, means in relation to achievement.
2. There may be confusion about which end of the scale represents high or low achievement. (Is one (1) high or low?)
3. A numerical mark fails to communicate specific student strengths and weaknesses.
4. The value of a numerical mark depends on the factors considered when arriving at the mark and communication of those factors to users of the marks.
5. The meaning of numerical marks varies from one situation to another.

Pass/Fail Marks

Pass/fail (P or F), satisfactory/unsatisfactory (S or U), credit/no credit (CR or NCR), pass/no grade (P or NG), and honors/satisfactory/unsatisfactory (H or S or U) as options to the letter mark plan are usually limited to particular subjects or courses. Pass/fail marks are rarely used separately from another marking system, particularly the conventional four- or five-letter mark system. These marks provide less information than other more conventional marking plans, but may be most satisfactory for some situations.

The two-category system is used at the college level so that a student may enroll in a course outside the major and minor areas without affecting overall performance as represented by a grade-point average. Students have an opportunity to explore new areas of interest in a less threatening situation. However, in some cases students may put forth less effort when enrolled on a pass/fail option. Some students may do minimum work just to complete the course when they know that there will be no indication of the degree of satisfactory achievement.

The pass/fail option provides less information concerning student achievement than the letter or numerical marking plan. The idea behind a system that encourages university students to enroll in untried areas of studies is good; however, the performance of students may be idiosyncratic in relation to their performance in a pass/fail marking plan.

Strengths of pass/fail marks

1. Students feel that there is less competition; therefore, they may be more relaxed and less anxious.
2. A freer learning atmosphere provides older students an arena for taking risks, disagreeing with a teacher, and exploring a subject in their own ways.
3. Students may work to meet the requirements for successful course completion without the pressures of traditional marking.

4. The teacher and student together may work out the criteria for passing.

Weaknesses of pass/fail marks

1. The pass/fail mark provides less information since it does not distinguish the degree of satisfactory student accomplishment.
2. This plan of marking relieves the teacher of the typical evaluation but deprives the student of helpful feedback.
3. Some students do less work than others for a passing mark and large variations may exist in standards for passing from one instructor to another.
4. The student not doing well may experience the pressure associated with failing in any marking plan.
5. A pass/fail mark fails to communicate specific student strengths and weaknesses.
6. The value of a pass/fail mark depends on factors considered when arriving at the mark and communication of those factors to users of marks.
7. The meaning of pass/fail marks varies from one class to another.

Percentage Marks

Marks can be assigned using percentages to report the level of student achievement. Teachers can assign a number between 0% and 100% which corresponds to the percentage of material learned by the student. A mark of 100% represents total achievement of material covered and a 0% represents complete lack of achievement. Percentage marks extend the 0 to 100 scale concept of grading by placing the scaling into percentage units. Percentage marks continue to be popular among teachers and school administrators who establish this plan for entire schools.

A modified approach to percentage marks has been to provide a percentage scale that corresponds to letter grades. A variety of designations of percentage ranges relative to letter marks is used. Some teachers find conversion tables a convenience in assigning letter marks. A teacher keeping good records of student achievement can determine percentages and then convert to letter or numeral marks. For example, the designations may be as follows:

Percentage Mark	Letter Mark	Numerical Mark
96–100	A	4
85– 95	B	3
75– 84	C	2
60– 74	D	1
Below 60	E	0

The percentage may be based on a portion of the total possible points for a marking period, on the percentage of the top score obtained by a student in the class on each observation, or on a point arbitrarily set by the teacher.

Strengths of percentage marks

1. The percentage mark can provide an efficient summary indication of achievement.
2. The percentage mark may correspond to the percent of the material that the student has learned in relation to the objectives for instruction.
3. Percentage marks may be converted to letter marks or numerical marks if a plan for such conversion is set up.
4. Percentages may be easier for some teachers to understand than other marking plans and easier for teachers to interpret to parents.

Weaknesses of percentage marks

1. Percentage marks do not communicate strengths and weaknesses of student performance in terms of what has been learned and what a student can do.
2. The value of the mark depends on how the percentage is calculated. It could be based on a perfect performance for 100%, 100% as based on the best performance of any one student in the class, or some arbitrary percentage set by the teacher.
3. A percentage mark fails to communicate specific student strengths and weaknesses.
4. The value of a percentage mark depends on factors considered when arriving at the mark and communication of those factors to users of marks.
5. The meaning of percentage marks varies from one class to another. (See Figure 15.2)

ALTERNATIVES TO MARKS

Through the years teachers have found need to report student appraisal with something other than a mark to supplement a marking plan with additional information. Some major thrusts for changes in marking came in the 1970s as groups wrestled with the question "Is the traditional system of grading . . . the most educationally useful system of evaluation?" (Kirschenbaum, Simon, Napier, 1971, p. 14). Self-evaluation, self-marking, marks by contract, blanket marks (all students receive the minimum mark) and other plans have been tried and are still used although none of these has been widely accepted. Some others seem to be used more and are presented in this section.

Possible Strengths	Letter marks	Number marks	Pass/fail marks	Percent marks
Efficient summary of achievement	XXXX	XXXX		XXXX
Easy for parents to understand	XXXX			XXXX
Widely used and clear hierarchy	XXXX			
Promotes study and enhances learning	XXXX	XXXX		XXXX
Optimal number (5–8) of points	XXXX	XXXX		
Convertible to grade-point average	XXXX	XXXX		XXXX
Less competitive atmosphere for learning			XXXX	
Criteria for passing may be joint decision of student and teacher			XXXX	
Corresponds to the amount learned			XXXX	XXXX
Freer atmosphere for exploration			XXXX	
Possible Weaknesses				
Fails to communicate specific student strengths and weaknesses	XXXX	XXXX	XXXX	XXXX
Value depends on factors considered in arriving at the mark	XXXX	XXXX	XXXX	XXXX
Student may feel competitive pressure	XXXX	XXXX	XXXX	XXXX
Meaning varies from one class to another	XXXX	XXXX	XXXX	XXXX
Temptation of teacher to avoid low marks	XXXX	XXXX		
Deprives the student of helpful feedback			XXXX	
Large variation in work to pass			XXXX	
Must convert scores to determine average	XXXX		XXXX	XXXX
Confusion about which end of the scale represents high or low achievement		XXXX		
Difficult for parent to know what score means in relation to achievement		XXXX	XXXX	

FIGURE 15.2. Strengths and weaknesses of four types of marks for reporting school achievement

Letters to Parents

Descriptive evaluation can be communicated in letters to parents that give additional information regarding student achievement in relation to other factors. A typical letter employs qualitative descriptions of learning, skills, and abilities that typify a student's growth to convey to parents how well a student is progressing. The teacher in a single course or at a grade level in a self-contained classroom can write a letter concerning a student's strengths, weaknesses, and learning needs and may include plans for improvement through future educational sequences. Recommendations to assist parents in helping their child at home may also be included in the written report.

Some reporting systems employ the written letter to parents as a supplement to another marking plan. For example, the letter mark may give a broadly based report and the specifics reported in a descriptive written report of student achievement in context of other factors.

Strengths of letters to parents

1. A letter can be written to reflect the uniqueness of an individual student and associated strengths and weaknesses.
2. When help from home is desired, the teacher may suggest ways this can be accomplished.
3. Letters may open communication between the home and school and parent comments should be encouraged through letters to the teacher.
4. The teacher is obligated to think about each student's individual traits while assigning marks and recording them in the roll book.

Weaknesses of letters to parents

1. Composing meaningful letters is time consuming and writing becomes difficult.
2. Letters are subjective and contents may be affected unknowingly by how the teacher feels personally about the student.
3. Generalized statements and terminology employed by the teacher may be vague.
4. The usefulness of the evaluations is a function of the ability of the teacher to write meaningful letters.
5. Letters lack a cumulative view as a student moves through a particular grade level or school. Continuity in a series of written reports is difficult to achieve.

Parent-Teacher Conferences

In elementary schools, particularly at the primary level, parent-teacher conferences in addition to a report card indicating student marks have been quite popular. Teachers in some school systems routinely conduct parent-teacher conferences for all parents during the regular school day. In some schools students are dismissed for a day or half a day for parent conferences.

Conferences in which the student is included for all or part of the conference may be beneficial for all concerned. The student will not have the feeling of being left out or perceive that there is secret dialogue between the parent and teacher. By having student-parent-teacher conferences a cooperative, trusting atmosphere may exist among the three parties.

Strengths of parent-teacher conferences

1. A conference provides an opportunity for a face-to-face discussion of student progress and plans for future instruction, as well as to develop plans for parents to assist students at home.
2. Rapport can be established and two-way communication developed between home and school.
3. Parents have an opportunity to provide information concerning out-of-school experience and behavior which may be helpful to the teacher.

Weaknesses of parent-teacher conferences

1. Parent-teacher conferences are time consuming.
2. Parent-teacher conferences alone fail to provide a systematic record of student achievement or educational development.

Checklists

The descriptive checklist is one form of marking that provides specific information concerning what a student can do. This reporting technique has been used extensively with communication of information concerning students' skill performance—physical and cognitive. The information provided through checklists also may include personal growth, work-study habits, responsibility, social maturity, effort, attitude, willingness, and such, and be used in addition to a letter or numerical mark for achievement. They are especially useful at elementary school levels where concern centers upon social, emotional, and basic skills development. Statements are provided in list format and the teacher reacts to each one by checking the degree to which the statement is applicable or if improvement is needed. Various alternatives to this procedure are available. Examples of descriptive checklists are illustrated in Figure 15.3. The examples illustrate uses of the checklist and two of the various response modes that can be used with the descriptive checklist.

Checklists may also be utilized for evaluation of aspects of academic performance or achievement in subject areas. Such a checklist may break some skill or course down into component parts of instructional objectives taught during the period and an indication of achievement given for each part. In

Social and Emotional Development (Check (✓) shows child's performance)	Most of the time	Part of the time	Not at this time
Gets along well with others	✓		
Is willing to take responsibility		✓	
Shows self-confidence	✓		
Takes part in many activities			✓

Informal Reading Readiness Checklist (To be checked (X) at the end of each semester)	Yes	No
Enjoys stories and looking at books	X	
Can see likenesses and differences	X	
Can hear likenesses and differences		X
Uses left to right sequences	X	
Speaks in sentences		X

FIGURE 15.3. Two examples of descriptive checklists

addition, a letter grade may be given for the overall achievement for the skill or course studied. When this is the case, statements included under each area are usually numerous, and teachers consume considerable time and energy in reporting student achievement or academic progress in order to accomplish the goal of reporting reliable and valid data.

Strengths of checklists

1. Checklists are detailed and can provide much information concerning student achievement and other nonacademic characteristics.
2. Checklists communicate clear areas of student strengths and weaknesses and are easy for parents to understand.
3. Completing a checklist requires that the teacher spend considerable time and thought concerning the strengths and weaknesses of each individual student.

Weaknesses of checklists

1. When a checklist is used to report student achievement many specific statements are needed and many judgments must be made by the teacher.
2. Detailed checklists take considerable time to complete.

3. Information on checklists cannot be averaged to provide a summary record.
4. An overly detailed checklist may provide too much information. A balance should be struck between too little and too much information.
5. Terminology that is not meaningful to the consumer may appear on checklists (see Figure 15.4).

MULTIPLE MARKING AND REPORTING SYSTEMS

A multiple marking plan provides for the conversion of data collected through all types of observations into a traditional marking plan that uses letter or numerical marks to report achievement and a checklist or additional marks to report other factors. A multiple reporting system utilizes the mark (usually a letter) for reporting achievement and reports other information through additional marks (usually numerals), a checklist, letter to parents, or parent-teacher conference. The establishment of a multiple marking or reporting system provides a uniform and systematic procedure for reporting other student behaviors along with the report on achievement. Some schools use the traditional marking system consisting of letter or numerical marks to express academic achievement and supplement the mark with checklists or ratings of psychological and other nonacademic characteristics deemed important. In this way a letter mark can be awarded for pure achievement in a subject while supporting information about other important factors may be clearly exhibited. In addition to the achievement mark, attributes such as persistence, effort, improvement, or growth may be communicated in the reporting system without confounding the meaning of the achievement mark.

Norman E. Gronlund (1981, pp. 518–20) provides a discussion of the principles for development of a multiple marking or reporting system and suggests that any system should be: *(a)* guided by the functions to be served, *(b)* developed cooperatively by parents, students, and school personnel, *(c)* guided by clearly stated educational objectives, *(d)* based on adequate evaluation, *(e)* detailed enough to be diagnostic and compact enough to be practical, and *(f)* provide for parent-teacher conferences as needed. As you read this section of the chapter and study the examples of reports being utilized, reflect upon Gronlund's stated principles in relation to the examples.

The nature of the classroom, the subject, and the set of objectives should provide direction for organizing the marking or reporting plan. In addition, a plan of reporting should establish what factors are taken into consideration when determining marks and thus provide for added understanding regardless of the type of report utilized. The system of written communication to students and parents is commonly through a report card which may take one of many different forms. Figure 15.5 is an example of a report card used for grades 4, 5, and 6 that utilizes single letter marks: A, B, C, D, or E for academic achievement in reading, language, spelling, mathematics, social studies, and science-health. A numerical scale for student effort also is employed for rating

Possible Strengths	Letters to parents	Parent/ teacher conferences	Checklists
Careful attention and thought must be given to each student	XXXX	XXXX	XXXX
Reflect the strengths, weaknesses, and uniqueness of the student	XXXX	XXXX	XXXX
Communicate how parent may help the student	XXXX	XXXX	
Open communication between home and school	XXXX	XXXX	
Provide for face-to-face discussion		XXXX	
Parents may provide input		XXXX	
Detailed and provide a variety of information including nonacademic traits			XXXX
Possible Weaknesses			
Information may not be averaged to provide a summary record	XXXX	XXXX	XXXX
Time consuming	XXXX	XXXX	XXXX
Good writing skills needed (clear report)	XXXX		
Lack of a systematic record of progress	XXXX	XXXX	
May provide too much detailed information			XXXX
May use vague statements and confusing terminology	XXXX	XXXX	
Teacher biases concerning student personality may affect evaluation	XXXX	XXXX	
Lack a cumulative view of the students as they move through the school grades	XXXX	XXXX	
Many specific statements require teacher judgments			XXXX

FIGURE 15.4. Strengths and weaknesses of three types of alternatives to marks for reporting school achievement

each academic subject, and a ($\checkmark$) for any subcategory indicates a need for improvement.

The special subjects of art, music, physical education, and categories of personal growth are marked on a basis of: O—Outstanding, S—Satisfactory, U—Unsatisfactory. Deficiencies in the subcategories of personal growth under work study habits, responsibility, and social maturity are marked with a check ($\checkmark$) that indicates a need to improve. The use of these marks is illustrated in Figure 15.5 where the first grading period marks are reported. This type of multiple marking plan has proven to be well accepted by parents as well as other users of student reports. This type of multiple marking plan vividly illustrates the separation of academic achievement from the attributes which deal with personal growth. The report is meaningful and provides clarity for reporting important aspects of student progress and development. Provision for information not discernible from a single mark stimulates better communication, interpretation, and understanding. A comprehensive report of achievement and personal traits should have more meaning for everyone concerned. The report supports teacher interest in and concern for the cognitive, affective, and psychomotor development of students.

The reading section of a report card at the primary level which employs a mark for achievement, an explanation of effort, and areas in need of improvement is illustrated in Figure 15.6. For reporting periods 1 and 2, marks of B and A respectively were awarded for reading. The number following the letter mark indicates the level of effort put forth where 1 in the example indicates "tries consistently." The grade level of instruction is indicated by the number 4 in the box for recording the level of instruction. The ($\checkmark$) indicates that during the first marking period the student needed to improve by making use of phonics. Apparently improvement was made during the next period because it was not checked at the end of the second recording period. In early childhood classes checklists may be the only form of report card given.

The example of Figure 15.7 represents a checklist used at the kindergarten level. This checklist is the only report given and it provides for marking in each semester of the academic year. The readiness checklist which is completed at the end of the second semester provides information for developing teaching plans for first grade. The main aspects of progress and growth are divided into social and emotional development, language development, creative expression, work habit development, physical skill development, and health observation. The teacher reports student progress and growth by checking one of three categories: *(a)* most of the time, *(b)* part of the time, or *(c)* not at this time, for each category listed.

The four-period primary level report card in Figure 15.8 provides for appraisal of achievement by a letter mark: O for outstanding, S for satisfactory, N for needs improvement, and L for satisfactory for ability, but below grade level. The letter marks are utilized in reporting progress in reading, language, mathematics, art, music, and physical education. Letter marks are also used in reporting personal growth and work habits. Numerals: 1 for "tries consistently to do his best," 2 for "tries most of the time," and 3 for "tries very little"

Name Sam Bellingham

EXPLANATION OF MARKS

SCHOLASTIC ACHIEVEMENT
A Outstanding   D Poor
B Very good   F Unsatisfactory
C Satisfactory ✓ ✓ Needs to Improve

EFFORT
1. Tries consistently
2. Tries most of the time
3. Tries very little

	1	2	3	4	Final Mark
READING					
Level of Instruction	B1				
Understands what he reads	m				
Makes use of phonetic skills	✓				
Reads well orally					
Shows growth in vocabulary development					
LANGUAGE	C1				
Oral					
Expresses ideas well					
Practices correct word usage					
Uses good diction					
Written					
Expresses ideas well	✓				
Shows growth in mechanics of writing	✓				
Shows skill in using reference materials	✓				
Can identify parts of speech	A1				
SPELLING	C2				
Learns assigned words	3				
Spells well in written work					
MATHEMATICS	C3				
Level of Instruction					
Masters basic number facts					
Is accurate in number operations					
Understands four number operations					
Reasons well in written problems	✓				
Completes assigned work	✓				
SOCIAL STUDIES	C3				
Is developing skill in using maps, globes, charts, graphs	✓				
Contributes to class discussion	✓				
Performs well in written work and on tests	✓				
Contributes to project and committee work					
SCIENCE-HEALTH	A1				
Contributes to class discussion					
Performs well on written tests					
Contributes to project and committee work					

EXPLANATION OF MARKS
O Outstanding
S Satisfactory
U Unsatisfactory
✓ Needs to Improve

SPECIAL SUBJECTS	1	2	3	4	Final Mark
ART	S				
MUSIC	S				
PHYSICAL EDUCATION	O				

PERSONAL GROWTH	1	2	3	4	Final Mark
WORK STUDY HABITS	S				
Listens and follows directions					
Works steadily and quietly					
Uses time wisely	✓				
Completes work on time					
Does written work neatly					
Shows growth in independent study					
Makes consistent effort to improve	✓				
RESPONSIBILITY	S				
Uses books and materials with care					
Brings necessary materials to class					
Obeys school and safety rules					
Practices good health habits					
SOCIAL MATURITY	S				
Works and plays well with others					
Respects rights of others					
Respects proper authority					
Uses reasonable self-control					
Accepts suggestions					
Is courteous in speech and action					

ATTENDANCE RECORD	1	2	3	4	Years Total
Days Present	44				
Days Absent	1				
Times Tardy	0				

Child's classification for next year.   Grade

FIGURE 15.5. Report card for grades 4, 5, and 6

ACHIEVEMENT   EFFORT

A Outstanding   1. Tries consistently
B Very good   2. Tries most of the time
C Satisfactory   3. Tries very little
D Poor
E Unsatisfactory
                      ✓ Needs to improve

	1	2	3	4	Final Mark
Reading	B1	A1			
Level of instruction	4	4			
Understands what he reads					
Makes use of phonetics	✓				
Reads well orally					
Shows growth in vocabulary development					

FIGURE 15.6. Reading section of a report card

are used to report the level of effort expended. A check (✓) is utilized below the letters and numbers to indicate when improvement is needed in an area. An asterick (*) indicates "not applicable."

The student evaluation report in Figure 15.9 employs symbols: [+] strength in this area, [✓] satisfactory in this area, [−] weakness in this area, and [ ] does not apply at this time, that inform parents of an elementary school student's progress in the areas of reading, language, spelling, handwriting, mathematics, science and health, social studies, personal growth, and study skills. The subcategories under each of the areas provide information pertinent to how the student functions and is able to perform in the particular concern. The notice to parents stated on the report form indicates that "progress is determined by each child's ability—it is continuous." Special subjects of art, music, and physical education are not covered on this particular report. In this reporting system as with many others the teacher must know each student well and keep good records to adequately report student progress.

In elementary schools combinations of traditional marking plans and alternative marking plans are numerous. Checklists are often the only report given in elementary schools, particularly in kindergarten and the primary grades. At the secondary school level, alternative marking plans are used to supplement other marks but less often than at the elementary school level. The alternative marking plans provide information not discernible from the single

KINDERGARTEN

PROGRESS AND GROWTH OF

Name _Rich_

1st Semester- 2nd Semester

	Most of the time	Part of the time	Not at this time	Most of the time	Part of the time	Not at this time
Social and Emotional Development *check (✓) shows child's performance*						
Gets along well with others		✓			✓	
Is willing to take responsibility		✓			✓	
Shows self confidence		✓				
Readily takes part in a variety of activities	✓					
Language Development						
Speaks clearly	✓					
Participates in group discussions		✓			✓	
Listens well when others are speaking		✓			✓	
Creative Expression						
Expresses ideas easily with art materials			✓		✓	
Participates in music activities			✓		✓	
Work Habit Development						
Follows group instruction		✓			✓	
Completes work within a reasonable length of time			✓		✓	
Is able to work independently			✓			✓
Has adequate attention span			✓		✓	
Takes responsibility in care of materials		✓			✓	
Physical Skill Development						
Shows good large muscle coordination as in skipping and hopping		✓				
Shows good small muscle coordination as in cutting, coloring and buttoning			✓		✓	
Health Observations						
Appears to be alert and well	✓			✓		
Practices good health habits	✓			✓		

2nd semester

	Most of the time	Part of the time	Not at this time
Readiness check list *(to be checked (X) the second semester)*			
Enjoys books and stories		✓	
Can see likenesses and differences		✓	
Can hear likenesses and differences			✓
Uses left to right sequence		✓	
Speaks in sentences	✓		
Remembers and identifies: numerals ($1^{to}10$)		✓	
simple shapes		✓	
colors		✓	
letters		✓	
Relates group of objects to numerals		✓	

Attendance Record

	1st sem	2nd sem	Years total
Days Present	83	84	167
Days Absent	1	3	4
Times Tardy	0	0	0

Parent's Signature _____

Classification for next year _first grade_

FIGURE 15.7. Example of a report card for kindergarten

NAME __Stephanie Johnson__

EXPLANATION OF MARKS

O Outstanding
S Satisfactory
N Needs Improvement
L Satisfactory for ability, but below grade level

1. Tries consistently to do his best
2. Tries most of the time
3. Tries very little
✓ Area needing improvement
* Not applicable

SCHOLASTIC PROGRESS

	1	2	3	4
READING ✓				
Understands what he reads	O 1			
Makes use of phonetic skills				
Reads well orally				
Masters basic vocabulary				
LANGUAGE	O 1			
Oral expression				
Written expression				
Writing legibility				
Spelling skill				
MATHEMATICS	S 2			
Is learning to count in many ways				
Can read and write numbers correctly				
Knows number facts	✓			
Is learning to solve story problems	✓			
Works accurately				
ART	S			
MUSIC	S			
PHYSICAL EDUCATION	S			

PERSONAL GROWTH

	1	2	3	4
WORK HABITS				
Listens attentively	O			
Follows directions				
Works quietly				
Uses time wisely				
Finishes work on time				
Checks work for mistakes				
Takes pride in neat work	S			
Works well independently				
PERSONAL GROWTH				
Respects property				
Uses books and materials carefully				
Respects rights of others				
Obeys school rules				
Accepts suggestions				
Relates well to others	✓			
Is growing in self-control				
Avoids unnecessary talking	✓			
Note enclosed with card	✓			

In addition to the listed subjects your child is receiving instruction in the following integrated learnings:

Social Studies to develop a growing knowledge and understanding of the family, school, community, country and world.

Science to teach a growing knowledge of nature and the world about us.

Health to encourage a growing knowledge of healthful living and the application of this knowledge in daily habits.

S 1003

FIGURE 15.8. Report card for primary level

STUDENT'S NAME:

SCHOOL

Year in School

STUDENT EVALUATION REPORT

NOTICE TO PARENTS

This report is to inform you of your child's progress. It is NOT a comparison with achievement of other children. Progress is determined by each child's ability—its continuous.

⊞ Strength in this area
⊠ Satisfactory in this area
⊡ Weakness in this area
☐ Does not apply at this time

TEACHER'S NAME:

Your child's elementary years are most important to his school life. Your utmost cooperation is needed.

READING

	Quarter			
	1	2	3	4
Level of instruction				
Uses word attack skills				
Shows growth in vocabulary				
Reads with understanding				
Reads orally with expression				
Reads and follows directions				
Skims and locates information				
Reads for enjoyment				
Completes assignments				
Puts forth effort				
Final Evaluation				

LANGUAGE

ORAL
  Expresses ideas well
  Practices correct word usage
WRITTEN
  Expresses ideas w⸱⸱⸱

SPELLING

	Quarter			
	1	2	3	4
Spells correctly in written work				
Spells assigned words correctly				
Completes assignments				
Puts forth effort				
Final Evaluation				

HANDWRITING

Manuscript ☐
Cursive ☐
  Writes legibly
  Practices correct letter formation
  Completes assignments
  Puts forth effort
Final Evaluation

MATHEMATICS

☐ Whole numbers   ☐ Fractions
Level of instruction
  Can count
  Understands numerals and their meanings
  Knows addition facts
  Knows subtraction facts
  Knows Multiplication Facts
  Knows division facts
  Solves story problems
  Understands units of measure
  Recognizes geometric shapes
  Understands graphs, tables, and scale drawings
  Works accurately
  Completes assignments
  Puts forth effort
Final Evaluation

SCIENCE AND HEALTH

Contributes to project and committee work
Shows scientific curiosity
Participates in class discussion

SOCIAL STUDIES

	Quarter			
	1	2	3	4
SKILLS AND CONTENT				
Uses variety of reference materials				
Is gaining knowledge of other cultures				
Is gaining in skills of observation				
Is skillful in using maps, globes, and charts				
Organizes information				
Understands unit being presented				
Participates in current events discussion				
Contributes to project and committee work				
Completes assignments				
Puts forth effort				
Final Evaluation				

PERSONAL GROWTH

Assumes responsibility
Respects personal and school property
Relates well to others
Respects authority
Observes school and safety rules
Is courteous in speech and action
Displays growth in self-control
Displays good sportsmanship
Respects rights of others

Final Evaluation

STUDY SKILLS

Listens attentively
Reads and follows directions
Works quietly
Uses time wisely
Finishes work on time
Checks work for mistakes
Takes pride in neat work
Works well independently

FIGURE 15.9. Student evaluation report (partial)

mark and aid in providing information used to clarify what marks mean. Careful wording of checklists makes the teacher's job of reporting student progress easier. Basing reports on adequate data makes them valid for further decision making.

COMPUTERIZED REPORTING OF MARKS

Many school corporations utilize computers to report marks and calculate grade-point averages. The computational capacity and capability of handling large volumes of quantitative data with speed and accuracy makes the computer an administrative asset in mark reporting and record keeping. An illustration of one type of computer recording scheme currently utilized in junior and senior high schools is illustrated in Figure 15.10. The continuous interfold sheet on the left hand side of the mark-sense card is completed by the teacher for each class taught by first penciling in the information requested

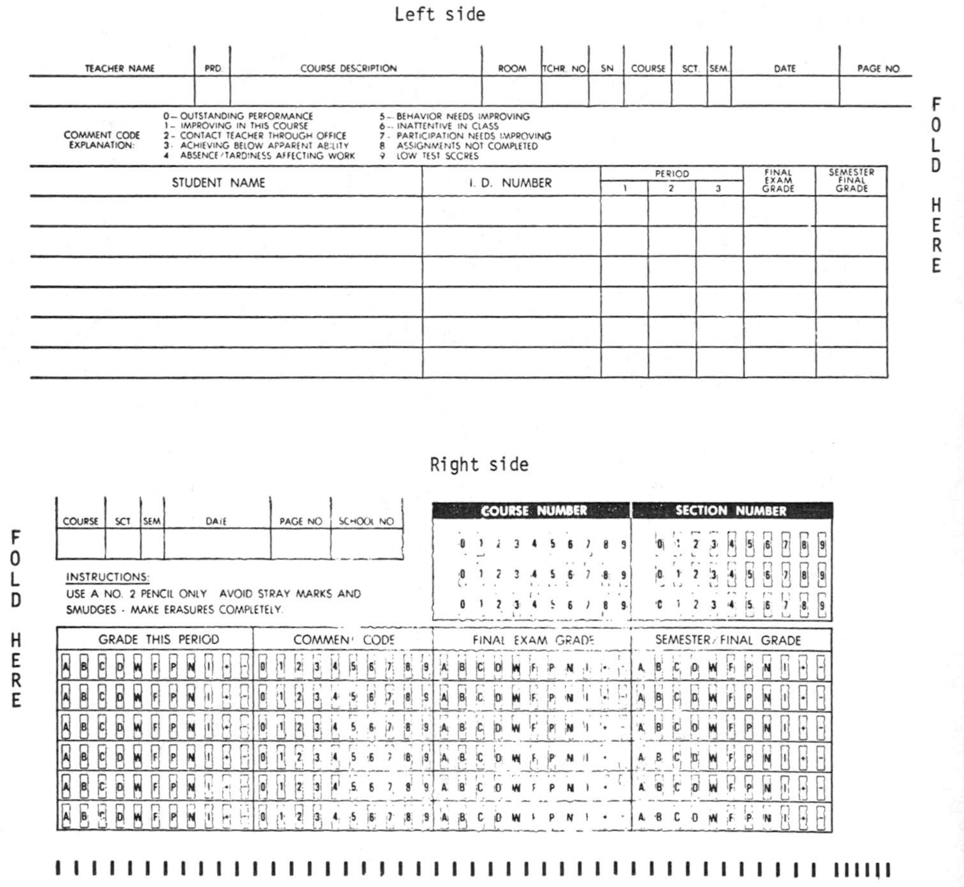

FIGURE 15.10. Continuous interfold sheet for a class. (The two cards are attached and folded where indicated)

concerning the teacher's name, period, course description, and such for each class. The teacher then records each student's name, ID number, a mark for each period, final examination mark, and semester mark.

Each line on the right hand side of the interfold sheet of the card contains the information to be reported for the student listed on that line on the left hand page. Letter marks and comments are recorded according to the code provided. The continuous interfold sheet and corresponding cards are returned to the central office for processing where the computer collects a student's marks for all classes and records them on that student's report card (See Figure 15.11). The report card is distributed to the student and two copies are retained for the school office. This type of computer output provides for a cumulative report for each marking period during the semester. Parents are not required to sign the report nor do students return the report to the school.

Other similar arrangements are used with computer assisted reports. Data can be quickly called for and utilized in many ways in administrative offices. When a school system utilizes the computer to report school marks, data are readily accessible and easy to retrieve for further analysis. For example, a teacher can compare his or her pattern of mark assignment with other teachers, marks given in one department can be compared to marks given in other departments, and any inconsistency investigated for correction if needed.

TECHNICAL ISSUES

A marking system requires a teacher to make decisions about student differences and individuality. The many purposes of classroom instruction preclude development of a single best way of deriving marks; however, certain principles underlie all marking systems. By combining a basic philosophic view, type of instruction, and uniqueness of student groups with the following principles a unique marking system can be tailored for a specific classroom. This is not a cookbook approach and each teacher should modify, add to, or delete to meet special needs. Most important is the awareness of the need for "good" procedures.

1. Use a broad data base. Collect information from a variety of observational procedures.
2. Record all data in a systematic way over the reporting period.
3. Quantify the information to be used in deriving marks. Value judgments should be reserved for the final evaluations.
4. Place most of the weight for interpretation on data that are collected near the end of the reporting period. The focus for marking is on what the student can do terminally.
5. Use only information about achievement as input data for the mark. Reports on other traits should be made separately on checklists or rating scales.
6. Ask yourself if the value judgments reflected in the marks are valid for making important decisions about or by students.

Hazelpine, Christopher Mr. & Mrs. Ralph Hazelpine	CLASS STUDENT NO. 770050 8 SECTION COUNSELOR	PRINCIPAL Billings Jr. H. S. PHONE Mr. Sting 238-4496

PERIOD ENDING 01 14 85

SUBJECT	PERIOD			SEMESTER			TEACHER	ROOM NO.
	1	2	3	EX	GR	CR		
Mathematics	B	C	C+	B	B-	1.0	Belltone 88102	
English	C-	C	C	D+	C-	1.0	Heartline 83609	
Physical Education	B	B	B	B	B	1.0	Brevortine 48904	
General Music	B	B	B+	D	B-	1.0	Melodie 67845	
Social Studies	C	C	C	C	C	1.0	Kranely 88903	
Science	D	D	D	D	D	1.0	Jesseky 86868	
Art	C	C	C	C	C	1.0	Rolfee 84565	

I = INCOMPLETE P = PASS FP = FAILURE AU = AUDIT W = WITHDRAWAL	PRESENT G.P.A. CUM. G.P.A. CUM. CREDITS	TARDY THIS REPORT TARDY TO DATE	DAYS ABSENT THIS REPORT TOTAL DAYS ABSENT TO DATE

FIGURE 15.11. Student report form

CONSIDERATIONS IN DETERMINATION OF MARKS AND WRITING REPORTS

Regardless of the type of mark or reporting plan being utilized, several important considerations should be kept in mind when summarizing student performance.

1. The function of marks and marking plans is to communicate effectively the degree of student achievement over a specified period of time or course for those who complete an educational sequence.

2. A reported mark should be an accurate and meaningful representation of what a student has learned in relationship to what was learned by other students (using norms), to how the student met the objectives (using a priori standards), or the amount of academic growth during the educational sequence (using growth).

3. A mark should have minimum of error and be reported concisely as a symbol.

4. The basis for assigning marks should be clear. Evidence should be available to explain the input used in forming the mark awarded.

5. The content of each mark should function to report achievement in a specific subject area, because the mark may become meaningless if too wide an area is considered.

6. The highest mark should be awarded to the highest demonstrated achievement and so on until the lowest mark is awarded to the lowest level of achievement.

7. The mark should not be used as a form of punishment.

8. Marks have a secondary impact on students by increasing their motivation.

9. Much attention should be given to improving the precision of marks to minimize misrepresentation and misinterpretation.

10. A well developed and uniform reporting plan for a school should lead to meaningful information and limit to a minimum interpretation problems by consumers.

11. The reporting plan should balance between an attempt to report too much detail and a report that contains too little information.

12. Many aspects of student achievement and personality are involved in the classroom milieu, making it impossible to give a total report with a single symbol that includes multiple aspects of cognitive, affective, and psychomotor behavior thus necessitating a multiple marking plan to communicate adequately for some levels of education.

13. The use of a multiple report plan provides an opportunity for the teacher to focus on a mark for pure achievement, and then report separately other factors concerning personal characteristics.

14. Teachers within a school or high-school department should decide with input from parents how report cards should be organized and what information to report. If the uniqueness of the situation is considered the report card is also likely to be unique in its makeup and the information that it communicates.

SUMMARY

Marks are employed to summarize cognitive achievement or skill performance over a specified period of time. Controversy concerning the awarding of marks is involved, with many opinions expressed by the various audiences to which marks are reported. One main factor in the marking controversy is the lack of uniformity in the meaning of a mark since different teachers may judge and include other factors than pure achievement in their reporting of marks. The meaning of a particular mark tends to vary from one teacher to another and the source of variation is rarely communicated to the consumer.

The purpose of marking is generally to inform students, parents, other teachers and school personnel, and potential employers of students about achievement and related academic performance. Marks facilitate student learning and development. Parents use marks to support and encourage student study. Marks can help to establish a dialogue between home and school. Other teachers and school personnel look to marks when directing future learning experiences and in determining whether instructional objectives have been met. Administrators use marks in administrative decisions regarding eligibility for extracurricular activities, reporting academic performance for admission to postsecondary programs, and to provide prospective employers with information for employment decisions. The diverse use of marks makes it impossible to find one universal marking procedure or plan.

The traditional types of marks and reporting were discussed providing strengths and weaknesses of each to aid in making decisions about what mark to use when reporting school performance: letter, numerical, pass/fail, or percentage. In addition alternatives to marks: letters to parents, parent-teacher conferences, and checklists, along with their strengths and weaknesses, were discussed.

The discussion of traditional and alternative reports provides an understanding of the use of multiple marking and reporting plans which can reduce if not eliminate the difficulties founded in a single marking program. Examples of several actual report forms in use were presented to illustrate the detail that can be addressed to report student learning. An example of computerized mark reporting was provided. The chapter was highlighted by a list of important considerations which should be remembered when assigning marks.

NEW TECHNICAL TERM LISTED IN THE GLOSSARY

Marking plan

ACTIVITY EXERCISES

1. Prepare a short questionnaire that could be sent to parents that would allow them to give input for a new report card to be used next year. Try to collect information that could be developed into a list of "What our parents want to know."
2. Consider a school system (K–12) that has reported secondary school marks by the computer for five years. List as many uses of these data that have accumulated over this time as you can think of. How could they contribute to support of literacy of future students?
3. List the criteria of a good reporting plan from the viewpoint of:
   A. students
   B. parents

C. teachers
D. all three collectively

4. Obtain a report card for an elementary or secondary school and study the information communicated by the report. Interview two or three parents with children in the school using the report card and list their feelings of the report card and what it communicates to them.

5. Develop a marking plan you feel would provide valid and reliable information for students, parents, and others in the community. Visit with a school principal and two teachers and record their opinions of the marking plan you developed.

FOR DISCUSSION

1. Describe the advantages of a multiple system of reporting student progress in the elementary school.

2. Assume that you are teaching in a state that requires students to pass competency tests to qualify for high school graduation. How can marking and reporting plans aid preparation of students throughout the first 11 grades and support student success on the competency tests?

3. Explain why marks should be based exclusively on information about achievement and not on attendance, effort, attitude, or deportment.

4. How could reports to parents be improved by involving students in preparation of written reports about student achievement? At what age do you think students should participate?

REFERENCES AND KNOWLEDGE EXTENDERS

ANTES, C. A., & ANTES, R. L. *The role of classroom teachers in student self-concept development.* Terre Haute, IN: Curriculum Research and Development Center, Indiana State University, 1976.

EBEL, R. L. *Essentials of educational measurement* (3rd ed.). Englewood Cliffs, NJ: Prentice-Hall, 1979. Chap. 12, pp. 227–257.

GEISINGER, K. F. Marking systems. In H. E. Mitzel (Ed.), *Encyclopedia of educational research, 3,* 1139–1149. New York: Free Press, 1982.

GRONLUND, N. E. *Measurement and evaluation in teaching* (4th ed.). New York: Macmillan, 1981. Chapter 19, pp. 509–534.

KIRSCHENBAUM, H., SIMON, S. B., & NAPIER, R. M. *Wad-ja-get? The grading game in American education.* New York: Hart, 1971.

KUNDER, L. H., & PORWOLL, P. J. *Reporting pupil progress: Policies, procedures, and systems.* Arlington, VA: Educational Research Service, 1977.

MILTON, C., & EDGERLY, J. W. The testing and grading of students. New Rochelle, NY: *Change Magazine,* 1976.

SIMON, S. B., & BELLANCA, J. A. (Eds.). *Degrading the grading myths: A primer of alternatives to grades and marks.* Washington, D.C.: Association of Supervision and Curriculum Development, 1976.

TERWILLIGER, J. S. *Assigning grades to students.* Glenview, IL: Scott, Foresman, 1971.

TERWILLIGER, J. S. Assigning grades—Philosophical issues and practical recommendations. *Journal of Research and Development in Education,* 1977, *10*(3), 21–39.

Chapter 16. Published Tests

After study of Chapter 16, you should be able to:

1. State the criteria a test must meet to be considered standardized.
2. List the types of standardized achievement tests and tell how they are used in the classroom.
3. Outline the procedures for development of a standardized achievement test.
4. Differentiate between standardized achievement tests and aptitude tests.
5. Describe the purpose of screening tests and their use in the classroom.
6. List the sources of information about standardized tests.
7. Locate tests in the *Mental Measurements Yearbook* series.
8. Evaluate standardized tests for specific classroom measurement.
9. List and describe the types of norms associated with standardized tests.
10. Discuss the notion that "norms are not necessarily standards to be met."
11. Choose the proper norm for a specific situation or audience.
12. Discuss why test scores are many times reported as bands rather than specific points.
13. Explain how each glossary term listed at the end of the chapter is used in classroom measurement and evaluation.

Published tests can be used to complement teacher-made classroom tests. Published tests like teacher-made tests measure student progress and attainment, thus aiding in the determination of how well students have achieved or acquired skills. Use of published tests should be an integral part of the ongoing instructional program and evaluation process. They provide the teacher with an independent, objective frame of reference for evaluating a class based on external norms. A combination of teacher-made tests and observation along with carefully selected published tests provide a comprehensive program of student appraisal and program assessment in education.

School systems need information about students which may best be gathered through administration of well-prepared tests published by persons outside that school system. Some of the reasons for using such tests are determination of a student's progress from year to year, determination of how to deal with the idiosyncratic features of a student, and comparison of how students collectively compare to other like groups throughout the country.

Because coverage of published tests is general in nature and deals with performance in a wide geographical region, results cannot be used to judge a teacher's effectiveness in dealing with a set of objectives for an individual student or a specific classroom of students. A teacher's effectiveness should not be judged on information supplied from a published test for a group of students who come to school with special needs and predetermined conditions over which the teacher has little or no control. In other words, a school program serves a special set of objectives, and norms for published tests should not become standards for all students. For some students and some classrooms average attainment may be far more than teachers should expect while that for other students and other classrooms the average may be far below what the teacher should expect. Although published test results, especially in academic and skills areas, are often compared to the norm group as if the norm group performance is a standard, this procedure is not recommended by test publishers or specialists in testing. However, standardized tests can provide information not obtainable in any other way, and their use is needed for completely integrated school program evaluation.

Appendix E provides an outline of a schoolwide standardized testing program which indicates the grade and time of year tests are administered, whether the test scores are scholastic aptitude measures or achievement measures, the purpose, and the use to be made of test results. Every teacher employed in a school system that has a testing program should be supplied with this information. Standardized testing programs may vary widely depending on the purpose and use to be made of test results, and the outline is presented as illustrative, not as a model, for all school systems. Tests administered to individual students by school psychometrists, psychologists, and school counselors are not included in the illustrative outline of a schoolwide testing program because they are incorporated as needed. Generally the testing program for all students capable of taking group-administered tests consists of periodic measurement of scholastic aptitude and yearly achievement testing in grades one through six or through junior high school. At the senior high school level measurement of scholastic aptitude and achievement in specific subjects is carried out to support instruction. Throughout the school system competencies may be checked by both teacher-made and standardized tests to support remediation by corrective teaching for identified deficiencies. These may be incorporated into the overall plan, selected school by school, or chosen by a classroom teacher who decides what tests are needed.

CLASSIFICATION OF PUBLISHED TESTS

Published tests come from many sources. Some are produced by individuals who have developed a particular test for their own use and later made it available for others, some by companies which do nothing except publish tests, some by companies that publish many kinds of materials and have a division which publishes tests, and others by companies that publish textbooks and include tests to be used with a specific book or series of books. Published materials vary widely in purpose and the proper ways to use and interpret them.

Tests That Accompany Textbook Series

Many textbooks and textbook series make available supplementary materials which include tests that can be administered to students who use the books. The purpose of such tests is to assess the extent that each student and the class as a whole have achieved mastery of the content or met the objectives set by the authors of the book who either prepared the tests or approved them as being appropriate for the content.

Since the tests are to be for mastery of a body of content, norms are neither supplied nor needed. Furthermore, the teacher is allowed to use each test as desired. If directions are included, they are very general, often without specific directions for the student. Time limits can be set by the teacher or disregarded. If the teacher chooses to do so, some tests can be completed outside of class as a student learning experience. No predetermined ways of using the tests restrict how the tests are administered, how they are scored, or how the scores are to be interpreted. The tests which accompany textbooks and textbook series are *not standardized.*

Since the purpose of these tests is to assess the students' grasp of material presented in the book(s) being used, the information is good immediate feedback for formative evaluation and can be used to direct further instruction or reteaching. For skill development, direction for remediation exercises may be discerned from individual student performance, and a certain amount of diagnostic information about successes and failures may be obtained from tests where procedure is important.

Textbook tests may be used flexibly by the teacher and can become a valuable tool for data collection if used properly. However, the test does *not* give a measure of attainment of objectives attached to what the teacher used to supplement the textbook or any serendipitous outcomes of the study. Maybe a better name for these "tests" would be instructional materials, since their use is more directly pointed to instruction and corrective teaching than to testing. In any event, they should not be used as tests to replace either teacher-made or standardized tests which serve other purposes. The technical qualities, reliability, and validity of textbook tests usually are not reported and their uses are specific to a book or series of books.

Standardized Tests

To meet criteria for being a standardized test a prescribed set of tasks must be presented in such a way that anyone taking the test must give reactions to the same items, the test must be administered according to guidelines set by the test authors, the student responses scored according to the authors' instructions, and the scores interpreted through norms made available with the test. To be acceptable to measurement and subject-matter specialists it should meet certain standards set for widely used published tests.

A myriad of standardized tests available for teachers, other educators, and psychologists allows for selection of appropriate testing instruments. The broad categories of tests commonly used in schools include: *(a)* achievement, *(b)* aptitude, *(c)* mental ability, and *(d)* personality tests. These tests are designed to measure characteristics associated with student performance in school subjects and school-related behavior.

The large number and variety of published standardized tests available for a multitude of uses necessitate that teachers be knowledgeable concerning types of tests available, how to select a test best suited to their needs, and the strengths and limitations of tests relevant to different educational levels. Figure 16.1 is a list of test categories taken from a classified index of test titles listed in *The Eighth Mental Measurements Yearbook* (Buros, 1978). The 1,184 tests classified into 15 categories has been further broken down by each of the classifications to illustrate the number of titles for each category (Buros, 1978, pp. 1–1189). The ensuing presentation concerning standardized achievement, standardized aptitude, and screening tests refers to types of tests classified in Figure 16.1. The examples of components of standardized achievement and aptitude tests refer to various tests and specific test names are not provided since it would be impossible to list components for each specific test available. The purpose in the presentation is to bring attention to the type of coverage of typical standardized tests. The reader wishing more specific information may explore sections of *The Eighth Mental Measurements Yearbook* to become familiar with tests listed in each category of interest.

STANDARDIZED ACHIEVEMENT TESTS

The procedure for development of standardized achievement tests provides insight into understanding their intended function. A need expressed by school personnel for some particular type of test information may eventually lead to the construction of a standardized test if a feasibility study indicates a potential market sufficient to support the test's development. An example of a potential market for a published standardized test is related to the concern with and movement to competency examinations. When need for this type of testing generated a market, competency-based tests were developed.

In building a standardized achievement test a country-wide analysis of curriculum is undertaken. Careful study and review of the content of a representative number of widely accepted textbooks, representative courses of study, recommendations of curriculum specialists, and research literature in the subject area help establish content areas. Teachers, test experts, curriculum specialists, and other school personnel are also called upon to determine the learning outcomes which should be assessed in the subject and skill areas. Trends in curriculum are ascertained from curriculum experts. When the preliminary overview is completed, the emphasis to be given each objective is

Classification	Listed	Classification	Listed
Achievement Batteries	38	Test Programs	12
English	24	Multi-Aptitude Batteries	12
Literature	10	Personality	220
Spelling	5	Reading	34
Vocabulary	6	Diagnostic	32
Fine Arts		Miscellaneous	3
Art	6	Oral	11
Music	12	Readiness	17
Foreign Languages	1	Special Fields	3
English	10	Speed	1
French	14	Study Skills	9
German	12	Science	7
Greek	1	Biology	6
Hebrew	2	Chemistry	25
Italian	3	Physics	6
Latin	3	Sensory-Motor	14
Russian	6	Vision	4
Spanish	21	Social Studies	8
Intelligence	32	Economics	10
Group	32	Geography	2
Individual	29	History	11
Specific	26	Political Science	8
Mathematics	45	Sociology	3
Algebra	5	Speech and Hearing	4
Arithmetic	8	Hearing	22
Calculus	1	Speech	26
Geometry	2		
Special Fields	1	Vocations	7
Statistics	1	Careers and Interests	44
Trigonometry	2	Clerical	8
Miscellaneous	3	Manual Dexterity	1
Agriculture	1	Mechanical Ability	7
Blind	2	Miscellaneous	11
Business Education	9	Selection and Rating Forms	4
Courtship and Marriage	27	Vocations: Specific	
Driving and Safety Education	2	Accounting	13
Education	47	Computer Programming	5
Health and Physical Education	9	Dentistry	6
Home Economics	3	Engineering	3
Industrial Arts	2	Law	7
Learning Disabilities	30	Medicine	8
Listening	3	Miscellaneous	3
Philosophy	3	Nursing	15
Psychology	5	Sales	4
Record and Report Forms	1	Skilled Trades	44
Religious Education	4	Supervision	17
Socioeconomic Status	1		

FIGURE 16.1. Classification index of tests from *The Eighth Mental Measurements Yearbook* **(Buros, 1978)**

analyzed to provide the approximate percent of test items to be written to measure each objective and a table of specifications is built to reflect content and behaviors as emphasized in instruction. Content validity is built into the instrument using this direction.

In preparing test items, subject-matter specialists and test experts develop a large pool of items usually of the multiple-choice format, however the trend in standardized testing today is to incorporate many different kinds of tasks as suggested by what is being measured. The pool of items written to measure the instructional objectives and content as indicated in the table of specifications is edited by professional item writers. The professional team of item writers may consist of test authors, teachers employed to write items, and members of the publisher's staff. After careful review and editing of each task in the pool of items, preliminary test booklets are compiled.

The preliminary form(s) of the test are administered to a group of students as similar as possible to those to be tested with the final form of the test. This procedure is known as **field testing.** Separate testing for each grade level in different geographical areas may be undertaken. Field testing provides information relevant to the effectiveness of response options, the equivalence of items on the various forms of the test, and the adequacy of the directions, time limits, and test format. The appropriateness of each item for use in the test is also determined. After results of field testing are analyzed, revisions are made to improve the items, the final set of items to be used is selected, and the test is assembled in final form. Items not used in the final form of the test may be employed to develop alternative test forms and to allow for replacement of items when needed.

The final form of the test attempts to maximize content sampling while providing a test which does not take too much time to administer. Time limits for standardized tests are set so that they can be administered in time sequences which correspond to student attention span or to the average length of a school class period. For a very long test or **battery** of tests, the divisions for test sessions are made to fit within typical school class periods or to student attention span. The question is asked, "How can the test be developed so that it is not too long and yet adequately sample the topics and content of concern?" The table of specifications assists test developers to include the percentage of items appropriate for each behavioral domain taking into account the importance of content topics.

The test in its final form is administered to a representative group of students for the purpose of establishing norms. Care and attention must be given to the selection of truly representative students for whom the test is intended if comparisons are to be made between scores made by students administered the test and scores made by the **norm population.** Norms for groups with specific sets of characteristics (geographical regions, rural, inner-city, and such) can be established for the test by administration to each separately. Preparation of accessory materials such as the test manual, scoring sheets, scoring stencils, and associated aids is completed prior to marketing the test. An itemization of the procedure for development of a standardized achievement test is as follows:

1. The content area to be assessed is defined and behaviors listed.
2. A table of specifications is developed.
3. Potential test items are constructed.
4. The test items are field tested.
5. The field test results are analyzed.
6. The final test is constructed.
7. Data are collected from a representative group of students.
8. Norms are established for the test.
9. The reliability and validity of the test are determined.
10. The standardized procedures for administration and scoring are established.
11. The test manual and accessory materials are developed.

Achievement tests measure the effects of school instructional learning experiences and provide information about what a student knows and can do at the time of testing. The sampling of course content is based on common topics and student accomplishment or level of success in general learning. An achievement test may be classified as diagnostic, single-subject, or battery.

Diagnostic Tests

A diagnostic test is administered to isolate specific weaknesses in a restricted range of achievement and skill development in a subject. The nature of any weakness is suggested by careful analysis of individual item responses or calculation. The diagnostic test provides information for the teacher regarding a deficit or weakness in an en route, or enabling skill, or knowledge needed in a learning sequence. Strengths are also identified to enhance instructional effectiveness. Diagnostic tests are available for many subjects to help the teacher determine student ability in the essentials of learning, and cover specific skills better than a general achievement test. For example, Figure 16.1 indicates that Buros (1978) lists 32 diagnostic tests which are designed to direct remediation by corrective teaching. The items of some achievement tests can be clustered to give diagnostic information, but they are generally not specific enough to allow for the needed identification of specific deficiencies.

Diagnostic reading tests measure the major components of the reading process and identify strengths and weaknesses in reading through such factors as comprehension, auditory discrimination, visual discrimination, reading rate, vocabulary, and motor skills. Subtests in areas such as syllabication, beginning and ending sounds, blending, sound discrimination, comprehension (literal, inferential), blending rate, oral reading, word pronunciation, knowledge of word parts, vowels, and naming capital letters allow identification of deficiencies.

Generally from 8 to 20 separate subtests and scores are available in a diagnostic reading test depending on the specific test. The administration time varies from one to two-and-a-half hours and may be broken into a series of short sessions. A diagnostic reading test is usually administered on an individual basis working at the speed appropriate for the student except for a flashcard presentation for word pronunciation and phrases.

Diagnostic tests in other areas follow the same basic pattern of breaking down skills and knowledge into specifics. For example, a diagnostic test in arithmetic may include subtests on basic facts, fundamental operations with whole numbers, operations with percentages, fundamental operations with decimal fractions, operations with measures, computation, problem solving, and fundamental operations with common fractions.

Through identification of the difficulties or weaknesses, the teacher can determine where special remediation is needed and introduce corrective teaching. It should be kept in mind that diagnostic tests do not reveal the causes of deficiencies. The information obtained through careful study of test results may be helpful in recognizing the possible antecedents to the student's deficiency.

Single-Subject Tests

Single-subject tests measure specialized areas included in the curriculum and separate tests are available in nearly every subject at the appropriate grade level as can be seen from Figure 16.1. Single-subject tests contain more items and assess the subject area from a wider spectrum than found in subtests of **a survey battery.** A school may use a single-subject subtest from a battery or a specially prepared single-subject test to assess level of achievement. Single-subject tests provide for a wider sample of the subject and better represent the instructional objectives of a particular course or grade level. For this reason, a single-subject test will provide better coverage of the instructional objectives in a particular class or school. Often subject tests are given at the end of a course to compare students individually or as a class with national norms. The teacher can determine the students' level of achievement and general strengths and weaknesses in the specific subject as well as evaluate the effectiveness of the teaching procedure to meet those objectives considered by the test authors to be important. In selecting a single-subject or skills test, the teacher will want to choose one which has a close match between test items and objectives set for the students during prior instruction.

Coverage of single-subject tests

The diversity of single-subject tests in various areas is illustrated in Figure 16.1 above. The following six tests provide examples of the coverage of typical single-subject achievement tests.

1. A language arts achievement test for the primary grades requires students make appropriate pictures in the test booklet in response to words, sentences, stories, and poems read by the teacher. These responses provide an achievement score for the areas of comprehension, recall, interpretation, evaluation of, and inference from the spoken word.

2. A social studies achievement test for grades four through eight mea-

sures the relevant knowledge which students have acquired in elementary social studies. The scores represent the measurement of American heritage, people of our land and times, geography, and basic social process.

3. An English achievement test for grades 9 through 12 measures achievement in two fundamental areas of reading comprehension and written expression. Reading comprehension consists of scores for vocabulary, level of comprehension, speed of comprehension, and total reading comprehension. Written expression consists of two parts: effectiveness and mechanics. Standardized English tests usually stress the fundamentals of English grammar, sentence structure, spelling, punctuation, errors in usage, and capitalization. In addition, English tests are available to measure knowledge and appreciation of literature, spelling and writing ability, and writing or composition ability.

4. A series of mathematics achievement tests for secondary grades measures understanding of mathematical concepts in either arithmetic or the structure of the number system depending upon which test is administered. At grades eight and nine algebra I or algebra II tests are available. Geometry and trigonometry tests are available for grades 10 to 12. Supplemental tests in algebra III, analytic geometry, and calculus are available through the college level. Titles assigned to mathematics tests often correspond with titles of math courses offered in most secondary schools.

5. An industrial arts achievement test for use in grade levels seven through nine covers five areas of the industrial arts curriculum: general industrial arts, drawing, electricity/electronics, metals, and woods. These tests are designed for students who have had two semesters of general industrial arts and students at the same grade level who have taken one semester in woods, metals, drawing, or electricity/electronics. A general industrial arts test measures knowledge and understanding in six specific areas: comprehension and application in woods, metals, drawing, electricity/electronics, general industrial arts, and industry.

6. A physical fitness achievement test to be administered in grades 10 and up provides an overall measure of physical fitness which reflects the instructional objectives of the physical education program. The physical measurements for the 10 subtests include: extent flexibility, dynamic flexibility, shuttle run (explosive strength), softball throw (explosive strength), hand grip (static strength), pull-ups (dynamic strength), leg-lifts (trunk strength), cable jump (coordination), balance (equilibrium), 600-yard run-walk (stamina).

Reading tests

One of the most important reasons for school failure is difficulty in reading, and many academic problems in the school can be traced to reading deficiencies. The continuing publicity concerning reading has stimulated the use of reading tests to the point where they may be the most widely used type of published test in elementary schools. The publication of *Reading Tests and Reviews II* (Buros, 1975) and the 110 reading tests listed in *The Eighth Mental Measurements Yearbook* (Buros, 1978) illustrate the concern for reading and the need for a variety of standardized instruments to help assess this skill and improve reading. Reading tests are designed to: *(a)* determine readiness, *(b)* measure achievement, or *(c)* diagnose problem areas.

Reading achievement tests typically assess vocabulary, reading comprehension, and rate (speed) of reading. According to publishers some reading tests are of value as predictive, screening, and diagnostic instruments. The nature of the reading materials in reading tests and the demands made on students differ widely from test to test. The skills tested, the method of their assessment and the extent of sampling also vary widely as illustrated by the following examples.

1. A reading achievement test with six levels (primary-1, primary-2, primary-3, primary-2.5–3, survey 4–6, and survey 7–9) covers grades one through nine. The first three levels assess the areas of vocabulary and comprehension. The fourth level provides a measure for speed and accuracy. The fifth and sixth levels provide scores for the area of speed and accuracy, vocabulary, and comprehension.

2. A reading achievement test in silent reading for grade level two, provides scores in the areas of words in use, multiple word meanings, and comprehension. On the basis of student performance on this test, the classroom teacher can tailor the reading program to meet student needs.

3. A reading achievement test at three levels (1–2.5, 2–4, and 4–9) is designed to measure students' ability to understand the overall theme of a story, identify the main idea in a paragraph, infer logical ideas, retain significant details, and understand the meaning of words in context. The first level provides scores in the areas of verbal-pictorial association, language perception, comprehension, and vocabulary. The second and third levels provide scores in comprehension and vocabulary.

Different philosophies about how to measure reading comprehension are reflected in how the student is presented tasks to measure comprehension. Some tests contain 75- to 100-word vocabulary tests to measure student ability to comprehend meaning. Others measure comprehension by measuring student ability to understand the general significance of a paragraph, note important details, and predict outcomes.

Batteries

Achievement test batteries consist of a cluster of tests in different subjects standardized on the same population thus making comparisons across subjects possible for a student. Achievement batteries are popular at the primary and elementary levels because of the uniformity in content and objectives, but use of batteries extends into secondary levels. Each specific test battery provides different emphases to topics, thus careful consideration is necessary in selection and adoption of a test battery which best parallels the curricular emphasis of the school. There are similarities among test batteries.

A typical achievement battery consists of four or more subtests which provide scores for each subtest as well as a total battery score. Survey batteries are available for various grade levels which allow for varying levels and emphases from one grade level to another. In general, all batteries at the same level cover much the same content, but the orientation of the test writers and publishers in regard to what they feel a particular battery should do causes batteries to differ in some ways. Batteries are keyed to knowledge and skills common to textbooks and courses of study and they measure basic components essential to success in schoolwork. The individual subtests of achievement batteries for the first four grades usually assess levels of reading, spelling, language, and arithmetic attainment. A battery for grades five and six, in addition to the areas covered in the earlier grades, may include subtests in study skills, literature, history, civics, geography, or science. Examples of coverage of test batteries follow.

1. A general achievement battery at six levels includes grades kindergarten through 9.5. The purpose of the battery is to measure the essentials of reading, mathematics, language, and study skills at the grade level specified. The primer level (kindergarten–1.4) includes three areas and scores: listening for sounds, reading, and numbers. Primary I (1.5–2.4) includes four areas and scores: reading, word knowledge, word analysis, and mathematics. Primary II (2.5–3.4) includes five areas and seven scores: reading, word knowledge, language, spelling, mathematics (computation, concepts, problem solving).

Science and social studies content are added at the intermediate (5.0–6.9) and advanced (7.0–9.5) levels of this battery giving subtest scores for these levels. This test covers the subject matter areas usually taught at each grade level in the elementary and junior high schools. The content reflects what is widely taught in the classroom at the appropriate level, and emphasis is placed on facts and understandings. This test, like most batteries is set up so that the teacher and other school personnel can make a decision about which subtests to use. For example, the intermediate battery includes subtests for science and social studies which may be omitted if these subjects were not taught at that level. The teacher and other interested personnel choose subtests that are valid tests for the classes to be tested, or the total battery if it is valid for the instruction given.

2. A general achievement battery at three levels: grades 1–2 provides scores for the areas of reading (verbal pictorial association, language perception, comprehension, vocabulary), arithmetic (concepts, reasoning, computation): grades 2–4 provides scores for the areas of language arts (capitalization, punctuation, grammatical usage, spelling), arithmetic (concepts, reasoning, computation), reading (comprehension, vocabulary): and grades 4–9 provides scores for the areas of social studies, science, language arts (capitalization, punctuation, grammatical usage, spelling), arithmetic (reasoning, concepts, computation), and reading (comprehension, vocabulary), plus optional work-study skills (references, charts).

This battery provides an overlapping of items from level to level which makes provision for continuity of the series and offers an advantage when comparing results of different levels which have been administered in the same classroom. Emphasis in this battery is placed on measuring the student's development of understanding and the application of learning rather than merely measuring the acquisition of knowledge.

3. A basic skills battery developed specifically for those who prefer batteries which do not attempt to cover all subjects and oriented to skill development for grades 3–9 provides scores for the areas of vocabulary, reading comprehension, language skills (spelling, capitalization, punctuation, usage), work-study skills (map reading, reading graphs and tables, knowledge and use of reference materials), and arithmetic skills (arithmetic concepts, arithmetic problem solving).

This battery is directed to measuring student achievement in several of the more basic areas and concentrates on the fundamentals of elementary school instruction and the basic skills essential to day-to-day learning in the classroom. The battery requires students to use their acquired skills and measures their ability to do so in addition to measuring knowledge of formal rules and facts. Some individuals feel that the broader sampling of the basic skill areas tested makes this type of battery more valuable than the general achievement batteries which sample more subject areas.

In choosing an achievement battery a perusal and comparison of subtests of different achievement batteries, grade level coverage, number of individual subtest scores, administration time, and an actual review of the individual items for each subtest is necessary to make adequate choices of a battery for a particular school situation. In examples 1 and 2, the general achievement batteries include academically oriented, subject content in addition to basic skills. Some tests add separate subtests on science and social studies which are considered by some as essentially tests of reading and study skills rather than of subject matter. The basic skills achievement battery, example 3, covers the basic skills and requires deeper mastery. The examples given here exemplify some of the differences among batteries. While these differences are important in making initial decisions about which batteries will be given further consideration, only a detailed study of the test, manual, and items will answer the question of appropriateness of any particular battery to any specific classroom or school.

The popular movement for individualization of instruction, nongraded classes, and nongraded instructional materials has stimulated test developers and publishers to provide for individualized testing which allows simultaneous administration of more than one level of the test within the same classroom. Test publishers have batteries available from grades 1–14 which are designed for the dual purposes of facilitating educational measurement and individual diagnosis. These tests indicate the level of performance of each student in the attainment of basic curricular objectives including reading, arithmetic, and language.

Secondary school level batteries are used to assess students' knowledge and skill in reading (vocabulary and comprehension), language (mechanics, expression, and spelling), arithmetic (computation, concepts, and applications), and study skills (using reference and graphic materials). Other content subjects are not included in secondary batteries because students tend to specialize more in the upper grades. Examples of coverage of secondary test batteries follow.

1. A general achievement battery at one level, grades 9–12 provides scores for the areas of English, numerical competence, mathematics, reading, science, social studies, and spelling subtests (English and spelling combined or available as separate tests). Three supplementary tests (arts and humanities, business and economics, and technical comprehension) are available as separate tests or as part of the battery. The common areas of study measured by this battery are the common core subjects taught at the high school level although the content and emphasis may vary widely from school to school.

2. A general achievement battery at one level, grades 9–13 provides scores for the areas of language arts (reading, spelling, language, study skills), social studies (study skills, vocabulary, information), mathematics (computation and concepts, analysis and problem solving), and science (concepts and understandings, information). Each subtest is available as a separate test. The publisher is hoping to capitalize on the availability of each separate test and the four subtests together as a battery to provide for comparability of students across the tests.

3. A general achievement battery at one level, grades 8–12, provides scores for the areas of aptitude (verbal, quantitative) and achievement (reading, mathematics, and English). The battery measures interpretive and applicative abilities related to subject areas. The aptitude and achievement subtests combine into a total score.

In general, batteries for high school cover the subjects of English, social studies, science, and mathematics. High school achievement batteries are developed to include a range of difficulty wide enough to cover from lower to higher ability students. The particular areas assessed may vary widely. For example, some mathematics tests include only elementary algebra and geometry while others may measure additional advanced knowledge such as advanced algebra, trigonometry, probability, and set theory. Social studies usually includes American history and world history with many variations needed to correspond to different classroom emphasis. Supplementary single subtests for batteries are not usually as thorough in the range or depth of measurement in the subject as single-subject tests. Subtests of batteries are shortened to provide an overall assessment in the form of a composite score for the battery. When in-depth information about achievement in a specific content area is desired, additional information may be acquired through a single-subject achievement test. The amount of emphasis given to topics in subtests and the skills measured differ among subtests of the same subject area on different tests. Therefore, careful consideration must be given to the selection of the test which best measures what is stressed in a particular classroom.

Achievement test batteries provide supplemental data for purposes of grade placement, grouping, and promotion. Students' scores provide a measure of general educational development or essential skill development as well as direct evidence of learning progress and usually serve summative evaluation. As further indication of attainment, comparisons are made of students' scores with test norms. Information concerning students' levels of educational development and competence in the basic skill areas can aid in grouping students and provide an idea of where diagnostic testing should be implemented. Diagnostic tests can be employed in follow-up to identify specific weaknesses and strengths. All types of data should be carefully considered and weighed in light of the students' classroom performance and scores on teacher-made tests, as well as on standardized achievement tests.

STANDARDIZED APTITUDE TESTS

Standardized aptitude tests include: *(a)* mental abilities tests which are also known as general scholastic aptitude or intelligence tests, *(b)* multiaptitude tests or aptitude test batteries, and *(c)* specific aptitude tests or single-subject aptitude tests. Aptitude tests predict success in general academics, a subject, or a special occupational area. These tests measure innate abilities of students or abilities obtained as a result of general experience.

A clear distinction between aptitude and achievement tests does not exist, since prior learning is involved and influences current behavior. The same test item could appear in either an achievement or aptitude test or both. Since both are measures of prior learning the use of the results largely determines whether a test is for measuring achievement or aptitude; however, there are differences in what each type of test asks students to do in the tasks. Anastasi (1982, pp. 393–396) presents a discussion of the nature and uses of aptitude and achievement tests which incorporates the following ideas. Achievement tests measure: *(a)* the effects of a specific program; *(b)* effects of a relatively standardized set of experiences; *(c)* effects of learning that occur under partially known and controlled conditions; *(d)* and what the individual can do at the time. Aptitude tests measure: *(a)* the effects of the cumulative influence of experiences, *(b)* effects of learning under relatively uncontrolled and unknown conditions, and *(c)* predict what the individual can do in the future.

If a school instructional program is geared to student potentials, classroom teachers continually make judgments of students' scholastic abilities to aid in formation of educational goals. Through aptitude testing teachers can become aware of an individual's general ability and potential for cognitive functioning in different areas of learning. Since aptitude tests predict the degree of potential success, high performance indicates potential success, and poor performance indicates potential difficulty in the endeavor.

One excellent indicator of future performance is past performance or achievement. Daily recitation, daily assignments, and class performance provide information concerning aptitudes. That information can be supplemented by results of standardized aptitude tests which provide objective and meaningful data not otherwise obtainable. Standardized aptitude tests are particularly helpful when information about past performance is not available for making aptitude assessment. For example, when young children enter school for the first time, information about past performance is not available so aptitude tests may be employed in appraisal of these students. A transfer student from a distant school system usually has a grade card which provides an indication of past achievement while aptitude tests provide additional information about the student's capabilities and potential. By being aware of student potential, the teacher may plan experiences to aid in the development of skills necessary for success by anticipating and possibly avoiding learning difficulty. The information from tests may aid counselors in advising students concerning possible choices in course and curriculum selection.

Testing Mental Abilities

Scholastic aptitude, academic aptitude, mental abilities, mental functioning, and intelligence as related to standardized tests refer to measurement of students' capabilities to learn. The lack of a commonly accepted definition of these terms has led to variations in opinions and definitions which result in a wide divergence in the tests developed and employed to assess mental ability.

The classroom teacher's reference to intelligence relates to what is actually measured by mental ability tests. Intelligence may be defined as the aggregate or global capacity of an individual to act purposely, to think rationally, and to deal effectively with the environment. Most individuals agree that intelligence is known by its effects or properties, so it is the capacity to learn, adapt, and reason—the ability to learn. In some situations intelligence may even be a reflex or automatic action involving insight and ratiocination. Since mental ability scores have been found to be closely related to academic success, predictions are made of the students' global mental ability to function in an academic environment as well as in everyday life.

Mental ability testing can be done individually or by groups. Group tests are administered as paper-and-pencil tests and generate a verbal score that is interpreted by norm tables. Typically, individually administered mental ability tests generate: *(a)* a verbal score, *(b)* a nonverbal score, and *(c)* a total test score. Both the verbal and nonverbal components of the test attempt to measure the same construct through two separate procedures, and combined give a total score that is a better predictor than the single verbal score from a group test.

Individual tests

Individual mental ability tests are administered on a one-to-one basis, one examiner and one student. The examiner must have special training and experience in administering the test before testing in a clinic or school. Typically the individual test is employed as a clinical device to screen students for special purposes or when wide variations exist in scores on group tests for an individual. The individually administered test provides for strict observation of behavior and leads to highly reliable measures. A widely employed individually administered test consists of 20 levels of tests for age two through adult: *(a)* ages two to four and a half at half-year intervals, *(b)* tests for ages 5 to 14 at yearly intervals, and *(c)* tests for those above 14 years of age, designated as average adult and superior adult I, II, and III. This is primarily a verbal test which deals with vocabulary, general information, comprehension, and similar tasks requiring verbally presented responses.

Another individual intelligence scale which is employed for 16- to 25-year-olds yields three scores: *(a)* verbal, *(b)* performance, and *(c)* total IQ, which is a composite of the verbal and performance scales. The verbal section is composed of six scales: general information, comprehension, arithmetic reasoning, memory span, similarities, and vocabulary. The performance section is composed of five scales: picture completion, picture arrangement, block design, object assembly, and digit-symbol manipulation.

Since an examiner must be extensively trained to administer this type of test, only a brief introduction is provided here. In Figure 16.1, above, *The Eighth Mental Measurements Yearbook* classification of tests information regarding 29 individual intelligence tests is available. Additional examples of coverage of those tests may be viewed in Buros (1978). The results of individual testing are available to teachers from school testing personnel and records. When differences exist between group and individual scores, the individual testing information should be given greatest confidence.

Group tests

Group tests for mental abilities are administered to several students at the same time, either by the classroom teacher or a testing specialist. Group tests have levels for different ages, although some are available for multiple levels such as K–8, 3–12, 4–14, and other combinations. Group administration is more economical than individual administration, as the time required for testing is less, and group tests do not require a clinically trained person to administer them. Classroom teachers with a minimum of direction or inservice training are able to handle comfortably the administration of group mental ability tests. Group administered tests produce essentially the same results as individually administered tests but are considered to be less accurate especially for very low functioning students and very high functioning students. Scores on a group test which are very low or high and those which seem to differ from the teacher's assessment may indicate students who should receive an individually administered intelligence test. The multilevel test has an advantage of measuring the same construct at all levels of the tests, and norm groups should be comparable among all levels.

Group testing is typically not used with children under six years of age, since these children would have difficulty following directions and instructions. Paper-and-pencil instruments for assessing mental abilities are widely used in grade one and up.

Figure 16.1 reveals 32 group intelligence tests listed in Buros (1978). Examples of coverage of group tests of mental ability follow.

1. A multilevel cognitive abilities test which consists of two primary levels and eight different but overlapping levels for 3–12, gives coverage for K–12. The kindergarten–grade 1 and grade 2–3 levels provide scores for the subtests: oral vocabulary, relational concepts, multimental concepts, and quantitive concepts. The two primary tests (K–1 and 2–3) use pictorial materials and oral instructions, eliminating the influence of reading skills on performance. At the primary level it is recommended that the subtests be given on separate days. The verbal subtests and the quantitative subtests function as the verbal score component of the test for grades 3–12. The nonverbal set of subtests provides the nonverbal score.

The eight levels serving grade levels 3–12 provide three scores: *(a)* verbal battery consisting of vocabulary sentence completion, verbal classification, and verbal analogies, *(b)* quantitative battery consisting of number series, quantitative relations, and equation building, and *(c)* nonverbal battery consisting of figure classification, figure analogies, and figure synthesis. The advantages of the multilevel format are the optional spread of item difficulties for each grade level, the flexibility of adapting tests to the type of group tested, and sufficient overlap in content from level to level to provide a common basis for equating scores at successive levels.

2. A test of mental abilities at four levels (grades K–2, 3–6, 6–9, and 9–12) provides one score for a series of subtests. The test for K–2 provides scores for listening, picture vocabulary, size, and number. The influence of reading skills on the K–2 battery is eliminated through an oral reading of the test to which students respond by marking appropriate pictures or symbols. The pace of item presentation is controlled by the characteristics of the group being tested. A test for 3–6, 6–9, or 9–12 provides one score for the subtests of vocabulary, sentence completion, opposites, general information, verbal analogies, verbal classification, verbal inference, number series, arithmetic reasoning, and figure analogies. The overlap on the three latter levels permits the use of the lower of two levels for classes suspected to be below average in ability.

Group tests used in measurement of general mental ability or scholastic aptitude attempt to sample a broad range of cognitive abilities. Generally a number of subtests make up the verbal, nonverbal, and total score on the basis that a variety of abilities are combined to produce one score. Total scores are usually transformed into intelligence quotients (IQ). Test companies have moved in the direction of providing tests of different levels which can be used in kindergarten to grade 12 in group testing. Some of the tests also extend beyond high school to adult levels.

There are many group tests, and they differ somewhat with respect to the kinds of items they include. Tests contain some or all of the subtests in vocabulary, sentence understanding, general information, analogies, arithmetic reasoning, following directions, and perception of similarities and differences. The *Eighth Mental Measurements Yearbook* contains reviews of over 30 different group intelligence tests.

Multiaptitude Batteries

In the development of multiaptitude batteries it is assumed that several abilities are measurable based on the degree of possession of characteristics needed for different academic performance or vocations. Each of the subtests is standardized on the same group of individuals, making comparisons among subtests possible. Performance on multiaptitude batteries is usually interpreted by factor analysis which permits the use of subtests in various combinations to predict success in a number of different subjects and occupations.

Figure 16.1 reveals 12 multiaptitude tests in Buros (1978). Examples of coverage of multiaptitude batteries follow.

1. A multiaptitude battery which consists of one level for grades 7–12 provides scores in the areas of verbal reasoning, numerical ability (the sum of these two scores indicates general scholastic aptitude), abstract reasoning, clerical speed and accuracy, mechanical reasoning, space relations, spelling, and language usage. This test is an integrated battery of aptitude tests designed for educational and vocational guidance in the junior and senior high school. Of the nine scores, one provides an index of scholastic ability. The scores provide a basis for identification of intellectual promise and for planning a student's academic program. Information concerning the strengths and weaknesses of the student in each of eight abilities areas may be attained through the battery. The test also claims effective prediction of course grades.

2. A multiaptitude battery for the age of 16 years and over provides scores in the areas of intelligence; verbal, numerical, spatial, form perception; clerical perception; eye-hand coordination; motor speed, finger dexterity; and manual dexterity. A measure of mental ability and occupational ability is provided. The nine tests measure ability in assembling and disassembling materials, three-dimensional space, arithmetic reasoning, vocabulary, form matching, tool matching, name comparison, and computations.

Testing Other Aptitudes

Aptitude tests for specific areas are used to predict artistic, musical, creative, clerical, and mechanical success. This type of aptitude test helps predict whether students will do well or poorly in a specific class or skill. Some subject areas with fixed content should be avoided by students not possessing the skills and knowledge needed. To attain success, students who score poorly on a specific aptitude test may be encouraged to select a different area for study.

A large number of specific aptitude tests (see Figure 16.1) are available, representing a diversity of subject and vocational areas. Some subtests from aptitude batteries are published as separate tests, but they usually do not provide the depth found in specific tests. Examples of coverage of specific aptitude tests follow:

1. A musical talent aptitude test which consists of one level for grades 4–12 provides scores for the areas of pitch, loudness, time, timbre, rhythm, and tonal memory. Each of the subtests is presented by a phonograph record or

tape recording. The abilities measured are considered to be fundamental to development of musical proficiency. The scores are intended to be unrelated to the amount of former musical training. All items on the test consist of pairs of stimuli; for example, that for pitch requires a judgment of which of two sounds is higher or lower, and timbre involves the discrimination of the difference in quality of two notes. The time subtest requires determining which of two time intervals is longer. Tonal memory requires an indication of whether two sequences of notes are the same or different.

A high score on this test, as on other musical aptitude tests, may be indicative of a greater chance of success in music for an individual than a low score. Musical aptitude tests simply provide an indication of the aptitude for music. With appropriate instruction, personal motivation, and other pertinent factors or characteristics, an individual with a high score is expected to be relatively successful in the music area.

2. A mechanical aptitude test, which consists of one level for grades 9–12, measures spatial perception based upon the ability to visualize the assembly of two-dimensional shapes into a whole design. The test consists of over 60 three-dimensional geometric figures disarranged into two-dimensional figures. There are five figures to select from to assemble each disassembled figure correctly. The abilities required in this test involve engineering, mechanical drawing, machine drafting, descriptive geometry, and art.

3. A clerical aptitude test which consists of one level for grades 7–12 provides scores for the areas of alphabetizing-filing, arithmetic, clerical speed and accuracy, coding, eye-hand accuracy, grammar and punctuation, spelling, spelling-vocabulary, vocabulary, and word fluency. The test is designed to assess aptitude in performing clerical skills as demonstrated by the subtests outlined. The tests relate well to general office work, clerking, and accounting. Additional subtests in typing and shorthand make the test adaptable for additional related positions.

These three specific aptitude tests are employed to predict the probability of musical, mechanical, and clerical success. Additional specific aptitude tests are available in other areas such as art, creativity, commerce and business, and foreign language. The area of mechanical aptitude includes numerous tests to measure skills such as hand-tool dexterity, mechanical comprehension, small-parts dexterity, mechanical insights, and others.

In the clerical area separate tests are available for checking, classifying, language skills dictation, number checking, and knowledge tests for bookkeeping, office machines, typing, and others. Each of these attempts to determine aptitudes of the clerical office worker in a specific skill or aptitude. These types of tests relate to general office work, typewriting, bookkeeping, or shorthand. In general, specific aptitude tests go into greater depth than aptitude batteries and emphasize abilities important to success in a particular job assignment or area of study in an occupationally oriented school subject. Results of tests of special abilities are most valuable for counselors and teachers in directing students toward possible areas of study where they can expect to be successful.

READINESS TESTS

Readiness tests measure a student's preparedness to undertake a new study. They are intended to predict how well the student will profit from instruction in a new undertaking. These tests help the teacher recognize skills with which students need help in order to avoid difficulty. Although readiness tests can be developed for all subjects and all levels, readiness testing is most used at the primary level for reading and mathematics. Tests used to predict success in advanced courses are usually referred to as **prognostic tests** but serve essentially the same role as a readiness test.

The preschool reading readiness test measures the child's development of experiential background and physical maturity considered essential for undertaking the important task of learning to read. It is important to determine in kindergarten or early first grade if a student has those things necessary to undertake learning this process. Knowledge about a child's readiness helps the teacher to sequence individual experiences to develop those reading potentials which are not based on physical maturation and to delay reading instruction until the physical development takes place. Some schools offer a transition class between kindergarten and first grade to accommodate students who do not exhibit sufficient readiness to do first grade work, especially in the area of reading, and readiness tests help the teacher identify students who need the transitional class.

Usually the first published test that a student meets is a reading readiness test administered in kindergarten or early first grade. Although reading readiness tests may indicate weaknesses in certain broad areas, they are not designed to isolate specific deficiencies. Reading readiness tests use differing approaches but draw on information about students': *(a)* motor skills, *(b)* auditory discrimination, *(c)* visual discrimination, *(d)* vocabulary, and *(e)* memory. Figure 16.1 points up 17 reading readiness tests listed in Buros (1978). Examples of reading readiness tests follow.

1. A reading readiness skills test administered at the end of kindergarten-beginning of first grade in four sessions provides scores in the areas of listening comprehension, auditory discrimination, visual discrimination, following directions, letter recognition, visual motor coordination, auditory blending, and word recognition. The purposes of the test are to determine which children are ready to begin reading, to predict generally how rapid their progress is likely to be, and to indicate which areas of abilities required in learning to read (motor, visual, and auditory) need development.

2. A reading readiness and number readiness test for kindergarten-grade 1, provides scores in the areas of word meaning, listening, matching, alphabet, numbers, copying, and (optional) draw-a-man. The test predicts readiness for reading and number concepts. The numbers subtest, which provides an index of mathematical readiness, requires the child to count and apply simple numerical concepts.

Reading readiness tests employ oral directions and a sample of practice exercises to make sure that each student understands what is expected and how responses are to be recorded in the test booklet. Most of the tests are untimed even though an approximate time for each subtest is indicated. Close supervision must be provided to make sure that students follow directions.

SCREENING TESTS

The Education for All Handicapped Children Act, Public Law 94-142, became effective in 1975 and required each state to insure that a free appropriate education be available to all handicapped children ages 3 through 21. Handicapped children are identified as the mentally retarded, hard of hearing, deaf, orthopedically impaired, other health impaired, speech impaired, visually handicapped, or seriously emotionally disturbed, or children with specific learning disabilities. With this direction school officials and teachers found need for types of tests to identify handicapped youths.

Increased attention has been given to students who are in need of special instruction in the regular classroom. Without special learning sequences it would be difficult for these students to be successful in school. Students, who by all indications should perform as average or above average but who show a vast discrepancy between expected achievement and actual achievement, are classified as having a **learning disability.** Special activities and programs are being developed to serve learning disabled students and teachers are increasingly being called upon to identify these students through direct observation and screening devices.

Depending upon the criteria employed to identify learning disabilities, estimates of the prevalence of learning disability range from 1 to 20 percent of the school population, with more boys than girls being disabled. A regular classroom usually has at least one or two learning disabled students which places this as the number one handicap in schools today (Faas, 1976, p. 4; Learner, 1971, pp. 11–12).

Detection of learning disabilities can help prevent a student from becoming an educational casualty in school. Teachers have a responsibility to identify students who might have one or more learning disabilities. Referrals may then be made to support personnel for diagnosis and follow-up with appropriate remedial instruction. The earlier learning disabilities are recognized the greater the chances of successful remediation. Schiffman and Goldberg (1972, p. 25) found that when learning disabilities were diagnosed in the second grade, remediation was successful in 82 percent of the cases. If discovered, however, between the sixth and ninth grades, the incidence of success was reduced to 6 to 11 percent.

Educators are becoming more aware of the number of cases of learning disability and the need for its detection at all levels. The classroom teacher through observation and testing is in the key position to make judgments concerning a student's potential for learning and the degree of attainment of that potential. Continuous and systematic efforts of the teacher through the use of effective screening instruments, as well as observation, are crucial to early identification of cases of learning disability. Teachers in schools that have established special programs are called upon to refer those students they suspect have learning difficulties for additional diagnosis and possible inclusion in these programs.

What Are Learning Disabilities?

The learning disabled student is identified through discrepancies between observed development and normal expected development as related to school progress. For our discussion learning disability is defined as:

> A discrepancy between expected and actual achievement or one or more deficits in the learning process, such as delayed development in speech, language, reading, spelling, or arithmetic.

The overt manifestations of learning disabilities vary in number and severity and may be discovered by the classroom teacher through observation of student behavior. Learning disorders may be present in any of the following areas: motor skills, perception, memory, language, cognitive skills, maturational factors, psychological factors, and social factors. Learning disabled students are generally described as exhibiting one or more of the following characteristics: *(a)* academic difficulties in reading, writing, spelling, or arithmetic; *(b)* an activity level which is overactive or underactive in energy level; *(c)* an attention span of very short duration or a fixation on a single task which is continually repeated; *(d)* auditory perceptual difficulties which may involve a lack of sound discrimination, failure to cope with spoken words and sounds, inability to attend to auditory stimuli, and inability to remember what has been heard; *(e)* fine motor, gross motor, and tactile discrimination well below expectations; *(f)* underdeveloped orientation to spatial organization and temporal concepts; *(g)* social-emotional behavioral problems such as impulsive or explosive behavior, lack of social competence, slow adjustment to change, and widely varying moods; *(h)* visual perceptual difficulties such as visual discrimination, figure-ground, closure, and memory; and *(i)* work habits characterized by poor organization, slow work, and carelessness (Faas, 1976, pp. 23–25).

Teacher-Administered Screening Tests

Wide diversity is observed among students with learning disabilities and they form a heterogeneous group. While symptoms may be similar, the degree and type of learning disabilities vary widely necessitating individual remedial and learning programs based on each student's needs. A number of instruments which can be administered by the teacher are available as well as those instruments requiring administration by a trained and experienced individual. From Figure 16.1 it can be seen that 30 learning disabilities tests are listed in Buros (1978) and more have been developed since that time. The following sections are devoted to descriptions of specific devices which have been used to aid the classroom teacher to identify students with learning disabilities.

There is a limited number of screening tests which may be administered by the classroom teacher without special training; therefore, names of specific tests are provided.

Boehm Test

The *Boehm Test* (Boehm, 1970), grades K–2, is used to assess individual mastery of fundamental concepts essential for success in school. Children with insufficient development of the concepts of time, space, and quality needed to understand and follow directions necessary for beginning instruction can be identified. Children not familiar with the concepts essential to learning are likely to be handicapped in following classroom instruction when, in fact, they only lack experience with certain concepts. The test is administered in approximately half an hour, in one or two sessions, to small groups of individuals and can be quickly scored by the teacher.

The concepts measured by the test are grouped into four categories: *(a)* spatial concepts (location, direction, orientation, and dimensions), *(b)* quantitative concepts, *(c)* temporal concepts, and *(d)* miscellaneous concepts. Children with an overall low level of concept mastery, particular concepts not known to an individual child, and the proportion of children in a class who have not mastered any given concept are identified. The teacher may plan classroom activities to integrate and develop the concepts from the test according to individual needs, thus avoiding a pattern of failure and falling behind.

First-Grade Screening Test (FGST)

The purpose of the *First-Grade Screening Test* (Pate & Webb, 1969), administered near the end of kindergarten or early in the first grade, is to screen beginning or potential first grade children for identification of those who, without special assistance, will fail to make sufficient progress during the first grade to be ready for second grade. The test is administered in 30 to 45 minutes, in one or two sessions, to individuals or groups up to 25. The teacher can score the test objectively.

The test samples general information, body image, self-perception, perception of parental figures, visual-motor coordination, memory, and ability to follow directions. The teacher may base grouping of students for some classroom instruction on the basis of student's strengths and weaknesses in the areas tested in order to achieve a certain level of expectation.

Pre-Reading Screening Procedures Test

The *Pre-Reading Screening Procedures Test* (Slingerland, 1969) assesses the academic needs of kindergarten or beginning first-grade students who have average or above average intelligence to determine if they: *(a)* appear ready for conventional methods of instruction, *(b)* show indications of specific language disabilities through errors in perception and recall of language symbols, *(c)* should be observed for potential language and perceptual difficulties, or *(d)* need more time for chronological maturation or language development.

The test is administered in 30 minutes, in one, two, or three sessions, to a maximum of 20 students. The instrument contains seven perceptual motor tests and two optional, individually administered auditory tests which can be employed when the results of the first seven tests are inconclusive. The entire test constitutes a structured observational instrument, and performance is important. Difficulty with perceptual-motor skills which are needed for development of reading, writing, spelling, and other academic achievement is identified.

Meeting Street Screening Test

The *Meeting Street Screening Test* (Hainsworth & Siqueland, 1969), individually administered in 15 to 20 minutes, is employed as an aid in identifying kindergarten and first-grade children who do not possess the requisite language and visual-perceptual-motor skills and gross motor control to process adequately the symbolic information of the traditional school curriculum.

Subtest scores are obtained for: *(a)* motor patterning, which surveys bilateral sequential movement patterns and awareness of the body in space; *(b)* visual-perceptual-motor skills, which surveys visual discrimination, visual memory, reproduction of geometric and letter forms in correct spatial orientation and sequence, and the understanding of spatial and directional concepts on a piece of paper; and *(c)* language, which surveys how a student listens, remembers, sequences, and formulates language. A total score consisting of the three tests is also determined.

Screening Test for the Assignment of Remedial Treatments (START)

The *Screening Test for the Assignment of Remedial Treatments* (Ahr, 1968), designed for preschool and kindergarten age students, administered in approximately one hour to groups of students, screens for individual diagnosis and treatment based on their degree of success in visual memory, auditory memory, visual-motor coordination, and visual discrimination. Scores are provided to help the teacher make a judgment regarding a student's need for remediation.

Slingerland Screening Tests

The *Slingerland Screening Tests* (Slingerland, 1974) may be administered individually or in groups. The tests for each of the four forms require three sittings of approximately 20 minutes each or a total of 60 minutes. The purpose of the test is to identify students who display specific perceptual-motor behavior which may interfere with development in reading, writing, and spelling; identify children with probable perceptual-motor difficulty or visual, auditory, or kinesthetic deficiency interfering with written language; identify children functioning well below their capabilities; and identify for referrals, special class, or tutorials.

Eight subtests plus two additional auditory tests are contained in each of the four test forms (form A, grade one and beginning of grade two; form B, grade two and beginning of grade three; form C, grades three and four; and form D, grade five). The subtest scores disclose deficits that may exist in vital areas upon which receptive, expressive, and written language depend.

In addition to concerns about what students have learned, published tests deal with other human traits which have a bearing on how students perform in the classroom setting. In the day-to-day contact of teacher and students, the teacher develops impressions about students' levels of mental functioning, special aptitudes, interests, attitudes, and personality traits. Student performance on published tests in all areas provides objective supplemental data about students. Although the actual testing in some areas will be done by someone other than the classroom teacher (school psychologist, psychometrist, or other special testing person), the ultimate user of test data will be the classroom teacher in conducting the ongoing business of educating students. For this reason the following several sections discuss where to find information about standardized tests, their evaluation, and how to select the appropriate test for a given educational use.

SELECTING STANDARDIZED TESTS

Whether a standardized test which is used in a classroom or school meets the needs of that particular situation is determined to a large degree by the care taken in test selection. A test which is employed solely on the basis of a test title or on the recommendation of one teacher, counselor, or administrator may fail to accomplish the purpose for which it was intended and thus lose its validity and usefulness for that school. The involvement of interested school personnel, particularly classroom teachers, in test selection is of critical importance to the morale of teachers and to the utilization of test results to further the development of meaningful classroom activities. Test selection should be viewed as a cooperative enterprise involving all those who care, especially those closest to the classroom scene—the teachers.

Because of limited school funds many schools use the same standardized tests for several years before undertaking review and revision of the testing program. Therefore, careful initial selection of each test is important. Many times teachers administer standardized tests and complain about the time taken away from classroom activities, particularly when the results of testing are not reported to them or are not relevant to their needs. Cooperative planning can avoid these situations and supports maximum student benefit from a testing program.

Sources of Information about Tests

An early step in the selection of a published test is to raise questions in regard to what kind of student information is needed and how the information is to be utilized for the mutual benefit of students and teachers. The question of how the information can best be obtained, as well as a review of the information currently available from sources other than standardized testing, should be given careful consideration. The school staff must decide exactly what information is needed from standardized testing that is not available through other means. After the goals of the total testing program are set, a committee of individuals should be appointed to select the standardized test(s) which meet the school's needs. When primary considerations are disposed of, the question arises, "Where can information concerning standardized tests be found?" The following sections are devoted to explanation of some sources of information about standardized tests and their use in the classroom.

The Mental Measurements Yearbook series

The most widely known body of information regarding standardized tests is found in *The Mental Measurements Yearbook* series. Since 1938, eight *Mental Measurements Yearbooks* have been published. Figure 16.2 provides the dates of publication and the number of tests listed in the eight issues of the *Yearbook* published over the 41-year span.

The objectives of *The Eighth Mental Measurements Yearbook* are to

Title	Date	Number of Standardized Tests
The Nineteen Thirty-Eight Mental Measurements Yearbook	1938	312
The Nineteen Forty Mental Measurements Yearbook	1940	524
The Third Mental Measurements Yearbook	1949	705
The Fourth Mental Measurements Yearbook	1953	830
The Fifth Mental Measurements Yearbook	1959	957
The Sixth Mental Measurements Yearbook	1965	1,200
The Seventh Mental Measurements Yearbook	1972	1,155
The Eighth Mental Measurements Yearbook	1978	1,184*

FIGURE 16.2. Numbers of tests in the eight volumes of the *Mental Measurements Yearbooks*

*The companion publications *Reading Tests and Review: Including a Classified Index to the Mental Measurements Yearbooks* (1968) and *Personality Tests and Reviews: Including a Classified Index to the Mental Measurements Yearbooks* (1970) edited by Oscar K. Buros and published by Gryphon Press each list some tests not found in *The Eighth Mental Measurements Yearbook.*

provide: *(a)* information about tests published in the English-speaking world, *(b)* critical reviews of tests, *(c)* bibliographies of verified references on the construction, use, and validity of specific tests, *(d)* critical portions of test reviews appearing in professional journals, and *(e)* listings of new and revised books on testing as well as evaluative excerpts from reviews which appear in professional journals.

Tests in Print III

Tests in Print III (Mitchell, 1983) is an index to tests, test reviews, and literature on specific tests. This reference, which is a comprehensive bibliography of all tests published separately for use with English-speaking subjects, serves as a master index to the first eight *Yearbooks*. For each test listed by title, the following information is provided: population for which suitable; range of copyright dates; part scores; absence of a manual; questionable updating of test materials; authors; publisher; country if not the United States; and cross reference to more informative entries, test reviews, excerpted test reviews, and references.

Publishers' information

Catalog.   Test publishers' catalogs provide a means of finding out about new tests not included in *The Mental Measurements Yearbook* series or *Tests in Print III* and more information about those which are. Each company publishing tests provides free catalogs upon request. Usually each test available from the publishing company is listed by title followed by the author's name, range and level of the test, the approximate working time required, and scoring services which are available. Additional sales information such as the price of the materials and packaging is provided. Brief statements concerning intended use and standardization (norms) are usually available. The price of a **specimen set** or examination kit for a test will be stated, if one is available.

Specimen set.   The specimen set, which is usually available for reasonable cost, contains the test booklet, response sheet, administrator's manual, technical information, and further information about cost and any scoring services which may be available. Additional accessory material which is available may also be provided in the specimen set.

Test manual.   The publisher's manual which accompanies a particular test provides information concerning what the test is designed to measure, specific scoring instructions, evidence of reliability and validity, scales and norms, aids to interpretation of test results, and any other information concerning claims for the test. Sufficient information should be provided to assist in making judgments regarding the usefulness and interpretation of the test as specified by the American Psychological Association publication *Standards for Educational and Psychological Tests and Manuals,* 1974. (see Appendix F.)

Bulletins.   The California Test Bureau, the Psychological Corporation, Educational Testing Service, Harcourt Brace Jovanovich, and Houghton Mifflin Company publish bulletins on testing. Some of the bulletins are free while others are available at a minimum charge. Inquire to the company to obtain these bulletins.

Indexes.   The *Education Index, Current Index to Journals in Education,* and *Psychological Abstracts,* published monthly, contain listings of newly published tests, research reports on test use, and sources of information about testing practices. Articles regarding standardized tests and testing are catalogued in these indexes.

Journals.   Professional journals in education and psychology provide current information about tests related to their respective areas of concern. For example, the *Journal of Educational Measurement,* a quarterly publication, contains original research articles and reports test reviews in each issue. Some additional references include: *American Educational Research Journal, American Psychologist, Educational and Psychological Measurement, Journal of Counseling Psychology, Measurement and Evaluation in Guidance, Psychological Bulletin,* and *Review of Educational Research.*

Guidelines for Evaluating Standardized Tests

In the selection of a standardized test the relative importance of various aspects of the test must be taken into account. The number and variety of tests available make selection of the most appropriate one difficult unless some type of test evaluation form is utilized. A test evaluation form provides a systematic summary description of each test for convenience in comparing and reviewing tests. Appendix G— "Information Needed to Evaluate a Standardized Test" —lists essential criteria in evaluating a test. The following discussion of the information needed to evaluate a standardized test abridges the standards set forth by the Joint Committee of the APA, AERA, and NCME and should be adequate for classroom needs.

1. Name of test, date, and author. The type of test should be stated and a description of the test and subtests should be given.
2. Purpose of the test. The purpose and application for the test should be clearly stated.
3. Grade levels or ages. The students' ages and grade levels and other related information should be described.
4. Equivalent forms. The number of equivalent or alternate forms should be specified. A statement of the comparability should be made.
5. Publisher and cost. The packaging of the test, directions, scoring sheets, specimen sets, and other materials should be stated with the cost for each item specified.
6. Content of the test. The areas of concern of the test and method of selecting content along with its applicability to grade levels or ages should be specified.
7. Time for administration. The length of time needed to administer the test and various alternatives in administration should be clearly stated.
8. Directions for administration. Clear and precise procedures for ad-

ministration of the test should be available. How are students given directions for taking the test?

9. Validity. A complete validity section should be available which assures that the test measures what it is intended to measure. The sample employed in the validity study and the conditions under which the testing is done should be described sufficiently for the user to judge whether the reported validity is pertinent to the situation.

10. Reliability. The methods for obtaining reliability coefficients and standard errors of measurement should be in sufficient detail and should be recorded for comparison to other tests.

11. Norms. The appropriate and accurate norms in the form of age, grade, percentile rank, standard score, or any other type should be reported. The measures of central tendency and variability should be reported. What norms are reported for the test?

12. Format of the test. The format of the test should be described in detail.

13. Scoring procedures available. The test items should be relatively objective and simple to score. What procedures are available for hand scoring or machine scoring?

14 and 15 call for the evaluator's judgment regarding the completeness and usability of the manual and the reaction to the whole test, while 16 gives reactions of others who have critically reviewed the test.

These 16 points are minimum considerations for standardized test evaluation, and test selectors may wish to include other concerns. When information has been gathered on several tests, the data for each should be compared to previously determined criteria established by the reviewing teacher or committee. Before a particular test or test battery is selected for administration, it is essential that a teacher review the actual test items to determine if they are appropriate for objectives formed for a specific set of students. The teacher should actually take the test to determine if the content and level are appropriate for the students who will be taking the test. Although the publisher is interested in providing the potential customer with information which will stimulate the purchase of the test, what is provided in manuals is usually objective and reliable. Information collected from the test manual supplements data from other sources and includes information which may not be available elsewhere. This information, when combined with the teacher's judgments based on knowledge of the students and objective review of the test and test items, provides a good basis for making a decision about use of a particular standardized test. Final selection will be based on conditions of practicality, cost, and the ability of the test to exceed the specified minimum standards established.

NORMS FOR STANDARDIZED TESTS

Raw scores on a standardized test have no meaning unless interpreted in relationship to some reference or norm group provided by the test publisher. Norms may also be established for the local area by a test publisher or school corporation. Norms provide a reference against which to compare performances and indicate where students stand in relation to the students in the norming population. A norm is descriptive of the average or typical performance obtained by a group of students and provides a point to anchor the range of scores for score interpretation. For example, on a reading test the nationwide fourth grade average raw score was 53 points. The fourth grade norm score is 53, based on the fourth graders who took the test. Scores above and below 53 are interpreted in relation to positions relative to that point. Percentile ranks are formed somewhat differently in that they report the percentage of students in the norming group who fall below each possible test score.

It is important that a distinction between a norm and a standard be made, since these terms at times are incorrectly used interchangeably. A *norm* is the average or typical performance obtained on a test by a specified group of students. A norm is not intended to be used as a standard for everyone to meet. A group of students whose performance on a test is at the norm for their age are average or typical students. For some students attainment higher than the norm may be expected, and for some students attainment lower than the norm may be expected. Certainly not all students are expected to fall at the exact average made by any group which in itself had different scores. Comparisons to norms are best made on a class or group basis. Individuals should be compared to norms only for diagnostic purposes or in development of a student profile to compare relative standing in the several areas tested.

The test manual for a standardized test contains a norm table(s) for reference so that classroom teachers may compare their students' performance with an external criterion group. The average score of 53 in the example of fourth graders was computed by administering the test to a sample of fourth graders selected to represent the entire country at the time the norms were computed. The example focuses on the fourth grade, but the reading test was given to a sample of students from grades three, four, and five, and norms are reported in the manual for each grade level. Further extrapolation of these results extends the norms to grades one, two, six, and seven.

A test manual may contain several sets of tables which report different types of norms and may include information about performance for different geographical regions or student samples with different sets of characteristics. Teachers usually have a choice of several sets of norm tables and must decide upon norms appropriate for their students based upon how the data will be used. The most common types of test norms are age, grade, percentile rank, and standard score.

Age Norms

Age norms are based on the average or typical scores of students at different chronological ages. A set of age equivalents to be used as norms can be developed for any trait which changes progressively with age. Weight of public school students, for example, increases with age. A table of age norms for weight would provide the average weight for students of a specific age. By comparing a student's current weight and age to the table, teachers could judge if a student's weight was higher or lower than the average weight of a student at that age. As applied to average weight, age norms are most applicable in the elementary school years. In the elementary school, age norms are convenient for reporting information about progress, since subjects such as reading and arithmetic are studied at increasing levels of complexity as one progresses through grades one to six.

Age equivalents divide the calendar into 12 parts corresponding to the months of the year. For example, the age equivalents for seven-year-olds range from 7–0 to 7–11, the first figure representing the year and the second the month. Academic achievement and ability comparisons can be made for children in the elementary schools. Consideration should be given to the fact that two students may score at the same age-norm equivalent and have different characteristics. They may show different strengths in areas of ability and achievement. For example, a high achieving student in grade four (10 years old) and a low achieving student in grade seven (13 years old) may obtain the same equivalent scores of 11.0 (or the average performance of an 11-year-old) on the test. These equal scores may be obtained in different ways and obviously reflect different levels of performance relative to their specific age group. Certainly the fourth grader who is 10 years old and scores the average of an 11-year-old is different from the seventh grader who is 13 years old and scores the average of an 11-year-old.

Grade Norms

Grade norms are very similar to age norms. Grade equivalents are based upon the average scores of students at different grade levels rather than on average scores of students of different ages. Grade equivalents are based on the nine-month school year and range from .1 to .9 corresponding with the first month through the ninth month of the school year. The other 10th is assumed to take care of advancement during summer vacation. Grade equivalents for a second-grade class range from 2.0 to 2.9; the first figure denotes the school grade and the second figure the month. For example, a 2.6 is second grade, sixth month.

Grade equivalents, like age equivalents, have been popular in interpreting academic performance or attainment of children in the elementary school. School personnel feel that parents can easily understand grade norms. However, some persons who do not fully understand how the grade norms are obtained are inclined to interpret the grade norm as indicating the grade level where the student should be receiving instruction. Since this is not true, some confusion has been observed. For example, the following grade equivalents are for Rich, who is a second-grade student in the fifth month of school.

Language Arts	2.3
Reading	2.5
Arithmetic	3.1

Rich is average in reading, two grade equivalent months behind in language arts, and six grade equivalent months ahead in arithmetic. Grade norms are especially misleading at the extreme ends, for example, a second grader who scores 6.0 in reading could not begin to function in a sixth-grade class or actually read with ease in a sixth-grade reading book.

There are limitations to grade norms which can lead to misunderstanding. Grade norms are influenced by the age spread of students at each grade level, and age variation within a class may be sizable. Due to retainment or early or late entrance to school, ages within any elementary grade may vary two to three years and even more in secondary grades. Increased age may account for some increases in performance over other classmates but is not taken into consideration by grade norms. The wide range of ages within one grade level can be controlled for by not including in the norming group any student who is atypical in age for the grade level. A limited range is set for students to be included as typical in creating norms. Grade equivalents so created are referred to as **modal age norms.**

For both age and grade norms the assumption is made that the student tested is studied consistently from year to year and that the test employed adequately reflects the student's progress at each level for which norms are reported. Different rates of intellectual development occur at each grade and age level. An illustration of grade and age norms is provided in Figure 16.3.

Percentile Rank Norms

Percentile rank norms indicate a student's relative standing in a set of scores obtained from the norming population. The norming group is selected on certain characteristics, and the scores as well as the characteristics are reported for comparison purposes. Test publishers provide tables which show the raw scores in one column and percentile rank equivalents in another. A percentile rank of 80 tells us that a student scoring at this level has equaled or surpassed the performance of 80 percent of those students upon which the test was standardized. It is assumed that those students are representative of the students currently taking the test, and students scoring at this level are assumed to also exceed or equal 80 percent of those currently taking the test. The percentile ranks provide the relative position of each student or the percentage of students falling below each possible test score.

A set of norms must be obtained for each group within which a student is to be compared. The norm group must always be referred to in interpreting percentile rank. It is also important to keep in mind that differences in percentile ranks on different parts of the scale are not equal, since scores tend to cluster around the measure of central tendency. A difference of only a few raw-score points may exist between the 50th and 60th percentile ranks, but there may be a considerable distance in raw-score points between the 85th and 95th percentile ranks. The size of the percentile rank units (see Figure 16.4) is not constant in terms of raw score units.

Raw Score	Grade Equivalent	Age Equivalent
25	5.4	10–4
24	5.1	10–2
23	4.9	10–0
22	4.7	9–12
21	4.6	9–10
20	4.5	9–9
19	4.4	9–8
18	4.4	9–8
17	4.3	9–7
16	4.3	9–7
15	4.2	9–7
14	4.1	9–6
13	4.1	9–6
12	4.0	9–5
11	4.0	9–4
10	3.9	9–3
9	3.8	9–1
8	3.7	9–0
7	3.6	8–12
6	3.5	8–9
5	3.4	8–5
4	3.3	8–2
3	3.1	8–0
2	2.8	7–11
1	2.5	7–7
0	2.0	7–4

FIGURE 16.3. Grade and age norms for a fourth-grade reading test

Percentile Rank Bands

Many test publishers have moved to the preparation of norm tables in the form of percentile rank bands (see Figure 16.5). This procedure provides the range of scores which is expected to include the student's true score at a given probability level. Percentile rank bands take into consideration the inaccuracy of test scores in making comparisons. They prevent the test user from attaching too much precision to a test score while making the user aware of variability in performances. As explained in Chapter 14, the band usually reported extends one standard error of measurement on either side of the obtained score, giving a confidence level of 68 percent for that band.

Standard Score Norms

Standard score norms provide the student's relative position in a group expressed in terms of standard deviation units from the mean. Standard scores

Raw Score	Level 3–6 Grade PRs 3	4	5	6	Raw Score
90					90
89					89
88				99	88
87				98	87
86			99	96	86
85			98	94	85
84			98	92	84
83			97	89	83
82			96	87	82
81			94	84	81
80			93	81	80
79		99	91	78	79
78		98	90	75	78
77		98	88	72	77
76		97	86	69	76
75		97	84	66	75
74		96	82	63	74
73		95	80	60	73
72		94	78	57	72
71		94	75	54	71
70		93	73	52	70
69	99	92	71	50	69
68	99	90	68	48	68
67	98	89	66	46	67
66	98	87	63	44	66
65	97	86	61	42	65
64	97	84	59	40	64
63	96	83	57	38	63
62	96	81	55	36	62
61	95	79	53	34	61
60	95	77	51	33	60
59	94	75	49	31	59
58	93	74	47	29	58
57	92	72	45	28	57
56	91	70	44	27	56
55	90	68	42	25	55
54	89	66	40	24	54
53	88	64	38	23	53
52	87	63	37	22	52
51	86	61	35	21	51
50	85	59	34	20	50
49	84	57	32	19	49
48	82	55	31	18	48
47	81	54	30	17	47
46	80	52	29	16	46
45	79	50	28	15	45
44	77	48	27	15	44
43	76	47	26	14	43
42	75	45	24	14	42
41	73	44	23	13	41

Raw Score	Level 3–6 Grade PRs 3	4	5	6	Raw Score
40	72	43	22	12	40
39	70	41	21	12	39
38	69	40	20	11	38
37	67	39	19	11	37
36	66	37	18	10	36
35	64	36	17	10	35
34	63	35	16	9	34
33	61	33	15	8	33
32	59	32	14	8	32
31	58	30	13	7	31
30	55	28	12	6	30
29	53	27	12	6	29
28	51	25	11	6	28
27	49	24	10	5	27
26	47	22	9	5	26
25	45	20	8	5	25
24	43	19	8	4	24
23	41	18	7	4	23
22	38	16	6	3	22
21	36	15	5	3	21
20	33	13	5	3	20
19	30	12	4	2	19
18	27	11	3	2	18
17	24	9	3	1	17
16	21	8	2	1	16
15	18	7	2		15
14	16	6	1		14
13	14	5	1		13
12	12	4			12
11	9	3			11
10	8	3			10
9	6	2			9
8	5	2			8
7	4	1			7
6	3				6
5	2				5
4	1				4
3					3
2					2
1					1

FIGURE 16.4. Percentile ranks of raw scores by grade and test level

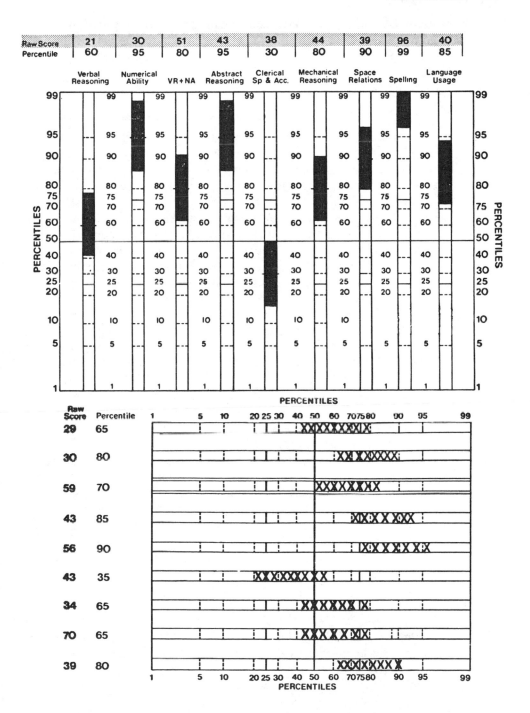

FIGURE 16.5. Two ways to present percentile rank bands

(*z* score, *Z* score, *T* score, etc.) and stanines have been discussed in Chapter 14. Norm charts which report standard scores for raw test scores are included in most standardized test materials when needed for raw score interpretation.

Which Norm to Use?

In selecting a test, consideration should be given to the adequacy of the norms to interpret scores for the group to be measured. Test norms should be appropriate for students being tested and for judgments to be made from test data. If the teacher wishes to know how students compare in language areas with students in the nation, then national norms may be appropriate. The relevance of these norms depends upon how closely the characteristics of the national sample approximates a particular school's students, unless the goal is just to compare a group with the national norms. Test norms should be current. Out-of-date norms are not necessarily relevant for interpreting scores today. They may not reflect changes in school curriculum, instructional methods, and students. Comparison of students' scores to out-of-date norms may result in inappropriate data concerning their test performance.

Norms may be developed based upon a group with special characteristics —high school students successful in college, national aptitude testing programs for college admissions, business colleges, suburban schools, inner city schools, and others. Placement for the instructional programs in a local school system may call for **local norms** which are established in a school system or at the state level. These are established by administering the instrument to the local student population and then developing the norm tables from the data. If accumulated over a period of time, these local norms will convey the average performance of students in the particular school system.

A norm should be representative of the students it purports to represent, particularly the various subgroups of the population. Norms at the national level should be developed on a base which is proportionally representative of the sexes, geographical areas, socioeconomic levels, and so on of the students to whom the test will be given. The test manual or report of norms for a test will supply information concerning the makeup of the norm group for a test, and decision can be made based on the match between the group to be tested and the norm group.

SUMMARY

Published tests vary widely in their intended use. Teacher-made and published tests complement each other in providing a breadth of information concerning student learning and progress. Teachers' editions of textbooks and textbook series may include as supplementary materials tests to be employed when working with students in mastery of content covered by the textbook. These instructional materials or tests are not standardized and the teacher is at liberty to use them at will to help students master content.

The large number and variety of standardized tests available and their many uses necessitate that the teacher know about development, selection, sources of information, and guidelines for evaluation of tests. It is important that extreme care be taken in the selection of a test which is appropriate for the specific situation for which it is being used. Sources of information about standardized tests include *Mental Measurement Yearbooks, Tests in Print III,* publishers' information (catalogs, specimen sets, test manuals, bulletins), indexes, and journals.

Test publishers follow a code of ethics published under the title *Standards for Educational and Psychological Tests and Manuals,* which serves as a guide for those involved in test development, production, and use (see Appendix F). The standards used in conjunction with a test evaluation form assist school personnel in making sound judgments about tests being considered for selection. Final selection of a test should be based on a thorough study of the complete test and accessory materials. In addition the teacher should take the test in order to review the items to determine if they are appropriate for students being tested.

Achievement tests are classified as diagnostic, single-subject, or batteries. Strengths and weaknesses in a particular limited undertaking are assessed by a diagnostic test. Single-subject tests assess achievement in one content area while the battery provides comprehensive coverage of the important aspects of achievement at the elementary or secondary level. All subtests of a battery are standardized on the same sample of students.

At the elementary school level, achievement tests tend to focus on the basic skills of operating with words and numbers as applied in the various skills and subject areas. At the primary level reading, spelling, language, and arithmetic attainment are the basic areas covered by achievement tests. There is a progressive shift in the nature of achievement tests to match the capabilities of student maturation. The reading skills and related language arts area are covered heavily in most elementary batteries.

At the secondary-school level standardized achievement tests shift emphasis to the subject matter of particular courses and curricular areas. For this reason secondary teachers find more use for single-subject tests than for batteries. Generally batteries at this level assess students' general knowledge and skill in reading and understanding material from different fields of knowledge. These tests provide a good prediction of later academic success. Numerous single-subject tests are available in the various subject areas of the curriculum.

Aptitude tests predict how well an individual will succeed in education or training. Predicting future performance depends to some degree on life experiences as well as school experiences. Through the administration of these tests educators are able to make inferences about future performance in general or in specific areas of instruction and skills required for a particular type of performance. Standardized aptitude tests include: mental ability (scholastic aptitude or intelligence), multiaptitude, readiness, and specific aptitudes such as musical, artistic, clerical, mechanical, and creative. Standardized aptitude tests are particularly helpful when information regarding past performance is not available.

Measurement of student capabilities to learn or level of general cognitive functioning through the use of mental ability tests is usually carried out by giving group tests to a whole class. Individually administered tests are used with children who cannot read and in situations where special testing is required based on wide discrepancies of earlier results of tests and student performance. Individual tests involve one student and one examiner who provides oral directions for each task presented and evaluates the examinee's performance on the task before moving on to another.

Multiaptitude batteries assess several abilities necessary for success in more than one area. Typically subtests include verbal reasoning, numerical ability, abstract reasoning, clerical speed and accuracy, mechanical reasoning, spelling, language usage, and others. Specific aptitude tests predict success in a single area and provide more depth than is found in multiaptitude batteries.

Early identification of preschool and school children who experience learning disabilities has become a national concern. Prevention programs stimulated by state and federal funds are multiplying. Estimates of the prevalence of learning disabilities in school children range from 1 to 20 percent of the school population with at least one or two students who are learning disabled in every classroom.

The key position for early identification and detection of learning disabilities lies with educators and at the school level with the classroom teacher. The younger a child is when identified as a potentially learning disabled individual, the better the chances for remediation. Many elementary children fall behind their age mates due to learning disabilities which have not been identified and remediated. The outcome of this situation many times contributes to a poor self-concept and related adjustment problems. Early detection relies heavily on screening tests and devices available for mass screening. After the first and second grades, detection of learning disabilities relies on the methods or devices such as observation, rating scales, and anecdotal records which are used by the classroom teacher in an effort to support cursory observations made in classroom contacts with students.

The definition of learning disability used in the chapter includes any child or student exhibiting a discrepancy between expected and actual achievement; one or more deficits in the learning process, such as delayed development in speech, language, reading, spelling, or arithmetic. A combination of learning disabilities as well as varying intensity of particular disabilities may be found; therefore, each particular situation must be judged individually.

Six screening tests which can be administered by the classroom teacher were presented. Early detection requires a knowledge of screening instruments. In addition to screening tests, direct observation structured by rating scales, checklists, and anecdotal records is employed in identification of learning disabilities. The classroom teacher's informal testing, formal testing, and observations can add information to the total screening process. The various identification approaches available complement each other in supplying information.

Norms provide a frame of reference for interpreting test results. A norm refers to the average performance for a particular group of students. Test manuals for standardized tests contain norm tables for reference in score interpretation. Age norms are based on the average score of students at different chronological ages. Grade norms are based on average scores of students at different grade levels. Percentile rank norms indicate a student's relative standing in a set of scores from the norming population. Standard score norms provide the student's relative position in a group expressed in standard deviation units from the mean.

NEW TECHNICAL TERMS LISTED IN THE GLOSSARY

Age norm	Norm population
Battery	Prognostic test
Field testing	Readiness test
Grade norm	Single-subject test
Learning disability	Specimen set
Local norms	Survey battery
Modal age norms	

ACTIVITY EXERCISES

1. Obtain the specimen set for a standardized achievement test and use the "Information Needed to Evaluate a Standardized Test" (see Appendix G) to appraise the test.
2. Obtain a set of norms for a standardized achievement test and establish for yourself the procedure for transforming raw scores to standard scores for selected test measures.
3. Select a standardized achievement test and a standardized aptitude test and look up the tests in the *Mental Measurements Yearbook* and *Tests in Print III,* and in one of the following sources: catalog, bulletin, index, or journal. React to the information provided in each reference.
4. Obtain the specimen set for a standardized achievement test and study the types of norms available for interpretation to various audiences. Explain the strengths and weaknesses of the following norms: *(a)* age norms, *(b)* grade norms, *(c)* percentile rank norms, *(d)* percentile rank bands, and *(e)* standard score norms.

FOR DISCUSSION

1. Using the criteria that establish a test as being standardized, show that most tests that accompany textbooks are not standardized.
2. Defend the position that standardized test results should *not* be used to evaluate the effectiveness of a teacher.
3. Give the purpose of screening tests and how a classroom teacher could utilize them in a classroom.

4. List the indexes for the *Eighth Mental Measurements Yearbook* and explain how each can aid in locating standardized tests.

REFERENCES AND KNOWLEDGE EXTENDERS

AHR, A. E. *Screening test for the assignment of remedial treatments.* Skokie, IL.: Priority Innovations, 1968.

AMERICAN PSYCHOLOGICAL ASSOCIATION. *Standards for educational and psychological tests.* Washington, D.C.: Author, 1974.

ANASTASI, A. *Psychological testing* (5th ed.). New York: Macmillan, 1982.

BOEHM, A. E. *Boehm test of basic concepts.* New York: Psychological Corporation, 1970.

BUROS, O. K. (Ed.). *Intelligence tests and reviews.* Highland Park, NJ: Gryphon Press, 1975.

BUROS, O. K. (Ed.). *The mental measurements yearbooks.* Highland Park, NJ: Gryphon Press, 1938, 1940, 1949, 1953, 1959, 1965, 1972, 1978.

BUROS, O. K. (Ed.). *Personality tests and reviews II.* Highland Park, NJ: Gryphon Press, 1975.

BUROS, O. K. (Ed.). *Reading tests and reviews II.* Highland Park, NJ: Gryphon Press, 1975.

BUROS, O. K. (Ed.). *Vocational tests and reviews.* Highland Park, NJ: Gryphon Press, 1975.

EBEL, R. L. *Essentials of educational measurement.* Englewood Cliffs, NJ: Prentice-Hall, 1979. Chap. 16, pp. 310–328; chap. 17, pp. 329–337; chap. 18, pp. 344–361.

EBEL, R. L. *The uses of standardized testing.* Bloomington, IN: Phi Delta Kappa Educational Foundation, 1977. (See Perrone, V.).

FAAS, L. A. *Learning disabilities: A competency approach.* Boston: Houghton Mifflin, 1976.

GLASER, K. *Learning difficulties.* Springfield, IL: Charles C Thomas, 1974. Chap. 1, pp. 3–16; chap. 3, 32–42.

GRONLUND, N. E. *Measurement and evaluation in teaching* (4th ed.). New York: Macmillan, 1981. Chap. 11, pp. 275–302; chap. 12, pp. 303–330; chap. 13, pp. 331–366; chap. 14, pp. 367–403.

HAINSWORTH, P. K., & SIQUELAND, M. L. *Early identification of children with learning disabilities: The meeting street school screening test.* Providence, RI: Crippled Children and Adults of Rhode Island, 1969.

HAMMILL, D. D. Evaluating children for instructional purposes. In D. D. Hammill & N. R. Bartel (Eds.), *Educational perspectives in learning disabilities.* New York: John Wiley, 1971. Chap. 9, pp. 119–131.

HOPKINS, C. D., & ANTES, R. L. *Classroom testing: Administration, scoring, and score interpretation.* Itasca, IL: F. E. Peacock, 1979. Chap. 5, pp. 81–98; chap. 6, pp. 99–107.

JOHNSON, D. J., & MYKLEBUST, H. R. *Learning disabilities: Educational principles and practice.* New York: Grune & Stratton, 1967. Chap. 3, pp. 48–63.

KASS, C. E. Introduction to learning disabilities. In D. D. Hammill & N. R. Bartel (Eds.), *Educational perspectives in learning disabilities.* New York: John Wiley, 1971. Chap. 2.

LEARNER, J. W. *Children with learning disabilities* (2nd ed.). Boston: Houghton Mifflin, 1971. Chap. 1, pp. 2–44; chap. 2, pp. 72–102.

MEHRENS, W. A., & LEHMANN, I. J. *Measurement and evaluation in education and psychology* (2nd ed.). New York: Holt, Rinehart & Winston, 1978. Unit IV, pp. 389–589.

MITCHELL, J. V., Jr. (Ed.). *Tests in print III.* Lincoln: University of Nebraska Press, 1983.

PATE, J. E., & WEBB, W. W. *First-grade screening test manual.* Pines Circle, MN: American Guidance Service, 1969.

PERRONE, V. *The abuses of standardized testing.* Bloomington, IN: Phi Delta Kappa Educational Foundation, 1977. (See Ebel, R.L., 1977).

REGER, R. (Ed.). *Preschool programming of children with disabilities.* Springfield, IL: Charles C Thomas, 1970. Chap. 3, pp. 17–28; chap. 4, pp. 29–34.

SAX, G. *Principles of educational and psychological measurement and evaluation* (2nd ed.). Belmont, CA: Wadsworth, 1980. Chap. 11, pp. 311–355; chap. 12, pp. 356–399; chap. 13, pp. 400–435.

SCHIFFMAN, G. B., & GOLBERG, H. K. *Dyslexia—Problems of reading disabilities.* New York: Grune & Stratton, 1972.

SLINGERLAND, B. H. *Pre-reading screening procedures.* Cambridge, MA: Educators Publishing Service, 1969.

SLINGERLAND, B. H. *Slingerland screening tests.* Cambridge, MA: Educators Publishing Service, 1974.

SPROULL, L., & ZUBROW, D. Standardized testing from the administrative perspective. *Phi Delta Kappan,* 1981, *62,* 628–631.

THORNDIKE, R. L., & HAGEN, E. *Measurement and evaluation in psychology and education* (4th ed.). New York: John Wiley, 1977. Chap. 9, 10, and 11, pp. 273–393.

WALLACE, G., & KAUFFMAN, J. M. *Teaching children with learning problems.* Columbus, OH: Charles E. Merrill, 1973. Chap. 1, pp. 4–15; chap. 3, pp. 61–92.

WICK, J. W. *Educational measurement.* Columbus, OH: Charles E. Merrill, 1973. Chap. 7, pp. 141–174.

Glossary

Since this book, *Classroom Measurement and Evaluation,* 2nd ed., is somewhat technical in nature, certain words may be new to the reader. Other commonly used words take on special meaning when applied to measurement and evaluation in education. For these reasons certain words have been selected and explained for the reader in the following glossary.

Although you may feel that you understand the meaning and usage of a listed word, a check of the glossary explanation can reinforce that understanding or clarify the authors' use in this book. Usage here is intended to conform with general use, but since precise definitions are not agreed on for all terms, somewhat different explanations can be found in other places.

Furthermore, this is not intended to be a dictionary of measurement and evaluation terms but an aid to persons reading this book. When a word which is listed in the glossary appears for the first time in the book it is printed in **boldface type.** If a word used in a denotation is also denoted in the glossary, it will appear in **boldface type** in the denotation.

Accordion key: A **device** containing the correct responses to objective **test** items arranged so that the answers on any page or in any column of a test appear in a strip or column. The response sheet can be folded vertically and used in **scoring** each column.

Accountability: A system of holding the school administration and teachers responsible for student attainment of **educational objectives.**

Achievement test: A **published** or **classroom test** used to **measure** the degree of attainment of **educational objectives** in a content subject or series of subjects.

Action: A part of a **behavioral objective** statement. The behavior to be observed when determining whether a student or students have attained the goal of an **educational objective** stated in terms of actions to be exhibited in **measurement.**

Affective domain: The area of human action which emphasizes the internalized processes such as emotion, feeling, interest, attitude, value, character development, and motivation.

Age norm: An average **score** on a **test** for students of a specified age. Extended **norms** are listed in tables for **standardized tests** for score interpretation.

Alternative: One of the responses used for the stem-option type of **multiple-choice item.** One **alternative** is the correct answer and the others are **distracters.**

Ambiguity: Confusion on the part of the test taker about what to do or indecision about the correct response. (See **Apparent ambiguity** and **Intrinsic ambiguity.**)

Analytical procedure: A **scoring** technique using a detailed guide to score **essay item** responses by identifying crucial elements of the ideal response and their relative weights. The student's essay is then compared to the elements of the ideal response and weighted accordingly. (See **Global procedure.**)

Anecdotal record: An objectively written description of a student's behavior, what was said or done in a specific situation recorded as being typical or unusual behavior.

Apparent ambiguity: Uncertainty about the task being presented or the expected response in a test item which results from the test taker's lack of knowledge about the subject area.

Appraisal: Identification of the level of knowledge or skill of students to allow initiation points for instruction to be established.

Attribute: Characteristic or trait that is either present to some degree or absent in a person or thing being observed.

Balance: The selection and provision of test items such that subject-matter topics and behaviors are sampled in the **test** in accordance with established relative weights.

Battery: A set of **tests** intended to be administered together. By using one **norm group,** the separate **tests** are designed to generate comparable **scores** for comparison of student attainment in the several areas measured. A composite **score** for the complete **battery** may be computed to estimate overall attainment.

Behavioral objective: A statement which describes what students should be able to do after completing a prescribed unit of instruction. The statement represents aims of education stated as observable descriptions of measurable behavior.

Central tendency: A point in an array of **scores** or distribution of scores around which the scores tend to center.

cf: Symbol for cumulative frequency. A column of *cf* shows for any score interval the number of **scores** in the distribution that lie below the upper limit of that interval. Obtained in a **frequency distribution** table by adding the frequency in an interval to all the **scores** below that interval.

Chance level: The theoretical or expected frequency of occurrence of some event based on the concepts of random probability. The result expected to form from occurrences which are based in randomness. Blind guessing of responses to multiple-choice and true-false items would be expected to generate correct responses at this level.

Checklist: A list of points to notice in **direct observation.** It is used to focus the observer's attention to the presence, absence, or frequency of occurrence of each point of the prepared list as indicated by checkmarks.

Classification item: A type of test item in which a premise is presented as a word, incomplete statement, or sentence. The response of the student is then limited to the set of classes which have been given to the test taker. The test taker selects one of the classes to categorize each premise.

Classroom test: A measuring **device** which has been developed by a classroom teacher for use with a specific classroom as opposed to a **standardized test** which is used widely. Syn.: Informal **test.**

Coefficient of validity: A **correlation** between a set of scores on a **test** with a criterion (some external **measure**) established as representative of exhibiting the trait the **test** is designed to **measure.** (See **Criterion-related validity.**)

Cognitive domain: The area of human action which pertains to mental processes such as intellectual, learning, and problem solving.

Completion item: A type of test item that asks the student to supply one or more missing words purposely omitted from a sentence.

Computer-assisted testing (CAT): A data-processing procedure which **scores** and analyzes student responses to items electronically. The component of testing may be a supplement to a programmed instructional sequence.

Concurrent validity: Describes how well test scores correspond to measures of present criterion performance or status. Based upon **correlation** with a criterion variable that is measured at about the same time that the test is administered. (See **Criterion-related validity.**)

Conditions: A part of a **behavioral objective** statement. Circumstances under which the behavior is to be performed. It includes the restrictions imposed on the learner when demonstrating the behavior.

Conference: A meeting of two or more persons to discuss some common interest. In education, the meeting usually involves two or more of the following persons: student, parent, teacher, administrator.

Confidence interval: A **range** of possible values which has a particular probability of including a student's **true score.** As the probability is increased, the range of the **confidence interval** is increased. Likewise, if the probability is decreased the interval set for confidence will decrease. The **standard error of measurement** is used to set a **confidence interval** for placement of the **obtained score** in relation to the student's **true score.**

Construct: An idea or concept invented to explain an aspect of human behavior or some other idea. It primarily exists to name certain nonphysical characteristics. Example: hostility.

Construct validity: Indicates the degree to which certain explanatory conceptualizations account for performance on a **test.**

Constructed-response item: An item that requires the student to create a response within the structure provided by the item (completion, short answer, essay).

Content sampling: Method of selecting items for an **achievement test** over a body of content when not all questions or tasks can be presented.

Content validity: Describes how well the content of the **test** samples the subject matter that the course of instruction aimed to teach.

Correction factor: An adjustment made for a test **score** which changes the

score by the amount of expected correct answers obtained by pure guesses. It may be either additive or subtractive.

Correction for guessing: An alteration of test **scores** used to increase the **reliability** of the **scores** by removing the chance factors involved with guessing blindly to responses to multiple-choice and true-false test items.

Correlation: A study of the relationship which exists between two sets of **scores** taken from one set of students. The tendency of one set of **scores** to vary concomitantly with the other set.

Correlation coefficient: A pure number, limited by the values of −1.00 and +1.00, that expresses the degree of relationship between two sets of **scores** obtained from one set of subjects. **Correlation coefficients** range from .00, denoting a complete absence of relationship, to +1.00, indicating perfect positive correspondence and from .00 to −1.00, which indicates perfect negative correspondence.

Criterion groups: Two sets of test papers used in **item analysis.** One set is selected from the highest scoring subjects while the other set is selected from the lowest scoring subjects. Each group has the same number of papers.

Criterion keying: A method of **scoring** or interpreting a student's set of responses to another response pattern. Widely used for self-report devices to define likes or dislikes.

Criterion-referenced: A way of interpreting a test **score** that compares an individual's performance to a defined behavior domain.

Criterion-related validity: Determined by comparing the test **scores** with one or more external variables considered to provide a direct **measure** of the characteristic or behavior in question. For **predictive validity** the criterion is future performance. For **concurrent validity** the criterion is present performance.

Decile: One of nine points that divide an ordered distribution of **scores** into 10 equal parts.

Descriptor set: A collection of ordered classes which establishes the degrees of worthiness of student performance. Used with **criterion-referenced** procedures.

Device: A plan, scheme, **test,** or mechanical instrument employed to obtain information about students.

Diagnosis: Identification of specific deficiencies in a learning sequence. Corrective teaching is administered for remediation.

Diagnostic evaluation: Judgment designed to point out specific strengths and weaknesses or failures of a student to learn a specified skill or procedure.

Diagnostic test: An examination which focuses on a specific skill or limited subject field designed to reveal specific deficiencies to direct remedial action. Used primarily in skill development.

Difficulty: The degree of arduousness of a **test** task for students as opposed to the easiness of the **test** task. **Difficulty** is measured by the **difficulty index (P).**

Difficulty index: A **measure** of the percentage of incorrect responses determined by dividing the number getting the item wrong by the number who tried the item. Used to establish how difficult an item was for the group who took the **test**. (See **Easiness index.**)

Direct observation: Noticing of phenomena without any intervening factor between the observer and that which is being observed. A record of the situation is made.

Discrimination: Ability of a **true-false** or **multiple-choice** item to make distinction between high and low scoring students based on the total **test score.** **Discrimination** is measured by the **discrimination index.**

Discrimination index: A value which indicates the ability of an item to separate high achieving students from low achieving students. The most commonly used index is obtained by comparing the number in the highest 27 percent of the group who responded correctly with the number in the lowest 27 percent who responded correctly.

Distracter: A **multiple-choice item** response which is classed as an incorrect **alternative.** It is a plausible wrong answer designed to be attractive to a student who does not know the correct answer.

Domain: A sphere of human activity. The three major categories are cognitive, affective and psychomotor. (See **Cognitive domain, Affective domain, Psychomotor domain.**)

Domain-referenced: The referencing of an examinee's performance to a definite set of learner behavior. This term was antecedent to wide use of the contemporary definition of criterion-referenced. Today domain-referenced may be used as a synonym for criterion-referenced.

Easiness index: A **measure** of the percentage of correct responses determined by dividing the number of students getting the item right by the number who tried the item. Used to establish how easy an item was for the group who took the **test.** [See **Difficulty index.**]

Educational measurement: The use of **devices** as measuring instruments to **quantify** certain student **attributes.** In the classroom **educational measurement** deals primarily with achievement in content subjects and skill development.

Educational objective: A statement of a goal for the process of education which is based on the need of students.

Equivalence: Reflects the extent that one **test** samples the same content and behaviors that a second **test** samples.

Equivalent-forms reliability: Reliability of a test as estimated by comparing the **scores** made by a set of students who took two **tests** either concurrently or at different times. It is a **correlation** of **equivalence** if the two **tests** were taken concurrently and a **correlation** of **stability** and **equivalence** if the two tests were taken at different times.

Error: Variation produced by the inaccuracies of **measurement.** The source of the variation may be within the test instrument, within the subjects of **measurement,** or in the way the **test** was administered.

Essay item: A question or situation with instructions which require the test taker to organize a complete thought in one or more written sentences.

The freedom allowed in the response generates responses which must be assessed by a scorer who is knowledgeable in the subject area.

Evaluation: The continuous inspection of all available information concerning the student, teacher, educational program, and the teaching-learning process to ascertain the degree of change in students and form valid judgments about the students and the effectiveness of the program.

Event sampling: Observation of occurrences of a particular kind of incident as related to an individual or interaction between and among individuals.

Exact limits: See **Real limits.**

Examinee reliability: A **measure** of the consistency of a person's reactions to test tasks. It is established by **correlation** of **scores** obtained by students who take the same **test** on two different administrations.

Extended response: The answer to an **essay item** which asks or implies a question which has no definite limits to restrict the student response. The response set is **open-ended.**

Field testing: A trial administration of a preliminary form of a **standardized test.** The examinees' responses are analyzed to point up well-functioning items and items which need to be improved. Test directions, time limits, and format are evaluated in terms of the trial run and student reactions.

Formative evaluation: A judgment of an ongoing program used to provide information for product or program review, identification of the effectiveness of the instructional process, and the assessment of the teaching process.

Frequency distribution: A systematic arrangement of **scores** in a series of intervals showing the number of individuals who had **scores** in each of the intervals.

Frequency polygon: A graphical representation of the frequency of **scores** associated with designated points on the baseline. The mid-point of each interval is recorded by a dot representing the **scores** falling in each interval. Adjacent points are connected by lines.

General educational objective: Description in broad terms of what is to be accomplished, reflecting concern in education as developed at the national or state levels through committees of educators. A general **objective** may be stated at the local level to direct more specific classroom **objectives.**

Global procedure: A technique of **scoring** essay responses using overall impression ratings of responses. The assessment is based on standards as determined by the overall student response to a test task rather than an analytical division into important factors. (See **Analytical procedure.**)

Grade norm: An average **score** on a **test** for students of a specified grade. Extended **norms** are listed in tables for **standardized tests** for score interpretation.

Grouped data: Scores arranged in intervals in a systematic way. The **scores** are condensed into a smaller number of categories which aid interpretation of a large **range** of scores or groups where gaps appear in the ordering of the original scores.

Halo effect: A bias in rating of specific traits arising from the rater being influenced by overall or general impressions or previously formed opinion of the individual or object being rated.

Hand scoring: Checking of students' responses to **objective tests** by the teacher or a helper with the use of a **key,** scoring stencil, or other tool.

Histogram: A graph of a distribution of **scores** or **frequency distribution** prepared by placing score values on a **horizontal axis** or baseline with the scores increasing from left to right. The **vertical axis,** representing frequency, begins with zero and continues to the highest frequency for any interval. Frequencies are recorded across intervals thus forming rectangles.

Horizontal axis: As related to a graph or **scattergram,** this axis represents the values of one set of **scores** as they increase from left to right on the graphical representation.

Instructional evaluation: A kind of **formative evaluation.** Judgments are made about the effectiveness of the teaching-learning process.

Instructional objective: Indicates what is desired at the end of learning. It directs student learning toward development of clearly described attitudes, skills, knowledge, or understandings.

Instrumentation: The use of apparatus and **devices** for measuring or recording behavior and performance.

Internal consistency: Analysis of interrelatedness of student responses among items of a **test** which gives an estimate of consistency at one point in time. The most frequently used **measure** of **internal consistency** for classroom tests is an odd-even division of test items. The r is found for the two halves and corrected for longer length by the **Spearman-Brown formula.**

Intrinsic ambiguity: Uncertainty about the task on a test item which results from the way the item is worded or otherwise presented.

Isomorphic: Something similar or identical in structure or appearance to something else.

Item analysis: An examination of student performance for each item on a **test.** It consists of reexamination of the responses to items of a test by applying mathematical techniques to assess two characteristics—difficulty and discrimination—of each objective item on the test.

Key: A solution set containing the correct responses to objective **test** items.

Kuder-Richardson (K-R) formulas: Formulas (See Appendix D) for estimation of the **internal consistency** of a test from a single administration of a **test.** Estimation of the **reliability** of a test from right and wrong responses about the individual **items** in the test, number of **items** in the test, and the **variance** of the test scores. Some derivations of K-R formulas use other values from the test.

Kurtosis: The flatness or peakedness of a distribution. A distribution is classified as **platykurtic** (flat), **leptokurtic** (peaked), or **mesokurtic** (neither flat nor peaked).

Learning disability: A discrepancy between expected and actual achievement;

one or more deficits in the learning process, such as delayed development in speech, language, reading, spelling, or arithmetic.

Leptokurtic: A characteristic which describes the peakedness of a **frequency polygon** which is more peaked than the **normal curve.** (See **Kurtosis.**)

Limited response: Essay item which asks a question or gives instructions for restricting the area to be covered in responding to the stated tasks. The coverage expected is well fenced-in for the student.

Linear tendency: An inclination for data to reveal a linear form when graphed in a **scattergram,** as opposed to a curvilinear form or no discernible form. (Syn.—Rectilinear.)

Local norms: A numerical basis for interpreting a **score** on a **test.** The base may be for a particular school, locality, section of a state, state, or other limited geographical region.

Machine-scoring: The **scoring** of **tests** by means of electrical contacts, optical scanning, and other **devices** that eliminate or minimize the handwork usually involved in marking, counting, and assembling credits.

Mark: Value or rating in the form of a symbol which indicates an estimate of a student's work or an assessment of accomplishment in a course of study.

Marking plan: An arrangement scheme for reporting student achievement using a set of symbols called **marks.**

Mastery test: A **test** designed to **measure** the knowledge and skills that every student in the class should have acquired. Students' **scores** are compared to predetermined exterior standards rather than to position relative to others in the group who took the test or to **norms of a standardized test.** A **mastery test** may be used for a single student in an individualized program.

Matching item: Presents a list of premises and a list of responses. The student is asked when given a premise word to select from the possible responses one which is related to that premise.

Mean: The arithmetical average of a set of values. The sum of the **scores** is divided by the number of **scores.**

Measure (noun): The number value obtained from the process of **measurement.** The value, extent, dimensions, capacity of anything as reported in terms of some **unit.**

Measure (verb): The process of **measurement.**

Measurement: A process that assigns by rule a numerical description to **observation** of some **attribute** of an object, person, or event.

Measures of variability: Measures of the spread or dispersion of test **scores.** **Educational measurement** procedures usually use the **standard deviation.**

Mechanical instrument: An apparatus used to collect data.

Median: The midpoint (sometimes the middle score) of a distribution of **scores.** It is the point above and below which 50 percent of the **scores** fall.

Mesokurtic: A characteristic form of kurtosis that is neither **leptokurtic** nor **platykurtic.** The form is like that of the unit normal distribution.

Minimum acceptance: A part of a **behavioral objective** statement. Specifies the lowest level of accepted learner performance in terms of the quality or quantity.

Modal age norms: Averages to be used to interpret test performance, but students who are atypical in age for the **norm population** are not included in the computation of the average. Students who are too young or too old for a stated limited age range are excluded from the **norm group.**

Mode: The most frequently occurring score in a distribution.

Multiple-choice item: A task consisting of some premise and a series of possible responses. The student chooses a response which is considered to be the correct one from the listed **alternative** choices.

Norm: A value or set of values reflecting performance of a defined group on a **test** or inventory. Used in testing to aid in interpretation of **scores** on **standardized tests.**

Norm group: Synonymous with **norm population.**

Norm population: The set of subjects used to establish the averages to be used to interpret student **scores** on a **standardized test.**

Normal curve: The unit normal. A bell-shaped **frequency polygon** that is used as a model to study proportions and number of cases for intervals on the abscissa of a **frequency polygon.**

Normalize: A transformation or modification procedure which gives a distribution the properties of the **normal curve** (used with **T scores**).

Norm-referenced: A form of interpreting test **scores** which employs the practice of comparing a student's performance to the class performance or to some exterior average performance, such as local, state, or national averages.

Objective: A goal or end. It describes what is to be accomplished. In most cases the objective directs attention or mirrors a concern regarding something.

Objective item: A test item that can be scored without knowledge of the subject matter.

Objectivity: The degree to which the task to be performed is clear and the correct response is definite. Most experts in the content or subject area covered by the **test** would select the same **alternative** as the best response.

Observation: The process of collecting information that will be used as a basis for evaluation. Also, any fact that is used as a basis for evaluation. Thus, observation (the process) generates observations (the results of the process).

Observe: The act of gathering data. In education the results of observation are used to make **evaluations.**

Obtained test score: The value or number of points which a student gets on a test. A **raw score** made up of the **true score** and an **error** component.

Open-ended test: Some educational **tests** are built to **measure** the complete **range** of expected values. These are referred to as being open-ended and have a top possible **score** so high that rarely if ever will a student have a **score** at the ceiling.

Operational definition: A description which gives meaning to a concept **(construct)** by specifying in terms of tasks how the **attribute** is to be measured. The operational definition gives meaning by describing in operations how someone exhibits the property being defined.

Ordering: Arranging scores in order of size from the highest to lowest. This procedure places each **score** in a position such that all larger scores are to one side of it and all smaller scores are on the other side of it.

Ordinal data: Information that contains an order but is not reported in equal intervals. [e.g. 1st, 2nd, 3rd, etc.]

Pearson product-moment correlation (*r*): A coefficient of correlation obtained from the Pearson product-moment formula. It is used to **measure** concomitant variability for two sets of values.

Percentile: One of 99 points which divide an ordered distribution into 100 equal parts. Each percentile shows the place in the distribution where a designated proportion of the total distribution falls below. For example, P_{70} is a score value where 70 percent of the scores are less than the P_{70} value.

Percentile rank: The percentage of **scores** in a distribution equal to or lower than the **score** corresponding to the given rank. Each percentile rank indicates the percentage of all the **scores** in a **frequency distribution** that fall below a given **raw score.**

Performance evaluation: An **appraisal** of accomplishment for student's attainment in skill and physical development.

Performance test: A sequence of tasks used to appraise an individual's level of skill or manual development. The **test** requires demonstration of the facility through overt manipulation of objects or instruments or demonstration of a developed skill.

Physical measurement: Quantification of physical **attributes** of subjects or objects such as height or weight as opposed to hidden **attributes** such as motivation or achievement.

Platykurtic: A characteristic which describes the peakedness of a frequency polygon which is flatter than the **normal curve.** (See **Kurtosis.**)

Power test: A **test** in which the tasks are arranged in order of increasing difficulty. It is intended to **measure** the level of maximum achievement or ability of the student.

Predictive validity: The degree to which predictions made from the test are confirmed by evidence gathered at some later time.

Problem item: A challenging situation posed to a student which requires reflective thinking for solution in technical terms, or a mathematical task presented in algorithmic form.

Procedure: The **process** or set of actions used to create a **product.**

Process: A set of actions used in the forming of a **product.**

Product: (1) A part of a **behavioral objective** statement. The **result** of the behavior which is evaluated to determine if the **objective** has been achieved. (2) The **result** of performance. A product could be intangible such as recitation of a poem or climbing a ladder. A product could be tangible such as a ceramic vase or a 500-word essay.

Product scale: An achievement **measure** consisting of graded samples of performance against which student behavior is compared as a **measure** of standard.

Prognostic test: A **device** designated to identify characteristics and abilities to estimate future success on a new undertaking.

Psychological measurement: Quantification of hidden **attributes** of human subjects. It deals with the **measurement** and **quantification** of the factors of intelligence, emotions, and personality.

Psychomotor domain: The area of human action which emphasizes all types of body movements which are involuntary or voluntary.

Published test: A commercially printed **test** for which content has been selected and checked empirically. The test may serve to cover content of a specific textbook or textbook series as a **measure** of achievement and a diagnostic tool for that content. Also includes tests which have been standardized. (See **Standardized test.**)

Quantification: The assignment of numbers to **attributes** of objects, persons, or events. It requires the specification of operations or the creation of an instrument by means of which appropriate numbers can be attached to various amounts of the characteristic or property.

Quantify: To indicate the extent of something by assigning a value to it.

Quartile: One of three points that divide the scores in an ordered distribution into four equal groups—25 percent of the scores fall below Q_1, 50 percent fall below Q_2 **(median)**, and 75 percent fall below Q_3.

Quartile deviation: The value which is equal to one-half of the distance from the 25th percentile, P_{25} (first quartile, Q_1) to the 75th percentile, P_{75} (third quartile Q_3). $Q = (Q_3 - Q_1)/2$

Range: The difference in score **units** between the highest and lowest **scores** in a distribution. Range $= X_h - X_l$ [If the data are continuous and reported in **units** of one rather than fractions, the range can be defined as being equal to $(X_h - X_l) + 1$]

Rank: The position of a **score** or individual in relation to others in the group. The highest **score** is usually given a rank of one, the next a rank of two, and so on.

Ranking: An arrangement of a set of **scores** in sequential order of magnitude (size) and assignment of a rank to each score. All scores are ranked by assigning a rank of one to the first score, the second score a two and so on until all scores are given a ranked number. When more than one score is recorded for a point on the original scale, the average rank for all the scores which are the same is assigned to each of those numbers.

Rating scale: A **device** that permits an observer an opportunity to record the intensity or degree of impressions while observing a subject or setting. It can also be used by an individual to report personal **attributes.**

Raw score: The first **score** given to a test paper. It may include weighting and a **correction for guessing,** but no other transformation.

Readiness test: A **device** designed to investigate abilities of students for the purpose of assessing preparedness to undertake a new learning experience. Most used for reading and mathematics instruction at the primary school level.

Real limits: Points on the continuum used to designate the terminal points of the intervals used to record frequency of occurrence. They are used when the data are continuous.

Reliability: Consistency of **observation.** The consistency with which a data collection device **measures** whatever it is that the device **measures.** The degree of reliability may be reported as a **correlation coefficient.** It may be interpreted by the **standard error of measurement.**

Representative sample: A **sample** possessing the same inclinations as the total group or population with some reference to a characteristic or characteristics. In testing, the test instrument is composed of tasks which are intended to reflect the characteristics of the larger population of possible test tasks which could be asked as to subject matter and behaviors.

Result: Product of the actions associated with performance in skill and manual development.

Rho (ρ): A **measure** of the relationship existing between the rank orders of the **observation** of two variables. An adaption of the Pearson technique made by Spearman where equal interval between ranks is assumed.

Sample: Any subset of persons or items selected to represent a larger group or population. (See **Representative sample.**)

Sampling distribution: A theoretical **frequency distribution** containing data representative of possible **samples** rather than values obtained from an individual or a group of individuals.

Scattergram: A graphical representation made by plotting a point for each pair of **scores** that has been obtained for the set of subjects. A double entry table used as a visual display of the relationship of two sets of scores. It is made up of a series of dots each of which represents two values from one subject. If the **scores** on the two variables being measured are highly related, then the dots will tend to form a line.

Score: A number assigned to a test taker to provide a quantitative description of performance on the test.

Scorecard: A **device** that extends the concept of a **checklist** to include a weighting of each aspect rather than merely noting presence or absence of an item.

Scorer reliability: A measure of agreement of **scores** for two readers or scorers. The raters agree on the number of points to be given to a perfect response; then each reader or scorer assesses responses according to his **evaluation.** The higher the agreement, the higher the **correlation coefficient** used to **measure** the agreement.

Scoring: The act or process of marking responses to **objective test** situations or evaluating written responses for essay tasks.

Selected-response item: An item which requires the student to choose from provided alternatives (**classification, true-false, multiple-choice,** and **matching**).

Self-scoring: A method of marking responses to **objective test** items in such a way that the test taker knows immediately whether the response is correct or incorrect. An incorrect response usually requires another selection. The number of trials needed to get agreement is considered as the **score**. The more trials needed, the lower the **score**.

Short-answer item: A **constructed-response item** that asks for a response from the student which is usually more than one word but not a complete statement.

Single-subject test: A **device** which **measures** achievement in one subject or limited scope of a larger discipline.

Skewness: The tendency of a distribution to depart from symmetry or balance about the mean. The degree of symmetry attached to the occurrence of the scores along the **score** interval.

Spearman-Brown formula: A formula expressing the relationship between the **reliability** of a **test** and its length, used to estimate the **reliability** of a **test** when it is lengthened. For classroom use the special case of doubling the length of a **test** is used for the **split-half** technique of estimating **internal consistency.**

Specific determiner: A word or characteristic in a **selected-response item** that gives the test taker an unintended clue to the correct response.

Specificity: The selection and provision of test items which actually require knowledge in the content or subject areas covered by the test. Someone who has not studied in the area being tested should **score** very low if the **test** is high in **specificity.**

Specimen set: Information about a **standardized test.** Includes a copy of the **test** instrument, test manual, and other materials and information about the test. Offered at a nominal fee by the test publisher.

Speededness: The extent to which a student's **score** is dependent on the quickness exhibited in responding to test tasks. This should not be a major factor in **scoring** well on most classroom **tests.** Tests of performance, such as race running or typing, should have a large component of speededness in the **measure.**

Split-half reliability: Reliability of a **test** performed by splitting it into comparable halves (such as the odd-numbered and even-numbered items) and correlating the **scores** of the two halves. It is a **correlation** of **internal consistency.**

Stability: Refers to the consistency of the **test** results over a period of time as **measured** by the **reliability** estimates using the **test-retest** method when a set of subjects takes the same **test** twice with a time interval between testings.

Standard deviation: A **measure of variability** or dispersion of a set of **scores.** It is the square root of the **mean** of the squared deviations of **scores** from the **mean.**

Standard error: The **standard deviation** of some **sampling distribution.** The **standard deviation** of the theoretical distribution of **scores** from repeated **measurement.** It **measures** fluctuation of **statistics** over repeated sampling. **Standard error of measurement** is an estimate of the dispersion of a group of **obtained scores** from the corresponding set of **true scores.** The standard error of measurement is a measure of deviations of obtained scores from associated true scores.

Standard error of measurement: See Standard error.

Standard score: A score which expresses each individual's score in terms of the number of standard deviation units of the score from the mean or a transformation thereof.

Standardized test: A commercially printed test for which content has been selected and checked empirically. The test is standardized so that administration and scoring procedures are the same for all test takers. Score interpretation is made to averages of performances of groups of test takers whose scores are then used for making comparison to interpret obtained scores.

Stanine: Short for standard nine—a scale with nine standard divisions. A distribution is broken into nine groups (1 through 9) based on intervals of one-half a standard deviation except for stanines 1 and 9 which cover more of the continuum but contain very few obtained scores.

Statistics: Procedures which deal with the classification and occurrence of different attributes or things. As applied to classroom testing procedures, uses mathematical techniques to collect, analyze, interpret, and present data.

Stem: The portion of a multiple-choice item which serves as a premise to set the task for the student's selection of a correct response from several presented alternatives.

Strip key: A device containing the correct responses to objective test items arranged so that the answers on any page or in any column of a test appear in a strip or column that may be placed alongside a student's responses for scoring.

Summative evaluation: A terminal evaluation employed in the general assessment of the degree to which the larger outcomes have been obtained over a substantial part of or all of a course. It is used in determining whether or not the learner has achieved the ultimate objectives for instruction which were set up in advance of the instruction.

Survey battery: Assesses student knowledge, skills, or other learning outcomes when instruction is structured so that all students have the same exposure, but they achieve at different levels. Contrasted with a diagnostic test which is intended to identify weaknesses in attainment and with a mastery test which is concerned with measuring attainment of a limited body of content.

Symmetrical: If the graph of a distribution could be folded along an ordinate at the middle in such a way that the two halves coincide perfectly, the distribution is symmetrical. Equal frequencies at equal distances from a central location are found. The normal curve is an example of a symmetrical distribution.

T score: Normalized standard scores with a mean of 50 and a standard deviation of 10. Determined by multiplying the z score by 10 and adding 50 points to the product and normalizing the transformation for symmetry.

Table of specifications: A two-dimensional chart which is used to direct the writing of **test** items and construction of a **test** so that the subject topics and behaviors are emphasized in their relative degrees of importance as reflected by **objectives** and classroom emphasis. (See **Test blueprint.**)

Taxonomy: A system of classification and the concepts of identification, naming, and categorization underlying the coordination.

Test: An instrument, **device,** or procedure which proposes a sequence of tasks to which a student is to respond. The results are then used as **measures** to define relative value of the trait to which the **test** relates.

Test appraisal: Analyzing the characteristics of a **test** and test results to determine its adequacy. Includes **item analysis** data to study each item and its contribution to the test results and inspection of **specificity, objectivity,** and **balance** of the test instrument.

Test assembly: Organization of directions and items into an order of tasks and reproduction into a **test** instrument.

Test blueprint: Synonymous with **table of specifications.** A two-way chart relating **test** items to the course content and the desired learning outcomes. (See **Table of specifications.**)

Test directions: Test-taking information for the student about what is to be done, how it is to be done, and how answers are to be recorded. They usually appear as a set of general instructions about how to proceed and specific procedures about responding to each different type of item.

Test-item file: A collection of individual items on cards which are arranged by content areas for future use in **test assembly.**

Test reliability: The accuracy with which a measuring device **measures** what it **measures.** Consistency of **measurement.**

Test-retest: A method of estimating the **reliability** of a **test** by correlating the **scores** made by the same individuals on two administrations of the **test.**

Test wiseness: A talent that test-takers may have that allows them to outwit an inept test constructor. Correct responses may be identified for selected-response items from clues in the item rather than from knowledge.

Time sampling: Data collection that systematically selects different points in time or time intervals for recording observations.

Trait sampling: Observation of occurrences as specific behaviors of an individual or interaction between and among individuals.

True limits: See **Real limits.**

True-false item: A statement given to the test taker who is to identify it as being essentially true or essentially false.

True test score: An average of a very large number of possible **scores** that an individual could conceivably **score** on the administration of a **test.** The value of an **observation** entirely free from **error.** The mean of an infinite number of **observations** of a quantity.

Unit: A single, indivisible entity. A fixed quantity or amount. In testing any specified amount or quantity to be counted to a composite **test score.**

Unobtrusive observation: Instances of noticing made in such a way that the persons being observed do not know that they are being observed.

Validity: The degree to which **observation** describes accurately what is being observed.

Variance: A measure of variability. A mean square obtained by squaring each score's deviation from the **mean** and dividing by the number of **scores**. The square root of the **variance** is the **standard deviation.**

Vertical axis: As related to the **scattergram** this axis represents the **scores** of one set of **scores** as they increase from bottom to top on the graphical representation.

Who: A part of a **behavioral objective** statement. The learner or student designated in an **educational objective.** It is necessary to clearly state **who** is to perform the desired behavior.

Written assignment: A task given to a student in which the student is to create a response from information available to him. The assignment is usually used as a learning experience for the student.

z score: A standard score having a **mean** of 0 and a **standard deviation** of 1.00. It indicates the number of **standard deviations** an individual **score** is from the **mean** of the distribution.

Z score: A standard score with a **mean** of 50 and a **standard deviation** of 10. Determined by multiplying the **z** score by 10 and adding 50 points to the product. This distribution has the same degrees of **skewness and kurtosis** as the original distribution.

Appendix A Affective and Psychomotor Domains

Although classroom instruction is directly related to establishing student literacy, teachers deal with students' affective and psychomotor attributes in the classroom. A description of the major levels, illustrative behavioral terms for stating specific learning outcomes, and illustrative educational objectives focuses attention on the major levels of the affective and psychomotor domains.

Affective Domain

The affective domain* has five levels in hierarchical order moving from "receiving" to "characterization by a value or value complex." Each major category is further subdivided as indicated.

Affective Domain

1. Receiving (attending)
   1.1 Awareness
   1.2 Willingness to Receive
   1.3 Controlled or Selected Attention
2. Responding
   2.1 Acquiescence in Responding
   2.2 Willingness to Respond
   2.3 Satisfaction in Response
3. Valuing
   3.1 Acceptance of a Value
   3.2 Preference for a Value
   3.3 Commitment
4. Organization
   4.1 Conceptualization of a Value
   4.2 Organization of a Value System
5. Characterization by a Value or Value Complex
   5.1 Generalized Set
   5.2 Characterization

---

*From David R. Krathwohl, Benjamin S. Bloom, and Bertram B. Masia, *Taxonomy of Educational Objectives—The Classification of Educational Goals, Handbook II: Affective Domain* (New York: David McKay Company, Inc., 1964), pp. 95–193.

The affective domain includes the internalized processes such as emotion, feeling, interest, attitude, value, character development, and motivation. Objectives based on the five levels of the affective domain contain behaviors and objectives based on personal-social aspects of development. Discussion of the five levels follows.

1. Receiving (attending), the lowest level of the learning outcomes of the domain refers to willingness of students to receive the teacher's attention. Students must be able to accept stimuli and attend.

Illustrative behavioral terms for stating specific learning outcomes include:

ask	choose	describe	follow
give	hold	identify	locate
name	point to	select	sit erect
reply	use		

Illustrative educational objectives:

—Asks questions of a guest speaker.
—Gives attention to others when in direct conversation.

2. Responding involves the active participation on the part of the student in attending and reacting to a particular phenomenon. Seeking out and enjoyment of particular activities.

Illustrative behavioral terms for stating specific learning outcomes include:

answer	assist	comply	conform
discuss	greet	help	label
perform	practice	present	read
recite	report	select	tell
write			

Illustrative educational objectives:

—Complies with playground regulations.
—Selects music for self-expression and a means of personal satisfaction.

3. Valuing is the worth or value a student attaches to a particular phenomenon, object, or behavior.

Illustrative behavioral terms for stating specific learning outcomes include:

complete	describe	differentiate	explain
follow	form	initiate	invite
join	justify	propose	read
report	select	share	study
work			

Illustrative educational objectives:

—Forms a desire for good literature.
—Invites members of an outside group into a discussion.

4. Organization is the beginning of building of a value system and is concerned with comparing, relating, and synthesizing values.

Illustrative behavioral terms for stating specific learning outcomes include:

adhere	alter	arrange	combine
compare	complete	defend	explain
generalize	identify	integrate	modify
order	organize	prepare	relate
synthesize			

Illustrative educational objectives:

—Identifies ideas about the conduct of life from reading materials.
—Defends personal rationale for a place as a citizen in the community.

5. Characterization by a value or value complex. The individual's behavior as related to the life style is under the control of the value system. The behavior is consistent, pervasive, and predictable.

Illustrative behavioral terms for stating specific learning outcomes include:

act	discriminate	display	influence
listen	modify	perform	practice
propose	qualify	question	revise
serve	solve	use	verify

Illustrative educational objectives:

—Displays a consistent philosophy of life.
—Modifies judgments in relation to new evidence.

The affective domain is categorized from the "receiving" subcategory through "characterization by a value or value complex" and each higher level requires attainment at each level beneath it. The levels of receiving, responding, and valuing can be obtained through experiences provided in class. The organizational level, if it is to be obtained, requires that teachers help students organize and clarify their own value systems. Teachers must provide direction and assistance even though only a few students move to the fifth level—characterization by value or value complex. The illustrative behavioral terms for stating specific learning outcomes and the illustrative educational objectives facilitate the writing of affective behavioral objectives.

Psychomotor Domain

The psychomotor domain* consists of six major levels arranged in hierarchical order moving from "reflex movements" to "nondiscursive communication" as shown in the summary outline of the domain. Each major category is further subdivided as indicated.

Psychomotor Domain

1. Reflex Movements
   1.10 Segmental Reflexes
   1.20 Intersegmental Reflexes
   1.30 Suprasegmental Reflexes
2. Basic-Fundamental Movements
   2.10 Locomotor Movements
   2.20 Nonlocomotor Movements
   2.30 Manipulative Movements
3. Perceptual Abilities
   3.10 Kinesthetic Discrimination
   3.20 Visual Discrimination
   3.30 Auditory Discrimination
   3.40 Tactile Discrimination
   3.50 Coordinated Abilities
4. Physical Abilities
   4.10 Endurance
   4.20 Strength
   4.30 Flexibility
   4.40 Ability
5. Skilled Movements
   5.10 Simple Adaptive Skill
   5.20 Compound Adaptive Skill
   5.30 Complex Adaptive Skill
6. Nondiscursive Communication
   6.10 Expressive Movement
   6.20 Interpretive Movement

Objectives based on the six levels of the psychomotor domain assist educators in categorizing observable movement phenomena into one of the hierarchical levels of the domain. Discussion of the six levels follows.

1. Reflex movements are movements which are involuntary in nature. They are the forerunners and essential for basic or fundamental movement.

_____

*From Anita J. Harrow, *A Taxonomy of the Psychomotor Domain* (New York: David McKay Company, Inc., 1972), pp. 44–99.

Illustrative behavioral terms for stating specific learning outcomes include:

flexing   extending   stretching   postural adjustments

Illustrative educational objectives:
Behavioral objectives for this classification level are not a concern of educators. It is included because reflex movements are prerequisite to development of the classification levels at the higher levels.

2. Basic-fundamental movements are inherent movement patterns which form the basis for specialized complex skilled movements. The movements are inherent motor patterns based upon reflex movements which emerge without training.

Illustrative behavioral terms for stating specific learning outcomes include:

walking	running	jumping	sliding
hopping	rolling	climbing	pushing
pulling	swaying	stooping	handling objects

Illustrative educational objectives:

—Perform sliding, walking, running, and jumping activities.
—Perform a two-footed jump.

3. Perceptual abilities refer to all perceptual modalities where data are provided which are then utilized by the brain centers when making a response decision.

Illustrative behavioral terms for stating specific learning outcomes include:

(visual) dodging a moving ball, (auditory) following verbal directions, (tactile) differentiating by feel between objects, (kinesthetic) making bodily adjustments in activity, (coordinated abilities) jumping a rope, punting, and catching.

Illustrative educational objectives:

—Walk forward and backward the length of a balance beam and balance on one leg for 15 seconds.
—Catch a playground ball thrown in the air.

4. Physical abilities are functional characteristics of organic vigor which lead to making skilled movements a part of the movement repertoire.

Illustrative behavioral terms for stating specific learning outcomes include all strenuous activities which require endurance and quick, precise movements such as distance running, weight lifting, and wrestling.
Illustrative educational objectives:

—To improve the cardiovascular endurance of eighth-grade boys and girls through running.
—To develop and increase the trunk-hip flexibility of fourth, fifth, and sixth-grade students.

5. Skilled movements are learned and reasonably complex skills which result from the degree of efficiency when performing a complex task.

Illustrative behavioral terms for stating specific learning outcomes include:

hurdle run, catching and batting, back handsprings, and back somersaults.

Illustrative educational objectives:

—To improve typing skills of typing students on a 10-minute exercise.
—To improve the ability of boys and girls to run the 50-yard hurdle run.

6. Nondiscursive communication is composed of forms of movement communication and ranges from facial expressions to modern dance choreographies.

Illustrative behavioral terms for stating specific learning outcomes include:

body posture, gesture, facial expression, all effeciently executed dance movements, and choreographies.

Illustrative educational objectives:

—To develop in elementary children the ability to demonstrate rhythmic creative movement.
—To develop in children the ability to perform in free-response activities.

The psychomotor domain is categorized from the "reflex movements" subcategory through "nondiscursive communication" and each level requires attainment of each level beneath it. The psychomotor domain relies on activities which develop through kinesthesia which involves the perception of muscular movement derived from the functioning of afferent nerves connected with muscular tissue, skin, joints, and tendons. All students are involved in muscular movement and the associate movements to different degrees. Age and maturation greatly affect the psychomotor activities that may be accomplished. As students grow and mature the skills they are capable of performing become more complex and may even depend on affective and cognitive factors. The psychomotor domain is involved in most activities students engage in.

Appendix B Writing Behavioral Objectives

You are now ready to learn to identify each element in writing or evaluating statements of behavioral objectives. Through your efforts you will develop an understanding of how to construct and critique behavioral-objective statements.

In view of the fact that classroom teachers write behavioral objectives, it is important to explain precisely what the term means. A behavioral-objective statement includes the following elements: **who, action, product, conditions,** and **minimum acceptance,** and presents in terms of performance what a student is expected to do. The following are examples of behavioral objectives for elementary school mathematics:

Example 1

Using a place-value chart, a third-grade student can identify how many hundreds, tens, and ones are represented by any numeral and score at least 80 percent in an examination over the area.

Example 2

Given arabic numerals 1 through 20, a fourth-grade student can compare those numerals with roman numerals by writing on paper the numbers from I through XX with no errors.

The examples help to point out that in the development of a plan for instruction and evaluation, statements of objectives must describe what students should learn in specific and limited units of instruction. The following pages require your reaction to objectives to help your study of objective writing.

ELEMENT 1: WHO

One may assume that the learner or student is implied in any educational objective. Nevertheless, when writing behavioral objectives, it is necessary to state clearly **who** is to perform the desired behavior. The learner should be distinctly designated by the subject of the action to avoid ambiguity. Alternative words or phrases may be employed for the term "learner." Examples of synonyms for the learner are: the student, the pupil, the class, fifth-grade children, each member of the class, 15-year-old girls, youth, and similar descriptive words.

Application 1—Identifying the Learner: Who

(WHO)

Place a check beside the number of each item that specifies who is expected to meet the objective. Circle the word which indicates who is to perform the objective.

1. _____ The fourth-grade math student can identify the dollar and cents notation in addition and subtraction problems.
2. _____ The fifth-grade pupil will be able to identify measures of objects when presented with a map or blueprint drawn to scale.
3. _____ To be able to point north, south, east, and west.
4. _____ Identify where clothing comes from.
5. _____ The eighth-grade student will be able to focus a microscope so that a cell can be seen.

Discussion of application 1: Who

(WHO)

1. __✓__ Who is to do the identifying? The (fourth-grade math student.) He or she is specified which meets element one's standard, and the statement should be checked.
2. __✓__ Who will identify? The (fifth-grade student.) He or she is specified which meets element one's standard, and the statement should be checked.
3. _____ The subject of the verb is not stated. If the learner is to point to the directions, he or she should be named. Element one's standard is not met in this statement, and it is not checked.
4. _____ The statement does not specify who is to identify; therefore, it does not meet element one's standard, and the statement is not checked.
5. __✓__ Who will focus? The (eighth-grade student.) He or she is specified which meets element one's standard, and the statement should be checked.

ELEMENT 2: ACTION

In writing behavioral objectives the behavior to be observed is stated in **action** verbs. The verb answers the question, "What does the learner do?" in terms of observable behavior. The verbs should be free of ambiguity. Some words which are open to many interpretations and to be *avoided* as indicating the actual behavior to be observed are: know, understand, appreciate, master, acquire, use, grasp the significance of, believe, enjoy, analyze, interpret, perceive, synthesize, learn, and apply. As you can see, it is nearly impossible to observe, measure, and determine the actual behavior when the verb is open to many interpretations.

When writing behavioral objectives the behavior to be observed *is stated* in action verbs such as:

1. Apply	6. Distinguish	11. Predict
2. Compare	7. Identify	12. Rename
3. Compute	8. List	13. Solve
4. Construct	9. Name	14. State
5. Describe	10. Order	15. Write

The taxonomies provide under each subcategory of the domains illustrative behavioral terms for stating specific learning outcomes. For example, knowledge (a major cognitive domain) provides illustrative behavior terms for stating specific learning outcomes as: defines, describes, identifies, labels, matches, names, outlines, reproduces, selects, and states. Reference to the subcategories of the taxonomies provides useful information in developing and writing as well as identifying behavioral objective statements. Illustrative educational objectives are also provided which illustrate the use of an action word.

Application 2: Action

(WHO)   ACTION

Place a check beside the number of each item which states the action of the learner. Circle the word which indicates who is to perform the objective and underline the action word.

1. _____ The sixth-grade student can list the names of the states and the capital of each.
2. _____ The fourth-grade student can learn the multiplication facts.

3. _____ The third-grade students can solve problems using multiplication and division with factors one to nine.
4. _____ Fifth-grade students can identify the background of the American Revolution by being able to write about the events and their relationships to the area that is now Indiana.
5. _____ The third-grade student can identify tone patterns and phrases as same or different.

Discussion of application 2: Action

(WHO)   ACTION

1. ___✓___ The action word <u>list</u> is specified which meets element two's standard, and the statement should be checked. The sixth-grade student indicates who will list the names of states and capitals.

2. _____ The verb, "will learn," is ambiguous and element two's standard is not met, since "will learn" cannot be observed. The statement is not checked. The (fourth-grade student) answers the question "Who?"

3. __✓__ The action <u>solve</u> is specified which meets element two's standard, and the statement should be checked. The (third-grade students) answer the question "Who?"

4. __✓__ The action <u>identify</u> is specified which meets element two's standard, and the statement should be checked. (Fifth-grade students) answer the question "Who?"

5. __✓__ The action <u>identify</u> is specified which meets element two's standard, and the statement should be checked. The (third-grade student) answers the question "Who?"

ELEMENT 3: PRODUCT

The **product** or the result of the behavior is evaluated to determine if the objective is mastered. It answers the question, "What is the product, result, or performance of the behavior?"

Application 3: Product

(WHO)   ACTION   PRODUCT

Place a check beside the number of each item which states the result of the behavior. Circle the word which indicates who is to perform the objective, underline the action, and underline with a double line the product.

1. _____ The seventh-grade student can write a paper concerning electricity.

2. _____ The fifth-grade student can construct a paper describing the life of Abraham Lincoln.

3. _____ The fourth-grade class members can solve a problem by computation of the area of a square given the dimensions.

4. _____ To develop an understanding of the body's functions and mechanics of maintaining these functions.

5. _____ The ninth-grade students can identify the names of representative folk music from the United States.

Discussion of application 3: Product

(WHO)   ACTION   PRODUCT

1. __✓__ The product is the <u>paper</u> which meets element three's standard, and the statement should be checked. The

(seventh-grade student) answers the question "Who?" and the action is <u>writes.</u>

2. __✓__ The product is the <u>paper</u> which meets element three's standard, and the statement should be checked. The (fifth-grade student) answers the question "Who?" and the action is <u>construct.</u>

3. __✓__ The product or result is the <u>computation</u> which meets element three's standard, and the statement should be checked. (Fourth-grade class members) answer the question "Who?" and the action is <u>solve.</u>

4. _____ The product is not stated, and the statement does not meet element three's standard and will not be checked. The learner is not stated and the action "understanding" is ambiguous.

5. __✓__ The product is the <u>names</u> which meets element three's standard, and the statement should be checked. (Ninth-grade students) answers the question "Who?" and the action is <u>identify.</u>

ELEMENT 4: CONDITIONS

The **conditions** under which the behavior is to be performed states the restrictions imposed on the learner when demonstrating the behavior. The identification of the situation in which the behavior occurs may be stated, or in some cases no special conditions are specified.

Application 4: Conditions

(WHO)   <u>ACTION</u>   <u>PRODUCT</u>   <u>CONDITIONS</u>

Place a check beside the number of each item which states the conditions under which the behavior is to be performed. Circle the word which indicates who is to perform the objective, underline the action, underline with a double line the product, and draw a broken line under the conditions.

1. _____ A ninth-grade student can add apostrophes to words in 10 sentences to show correct possessives in a 15 minute quiz.

2. _____ Fourth-grade students can state the steps taken for Indiana Territory to become a state by giving an oral presentation in front of the class.

3. _____ The home-economics student will construct a skirt using the sewing machines available in the home economics classroom.

4. _____ The advanced learner will design and construct a table from wood using the woodworking tools available in the school's workshop.

5. _____ Each student in beginning speech will prepare and present a 10 minute persuasive speech before the class.

Discussion of application 4: Conditions

(WHO)   ACTION   PRODUCT   CONDITIONS

1. ___✓___ The condition is in a 15-minute quiz which meets element four's standard, and the statement should be checked. (Ninth grade student) adds apostrophes.

2. ___✓___ In front of the class is the condition, it meets element four's standard and the statement should be checked. (Fourth-grade students) state the steps.

3. ___✓___ The condition is sewing machines available in the home economics classroom which meets element four's standard, and the statement should be checked. (Home economics student) construct skirt.

4. ___✓___ Woodworking tools available in the school's workshop is the condition, it meets element four's standard, and the statement should be checked. (Advanced learner) design and construct wood table.

5. ___✓___ The condition is before the class which meets element four's standard, and the statement should be checked. (Student in beginning speech) prepare and present persuasive speech

ELEMENT 5: MINIMUM ACCEPTANCE

This element specifies the **minimum acceptance** level of learner performance in terms of the quality or quantity. The standard is employed to evaluate the success of the performance. Standards are stated in many ways and provide the evaluator with the quality, quantity, or time.

Application 5: Minimum Acceptance

(WHO)   ACTION   MINIMUM
               ACCEPTANCE   PRODUCT   CONDITIONS
               X X X X X X X

Place a check beside the number of each item which states the minimum acceptance employed to evaluate the success of the performance. Place X's under the minimum acceptance. Circle the word which indicates who is to perform the objective. Underline the action, underline with a double line the product (result), and place a broken line under the conditions.

1. _____ Given 10 words beginning with different letters the fourth-grade student will number them in alphabetical order with no errors.
2. _____ The eighth-grade learner can locate on the map provided 10 out of 15 different main roads and canals which were used during the American Revolution.
3. _____ The seventh-grade student can distinguish how solids, liquids, and gases are alike and different.
4. _____ Have a repertory of songs, which includes works by master composers.
5. _____ A sixth-grade student can compute the area of a right triangle given the measures and the sides with no errors.

Discussion of application 5: Minimum Acceptance

(WHO)   ACTION   MINIMUM
                 ACCEPTANCE   PRODUCT   CONDITIONS
                 X X X X X X X

1. ___✓___ The minimum acceptance is no errors which meets element
                 X X X X X
five's standard, and the statement should be checked. (Fourth-grade student) number alphabetical order given 10 words beginning with different letters

2. ___✓___ The minimum acceptance is 10 out of 15 different which
                 X X X X X X X X X X X
meets element five's standard, and the statement should be checked. (Eighth-grade learner) locate roads and canals on the map provided

3. _____ The minimum acceptance to be employed to evaluate is not specified, and the statement should not be checked. (Seventh-grade student) distinguish how solids, liquids, and gases are alike or different. No conditions are stated.

4. _____ The statement should not be checked, since the minimum acceptance is not specified. The question "Who?" is not answered. The action in ambiguous. repertory of songs

5. __✓__ The minimum acceptance is with no errors which meets
X X X X X X X X X X X
element five's standard, and the statement should be
checked. (Sixth-grade students) compute area of a right
triangle given the measures and the sides

The following two critiques of the components identifiable for the behavioral objectives in the two mathematics objectives provides a brief review of the five elements you have just studied. You may wish to identify the elements for each example on a sheet of paper in order to check your work against answers that follow the examples.

Example 1

Using a place-value chart, a third-grade student can identify how many hundreds, tens, and ones are represented by a numeral and be able to score at least 80 percent in an examination over the area.

1. Who	— a third-grade student
2. Action	— identify
3. Product	— numerals on an examination
4. Conditions	— using a place-value chart
5. Minimum acceptance	— score at least 80 percent

Example 2

Given arabic numerals, 1 through 20, a fourth–grade student can compare those numerals with roman numerals by writing on the paper the numbers from I through XX with no errors.

1. Who	— fourth-grade students
2. Action	— compare
3. Product	— numerals
4. Conditions	— by writing on paper given numerals, 1 through 20
5. Minimum acceptance	— no errors

In summary, a behavioral objective: (a) is characterized by specificity and lack of ambiguity, (b) is stated in terms of behavior, (c) is interpreted in the same manner by most people, (d) is evaluated in the same manner by most people, and (e) tells the learners what they will be doing when the objective is reached.* Behavioral objectives are deemed to be completed if they contain the following elements: The first element to be considered is *who* is to perform the desired behavior. The objective includes the *action* of the observable behavior to be employed. Whether or not the objective is mastered is indicated by evaluation of the *product* which is clearly stated in the objective. The *conditions* under which the behavior is performed are stated as is the *minimum acceptance* to be employed to evaluate the success of meeting the objective.

---

*John W. Wick. *Educational measurement.* Columbus, OH: Charles E. Merrill, 1973, p. 22.

Appendix C Correction for Guessing

If in the planning stage a decision was made to correct responses to selected-response items for guessing the responses, a formula must be applied to the students' scores. Students will have been informed that they should mark only those items that they feel they know and not guess blindly as they mark the responses. The **correction for guessing** is used to increase the reliability of the test scores by removing the chance factors involved with guessing blindly to responses, or to adjust for correct responses that students could get by marking responses for items that they do not have time to work through logically. The popularity of the correction procedure stems from published tests where students do not have sufficient time to complete all items. Correction for guessing in a classroom testing situation may be appropriate, for example, when a teacher feels that it is important to assess the ability of students to complete fundamental problems, but no student is expected to have time to complete every item on the test. In this situation the number of right answers may provide the rapid, careless student, or a student who marks an answer for every item, with an advantage even though each item is not read. By chance the student may receive a good score but a slower, more careful student who does well on the items completed but does not mark all the items may do less well.

Use of one correction formula requires counting the number of right and wrong answers but not those of items that are omitted. This formula to correct for guessing subtracts from the student's correct responses those which conceivably were answered correctly by blind guessing. If some items were missed, it is assumed that since the student did not know these items, the student surely did not know some that were answered correctly (that the student guessed at those that were missed and some more that were right). This general formula reduces the total "correct right score" by subtracting a **correction factor** based on the number of items missed. Another formula adds to the number of correct responses a proportion of the items omitted.

Correction Formulas

No mathematical formula can adjust scores for responses which each student receives through blind guessing. The formula is based on probabilities associated with guessing correctly, taking into account the number of alternatives provided by the item. The formula for guessing is based on the assumption that when guessing a student has no idea at all about any of the possible responses and their correctness or incorrectness. Thus all options are equally attractive. In a true-false test a student could expect to get about half of the items correct without even reading them by blindly marking responses for each item. A score of 50 percent correct on true-false tests is referred to as a score at **chance level** because that percentage is expected by chance guessing. For a multiple-choice test with four alternatives the chance level is 25 percent, and with five alternatives the chance level is 20 percent.

The general formula for correction is as follows:

$$S = R - \frac{W}{N - 1}$$

Or

$$\text{Score} = \frac{\text{Number}}{\text{right}} - \frac{\text{Number wrong}}{N - 1}$$

S = score
R = number of correct responses
W = number of incorrect responses (exclude omitted items)
N = number of alternatives for each item

When applying the formula to true-false items the N (number of possible responses) is 2, thus

$$S = R - \frac{W}{2 - 1}$$
$$S = R - W$$

Or

$$\text{Score} = \text{Right} - \text{Wrong}$$

The correction formula for multiple-choice scoring varies according to the number of alternatives provided by the items:

Three alternatives $\quad S = R - \dfrac{W}{3 - 1} \quad or \quad S = R - \dfrac{W}{2}$

Four alternatives $\quad S = R - \dfrac{W}{4 - 1} \quad or \quad S = R - \dfrac{W}{3}$

Five alternatives $\quad S = R - \dfrac{W}{5 - 1} \quad or \quad S = R - \dfrac{W}{4}$

R = number of right answers
W = number of wrong answers (exclude omissions)
N = number of alternatives
S = score corrected for guessing

Another approach to reducing guessing on classroom tests may be more acceptable to students. The **correction factor** adds something to the score rather than reducing the score, although the same concept of probabilities is used. Students are asked to omit the items that they must guess blindly on and informed that they will be given credit for a certain percentage of those items omitted. The score is increased by the amount of expected correct responses at the chance level for the type of item being used.

For true-false items the additive factor is 50 percent of those items omitted. For each two omissions the student's score is augmented by one point. Multiple-choice items use the appropriate chance level to determine how much will be added. The general formula is:

$$S = R + \frac{O}{N}$$

S = score corrected for guessing
R = number of correct responses
O = number of omissions
N = number of alternatives

The correction formula for true-false items is: $S = R + \dfrac{O}{2}$

The correction formulas for multiple-choice items are:

3 alternatives	$S = R + \dfrac{O}{3}$
4 alternatives	$S = R + \dfrac{O}{4}$
5 alternatives	$S = R + \dfrac{O}{5}$

Should Correction be Used?

Because of the psychological implications of adding to a score rather than taking away from a score, the additive formula is suggested as a better way to correct for guessing on a classroom test. Do not interpret this to mean that the authors suggest that correction for guessing should be built into scoring of all selected-response tests. In general, the best approach seems to be to have each student respond to each item with a best idea. By eliminating alternatives that the student knows to be incorrect, probabilities of correct response are enhanced and should be reflected in higher test scores. For this reason rational guessing should be encouraged rather than discouraged. The following points should be considered when making a decision about how to handle guessing for your tests.

The wide use of selected-response items has continued to raise questions in regard to whether or not students should be informed that they should respond to each item or skip items when they are not reasonably sure of the correct response. Some students guess blindly on tests when: (a) they have no knowledge of the subject material pertaining to a question, (b) test time is about to terminate, or (c) they for one reason or another do not attempt logical thought processes to respond to items. A student willing to guess may by chance score higher on a test than a student who fails to guess blindly. A student who is hesitant to gamble on items may be placed at a disadvantage by following directions which indicate a correction for guessing, while a student gambling on items may be at the advantage in guessing if good luck results in getting many items correct by guessing.

There are numerous opinions regarding correction for guessing,* and sooner or later the person employing tests must make a decision whether or not to correct for guessing. Correction for guessing achieves little or no purpose in classroom situations, particularly since it works to the disadvantage of students who are insecure in the test situation. It seems logical to conclude that more capable students benefit more than the less able students in guessing. The concept of a correction formula makes the basic assumption that when a student does not know the answer, a blind guess will be made. This rarely occurs, and the assumption is only partially met. Usually some knowledge can be brought to bear on the task at hand, and for multiple-choice items a process of elimination can be employed. Gronlund* speaks to this point when he states that the correction formula undercorrects for chance success when some of the alternatives can be eliminated, and the formula overcorrects for chance success when incorrect alternatives are selected because of misinformation or the plausibility of distracters. When employed in classroom testing, an unknown amount of error is introduced into the scoring.

Within the field of measurement and evaluation there is general agreement that students should be instructed to respond to each item on classroom tests with ample testing time provided. Gronlund states in reference to answering questions about use of correction for guessing:

> Because of the questionable assumption on which the correction for guessing formula is based, it is recommended that it not be used with the ordinary classroom test. The only exception is where the test is speeded to the extent that pupils complete different numbers of items. Here its use is defensible, since pupils could increase their scores appreciably by rapidly (and blindly) guessing at the remaining untried items just before the testing period ended. (p. 253)

Based upon the information and opinions available concerning correction for guessing, it is suggested that it not be used in classroom testing except as noted. The formula is of no practical value when all students have ample opportunity to read and respond to every item as in typical classroom testing situations. Therefore, students should be instructed to respond to all items on a classroom test even though it is through a process of elimination and rational guessing. The test score should be augmented by rational guessing to the degree that the student is knowledgeable on the topics.

---

*Rowly, G.L., & Traub, R.E. Formula scoring, number-right scoring, and test-taking strategy. *Journal of Educational Measurement,* 1977, *14,* 15–22.
*Gronlund, N.E. *Measurement and evaluation in teaching* (4th ed.). New York: Macmillan, 1981, p. 253.

Appendix D Kuder-Richardson Formulas for Test Reliability

Kuder-Richardson 20 (KR 20)

$$r_{\text{KR } 20} = \frac{n}{n-1}\left(1 - \frac{\Sigma pq}{\sigma^2}\right)$$

Where:

n = the number of items on the test
p = the proportion of test takers who scored 1 on a particular item
q = the proportion of test takers who scored 0 on a particular item
σ^2 = the variance of the total scores of the test.
Σ is the sum of

When X_i is a score on the test:

$$\sigma^2 = \frac{\Sigma X^2 - \frac{(\Sigma X)^2}{n}}{n}$$

Kuder-Richardson 21 (KR 21)

$$r_{\text{KR } 21} = \frac{n}{n-1}\left[1 - \frac{\bar{X}\left(1 - \frac{\bar{X}}{n}\right)}{\sigma^2}\right]$$

Where:

n = the number of items on the test
$\bar{X}$ = the mean of the set of test scores
σ^2 = the variance of the total scores of the test

Appendix E

Outline of a schoolwide standardized testing program

Grade and Time of Testing	Scholastic Aptitude Measures	Achievement Measures	Purpose and Use
Elementary			
Kindergarten — first two weeks of March at the .6 grade placement level	*Metropolitan Readiness Tests,* Form P, Level II		To obtain an evaluation of those cognitive skills which are important in early reading and mathematics skills. To provide information for planning the first grade experience.
One — first two weeks of October	*SRA Primary Mental Abilities Test,* K–1		To aid in planning for individual and group instruction. The test gives a diagnostic picture of the strengths and weaknesses of pupils.
One — First two weeks of March at the .6 grade placement level		*Metropolitan Achievement Tests,* Survey Battery, Primary I	The primary purpose of the test is to measure how well each student has mastered the basic skills. The results should serve as an aid in fitting the instruction to the needs of the individual students. Various other instructional and guidance values stem from this.
Two — First two weeks of March at .6 grade placement level		*Iowa Tests of Basic Skills,* Level 8	To measure how well each student has mastered the basic skills. Any student whose performance is a 1 or 2 stanine score in any of the basic skill areas will have a remedial program outlined for the year in the deficient skill area(s).
Three — First two weeks of October	*Cognitive Abilities Test*		To measure how well each student has developed cognitive skills. The results

Grade and Time of Testing	Scholastic Aptitude Measures	Achievement Measures	Purpose and Use
			should serve as an aid in fitting the instruction to the needs of individual students.
Three — First two weeks of March at .6 grade placement level		*Iowa Tests of Basic Skills,* Level 9, plus social studies and science supplement	Continue the evaluation of the mastery of basic skills.
Four — First two weeks of March at .6 grade placement level		*Iowa Tests of Basic Skills,* Level 10, plus social studies and science supplement	To evaluate the individual mastery of basic skills. Any student whose performance is a 1 or 2 stanine score in any of the basic skill areas will have a remedial program outlined for the following year in the deficient skill area(s).
Five — First two weeks of March at .6 grade placement level		*Iowa Tests of Basic Skills,* Level 11, plus social studies and science supplement	Continue evaluation of the mastery of basic skills.
Six — First two weeks of March at .6 grade placement level		*Iowa Tests of Basic Skills,* Level 12, plus social studies and science supplement	Continue the evaluation of basic skills mastery. Any student whose performance is a 1 or 2 stanine score in any of the basic skill areas will have a remedial program outlined for the following year in the deficient skill area(s).

Junior High School

Eight — First two weeks of March at the .6 grade placement level		*Sequential Tests of Educational Progress,* Level I	To be used for the continuing assessment of individual mastery of the basic skills. Any student whose performance is 1 or 2 stanine score in any of the basic skill areas will have a remedial program

Grade and Time of Testing	Scholastic Aptitude Measures	Achievement Measures	Purpose and Use
			outlined for the following year in the deficient skill area(s).
Eight (or accelerate seven and eight) — Middle of March to Middle of April	*Orlearns Algebra Prognosis and Orleans Geometry Prognosis*		To aid in high school planning.
Any grade — When necessary on an individual basis	*Otis-Lennon Mental Abilities,* Intermediate		To provide a measure of scholastic ability for students who are new enrollees and have no records of scholastic aptitude.
Senior High School			
Ten — First two weeks of March at the .6 grade placement level		*Sequential Tests of Academic Progress,* Level 3	To be used for the continuing assessment of individual mastery of the basic skills. Any student receiving a 1 or 2 stanine score in any of the basic skills will have a remediation program outline for the following year in the deficient skill area(s).
Any Grade — When necessary on an individual basis	*Otis-Lennon Mental Abilities,* Advanced		To provide a measure of scholastic ability for students who are new enrollees and have no record of scholastic aptitude.
Eleventh — Date set by Educational Testing Service; usually in late October	*Preliminary Scholastic Aptitude Test*		To screen for scholarships
Twelfth — November, December, March, May, June	College Entrance Examination Board, *Scholastic Aptitude Test (SAT)*		

Appendix F Ethics Code—Standards for Published Tests

Even though testing is a very competitive and profitable business, test publishers adhere to a code of professional ethics. In 1974 the American Psychological Association, the American Educational Research Association, and the National Council on Measurement in Education updated *Standards for Educational and Psychological Tests and Manuals.* This publication reports standards that should be adhered to in every published test and manual. The standards are intended to serve as a guide for *(a)* test developers, *(b)* publishers, and *(c)* test users. The report includes a list of essential, very desirable, and desirable features that should be included in all published tests and manuals. Six major categories provide comprehensive criteria by which tests may be evaluated. Those six categories including a summary of the essential requirements are given below for the reader's reference. (A revised edition is now being prepared as an updated reference for test standards.)

Standards for Tests, Manuals, and Reports*

 I. Dissemination of Information
- 1. A test should be accompanied by a manual which follows the recommended standards.
- 2. The test manual should describe fully the specifications in the development of the test.

 II. Interpretation
- 1. The test, manual, and other related materials should help users interpret test results.
- 2. The test manual should state the purposes for which the test is recommended.
- 3. The test manual should describe the reasoning underlying the test and what it is intended to measure.
- 4. The test manual should specify special qualifications to administer, score, and interpret the test.
- 5. Validity and reliability evidence should be available to support the claims made.

---

*Adapted from: Joint Committee of the APA, AERA, and NCME, *Standards for Educational and Psychological Tests and Manuals.* Washington: American Psychological Association, 1974).

0. Computer score interpreters should provide written material concerning evidence in reference to computer-based scores interpretation.

III. Administering and Scoring
1. The directions for administering the test should encourage uniformity in test situations.
2. Scoring error should be reduced by clearly stated directions.

IV. Norms and Scales
1. Norms should be published and available when the test is released.
2. Norms should be defined in reference to the appropriate populations.
3. Norms should be reported using percentiles or standard scores for one or more reference groups. Measures of variability and central tendency should be reported.
4. Derived scales should be described for accurate interpretation.
5. Normative data based on group summary statistics should be available.

V. Validity
1. The manual should report the validity for each type of inference for which the test is recommended.
2. Evidence in support of validity and reliability should be reported.
3. (Criterion-Related Validity) All measures of criteria should be described completely and accurately. The adequacy of the criterion should be reported.
4. (Criterion-Related Validity) The sample used in the validity study and conditions of testing should be consistent with the recommended test use.
5. (Criterion-Related Validity) Collection of data for a validity study should follow procedures consistent with test purposes.
6. (Criterion-Related Validity) Any statistical analysis of criterion-related validity should be presented in order for adequate judgments or predictions to be made.
7. (Criterion-Related Validity) There should be an investigation of possible differences in criterion-related validity for ethnic, sex, and other subsamples identified when the test is given.
8. (Criterion-Related Validity) Validity statements should not be based on the original samples, and independent cross-validation samples should be reported.
9. (Content Validity) The test manual should give a clear definition of the universe represented and describe the procedures for sampling from it.
10. (Construct Validity) Proposed interpretation of scores on a test measuring a theoretical variable (ability, trait, or attitude) should be stated fully.

VI. Reliability and Measurement Error
1. Evidence of reliability and estimates of the standard error of measurement should be presented which permit the test user to judge how dependable the scores are for the intended use of the

test. Absence or the lack of availability of these data should be stated.

2. Procedures and samples used to determine reliability coefficients or standard errors of measurement should be described sufficiently.
3. Reliability studies should be reported in terms of variances of error components, standard errors of measurement, or product-moment reliability coefficients.
4. (Comparability of Forms) Data regarding the equivalence of forms should be provided including means, variances, and characteristics of items.
5. (Internal Consistency) Evidence of internal consistency should be reported.
6. (Comparisons Over Time) The extent test scores are stable and how constant in parallel forms should be reported after a time lapse in test administration.

Appendix G Information Needed to Evaluate a Standardized Test

1. Name of test, date, and author.
2. Purpose of the test.
3. Grade levels or ages.
4. Equivalent forms? How many?
5. Publisher and cost.
6. Content of test.
7. Time for administration.
8. Directions.
9. Validity.
10. Reliability.
11. Norms.
12. Format of the test.
13. Scoring procedures available.
14. Manual (your own reaction to completeness and usability).
15. Evaluation, including reaction to specific points above and personal reaction to the test as a whole.
    Example for reaction:
    a. What acceptable evidence is offered to substantiate claims in regard to the purpose?
    b. What is the universe of content from which items were drawn? What criteria were used in choosing items?
16. Critique of reviews from Buros's *Mental Measurements Yearbook* series.

Appendix H Data Collection Procedures

I. Testing procedures
 A. Standardized tests (Formal)
  1. Achievement tests—designed to indicate degree of success in some past learning activity
   a. Achievement tests in specific courses
   b. Achievement survey
    Examples of subjects covered:
     Fine arts: art and music
     Foreign languages: Arabic, Chinese, English, French, German, Greek, Hebrew, Italian, Latin, Russian, and Spanish
     Reading: diagnostics, oral, readiness, special fields, and study skills
     English: literature, spelling, and vocabulary
     Mathematics: algebra, arithmetic, calculus, geometry, and trigonometry
     Science: biology, chemistry, geology, and physics
     Social studies: economics, geography, history, political science, and sociology
     Miscellaneous: business education, driving and safety education, health and physical education, home economics, industrial arts, philosophy, and psychology
  2. Mental abilities tests—designed to determine learning capabilities
   a. Group and individual intelligence tests
   b. General mental ability tests
   c. Tests of special mental abilities
   d. Multifactor tests of mental abilities
   e. Performance tests of mental abilities
  3. Aptitude tests—primarily designed to predict success in some future learning activity
   a. Aptitude test batteries
    Examples of aptitudes covered:
     Mechanical, clerical, musical, art, and foreign language
   b. Specific aptitudes

B. Classroom tests (teacher-made achievement tests applied to teaching areas—informal)
1. Oral
2. Written
   a. Constructed—e.g., essay, short answer
   b. Selected—e.g., true-false, multiple-choice
3. Diagnostic tests—reveal specific disabilities in achievement
4. Mastery tests—measure knowledge, skills, and other learning outcomes by criteria
5. Survey tests—emphasize general achievement
C. Tests for textbook series

II. Nontesting procedures
A. Self-report techniques—to obtain information from an individual about self
1. Interview—face-to-face relationship between interviewer and another individual. May obtain information concerning the individual's attitudes, opinions, interest, etc.
2. Questionnaire—obtaining information from individuals in a systematic attempt to evaluate interests, attitudes, and other aspects of personal and social adjustments
B. Observational techniques—obtain information by direct observation of behavior
1. Anecdotal record—short verbal picture of an incident
2. Checklist—prepared list of statements relating to behavior traits
3. Rating scale—device for systematically recording observers' judgment concerning the degree to which a quality or trait is present
4. Scorecard—a device which weights component parts into a total score for a complex situation
5. Sociometric technique—method of evaluating the social relationships existing in a group
6. Mechanical instruments—used to record a situation or part of the classroom environment for an in-depth study
7. Unobtrusive observation—method of gathering information through a secondary source
C. Character and personality inventories—designed to determine character and personality traits of individuals
1. Projective
2. Nonprojective
D. Vocational interest inventories—designed to determine interests in specific vocations
1. Examples of specific vocations covered:
    Accounting, business, computer programming, dentistry, engineering, law, medicine, nursing, selling, skilled trades, supervision, and transportation

      2. Examples of vocational skills covered:
         Clerical, manual dexterity, and mechanical ability

E. Performance measures
    1. Skill development
    2. Physical activity

F. Technical problem
    1. Mathematical
    2. Engineering

Appendix I

Areas of the normal curve in terms of x/σ

(1) z Standard Score $(\frac{x}{\sigma})$	(2) A Area from Mean to $\frac{x}{\sigma}$	(1) z Standard Score $(\frac{x}{\sigma})$	(2) A Area from Mean to $\frac{x}{\sigma}$	(1) z Standard Score $(\frac{x}{\sigma})$	(2) A Area from Mean to $\frac{x}{\sigma}$
0.00	.0000	0.34	.1331	0.68	.2517
0.01	.0040	0.35	.1368	0.69	.2549
0.02	.0080	0.36	.1406	0.70	.2580
0.03	.0120	0.37	.1443	0.71	.2611
0.04	.0160	0.38	.1480	0.72	.2642
0.05	.0199	0.39	.1517	0.73	.2673
0.06	.0239	0.40	.1554	0.74	.2703
0.07	.0279	0.41	.1591	0.75	.2734
0.08	.0319	0.42	.1628	0.76	.2764
0.09	.0359	0.43	.1664	0.77	.2794
0.10	.0398	0.44	.1700	0.78	.2823
0.11	.0438	0.45	.1736	0.79	.2852
0.12	.0478	0.46	.1772	0.80	.2881
0.13	.0517	0.47	.1808	0.81	.2910
0.14	.0557	0.48	.1844	0.82	.2939
0.15	.0596	0.49	.1879	0.83	.2967
0.16	.0636	0.50	.1915	0.84	.2995
0.17	.0675	0.51	.1950	0.85	.3023
0.18	.0714	0.52	.1985	0.86	.3051
0.19	.0753	0.53	.2019	0.87	.3078
0.20	.0793	0.54	.2054	0.88	.3106
0.21	.0832	0.55	.2088	0.89	.3133
0.22	.0871	0.56	.2123	0.90	.3159
0.23	.0910	0.57	.2157	0.91	.3186
0.24	.0948	0.58	.2190	0.92	.3212
0.25	.0987	0.59	.2224	0.93	.3238
0.26	.1026	0.60	.2257	0.94	.3264
0.27	.1064	0.61	.2291	0.95	.3289
0.28	.1103	0.62	.2324	0.96	.3315
0.29	.1141	0.63	.2357	0.97	.3340
0.30	.1179	0.64	.2389	0.98	.3365
0.31	.1217	0.65	.2422	0.99	.3389
0.32	.1255	0.66	.2454	1.00	.3413
0.33	.1293	0.67	.2486	1.01	.3438

Areas of the normal curve in terms of x/σ (continued)

(1) z Standard Score $(\frac{x}{\sigma})$	(2) A Area from Mean to $\frac{x}{\sigma}$	(1) z Standard Score $(\frac{x}{\sigma})$	(2) A Area from Mean to $\frac{x}{\sigma}$	(1) z Standard Score $(\frac{x}{\sigma})$	(2) A Area from Mean to $\frac{x}{\sigma}$
1.02	.3461	1.39	.4177	1.76	.4608
1.03	.3485	1.40	.4192	1.77	.4616
1.04	.3508	1.41	.4207	1.78	.4625
1.05	.3531	1.42	.4222	1.79	.4633
1.06	.3554	1.43	.4236	1.80	.4641
1.07	.3577	1.44	.4251	1.81	.4649
1.08	.3599	1.45	.4265	1.82	.4656
1.09	.3621	1.46	.4279	1.83	.4664
1.10	.3643	1.47	.4292	1.84	.4671
1.11	.3665	1.48	.4306	1.85	.4678
1.12	.3686	1.49	.4319	1.86	.4686
1.13	.3708	1.50	.4332	1.87	.4693
1.14	.3729	1.51	.4345	1.88	.4699
1.15	.3749	1.52	.4357	1.89	.4706
1.16	.3770	1.53	.4370	1.90	.4713
1.17	.3790	1.54	.4382	1.91	.4719
1.18	.3810	1.55	.4394	1.92	.4726
1.19	.3830	1.56	.4406	1.93	.4732
1.20	.3849	1.57	.4418	1.94	.4738
1.21	.3869	1.58	.4429	1.95	.4744
1.22	.3888	1.59	.4441	1.96	.4750
1.23	.3907	1.60	.4452	1.97	.4756
1.24	.3925	1.61	.4463	1.98	.4761
1.25	.3944	1.62	.4474	1.99	.4767
1.26	.3962	1.63	.4484	2.00	.4772
1.27	.3980	1.64	.4495	2.10	.4821
1.28	.3997	1.65	.4505	2.20	.4861
1.29	.4015	1.66	.4515	2.30	.4893
1.30	.4032	1.67	.4525	2.40	.4918
1.31	.4049	1.68	.4535	2.50	.4938
1.32	.4066	1.69	.4545	2.60	.4953
1.33	.4082	1.70	.4554	2.70	.4965
1.34	.4099	1.71	.4564	2.80	.4974
1.35	.4115	1.72	.4573	2.90	.4981
1.36	.4131	1.73	.4582	3.00	.4987
1.37	.4147	1.74	.4591		
1.38	.4162	1.75	.4599		

Appendix J

Squares and square roots of numbers from 1 to 120

N	$\sqrt{N^2}$	N	N	$\sqrt{N^2}$	N	N	$\sqrt{N^2}$	N
1	1	1.0000	41	1681	6.4031	81	6561	9.0000
2	4	1.4142	42	1764	6.4807	82	6724	9.0554
3	9	1.7321	43	1849	6.5574	83	6889	9.1104
4	16	2.0000	44	1936	6.6332	84	7056	9.1652
5	25	2.2361	45	2025	6.7082	85	7225	9.2195
6	36	2.4495	46	2116	6.7823	86	7396	9.2736
7	49	2.6458	47	2209	6.8557	87	7569	9.3274
8	64	2.8284	48	2304	6.9282	88	7744	9.3808
9	81	3.0000	49	2401	7.0000	89	7921	9.4340
10	100	3.1623	50	2500	7.0711	90	8100	9.4868
11	121	3.3166	51	2601	7.1414	91	8281	9.5394
12	144	3.4641	52	2704	7.2111	92	8464	9.5917
13	169	3.6056	53	2809	7.2801	93	8649	9.6437
14	196	3.7417	54	2916	7.3485	94	8836	9.6954
15	225	3.8730	55	3025	7.4162	95	9025	9.7468
16	256	4.0000	56	3136	7.4833	96	9216	9.7980
17	289	4.1231	57	3249	7.5498	97	9409	9.8489
18	324	4.2426	58	3364	7.6158	98	9604	9.8995
19	361	4.3589	59	3481	7.6811	99	9801	9.9499
20	400	4.4721	60	3600	7.7460	100	10000	10.0000
21	441	4.5826	61	3721	7.8102	101	10201	10.0499
22	484	4.6904	62	3844	7.8740	102	10404	10.0995
23	529	4.7958	63	3969	7.9373	103	10609	10.1489
24	576	4.8990	64	4096	8.0000	104	10816	10.1980
25	625	5.0000	65	4225	8.0623	105	11025	10.2470
26	676	5.0990	66	4356	8.1240	106	11236	10.2956
27	729	5.1962	67	4489	8.1854	107	11449	10.3441
28	784	5.2915	68	4624	8.2462	108	11664	10.3923
29	841	5.3852	69	4761	8.3066	109	11881	10.4403
30	900	5.4772	70	4900	8.3666	110	12100	10.4881
31	961	5.5678	71	5041	8.4261	111	12321	10.5357
32	1024	5.6569	72	5184	8.4853	112	12544	10.5830
33	1089	5.7446	73	5329	8.5440	113	12769	10.6301
34	1156	5.8310	74	5476	8.6023	114	12996	10.6771
35	1225	5.9161	75	5625	8.6603	115	13225	10.7238
36	1296	6.0000	76	5776	8.7178	116	13456	10.7703
37	1369	6.0828	77	5929	8.7750	117	13689	10.8167
38	1444	6.1644	78	6084	8.8318	118	13924	10.8628
39	1521	6.2450	79	6241	8.8882	119	14161	10.9087
40	1600	6.3246	80	6400	8.9443	120	14400	10.9545

Name Index

Ahmann, J. S., 185
Ahr, A. E., 448, 464
Algina, J., 295, 339
Anastasi, A., 295, 438, 464
Antes, C. A., 394, 423
Antes, R. L., 28, 72, 100, 129, 167, 185, 205, 233, 339, 391, 394, 423, 464
Ayres, L. P., 58, 72

Babbie, E. R., 56, 72
Bagford, L. W., 40, 41
Baker, F. B., 225, 233
Bartel, N. R., 464
Beck, M. D., 63, 72
Beggs, D. L., 263
Bellanca, J. A., 423
Berk, R. A., 41, 295, 338, 344, 391
Bloom, B. S., 9, 23, 28, 36, 41, 115, 129, 169, 185, 482
Boehm, A. E., 447, 464
Braden, W. W., 100
Brennan, R. L., 295
Brown, C. M., 100
Brown, F. G., 205
Buros, O. K., 33, 41, 428, 431, 433, 440, 442, 444, 446, 464

Campbell, D. T., 59, 72
Cartwright, C. A., 72
Cartwright, G. P., 72
Castaldi, B., 213, 233
Chapman, J. C., 83, 100
Chase, C. I., 305, 314
Cliff, N., 58, 72
Coffman, W. E., 166, 185, 227, 233
Colwell, R., 100
Cooper, J. O., 100
Coulson, D. B., 295, 339
Cronbach, L. J., 41, 295, 302, 308, 312, 314
Cureton, E. E., 315

Davis, R. A., 30, 42
Downie, N. M., 263

Ebel, R. L., 20, 28, 120, 123, 129, 135, 166, 185, 218, 233, 236, 237, 263, 295, 310, 315, 397, 423, 464
Edgerly, J. W., 423
Erickson, R. C., 100

Faas, L. A., 445, 446, 464
Ferguson, G. A., 373, 391
Fitzpatrick, R., 74, 100
Fredericksen, N., 100

Garvin, A. P., 335, 339
Geisinger, K. F., 423
Gilman, D. A., 303, 315, 318, 339
Glaser, K., 464
Glaser, R., 41
Glock, M. D., 185
Goldberg, H. K., 445, 465
Gronlund, N. E., 48, 72, 115, 129, 166, 233, 263, 295, 315, 391, 410, 423, 464, 501

Hagen, E., 20, 28, 60, 72, 295, 315, 391, 465
Hainsworth, P. K., 448, 464
Hambleton, R. K., 295, 339, 342, 391
Hammill, D. D., 464
Harrow, A. J., 28, 485
Hastings, J. T., 23, 28, 36, 41, 115, 129
Hoffman, B., 120, 129
Hopkins, C. D., 28, 72, 100, 129, 167, 185, 205, 233, 339, 391, 464

Johnson, D. J., 464
Jones, A. S., 40, 41
Jones, L. V., 14, 28, 72

Kass, C. E., 464
Kauffman, J. M., 465
Kearney, N. C., 6, 28
Kelley, T. L., 246, 263
Kirschenbaum, H., 405, 423
Krathwohl, D. R., 28, 482
Kunder, L. H., 423

Larsen, S. C., 42
Learner, J. W., 445, 464
Lehmann, I. J., 72, 100, 129, 167, 185, 233, 391, 464
Lewis, E. L., 263
Lien, A. J., 100, 391
Lien, J. S., 100
Likert, R. A., 56, 72
Lindquist, E. F., 42, 100, 129, 234, 295, 315
Lippy, G., 214, 233
Lorge, I., 72

Lyman, H. B., 391

Madaus, G. F., 23, 28, 36, 41, 115, 129
Mager, R. F., 36, 41
Mann, P. H., 41
Masia, B. B., 28, 482
Masling, J., 59, 72
McClung, R. M., 41
Meehl, P. E., 302, 308, 314
Mehrens, W. A., 72, 100, 129, 167, 185, 233,
Milton, C., 423
Mitchell, J. V., 33, 41, 451, 464
Mitzel, H. E., 423
Morrison, E. J., 74, 100
Murdoch, K., 100
Myklebust, H. R., 464

Napier, R. M., 405, 423
Nitko, A. J., 41
Noll, V. H., 6, 28, 233, 391

Oppenheim, A. N., 56, 72

Pate, J. E., 447, 465
Perrone, V., 465
Popham, W. J., 41, 42, 263, 339
Porwoll, P. J., 423
Purnell, R. T., 30, 42

Reger, R., 465
Richardson, M. W., 129
Ross, E. T., 234
Rowly, G. L., 129, 234, 501
Rush, G. P., 83, 100
Ryans, D. G., 100

Sanders, J. R., 22, 28
Sax, G., 254, 263, 295, 315, 391, 465
Scannell, D. P., 6, 28, 233, 336, 339, 391
Schiffman, G. B., 445, 465

Schwartz, R. D., 59, 72
Sechrest, L., 59, 72
Simon, S. B., 405, 423
Sigueland, M. L., 448, 464
Slingerland, B. H., 447, 448, 465
Snow, R. E., 41
Spaulding, G., 234
Sproull, L., 465
Staib, J. H., 190, 205
Stalnaker, J. M., 129
Stetz, F. P., 63, 72
Stufflebeam, D. L., 20, 28
Subhoviak, M. J., 295
Suiter, P. A., 41
Swaminathan, H., 295, 339

Tanur, J. M., 72
Terwilliger, J. S., 394, 396, 423
Thorndike, R. L., 20, 28, 41, 60, 72, 100, 129, 166, 167, 185, 233, 234, 295, 314, 315, 391, 465
Tinkleman, S. N., 234
Tracey, D. B., 336, 339
Traub, R. E., 129, 501
Traxler, A. E., 234
Tyler, R. W., 30, 37, 42, 216, 234

Vaughn, K. W., 129

Wallace, G., 42, 465
Wallen, E. A., 40, 41
Webb, E. J., 59, 72
Webb, W. W., 447, 465
Wentling, T. L., 100
Wesman, A. G., 125, 129, 167, 234
White, S. H., 37, 42, 216, 234
Wick, J. W., 315, 465, 497
Worthen, B. R., 22, 28

Zubrow, D., 465

Subject Index

Accordian key for scoring tests, 220, 466
Accountability of school programs, 2, 22, 466
Achievement battery, 436–7
 choosing, 436
 for secondary schools, 436–7
Achievement test, 111, 466
Action: element of a behavioral objective, 466, 489, 490–1
Activity exercises, (see end of each chapter)
Adequate sample, 93–4
Affective domain: writing behavioral objectives, 8, 466, 482–5
Age equivalents, 455
Age norms for standardized tests, 454–5, 466
Algorithm, 188
"All of the above" in multiple-choice items, 145
Alternatives, 140, 466
Ambiguity in test items, 135, 138, 467
 apparent, 139
 intrinsic, 139
American Educational Research Journal, 452
American Psychologist, 452
Analysis: of a test
 criterion-referenced tests, 240–5
 distracters, 251–2
 forming criterion groups, 241–2
 interpretation, 244–5, 252–5
 procedure, 242–7, 247–51
 student selections, 257
Analytical procedure for essay scoring, 227, 228, 467
Anecdotal records, 60–1, 467
 examples, 61
 value to evaluation, 61
Anxiety: over classroom tests, 124
Apparent ambiguity, 139, 467
Appraisal, 2, 30, 467
 entry for instruction, 32
 information for, 31
 source of data, 31–2
 student progress, 1
Appraisal, test: *See* Test appraisal
Aptitude tests: specific areas, 438
Artificial test situation, 46–7, 49

Assessment, 2
 instruction effectiveness, 1
Attribute, 16, 467
Average: as reference points, 329
Averaging scores, 375–8

Balance of tests, 235–6, 237–8, 467
Battery, test, 430, 434–8, 467
Behavioral objectives, 7–12, 467
 examples, 7
 elements of, 7
 writing of, 489–97
Boehm Test, 447
Bulletin, test, 451

Cardinal Principles of Secondary Education, 5
Cause-effect, 139
Central tendency, 353, 467
 comparison of, 359
 computing, 359
 cf. 350, 467
Chance error, 266
Chance level, 117, 467, 499
Checklist, 51–4, 79–81, 84, 88, 408–10, 467
 constructing, 51–2
 examples, 52
 strengths, 409
 using, 51–4
 weaknesses, 409–10
Chess moves: as multiple-choice selections, 132
Classification items, 467
 categories, 160
 guides for writing, 161
 for recall, 160
 strengths, 160
 weaknesses, 161
Classification of objectives, 6–12
Classroom measurement, 16–17
 shortcomings, 25–6
Classroom tests, 468
 improving validity, 311–12
Clinical help, need for, 33
Coefficient of validity, 306, 468
Cognitive domain, 9–12, 468
Collecting data, 79–81, 85–91

Completion items, 468
    guides for writing, 173–5
    placement of blanks, 174
    strengths, 172
    weaknesses, 173
Computer-assisted testing, 214, 468
Computer reporting, 418–9
Concurrent validity, 282, 299, 300–1, 306,
    468
Conditions: element of a behavioral objec-
    tive, 468, 489, 493–4
Conference, 24, 468
Confidence interval, 285, 468
Consistency: in measurement, 266
Construct, 16, 468
Constructed-response items, 118, 468
    strengths, 170
    types of, 119
    weaknesses, 171
Construct validity, 299, 301–2, 306–9, 468
    evidence for, 308
Content sampling, 66, 468
Content validity, 105, 299–300, 303–5, 468
    criterion-referenced, 303
    norm-referenced, 303
    published tests, 305
Cooperative Social Studies Test, 19
Correction factor, 468, 498, 499
Correction for guessing, 469, 498–501
Corrective teaching, 33, 34
Correlation, 269, 469
    measuring relationships, 269–75
    and reliability, 268–9
    scattergrams, 269
    using, 268–9
Correlation coefficient, 269, 469
Counting average, 357
Criterion: establishment of, 319–20
Criterion group, 242, 469
Criterion keying, 113, 469
Criterion-referenced, 105, 114–5, 343–4,
    469
    in certification, 38–9
    descriptive explanation, 323
    difference from norm-referenced, 319
    difficulty index, 243
    discrimination index, 243
    examples of, 323–5
    interpreting analysis, 244
    item analysis, 240–5
    strengths, 327
    using, 334
    weaknesses, 328
Criterion-related validity, 300, 305–6, 469
Current Index to Journals in Education,
    452

Data-collecting devices: improving validity,

311–13
Data-collection fluidity, 40
Decile, 360, 469
Decision errors: in criterion-referencing,
    320–1
Decision-making, 2–3, 21, 22, 25, 44
Descriptor set, 323, 469
Device, 51, 469
Diagnosis, 30, 469
    by computer, 35
    done by individual, 33
    specific, 33
Diagnostic evaluation, 25, 469
Diagnostic test, 30, 111, 431–2, 469
    construction, 33–4
    selection, 33–4
Difficulty index, 236, 469
    formula, 243, 249
Difficulty level:
    mastery tests, 116
    open-ended tests, 116
    power tests, 116
    of tasks, 116
    understanding the principle, 118
Difficulty level of tasks on tests, 134, 235,
    253, 469
    control of, 147
    mastery tests, 116
    open-ended tests, 116
Directions, test:
    adults, 211
    clarifying, 211
    older students, 211
    primary grades, 208–11
Direct observation, 49–51, 470
    data-collection devices, 51–8
    reliability checks, 68
    strengths, 49–50
    supplementing, 61–3
    validity checks, 68–9
    validity factors, 67
    weaknesses, 50–1
Discrimination, 136, 235, 253, 470
Discrimination index, 236, 470
    formula, 243, 250
Distracter, 140, 470
    effectiveness, 251–2, 256–7
Domain, 7, 470
Domain-referenced, 111, 470

Easiness index, 249, 470
Education for All Handicapped Children
    Act, 445
Educational and Psychological Measure-
    ment, 452
Educational Index, 452
Educational measurement, 24, 317, 470
Educational objective, 4, 470

for general outcomes, 48
as instructional objective, 5
at levels of education, 6
by domains, 7
sounding board for evaluation, 12
The Eighth Mental Measurements Yearbook, 428, 433, 441, 450
Elementary School Objectives, 6
Equivalence, 281, 470
Equivalent forms reliability, 267, 276, 470
standardized tests, 276
Error, 15–6, 470
Error score, 267
Essay items, 470
extended response, 179
guides for writing, 181–2
limited response, 179
response freedom, 180
scoring freedom, 181
strengths, 180
weaknesses, 181
Essay responses: scoring, 229–31
Establishing norms, 330–1
Establishing the criterion, 319–20
Ethical test practices, 506–8
Evaluating procedure, 77–8
Evaluating products, 84–5
Evaluating standardized tests, 452–3
Evaluation, 471
to assign marks, 25
bases for, 24
definition, 21
as feedback, 22
focus of, 21
functions of, 3
grouping students, 25
prerequisites to, 3
purpose of, 21–2
reason for, 21–2
support of literacy, 40
types of, 23–4
Event sampling, 65, 471
Exact limits, 352, 471
Examinee reliability, 275, 471
Extended response, 179, 471

False-negative errors, 321
False-positive errors, 321
Field testing, 430, 471
First-Grade Screening Test, 447
For discussion, (*See* end of each chapter)
Formative evaluation, 21, 23, 471
and curriculum development, 23, 35–6
frequency of testing, 37
in learning, 23
principle of, 35
using objectives, 36
Freedom: in constructed-response items, 170
Frequency distribution, 348, 471
grouped data, 350–1
steps to set up, 348
Frequency polygon, 352–3, 471
Frequency of testing, 123

Global scoring for essay responses, 227, 228–9, 471
Glossary terms, 466–81 (Also listed at end of chapters where they first appear)
Grade, 396
Grade equivalents, 455
using, 456
Grade norms for standardized tests, 455–6, 471
Grouped data, 350, 471
Guessing, 122
Guessing: correction for, 498–501
formulas, 498–500
use of, 500–1

Halo effect, 49, 472
Hand scoring, 220–2, 472
Histogram, 351–2, 472
Horizontal axis, 269, 472

Illusions, 45
Improving test quality: by appraisal, 258–9
Individualized instruction, 115
and mastery tests, 113
Instructional evaluation, 25, 472
Instructional objectives, 4–5, 43, 472
examples, general, 6
Instrumentation, 45, 472
Internal consistency, 267, 277, 472
Interpretation: of test performance, 325–7, 332
Interpreting scores, 266
Intrinsic ambiguity, 139, 472
Isomorphic, 18, 472
Item analysis, 245, 472
Item arrangement, 212–14
hierarchy, 213
item difficulty, 212
item type, 212
subject topics, 212
Item examples:
classification, 162–5
completion, 176–7
essay, 183
matching, 156–60
multiple-choice, 148–9
problem, 195–8, 200–3
short answer, 178–9
true false, 139–40
Item stem, 140
Item writing:

an art, 125
  guides for writing, 125
Journal of Counseling Psychology, 452
Journal of Educational Measurement, 452
Judging performance:
  in learning sequence, 96
  procedure-product interdependence, 95

Key, 472
Knowledge extenders, (*See* end of each chapter)
Kuder-Richardson (K-R) formulas, 267, 279-80, 472, 502
Kurtosis, 367-8, 472

Learning:
  test directed, 3, 6, 102
  by selection, 132-3
Learning disability, 445-6, 472
  characteristics, 446
  definition, 446
Length, test, 288-9
Leptokurtic, 368, 473
Letter marks, 399-401
  strengths, 400-1
  weaknesses, 401
Letters to parents, 407
  strengths, 407
  weaknesses, 407
Levels of passing, 323
Limited response, 180, 473
Linear tendency, 275, 473
Local norms, 460, 473

Machine scoring, 224-5, 473
Manual, test, 451
Mark, 25, 473
  basis for, 393
  general considerations, 420-1
  summative evaluation, 38
  technical considerations, 419
Marking plans, 394, 473
  philosophies for, 394-6
  shortcomings, 397
Marks, use of:
  employers, 399
  parents, 398
  school personnel, 398-9
  students, 397
Mastery, 111
  need for, 328-9
Mastery measurement, 112-3
Mastery test, 111, 112-3, 336, 473
  instructional objectives, 113
  need for, 114
Matching items, 473
  guides for writing, 150

homogeneous lists, 152
premises, 149
responses, 149
strengths, 150
using, 149
weaknesses, 150
Mathematical problem:
  application of principles, 190
  guides for writing, 192-5
  natural situations, 191
  need for, 189
  scoring, 192
  strengths, 190
  weaknesses, 191
Maximum development, 115
Mean, arithmetic, 357-8, 473
Meaningful data, 12-3
Measure, 14, 473
  as a number value, 14
  as a process, 14
Measurement, 317, 473
  of constructs, 16
  definition, 15
  of extraneous factors, 103
  function in schools, 24
  functions of, 3
  as observation, 15
  as quantification, 17
  two aspects, 18
Measurement and Evaluation in Guidance, 452
Measurement as quantification, 17-8
Measures:
  meaning of, 318
  uses for, 318
Measures of variability, 361, 365, 473
Measuring achievement, reason for, 102
Measuring devices: criterion-referencing, 321-5
Measuring units, 18-9
Mechanical devices, 62, 79, 84, 473
  use in observation, 62, 96-8
Median, 357, 473
Meeting Street Screening Test, 448
Mental abilities tests, 438
  divergence in tasks, 439
  group, 439, 440-1
  individual, 439-40
Mental Measurement Yearbook series, 33, 450, 451, 461
Mesokurtic, 368, 473
Minimum acceptance: element of a behavioral objective, 466, 489, 490-1
Minimum essentials, 115
Minimum standards, 112
Modal age norms, 456, 474
Mode, 355-7, 474

Multiaptitude test battery, 442
Multiaptitude tests, 438
Multiple-choice item, 474
  effective distracters, 251
  guessing responses, 141
  guides for writing, 142–7
  strengths, 141
  using, 140
  weaknesses, 141–2
Multiple reports, 410–8

National Education Association, 5–6, 28
Natural situation:
  simulation of, 74–5
  for testing, 46–7
Negative statement: in true-false items, 137
Norm, 30, 474
  which one to use, 460
Normal curve, 474
  properties, 374
  theoretical, 374
  unit normal, 373
Normalize, 373, 474
Norm group, 298, 474
Norm population, 430, 474
Norm-referenced tests, 115
  difficulty index, 248–250
  discrimination index, 250–1
  interpreting analysis, 252–5
  item analysis, 245–55
Norm-referencing, 345, 474
  classroom tests, 329
  comparison used, 329
  difference from criterion-referencing, 318
  measuring devices, 331
  strengths, 333
  using, 334
  weaknesses, 333–4
Norms, 453–60
  establishment of, 330
  levels of achievement, 330
  as referents, 330
  not standards, 454
Norms as referents, 330
Numerical marks, 401–3
  strengths, 402
  weaknesses, 403

Objective, 5, 474
Objective items, 132, 133, 474
Objectives:
  classification, 6–12
  as referents, 319
Objectives and data-collecting procedures, 47–8
Objectives as referents, 319
Objectivity, test, 235–6, 239–40, 474

verification, 239
Observation, 14, 474
  classroom, 44
  frame of reference, 46
  planning for, 63–4
  as process, 43
  nature of, 44
  need to structure, 48
  as product, 43
  sampling behavior, 64
  teachers' use, 48
  tools for, 70
  by testing, 63
  unrecorded, 45
Observational procedures: planning for, 47–8
Observe, 15, 474
Observer effects: in performance, 94–5
Obtained test score, 266, 474
  understanding, 266
Odd-even division, 277
Open-ended measurement, 111–2
Open-endedness:
  for learning, 111
  for testing, 110–1
Open-ended or mastery, 110–1
Open-ended test, 111–2, 474
  need for, 114
  setting standards, 115
  use of easy items, 118
Operational definition, 18, 19, 474
  example, 19
  from tests, 18
  validity check, 310–1
Optical illusions, 45
  and observation, 45–6
Optional responses, 182
Ordering, 345–6, 475
Ordinal data, 363, 475

Parent/teacher conferences, 407–8
  strengths, 408
  weaknesses, 408
Pass/fail marks, 403–4
  strengths, 403–4
  weaknesses, 404
Pearson correlation:
  basic formula, 271
  computational formulas, 272–3
Pearson product-moment correlation, 271, 475
Percentage marks, 404–5
  strengths, 405
  weaknesses, 405
Percentile, 360, 475
  calculation, 360
  formula, 360

Percentile rank bands, 330, 457
Percentile rank norms, 456–7, 475
Performance:
  evaluation of, 76
  getting a sample, 93
  standards for judging, 76–7
  two parts, 73, 75, 76
  valid evaluation, 93
Performance evaluation, 74, 475
  for psychomotor domain, 74
  use of, 74
Performance test, 74, 475
  in the classroom, 74–5
Physical measurement, 15–6, 475
  shortcomings, 16
Platykurtic, 368, 475
Power test, 116–7, 475
  example, 117
Predictive validity, 299, 301, 306, 475
Pre-Reading Screening Procedures Test,
  447–8
Prerequisites: to other learning, 328
Problem items, 118, 189, 475
Presentation, 187, 188
  types of, 119
Problem solving:
  in 1980 NCTM Yearbook, 189
  as an objective, 189
Procedure, 73, 77–83, 475
  actions of, 77
  collecting data, 79–81
  evaluating, 77–8
  recording data, 81–3
  relationship to product, 77
  setting standards, 78–9
Procedure as process, 76
Procedure-product interdependence, 95–6
Procedures, data collection, 510–2
Process, 43, 73, 475
Product: element of a behavioral objective,
  475, 489, 492–3
Product as result, 76
Products, 43, 73, 83–91, 475, 489, 492–3
  collecting data, 85
  criterion for judging, 84
  evaluating, 84–5
  importance, 83
  recording data, 91
  setting standards, 85
Product scale, 58, 84, 90, 475
Prognostic test, 444, 476
Program assessment, 425
Program evaluation, 24, 326–7
Psychological Abstracts, 452
Psychological Bulletin, 452
Psychological measurement, 24, 476
Psychological test, 102

Psychomotor domain, 8, 485–8, 476
Public Law, 94–142, 445
Published test, 20, 476

Quantification, 17, 476
  two aspects, 18
Quantify, 15, 476
Quartile, 360, 476
Quartile deviation, 363–5, 476

Range, 361–2, 476
Rank, 346, 476
Ranking, 346–8, 476
Rating scale, 54–8, 79–81, 84, 88, 476
  constructing, 56–8
  examples, 56, 58
  reasons to use, 56
  using, 58
Rational choices: from selected-response
  items, 132
Raw score, 341, 476
Readiness test, 444, 476
Reading Tests and Reviews II, 433
Real limits, 352, 477
Recording data, 81–3, 91
References, (*See* end of each chapter)
Reference system: choosing, 334–7
Relative performance, 387–8
Reliability, 13, 477
  definition, 13
  factors that effect, 292
  guessing, 134
  relationship to validity, 13
Reliability checks, 68
Reliability coefficient:
  to estimate consistency, 267
  factors affecting, 287–92
  interpretation, 274–5
Report cards, 410–8
Representative sample, 64, 105, 477
Requisites: to special functioning, 328
Responses, recording, 219
Result, 73, 477
Review of Educational Research, 452
Revision of items, 255–7
  analyzing responses, 257
  distracters, 256
  using D values, 255
  using P values, 255
Rho, 477
  formula, 273

Sample, 64, 104, 477
Sampling:
  for norm-referenced tests, 105
  graphic representation, 104, 105
  observation, 64–7

Sampling distribution, 283, 477
*A Scale for Measuring the Quality of Hand-
    writing of School Children,* 58
Scales, absolute, 343–4
Scaling scores, 113
Scattergram, 269, 477
Score, 477
    criterion-referenced, 342
    meaning of, 341–2
    norm-referenced, 342
Scorecard, 54, 86, 477
    use in schools, 54
Score interpretation, 124
    frequency polygon, 352–3
    histogram, 351–2
    by ordering, 345–6
    by ranking, 346–8
    relative performance, 387–8
Scorer reliability, 267, 280, 477
Scoring items:
    constructed-response, 225–31
    essay, 227–231
    selected-response, 225
Scoring key, 133
Scoring procedures, 219–220
Scoring tests, 124, 219–31
    hand scoring, 220–2
    item types, 225–8
    machine scoring, 224–5
    self-scoring, 222–4
*Screening Test for Assignment of Remedial
    Treatment,* 448
Screening tests, 446–9
    teacher-administered, 446–9
Selected-response items, 117–8, 477
    strengths, 133
    types of, 119
    weaknesses, 134
Selection: as an objective, 132–3
Self-scoring, 222–4, 477
Sense data and observation, 45–6
Short-answer items, 477
    guides for writing, 178
    strengths, 177
    weaknesses, 178
    written expression, 177
Simultaneous variation, 269
Single-subject tests, 432–4, 478
    coverage, 432–3
    reading tests, 433–4
Skewness, 366–7, 478
Slingerland Screening Tests, 448–9
Spearman-Brown formulas, 278, 478
    estimating reliability, 288
    general, 278
    split-halves, 279
Specific determiner, 137, 478

as a clue, 127
Specificity, test, 235–6, 238–9, 478
    verification, 239
Specimen set, for tests, 451, 478
Speededness of a test, 291–2, 478
Speed test, 117
    example, 117
Split-half procedure for estimating reliability,
    267, 277–9, 282, 478
Stability of tests, 281, 478
Standard deviation, 478
    calculation, 363
    formula, 362
Standard error, 283, 478
Standard error of measurement, 282–7, 479
    formula, 283
Standardized test, 30, 479
Standardized testing program, 426
    example, 503–5
Standardized test evaluation, 509
Standardized tests:
    categories, 428
    criteria for, 427
    development procedure, 430–1
Standards:
    external, 115
    setting, 78–9, 85
Standard score, 330, 479
Standard score norms, 457–60
*Standards for Educational and Psychologi
    cal Tests and Manuals,* 461
Stanine, 479
    as bands, 383
    to interpret scores, 383
    percentages, 383
Statistics, 332, 345, 479
Stem, 140, 479
Strip key, 220, 479
Student appraisal, 425
Student developmental level, 123
Student evaluation, 24, 325–6
Student needs: appraisal, 32
Summative evaluation, 21, 23, 479
    program effectiveness, 39
    terminal judgment, 23
    uses, 38
Survey battery, 432, 479
Symmetrical, 366, 479

Table of specifications, 105–10, 479
    allotting tasks, 107
    as a blueprint, 106
    building, 106–8
    distributing topics and behaviors, 107–8
    for an essay test, 108–9
    matrix dimensions, 106
    skeleton table, 106

using, 109–10
   for validity, 109
Tasks, selection of, 119–22
Taxonomy, 7, 480
   affective domain, 8
   cognitive domain, 7, 9–11
   psychomotor domain, 8
Teacher-made test: advantage over published test, 102
Technical problem:
   guides for writing, 199–200
   indepth investigation, 199
   natural situations, 198
   special study, 198
   strengths, 198
   weaknesses, 199
Test, 480
   definition, 102
   frequency, 123
   as a measuring instrument, 317–8
   as an operational definition, 62
   purpose, 103
   scoring of, 111
   as a sample, 104–5
   selecting tasks, 104, 124
   validity of, 103
Test anxiety, 124
Test administration:
   acclimatization, 217
   heating/ventilation, 217
   lighting, 217
   noise, 217
   physical conditions, 216
   psychological aspects, 218
Test appraisal, 480
   contributions to teacher/students, 260
   reasons for, 236
Test assembly, 207, 480
Test blueprint, 106, 480
Test directions, 208, 480
Test information, sources of, 450–2
Test-item file, 122, 480
Test items:
   building quality, 132
   clues in, 127
   construction guidelines, 125–7
   preliminary form, 126
   tied to objectives, 126
   writing as art, 125
Test manual, 208
Test performance:
   class, 325
   program evaluation, 326
   student, 325
   student evaluation, 325
Test planning: need for, 103
Test publisher's catalog, 451

Test reliability, 266, 480
Test reproduction, 214–6
Test-retest, reliability, 267, 275–6, 480
Test scores:
   interpretation, 332
   making comparable, 374
Test tasks, 119–22
   choosing, 119
   types of, 119
Testwiseness, 218, 480
Testing:
   in an artificial situation, 46
   choosing types of items, 119–20
   disturbing factors, 123
   fitting to schedules, 123
   frequency, 123
   generalizing to real world, 46
   levels of achievement, 111
   measuring minimums, 112
   as observation, 63
   recall of facts, 109
   and student opinion, 122
   time for, 123
   as a tool of learning, 37–8
Testing fluidity, 40
Testing mental abilities, 439–42
   group tests, 440–1
   individual tests, 439–40
Tests as operational definitions, 19–20
Tests in Print III, 33, 451, 461
Textbook tests, 426–7
Time sampling, 64–65, 480
Trait sampling, 66, 480
Transition class, 444
True-false items, 480
   correction by test-taker, 134
   criticism of, 135
   guides for writing, 136–9
   strengths, 135
   weaknesses, 136
True limits, 352, 480
True test score, 266, 267, 480
T score, 373, 479

Unit, 16, 480
Unobtrusive observation, 58–60, 480
   reason to use, 59
   when to use, 60
Using reliability and validity, 13–4

Validity, 481
   content, 105, 110
   definition, 13
   determination of, 302
   emphasis, type, 309–10
   matter of degree, 299
   published tests, 298

sampling behaviors, 310
for specific use, 299
for test results, 299
relationship to validity, 13
Validity checks, 68–9
Variability:
comparison of measures, 365
measures of, 361–5
Variance, 283, 481
Vertical axis, 269, 481

Who: element of a behavioral objective, 481

489–90
Words, glossary, 466–81
Written assignment, 24, 481
Written expression:
in lists of objectives, 170
as an objective, 170

z scores, 481
use of, 375–8
Z scores, 481
use of, 379–80

THE BOOK MANUFACTURE

Classroom Measurement and Evaluation, Second Edition, was typeset by Com/Com, Allentown, PA. It was printed and bound at Kingsport Press, Kingsport, Tennessee. Cover design was by Willis Proudfoot. Internal design was by the F.E. Peacock Publishers' art department. The typeface is Times Roman with Avant Garde display.